Lecture Notes in Computer Science   15261

Founding Editors

Gerhard Goos
Juris Hartmanis

AF167601

Editorial Board Members

Elisa Bertino, *Purdue University, West Lafayette, IN, USA*
Wen Gao, *Peking University, Beijing, China*
Bernhard Steffen, *TU Dortmund University, Dortmund, Germany*
Moti Yung, *Columbia University, New York, NY, USA*

The series Lecture Notes in Computer Science (LNCS), including its subseries Lecture Notes in Artificial Intelligence (LNAI) and Lecture Notes in Bioinformatics (LNBI), has established itself as a medium for the publication of new developments in computer science and information technology research, teaching, and education.

LNCS enjoys close cooperation with the computer science R & D community, the series counts many renowned academics among its volume editors and paper authors, and collaborates with prestigious societies. Its mission is to serve this international community by providing an invaluable service, mainly focused on the publication of conference and workshop proceedings and postproceedings. LNCS commenced publication in 1973.

Nils Jansen · Sebastian Junges ·
Benjamin Lucien Kaminski · Christoph Matheja ·
Thomas Noll · Tim Quatmann ·
Mariëlle Stoelinga · Matthias Volk
Editors

Principles of Verification: Cycling the Probabilistic Landscape

Essays Dedicated to Joost-Pieter Katoen on the Occasion of His 60th Birthday, Part II

 Springer

Editors
Nils Jansen [iD]
Ruhr University Bochum and Radboud
University Nijmegen
Bochum, Germany

Benjamin Lucien Kaminski [iD]
Saarland University and University College
London
Saarbrücken, Germany

Thomas Noll [iD]
RWTH Aachen University
Aachen, Germany

Mariëlle Stoelinga [iD]
University of Twente and Radboud
University Nijmegen
Enschede, The Netherlands

Sebastian Junges [iD]
Radboud University Nijmegen
Nijmegen, The Netherlands

Christoph Matheja [iD]
University of Oldenburg
Oldenburg, Germany

Tim Quatmann [iD]
RWTH Aachen University
Aachen, Germany

Matthias Volk [iD]
Eindhoven University of Technology
Eindhoven, The Netherlands

ISSN 0302-9743 ISSN 1611-3349 (electronic)
Lecture Notes in Computer Science
ISBN 978-3-031-75774-7 ISBN 978-3-031-75775-4 (eBook)
https://doi.org/10.1007/978-3-031-75775-4

© The Editor(s) (if applicable) and The Author(s), under exclusive license
to Springer Nature Switzerland AG 2025

This work is subject to copyright. All rights are solely and exclusively licensed by the Publisher, whether the whole or part of the material is concerned, specifically the rights of translation, reprinting, reuse of illustrations, recitation, broadcasting, reproduction on microfilms or in any other physical way, and transmission or information storage and retrieval, electronic adaptation, computer software, or by similar or dissimilar methodology now known or hereafter developed.
The use of general descriptive names, registered names, trademarks, service marks, etc. in this publication does not imply, even in the absence of a specific statement, that such names are exempt from the relevant protective laws and regulations and therefore free for general use.
The publisher, the authors and the editors are safe to assume that the advice and information in this book are believed to be true and accurate at the date of publication. Neither the publisher nor the authors or the editors give a warranty, expressed or implied, with respect to the material contained herein or for any errors or omissions that may have been made. The publisher remains neutral with regard to jurisdictional claims in published maps and institutional affiliations.

The cover image was created with the assistance of AI.

This Springer imprint is published by the registered company Springer Nature Switzerland AG
The registered company address is: Gewerbestrasse 11, 6330 Cham, Switzerland

If disposing of this product, please recycle the paper.

Preface

We are very excited to publish these *three* Festschrift volumes to celebrate the 60th birthday of our valued colleague and mentor Joost-Pieter Katoen, a.k.a. JP, or Prof. Dr. Ir. Dr. h.c. Joost-Pieter Katoen (PDEng).

The scientific journey of Joost-Pieter is long, versatile, and rich.

Career. Joost-Pieter studied Computer Science at the University of Twente and obtained his M.Sc. with distinction in 1987. He obtained a Professional Doctorate in Engineering (EngD) from Eindhoven University of Technology in 1990 and afterwards worked for two years as a Research Scientist at Philips Research Labs in Eindhoven. Joost-Pieter then returned to Enschede and obtained a Ph.D. in Computer Science from the University of Twente in 1996 with a thesis on *Quantitative and Qualitative Extensions of Event Structures*. As a postdoctoral researcher, Joost-Pieter worked at the University of Erlangen-Nürnberg for two years. During this time, he developed the new graduate course on *mechanized validation of parallel systems*, and started research into the topic of model checking. In 1999, he returned to the University of Twente as an Associate Professor, and chaired the Formal Methods and Tools group from 2002 on. Since 2004, he chairs the Modeling and Verification (MOVES) group at RWTH Aachen University as a full professor.

Research. Joost-Pieter is a prominent member of *the founding family of the area of probabilistic model checking*. Probabilistic model checking is a very successful research field and the state-of-the-art for formally evaluating systems with stochastic behavior. Applications range from robotics and cyber-physical systems to demographic models and systems biology. Probabilistic model checking techniques empower these fields with effective modeling techniques and efficient algorithms for analyzing their stochastic behavior.

Numerous applications have been analyzed, leading to better engineering solutions, such as optimized maintenance schedules for railroad tracks, energy-efficient schedules in satellites, safer airbag controllers and cardiac pacemakers, secure encryption schemes, efficient robot planning and reliable quantum computing. Recently, probabilistic model checking has made the first and solid steps towards the grand challenge of verified AI, providing hard guarantees about the correctness of AI algorithms.

It is, therefore, no surprise that various entities – including NASA, ESA, Siemens – have adopted probabilistic model checking as a key technology in their validation and verification cycle.

Joost-Pieter played a key role in the success of this field. He made major contributions to its foundations, developing the semantic foundations of various stochastic models and numerous foundational algorithms to analyze such models, ranging from classical models like Markov chains to sophisticated models like probabilistic timed automata. His work on model checking algorithms for continuous-time Markov chains (CTMCs) was particularly influential and has been recognized by a *CONCUR test-of-time award* and *the Jean-Claude Laprie Award on Dependable Computing*. Furthermore, his book

Principles of Model Checking, co-authored with Christel Baier, has become the standard reference textbook in the field, used by students, researchers, and professionals all over the world.

More recently, he delved into the world of probabilistic programming, a novel programming paradigm to define and analyze probabilistic models that underly machine learning, data analysis, and artificial intelligence. Fueled by an ERC Advanced Grant, Joost-Pieter made numerous and significant contributions to analyzing probabilistic programs, such as deductive verification, synthesis, termination, complexity, semantics, and correctness.

Joost-Pieter's work has received widespread recognition. He became a distinguished professor at RWTH Aachen University in 2013 and received an honorary doctorate from Aalborg University in 2017. He is a member of Academia Europea, an ACM Fellow, a member of the Royal Holland Society of Science and Humanities (KHMW), a member of the North Rhine-Westphalian Academy of Science, Humanities and the Arts, and a member of the German National Academy of Sciences Leopoldina.

Tools. Throughout his research, Joost-Pieter has always emphasized the need for efficient, usable tools that make the research results available to a broader audience. Joost-Pieter advocates "push-button technology" which should provide efficient computations with minimal user knowledge necessary. One of Joost-Pieter's first tools was the *Erlangen-Twente Markov Chain Checker (E-MC^2),* the first model checker for CTMC, in 2000.

The *Markov reward model checker (MRMC)* was developed from 2005 on and supports a range of Markov models – such as DTMCs, CTMCs, CTMDPs – and logics – such as PCTL, CSL. In the last decade, the next generation model checker *Storm* has been developed – with the initial development in the MOVES group and nowadays spreading development across borders.

The *COMPASS* toolset was developed in a successful industrial collaboration with the European Space Agency (ESA) and targets on-board computer-based aerospace systems. In particular, the toolset brings model checking techniques into the engineering process of aerospace systems.

Recently, Joost-Pieter's research on probabilistic programs has led to the development of the deductive verifier *Caesar.*

Leadership. Joost-Pieter Katoen has served the academic community in numerous ways. Amongst others, he is a founding member of the *IFIP Working Group 1.8 on Concurrency Theory* and played a leading role in establishing the *QEST* conference, merging the *TOOLS, PNPM,* and *PAPM-PROBMIV* communities. In 2011, he organized the *Aachen Concurrency and Dependability Week*, encompassing the conferences *QEST, CONCUR,* and *TGC* in Aachen. From 2015 to 2019, he chaired the Steering Committee of the *European Joint Conferences on Theory and Practice of Software (ETAPS)* and was President of the *ETAPS* association. Under his leadership, *ETAPS* adopted a *Gold Open Access policy* in the LNCS proceedings so that the results published at the ETAPS conferences are available to anyone without any charges.

Joost-Pieter has been an inspiring colleague and mentor for many young scientists. He organized the first *Young Researchers Workshop on Concurrency Theory (YR-CONCUR)* in 2009. He co-organized PhD schools on *Quantitative Model Checking* and the *Foundations of Probabilistic Programming*. For his commitment to work-life balance, especially for young Ph.D. students with children, he was awarded the *FAMOS Prize* by RWTH Aachen University in 2017. Since 2017, he chairs the Research Training Group on *Uncertainty and Randomness in Algorithms, Verification and Logic (UnRAVeL)*.

Colleague. Apart from his scientific contributions, we also know Joost-Pieter as an energetic, pleasant, and fun colleague. He is an active sports person, using summer holidays to climb the Alps on his bicycle, combining winter workshops with downhill skiing, and keeping speed skating skills up to date in the hope of another iteration of Elfstedentocht. Joost-Pieter's active cycling cannot only be observed by the hundreds of kilometers per month on Strava but also in person during summer when he occasionally switches to the bicycle to commute from Maastricht to Aachen.

While Joost-Pieter probably has the most visits to venues such as *ETAPS*, *CAV*, *LICS*, or *POPL*, visits to venues such as *Pinkpop* follow closely, and he not only avidly follows new paper publications but is also always up to date when it comes to new releases from, for example, Red Hot Chili Peppers and Twenty One Pilots.

Last but not least, Joost-Pieter is always up for and on the lookout for good coffee/espresso, and many discussions and new research ideas have been fueled by fresh coffee beans. One of these results still goes by the name *The Starbucks Algorithm*.

These Festschrift volumes contain 56 contributions of (former) colleagues, PhD students, and collaborators of Joost-Pieter. The papers exemplify his long, versatile, and rich journey through the landscape of probabilistic model checking. For these volumes, we organized a thorough review process that involved all contributing authors and other experts. We thank everyone who contributed an article or helped with the reviewing.

We celebrated the birthday of Joost-Pieter at the *Colloquium on Principles of Verification: Cycling the Probabilistic Landscape* in Aachen in November 2024.

Happy birthday, Joost-Pieter!

September 2024

Nils Jansen
Sebastian Junges
Benjamin Kaminski
Christoph Matheja
Thomas Noll
Tim Quatmann
Marielle Stoelinga
Matthias Volk

Organization

Program Committee

Nils Jansen	Ruhr University Bochum and Radboud University Nijmegen
Sebastian Junges	Radboud University
Benjamin Lucien Kaminski	Saarland University and University College London
Christoph Matheja	University of Oldenburg
Thomas Noll	RWTH Aachen University
Tim Quatmann	RWTH Aachen University
Marielle Stoelinga	University of Twente
Matthias Volk	Eindhoven University of Technology

Additional Reviewers

Erika Abraham
Thom Badings
Christel Baier
Ezio Bartocci
Kevin Batz
Dirk Beyer
Eline Bovy
Carlos E. Budde
Milan Ceska
Mingshuai Chen
Alessandro Cimatti
Andrea Corradini
Philipp Czerner
Pedro R. D'Argenio
Clemens Dubslaff
Javier Esparza
Bernd Finkbeiner
Martin Fränzle
Hubert Garavel
Jürgen Giesl
Radu Grigore
Jan Friso Groote
Timo P. Gros

Radu Grosu
Kim Guldstrand Larsen
Thomas Haas
Ichiro Hasuo
Boudewijn Haverkort
Linus Heck
Holger Hermanns
Falk Howar
Marieke Huisman
David N. Jansen
Einar Broch Johnsen
Taylor T. Johnson
Eduard Kamburjan
Jan-Christoph Kassing
Panagiotis Katsaros
Bram Kohlen
Laura Kovács
Stefan Kowalewski
Jan Kretinsky
Antonín Kučera
Marta Kwiatkowska
Rom Langerak
Sander J. J. Leemans

Alberto Lluch Lafuente
Anirban Majumdar
Rupak Majumdar
Mieke Massink
Annabelle McIver
Marius Mikučionis
Carroll Morgan
Daniel Neider
Gethin Norman
Petr Novotný
Federico Olmedo
Muhammad Osama
Raúl Pardo
Dave Parker
Corina Pasareanu
Guillermo Perez
Annabell Petri
Jakob Piribauer
Francesca Randone
Jean-Francois Raskin
Anne Remke
Arend Rensink
Theo Ruys
Gabriel Santos

Philipp Schröer
Arpit Sharma
Ana Sokolova
Marnix Suilen
Stefano Tonetta
Andrea Turrini
Nikos Tzevelekos
Frits Vaandrager
Wil van der Aalst
Sören van der Wall
Tom van Dijk
Erik Voogd
Andrzej Wasowski
Kazuki Watanabe
Anton Wijs
Tim Willemse
Tobias Winkler
Verena Wolf
Mustafa Yalciner
Naijun Zhan
Lijun Zhang
Zhen Zhang
Lenore Zuck

Contents – Part II

Model Checking Applications

On Woolhouse's Cotton-Spinning Problem

Jan Friso Groote$^{(\boxtimes)}$ and Tim A.C. Willemse

Department of Mathematics and Computer Science, Eindhoven University of
Technology, P.O. Box 513, 5600 Eindhoven, MB, The Netherlands
{J.F.Groote,T.A.C.Willemse}@tue.nl

Abstract. In 1864 W.S.B. Woolhouse formulated the Cotton-Spinning
problem [12]. This problem boils down to the following. A piecer works
at a spinning mule and walks back and forth along the mule to repair
broken threads. The question is how far the piecer is expected to walk
when the threads break at random. This problem can neatly be solved
using process modelling and quantitative model checking, showing that
Woolhouse's model led to an overestimation of the walking distance.

1 Introduction

The Industrial Revolution, which started in Great Britain in the 18th century,
saw the rise of mechanised factory systems and efficient manufacturing processes.
Textile production was among the first to profit, with machines called *spinning
mules* for spinning cotton and other fibres being used extensively. These mules,
which could be operated by a *minder* – also known as a mule spinner – and two
piecers, allowed for a huge reduction in required labour and led to significant cost
reductions of spinning. The machines consisted of a carriage that was able to
carry up to 1,320 spindles and could be up-to 46 m long. The carriage would move
back and forth, to and from the unspun cotton, over a distance of 1.5 m, four
times a minute [2]. The spindles would twist the threads when the mule would
move away from the unspun cotton and they would take up the spun threads as
the carriage would return towards the cotton. Figure 1 gives an impression of a
factory with spinning mules (the picture originates from [1]).

Piecers, typically young girls or
boys, would repair the sporadic yarn
breakages. They would walk with
and along the mule as it moved,
catch ending or broken threads and
piece them. The quality of the roving
greatly impacted the number of yarn
breakages, with 5 to 6 breakages a
minute being typical of machines in
the early 20th century. While repair

Fig. 1. Spinning mules in a factory.

could be done in a few seconds, requiring only a slight rolling of the forefinger
against the thumb, it had to be done while the mule was moving.

© The Author(s), under exclusive license to Springer Nature Switzerland AG 2025
N. Jansen et al. (Eds.): Principles of Verification: Cycling the Probabilistic Landscape,
LNCS 15261, pp. 3–17, 2025.
https://doi.org/10.1007/978-3-031-75775-4_1

The actuary W.S.B. Woolhouse, seemingly concerned with the welfare of the factory workers, set out to investigate the average distance piecers walked in a given day. After taking note of the various dimensions of the mules typically found in the greater Manchester district, the number of strokes of a machine per minute, and the expected number of breakages of the threads at each stroke, he computed that distances travelled in excess of 30 mi (>45km) would not be uncommon.

In 1864 Woolhouse presented the problem from a mathematical point of view as follows in a publication in *The Assurance Magazine and Journal of the Institute of Actuaries* [12]. We henceforth refer to the problem to determine the walking distance of a piecer as *Woolhouse's problem*. Woolhouse solves the problem using a model where the piecer starts at a uniformly chosen point behind the mule and calculates the required walking distance during one stroke of the mule with N uniformly distributed broken threads. In his words [12]:

> "*Supposing n points to be taken promiscuously on a line of a given length, and that a person stationed somewhere on the line is required to proceed to all the points by the shortest route, determine the average distance that he may be expected to travel*".

As Woolhouse's model only considers one stroke of the mule, the model only describes the actual behaviour of the piecer in a limited way, which reduces the adequacy of his results. It would be nicer to model the situation where the piecer walks back and forth the mule a number of times. However, this is tricky to model with classical probability theory.

The actual behaviour of the piecer can, instead, be very neatly modelled using probabilistic process formalisms. In this particular case, we use mCRL2 [3]. Using a recently developed quantitative modal logic [6] the average walking distances can be easily expressed. By solving the modal formulas on the behavioural models the required results are obtained.

In Sect. 2 of this paper, we set out to reformulate Woolhouse's model with a small change, which we believe mends a minor aberration of the original model. We give an equivalent process description for this model, which additionally enables us to analyse the situation where a piecer walks back and forth along the mule during multiple strokes.

Woolhouse's approach is not truly natural as he assumes a fixed number N of broken threads per stroke. Therefore, in Sect. 3, we consider a more natural model where each thread can break with equal probability. This may lead to the situation that sometimes no threads break, and, very rarely, every thread breaks. This model is computationally expensive because exponentially many breakage patterns must be considered. To cope with the complexity of this new model, we introduce an alternative model that is more optimal, yet remains strongly probabilistically bisimilar to the expensive model. Using this equivalent model we can make nice assessments of the average walking distances of the piecers. Our analysis, reflected upon in the last section, indicates that Woolhouse's model tends to overestimate the walking distances.

We provided an analysis in this paper using mCRL2 and quantitative modal formulas. However, there are other probabilistic process tools using which similar analyses can be done. Typical tools are Storm [8], Prism [9] and Modest [7].

Katoenpoets. This paper is especially written for the 60th birthday of Joost-Pieter Katoen. Joost-Pieter's last name in Dutch is not common and means 'cotton'. This is one motivation for re-investigating the cotton-spinning problem of 1864. Another is that this problem is about both behaviour and probabilities, which are the most important ingredients in the research of Joost-Pieter.

2   Woolhouse's Model

Woolhouse provides an answer to his problem in [12]. We explain Woolhouse's approach but give our own probabilistic model which deviates from Woolhouse's formulation as he slightly miscounts the number of breakage patterns. But the models are very close, especially for large mules. The probabilistic model is quite technical and is not essential to understand the rest of the paper. Subsequently, we provide a model in mCRL2, analysed by quantitative modal formulas, and show that this model exactly coincides with our probabilistic model. The mCRL2 model is more suitable to study the actual distance the piecer walks.

2.1   A Probabilistic Model

Assume the spinning mule has a width *width* of positions and at exactly N of these positions threads break. The piecer stands at a position *pos* and walks either to the left, to the right, or in both directions to repair all broken threads. Following Woolhouse we concentrate on the longitudinal walking distance and ignore that the piecer may also walk back and forth along the threads. Woolhouse uses the letters a, n and P for respectively *width*, N and *pos*. The four situations that can occur are depicted in Fig. 2.

We first consider the situation where the piecer only needs to walk a distance β to the left as all broken threads occur at *pos* or to the left of *pos* and the furthest is exactly β away. This corresponds to the upper diagram in Fig. 2. Note that $\beta \geq N - 1$ as all broken threads must be situated at distinct positions. The probability corresponding to this situation is

$$\binom{\beta}{N-1} \Big/ \binom{width}{N}.$$

If we let β range from $N - 1$ to *pos*, we get the expected distance that the piecer needs to walk in this case:

$$\Delta_1 = \sum_{\beta=N-1}^{pos} \frac{\beta\binom{\beta}{N-1}}{\binom{width}{N}} = \frac{(pos - N + 2)(N\,pos + N - 1)\binom{pos+1}{N-1}}{N(N+1)\binom{width}{N}}.$$

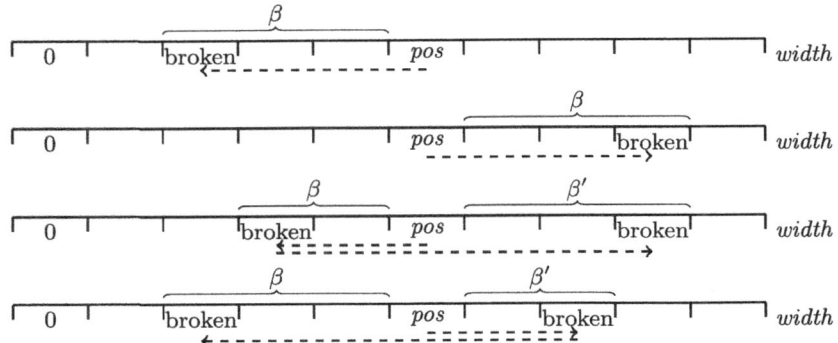

Fig. 2. The four possible walking patterns of the piecer.

The probability that all broken threads are at *pos* or to the right of the piecer, and the furthest thread is at distance β, is the same as above. In this case the expected distance to walk to the right is the following:

$$\Delta_2 = \sum_{\beta=N-1}^{width-pos-1} \frac{\beta\binom{\beta}{N-1}}{\binom{width}{N}} = \frac{(pos + width - N + 1)(aN - Npos - 1)\binom{width-pos}{N-1}}{N(N+1)\binom{width}{N}}.$$

In situations where the piecer finds a broken thread to his/her left at distance β and to his/her right at distance β' and all other threads are in between, has probability:

$$\binom{\beta + \beta' - 1}{N - 2} / \binom{width}{N}.$$

If $\beta \leq \beta'$, this corresponds to the penultimate diagram in Fig. 2. The piecer walks $2\beta + \beta'$. So, the expected walking distance is:

$$\Delta_3 = \sum_{\beta=1}^{pos} \sum_{\beta'=\max(\beta,N-1-\beta)}^{width-pos-1} (2\beta + \beta')\binom{\beta + \beta' - 1}{N - 2} / \binom{width}{N}.$$

Reversely, if $\beta > \beta'$, corresponding to the final diagram in Fig. 2, the piecer walks $\beta + 2\beta'$. So, the expected walking distance is:

$$\Delta_4 = \sum_{\beta=1}^{pos} \sum_{\beta'=\max(1,N-\beta)}^{\min(width-pos-1,\beta-1)} (\beta + 2\beta')\binom{\beta + \beta' - 1}{N - 2} / \binom{width}{N}.$$

The total expected walking distance $\Delta = \Delta_1 + \Delta_2 + \Delta_3 + \Delta_4$ as a fraction of the width of the mule is given in Table 1. The table lists the relative walking distance as a fraction of the width of the mule, when N threads, indicated in the left column, break, and the piecer starts at the relative position indicated at the top. So, if the piecer starts at distance $0.3width$ from the left and 3 threads break, the piecer walks on average a distance $0.6580\,width$. This table is almost the same as the table given in [12] despite the different calculation. It is calculated with $width = 10000$.

Table 1. Walking distances relative to the width of the mule according to the probabilistic model in Sect. 2.1 ($width = 10000$).

N	Relative starting point of the piecer, i.e., $pos/width$					
	0.0	0.1	0.2	0.3	0.4	0.5
1	0.5000	0.4100	0.3400	0.2900	0.2600	0.2500
2	0.6666	0.5853	0.5360	0.5107	0.5014	0.5000
3	0.7500	0.6779	0.6524	0.6580	0.6765	0.6876
4	0.8000	0.7362	0.7302	0.7605	0.8025	0.8251
5	0.8333	0.7772	0.7871	0.8357	0.8952	0.9272
6	0.8571	0.8081	0.8313	0.8931	0.9651	1.0046
7	0.8750	0.8327	0.8670	0.9385	1.0190	1.0646
8	0.8889	0.8528	0.8966	0.9752	1.0617	1.1121
9	0.9000	0.8698	0.9216	1.0055	1.0960	1.1505
10	0.9091	0.8844	0.9430	1.0309	1.1242	1.1821

From this table Woolhouse concludes that the piecer must walk substantial distances. In particular he concludes that the piecer may have to walk more than the length of the spinning mule if the number of broken threads N is high and the piecer starts in the middle. Woolhouse observes that "when this is the case, the piecer would do well to walk backwards and forwards alternately the entire distance" [12].

This indicates a prime weakness in Woolhouse's analysis. He assumes that the piecer starts either at a fixed position, or uniformly distributed over all starting points. But in reality the piecer will start at the position where he or she stopped in the previous round which is unlikely to be uniformly distributed. We provide a model in mCRL2 which allows us to investigate the behaviour of the piecer during multiple rounds.

2.2 Woolhouse's Model in mCRL2

Woolhouse's model in mCRL2 is given in Fig. 3. The process $Mule(pos)$ describes how the piecer repeatedly walks back and forth along the spinning mule to repair broken strands of yarn, where pos indicates the position where the piecer stands between two repair sessions. The action $threads(l)$ with l a list of threads, indicates the current threads of which N are broken according to a uniform distribution. The position of the leftmost broken thread is indicated by $lbt(l)$ and the rightmost broken thread by $rbt(l)$. Our piecer walks left, right-left, left-right,

sort *Thread* = **struct** *fine* | *broken*;

map *N, initial_position, width* : $\mathbb{N}$;
    count_broken_threads, lbt, rbt : *List(Thread)* → $\mathbb{N}$; %*lbt* : leftmost broken thread;
                                                                          %*rbt* : rightmost broken thread.
    no_broken_thread : *List(Thread)* → $\mathbb{B}$;
    binomial : $\mathbb{N} \times \mathbb{N} \to \mathbb{R}$;
    fac : $\mathbb{N} \to \mathbb{N}$;

eqn *width* = 20;
    N = 1;
    initial_position = 10;

var *n, m* : $\mathbb{N}$;
eqn *fac*(0) = 1;
    $n > 0 \to fac(n) = fac(\max(0, n-1)) * n$;
    binomial(*n, m*) = *fac*(*n*)/(*fac*(*Int2Nat*(*n − m*)) * *fac*(*m*));

var *l* : *List(Thread)*;
eqn *lbt*([]) = 0;
    lbt(*fine*▷*l*) = 1+*lbt*(*l*);
    lbt(*broken*▷*l*) = 0;
    rbt(*fine*▷*l*) = 1+*rbt*(*l*);
    rbt(*broken*▷*l*) = *if*(*no_broken_thread*(*l*), 0, 1+*rbt*(*l*));
    no_broken_thread([]) = *true*;
    no_broken_thread(*fine*▷*l*) = *no_broken_thread*(*l*);
    no_broken_thread(*broken*▷*l*) = *false*;
    count_broken_threads([]) = 0;
    count_broken_threads(*fine* ▷ *l*) = *count_broken_threads*(*l*);
    count_broken_threads(*broken* ▷ *l*) = 1 + *count_broken_threads*(*l*);

act *threads* : *List(Thread)*;
    walk : $\mathbb{Z}$;

proc *Mule*(*pos* : $\mathbb{N}$) =
        dist *l*:*List(Thread)*[*if*(#*l* ≈ *width* ∧ *count_broken_threads*(*l*)≈*N*,
                                          1/*binomial*(*width, N*), 0)].
            threads(*l*)·
            ((*pos*≤*lbt*(*l*))→*walk*(*rbt*(*l*)−*pos*)·*Mule*(*rbt*(*l*)) +
            (*pos*≥*rbt*(*l*))→*walk*(*pos*−*lbt*(*l*))·*Mule*(*lbt*(*l*)) +
            (*lbt*(*l*)<*pos*∧*pos*<*rbt*(*l*)) →
                    (*walk*(*pos*+*rbt*(*l*)−2∗*lbt*(*l*))·*Mule*(*rbt*(*l*)) +
                    walk(2∗*rbt*(*l*)−*pos*−*lbt*(*l*))·*Mule*(*lbt*(*l*))));

init *Mule*(*initial_position*);

Fig. 3. Woolhouse's model in mCRL2.

or only to the right to repair the broken strands. The action $walk(d)$ indicates the distance d that the piecer traverses. The process allows the piecer to walk left-right or right-left without enforcing that the shortest distance is taken.

map $Max : \mathbb{N}^+$;
eqn $Max = 50$;

form $1/(Max*width)*\nu X(n{:}\mathbb{N} = 0).$ (
$\qquad\qquad (n \approx Max \wedge 0) \vee$
$\qquad\qquad (n < Max \wedge [true]\ \textbf{inf}\ d{:}\mathbb{Z}.[walk(d)](d{+}X(n{+}1))));$

Fig. 4. The minimal distance covered by the piecer for Max repair rounds.

Table 2. Walking distances relative to the width of the mule according to Woolhouse (i.e., the model in Fig. 3 with $width = 10$ and $Max = 1$).

N	Relative starting point of the piecer, i.e., $pos/width$					
	0.0	0.1	0.2	0.3	0.4	0.5
1	0.4500	0.3700	0.3100	0.2700	0.2500	0.2500
2	0.6333	0.5711	0.5378	0.5244	0.5222	0.5222
3	0.7250	0.6850	0.6883	0.7150	0.7417	0.7417
4	0.7800	0.7600	0.7929	0.8524	0.9057	0.9057
5	0.8167	0.8167	0.8722	0.9532	1.0262	1.0262
6	0.8429	0.8629	0.9362	1.0291	1.1148	1.1148
7	0.8625	0.9025	0.9892	1.0875	1.1808	1.1808
8	0.8778	0.9378	1.0333	1.1333	1.2311	1.2311
9	0.8900	0.9700	1.0700	1.1700	1.2700	1.2700
10	0.9000	1.0000	1.1000	1.2000	1.3000	1.3000

In Fig. 4 a quantitative modal formula is given that provides the minimal average distance, relative to the width of the mule, that the piecer needs to cover to do one round of repairs when performing Max rounds of repairs in total. This is the only formula that we need in this paper, but the quantitative modal mu-calculus is a very expressive formalism using which a large variety of properties can be expressed [6].

Basically, the formula recursively accumulates the distances d in Max consecutive $walk(d)$ actions and divides that by $Max*width$. Our use of a maximal fixed point to specify the recursion is of no relevance and it can be replaced by a minimal fixed point operator since the recursion is guaranteed to stop when n reaches Max.

In quantitative modal logic boolean values $true$ and $false$ are represented by $+\infty$ or $-\infty$. This works fine in this setting as $\vee$ stands for maximum and $\wedge$ for minimum. So, the subformula $n \approx Max$ evaluates to either $+\infty$ or $-\infty$, depending on whether n is equal to Max or not. In the same vein, $n < Max$ evaluates to $+\infty$ or $-\infty$. So, $n \approx Max \wedge 0$ equals 0 or $-\infty$ depending on whether n is equal to Max or not. So, if n equals Max the part after the dot in the formula in Fig. 4 is equal to 0, and if n is smaller than Max it equals $[true]$ $\mathbf{inf}$ $d{:}\mathbb{Z}.[walk(d)](d{+}X(n{+}1))))$.

In this quantitative setting, for an action a and formula ϕ, the box-operator $[a]\phi$ gives the smallest value of evaluating ϕ in target states that can be reached by performing a multiplied by the probability that such an action can happen. This is a natural extension of the box operator in Hennessy-Milner logic. Similarly, $\langle a \rangle \phi$ gives the largest value of evaluating ϕ in states reachable via non-deterministic actions a multiplied by the probability. Following common practice in mCRL2, the expression $true$ in $[true]\phi$ stands for any possible action.

We quantify over data values using the infimum (**inf**) and supremum (**sup**) operators. The expression $\mathbf{inf}$ $d{:}\mathbb{Z}.\phi$ is the infimum of all values of ϕ, which can contain the bound variable d, over all values of d taken from the domain $\mathbb{Z}$.

So, formula $[walk(d)](d{+}X(n{+}1))))$ equals the smallest value of $d{+}X(n{+}1)$ evaluated in the states reached by action $walk(d)$. That is, this subformula optimises on the end position of the piecer after the action $walk(d)$ such that the concrete walking distance d plus the distance still to be covered in rounds $n{+}1, \ldots, Max{-}1$.

The formula $\mathbf{inf}$ $d{:}\mathbb{Z}.[walk(d)](d{+}X(n{+}1))$ equals the smallest value for all such distances d optimising the distance travelled from round n onwards. Prefixing this formula with $[true]$, which matches the action $threads(l)$, the value associated with this subformula is multiplied by the probability of a certain breakage pattern l. So, $[true]\mathbf{inf}$ $d{:}\mathbb{Z}.[walk(d)](d{+}X(n{+}1)))$ expresses the expected smallest distance the piecer walks in round n over all breakage patterns l added to the residual walking distance from the point where the piecer ends up.

The whole formula can now be recognised as a standard recursive pattern accumulating the minimal walking distance of the piecer over Max strokes over the mule, and dividing this distance by Max and $width$ to obtain the relative distance compared to the width of the mule per stroke of the mule.

When setting $width = 10$, we can redo Woolhouse's analysis by setting $Max = 1$. The results are listed in Table 2. We make two observations. Compared to Table 1, with $width = 10000$, the distances in Table 2 are more extreme. This is caused by the more even distribution of the broken threads when $width$ is larger. Furthermore, columns 0.4 and 0.5 are equal, as with 10 strands they are symmetrical as no strands exist between strands 4 and 5. We would like to stress that with $Max = 1$ the walking distances predicted by the mCRL2 model coincide exactly with those of our probabilistic model of Sect. 2.1.

It is interesting to see what happens if our piecer repeatedly repairs strands. For this we let the piecer, rather arbitrarily, repair the strands during 50 rounds, i.e., $Max = 50$ in the formula in Fig. 4. The results are listed in Table 3. We observe that, as expected, the initial position is hardly of relevance anymore, and the expected walking distance of our piecer is slightly above the minimal distances of Woolhouse, but well below the maximal distances. Especially, when a large number of threads break, the piecer will automatically walk back and forth to optimise the distance.

Table 3. Walking distances relative to the width of the mule following Woolhouse for 50 strokes of the mule (model in Fig. 3 with $width = 10$ and $Max = 50$).

N	Relative starting point of the piecer, i.e., $pos/width$					
	0.0	0.1	0.2	0.3	0.4	0.5
1	0.3324	0.3308	0.3296	0.3288	0.3284	0.3284
2	0.5664	0.5652	0.5646	0.5645	0.5646	0.5646
3	0.7091	0.7083	0.7083	0.7088	0.7093	0.7093
4	0.7898	0.7894	0.7900	0.7910	0.7920	0.7920
5	0.8358	0.8358	0.8369	0.8383	0.8396	0.8396
6	0.8634	0.8638	0.8653	0.8670	0.8685	0.8685
7	0.8807	0.8815	0.8832	0.8851	0.8867	0.8867
8	0.8916	0.8928	0.8947	0.8967	0.8984	0.8984
9	0.8978	0.8994	0.9014	0.9034	0.9053	0.9053
10	0.9000	0.9020	0.9040	0.9060	0.9080	0.9080

3   A More Natural Model

Woolhouse's model assumes that the number of threads that break at each stroke is fixed. But it seems more natural that every thread has an equal probability to break. This can make quite a difference as sometimes no threads break, and at other times all threads are broken, with a substantial impact on how far the piecer must walk on average. In this section we study this more natural model and find that this further reduces the estimation of the distance the piecer must walk.

map $p : \mathbb{R}$;
$\quad$ *probability* : *List*(*Thread*) $\rightarrow \mathbb{R}$;

eqn $p = 1/10$;

var $l : List(Thread)$;
eqn $probability([]) = 1$;
$\quad probability(fine \triangleright l) = (1 - p) * probability(l)$;
$\quad probability(broken \triangleright l) = p * probability(l)$;

proc $Mule(pos : \mathbb{N}) =$
$\quad\quad$ **dist** $l{:}List(Thread)[if(\#l{\approx}width, probability(l), 0)]$.
$\quad\quad\quad threads(l)$.
$\quad\quad\quad (no\_broken\_thread(l))$
$\quad\quad\quad\quad \rightarrow walk(0){\cdot}Mule(pos)$
$\quad\quad\quad\quad \diamond \ ((pos{\leq}lbt(l)) \rightarrow walk(rbt(l){-}pos){\cdot}Mule(rbt(l)) +$
$\quad\quad\quad\quad\quad (pos{\geq}rbt(l)) \rightarrow walk(pos{-}lbt(l)){\cdot}Mule(lbt(l)) +$
$\quad\quad\quad\quad\quad (lbt(l){<}pos{\wedge}pos{<}rbt(l))$
$\quad\quad\quad\quad\quad\quad \rightarrow (walk(pos{+}rbt(l){-}2{*}lbt(l)){\cdot}Mule(rbt(l)) +$
$\quad\quad\quad\quad\quad\quad\quad walk(2{*}rbt(l){-}pos{-}lbt(l)){\cdot}Mule(lbt(l))))$;

init $Mule(initial\_position)$;

Fig. 5. A more natural model in mCRL2.

3.1   A Simple Natural Model

In this section we present a model where each thread has a probability p to break during a stroke of the mule. This model is depicted in Fig. 5. Note that we have omitted those data types and action declarations that are shared with the mCRL2 model in Fig. 3.

The essence of the model lies in the function *probability*, that for a list of threads calculates the likelihood of the pattern represented by the list occurring. This probability is an easy multiplication of the probabilities p for a thread that is *broken* and $1 - p$ for a thread that is *fine*. The model chooses repeatedly a list of threads l with the indicated probability. The piecer then walks from the current position *pos* to the leftmost broken thread ($lbt(l)$) and the rightmost broken thread ($rbt(l)$) either in a straight or in a back and forward manner, except if no threads are broken, in which case the piecer stays put.

In Table 4 we show the relative walking distance for our piecer as generated by the more natural model for 50 strokes of a spinning mule of width 10. Here we take the probability of a strand of yarn breaking $p = \frac{N}{10}$, which leads to, on average, N threads being broken per stroke to make this model comparable to that of Woolhouse. It should be noted that especially for smaller probabilities of a yarn breaking, i.e., for small values of N, the estimation is up to 10% below that of Woolhouse, while for large probabilities, the differences between the two

Table 4. Walking distance for the more natural model where a thread breaks with probability $p = \frac{N}{10}$ (model in Fig. 5 with $width = 10$ and $Max = 50$).

N	Relative starting point of the piecer, i.e., $pos/width$					
	0.0	0.1	0.2	0.3	0.4	0.5
1	0.2919	0.2915	0.2906	0.2902	0.2901	0.2901
2	0.5095	0.5084	0.5080	0.5080	0.5082	0.5082
3	0.6610	0.6602	0.6602	0.6607	0.6612	0.6612
4	0.7601	0.7597	0.7601	0.7610	0.7619	0.7619
5	0.8212	0.8212	0.8221	0.8234	0.8246	0.8246
6	0.8576	0.8580	0.8593	0.8608	0.8622	0.8622
7	0.8789	0.8797	0.8813	0.8831	0.8846	0.8846
8	0.8912	0.8924	0.8942	0.8962	0.8978	0.8978
9	0.8978	0.8994	0.9014	0.9033	0.9052	0.9052
10	0.9000	0.9020	0.9040	0.9060	0.9080	0.9080

models is negligible. The computation of these probabilities is expensive, as there are 2^{width} breakage patterns to be considered for each stroke. In the next section we show how this can be optimised.

3.2   An Optimised Natural Model

We optimise the model from the previous section using the observation that, for the purpose of analysing the distance traversed by the piecer, only the leftmost and rightmost threads that are broken are relevant for our piecer. So, instead of exploring all possible patterns of broken threads we only want to know what the probability $probability(l, r)$ is that the leftmost thread is at position l and the rightmost thread is at position r. The situation with no broken threads is represented by $r = 0$ and $l = width - 1$, whereas the situation with exactly one broken thread is represented by $l = r$. The function $probability(l, r)$ is given by:

$$
probability(l, r) = \begin{cases} (1-p)^{width} & \text{if } r = 0 \text{ and } l = width - 1, \\ & \text{i.e., no thread broken,} \\ (1-p)^{(width-1)}p & \text{if } l = r, \\ & \text{i.e., exactly one thread broken, and} \\ (1-p)^{(l-1+width-r)}p^2 & \text{if } l < r, \\ & \text{i.e., two or more threads broken.} \end{cases}
$$

For the case where two or more threads are broken, we observe that the probability has a factor p^2 because both the thread at position l and the thread at position r must be broken. Furthermore, all threads before l and after r must be fine. There are $width - r + l - 1$ such threads. All threads between positions l and r can be either broken or fine and therefore do not occur in the term. Note

map *probability* : $\mathbb{N} \times \mathbb{N} \to \mathbb{R}$;

var *l, r* : $\mathbb{N}$;
eqn *probability(l, r)* =
        if(l<width $\wedge$ *r<width,*
            *if(l<r, exp(1 − p, l − 1 + width − r) * p * p,*
            *if(l≈r, exp(1−p, width−1) * p,*
            if(l+1≈width∧r≈0, exp(1−p, width), 0))), 0);

proc *Mule(pos* : $\mathbb{N}$) =
        dist *l, r:*$\mathbb{N}$*[probability(l, r)].*
        threads(l, r)·
            $((l{>}r) \to walk(0)·Mule(pos) +$
            $(l{\leq}r{\wedge}pos{\leq}l) \to walk(r{-}pos)·Mule(r) +$
            $(l{\leq}r{\wedge}l{<}pos{\wedge}pos{<}r) \to$
                $(walk(pos{+}r{-}2{*}l)·Mule(r) +$
                $walk(2{*}r{-}pos{-}l)·Mule(l)) +$
            $(l{\leq}r{\wedge}pos \geq r) \to walk(pos{-}l)·Mule(l));$

init *Mule(initial_position);*

Fig. 6. An optimised natural model in mCRL2.

that the probabilities for one and zero broken threads are independent of the values for *l* and *r*.

This leads to a straightforwardly adapted model which can be found in Fig. 6. Again we leave out those parts of the mCRL2 specification that can be found in other tables.

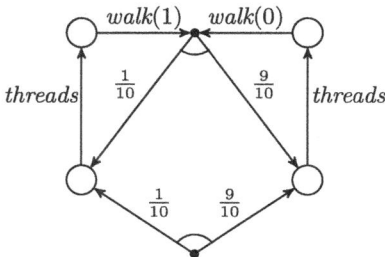

Fig. 7. Explicit walking behaviour of the piecer reduced modulo strong probabilistic bisimulation according to the more natural model (*width* = 2 and *init* = 0).

Although we carefully derived the optimised model, and the calculations are not particularly difficult, we may want to get extra assurance that the natural model and its optimisation are actually the same. Note that the parameters of the action *threads* in both models are different and therefore we remove the parameters altogether so that the models are comparable. Subsequently, we establish that the probabilistic state spaces of both models are strongly probabilistically bisimilar for various instances of the parameters using the algorithm from [4]. This shows that the behaviours of the spinning mules are indeed equal. In order to get an impression of what such a state space looks like we depict the behaviour of a spinning mule of width 2 and a probability of $\frac{1}{10}$ that a thread breaks modulo strong probabilistic bisimulation in Fig. 7. The probabilistic state at the bottom is the initial state, which is bisimilar to the probabilistic state at the top. With probability $\frac{1}{10}$ the thread where the piecer is not standing breaks. Recall that the action *threads* represent a stroke of the mule. This explains why the piecer has to walk a distance 1, indicated by the action *walk*(1), with probability $\frac{1}{10}$ whereas the piecer can stay put, i.e., do the action *walk*(0), with probability $\frac{9}{10}$. As stated above the parameter of action *threads* has been removed.

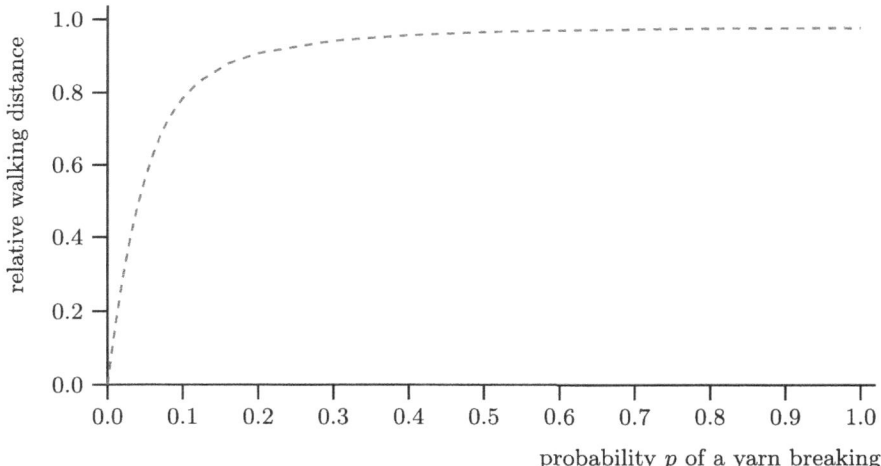

Fig. 8. Relative walking distance according to the more natural model (*width* = 50, *Max* = 50 and *init* = 0).

It is now possible to analyse this model for substantially larger widths of spinning mules. In Fig. 8 we depict the relative walking distance with increasing failure probability per thread for a mule of 50 threads wide. As the initial position is hardly of relevance, we only provide the numbers for the piecer starting at the leftmost position. As in Table 4 we iterate 50 times.

We observe that, compared to Table 4, when on average the same number of threads break, this model of a wider mule predicts slightly shorter walking distances for lower probabilities of breaking. That is, for one yarn breaking on average per stroke, we compare the walking distance with $p = \frac{1}{10}$ for a mule of 10 threads wide, with that for $p = \frac{1}{50}$ for the mule that is 50 threads wide. The values are respectively, ≥ 0.2901 for a mule of 10 threads, whereas this value is ≤ 0.2871 for a mule of 50 threads depending on the initial position of the piecer. This can be understood by noting that for mules with more yarns, broken threads can be closer together.

The walking distances for higher probabilities of yarn to break increase with more strands. This is due to the fact that the relative maximum walking distance for *width* strands is $\frac{width-1}{width}$, which for *width* = 10 is 0.90 and for *width* = 50 is 0.98. If we were to compensate for this the walking distance for lower breaking probabilities would reduce further.

4   Conclusion

We modelled Woolhouse's Cotton-Spinning problem using a process formalism and analysed it using quantitative modal formulas. Our models are quite straightforward and describe the problem in a natural, adequate way. Woolhouse concludes *"the distances travelled (by piecers) exceeded thirty miles (>45km) per day"* [12]. Our models predict shorter walking distances for the piecers, and we must conclude that Woolhouse's approach leads to an overestimation.

This seems in line with the observation by John Fielden, a British industrialist and Radical Member of Parliament for Oldham, around 1825 who stated in a speech *"At a meeting in Manchester a man claimed that a child in one mill walked twenty-four miles a day. I was surprised by this statement, therefore, when I went home, I went into my own factory, and with a clock before me, I watched a child at work, and having watched her for some time, I then calculated the distance she had to go in a day, and to my surprise, I found it nothing short of twenty miles"*.[1]

Based on the data mentioned in the introduction, which stems from the early 20th century, we assume 6 ruptured yarns per 1,320 lines per 15 s, which corresponds to $p = \frac{1}{220}$. Our last model gives a relative walking distance of 0.0761, which, for a mule of 46 m wide, would lead to a walking distance of 8.4km during a 10 h working day. Such estimations depend on the quality of the machines and the cotton, as well as the width of the mule. Although one must be careful to draw conclusions with such uncertainty of the elementary data, it appears that working conditions, especially the average walking distances, of piecers in the early 20th had improved based on technological improvement alone.

It is interesting to reflect a little on the process description languages, quantitative modal logic and the supporting mCRL2 toolset. All models and the modal formula in this paper are available in the example directory of the mCRL2 toolset (www.mcrl2.org). Most calculations have been carried out with exact arithmetic, i.e., using precise fractions, which is very time consuming. The modal formula and the respective process descriptions have been transformed to parameterised

---

[1] https://spartacus-educational.com/IRpiecers.htm.

real equation systems (PRES) that have been solved using numerical approximation. This approach is very comparable to solving modal formulas via parameterised boolean equations (PBES, [3,5]). As it stands the algorithms to solve PRESs are not very mature and are expected to substantially improve in the coming years. A particularly interesting avenue is to solve the PRESs symbolically, which is very successful for PBESs [10], and which is also available in probabilistic model checking tools such as Storm [8] and Prism [9]. Also a similar use of counter examples for PBESs in the context of PRESs may help to understand how the models lead to particular numerical outcomes [11].

References

1. Baines, E.: History of the Cotton Manufacture in Great Britain. H. Fisher, R. Fisher, and P. Jackson, London (1835)
2. Catling, H.: The Spinning Mule. Lancashire County Library (1986)
3. Groote, J.F., Mousavi, M.R.: Modeling and Analysis of Communicating Systems. MIT Press (2014)
4. Groote, J.F., Rivera Verduzco, J., de Vink, E.P.: An efficient algorithm to determine probabilistic bisimulation. Algorithms **11**(9), 131 (2018)
5. Groote, J.F., Willemse, T.A.C.: Parameterised boolean equation systems. Theor. Comput. Sci. **343**(3), 332–369 (2005)
6. Groote, J.F., Willemse, T.A.C.: Real equation systems with alternating fixed-points. In: G.A. Pérez and J.-F. Raskin, editors, *34th International Conference on Concurrency Theory, CONCUR 2023, September 18-23, 2023, Antwerp, Belgium*, volume 279 of *LIPIcs*, pp. 28:1–28:17. Schloss Dagstuhl - Leibniz-Zentrum für Informatik (2023)
7. Hartmanns, A.: An overview of modest models and tools for real stochastic timed systems. In: Dubslaff, C., Luttik, S.P., eds, Proceedings Fifth Workshop on Models for Formal Analysis of Real Systems, MARS@ETAPS 2022, Munich, Germany, 2nd April (2022)
8. Hensel, C., Junges, S., Katoen, J.-P., Quatmann, T., Volk, M.: The probabilistic model checker storm. Int. J. Softw. Tools Technol. Transf. **24**(4), 589–610 (2022)
9. Kwiatkowska, M., Norman, G., Parker, D.: PRISM 4.0: verification of probabilistic real-time systems. In: Gopalakrishnan, G., Qadeer, S. (eds.) CAV 2011. LNCS, vol. 6806, pp. 585–591. Springer, Heidelberg (2011). https://doi.org/10.1007/978-3-642-22110-1_47
10. Laveaux, M., Wesselink, W., Willemse, T.A.C.: On-the-fly solving for symbolic parity games. In: TACAS 2022. LNCS, vol. 13244, pp. 137–155. Springer, Cham (2022). https://doi.org/10.1007/978-3-030-99527-0_8
11. Wesselink, W., Willemse, T.A.: Evidence extraction from parameterised boolean equation systems. In: Ch. Benzmüller and J. Otten, editors, Proceedings of the 3rd International Workshop on Automated Reasoning in Quantified Non-Classical Logics (ARQNL 2018) affiliated with the International Joint Conference on Automated Reasoning (IJCAR 2018), Oxford, UK, July 18, 2018, volume 2095 of CEUR Workshop Proceedings, pp. 86–100. CEUR-WS.org (2018)
12. Woolhouse, W.S.B. : Cotton-spinning problem. Assurance Mag. J. Inst. Actuaries **11**, 224–229 (1864)

Algorithms for Robbins' Problem Using Markov Decision Processes

Léonard Brice⬤, F. Thomas Bruss, Anirban Majumdar$^{(\boxtimes)}$⬤,
and Jean-François Raskin⬤

Université Libre de Bruxelles (ULB), Brussels, Belgium
anirban.majumdar@ulb.be, jraskin@ulb.ac.be

Abstract. In this paper, we consider Robbins' problem, which is a full information variant of the well-known *secretary selection problem*. In this version of the problem, the goal is to minimize the expected rank of the selected candidate among n that are interviewed sequentially, and a decision to select or not the mth candidate needs to be taken right after the interview (so without seeing the last $n - m$ candidates and without recall). We first show how to model instances of Robbins' problem as infinite Markov Decision Processes (MDPs). Then we propose several finite-state abstractions of these MDPs that allow us to approximate the value of the problem for fixed n. While it is known that the full memory of past candidates' values is necessary for optimal expected rank minimization, making the analysis of the problem challenging, we highlight simple memory structures that are sufficient for obtaining near-optimal selection strategies. Additionally, we provide approximate values for Robbins' problem for numbers of candidates n up to 100 for which no good approximations were previously known (the exact value is only known for instances where $n \leq 4$ and numerical approximations were for small values of n not exceeding one digit), for all $n : 5 \leq n \leq 100$, we give better approximation than what was previously known.

Keywords: Robbins' problem · Secretary problem · Markov decision Processes

1 Introduction

Imagine the high-stakes world of professional cycling, where a director of a top-tier team is on the hunt for the perfect new team member. There are a known number n of candidates, and the director must interview them one by one. During the interview, the director asks questions about the candidate's weight, FTP number (Joost-Pieter Katoen, to whom this paper is dedicated, will know what this acronym means), VO$_2$max value, and more. The director is exceptionally

Professor Jean-François Raskin receives support from the Fondation ULB, and Dr. Anirban Majumdar's post-doctoral research is funded by a grant from the same foundation. Léonard Brice is supported by the FNRS through an FNRS aspirant grant.

© The Author(s), under exclusive license to Springer Nature Switzerland AG 2025

N. Jansen et al. (Eds.): Principles of Verification: Cycling the Probabilistic Landscape,
LNCS 15261, pp. 18–45, 2025.
https://doi.org/10.1007/978-3-031-75775-4_2

precise and has a function that maps the candidate's skills and attributes to the interval $[0, 1)$, and this function returns small values for the best cyclists, and it allows to compare the cyclists in a fine-grained way[1]. For example, this allows him to *rank* the current candidate against all previous ones, and as a specialist (the best candidate having rank 1, and the worst one having rank n), he also knows the probability distribution of these values among the set of candidates being interviewed as they are assumed to be randomly taken from a set of cyclists with world tour level.

Because other teams are also looking for the best cyclists, after each interview, the director must make an immediate decision about whether to hire the cyclist and add this candidate to his team, with no opportunity for second-guessing. Furthermore, if the first $n - 1$ candidates are rejected, the director is obliged to hire the last one.

The challenge is to devise a *selection strategy* that minimizes the expected rank of the selected cyclist among the n cyclists that he may potentially interview. In essence, how can the director ensure he is getting the best possible additional team member based on the candidate's rank in expectation among the n cyclists that he can review? And for the more mathematically oriented director (like Joost-Pieter Katoen would be), he might intriguingly ask: what is the limiting value of this expected rank as the number of candidates becomes large, *i.e.*, tends to infinite?

The problem that we sketched above not only tests the director's decision-making skills, but also his ability to strategize under pressure, ensuring the team gets a top-notch cyclist who can help them race to victory. This is a variant of the *secretary selection problem* (the fourth variant [3]), and it is also known as *Robbins' problem*. It still remains open to find an optimal strategy for this problem, as well as to determine the limiting value when n tends to infinity.

Robbins presented this problem at the end of his memorable talk on the International Conference on Optimal Stopping and Selection in 1990 (U. of Massachusetts). It is deep and an easy-to-describe representative of a whole class of problems in Probability Theory, which attract interest for several reasons. This is the class of problems of full history-dependence. Before formally defining Robbins' problem, let us intuitively explain the notion of a strategy on the previous example of selecting the best cyclist.

Here we could assume that the director will apply the following strategy: when interviewing the i-th candidate (with $1 \leq i \leq n$), if the *measure* of the candidate is less than or equal to $2/n - i + 2$, then select that candidate. The above strategy is an instance of a more general class of strategies σ_n^c: select the first candidate whose measure is less than or equal to $c/n - i + c$. Let us elaborate this strategy on a particular instance of the cyclist-selection problem described above.

Assume that the director has 4 interviews scheduled. At the first interview, assume that the value of the candidate is 0.7. Recall that small values in $[0, 1)$

---

[1] Candidates like M(v)DP, pun intended, would be mapped very close to 0 (best value) and should hopefully be selected by the director.

are associated to the best cyclists, this one is rather average and as

$$0.7 > 2/4 - 1 + 2 = 2/5,$$

the director bets to see a better candidate in the remaining 3 interviews, and therefore decides to "not stop".

Now assume that the measure of the second candidate is 0.55. Again, since

$$0.55 > 2/4 - 2 + 2 = 2/4,$$

the director decides to "not stop" and wait for hopefully better candidates to come.

Finally, assume that the third candidate has measure $1/3$. Since

$$1/3 < 2/4 - 3 + 2 = 2/3,$$

the team director decides to "stop" and select this candidate.

Let us note a few remarks. First, let us note that, by stopping now, the director chooses the best candidate seen so far (in this example), so the candidate's *relative rank* is 1. However, the team director has not seen the last candidate, and hence, the right question to ask is the following: what is the expected rank of the selected (3rd) candidate knowing that the last candidate is taken uniformly at random from $[0, 1)$. According to that, the probability that the last candidate is better than the selected one is $1/3$ (in that case, the *absolute rank*, or simply, *rank* of the selected candidate is 2), and the probability that it is worse than the selected one is $2/3$ (in that case, the rank of the selected candidate is 1). Therefore, the expected rank of the selected candidate is:

$$1/3.2 + 2/3.1 = 4/3 = 1.33.$$

Now, let us take the time here to note that it is also mathematically relevant to ask the following question: what is the expected rank of the candidate selected by the strategy $\sigma_n^{c=2}$. Further, one can also ask how this expected rank evolve as $n \to \infty$. Both of these problems for the class of strategies σ_n^c have been studied in details in the paper [5]. We also note that the straightforward strategy described above does not utilize the entire history of the values of the candidates observed so far. Consequently, this strategy cannot be optimal regardless of the value of c, since, as shown in [6], an optimal strategy for the Robbins' problem needs to fully depend on the history of the measure of the candidates seen so far.

We now formally define the Robbins' problem and the relevant notations.

Definition of Robbins' Problem. Let $n \in \mathbb{N}$ be a fixed natural number, and let $X_1, X_2, \cdots, X_n$ be independent and identically distributed (i.i.d.) random variables uniform on $[0, 1)$. We can observe them sequentially, *i.e.*, in the order $X_1, X_2, \cdots$, and we must select *exactly one* of them. A selection is only possible at the time of observation, and if X_m is selected, then the decision is irrevocable and the game is finished. At step n we see the whole picture, and if we have selected X_m, with $1 \leq m \leq n$, then we occur the loss

$$L_m = \sum_{j=1}^{n} \mathbb{1}\{X_j \leq X_m\}, \tag{1}$$

where $\mathbb{1}\{A\}$ is the *indicator function* of the event A, formally: $\mathbb{1}\{x\} = 1$ if $x \in A$, and otherwise $\mathbb{1}\{x\} = 0$.

In other words, if we denote the increasing order statistics of the X_j by

$$X_{1,n} \leq X_{2,n} \leq \cdots \leq X_{n,n} \tag{2}$$

and if we have chosen $X = X_{j,n}$, then our loss is j.

Note that we see the *values* and not only their relative ranks, but the *loss is the rank* of the accepted observation! At time n, the random variable L_m becomes deterministic, taking as value the final rank of X_m among the whole sample $X_1, X_2, \cdots, X_n$. If we must choose exactly one variable, what sequential strategy will minimize the expected loss?[2]

A *strategy* σ_n, for a fixed $n \in \mathbb{N}$, is a function that, given a sequence of numbers from $[0,1)$ of length less than or equal to n, decides to accept the last value (or, to continue) using STOP (resp., ¬STOP), with the additional condition that σ_n must accept exactly one number along all possible n-length sequences. Formally,

$$\sigma_n : [0,1)^{\leq n} \rightarrow \{\text{STOP}, \neg\text{STOP}\},$$

such that $\forall x_1, \ldots, x_n \in [0,1)^n$: $\exists j \leq n : \sigma(x_1 \ldots x_j) = $ STOP; and for all $j' < j, \sigma(x_1 \ldots x_{j'}) = \neg$STOP. A *solution* of Robbins' problem is then an *optimal strategy* σ_n^* that minimizes the expected loss:

$$\mathbb{E}^{\sigma_n^*}(L) = \inf_{\sigma_n} \mathbb{E}^{\sigma_n}(L) = v_n.$$

We also note that solving Robbins' problem for the uniform distribution will also mean solving it for any absolute continuous distribution F. Indeed, then we have a one-to-one correspondence between $X_1, \cdots, X_n$ and $F(X_1), \cdots, F(X_n)$. Since $\mathbb{P}(F(X) \leq y) = \mathbb{P}(X \leq F^{-1}(y))$, and the latter follows the distribution function F, it equals $F(F^{-1}(y)) = y$, *i.e.*, $F(X)$ is uniform on $[0,1)$.

The Challenge of Robbins' Problem as a Secretary Problem. We briefly explain why Robbins' problem stands out in the class of so-called secretary problems. The overall probably best-known optimal stopping problem is the so-called (classical) secretary problem, or "first" secretary problem. This is to maximize the probability of selecting with a single choice, with no recall of preceding observations and with rank information, the "best" rank (rank one) from a sequence of n uniquely rankable objects. Its solution was published in [14].

---

[2] Robbins announced this problem by saying "Finally, here is the problem which I'd like to see solved before I die". Robbins' wish did not realize. He died February 12th, 2001, and unfortunately the main part of the problem is still open today.

The same problem with full information (*i.e.*, the values and not only their ranks could be observed) was solved in [11]. Minimizing the expected rank under rank information was proved to be harder, and was completely solved in [8]. The same problem under full information is the fourth secretary problem, rounding up this two-by-two design of optimization problems, and this is Robbins' problem. We know that its full solution is open, so the "fourth" problem already presents a particular challenge in the class of secretary problems.

Known Results for Robbins' Problem. Since for each n, we need only to take n decisions, by backward induction principle, for each n, an optimal strategy must exist. Let v_n denote the corresponding optimal value, *i.e.*, the minimal expected (final) rank.

The following results ((i) to (iv)) are proved in [1,5,8].

(i) v_n is increasing in n.
(ii) The sequence (v_n) is bounded below (trivially by $L = 1$) and bounded above by another known value from a related problem studied in [8], which is $3.869\cdots$. This is one of the variants of the secretary problem (as described in the previous paragraph), where only the rank of the new draw within the current history is revealed and not the exact value. Since seeing the numerical values of the random variables allows us to rank them, obtaining the numerical values provides at least as much information as rank information. Therefore, one cannot achieve better results with rank information than by seeing the X_j. The optimal expected rank for rank information is $\tilde{v} = 3.869\cdots$, which is the upper bound mentioned above. As a direct consequence, the following limit is known to exist:

$$\tilde{v} = \lim_{n\to\infty} \tilde{v}_n \quad \text{exists and} \quad v = \lim_{n\to\infty} v_n \leq \tilde{v}, \tag{3}$$

where $\tilde{v}_n$ denotes the optimal value for n draws under rank-information. Note that the same reasoning applies to obtain an upper bound using memoryless strategies. This approach is summarized in the next paragraph.

(iii) Smaller X_m have smaller ranks. Hence, it is intuitive that the values X_m and the corresponding final ranks L_m (which will be known at time n only) should be positively correlated. Recall that *correlation* is a measure of dependence of one random variable of another one. We can compute it and obtain ([5], (1.6) - (1.8)):

$$\text{as } n \to \infty, \ \forall 1 \leq m \leq n : \text{corr}(X_m, L_m) = \sqrt{\frac{n-1}{n+1}} \to 1. \tag{4}$$

The strong positive correlation described in Eq. 4 suggests proposing a strategy by just looking at time m at the observed value X_m and to select it if and only if X_m is smaller or equal to some threshold $\varphi(X_1, \cdots, X_{m-1}; X_m; n)$. This is a *threshold strategy*. If, moreover, we ignore at each step m all preceding values $X_1, \cdots, X_{m-1}$, then we speak of a *memoryless threshold* strategy[3], or in short ml-strategy. We denote the optimal value obtainable for n observations in this restrained class by $\bar{v}_n$. This strong positive correlation of the values $X_1, X_2, \cdots, X_n$ and their corresponding absolute ranks can be exploited to define a pattern of memoryless threshold strategies. The precise optimal memoryless strategy is complicated to compute (see [1]); however, it is known that a threshold strategy using the threshold function $\varphi(n, m) = \frac{c}{n-m+c}$, i.e., the mth is accepted if this draw is less than or equal to $\frac{c}{n-m+c}$, with $c = 1.9469\cdots$ yields a good approximation. The upper bound obtained with this memoryless strategy is equal to $2.3318\cdots$ when n tends to infinity. So this improves the upper bound that we obtain with $\tilde{v}$.

It is however important to note that it was shown that the memoryless optimal strategy can always be improved, see e.g., [15]. However, so far nobody has proved that the improvement will not disappear as $n \to \infty$. The author in [12] studied a related problem, namely *Poisson embedded Robbins' problem*, in which the optimal limiting strategy is indeed not a memoryless threshold strategy.

(iv) Lower bounds of different levels for v_n, and thus for v can be obtained by a truncation argument (see [5, Section 4]). We say we truncate the loss at level j with $1 \leq j \leq n$, $j \in \mathbb{N}$, if the loss generated by X_m is defined to be equal to $\min\{j, L_m\}$. Therefore, clearly,

$$\forall 1 \leq j \leq n : v_n(j) \leq v_n. \tag{5}$$

Truncating at the level $j = 5$, the authors in [5] obtained the lower bound $L \approx 1.908$.

Intrinsic Difficulties of Robbins' Problem. We seemingly cannot compute v_n for large n as we do not know the optimal strategy in general. It is trivial for $n = 1$, almost trivial for $n = 2$, and still easy for $n = 3$, but that's it as far as we can say "easy". The problem is that the optimal strategy is *fully history dependent*, which means that the optimal strategy depends at each step m on the complete preceding cloud of values $X_1, X_2, \cdots, X_{m-1}$. The order in which the points arrived is irrelevant. This is why it is the "cloud" $\{X_1, X_2, \cdots, X_{m-1}\}$ of the history which counts. The full history dependence is proved in [6].

From a decision-theoretical point of view, the interpretation of full history-dependence is as follows. There is no sufficient statistic for optimal decisions other than the whole history itself, that is, the cloud of all points in $[0, 1)$ seen so far. This is not necessarily a serious problem for classes of problems where the influence of the history on the currently observed process can be shown to become irrelevant sufficiently quickly. However, Robbins' problem is a representative in the class of fully history-dependent problems where this asymptotic irrelevance is not clear.

---

[3] In the community of applied probability, where Robbins' problem originates, such strategies are referred to as *memoryless threshold strategies*. However, in the Formal Methods community, we refer to them as *counting strategies*, as the threshold used depends on the round number.

To understand the difficulty to compute the optimal strategy for n points and the corresponding value v_n precisely, we refer to Figure 1-Figure 4 of [10]. The authors of [10] coped with the challenge to solve the problem precisely for $n = 4$. Their graphs for the composed acceptance regions of the corresponding optimal strategy are complicated and do not show an easy structure.

The idea to compute, for larger n, the v_n by the truncation method, described in (iv) of Sect. 1, is seemingly hopeless. As shown in [5], the storage demands to implement the truncation method increases exponentially in both the number n and the truncation level j. Under the hypothesis that the capacity of computers increases exponentially, this is far away from the double-exponential growth we would need.

These combined difficulties may explain why many authors have stopped working on Robbins' problem. Indeed, not much was contributed to Robbins' problem after the nineties.

In a recent paper [4], several aspects of this full history dependence, as well as their implications, are investigated in detail. The author concludes that the intricacies of the problem require a new approach and argues that deep learning is, for several reasons, a promising candidate for this goal. However, the paper does not contain a concrete description of the architecture of a suitable neural network. This contrasts our present paper essentially, because our approach, based on Markov decision processes, is *concrete* throughout, and enables us to obtain new values of Robbins' problem for a range of interesting n.

Contributions. In this paper, we consider several abstractions of Robbins' problem that lead to finite MDPs solvable with algorithms based on backward induction, as implemented in tools like STORM [9]. Note that, if we consider the clouds simply as the successive states of the decision process, then this sequence indeed forms an MDP. These finite MDPs are useful for at least two purposes. First, when n is fixed, they allow us to compute an upper bound of the value v_n. We will demonstrate in the experimental section that the upper bounds obtained this way are better than the currently known upper bounds, which are derived from memoryless strategies. Second, by solving the underlying MDPs, we obtain strategies that can be practically implemented and whose performances surpass those of the previously known memoryless strategies. Furthermore, from these abstractions, we will highlight some properties that are crucial in the history for playing a good strategy.

Discretization. The first abstraction is a straightforward discretization of the problem: we partition the interval $[0, 1)$ in $d \in \mathbb{N}$ intervals of length $\frac{1}{d}$ and we abstract the draws by the interval in which they fall, and histories by counting how many draws landed in each interval. We show that for a fixed n, when d tends to infinity, this approximation scheme is giving the value v_n. The number of states of the underlying MDP increase proportionally in the number of draws and the number of possible histories of draws, the latter is given by the binomial coefficient $\binom{n+d-1}{n}$. As a consequence, this abstraction can be used only to approach the optimal value v_n for small values of n and d. Still, this MDP can be used to closely approximate v_n for values of n for which no good approximations were known so far. We report on this in the experiments section of the paper.

Note that, $\binom{n+d-1}{n}$ corresponds to the number of possibilities to place, without constraints, n balls in d places. If we limit our interest to single occupations (*i.e.*, conflict-free) only, the number becomes $\binom{d}{n}$. Then it is easy to see that $\binom{d}{n}/\binom{n+d-1}{n} \to 1$ as d goes to infinity. In other words, as d grows, the non-conflict probability tends to 1. This argument can be used to show that this simple abstraction scheme preserves the limit value (see Theorem 2).

Limiting the History. In the second abstraction, we limit the histories, and so the memory, in the following way: instead of remembering the number of draws that fall into every interval in the history, we only consider the intervals of the k best previous draws. This results in an MDP whose size is bounded by $\mathcal{O}(n \cdot d^{k+1})$. While this MDP only achieves the precision of the first approach when $k = n$, we observe experimentally that the value obtained using this MDP, which is proven to over-approximate the true value of Robbins' problem, is close to the value computed with the first MDP even for small values of k (e.g., $k = 2$ or $k = 3$). This implies that remembering only the values of the k best previous candidates allows us to devise a good strategy for stopping on a candidate with a small expected rank.

Handling the Bad Draws Carefully. In the third abstraction, we limit the way we record bad draws. In the finite-state MDP that keeps track of the k-best draws seen so far, defined in Sect. 4, the number of states grows as $\mathcal{O}(n \cdot d^{k+1})$, making it difficult to consider large values for d. As n grows, d must also be reasonably large to approximate v_n sufficiently well. Otherwise, the probability of conflicts in histories increases, reducing precision. Therefore, computing the value for the underlying MDP may become infeasible. However, if we remember the k best draws, it is likely that the values in memory are "good candidates" (*i.e.*, in $[0, l)$). For instance, if we remember the $k = 2$ best draws and have seen j draws taken uniformly at random, the probability that one is above l becomes very small when j is growing. Thus, for large n, it is reasonable to remember only the exact interval of the "good candidates" seen so far. Our next abstraction uses a non-uniform partitioning of $[0, 1)$, with a precise partitioning for $[0, l)$ into intervals of size $\frac{1}{d}$, and only one interval for candidates in $[l, 1)$. This reduces the number of states of the MDP to $\mathcal{O}(n \cdot l^{k+1})$. In Sect. 6, we will report on values for several choices of l, showing that, in practice, as n grows, a relatively smaller l suffices for a reasonable approximation of the value v_n.

Structure of the Paper. In Sect. 2, we introduce the necessary preliminaries. In Sect. 3, we present the MDP of the first abstraction, which discretizes the interval $[0, 1)$ into intervals of length $\frac{1}{d}$. In Sect. 4, we introduce the second abstraction and its MDP formalization, in which only the interval of the k best candidates are memorized in the history. In Sect. 5, comes the third abstraction, in which only the interval of *good* candidates (those whose value is less than l) are precisely recorded. In Sect. 6, we present experimental results. In Sect. 7, we draw conclusions and hint on possible future works.

Missing proofs can be found in Appendix A. All values for $n = 1$ to 100 with $d = 500, 1000$ and $k = 2$, and for the memoryless strategy of [1] are also reported in Appendix A.

2   Preliminaries

We introduce here the definitions for Markov chains and Markov decision processes. The interested reader will find more about those models in [2,16].

A *probability distribution* on a finite set S is a function $\delta : S \to [0, 1]$ such that $\sum_{s \in S} \delta(s) = 1$. We denote the set of all probability distributions on set S by $\mathcal{D}(S)$. The support of a distribution $\delta \in \mathcal{D}(S)$ is $\mathsf{Supp}(\delta) = \{s \in S \mid \delta(s) > 0\}$.

Definition 1 (Markov chain). *A (discrete-time) Markov chain or an MC is a tuple $M = (S, s_{in}, P, \mathsf{Loss})$, where S is a set of states, $s_{in} \in S$ is the initial state, P is a mapping from S to $\mathcal{D}(S)$, and Loss is a partial mapping $\mathsf{Loss} : S \to \mathbb{R}$.*

For states $s, s' \in S$, $P(s)(s')$ denotes the probability of moving from state s to state s' in a single transition, and we denote this probability $P(s)(s')$ as $P(s, s')$. A state $s \in S$ for which the loss mapping Loss is defined is called *final*. We assume here that for all final states s, $P(s, s) = 1$ (*i.e.*, final states are *absorbing*). We denote by $\mathsf{Paths}_M^{\mathsf{Loss}}$ the following set of finite paths $s_0 s_1 \ldots s_n$ in M such that:

- $s_0 = s_{in}$,
- $P(s_i, s_{i+1}) > 0$, for all $i : 0 \le i < n$,
- s_n is a final state, *i.e.*, $\mathsf{Loss}(s_n)$ is defined.

So $\mathsf{Paths}_M^{\mathsf{Loss}}$ is the set of paths in M that start in the initial state of M, and reach a final state. The probability of a path in $\rho = s_0 s_1 \ldots s_n \in \mathsf{Paths}_M^{\mathsf{Loss}}$ is equal to $\mathsf{Prob}(\rho) = \prod_{i=0}^{n-1} P(s_i, s_{i+1})$. Given M, we are interested in the expected loss obtained when executing M, which is noted $\mathbb{E}^M(\mathsf{Loss})$ and equal to:

$$\sum_{\rho \in \mathsf{Paths}_M^{\mathsf{Loss}}} \mathsf{Prob}(\rho) \cdot \mathsf{Loss}(\mathsf{last}(\rho))$$

where $\mathsf{last}(\rho)$ denotes the final state of ρ.

Definition 2 (Markov decision process). *A Markov decision process or an MDP is a tuple $\mathcal{M} = (S, A, s_{in}, P, \mathsf{Loss})$, where S is a set of states, A is a finite set of actions, $s_{in} \in S$ is the initial state, P is a (partial) mapping from $S \times A$ to $\mathcal{D}(S)$, and Loss is a partial mapping $\mathsf{Loss} : S \times A \to \mathbb{R}$.*

$P(s, a)(s')$ denotes the probability that action a in state s leads to state s' and we denote this probability $P(s, a)(s')$ as $P(s, a, s')$. Therefore, if an action a is admissible from a state s, we will have $\sum_{s' \in S} P(s, a, s') = 1$. Otherwise, we will have $P(s, a, s')$ is undefined (denoted by $\bot$) for all $s' \in S$. A *finite path* $\rho = s_0 a_0 s_1 \ldots a_{i-1} s_i$ is a sequence of states and actions such that for all

$t \in [0, i - 1]$, we have $s_{t+1} \in \mathsf{Supp}(P(s_t, a_t))$. We denoted by $\mathsf{Paths}_{\mathcal{M}}$ the set of all finite paths in $\mathcal{M}$.

For an MDP $\mathcal{M}$, a *strategy* is a function $\sigma : \mathsf{Paths}_{\mathcal{M}} \to A$ that maps a finite path ρ to an action $a \in A$. Note that a strategy σ in an MDP induces an MC $\mathcal{M}_{\sigma}$. Intuitively, this MC is obtained by unfolding $\mathcal{M}$ using the strategy σ and using the probabilities in $\mathcal{M}$ to define the transition probabilities. Formally, $\mathcal{M}_{\sigma} = (\mathsf{Paths}_{\mathcal{M}}, s_{in}, P_{\sigma}, \mathsf{Loss})$ where for all $\rho \in \mathsf{Paths}_{\mathcal{M}}$, $P_{\sigma}(\rho)(\rho \cdot as) = P(\mathsf{last}(\rho), a)(s)$, if $\sigma(\rho) = a$, and equals to 0 otherwise. MDPs are sometimes coined as $1\frac{1}{2}$ player games in the literature. Accordingly, we call the agent that take the decisions, and so execute a strategy σ along the execution the *protagonist*.

For a history h, we write $\sigma_{\restriction h}$ for the strategy $h' \mapsto \sigma(hh')$. We also, abusing notation, write $\mathbb{E}(\sigma)$ for the expected loss $\mathbb{E}^{\mathcal{M}_{\sigma}}(\mathsf{Loss})$ obtained by the protagonist when using the strategy σ, that is, the expectation of loss in the MC $\mathcal{M}_{\sigma}$.

3 An MDP Abstraction for Full d-Discrete History

The Exact Robbins' Problem MDP. Robbins' problem can be formalized as an (uncountable infinite) MDP, denoted $\mathcal{M}_n$, where states are the histories of draws received so far, and the set of actions is $\mathsf{STOP}, \neg\mathsf{STOP}$. Whenever the $\neg\mathsf{STOP}$ action is played, a new point is drawn uniformly at random from the interval $[0, 1)$ and added to the history of draws. When the STOP action is played, or when the last draw has been drawn, the expected rank associated with the last draw is returned as a loss. Given a history h and the draw x_i where the action STOP is chosen, we can compute the expected loss by determining the current rank of x_i within the history and adding the expected number of remaining draws that will be better than x_i. Solving this MDP involves finding the best strategy to minimize this expected rank. A part of this MDP is shown in Fig. 1a.

Unfortunately, this MDP contains an uncountable number of possible states, making it impractical to solve directly. To obtain an MDP with a finite number of states that can be solved algorithmically, we partition the interval $[0, 1)$ into $d \in \mathbb{N}$ intervals of length $\frac{1}{d}$ and use the following function to discretize histories:

Definition 3. *Let $d, n \in \mathbb{N}$, the d-discretization function $\alpha_d : [0, 1)^{\leq n} \to \mathbb{N}^d \cap [0, n]^d$ maps histories with $l \leq n$ draws to vectors of d natural numbers as follows: let $h = x_1, x_2, \cdots, x_l$ in $[0, 1)^l$, $\alpha_d(h) := \vec{y}$, such that for every $1 \leq i \leq d$:*

$$\vec{y}[i] = \left| \left\{ j \mid 1 \leq j \leq l \text{ and } x_j \in [\frac{i-1}{d}, \frac{i}{d}) \right\} \right|.$$

In the finite discrete abstraction, each state of the MDP will be a vector $\vec{y} \in \mathbb{N}^d \cap [0, n]^d$ that abstracts the histories so far by counting, for each interval I of length $\frac{1}{d}$, the number of draws in I, along with the interval of the last draw received and the number of draws remaining. As with the infinite MDP, the set of actions is $\mathsf{STOP}, \neg\mathsf{STOP}$. We formally define the MDP as follows:

Definition 4. *For every $n, d \in \mathbb{N}$, we define the MDP $\mathcal{M}_{n,d} = (S, A, s_{in}, P,$ Loss) where:*

- $S = \{(r, \mathsf{last}, \langle y_0, \cdots, y_{d-1} \rangle) \mid 0 \leq r \leq n, \ 0 \leq \mathsf{last} \leq d-1, y_i \geq 0, \ \sum_{i=0}^{d-1} y_i = n - r\} \uplus \{s_{in}, t\}$, *with t being a final state;*
- $A = \{\neg\mathsf{STOP}, \mathsf{STOP}\}$;
- $s_{in} = (n, \vec{0})$ *is the initial state, where $\vec{0}$ is the vector with all entries 0;*
  - *for every $s = (n - 1, m, \vec{y}) \in S \setminus \{s_{in}, t\}$, such that $\vec{y}[m] = 1$ and for all $j \neq m$, $\vec{y}[j] = 0$:*
    $$P(s_{in}, \neg\mathsf{STOP}, s) = 1/d;$$
  - *for every $s = (r, \mathsf{last}, \vec{y}) \in S \setminus \{s_{in}, t\}$ with $r > 0$, and for every $0 \leq m \leq d - 1$,*
    $$P(s, \neg\mathsf{STOP}, s') = 1/d,$$
    where $s' = (r - 1, m, \vec{y'}) \in S \setminus \{s_{in}, t\}$, such that $\vec{y'}[m] = \vec{y}[m] + 1$, and for all $j \neq m$, $\vec{y'}[j] = \vec{y}[j]$;
  - *for every $s \in S \setminus \{s_{in}, t\}$: $P(s, \mathsf{STOP}, t) = 1$;*
  - *all other probabilities are 0;*
- *for every $s = (r, m, \vec{y}) \in S \setminus \{s_{in}, t\}$:*

$$\mathsf{Loss}(s, \mathsf{STOP}) = \sum_{i=0}^{m-1} \vec{y}[i] + \frac{\vec{y}[m] + 1}{2} + r \cdot \frac{2m + 1}{2d} \tag{6}$$

Intuitively, the first expression above counts the number of draws that are strictly before the current one, the second expression is the average of the number of draws in the same interval as the last draw, and the last expression is the expected number of draws that will be smaller among the remaining draws. Lemma 1 formalizes the correctness; the proof can be found in the Appendix A.1. Notice that, such an MDP is a directed acyclic graph. A part of this MDP with $d = 5$ is shown in Fig. 1b.

The *objective* then is to minimize the expected total loss in $\mathcal{M}_{n,d}$.

Lemma 1 (Correctness). *Fix n, d. Let $x_1, \cdots, x_{n-r}$ be the observations seen so far as in the description of Robbins' problem. Let $\vec{y}$ be the d-discretization of the sequence, i.e., $\vec{y} = \alpha_d(x_1, \cdots, x_{n-r})$ and let $x_{n-r} \in [m/d, (m + 1)/d)$. Let $\mathcal{M}_{n,d}$ be the MDP as defined in Definition 4 and let $s = (r, m, \vec{y})$. Then the conditional expected rank of X_{n-r} given history $(\vec{y}, m)$ is: $\mathbb{E}(L_{n-r}|(\vec{y}, m)) = \mathsf{Loss}(s, \mathsf{STOP})$.*

The following two theorems characterize the quality of the approximation that we obtain with this discretization scheme. The proof of the first one is a direct consequence of Lemma 1, whereas the proof of the second theorem is more involved and deserves a detailed argument.

Theorem 1 (Upper-bound). *For every n and $d \in \mathbb{N}$, the minimum expected loss in $\mathcal{M}_{n,d}$ is at least v_n.*

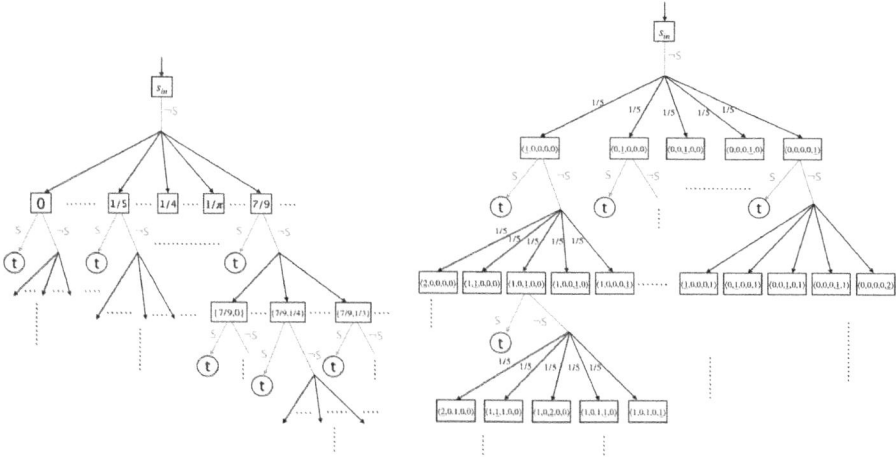

(a) A part of a continuous MDP for Robbins' problem.

(b) A part of a d-discrete MDP for Robbins' problem with $d = 5$.

Fig. 1. Illustration of two types of MDPs: on the left, a continuous one for the exact Robbins' problem, and on the right, a 5-discrete MDP. In both the MDPs, S (resp., $\neg S$) represents the protagonist's action STOP (resp., ¬STOP). For readability, we kept multiple copies of the final state t. In the states of the discrete MDP, the interval of the most recent draw "last" is marked with an underline; and further, for readability, the number of remaining draws "r" has been omitted from the states.

Theorem 2 (Limit-completeness). *For every n, as $d \to \infty$, the minimum expected loss in $\mathcal{M}_{n,d}$ converges to v_n.*

Let us briefly sketch a proof of Theorem 2. For a given $n \in \mathbb{N}$, both the exact and discretized Robbins' problems can be solved using backward induction. On complete branches of the tree of histories where no two draws fall in the same interval-let us call these cases *conflict-free*-the value attributed to the branch in both processes (the exact and the discretized) is the same: the number of points preceding x_n (the last draw) plus 1, and the number of occupied boxes before the box containing x_n plus 1. This result generalizes to conflict-free branches where we decide to stop, if we limit the remaining draws to conflict-free draws: in that case, the expected value when we stop is close in both processes (details are given in the formal proof in appendix). In technical terms, the conditional expectation for conflict-free draws is close in both processes. Thus, both problems start with the same value in the leaves of the tree. As d tends to infinity, the measure of conflict-free branches approaches 1. This implies that as d increases, the optimal losses in the two processes tend to the same value. The formal proof can be found in Appendix A.2.

4 Remembering the k Best Candidates only

The abstraction in Definition 4 keeps track of the full history of the observations seen so far. The number of states in this MDP grows roughly $\mathcal{O}(n \cdot d^n)$, and so it limits our ability to compute the value of the MDP to small n only. To be able to approximate the value v_n for larger values of n, we consider another abstraction that consists in remembering only the counts for the k smallest draws, *i.e.*, the k best candidates. In that case, the state space of the MDP grows only polynomially in n – the number of states is bounded by $\mathcal{O}(n \cdot d^k \cdot d) = \mathcal{O}(n \cdot d^{k+1})$. This second MDP abstraction is defined as follows.

Definition 5. *For every* n, d, *and every* $1 \leq k \leq n$, *we define the* MDP $\mathcal{M}_{n,d,k} = (S, A, s_{in}, P, \mathsf{Loss})$ *where*

- $S = \{(r, \mathsf{last}, \langle y_0, \cdots, y_{d-1}\rangle) \mid 0 \leq r \leq n, 0 \leq \mathsf{last} \leq d-1, y_i \geq 0, \sum_{i=0}^{d-1} y_i = \min(k, n-r)\} \uplus \{s_{in}, t\}$, *with* t *being a final state;*
- $A = \{\neg\mathsf{STOP}, \mathsf{STOP}\}$*;*
- $s_{in} = (n, \vec{0})$ *is the initial state;*
  - *for every* $s = (n-1, m, \vec{y}) \in S \setminus \{s_{in}, t\}$, *such that* $\vec{y}[m] = 1$ *and for all* $j \neq m$, $\vec{y}[j] = 0$:
    $$P(s_{in}, \neg\mathsf{STOP}, s) = 1/d;$$
  - *for every* $s = (r, \mathsf{last}, \vec{y}) \in S \setminus \{s_{in}, t\}$ *with* $n - r < k$, *and for every* $0 \leq m \leq d-1$,
    $$P(s, \neg\mathsf{STOP}, s') = 1/d,$$
    where $s' = (r-1, m, \vec{y'}) \in S \setminus \{s_{in}, t\}$, *such that* $\vec{y'}[m] = \vec{y}[m] + 1$ *and for all* $j \neq m$, $\vec{y'}[j] = \vec{y}[j]$;
  - *for every* $s = (r, \mathsf{last}, \vec{y}) \in S \setminus \{s_{in}, t\}$ *with* $n - r \geq k$, *let* $0 \leq \mathsf{maxi} \leq d-1$ *be the* maximum *index s.t.* $\vec{y}[\mathsf{maxi}] \neq 0$. *Then for every* $0 \leq m \leq d-1$,
    $$P(s, \neg\mathsf{STOP}, s') = 1/d,$$
    where $s' = (r-1, m, \vec{y'})$ *with* $\vec{y'}[m] = \vec{y}[m] + 1$ *and* $\vec{y'}[\mathsf{maxi}] = \vec{y}[\mathsf{maxi}] - 1$;
  - *for every* $s \in S \setminus \{s_{in}, t\}$: $P(s, \mathsf{STOP}, t) = 1$;
  - *all other probabilities are* 0;
- *for every* $s = (r, m, \vec{y}) \in S \setminus \{s_{in}, t\}$: *with* $0 \leq \mathsf{maxi} \leq d-1$ *being the* maximum *index s.t.* $\vec{y}[\mathsf{maxi}] \neq 0$, *the loss* $\mathsf{Loss}(s, \mathsf{STOP})$ *is defined as follows:*

$$
\begin{cases}
\sum_{i=0}^{m-1} \vec{y}[i] + \frac{\vec{y}[m]+1}{2} + r \cdot \frac{2m+1}{2d} & \text{if } m < \mathsf{maxi} \\
\sum_{i=0}^{m-1} \vec{y}[i] + \frac{\vec{y}[m]+1}{2} + \max(0, \frac{n-r-k}{2(d-m)}) + r \cdot \frac{2m+1}{2d} & \text{if } m = \mathsf{maxi} \\
1 + k + \max(0, (n-r-k-1) \cdot \frac{2m-2\mathsf{maxi}+1}{2(d-\mathsf{maxi})}) + r \cdot \frac{2m+1}{2d} & \text{if } m > \mathsf{maxi}
\end{cases}
\tag{7}
$$

The *objective* then is to minimize the expected total loss in $\mathcal{M}_{n,d,k}$.

Lemma 2. *For any* n, d, *the optimal loss of* $\mathcal{M}_{n,d}$ *of Definition 4 is the same as the optimal loss of* $\mathcal{M}_{n,d,n}$ *of Definition 5.*

We intuitively explain the loss function defined above. Here, in the first case, we have perfect information, and hence the loss is the same as in Definition 4. In the second case, we may have forgotten some history that had fallen into the same interval as the last draw, and to capture this, we add the expression $\frac{n-r-k}{2(d-m)}$ to the loss. However, notice that, this quantity is only added when we already have stored k histories, i.e., when $n - r > k$. Similarly, in the last case, we add $(n - r - k - 1) \cdot \frac{2m-2\mathsf{maxi}+1}{2(d-\mathsf{maxi})}$ to count for the draws that may have fallen between maxi and the current interval. Lemma 3 formalizes this intuition; the proof can be found in Appendix A.3.

Lemma 3 (Correctness). *Fix n, d and $1 \le k \le n$. Let $x_1, \cdots, x_{n-r}$ be the observations seen so far as in the description of Robbins' problem. Let $\vec{y}$ be the d-discretization of the sequence, i.e., $\vec{y} = \alpha_d(x_1, \cdots, x_{n-r})$ and let $x_{n-r} \in [m/d, (m+1)/d)$. Let $\mathcal{M}_{n,d,k}$ be the MDP as defined in Definition 5 and let $s = (r, m, \vec{y})$. Then, $\mathbb{E}(L_{n-r}|(\vec{y}, m)) = \mathsf{Loss}(s, \mathsf{STOP})$.*

5 Remembering the k Best Candidates in First l Intervals

In the finite-state MDP that keeps track of the k-best draws seen so far, defined in Sect. 4, the size grows as $\mathcal{O}(n \cdot d^{k+1})$, making it difficult to consider large values for d. Now, intuitively (as well as experimentally, cf. Table 1), as n grows, d should also be reasonably large to approximate v_n sufficiently well (otherwise, the probability of collisions in histories is high and this is when we lose precision), and thus, computing the value for the MDP $\mathcal{M}_{n,d,k}$ may be infeasible.

However, note that if we remember the k best draws, after a few rounds, it is likely that the values we have in memory are "good candidates". Let us say here that "good" means in $[0, l)$. For instance, if we remember the $k = 3$ best draws, and we have seen j draws taken uniformly at random, the probability that among the three best draws, one is above l, is bounded above by $(1-l)^{j-2} + (1 - l)^{j-1} + (1 - l)^j$. As a consequence, when n is large, it is intuitively reasonable to only remember the exact interval of only the "good candidates" seen so far. Therefore, our next abstraction will consider a non-uniform partitioning of $[0, 1)$, with a precise partitioning for $[0, l)$ into intervals of size $\frac{1}{d}$ as before, and only one interval for all the candidates that fall into $[l, 1)$. This significantly reduces the number of states of the MDP, which is $\mathcal{O}(n \cdot l^{k+1})$. In Sect. 6, we will report on the values for several choices of l, and show that, in practice, as n grows, a relatively smaller l suffices for a "reasonable" approximation of the value v_n. The (d, k, l)-abstraction is formally defined as follows.

Definition 6. *For every n, d, every $1 \le k \le n$, and every $0 \le l \le d - 1$, we define the MDP $\mathcal{M}_{n,d,k,l} = (S, A, s_{in}, P, \mathsf{Loss})$ where*

- $S = \{(r, \mathsf{last}, \langle y_0, \cdots, y_{l-1}, y_l \rangle) \mid 0 \le r \le n, 0 \le \mathsf{last} \le l, y_i \ge 0, \sum_{i=0}^{l} y_i = \min(k, n - r)\} \uplus \{s_{in}, t\}$, *with t being a final state;*
- $A = \{\neg\mathsf{STOP}, \mathsf{STOP}\};$

– $s_{in} = (n, \vec{0})$ is the initial state;
- for every $s = (n - 1, m, \vec{y}) \in S \setminus \{s_{in}, t\}$, such that $\vec{y}[m] = 1$ and for all $j \neq m$, $\vec{y}[j] = 0$:

$$P(s_{in}, \neg\mathsf{STOP}, s) = \begin{cases} 1/d & \textit{if } m < l \\ (d - l)/d & \textit{if } m = l \end{cases}$$

- for every $s = (r, \mathsf{last}, \vec{y}) \in S \setminus \{s_{in}, t\}$ with $n - r < k$, and for every $0 \leq m \leq l$,

$$P(s, \neg\mathsf{STOP}, s') = \begin{cases} 1/d & \textit{if } m < l \\ (d - l)/d & \textit{if } m = l \end{cases}$$

where $s' = (r - 1, m, \vec{y'}) \in S \setminus \{s_{in}, t\}$, such that $\vec{y'}[m] = \vec{y}[m] + 1$ and for all $j \neq m$, $\vec{y'}[j] = \vec{y}[j]$;
- for every $s = (r, \mathsf{last}, \vec{y}) \in S \setminus \{s_{in}, t\}$ with $n - r \geq k$, let $0 \leq \mathsf{maxi} \leq l$ be the maximum index s.t. $\vec{y}[\mathsf{maxi}] \neq 0$. Then for every $0 \leq m \leq l$,

$$P(s, \neg\mathsf{STOP}, s') = \begin{cases} 1/d & \textit{if } m < l \\ (d - l)/d & \textit{if } m = l \end{cases}$$

where $s' = (r - 1, m, \vec{y'})$ with $\vec{y'}[m] = \vec{y}[m] + 1$ and $\vec{y'}[\mathsf{maxi}] = \vec{y}[\mathsf{maxi}] - 1$;
- for every $s \in S \setminus \{s_{in}, t\}$: $P(s, \mathsf{STOP}, t) = 1$;
- all other probabilities are 0;

– for every $s = (r, m, \vec{y}) \in S \setminus \{s_{in}, t\}$: with $0 \leq \mathsf{maxi} \leq l$ the being maximum index s.t. $\vec{y}[\mathsf{maxi}] \neq 0$, and $0 \leq m \leq l$, the loss $\mathsf{Loss}(s, \mathsf{STOP})$ is defined as follows:

(i.) if $\mathsf{maxi} < l$ and $m < l$, then $\mathsf{Loss}(s, \mathsf{STOP})$ is (same as Equation (7)):

$$\begin{cases} \sum_{i=0}^{m-1} \vec{y}[i] + \frac{\vec{y}[m]+1}{2} + r \cdot \frac{2m+1}{2d} & \textit{if } m < \mathsf{maxi} \\ \sum_{i=0}^{m-1} \vec{y}[i] + \frac{\vec{y}[m]+1}{2} + \max(0, \frac{n-r-k}{2(d-m)}) + r \cdot \frac{2m+1}{2d} & \textit{if } m = \mathsf{maxi} \\ 1 + k + \max(0, (n - r - k - 1) \cdot \frac{2m-2\mathsf{maxi}+1}{2(d-\mathsf{maxi})}) + r \cdot \frac{2m+1}{2d} & \textit{if } m > \mathsf{maxi} \end{cases} \tag{8}$$

(ii.) if $m = l$, then $\mathsf{Loss}(s, \mathsf{STOP})$ is:

$$\begin{cases} (d - l) \cdot (\sum_{i=0}^{m-1} \vec{y}[i] + \frac{\vec{y}[m]+1}{2} + \max(0, \frac{n-r-k}{2(d-m)}) + r \cdot \frac{d+l}{2d}) & \textit{if } m = \mathsf{maxi} \\ (d - l) \cdot (1 + k + \max(0, (n\text{-}r\text{-}k\text{-}1) \cdot \frac{l+d-2.\mathsf{maxi}}{2(d-\mathsf{maxi})}) + r \cdot \frac{d+l}{2d}) & \textit{if } m > \mathsf{maxi} \end{cases} \tag{9}$$

The *objective* then is to minimize the expected total loss in $\mathcal{M}_{n,d,k}$.

Lemma 4. *For every n, d and every $1 \leq k \leq n$, the optimal loss of $\mathcal{M}_{n,d,k}$ of Definition 5 is the same as the optimal loss of $\mathcal{M}_{n,d,k,d-1}$ of Definition 6.*

We can prove the correctness of loss function as in the previous abstractions:

Lemma 5 (Correctness). *Fix $n, d, 1 \leq k \leq n$, and $0 \leq l \leq d - 1$. Let $x_1, \cdots, x_{n-r}$ be the observations seen so far as in the description of Robbins' problem. Let $\vec{y}$ be the d-discretization of the sequence, i.e., $\vec{y} = \alpha_d(x_1, \cdots, x_{n-r})$ and let $x_{n-r} \in [m/d, (m+1)/d)$. Let $\mathcal{M}_{n,d,k,l}$ be the MDP as in Definition 6 and let $s = (r, m, \vec{y})$. Then, $\mathbb{E}(L_{n-r}|(\vec{y}, m)) = \mathsf{Loss}(s, \mathsf{STOP})$.*

6   Experimental Results

Our experimental results have been obtained using an implementation of the backward induction algorithm in PYTHON3. In principle, we could have modelled our abstractions directly in tools like PRISM [13] or STORM [9], but the underlying MDPs are too large. Indeed, as we will report below, some of the MDPs we analysed have size (number of states plus number of edges) more than 10^{12}. Consequently, the running time for some of the largest MDPs in our ad hoc implementation ranges from several hours to a few days.

6.1   Experiments on d-Abstractions of Section 3

We have been able to achieve almost optimal values for small values of n with appropriate choices of d. For instance, it was shown in [1], that the optimal value for $n = 3$ is $v_3 = 1.3915 \cdots$; and with $d = 500$ and $d = 1000$, we have achieved the values $v_{3,500} = 1.391635988$ and $v_{3,1000} = 1.391593893$. Similarly, in [10], the authors show that $v_4 = 1.4932 \cdots$ (the method being reasonably complex); and we could achieve close values with, for example, $d = 500$ and $d = 1000$: $v_{4,500} = 1.493418067584$ and $v_{4,1000} = 1.493356615167$.

We conclude that our first abstraction is capable of computing (near) optimal rank for any n (number of draws), with appropriate choices for d. However, as noted earlier, the size of this MDP is roughly $\mathcal{O}(n \cdot d^n)$, which is a concern, since for larger n, the choice of d also should be 'reasonably' large (depending on n) for obtaining a 'reasonable' approximation of the optimal rank. It becomes almost infeasible to compute the value of this abstraction for $n \geq 6$, even with precision $d = 100$. In the following, we will see that our second abstraction is more tractable as well as can achieve 'good' approximations for larger n.

6.2   Experiments on (d, k)-Abstractions of Section 4

Consider the case $n = 4$ as discussed in the previous subsection. We observe that the optimal value for $n = 4$ is less than 2. This intuitively implies we can get a 'good' approximation even when we only store the 2 best draws seen so far. For instance, $v_{4,500,2} = 1.49433$ and $v_{4,1000,2} = 1.49423$. Based on this intuition, using (d, k)-abstraction, with smaller values of k (e.g., $k \in \{2, 3\}$), we can achieve values that are close to the optimal expected ranks for larger values of n. In the following, we first compare the optimal values for $n \leq 30$ with different values of

k (w.r.t. $d = 100$) (cf. Figure 2), and second, we report on the values for larger n with $k \in \{2, 3\}$ (cf. Table 1) and will see that, in most of the cases (for $n \leq 100$), we can achieve better values than the optimal values obtained by the memoryless strategy of [1].

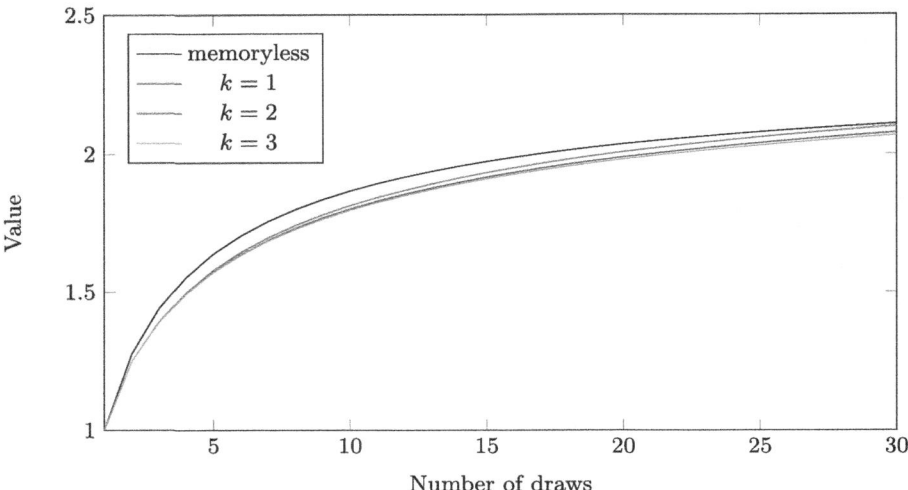

Fig. 2. Values for $1 \leq n \leq 30$ with the memoryless strategy of [1] with the parameter $c = 1.9469$; and for our (d, k)-abstraction – with the parameters $d = 100$ and $k = 1, 2, 3$ – are presented.

Having said the above, Fig. 2 shows a graphical comparison of the minimal expected ranks computed by the memoryless strategy of [1], with the (d, k)-abstraction, defined in Sect. 4, for the number of draws $n \leq 30$, with the precision $d = 100$, and for $k \in \{1, 2, 3\}$. Notice that, with this precision, we always achieve a better value than the memoryless one of [1], for all $k \in \{1, 2, 3\}$.

As mentioned earlier, we would like to clarify that the strategies considered in [1] are not truly "memoryless" in the classical sense. Rather, they are "counting" strategies, meaning they store the information about how many draws remain in the state space, denoted as r. Additionally, from this information, they infer that the ith draw (for all $i \leq n - r$) was in the interval $[\varphi(n, i), 1)$, where φ is the threshold function defined in Sect. 1.

In Table 1, we present values given by our (d, k)-abstraction for different n's and again compare with [1]. For all $n \leq 100$, we could achieve better values than [1] with an appropriate choice of d (e.g., $d = 100, 500$ or 1000) and even with relatively small k (e.g., $k \in \{2, 3\}$). For $n = 500$, with $d = 1000$, $k = 2$, we achieve a value close to that of [1]. Notice that, as described earlier, as n grows, d should also be larger - for instance, for $n = 500$, $d = 100$ is of not much help. All values for $n = 1$ to 100 with $d = 500, 1000$ and $k = 2$, and for the memoryless strategy of [1] are reported in Appendix A.4. From those values,

Table 1. Minimal expected rank for several choices of n, for $d = 100, 500$ with $k = 2, 3$; and for $d = 1000$ with $k = 2$ are presented. Additionally, we also report on the values achieved by the memoryless strategy of [1] to highlight the fact that we get better values with our abstractions for most n, with appropriate d, k.

n	$d = 100$		$d = 500$		$d = 1000$	ml [1]
	$k = 2$	$k = 3$	$k = 2$	$k = 3$	$k = 2$	
5	1.57347	1.57219	1.57231	1.57128	1.57217	1.63833
10	1.80133	1.79654	1.79912	1.79463	1.79886	1.86627
50	2.16781	2.15594	2.15293	2.14325	2.15155	2.17663
100	2.26683	2.25158	2.23382	2.22249	2.23077	2.23940
500	3.10808	3.10754	2.34799	2.33137	2.32697	2.30574

we conclude that we achieve better values for all $n \leq 100$ than the memoryless strategy of [1]. We would also like to mention that, for $d = 1000$ with $k = 3$, our system ran out of memory.

As mentioned earlier, some of the MDPs above are very large. For instance, the MDP $\mathcal{M}_{100,500,3}$ has size[4] roughly 6×10^{12}, and the time taken to compute the value for this set of parameters was 1.6×10^5 seconds ($\approx$ 45 hours). To take another example, the MDP $\mathcal{M}_{500,1000,2}$ has size around 5×10^{11}, and the computation time was approx. 1.3×10^5 seconds. This showcases the efficiency of our implementation.

6.3   Experiments on (d, k, l)-Abstractions of Section 5

The results of this section demonstrate, as described earlier, that for large n's, all k-best draws fall in the interval $[0, l)$ for reasonable choices of l, e.g., $l = d/10, d/5$ etc. with high probability. Therefore, while keeping track of the best draws in $[0, l)$ gives a good estimate of the optimal rank, on the other hand, it is much faster than our previous abstraction. Let us give an example. Consider $n = 500, k = 2$. With $d = 500$, the value is $v_{500,500,2} = 2.34799$ which took around 1.9×10^4 seconds, whereas $v_{500,2000,2,300} = 2.32791$, which is a better value than the previous, and the computation took only 2×10^3 seconds. The latter is still a 'good' over-approximation of $v_{500,1000,2} = 2.32697$ which took 1.3×10^5 seconds to compute. With $k = 3$, the computation of $v_{500,500,3}$ takes up to 11 days.

7   Conclusion

In this paper, we have studied several abstractions for Robbins' problem, modelling them as Markov Decision Processes. These abstractions have enabled us to compute approximate values for instances of Robbins' problem where no good

---

[4] The size here refers to the total number of states and transitions in the MDP.

approximations were previously known, specifically for all values between $n = 5$ and $n = 100$ for which we systematically obtain values that are better than the best previously known upper-bounds.

More importantly, our findings demonstrate that the memory of past draws can be concentrated on the few best draws while forgetting the less favourable ones. Specifically, when we remember the two or three best previous draws, our strategies are almost optimal. This indicates that even though the optimal strategy theoretically depends on the entire history, the optimal value may be effectively approximated with a relatively small number of draws seen so far.

Possible Future Works. First, it could be interesting to explore the problem of computing lower bounds numerically using MDPs, as this paper has primarily focused on methods for obtaining upper bounds. Second, another interesting question is to know whether our discretization approach may also give a new access to approximate the solution of a differential equation derived in [7]. In that article, n is thought to be the realization of a random variable N_n which is the count of i.i.d. events in a Poisson process of rate 1 on an interval $[0, n]$, $n = 1, 2, \cdots$. Hence, $\mathbb{E}(N)/N_n \to 1$ almost surely, and thus, it is somewhat intuitive that the corresponding optimal value should coincide in the limit with our searched value v of the original Robbins' problem. This is indeed true, however, we should mention that the proof is more complicated than one would think, and the complete proof is given in [7]. With this result, we are able to argue with increments of relative ranks on intervals of the form $[t, t + dt)$ and to express the limiting value v as the solution of a differential equation in two unknown functions, one of which is shown to tend to 0 as $t = n$ tends to ∞. The better we can estimate the latter, the closer we come to v. The difficulty of full history dependence therefore does not disappear, but this setting allows for an alternative closed-form approach.

Acknowledgements. We would like to thank Purba Das, lecturer in the Department of Mathematics at King's College London, for helpful discussions. We would also like to thank the anonymous reviewers of this paper for their valuable feedback and suggestions.

A   Appendix

A.1   Proof of Lemma 1

Lemma 1 (Correctness). *Fix n, d. Let $x_1, \cdots, x_{n-r}$ be the observations seen so far as in the description of Robbins' problem. Let $\vec{y}$ be the d-discretization of the sequence, i.e., $\vec{y} = \alpha_d(x_1, \cdots, x_{n-r})$ and let $x_{n-r} \in [m/d, (m+1)/d)$. Let $\mathcal{M}_{n,d}$ be the MDP as defined in Definition 4 and let $s = (r, m, \vec{y})$. Then the conditional expected rank of X_{n-r} given history $(\vec{y}, m)$ is: $\mathbb{E}(L_{n-r}|(\vec{y}, m)) = \mathsf{Loss}(s, \mathsf{STOP})$.*

Proof.

$$\mathbb{E}(L_{n-r}|(\vec{y}, m)) = 1 + \sum_{j<n-r} \mathbb{P}(X_j < X_{n-r} \mid (\vec{y}, m))$$

$$+ \sum_{j>n-r} \mathbb{P}(X_j < X_{n-r} \mid (\vec{y}, m)) \tag{10}$$

Now, for $j < n - r$,

$$\sum_{j<n-r} \mathbb{P}(X_j < X_{n-r} \mid (\vec{y}, m)) = \sum_{i=0}^{m-1} \vec{y}[i] + \frac{\vec{y}[m] - 1}{2} \tag{11}$$

And, for $j > n - r$,

$$\mathbb{P}(X_j < X_{n-r} \mid (\vec{y}, m)) = \mathbb{P}(X_j < X_{n-r} \mid X_{n-r} \in [m/d, (m+1)/d))$$

$$= \int_{m/d}^{(m+1)/d} \mathbb{P}(X_j < u) \cdot \frac{1}{1/d} du$$

$$= d \cdot \left. \frac{u^2}{2} \right|_{m/d}^{(m+1)/d}$$

$$= \frac{2m+1}{2d} \tag{12}$$

Thus, plugging Equations (11) and (12) into Equation (10), the lemma follows. □

A.2 Proof of Theorem 2

Theorem 2 (Limit-completeness). *For every n, as $d \to \infty$, the minimum expected loss in $\mathcal{M}_{n,d}$ converges to v_n.*

Proof. Let us fix $n \in \mathbb{N}$. In the exact Robbins' problem MDP for n, let $\sigma^\star$ be an optimal strategy. In the discretized MDP $\mathcal{M}_{n,d}$, let σ^d be an optimal strategy. By Theorem 1, we have $\mathbb{E}(\sigma^\star) \leq \mathbb{E}(\sigma^d)$. We now prove that $\mathbb{E}(\sigma^d) \leq \mathbb{E}(\sigma^\star) + \frac{(n-1)^2(n-2)}{d}$.

Let us consider the case where draws are *conflict-free*: for each i, we always have $\alpha_d(h)[i] \leq 1$. Let E be the event in which no conflict ever happens. Let us define the strategy σ using backward induction, with $\sigma(\alpha_d(h)) = \mathsf{STOP}$ for every h that already contains n draws, or such that:

$$\mathbb{E}(\sigma_{\restriction h, \mathsf{STOP}} \mid E) \leq \mathbb{E}(\sigma_{\restriction \alpha_d(h), \neg\mathsf{STOP}} \mid E)$$

and $\sigma(\alpha_d(h)) = \neg\mathsf{STOP}$ for every other h (let us recall that $\mathbb{E}(\sigma_{\restriction h, \mathsf{STOP}})$ and $\mathbb{E}(\sigma_{\restriction \alpha_d(h), \neg\mathsf{STOP}})$ are the expected losses if, after the history h, the protagonist stops or does not stop, respectively).

Intuitively: the strategy σ stops on the last draw, because it has to. At the previous draw, it stops if and only if the expected loss when stopping is better than or equal to the expected loss when not stopping. And so on back to the first draw. By construction, the strategy σ is optimal in $\mathcal{M}_{n,d}$ under the hypothesis that E occurs; but without that hypothesis, we have $\mathbb{E}(\sigma^d) \leq \mathbb{E}(\sigma)$, by optimality of σ^d.

We can prove by backward induction that $\mathbb{E}\left(\sigma_{\restriction \alpha_d(h)} \mid E\right) - \mathbb{E}\left(\sigma^\star_{\restriction h} \mid E\right) \leq \frac{1}{2d}$ for every conflict-free history h.

Indeed, let us first notice that, in the MDP $\mathcal{M}_{n,d}$, when the protagonist chooses to stop on the state $(r, m, \vec{y})$ with $\vec{y} = \alpha_d(h)$ such that h is conflict-free, the rank obtained is:

$$
\mathbb{E}\left(\sigma_{\restriction \alpha_d(h)} \mid E\right) = \sum_{i=0}^{m-1} \vec{y}[i] + \frac{\vec{y}[m]+1}{2} + r\frac{2\,m+1}{2d}
$$
$$
= \sum_{i=0}^{m-1} \vec{y}[i] + 1 + r\frac{2\,m+1}{2d}
$$

while the rank actually expected in the continuous MDP is (since the following draws can only reach intervals that are still empty):

$$
\mathbb{E}\left(\sigma^\star_{\restriction h} \mid E\right) = \sum_{i=0}^{m-1} \vec{y}[i] + 1 + r\frac{m - \sum_{i=0}^{m-1}\vec{y}[i]}{d-n+r}.
$$

We therefore find:

$$
\mathbb{E}\left(\sigma_{\restriction \alpha_d(h)} \mid E\right) - \mathbb{E}\left(\sigma^\star_{\restriction h} \mid E\right) = r\left(\frac{2\,m+1}{2d} - \frac{m - \sum_{i=0}^{m-1}\vec{y}[i]}{d-n+r}\right)
$$
$$
= \frac{d - (2\,m+1)(n-r) - 2d\sum_{i=0}^{m-1}\vec{y}[i]}{2d(d-n+r)}
$$
$$
\leq \frac{d - (2\times 0+1)(n-r) + 0}{2d(d-n+r)}
$$
$$
\leq \frac{1}{2d}
$$

This is true in particular for our base case, when $|h| = n$ and $r = 0$, in which case the protagonist has to stop.

Now, when $|h| < n$, i.e. $r > 0$, there are four cases to consider:

1. If $\sigma^\star(h) = \sigma(\alpha_d(h)) = \mathsf{STOP}$, then, as exposed above, we have:

$$
\mathbb{E}\left(\sigma_{\restriction \alpha_d(h)} \mid E\right) - \mathbb{E}\left(\sigma^\star_{\restriction h} \mid E\right) \leq \frac{1}{2d}.
$$

2. If $\sigma(\alpha_d(h)) = \neg\mathsf{STOP}$ and $\sigma^\star(h) = \mathsf{STOP}$, then by definition of σ, stopping was better than or equivalent to continue:

$$\mathbb{E}\left(\sigma_{\upharpoonright\alpha_d(h)} \mid E\right) - \mathbb{E}\left(\sigma_{\upharpoonright h}^\star \mid E\right) \leq \mathbb{E}\left(\sigma_{\upharpoonright\alpha_d(h),\mathsf{STOP}} \mid E\right) - \mathbb{E}\left(\sigma_{\upharpoonright h}^\star \mid E\right)$$
$$\leq \frac{1}{2d}$$

for the same reason as before.

3. If $\sigma^\star(h) = \sigma(\alpha_d(h)) = \neg\mathsf{STOP}$, then let $X \subseteq [0,1)$ be the set of real numbers that can still be drawn, i.e. that are not in an interval that has already been touched. Then, we have

$$\mathbb{E}\left(\sigma_{\upharpoonright\alpha_d(h)} \mid E\right) - \mathbb{E}\left(\sigma_{\upharpoonright h}^\star \mid E\right)$$
$$= \frac{1}{\int_{m \in X} dm} \int_{m \in X} \left(\mathbb{E}\left(\sigma_{\upharpoonright\alpha_d(h \cdot m)} \mid E\right) - \mathbb{E}\left(\sigma_{\upharpoonright h \cdot m}^\star \mid E\right)\right) dm$$
$$\leq \frac{1}{\int_{m \in X} dm} \int_{m \in X} \frac{1}{2d} dm \quad \text{(by induction hypothesis)}$$
$$\leq \frac{1}{2d}.$$

4. If $\sigma(\alpha_d(h)) = \mathsf{STOP}$ and $\sigma^\star(h) = \neg\mathsf{STOP}$, then by definition of σ, stopping was better than or equivalent to continue:

$$\mathbb{E}\left(\sigma_{\upharpoonright\alpha_d(h)} \mid E\right) - \mathbb{E}\left(\sigma_{\upharpoonright h}^\star \mid E\right) \leq \mathbb{E}\left(\sigma_{\upharpoonright\alpha_d(h),\neg\mathsf{STOP}} \mid E\right) - \mathbb{E}\left(\sigma_{\upharpoonright h}^\star \mid E\right)$$
$$\leq \frac{1}{2d}$$

for the same reason as before.

Therefore, in particular, under the hypothesis that the draws are conflict-free, we have $\mathbb{E}\left(\sigma \mid E\right) \leq \mathbb{E}\left(\sigma^\star \mid E\right) + \frac{1}{2d}$. Let us now bound the probability that the draws are *not* conflict-free. For each draw, the probability that one of the r later draws hits the same interval is exactly $\frac{r}{d}$. Therefore, the probability that such a conflict occurs in n draws is:

$$\mathbb{P}(\bar{E}) = \sum_{r=1}^{n-1} \frac{r}{d} = \frac{n(n-1)}{2d}.$$

Let us now note that in the case where conflicts can occur, we still have $\mathbb{E}\left(\sigma\right) - \mathbb{E}\left(\sigma^\star\right) \leq n - 1$, since the possible ranks are $1, \ldots, n$. Therefore, without conflict-freeness hypothesis, we have:

$$\mathbb{E}\left(\sigma^d\right) - \mathbb{E}\left(\sigma^\star\right) \leq \mathbb{E}\left(\sigma\right) - \mathbb{E}\left(\sigma^\star\right)$$
$$= \mathbb{P}(E)\left(\mathbb{E}\left(\sigma \mid E\right) - \mathbb{E}\left(\sigma^\star \mid E\right)\right) + \mathbb{P}(\bar{E})\left(\mathbb{E}\left(\sigma \mid \bar{E}\right) - \mathbb{E}\left(\sigma^\star \mid \bar{E}\right)\right)$$
$$\leq \left(1 - \frac{n(n-1)}{2d}\right)\frac{1}{2d} + \frac{n(n-1)}{2d}(n-1)$$
$$= \frac{n(n-1)^2 + 1}{2d} - \frac{n(n-1)}{4d^2}.$$

We find the inequality:

$$\mathbb{E}\left(\sigma^{\star}\right) \leq \mathbb{E}\left(\sigma^{d}\right) \leq \mathbb{E}\left(\sigma^{\star}\right) + \frac{n(n-1)^2+1}{2d} - \frac{n(n-1)}{4d^2},$$

which enables us to conclude to $\lim_{d\to\infty} \mathbb{E}\left(\sigma^{d}\right) = \mathbb{E}\left(\sigma^{\star}\right)$.   □

A.3   Proof of Lemma 3

Lemma 3 (Correctness). *Fix n, d and $1 \leq k \leq n$. Let $x_1, \cdots, x_{n-r}$ be the observations seen so far as in the description of Robbins' problem. Let $\vec{y}$ be the d-discretization of the sequence, i.e., $\vec{y} = \alpha_d(x_1, \cdots, x_{n-r})$ and let $x_{n-r} \in [m/d, (m+1)/d)$. Let $\mathcal{M}_{n,d,k}$ be the MDP as defined in Definition 5 and let $s = (r, m, \vec{y})$. Then, $\mathbb{E}(L_{n-r}|(\vec{y}, m)) = \mathsf{Loss}(s, \mathsf{STOP})$.*

Proof.

$$\mathbb{E}(L_{n-r}|(\vec{y}, m)) = 1 + \sum_{j<n-r} \mathbb{P}(X_j < X_{n-r} \mid (\vec{y}, m))$$

$$+ \sum_{j>n-r} \mathbb{P}(X_j < X_{n-r} \mid (\vec{y}, m)) \qquad (13)$$

Let $0 \leq \mathsf{maxi} \leq d-1$ be the *maximum* index s.t. $\vec{y}[\mathsf{maxi}] \neq 0$. Then, if $m < \mathsf{maxi}$, we have perfect (w.r.t. d-discretization) history, and thus the proof is the same as for Lemma 1. It is also the same when $n - r < k$.

When $n - r > k$, there are two possibilities:

(i) if $m = \mathsf{maxi}$, we may have forgotten some histories (w.r.t. d-discretization). Then, for $j < n - r$,

$$\mathbb{P}(X_j < X_{n-r} \mid (\vec{y}, m))$$

$$= \sum_{i=0}^{m-1} \vec{y}[i] + \frac{\vec{y}[m] - 1}{2} \qquad (14)$$

$$+ (n - r - k) \cdot \mathbb{P}(X_j < X_{n-r} \mid X_{n-r} \in [m/d, (m+1)/d); X_j > m/d)$$

The last probability above evaluates to:

$$= \int_{m/d}^{(m+1)/d} \mathbb{P}(X_j < u \mid X_j \in [m/d, (m+1)/d)) \cdot \frac{1}{1/d}$$

$$= d \cdot \int_{m/d}^{(m+1)/d} \frac{u - m/d}{1 - m/d} du$$

$$= \frac{1}{2(d-m)}. \qquad (15)$$

(ii) If $m > \text{maxi}$, again, we may have forgotten some histories. For $j < n - r$,

$$\mathbb{P}(X_j < X_{n-r} \mid (\vec{y}, m))$$
$$= k + (n - r - k - 1) \cdot \mathbb{P}(X_j < X_{n-r} \mid X_{n-r} \in [m/d, (m+1)/d); X_j > \text{maxi}/d) \tag{16}$$

Similar to the previous case, the last probability above evaluates to $\frac{2m - 2\text{maxi} + 1}{2(d - \text{maxi})}$.
Lastly, for both (i.) and (ii.), one can show that for $j > n - r$,

$$\mathbb{P}(X_j < X_{n-r} \mid (\vec{y}, m)) = \frac{2m + 1}{2d},$$

similar to the proof of Lemma 1. This concludes the proof of Lemma 3.

A.4 Experimental Results

Below, in Table 2 and 3, we present the values for $n = 1$ to 100 with $d = 500$, 1000 and $k = 2$, and for the memoryless strategy of [1] with the parameter $c = 1.9469$.

Table 2. Experimental results for $1 \le n \le 50$.

n	$d = 500, \ k = 2$	$d = 1000, \ k = 2$	ml [1]
1	1.0	1.0	1.0
2	1.2499999999999998	1.2500000000000002	1.275811749652425
3	1.3916359880000004	1.3915938930000002	1.4406553537397055
4	1.4943354630156864	1.4942292766819876	1.554231487592793
5	1.5723087548475956	1.5721659394269207	1.6383330315011604
6	1.6344823513487399	1.6343105674656457	1.7035992657834345
7	1.686172134541134	1.685981863167616	1.755981689668285
8	1.7297836238112014	1.7295734860288026	1.7991101490119972
9	1.76697396489574	1.7667368261168588	1.8353399442411704
10	1.7991230945455245	1.7988592862297756	1.8662733112166188
11	1.8272910253255565	1.8270040145651623	1.8930418652242904
12	1.8522528957634636	1.8519378867449332	1.9164696896925588
13	1.8745640590980146	1.874224452938298	1.9371724315418803
14	1.8946618448918564	1.8942880399765794	1.955620083731664
15	1.9128629244215691	1.912469614982583	1.9721781798256033
16	1.9294478151453334	1.929033113555414	1.9871356427648257
17	1.9446372244176986	1.9442008003839266	2.000724103173354
18	1.9586227440120254	1.958150441973076	2.0131316053179527
19	1.9715246546331406	1.971031895791245	2.0245125261168546
20	1.983506256178762	1.9829720564818833	2.0349948812329974

continued

Table 2. continued

n	$d = 500$, $k = 2$	$d = 1000$, $k = 2$	ml [1]
21	1.9946168335447256	1.9940766273998967	2.0446857921469492
22	2.0050126252872933	2.004429007754717	2.0536756356449932
23	2.0147173693490203	2.014113114384068	2.062041234034737
24	2.023820142205404	2.0231888014277133	2.069848336720526
25	2.0323804104347856	2.0317276626270973	2.0771535713006974
26	2.0404460915509004	2.039760355623614	2.0840059927096384
27	2.0480519382492663	2.047346308631722	2.0904483243764487
28	2.055253315368793	2.0545165201468136	2.096517960965898
29	2.06208187185613	2.0613137896711415	2.102247784792144
30	2.0685719367088833	2.067757442307411	2.107666835325425
31	2.074725546620756	2.073881232353291	2.1128008619181733
32	2.080552090798597	2.079715772444592	2.1176727829861313
33	2.0861324542984554	2.085268062249322	2.122303069719032
34	2.0914836026504333	2.0905692353602703	2.126710068493654
35	2.0965752795598043	2.0956356458969365	2.1309102731861964
36	2.1014658624003406	2.1004766720179333	2.134918556292427
37	2.1061101650196856	2.105115614550015	2.1387483659904847
38	2.110596788039435	2.109565837909762	2.1424118948965996
39	2.1148757196539156	2.1138301822128676	2.145920225175551
40	2.1190202503144295	2.1179304022088483	2.1492834538064725
41	2.1229810323778056	2.1218736663243685	2.152510801118974
42	2.1268059866429283	2.1256706784889094	2.1556107051654525
43	2.1304854284787837	2.1293242358747553	2.1585909040533426
44	2.134032347521156	2.132833017064226	2.1614585080030713
45	2.13747622844871	2.1362219755168406	2.1642200626062627
46	2.1407624248039046	2.139503475176765	2.1668816045206576
47	2.143947259608725	2.142680408893137	2.1694487106425955
48	2.147055594572068	2.145737152434097	2.171926541636693
49	2.1500380464592714	2.1486924123422817	2.174319880568634
50	2.1529295415335197	2.151552133002007	2.176633167275941

Table 3. Experimental results for $51 \leq n \leq 100$.

n	$d = 500$, $k = 2$	$d = 1000$, $k = 2$	ml [1]
51	2.1557396454186146	2.1543228280961673	2.1788705290187496
52	2.1584559348776926	2.1570154817019893	2.1810358078749115
53	2.161084374990729	2.159621468892033	2.1831325852783596
54	2.163638906199599	2.1621528943817827	2.185164204044484
55	2.1661360423984997	2.164600746007633	2.1871337881796253

continued

Table 3. continued

n	$d = 500,\ k = 2$	$d = 1000,\ k = 2$	ml [1]
56	2.1685455762131505	2.1669838446058245	2.189044260732053
57	2.17088052166434	2.1692927235554205	2.1908983599081324
58	2.173156975581998	2.17154464226942	2.1926986536484128
59	2.1753868074630205	2.173733743540678	2.194447552833746
60	2.1775580313757423	2.1758618646166585	2.196147323270252
61	2.1796539024262835	2.1779381497638695	2.197800096583713
62	2.181684624439103	2.1799527763240447	2.199407880138139
63	2.183671322526126	2.1819134618835685	2.200972566079641
64	2.185625664940774	2.1838237846732547	2.202495939594841
65	2.1875494899093324	2.1856892870308204	2.203979686462775
66	2.1894023170939043	2.1875183857519787	2.2054253999702604
67	2.1911918122871388	2.18929267351782	2.2068345872528328
68	2.192938048928508	2.1910205669424956	2.208208675116513
69	2.1946541480422255	2.1927152484466426	2.209549015389644
70	2.196351190908704	2.19436251693407	2.210856889848733
71	2.1980264943777943	2.1959741277496128	2.2121335147575847
72	2.199638990992517	2.1975551370165314	2.2133800450549295
73	2.201195468448455	2.1990979377684456	2.2145975782220644
74	2.2027167127907497	2.2006025251201864	2.2157871578588773
75	2.2042098404328647	2.2020746269975446	2.21694977699375
76	2.2056830630396034	2.2035241039015827	2.2180863811502745
77	2.2071427242962454	2.204929509280723	2.219197871191554
78	2.208586806232645	2.2063055634755595	2.2202851059607602
79	2.2099723195874885	2.207659567166601	2.221348904734892
80	2.2113220802261164	2.2089930212619016	2.2223900495070885
81	2.212638959237257	2.2102894802454824	2.2234092871113598
82	2.213931024081998	2.2115554172936966	2.2244073312024053
83	2.215201601334469	2.2127971269009685	2.225384864101958
84	2.216450741223749	2.214025083536994	2.2263425385221263
85	2.2176831196177855	2.215222600886031	2.227280979175232
86	2.21890853390639	2.216396082132078	2.2282007842788385
87	2.2201231708577858	2.2175472034019768	2.2291025269638842
88	2.2213018305735686	2.218679753554799	2.229986756593167
89	2.2224395504175263	2.219797600470205	2.2308539999968273
90	2.2235502739618855	2.2208814478953633	2.2317047626308755
91	2.2246364545163155	2.2219459487326625	2.232539529664348
92	2.225703217017416	2.222993377806948	2.233358767000202
93	2.226755182159646	2.2240270358827616	2.234162922234636
94	2.22779692784887	2.225049621939469	2.2349524255591584
95	2.2288278012809983	2.2260483368863495	2.2357276906093704

continued

Table 3. continued

n	$d = 500,\ k = 2$	$d = 1000,\ k = 2$	ml [1]
96	2.229854847099967	2.2270216289339064	2.236489115264133
97	2.2308791883475068	2.227978242294249	2.2372370823984697
98	2.231887015796814	2.228922541255891	2.237971960593348
99	2.2328644036886414	2.2298526426158514	2.2386941048051834
100	2.233816394952243	2.230774435151576	2.2394038569977424

References

1. Assaf, D., Samuel-Cahn, E.: The secretary problem: minimizing the expected rank with iid random variables. Adv. Appl. Probab. **28**(3), 828–852 (1996)
2. Baier, C., Katoen, J.: Principles of model checking. MIT Press (2008)
3. Bruss, F.T.: What is known about Robbins' problem? J. Appl. Probab. **42**(1), 108–120 (2005)
4. Bruss, F.T.: Mathematical intuition, deep learning, and Robbins' problem. Jahresbericht der Deutschen Mathematiker-Vereinigung, pp. 1–25 (2024)
5. Bruss, F.T., Ferguson, T.S.: Minimizing the expected rank with full information. J. Appl. Probab. **30**(3), 616–626 (1993)
6. Bruss, F.T., Ferguson, T.S.: Half-prophets and robbins' problem of minimizing the expected rank. In: Heyde, C.C., Prohorov, Y.V., Pyke, R., Rachev, S.T. (eds.) Athens Conference on Applied Probability and Time Series Analysis, pp. 1–17. Springer New York, New York, NY (1996). https://doi.org/10.1007/978-1-4612-0749-8_1
7. Bruss, F.T., Swan, Y.C.: A continuous-time approach to Robbins' problem of minimizing the expected rank. J. Appl. Probab. **46**(1), 1–18 (2009)
8. Chow, Y.S., Moriguti, S., Robbins, H., Samuels, S.M.: Optimal selection based on relative rank (the "secretary problem"). Israel J. Math. **2**(2), 81–90 (1964)
9. Dehnert, C., Junges, S., Katoen, J.-P., Volk, M.: A storm is coming: a modern probabilistic model checker. In: Majumdar, R., Kunčak, V. (eds.) Computer Aided Verification: 29th International Conference, CAV 2017, Heidelberg, Germany, July 24-28, 2017, Proceedings, Part II, pp. 592–600. Springer International Publishing, Cham (2017). https://doi.org/10.1007/978-3-319-63390-9_31
10. Dendievel, R., Swan, Y.: One step more in Robbins' problem: Explicit solution for the case n = 4. Mathematica Applicanda **44**(1), 135–148 (2016)
11. Gilbert, J.P., Mosteller, F.: Recognizing the maximum of a sequence. J. Am. Stat. Assoc. **61**(313), 35–73 (1966)
12. Gnedin, A.V.: Optimal stopping with rank-dependent loss. J. Appl. Probab. **44**(4), 996–1011 (2007)
13. Kwiatkowska, M., Norman, G., Parker, D.: PRISM: probabilistic symbolic model checker. In: Field, T., Harrison, P.G., Bradley, J., Harder, U. (eds.) Computer Performance Evaluation: Modelling Techniques and Tools, pp. 200–204. Springer Berlin Heidelberg, Berlin, Heidelberg (2002). https://doi.org/10.1007/3-540-46029-2_13

14. Lindley, D.V.: Dynamic programming and decision theory. J. Roy. Stat. Soc.: Ser. C (Appl. Stat.) **10**(1), 39–51 (1961)
15. Meier, M., Sögner, L.: A new strategy for Robbins' problem of optimal stopping. J. Appl. Probab. **54**(1), 331–336 (2017)
16. Puterman, M.L.: Markov Decision Processes: Discrete Stochastic Dynamic Programming. Wiley Series in Probability and Statistics, Wiley (1994)

Revisiting a Pioneering Concurrent Stochastic Problem: The Erlangen Mainframe

Hubert Garavel[1(✉)], Holger Hermanns[2(✉)], and David Parker[3(✉)]

[1] Univ. Grenoble Alpes, INRIA, CNRS, Grenoble INP, LIG, F-38000 Grenoble, France
`hubert.garavel@inria.fr`
[2] Saarland University, Saarland Informatics Campus, Saarbrücken, Germany
`hermanns@cs.uni-saarland.de`
[3] University of Oxford, Oxford, United Kingdom
`david.parker@cs.ox.ac.uk`

Abstract. The present article is an essay in research reproducibility after thirty years. We retrospectively consider a challenging problem proposed in 1994 by Ulrich Herzog and Vassilis Merksiotakis. This problem was about a multiprocessor computer, the Erlangen mainframe, that processes jobs of different priorities and is subject to hardware failures. Using the stochastic process algebra TIPP, a formal model of this mainframe was specified, which makes intensive use of parallel composition, multiway synchronisation between two or more concurrent processes, and compound transitions combining synchronised actions with rates of Continuous-Time Markov Chains. From this formal model, probabilistic results about availability, performability, and proper dimensioning of the mainframe were obtained using the TIPP software tools, which are no longer maintained. We investigate whether the same experiments can be reproduced today using state-of-the-art model checkers such as CADP, PRISM, and Storm.

1 Introduction

The present article was written in honour of Joost-Pieter Katoen and included in a collective *Festschrift* book offered to him on the occasion of his 60th birthday.

The topic of this article has a triple connection with the scientific works of Joost-Pieter Katoen. Firstly, it is about the formal modelling of stochastic systems, to which he has been contributing so actively [4] [20] [8] [9] [21] [29] [46] [32]. Secondly, it uses the Storm model checker, which has been developed by Joost-Pieter Katoen and his collaborators. Thirdly, it builds upon a case study proposed thirty years ago by the IMMD-7 team of Erlangen (Germany) headed by the well-known expert on performance analysis and queueing theory, Ulrich Herzog; at the time, Joost-Pieter Katoen was starting his postdoc in this team, which was striving for formal methods and tools able to overcome the inherent limitations of queueing network performance models, with a particular focus on process algebraic concepts to master complexity — a topic to which the PhD thesis of Joost-Pieter Katoen had substantially contributed [45].

© The Author(s), under exclusive license to Springer Nature Switzerland AG 2025
N. Jansen et al. (Eds.): *Principles of Verification: Cycling the Probabilistic Landscape*, LNCS 15261, pp. 46–74, 2025.
https://doi.org/10.1007/978-3-031-75775-4_3

Over the last three decades, the scientific field of formal methods for performance analysis has flourished, leading to a common understanding of the various ingredients that make up usable formal models of stochastic timed systems. Firstly, one or multiple *state-transition machines* are needed, which may each be extended with state variables and described in various ways, e.g., using process algebras. Secondly, these models often include *rate transitions*, each with some parameter $\lambda \in \mathbb{R}^+$ that corresponds to the elapse of a time period. For Continuous-Time Markov Chains (CTMCs, for short), which we use in this paper, the probabilistic duration of a transition is governed by an exponential distribution with parameter λ. Thirdly, a *parallel composition* operator supports running several of these machines concurrently, possibly forcing two or more machines to synchronise on certain transitions according to *actions* attached to the transitions.

Besides fundamental results, many modelling languages, compilers, and analysis tools have been developed[4] [30] [46]. It is therefore instructive to take a retrospective view and to try applying modern tools to early instances of formal stochastic modelling, in order to observe how science has progressed.

The publications made during the 1990s by the IMMD-7 team in Erlangen contain, in addition to pioneering ideas, many interesting case studies of formal methods for stochastic systems. From this list, we selected the "mainframe" example, which seems to be the oldest example they proposed. This example is described in two workshop papers published in 1994 [37, Sect. 4] and 1995 [35, Sect. 4]. It was formally described in the TIPP (Timed Processes and Performance Evaluation) process algebra and analysed with the TIPPtool software developed at Erlangen [34], which is no longer maintained. At first sight, the mainframe example exhibits suitable qualities: it sounds realistic; it seems detailed enough so that we do not need to invent missing information; its performance analysis generates eight figures that are tempting to reproduce using state-of-the-art tools.

Our challenge is thus formulated as follows: can we formally describe the mainframe example using more recent languages than TIPP, and can we reproduce in 2024 using modern tools the same experiments done thirty years ago with the TIPPtool? To this aim, we considered three well-known software tools:

- CADP[5] [25], which appeared before the TIPPtool, and has been developed since the late 1980s. For many years, CADP has been using LOTOS [43] as its input language (like TIPP, which was also based on LOTOS), but LOTOS has been progressively replaced by a more recent language named LNT. CADP provides most of the TIPPtool functionalities for analysing probabilistic and stochastic systems. CADP received the ETAPS Test-of-Time Tool Award in 2023.
- PRISM[6] [49], which appeared at the same time that the TIPPtool retired, and has been continuously developed since then. It is a widely-used and

---

[4] http://cadp.inria.fr/resources/zoo/
[5] https://cadp.inria.fr
[6] https://prismmodelchecker.org

versatile tool, with support for an extensive range of probabilistic/stochastic models, temporal logics and analysis techniques. PRISM received the ETAPS Test-of-Time Tool Award in 2024.
- Storm[7] [32], a more recent tool developed by Joost-Pieter Katoen and collaborators. Storm supports a broad range of probabilistic models, input formalisms and techniques, and has established itself as a high-performance and extendible tool for the verification of probabilistic/stochastic systems.

The present article is organised as follows. Section 2 presents the Erlangen mainframe, lists the minimal requirements that a specification language should satisfy to model this system properly, and discusses a few errors and ambiguities found in the original papers [37] [35]. Sections 3 and 4 report on the novel formal models that we developed for the Erlangen mainframe in the PRISM and LNT languages, respectively. Section 5 discusses to what extent we managed to reproduce the numerical experiments and the eight figures given in [37]. Finally, Sect. 6 provides concluding remarks and perspectives for future work.

2   The Erlangen Mainframe Modelled in TIPP

2.1   Description of the Erlangen Mainframe

The case study represents a multiprocessor mainframe that is designed to serve two purposes: (i) it has to maintain an important database and therefore has to process transactions submitted by a number of *users*, and (ii) it is used for program development and has to provide computing capacity to *programmers* for compiling and testing their programs. In addition, two interesting features are present:

- *Failures* may cause system downtimes, by making the mainframe become unavailable until it is repaired.
- Two types of *priorities* are built into the system. Database users need immediate reaction, so they *explicitly* have priority over the jobs issued by programmers. Failures cannot be preempted, which implies that they are neither buffered nor delayed; thus, they *implicitly* have the highest priority and take down the system immediately, until repair.

The description of the mainframe is highly modular and hierarchical (see Fig. 1). On the topmost level, the system is the parallel composition of three parts, the *Loads*, the *Queues*, and the *Processors*:

- *Loads*: There are three different arrival streams that put load on the system, namely the database *users*, the *programmers*, and *failures*. Each of these arrival streams produce events according to a given arrival rate. This rate however is not constant, but is instead modelled to vary according to a so-called Markov Modulated Poisson Process [22]. This means that each arrival stream

---

[7] https://www.stormchecker.org

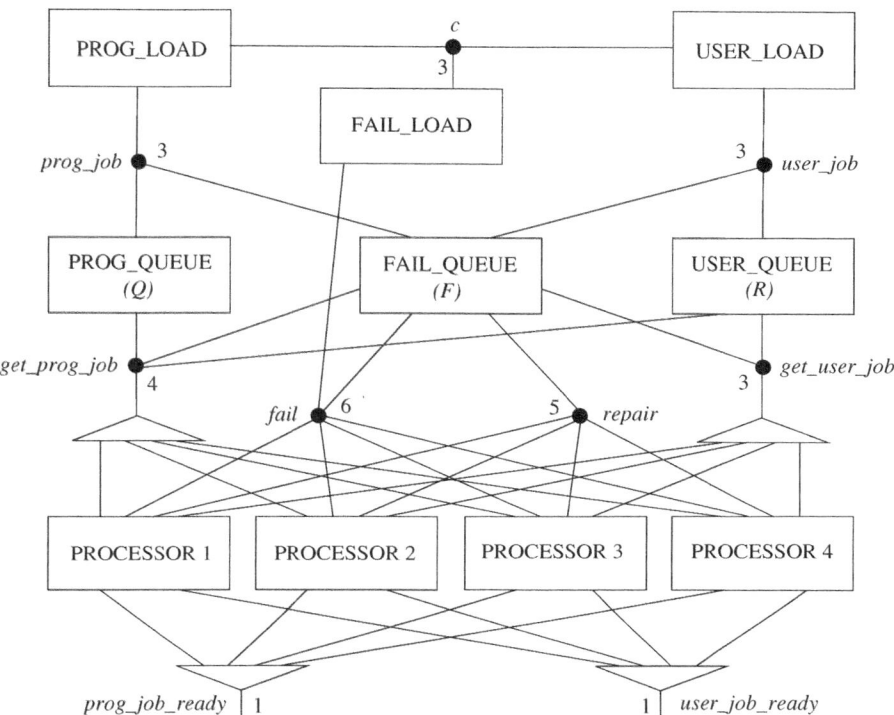

Fig. 1. Architecture of the Erlangen mainframe (black bullets represent n-ary synchronisations and white triangles represent 1-among-4 competitions for synchronisation)

has multiple phases (as in morning-afternoon-evening-night), and changing the phase comes with a change in arrival rate. The phase changes are governed by yet another rate, and happen synchronously across the streams; this is achieved by synchronising the three load processes, that otherwise run independently in parallel, on the phase change.

- *Queues*: The mediation between the events arriving from the loads and the processors is handled by three queues. The *user_queue* buffers the jobs generated by database users; the *prog_queue* buffers the jobs generated by programmers; the *fail_queue* reacts to failure events by triggering repairs. The priority mechanisms discussed above are implemented using clever synchronisations, ensuring that programmer jobs are only served if no user jobs are pending. Both types of jobs are, of course, processed only if the mainframe is not in a failure state.

- *Processors*: This part of the mainframe represents a multiprocessor consisting of four identical processors that run in parallel. The processors synchronise altogether on failures and repairs, meaning that failures affect the entire system, halting all processors, until repair.

The various interactions between the components described above (which will be represented by *processes* in our models) are shown in Fig. 1. Transitions performed simultaneously by multiple processes are modelled using *synchronisation*. In Fig. 1, the black bullets denote synchronisations, annotated by the number of processes participating and by an associated *action* (e.g., *prog_job* or *get_prog_job*). Furthermore, white triangles indicate situations where there is competition between several processes (here, always those modelling the four processors) to participate as a process in such a synchronisation.

2.2   Language Requirements for Modelling the Erlangen Mainframe

Because of its intrinsic features, the mainframe problem can only be modelled properly using languages that satisfy the following five requirements:

(a) It should be possible to express a parallel composition in which $n > 1$ client processes execute concurrently and compete together to establish binary synchronisations/communications with a server process. For instance, the four processors of the mainframe compete to communicate with the *Queues* process on actions *get_prog_job* and *get_user_job*.

(b) It should be possible to express multiway synchronisation (also known as n-party rendezvous), i.e., a parallel composition in which $n > 1$ execute concurrently and synchronise altogether on given actions. Multiway synchronisation is a powerful feature for modelling intricate systems [27] and, as such, is heavily used in the Erlangen mainframe, as illustrated by Table 1.

action	synchronisation pattern	rates
c	3-party rendezvous	φ
prog_job	3-party rendezvous	λ_1, λ_2
user_job	3-party rendezvous	μ_1, μ_2
fail	6-party rendezvous	δ_1, δ_2
repair	5-party rendezvous	β
get_prog_job	4-party rendezvous (3 queues, 1 processor)	α
get_user_job	3-party rendezvous (2 queues, 1 processor)	α
prog_job_ready	no rendezvous (interleaving)	ξ
user_job_ready	no rendezvous (interleaving)	ν

Table 1. Synchronised actions in the Erlangen mainframe

(c) It should be possible to express compound transitions of the form (a, λ), where a is an action (possibly synchronised with actions of other concurrent processes) and λ is the rate of an exponentially distributed delay. Indeed, all actions of the Erlangen mainframe are associated with a rate, as also shown by Table 1.

(d) It should be possible to express compound transitions of the form $(a, \mathbb{1})$, where a is an action and $\mathbb{1}$ denotes a neutral element that means "any rate". This neutral element, which exists in TIPP and other stochastic languages [39] [14] [10] as well, is such that the synchronisation of two transitions (a, λ) and $(a, \mathbb{1})$ results in a transition (a, λ). It is used in many places in the mainframe model, where one or multiple partners of synchronisation can be considered *passive*.

(e) It should be possible to mix, in the same sequential process, both types of transitions (a, λ) and $(b, \mathbb{1})$ — contrary to other formalisms, such as I/O automata, where active and passive actions must take place in different processes, as a means to avoid deadlocks. In the mainframe model, such a mix of transitions occurs in the three load processes and the four processors.

The three languages TIPP, PRISM, and LNT used to formally describe the Erlangen mainframe all satisfy these five requirements.

We have not yet discussed the semantics of synchronising two transitions (a, λ) and (a, μ). This has been a matter of debate at the times when stochastic process algebras like TIPP, PEPA [39], EMPA [10], and others [14] were conceived. Among the various approaches proposed, the TIPP semantics [37, rule $\langle \| \rangle$ of Fig. 1] states that the synchronisation of (a, λ) and (a, μ) produces a transition $(a, \lambda\mu)$. This "rate-product" semantics, which was also adopted by PRISM, TwoTowers [7], and GPA [15], generalises the above requirement (d) when $\lambda = \mathbb{1}$ or $\mu = \mathbb{1}$, assuming that $\mathbb{1}$ is understood as the rate 1.0 — yet, this semantics raises the issue of physical units, as rates λ and μ intuitively correspond to frequencies (i.e., the inverse of a duration), but their product does not.[8] Anyway, for the Erlangen mainframe, the rate-product semantics is not mandatory. Indeed, the mainframe model belongs to a particular subclass of TIPP models because it satisfies the following "one-to-many" property: in any n-party synchronisation (with $n > 1$), only one transition has the form (a, λ) while all other transitions have the form $(a, \mathbb{1})$. For instance, in the case of the *get_user_job* (resp. *get_prog_job*) transitions, the rate α is imposed by the *user_queue* (resp. *prog_queue*) processes, while the other processes (loads and processors) offer the neutral rate $\mathbb{1}$ for these transitions.

2.3   Issues in the Original Papers

While studying the mainframe model, we discovered various problems and ambiguities in the original papers. We briefly present these issues and explain how we addressed them:

(1) In the description of the processing unit [37, Sect. 4.2.2], there was a mistake: in the definition of PW_1, the action $(user\_job\_ready, \xi)$ should be replaced with $(prog\_job\_ready, \xi)$. This mistake was also present in the second paper [35, Sect. 4.2.2].

---

[8] There however is a "stoichiometric" interpretation (involving two reactants and a stochastic reaction constant) that can explain the phenomenon [28,14,11].

(2) The processes $ProgLoad_i$ and $FailLoad_i$ (where $i \in \{1, 2, 3\}$) are not specified in the original papers [37, Sect. 4.1] [35, Sect. 4.1]. As a first approximation, one may assume that they are pairwise similar to the processes $UserLoad_i$ (where $i \in \{1, 2, 3\}$), which are fully specified. Obviously, the rate parameters μ_1 and μ_2 of $UserLoad_i$ must be replaced by λ_1 and λ_2 for $ProgLoad_i$, and by δ_1 and δ_2 for $FailLoad_i$. The situation is more involved for the (c, φ) actions present in the $UserLoad_i$ processes. If one assumes that $ProgLoad_i$ and $FailLoad_i$ also propose these actions (c, φ), the "one-to-many" property is violated: the parallel composition of the load processes with 3-party synchronisation on c (which is explicitly mentioned in the original papers) should result, according to the TIPP rate-product semantics, in synchronised actions (c, φ^3). This does not seem realistic, given that $\varphi = 0.00334$: the value $\varphi^3 = 3.726 \times 10^{-8}$ is very small, and would be negligible compared to other rate transitions. By inspecting the source code of the TIPP models for the mainframe, to which we have access, we observed that $ProgLoad_i$ and $FailLoad_i$ propose actions $(c, \mathbb{1})$ instead of (c, φ), thus ensuring that 3-party synchronisations result in actions (c, φ) instead of (c, φ^3). Such a dissymmetry between the three load processes was not stated in the original papers; in our PRISM and LNT models for the mainframe (see Sect. 3 and 4), we use alternative modelling approaches that give the same results, but preserve the symmetry between the three load processes.

(3) There is a 5-party synchronisation on action $repair$ between the failure queue and the four processors. However, the two original papers differ in the way rates are associated to the $repair$ action. In the first paper [37, Sect. 4.2.1 and 4.2.2], the failure queue offers the action $(repair, \mathbb{1})$ while each processor proposes a $(repair, \beta/4)$ action; this violates the "one-to-many" property and, according to the semantics of TIPP, results in a synchronised action $(repair, (\beta/4)^4)$. In the second paper [35, Sect. 4.2.1 and 4.2.2], the failure queue offers the action $(repair, \beta)$ while each processor proposes a $(repair, \mathbb{1})$ action, leading to a synchronised action $(repair, \beta)$. We opted for the latter model, which is simpler and, based on the source code of the original TIPP models, seems to have been used for experiments.

(4) In both original papers, the machine is defined as a parallel composition involving four processors P, i.e., $Machine = Queues \parallel_B (P \parallel_C P \parallel_C P \parallel_C P)$, where B and C are sets of actions to be synchronised. However, in all the source TIPP files, the four processors are replaced by a single (equivalent) sequential process; the rationale behind such a simplification is exposed in [35, Sect. 4.3]: it reduces the size of the model's state space, but at the risk of potentially introducing errors if the modification is done manually. We found such a multiplicity of TIPP models annoying, making it harder to follow each experiment in detail. Instead, we opted for a unique model of the mainframe, with four processors composed in parallel.

```
 1   // phase: 1=low, 2=high, 3=idle
 2
 3   const int l_init; // initial phase (1, 2, or 3) for loads
 4
 5   module ProgLoad    // programmer (low priority) jobs
 6       pl : [1..3] init l_init;
 7       [prog_job] pl = 1 -> lambda1 : (pl' = 1); // prog job arrival
 8       [prog_job] pl = 2 -> lambda2 : (pl' = 2); // prog job arrival
 9       [c] true -> (pl' = mod (pl, 3) + 1);      // phase change
10   endmodule
11
12   module UserLoad    // user (high priority) jobs
13       ul : [1..3] init l_init;
14       [user_job] ul = 1 -> mu1 : (ul' = 1);    // user job arrival
15       [user_job] ul = 2 -> mu2 : (ul' = 2);    // user job arrival
16       [c] true -> (ul' = mod (ul, 3) + 1);     // phase change
17   endmodule
18
19   module FailLoad    // failures
20       fl : [1..3] init l_init;
21       [fail] fl = 1 -> delta1 : (fl' = 1);     // failure occurrence
22       [fail] fl = 2 -> delta2 : (fl' = 2);     // failure occurrence
23       [c] true -> (fl' = mod (fl, 3) + 1);     // phase change
24   endmodule
25
26   module LoadPhase   // rate for phase change of loads
27       [c] true -> phi : true;
28   endmodule
```

Fig. 2. PRISM model fragment specifying the load modules

3   Modelling the Erlangen Mainframe in PRISM

The PRISM modelling language provides a consistent formalism for specifying the various different types of probabilistic models that are supported by the tool. The language is also accepted by many other probabilistic verification tools, notably Storm, which we also make use of in the present article, and has established itself as a common format for model exchange and benchmarking [50,31].

It is inspired by the Reactive Modules formalism of Alur and Henzinger [1], taking a slightly simplified version of this language and extending it with support for models with probabilistic behaviour. PRISM models comprise the parallel composition of multiple *modules*, which are able to perform (binary or multiway) synchronisation, thus satisfying the requirements outlined in Sect. 2.2.

The state of a module is described by a set of finite-ranging variables and its dynamics by *guarded commands* of the form $[a]$ $g \to \lambda_1 : u_1 + \ldots \lambda_n : u_n$, which state that if guard g (a predicate over the global state of the model) is satisfied, then an a-labelled transition can occur in which module variables change according to one of the updates u_i. The values λ_i annotate each update u_i with the rate (for a CTMC, as here) or probability (for models with discrete probabilistic semantics) with which it occurs.

Fig. 2 shows a fragment of the PRISM model, namely, four simple modules that implement the *Loads* processes mentioned in Sect. 2.1. For instance, the module *UserLoad* describes the arrivals process for user jobs (i.e., the *UserLoad$_i$* processes described in Sect. 2). Variable *ul* tracks the phase, which increases periodically via a transition labelled with action c. This is specified by the third command, with the notation $ul'=expr$ denoting that the value of ul will be updated to $expr$ after the transition has occurred. The first two guarded commands, labelled with *user_job*, synchronise with another module representing the *user_queue*. The state of module *UserLoad* does not change when this transition occurs, but its state determines the rate attached to the transition (μ_1 or μ_2, depending on the phase).

In PRISM (as in TIPP), the combined rate of two synchronising transitions is taken to be the product of the individual rates. We often use the strategy, discussed earlier, of making one transition *passive*, with rate 1 (echoing the neutral element $\mathbb{1}$), with the other transition specifying the rate. For example, in Fig. 2, each c transition in modules *ProgLoad*, *UserLoad*, and *FailLoad* is passive (an omitted rate is assumed to be 1) and a separate module *LoadPhase*, without any local state, provides the rate φ. This approach is adopted in this case to permit multiple modules (the three load-related components) to engage in multiway synchronisation (since their phases change simultaneously) with the rate specified separately, for convenience and clarity.

The full model, including the properties, is 250-line long (150 lines if comments and blank lines are excluded)[9]. It comprises 11 modules, which are composed using the PRISM's default parallel composition operator ||, under which modules synchronise on their common actions and can transition asynchronously on others. In doing so, we deviate slightly from the original TIPP model, which composes the four processors asynchronously, allowing them to have common actions such as *get_user_job*, that synchronise only with other modules and not with each other. This is achievable with the ||| operator within PRISM's "**system...endsystem**" construct but, since this is not supported by all tools, we instead use || and include four copies (one for each processor) of actions such as *get_user_job*.

4 Modelling the Erlangen Mainframe in LNT

The PRISM modelling language is not considered as a process algebra, although its parallel composition operators are those of TCSP [12] [41]. As the Erlangen mainframe was originally specified in the process algebra TIPP, it makes sense today to reformulate it using a recent process algebra such as LNT.

LNT [26] [57] [17] is a modern language for describing complex concurrent systems, which derives from the international standards LOTOS [43] and E-LOTOS [44], and therefore combines the best ideas from TCSP and CCS [55] [56]. It also draws inspiration both from functional programming languages and imperative languages, such as CSP [40], Occam [54] [42] [6], and Ada [2].

The following LNT constructs are used to describe the Erlangen mainframe: "**par** $E_1...E_m$ **in** $B_1 \, ||...|| \, B_n$ **end par**" specifies the parallel composition of n

---

[9] The model has been added to the PRISM benchmark suite [50], under the name "erlangen", and all files needed for the analysis done in this paper are available from `https://www.prismmodelchecker.org/files/erlangen/`.

behaviours $B_1, ..., B_n$, which should all synchronise on m events $E_1, ..., E_m$; "**alt** B_1 []...[] B_n **end alt**" specifies the nondeterministic choice between n behaviours $B_1, ..., B_n$; "**loop** B **end loop**" and "**loop** L **in** B **end loop**" specify the infinite repetition of behaviour B, the latter being possibly interrupted by a "**break** L" construct; "**if** V **then** B **end if**" and "**case** V **in** ... **end case**" specify conditionals; "**var** $X : T$ **in** B **end var**" declares a variable X of type T that is local to behaviour B; variables can be modified using assignments of the form "$X := V$"; "E" specifies the occurrence of event E (pure synchronisation); "$E(V)$" and "$E(?X)$" specify, respectively, the emission of value V on event E, and the reception of some value in variable X on event E; finally, "**process** $P[E_1 : C_1, ..., E_m : C_m](X_1 : T_1, ..., X_n : T_n)$ **is** B **end process**" declares a process P of body B with m event parameters $E_1, ..., E_m$ having channel types $C_1, ..., C_m$, and n variable parameters $X_1, ..., X_n$ having types $T_1, ..., T_n$.

LNT, like LOTOS, has no built-in notion of probabilities or rates and, thus, cannot express DTMCs or CTMCs directly. It is nevertheless possible to use LOTOS or LNT to specify and analyse Markovian systems [23] [18] [53]. So far, this has been mostly done in the theoretical framework of *Interactive Markov Chains* (IMCs) [33] and *Interactive Probabilistic Chains* (IPCs) [19], in which the transitions labelled with a rate or a probability are clearly separated from ordinary transitions. The Erlangen mainframe is radically different from IMCs and IPCs since all its transitions are compound (see Sect. 2.2).

In our LNT model, we translate each TIPP transition (a, λ) with $\lambda \neq \mathbb{1}$ to an LNT transition "$a(\lambda)$", where a is an LNT event and λ a rate, meaning that λ is a value emitted on a. Intuitively, λ could be simply a real number but, for convenience, we defined instead a RATE type, the values of which are either real numbers or symbolic names (β, δ_2, μ_2) of rate parameters defined in [37].

In our LNT model, we also translate each TIPP transition $(a, \mathbb{1})$ to an LNT transition "a (**any** RATE)", meaning that some rate value is received on a. The synchronisation rules of LNT, which are those of TCSP and LOTOS, ensure that the synchronisation of $a(\lambda)$ and a (**any** *RATE*) gives $a(\lambda)$, which is the same result as in TIPP when (a, λ) is synchronised with $(a, \mathbb{1})$. Notice that we do not translate $(a, \mathbb{1})$ to "$a(1.0)$", which would probably cause a deadlock according to the synchronisation rules of LNT.

The complete LNT model for the Erlangen mainframe is 250-line long (200 lines if comments and blank lines are excluded)[10]. For instance, Fig. 3 shows how the three load processes are described in LNT.

Although the encoding of rates in compound transitions is radically different from the IMC theory, we get here the same benefits as for the IMC approach: to describe and analyse stochastic systems, we can apply a "classical" process algebra (i.e., LNT or LOTOS), keeping its semantics unchanged and reusing its software tools without modification. Such a systematic translation to LNT of the original TIPP model is only correct because two conditions hold:

---

[10] All files can be found in the demo example "demo_15" of CADP, which is available from https://cadp.inria.fr/demos.html

```
1   process LOADS [C, FAIL, PROG_JOB, USER_JOB: DELAY] (DELTA1, DELTA2,
2                  LAMBDA1, LAMBDA2, MU1, MU2, PHI: RATE, INIT_PHASE: PHASE) is
3      par C in
4         LOAD [C, FAIL] (DELTA1, DELTA2, PHI, INIT_PHASE)
5      ||
6         LOAD [C, PROG_JOB] (LAMBDA1, LAMBDA2, PHI, INIT_PHASE)
7      ||
8         LOAD [C, USER_JOB] (MU1, MU2, PHI, INIT_PHASE)
9      end par
10  end process
11
12  process LOAD [C, JOB: DELAY] (R1, R2, PHI: RATE, in var P: PHASE) is
13     loop
14        case P in
15           1 ->        -- low-load phase
16              loop PHASE1 in
17                 alt
18                    JOB (R1)
19                 []
20                    C (PHI);
21                    break PHASE1
22                 end alt
23              end loop;
24              P := 2
25           | 2 ->      -- high-load phase
26              loop PHASE2 in
27                 alt
28                    JOB (R2)
29                 []
30                    C (PHI);
31                    break PHASE2
32                 end alt
33              end loop;
34              P := 3
35           | 3 ->      -- idle phase
36              C (PHI);
37              P := 1
38        end case
39     end loop
40  end process
```

Fig. 3. LNT model fragment specifying the load processes

(1) The mainframe model satisfies the "one-to-many" property stated in Sect. 2.2, meaning that each $a(\lambda)$ may only be synchronised with wildcard receptions "a (**any** RATE)". The LNT semantics does not support the product of rates, so that a synchronisation of $a(\lambda)$ and $a(\mu)$ does not give $a(\lambda\mu)$ as in TIPP, but either **stop** if $\lambda \neq \mu$ or $a(\lambda)$ if $\lambda = \mu$. Notice that Fig. 3 exploits the latter property, as the parallel composition of the nearly identical load processes involves a 3-party synchronisation between three transitions (c, φ), which, in LNT but not in TIPP, has the same effect as synchronising one transition (c, φ) with two transitions $(c, \mathbb{1})$.

(2) The LNT compilers of CADP represent the transitions going out of each state using a multiset, rather than a set: for instance, the LNT behaviour "**alt** $a(\lambda)$ [] $a(\lambda)$ **end alt**" will not generate a single transition "$a(\lambda)$" (i.e., will not factorise identical transitions as permitted by the operational semantics of most process algebras), but a choice between two "$a(\lambda)$" transitions —

which are later merged into a single transition "$a(2\lambda)$" when applying strong or branching stochastic bisimulation.

To reproduce the numerical results of the original papers (see Sect. 5 below), one needs to express properties about certain state variables. In this respect, LNT follows the principles of process algebras and labelled transition systems: information is attached to transitions, not to states, so that the contents of states cannot be observed. The usual solution is therefore to add self-loop transitions (called "probes") to the LNT model, the labels of these transitions exporting information contained in the states they are attached to.

In the mainframe model, probes need to be introduced only in the three queue processes. In the *fail_queue*, we insert a *z_avail* probe that is attached to each global state of the CTMC in which the local state of the *fail_queue* is F_0 ("working") rather than F_1 ("failed"). In the *prog_queue*, we insert a *z_prog_queue(n)* probe that is attached to each global state of the CTMC in which the *prog_queue* contains n jobs. In the *user_queue*, we insert a similar *z_user_queue(n)* probe.

5 Numerical Solutions

5.1 Objectives and Methodology

The original paper [37, Sect. 4.3] provides eight figures, numbered from ③ to ⑩; we surround these numbers by square boxes to distinguish them from figure numbers of the present article. Two figures (Fig. ⑦ and ⑧) can also be found in [35]. Figures ③, ④, ⑤, and ⑥ are about steady-state probabilities (i.e., in the long term, after an equilibrium has been reached). Figures ⑦, ⑧, ⑨, and ⑩ are about transient probabilities (i.e., at specific time instants).

Our challenge, as we defined it, was to reproduce these eight figures by applying the CADP, PRISM, and Storm tools to our models of the mainframe.

Obtaining the same values as in the original paper was not an easy task, as several difficulties arose. As could be seen from the source TIPP files, the authors did many experiments, with different TIPP models (featuring different processor models), different queue sizes, and different rate parameters.

Such a variability has undesirable consequences: these experiments are difficult to follow because of their multiple experimental settings, and they are difficult to reproduce, as information is incomplete in places, with useful details and parameter values missing from the original paper.

In particular, numerical results do not always match across figures because of untold changes in models or parameters. For instance, Fig. ⑨ of [37], which assumes a couple of fixed values for the parameters β and δ_2, displays a steady-state availability result $A(\infty) = 0.981$, this value being independent from the phase in which the load processes are started. But in Fig. ⑤ of [37], which assumes that the load processes are started in phase 1 and explores various values of β and δ_2, none of the steady-state availability results displayed for $A(\infty)$ matches the value 0.981 of Fig. ⑨. Looking into the TIPP files, we presume that Fig. ⑨

was obtained by using a simpler processor model and different queue sizes (4, 4) than Fig. [5].

In a first attempt, we fought to reproduce exactly the same values as in the original paper by redoing the same experiments with various models, various queue sizes, and various sets of rate parameters. Using PRISM, we managed to reproduce the original results for Fig. [5]–[8] with good precision (from 3 to 6 decimal places).

We then considered that an exact reproduction of the original experiments was perhaps not the most suitable goal. Rather than mere imitation, we felt it would be better to recreate a simplified experimental setting that would be easier to understand, so that the mainframe example would get, hopefully, more chances to be studied by others and reused for various purposes, e.g., as a benchmark for performance analysis tools or as a lab exercise in university classrooms.

We therefore adopt the following simplifying assumptions, which will be detailed and justified below:

- We use a unique model of the mainframe, which is parameterized by the maximal sizes of the *prog_queue* and *user_queue*, and by the initial phase (1, 2, or 3) in which the three load processes are stated.
- Concerning the maximal queue sizes, the original paper [37, Sect. 3.4] observed that reducing them from (40, 10) to (10, 4) does not sacrifice model accuracy very much. We further reduce these sizes to (4, 4) by default, since larger sizes do not change the shape of figures (as justified below in Sect. 5.6), but increase the number of states of generated CTMCs and the execution time for computing steady-state and transient probabilities.
- Concerning the initial phase, we start all load processes in phase 1 (low load) by default. We verified that, despite the sophisticated behaviour of the three load processes (with three phases and different rates λ_1, λ_2, μ_1, μ_2, δ_1, δ_2, and φ), the long-run probability of being in each phase is identical (i.e., 1/3) for each of the three phases. This suggests that, when the three load processes are connected to the three queues, their sophisticated behaviour becomes more regular, just as a torrent loses its capricious flow when it pours into a reservoir lake with a barrage.
- Concerning the rate parameters, most of them have constant values, meaning that the impact of their modification is not studied in the experiments for producing Fig. [3]–[10]. We assign the following rate parameters the same default values as in the original paper [37]:

$$\alpha = 48 \quad \beta = 0.01 \quad \delta_1 = 0.00035 \quad \delta_2 = 0.0007 \quad \lambda_1 = 0.01667$$
$$\lambda_2 = 0.16 \quad \mu_1 = 0.033 \quad \mu_2 = 2 \quad \nu = 12 \quad \varphi = 0.00334 \quad \xi = 0.3$$

All these values are expressed in the same unit: min^{-1}. Only three of these parameters (β, δ_2, and μ_2) vary in the experiments.

Under these assumptions, and a few others to be stated hereafter, we obtain numerical results that are close to those of the original papers and, noticeably, preserve the shape of the curves of Fig. [3]–[10]. We now detail how to reproduce each of these eight figures in turn.

5.2   Reproduction of Figures ③ and ④ (Steady-State Analysis)

These two figures, which appear only in the first original paper [37], answer a dimensioning question: they explore how the size of queues impacts the probability that the mainframe system is blocked, waiting for new requests to be processed. Fig. ③ concerns the *prog_queue* (denoted Q in the original papers) for low-priority jobs. Fig. ④ concerns the *user_queue* (denoted R in the original papers) for high-priority jobs. Both figures vary two parameters: the queue size and the arrival rate μ_2 of user jobs. Fig. 4 displays the figures generated using CADP — those generated using PRISM being similar.

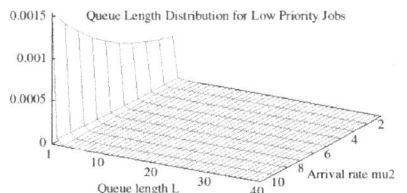 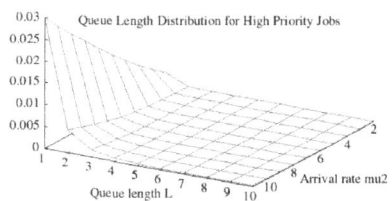

Fig. 4. Figures ③ and ④ generated using CADP

These two figures have been the most difficult ones to reproduce, because of ambiguities and lack of information. We briefly mention the issues we faced and the solutions we adopted:

(a) The z-axis of Fig. ③ and ④ are labelled $P(Q = l \mid \text{load} = \text{"high"})$ and $P(R = l \mid \text{load} = \text{"low"})$, respectively. Here, "l" does not denote the digit one, but the queue length indicated on the x-axis of both figures. To avoid any confusion, we hereafter denote queue length with a capital "L".

(b) In the original paper, the x-axes of Fig. ③ and ④ start at $L = 0$ and the shape of the curves gives the impression that there is a value on the z-axis when the queue length is zero — this value being the probability 0.002 for Fig. ③ and 0.051 for Fig. ④. This is not the case actually: the probabilities when $L = 0$ are very high (close to one) and would make the plots unreadable if displayed. To avoid such a misleading impression, the x-axes of our Fig. ③ and ④ explicitly start at $L = 1$ rather than $L = 0$.

(c) In Fig. ③, the x-axis displays the queue length L ranging from 1 to 40. This allows two possible interpretations: either (i) the mainframe system has a *prog_queue* Q of size 40, and the z-axis of Fig. ③ represents the distribution over L (and μ_2), i.e., the probability that the *prog_queue* has L elements, for all possible values of L but zero; or (ii) each value of L represents a different instance of the mainframe system in which the *prog_queue* has size L, and the z-axis represents the probability that the queue is full, i.e., contains L elements. Both interpretations are also plausible for Fig. 4, in which the size L of the *user_queue* R ranges from 1 to 10. We opted for the first interpretation, which seems compatible with the legends of Fig. 3 and 4, namely "Queue Length Distribution for Low Priority Jobs" and "Queue Length Distribution for High Priority Jobs". We implemented both interpretations in LNT and compared the results obtained using CADP: the probabilities are actually different, but the differences are so small that the shapes of Fig. 3 and 4 do not change.

(d) The z-axis labels of Fig. 3 and 4, namely, P(Q = L | load = "high") and P(R = L | load = "low") suggest that they express conditional probabilities, although the notion of conditional probability is not mentioned anywhere in the original papers. We first tried to interpret z-axis values this way by computing them according to the definition of conditional probabilities, i.e.:

$$P(Q = L \mid load = \text{"high"}) = \frac{P(Q = L \cap load = \text{"high"})}{P(load = \text{"high"})}$$

and:

$$P(R = L \mid load = \text{"low"}) = \frac{P(R = L \cap load = \text{"low"})}{P(load = \text{"low"})}$$

As mentioned already, we observed, using PRISM and CADP, that the steady-state probabilities P(load = "high") and P(load = "low") are both equal to 1/3. To compute the probabilities of both intersections, additional probes were introduced in the LNT specification to indicate when the phase of the load processes is high or low; these probes were then synchronised with the probes expressing the number of items in each queue, and their steady-state throughput was computed using CADP. Doing so, we obtained curves that were similar to those of the original paper, but with a visible difference in the z-axis values when $L = 1$. We thus decided to forget about conditional probabilities and to simply compute P(Q = L) and P(R = L) for the z axes; despite this simplification, we still obtain plausible curves.

Finally, we produced Fig. 3 and 4 (see Fig. 4) that closely resemble those of the original paper. Yet, the maximal values on the z-axis (when $L = 1$ and $\mu_2 = 10$) are not the same: in [37], these probabilities are approximately 0.002 for Fig. 3 and 0.051 for Fig. 4; on our figures, they are 0.0015 for Fig. 3 and 0.03 for Fig. 4. This probably arises from differences in mainframe models and rate parameters used for the various experiments.

5.3 Reproduction of Figures 5 and 6 (Steady-State Analysis)

These two figures describe the impact of failures and repairs on the processing of high-priority jobs. To do so, these figures vary the failure arrival rate δ_2 and the repair rate β and display, for each pair (δ_2, β), an availability value, denoted

$A(\infty)$, for Fig. 5 and a throughput value, denoted $M(\infty)$, for Fig. 6. Fig. 5 displays the figures generated using CADP, which are identical to those generated using PRISM, as well as those given in the original paper [37].

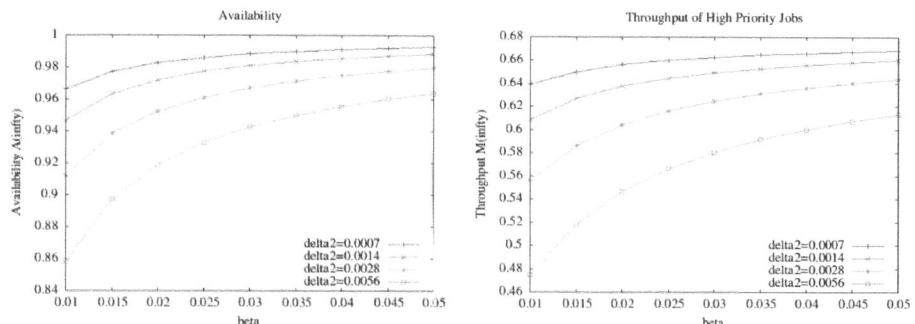

Fig. 5. Figures 5 and 6 generated using CADP

In Fig. 5, $A(\infty)$ is the steady-state limit of the *point availability* $A(t)$, which is defined [37, rule (2) of Sect. 3.2] as the probability that the mainframe is operational at time t; the intended meaning of "operational" here is that the failure queue process, which has two states F_0 and F_1, is in state F_0 where no failure is taking place. A different definition of "operational" (e.g., all processors are serving jobs) might produce different numerical results.

In Fig. 6, $M(\infty)$ is the steady-state limit of the *point throughput* $M(t)$ of the action *get_user_job* that occurs every time a high-priority job is submitted to the processors. $M(t)$ can be defined, according to [37, rules (9) and (10) of Sect. 3.2], as $M(t) = \sum_{i \in 1, \dots, n} r(s_i) P(X(t) = s_i)$, where s_i iterates over all reachable states of the CTMC, and where $r(s_i) = \sum_j \rho_j$ for all (get_user_job, ρ_j) transitions going out of state s_i.

5.4 Reproduction of Figures 7 and 8 (Transient Analysis)

These two figures bear similarity with Fig. 5 and 6 but display transient values for, respectively, point availability $A(t)$ and point throughput $M(t)$ instead of displaying their steady-state limits $A(\infty)$ and $M(\infty)$. Also, Fig. 7 and 8 assume a constant value (namely, 0.0007) for the parameter δ_2 and, rather than varying δ_2, consider 15 different time instants.

Fig. 6 shows the figures generated using CADP and PRISM. These figures are pairwise identical, and also identical to those given in the original papers [37] and [35].

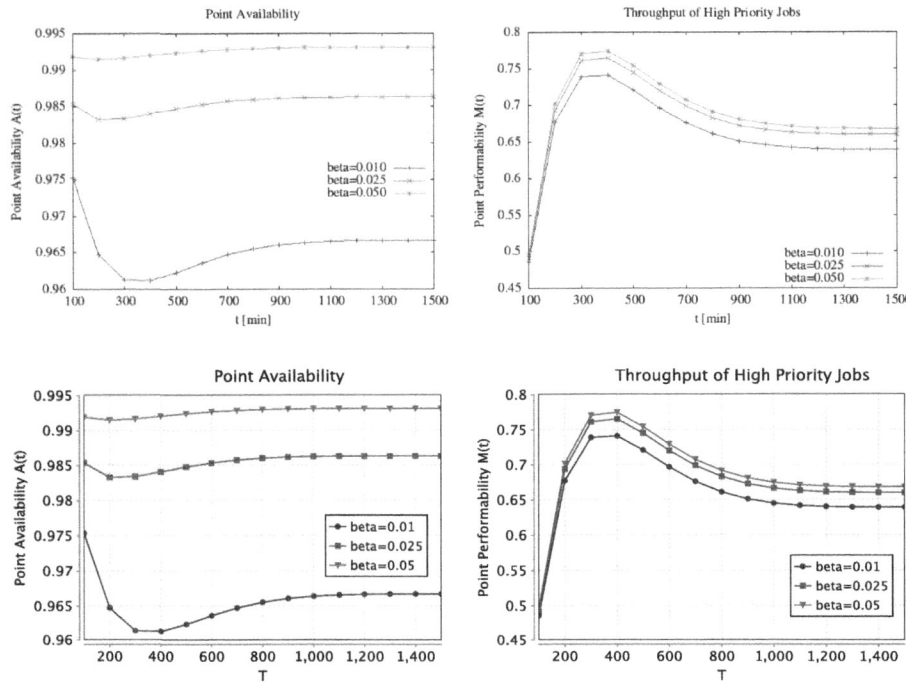

Fig. 6. Figures [7] and [8] generated using CADP (top) and PRISM (bottom)

5.5   Reproduction of Figures [9] and [10] (Transient Analysis)

These two figures are similar to Fig. [7] and [8], with the difference that they give the parameter β a constant value (namely, 0.01) and vary the *phase*, i.e., the initial state ("low", "load", or "idle") of the three load processes — these processes being all started in the same phase and modifying their phases simultaneously by means of a 3-party synchronisation on action c.

Fig. 7 shows the Fig. [9] and [10] generated using CADP. We felt that the top label of Fig. [9] in [37] ("Point Availability During High Load Phase") was misleading, as it suggests the use of conditional probabilities that are never evoked elsewhere in the original papers; we therefore changed this label to "Point Availability", while a longer, completely accurate label would be "Point Availability upon Initialisation in High Load".

The curves of Fig. [9] obtained using CADP and PRISM clearly have the same shape as those of the original paper. However, the values are slightly different. For instance, the steady-state limit $A(\infty)$ is 0.967 for CADP and PRISM, whereas it was 0.981 in [37]. We already discussed this issue in Sect 5.1 and believe that our Fig. [9] is coherent, as its value 0.967 matches the steady-state value of our Fig. [6] for $\beta = 0.01$ and $\delta_2 = 0.0007$ (see Fig. 5), which was not the case in the

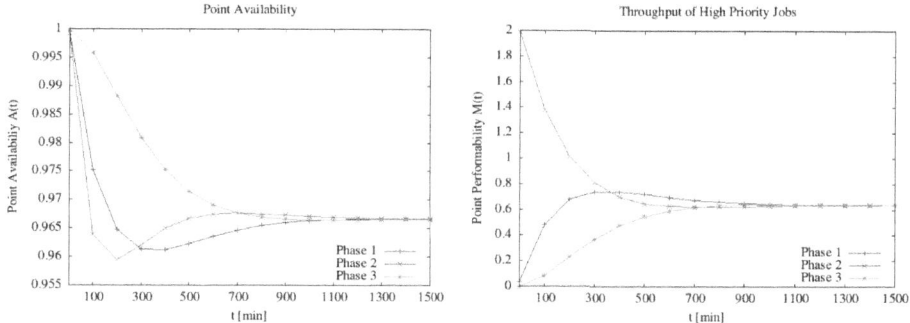

Fig. 7. Figures ⑨ and ⑩ generated using CADP

original paper. Interestingly, the value of β has a key influence on the shape of Fig. ⑨ (see Fig. 8 for a comparative view). Finally, our Fig. ⑩ is identical, in shape and values, to the one of [37].

5.6   Impact of Queue Sizes

The original paper [37] claims that reducing queue sizes from (40, 10) to (10, 4) has little impact on numerical results; we went further in this direction by reducing queue sizes to (4, 4). In this section, we present additional experiments that support these claims.

Table 2 summarises the experiments done with CADP for various sizes of the *prog_queue* and *user_queue*. For each experiment, the 2nd column of the table gives the number of states of the corresponding CTMC, after minimisation modulo stochastic strong bisimulation. The 3rd, 4th, and 5th columns quantify the loss of precision in the set of throughput values generated for Fig. ⑤–⑥, Fig. ⑦–⑧, and Fig. ⑨–⑩, respectively; the loss of precision for line (m, n) and column C is defined as the largest value, for $i \in \{1, ..., n\}$, of $2 |x_i - y_i|/(x_i + y_i)$, where $\{x_1, ..., x_n\}$ is the set of throughput values generated for queue sizes $(40, 10)$ and the figures of column C, and $\{y_1, ..., y_n\}$ the set of throughput values generated for queue sizes (m, n) and the figures of column C. From this table, we draw three conclusions:

- The numbers of CTMC states for queue sizes (40, 10) and (10, 4) are exactly those mentioned in [37, Sect. 4.3]. The fact that we obtain the same numbers is a clear indication that our LNT and PRISM models are compatible with those of the original paper.
- The losses of precision for queue sizes (10, 4) and (4, 4) are equal. Actually, all the throughput values for (10, 4) and (4, 4) are pairwise identical, except in two cases where a difference occurs at the 6th decimal position (0.63996 vs 0.639961). This retrospectively justifies our decision of reducing queue sizes to (4, 4).

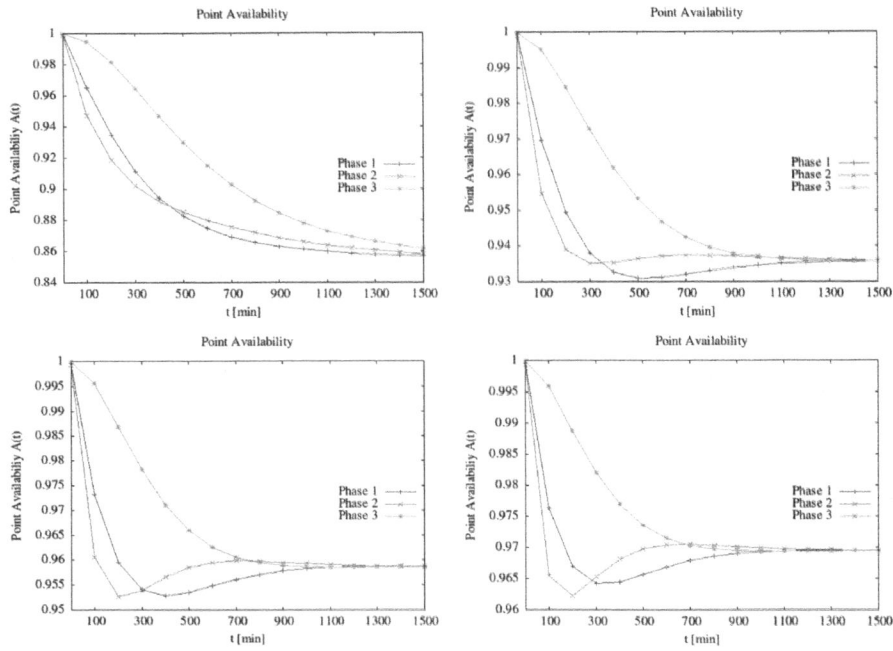

Fig. 8. Variants of Fig. 9 for $\beta = 0.002$, 0.005, 0.008, and 0.011

– Globally, the sizes of queues have negligible impact ($\approx 1.5\%$) on throughput values. This appears as a specific consequence of the chosen rate parameters and particular experiments for producing Fig. 5–10.

5.7   Using PRISM and Storm

We analysed the mainframe model using both the PRISM and Storm toolsets. There are differences in the two tools' overall functionality and focus (e.g., support for Markov automata only in Storm, and for stochastic games only in PRISM/PRISM-games), but there is a large common core of probabilistic model checking functionality, including what is needed for this exercise. The inputs to the two tools, in terms of model and property specifications, are identical for our purposes, since Storm accepts the PRISM modelling language (for which we activate the "PRISM-compatibility mode" of Storm) and the tools largely agree on the syntax for temporal logic queries.

Temporal logic. For property specifications, we use the temporal logic CSL (continuous stochastic logic) [3,4], which is a branching-time temporal logic for characterising transient and steady-state aspects of CTMCs. In the years since the mainframe example was first developed, CSL has established itself as widely used means to formally specify performance and reliability criteria of computer and

queue size	CTMC states	Fig. [5]–[6]	Fig. [7]–[8]	Fig. [9]–[10]
(40, 10)	21,648	—	—	—
(30, 8)	13,392	0.0031%	0.0032%	0.0032%
(20, 5)	6048	0.0186%	0.0187%	0.0196%
(10, 4)	2640	0.0312%	0.0314%	0.0326%
(4, 4)	1200	0.0312%	0.0314%	0.0326%
(3, 3)	768	0.0527%	0.0530%	0.0551%
(2, 2)	432	0.1121%	0.1126%	0.1167%
(1, 1)	192	1.4955%	1.4988%	1.5262%

Table 2. Impact of queue sizes

communication systems, bridging the fields of performance analysis and formal verification [5].

For the mainframe example, we use the following formulae:

(i) $\mathbf{S}_{=?}[\,ujq{=}l\,]$: long-run probability of queue length being l (Fig. [3] and [4])
(ii) $\mathbf{S}_{=?}[\,fq{=}0\,]$: long-run availability (Fig. [5])
(iii) $\mathbf{R}_{=?}^{thru\_hi}[\,\mathbf{S}\,]$: long-run throughput of high-priority jobs (Fig. [6])
(iv) $\mathbf{P}_{=?}[\,\mathbf{F}^{=T}fq{=}0\,]$: point availability (Fig. [7] and [9])
(v) $\mathbf{R}_{=?}^{thru\_hi}[\,\mathbf{I}^{=T}\,]$: point throughput of high-priority jobs at time T (Fig. [8])

The formula $\mathbf{S}_{=?}[\,\varphi\,]$ asks for the long-run (steady-state) probability that predicate φ is true. Here, we write φ in terms of the variables that make up the PRISM model: ujq is the current size of the *user_queue* and fq equals 1 if the mainframe has failed, 0 if not. Formula $\mathbf{P}_{=?}[\,\mathbf{F}^{=T}\varphi\,]$ is the transient equivalent, asking for the probability of φ being true at time instant T.

Formulae $\mathbf{R}_{=?}^{r}[\,\mathbf{S}\,]$ and $\mathbf{R}_{=?}^{r}[\,\mathbf{I}^{=T}\,]$ ask for the expected value of a reward r in the long-run and at time instant T, respectively. Here, *thru_hi* is a reward structure that, in any state, equals the total rate of outgoing (*user_job_ready*) transitions that correspond to a user job being processed. We note that the current exercise illustrates some of the benefits of temporal logic, conveying easily and precisely the properties being used, in a form directly accessible to multiple tools.

Solution methods and performance. CSL model checking [4] of the formulae above essentially reduces to either *steady-state* or *transient* solution of the CTMC. Steady-state analysis is done in [37] using iterative numerical techniques, in particular the Gauss-Seidel method. PRISM takes exactly the same approach. Storm's default technique here is also iterative: the generalised minimal residual method (GMRES) method, with ILU preconditioning.

Transient analysis in [37] is performed using the refined randomisation technique [52], which is very similar to the method known as *uniformisation*, proposed for CSL model checking in [4] and used by most probabilistic model checkers. In this sense, in contrast to the situation for other classes of probabilistic models, the default techniques used to solve core CTMC queries by modern probabilistic model checkers have not changed significantly.

Performance, however, has of course improved. While [37] reports numerical solution of the CTMC for queue sizes $(40, 10)$ taking about 165 seconds, PRISM and Storm build and solve the model in 2-3 seconds. Whilst the numerical solution part, which uses similar techniques to [37], is largely benefitting from hardware advances, other aspects of the process have changed. Techniques for model exploration and construction, for example, have improved. For the largest mainframe instance we considered here ($\sim$1.6 million states), both PRISM and Storm build the model in just a few seconds, the former with symbolic (binary decision diagram based) methods, the latter using explicit-state techniques.

As has been investigated at length [16], comparing the runtime of probabilistic verification tools needs to be done with considerable care when they use different solution methods offering different guarantees on the precision of their results. In this particular case, the methods and their configuration are very similar (for example, both tools by default terminate iterative numerical methods when they have converged to within a maximum relative difference of 10^{-6}). Whilst [16] showed Storm to generally perform better than other comparable tools across a broad range of benchmarks and model types, on these CTMCs, PRISM, and Storm exhibit very similar runtimes, e.g., both taking $\sim$34 seconds to solve the (steady-state) property (ii) above on a CTMC with 922,746 states.

Queue size	CTMC states		Transient (T=1000) time (s)			Steady-state time (s)		
	Full	Reduced	No bisim.	Bisim.	Change	No bisim	Bisim	Change
40,10	110,946	21,648	93.3	**19.0**	-80%	2.2	**1.1**	-50%
80,20	418,446	81,648	331.9	**78.7**	-76%	13.2	**11.0**	-17%
120,30	922,746	180,048	1,328.3	**492.5**	-63%	**33.8**	37.7	12%
160,40	1,623,846	316,848	1,949.1	**505.0**	-74%	**71.8**	125.2	74%

Table 3. Computation times (Storm) for transient and steady-state properties with and without bisimulation minimisation.

Bisimulation. Since strong bisimulation (lumping) for CTMCs [13,38,48] is known to preserve satisfaction of the logic CSL, a key result shown in [4], we also investigate applying bisimulation minimisation before model solution. Once such a minimisation has been applied (to the PRISM model described in Sect. 3), both PRISM and Storm produce models of exactly the same size as generated by CADP and as in [37]. Lumping is mentioned in [37] but does not seem to be applied. In fact, investigation shows that the reduction in size produced by minimising the PRISM model of Sect. 3 is solely due to redundancy in the representation of the state of the processors, and manually exploiting this at the modelling language level (by combining the processors into a single abstract process, already discussed at the end of Sect. 2.3) yields precisely the same reduced models. This suggest that applying bisimulation to the models of [37] may have yielded no further reductions anyway.

It is known, from practical investigations in [47] that minimisation can, but does not always, result in an overall reduction in computation time, depending on whether the benefits of solving a smaller, minimised CTMC outweigh the cost of performing minimisation. We measured times for representative CSL queries – (iv) and (ii) above – on CTMCs of various sizes, created by varying queue sizes. Although Section 5.6 showed that this has limited effect on the numerical results obtained, this provides a convenient way to examine the impact of the state space size on performance. To see this impact more clearly, we use larger models than in the earlier sections. Table 3 shows models sizes and times to run Storm (which has a larger range of minimisation options built in; here we use the default settings) with and without bisimulation. The faster of the two times are indicated in bold face.

We see that all models are reduced by the same amount: a factor of 5.25. Regarding computation time, we observe that minimisation yields significant gains (a factor 4 speed-up) for the transient property. On the other hand, for the steady-state property, the gain decreases with model size and using minimisation eventually becomes slower. This seems to be caused by an increase in the number of iterations required for numerical solution of the minimised model to converge, despite its smaller size (both in terms of the number of states and the average number of transitions for each state).

5.8   Using CADP

Unlike PRISM and Storm, which are integrated tools, CADP is rather a tool set, i.e., a collection of about fifty different tools that can be combined to achieve very diverse tasks. Only a small fraction of these tools is dedicated to the analysis of probabilistic and stochastic systems. CADP does not support a stochastic temporal logic such as CSL, but provides various tools that compute strong and branching stochastic bisimulations, steady-state probabilities, and transient probabilities [36] [18].

The CADP tools can be invoked directly from the command line or, in the case of involved scenarios, from verification scripts written in SVL language[11] [24] [51]. SVL eases the combination of the various CADP tools and plays a crucial role for the reproducibility of experiments. It provides high-level CADP-specific language constructs, which can be freely combined with POSIX shell commands. The latter, which are preceded by the escape symbol '%', provide for variable assignments and substitutions, "**if-then-else**" conditionals, "**for**" loops, parameterized procedures, etc.

The generation of Fig. [3]–[10] for the Erlangen mainframe is fully described by a 350-line SVL script (200 lines if not counting comments and blank lines). This script can either generate all figures, or only a specified subset of them (namely, [3], [4], [5]–[6], [7]–[8], or [9]–[10]). It contains three procedures:

---

[11] https://cadp.inria.fr/man/svl-lang.html

- Procedure *INITIALIZE* sets rate parameters, queue sizes, and initial phase to their default values.
- Procedure *GENERATE* takes the LNT description of the mainframe, replaces most rate parameters by their default values but keeps a few parameters in symbolic form (i.e., β, δ_2, and/or μ_2) that have to iterate over multiple values, replaces the queue sizes and initial phase by specified values, and generates a finite, explicit-state CTMC stored in a file (encoded in the BCG format of CADP). This CTMC contains compound action-rate labels on its transitions — some of these rates being still symbolic. Then, in this CTMC, every self-loop transition corresponding to a probe is either deleted if that probe is not useful for the particular figure to be generated, or is given the rate 1.0 otherwise (so that the throughput of the probe transition is equal to the probability of being in the state the probe is attached to).
- Procedure *INSTANTIATE* takes a CTMC with partially symbolic rates, replaces these rates by specified values, and minimises the CTMC modulo stochastic strong bisimulation using the BCG_MIN[12] tool of CADP. The resulting minimised CTMC is aperiodic, irreducible, has no deadlock state and no τ-transitions.

In the SVL script, the various code fragments for generating each figure are similar. First, they invoke the *INITIALIZE* procedure and, possibly, the *GENERATE* procedure. Then, they perform one loop or two nested loops to vary one or two rate parameters (β, δ_2, or μ_2) or the initial phase. The body of the innermost loop successively invokes the *GENERATE* procedure (if it has been called already before the loop), the *INSTANTIATE* procedure, and either the BCG_STEADY[13] tool or the BCG_TRANSIENT[14] tool of CADP for computing steady-state or transient probabilities.

Each invocation of the two latter tools appends to a text file a new line containing the transition throughputs (i.e., sum of transition rates multiplied by incoming state probabilities) of selected actions of the CTMC. For instance, the point availability values $A(t)$ and $A(\infty)$ defined in Sect. 5.2 are computed, using BCG_STEADY and BCG_TRANSIENT, as the throughput of self-loop transitions corresponding to the *z_avail* probe. Similarly, the point throughput values $M(t)$ and $M(\infty)$ of Sect. 5.2 are computed as the throughput of *get_user_job* transitions. Lastly, eight small Gnuplot scripts convert these throughput files to eight figures in PNG format.

The complete execution of the SVL script takes about 10 minutes on a standard laptop (Intel x64 processor, 16 GB RAM) running Linux.

Finally, we checked, using the BCG_CMP[15] tool of CADP, that, for the eight different queue sizes of Table 2, the CTMCs generated by PRISM are pairwise equivalent, modulo stochastic strong bisimulation, to the CTMCs (without probe transitions) generated by CADP.

---

[12] https://cadp.inria.fr/man/bcg_min.html

[13] https://cadp.inria.fr/man/bcg_steady.html

[14] https://cadp.inria.fr/man/bcg_transient.html

[15] https://cadp.inria.fr/man/bcg_cmp.html

6 Conclusion

The present work is an essay in research reproducibility. We revisited the Erlangen mainframe case study, a challenging example proposed thirty years ago [37] [35]. We improved this case study in two ways:

- *Corrections*: The original papers contained a few mistakes, which we found and fixed. Also, the explanations given in these papers were incomplete or ambiguous in places, but our collaborative thinking managed to recover the missing parts and provide the most plausible interpretations. When appropriate, we dug into the source TIPP files to get confirmation of our decisions.
- *Simplifications*: Some experiments for producing the eight figures displayed in [37] were unnecessarily complex. We addressed this issue by proposing a few simplifications that, while producing nearly identical results as in the original papers, are easier to understand and execute faster.

We developed two novel formal models for the Erlangen mainframe, one in the automata-based language PRISM, and another one in the process-algebra-based language LNT. The tools PRISM, Storm, and CADP performed all numerical experiments and successfully reproduced the same figures as in the original papers. This suggests that these tools could be used in combination to analyse other systems, especially critical ones, as the fact that different tools developed independently give identical results on the same model is a convincing argument for safety/security certification agencies.

As regards future developments, the present work could be reused and extended in several directions:

- The Erlangen mainframe is a suitable basis for lab exercises in university courses. Our paper gives hints on how using PRISM, Storm, and CADP on this case study in order to model the system, express its properties, and obtain performance numbers. Many more experiments could be proposed by varying other parameters than β, δ_2, and μ_2.
- The Erlangen mainframe could be specified using other languages and analysed using other tools, provided that the language requirements of Sect. 2.2 are satisfied. This example could also be used as a scalable model for software competitions since, by varying the size of queues, one easily obtains CTMCs of increasing complexity.
- Our modelling of the Erlangen mainframe relies on compound transitions that combine actions and rates. It would be interesting to investigate whether this problem can also be expressed in alternative formalisms without compound transitions, such as Interactive Markov Chains [33], in which transitions carry either an action or a rate.

Acknowledgements

We are grateful to the anonymous reviewers for their constructive remarks and to Nazareno Garagiola (Saarland University) for early experiments with Storm on the mainframe specifications.

70 H. Garavel et al.

References

1. Alur, R., Henzinger, T.A.: Reactive Modules. Formal Methods in System Design **15**(1), 7–48 (1999). https://doi.org/10.1023/A:1008739929481
2. ANSI: Ada Programming Language. Military Standard ANSI-MIL-STD-1815A, American National Standards Institute, New Year, USA (Jan 1983)
3. Aziz, A., Sanwal, K., Singhal, V., Brayton, R.K.: Verifying Continuous Time Markov Chains. In: Alur, R., Henzinger, T.A. (eds.) Proceedings of the 8th International Conference on Computer Aided Verification (CAV'96), New Brunswick, NJ, USA. Lecture Notes in Computer Science, vol. 1102, pp. 269–276. Springer (Jul 1996). https://doi.org/10.1007/3-540-61474-5_75
4. Baier, C., Haverkort, B.R., Hermanns, H., Katoen, J.: Model-Checking Algorithms for Continuous-Time Markov Chains. IEEE Transactions on Software Engineering **29**(6), 524–541 (2003). https://doi.org/10.1109/TSE.2003.1205180
5. Baier, C., Haverkort, B.R., Hermanns, H., Katoen, J.: Performance Evaluation and Model Checking Join Forces. Communications of the ACM **53**(9), 76–85 (2010). https://doi.org/10.1145/1810891.1810912
6. Barrett, G.: OCCAM 3 Reference Manual (Mar 1992), iNMOS Limited, Draft
7. Bernardo, M., Cleaveland, R., Sims, S., Stewart, W.: TwoTowers: A Tool Integrating Functional and Performance Analysis of Concurrent Systems. In: Budkowski, S., Cavalli, A.R., Najm, E. (eds.) Proceedings of the IFIP TC6/WG6.1 Joint 11th International Conference on Formal Description Techniques for Distributed Systems and Communication Protocols and 18th International Workshop on Protocol Specification, Testing and Verification (FORTE/PSTV'98), Paris, France. IFIP Conference Proceedings, vol. 135, pp. 457–467. Kluwer (Nov 1998)
8. Bohnenkamp, H., Pedro R. d'Argenio, Hermanns, H., Katoen, J.P.: MoDeST: A Compositional Modeling Formalism for Hard and Softly Timed Systems. IEEE Transactions on Software Engineering **32**(10), 812–830 (2006). https://doi.org/10.1109/TSE.2006.104
9. Bozzano, M., Cimatti, A., Katoen, J., Nguyen, V.Y., Noll, T., Roveri, M.: Safety, Dependability and Performance Analysis of Extended AADL Models. The Computer Journal **54**(5), 754–775 (2011). https://doi.org/10.1093/COMJNL/BXQ024
10. Bravetti, M., Bernardo, M.: Compositional Asymmetric Cooperations for Process Algebras with Probabilities, Priorities, and Time. In: Corradini, F., Inverardi, P. (eds.) Proceedings of the International Workshop on Models for Time-Critical Systems (MTCS'00), State College, PA, USA. Electronic Notes in Theoretical Computer Science, vol. 39, pp. 197–230. Elsevier (Aug 2000). https://doi.org/10.1016/S1571-0661(05)80749-2
11. Brinksma, E., Hermanns, H.: Process Algebra and Markov Chains. In: Brinksma, E., Hermanns, H., Katoen, J. (eds.) Revised Lectures on Formal Methods and Performance Analysis, First EEF/Euro Summer School on Trends in Computer Science, Berg en Dal, The Netherlands. Lecture Notes in Computer Science, vol. 2090, pp. 183–231. Springer (Jul 2000). https://doi.org/10.1007/3-540-44667-2_5
12. Brookes, S.D., Hoare, C.A.R., Roscoe, A.W.: A Theory of Communicating Sequential Processes. J. ACM **31**(3), 560–599 (Jul 1984). https://doi.org/10.1145/828.833
13. Buchholz, P.: Exact and Ordinary Lumpability in Finite Markov Chains. Journal of Applied Probability **31**(1), 59–75 (Mar 1994). https://doi.org/10.2307/3215235

14. Buchholz, P.: Markovian Process Algebra: Composition and Equivalence. In: Herzog, U., Rettelbach, M. (eds.) Proceedings of the 2nd Workshop on Process Algebras and Performance Modelling (PAPM'94), Regensberg/Erlangen, Germany. pp. 11–30 (Jul 1994)

15. Buchholz, P., Kemper, P.: Quantifying the Dynamic Behavior of Process Algebras. In: de Alfaro, L., Gilmore, S. (eds.) Proceedings of the Joint International Workshop on Process Algebra and Probabilistic Methods, Performance Modeling and Verification (PAPM-PROBMIV'01), Aachen, Germany. Lecture Notes in Computer Science, vol. 2165, pp. 184–199. Springer (Sep 2001). https://doi.org/10.1007/3-540-44804-7_12

16. Budde, C.E., Hartmanns, A., Klauck, M., Křetínský, J., Parker, D., Quatmann, T., Turrini, A., Zhang, Z.: On Correctness, Precision, and Performance in Quantitative Verification: QComp 2020 Competition Report. In: Proceedings of the 9th International Symposium on Leveraging Applications of Formal Methods, Verification and Validation (ISoLA'20), Rhodes, Greece. Lecture Notes in Computer Science, vol. 12479, pp. 216–241. Springer (Oct 2020). https://doi.org/10.1007/978-3-030-83723-5_15

17. Champelovier, D., Clerc, X., Garavel, H., Guerte, Y., McKinty, C., Powazny, V., Lang, F., Serwe, W., Smeding, G.: Reference Manual of the LNT to LOTOS Translator (Version 7.3) (May 2024), https://cadp.inria.fr/publications/Champelovier-Clerc-Garavel-et-al-10.html, INRIA, Grenoble, France

18. Coste, N., Garavel, H., Hermanns, H., Lang, F., Mateescu, R., Serwe, W.: Ten Years of Performance Evaluation for Concurrent Systems Using CADP. In: Margaria, T., Steffen, B. (eds.) Proceedings of the 4th International Symposium on Leveraging Applications of Formal Methods, Verification and Validation ISoLA 2010 (Amirandes, Heraclion, Crete), Part II. Lecture Notes in Computer Science, vol. 6416, pp. 128–142. Springer (Oct 2010). https://doi.org/10.1007/978-3-642-16561-0_18

19. Coste, N., Hermanns, H., Lantreibecq, E., Serwe, W.: Towards Performance Prediction of Compositional Models in Industrial GALS Designs. In: Bouajjani, A., Maler, O. (eds.) Proceedings of the 21th International Conference on Computer Aided Verification (CAV'09), Grenoble, France. Lecture Notes in Computer Science, vol. 5643, pp. 204–218. Springer (Jul 2009). https://doi.org/10.1007/978-3-642-02658-4_18

20. D'Argenio, P.R., Katoen, J.: A Theory of Stochastic Systems, Part I: Stochastic Automata. Information and Computation **203**(1), 1–38 (2005). https://doi.org/10.1016/J.IC.2005.07.001

21. Esteve, M., Katoen, J., Nguyen, V.Y., Postma, B., Yushtein, Y.: Formal Correctness, Safety, Dependability, and Performance Analysis of a Satellite. In: Glinz, M., Murphy, G.C., Pezzè, M. (eds.) Proceedings of the 34th International Conference on Software Engineering, (ICSE'12), Zurich, Switzerland. pp. 1022–1031. IEEE Computer Society (Jun 2012). https://doi.org/10.1109/ICSE.2012.6227118

22. Fischer, W., Meier-Hellstern, K.S.: The Markov-Modulated Poisson Process (MMPP) Cookbook. Performance Evaluation **18**(2), 149–171 (Sep 1993). https://doi.org/10.1016/0166-5316(93)90035-S

23. Garavel, H., Hermanns, H.: On Combining Functional Verification and Performance Evaluation using CADP. In: Eriksson, L.H., Lindsay, P.A. (eds.) Proceedings of the 11th International Symposium of Formal Methods Europe (FME'02), Copenhagen, Denmark. Lecture Notes in Computer Science, vol. 2391, pp. 410–429. Springer (Jul 2002). https://doi.org/10.1007/3-540-45614-7_23, full version available as INRIA Research Report 4492

24. Garavel, H., Lang, F.: SVL: a Scripting Language for Compositional Verification. In: Kim, M., Chin, B., Kang, S., Lee, D. (eds.) Proceedings of the 21st IFIP WG 6.1 International Conference on Formal Techniques for Networked and Distributed Systems (FORTE'01), Cheju Island, Korea. pp. 377–392. Kluwer Academic Publishers (Aug 2001). https://doi.org/10.1007/0-306-47003-9_24, full version available as INRIA Research Report RR-4223

25. Garavel, H., Lang, F., Mateescu, R., Serwe, W.: CADP 2011: A Toolbox for the Construction and Analysis of Distributed Processes. Springer International Journal on Software Tools for Technology Transfer (STTT) **15**(2), 89–107 (Apr 2013). https://doi.org/10.1007/s10009-012-0244-z

26. Garavel, H., Lang, F., Serwe, W.: From LOTOS to LNT. In: Katoen, J.P., Langerak, R., Rensink, A. (eds.) ModelEd, TestEd, TrustEd – Essays Dedicated to Ed Brinksma on the Occasion of His 60th Birthday. Lecture Notes in Computer Science, vol. 10500, pp. 3–26. Springer (Oct 2017). https://doi.org/10.1007/978-3-319-68270-9_1

27. Garavel, H., Serwe, W.: The Unheralded Value of the Multiway Rendezvous: Illustration with the Production Cell Benchmark. In: Hermanns, H., Höfner, P. (eds.) Proceedings of the 2nd Workshop on Models for Formal Analysis of Real Systems (MARS'17), Uppsala, Sweden. Electronic Proceedings in Theoretical Computer Science, vol. 244, pp. 230–270 (Apr 2017). https://doi.org/10.4204/EPTCS.244.10

28. Gillespie, D.T.: Exact Stochastic Simulation of Coupled Chemical Reactions. The Journal of Physical Chemistry **81**(25), 2340–2361 (Dec 1977). https://doi.org/10.1021/j100540a008

29. Hahn, E., Hartmanns, A., Hermanns, H., Katoen, J.P.: A Compositional Modelling and Analysis Framework for Stochastic Hybrid Systems. Formal Methods in System Design **43**(2), 191–232 (2013). https://doi.org/10.1007/S10703-012-0167-Z

30. Hartmanns, A., Hermanns, H.: In the Quantitative Automata Zoo. Science of Computer Programming **112**, 3–23 (2015). https://doi.org/10.1016/j.scico.2015.08.009

31. Hartmanns, A., Klauck, M., Parker, D., Quatmann, T., Ruijters, E.: The Quantitative Verification Benchmark Set. In: Vojnar, T., Zhang, L. (eds.) Proceedings of the 25th International Conference on Tools and Algorithms for the Construction and Analysis of Systems (TACAS'19), Prague, Czech Republic. Lecture Notes in Computer Science, vol. 11427, pp. 344–350. Springer (Apr 2019). https://doi.org/10.1007/978-3-030-17462-0_20

32. Hensel, C., Junges, S., Katoen, J., Quatmann, T., Volk, M.: The Probabilistic Model Checker Storm. International Journal on Software Tools for Technology Transfer **24**(4), 589–610 (2022). https://doi.org/10.1007/S10009-021-00633-Z

33. Hermanns, H.: Interactive Markov Chains: The Quest for Quantified Quality, Lecture Notes in Computer Science, vol. 2428. Springer (2002). https://doi.org/10.1007/3-540-45804-2

34. Hermanns, H., Herzog, U., Klehmet, U., Mertsiotakis, V., Siegle, M.: Compositional performance modelling with the TIPPtool. Performance Evaluation **39**(1-4), 5–35 (Feb 2000). https://doi.org/10.1016/S0166-5316(99)00056-5

35. Hermanns, H., Herzog, U., Merksiotakis, V.: Stochastic Process Algebras as a Tool for Performance and Dependability Modelling. In: Iyer, R.K. (ed.) Proceedings of the International Computer Performance and Dependability Symposium (IPDS'95), Erlangen, Germany. pp. 102–111. IEEE (Apr 1995). https://doi.org/10.1109/IPDS.1995.395813

36. Hermanns, H., Joubert, C.: A Set of Performance and Dependability Analysis Components for CADP. In: Garavel, H., Hatcliff, J. (eds.) Proceedings of the 9th International Conference on Tools and Algorithms for the Construction and Analysis of Systems (TACAS'03), Warsaw, Poland. Lecture Notes in Computer Science, vol. 2619, pp. 425–430. Springer (Apr 2003). https://doi.org/10.1007/3-540-36577-X_30

37. Herzog, U., Merksiotakis, V.: Stochastic Process Algebras Applied to Failure Modelling. In: Herzog, U., Rettelbach, M. (eds.) Proceedings of the 2nd Workshop on Process Algebras and Performance Modelling (PAPM'94), Regensberg/Erlangen, Germany. pp. 107–126 (Jul 1994), https://www.researchgate.net/publication/2731331

38. Hillston, J.: A Compositional Approach to Performance Modelling. Ph.D. thesis, University of Edinburgh, Scotland, United Kingdom (Dec 1994), https://hdl.handle.net/1842/15027

39. Hillston, J.: The Nature of Synchronisation. In: Herzog, U., Rettelbach, M. (eds.) Proceedings of the 2nd Workshop on Process Algebras and Performance Modelling (PAPM'94), Regensberg/Erlangen, Germany. pp. 143–160 (Jul 1994), https://www.researchgate.net/publication/2311019

40. Hoare, C.A.R.: Communicating Sequential Processes. Commun. ACM **21**(8), 666–677 (Aug 1978). https://doi.org/10.1145/359576.359585

41. Hoare, C.A.R.: Communicating Sequential Processes. Prentice-Hall, Englewood Cliffs, NJ (1985)

42. INMOS Limited: OCCAM 2 Reference Manual. International Series in Computer Science, Prentice-Hall (1988)

43. ISO/IEC: LOTOS – A Formal Description Technique Based on the Temporal Ordering of Observational Behaviour. International Standard 8807, International Organization for Standardization – Information Processing Systems – Open Systems Interconnection, Geneva (Sep 1989)

44. ISO/IEC: Enhancements to LOTOS (E-LOTOS). International Standard 15437:2001, International Organization for Standardization – Information Technology, Geneva (Sep 2001)

45. Katoen, J.P.: Quantitative and Qualitative Extensions of Event Structures. Ph.D. thesis, University of Twente, The Netherlands (Apr 1996). https://doi.org/10.3990/1.9789036507998

46. Katoen, J.: The Probabilistic Model Checking Landscape. In: Grohe, M., Koskinen, E., Shankar, N. (eds.) Proceedings of the 31st Annual ACM/IEEE Symposium on Logic in Computer Science, (LICS'16), New York, NY, USA. pp. 31–45. ACM (Jul 2016). https://doi.org/10.1145/2933575.2934574

47. Katoen, J., Kemna, T., Zapreev, I.S., Jansen, D.N.: Bisimulation Minimisation Mostly Speeds Up Probabilistic Model Checking. In: Grumberg, O., Huth, M. (eds.) Proceedings of the 13th International Conference on Tools and Algorithms for the Construction and Analysis of Systems (TACAS'07), Braga, Portugal. Lecture Notes in Computer Science, vol. 4424, pp. 87–101. Springer (Mar–Apr 2007). https://doi.org/10.1007/978-3-540-71209-1_9

48. Kemeny, J.G., Snell, J.L., Knapp, A.W.: Denumerable Markov Chains, Graduate Texts in Mathematics, vol. 40. Springer-Verlag, 2nd edn. (1976)

49. Kwiatkowska, M.Z., Norman, G., Parker, D.: PRISM 4.0: Verification of Probabilistic Real-Time Systems. In: Gopalakrishnan, G., Qadeer, S. (eds.) Proceedings of the 23rd International Conference on Computer Aided Verification (CAV'11), Snowbird, UT, USA. Lecture Notes in Computer Science, vol. 6806, pp. 585–591. Springer (Jul 2011). https://doi.org/10.1007/978-3-642-22110-1_47

50. Kwiatkowska, M.Z., Norman, G., Parker, D.: The PRISM Benchmark Suite. In: Proceedings of the 9th International Conference on Quantitative Evaluation of Systems (QEST'12), London, UK. pp. 203–204. IEEE Computer Society (Sep 2012). https://doi.org/10.1109/QEST.2012.14, https://prismmodelchecker.org/benchmarks

51. Lang, F.: Compositional Verification using SVL Scripts. In: Katoen, J.P., Stevens, P. (eds.) Proceedings of the 8th International Conference on Tools and Algorithms for the Construction and Analysis of Systems (TACAS'02), Grenoble, France. Lecture Notes in Computer Science, vol. 2280, pp. 465–469. Springer (Apr 2002). https://doi.org/10.1007/3-540-46002-0_33

52. Lindemann, C.: Employing the Randomization Technique for Solving Stochastic Petri Net Models. In: Lehmann, A., Lehmann, F. (eds.) Proceedings of the 6th GI/ITG Conference on Modelling, Measurement and Evaluation of Computing Systems (MMB'91), Neubiberg, Germany. Informatik-Fachberichte, vol. 286, pp. 306–319. Springer (Sep 1991). https://doi.org/10.1007/978-3-642-76934-4_21

53. Mateescu, R., Serwe, W.: Model Checking and Performance Evaluation with CADP Illustrated on Shared-Memory Mutual Exclusion Protocols. Science of Computer Programming **78**(7), 843–861 (Jul 2013). https://doi.org/10.1016/j.scico.2012.01.003

54. May, D.: OCCAM. SIGPLAN Notices **18**(4), 69–79 (1983). https://doi.org/10.1145/948176.948183

55. Milner, R.: A Calculus of Communicating Systems, Lecture Notes in Computer Science, vol. 92. Springer (1980). https://doi.org/10.1007/3-540-10235-3

56. Milner, R.: Communication and Concurrency. Prentice-Hall (1989)

57. Sighireanu, M., Catry, A., Champelovier, D., Garavel, H., Lang, F., Schaeffer, G., Serwe, W., Stoecker, J.: LOTOS NT User's Manual (Version 3.14) (Jun 2024), INRIA/CONVECS, Grenoble, France, https://vasy.inria.fr/ftp/traian/manual.pdf, 88 pages

A Probabilistic Analysis of Simplified Cluedo with STORM: The Birthday Cake Case

Ezio Bartocci[1] , Josée Desharnais[2(✉)] , Peter Lindner[3] ,
and Ana Sokolova[3]

[1] Technische Universität Wien, Vienna, Austria
ezio.bartocci@tuwien.ac.at
[2] Université Laval, Québec, Canada
josee.desharnais@ift.ulaval.ca
[3] Paris Lodron University of Salzburg, Salzburg, Austria
peter.lindner@plus.ac.at, ana.sokolova@cs.uni-salzburg.at

Abstract. We present a family of probabilistic models of a simplified version of the Cluedo game. In this version of the game, instead of a murder happening, a birthday cake has mysteriously disappeared. The aim of the game is to guess, from the clues that each player will collect while playing, what happened to the cake. The winner is the player that first guesses who has eaten the cake and the room where this has happened. We implemented several probabilistic models of the game encoding different playing strategies as Markov Decision Processes in the PRISM language. We investigate these strategies by comparing their effectiveness in winning the game using the PRISM and STORM probabilistic model checkers. In particular, we use PRISM for statistical results and STORM for exact computation. Since the generated state space is in general huge, we limit our models to only two players resulting in almost 15 billion states to check. We believe that this benchmark could serve to further improve the current state-of-the-art probabilistic model checking.

Keywords: Cluedo · Markov Decision Processes · Probabilistic Model Checking · Stochastic Games

1 Introduction

Prologue. *It is a stormy night in the Netherlands. Joost-Pieter is celebrating his birthday and has invited some of his dearest friends to arrive the night before the event. His friends brought a cake, a famous Limburg vlaai. In the morning, they all realize that a mysterious event happened: The cake has been eaten! After a short brainstorming, nobody recalls or admits eating the cake. They all decide on playing a game in order to find out who ate the cake and where it happened.*

This work was partially supported by the Vienna Science and Technology Fund (WWTF) [10.47379/ICT19018] (ProbInG).

© The Author(s), under exclusive license to Springer Nature Switzerland AG 2025
N. Jansen et al. (Eds.): Principles of Verification: Cycling the Probabilistic Landscape,
LNCS 15261, pp. 75–97, 2025.
https://doi.org/10.1007/978-3-031-75775-4_4

The game is deductive and probabilistic. It is closely connected to the traditional board game Cluedo, originally designed by Anthony E. Pratt in United Kingdom in 1943, see e.g., [23]. Cluedo is known as Clue in North America. One difference between our version and the original game is that nothing terrible happens in our situation – we are dealing only with an eaten cake, not with a serious crime. Remarkably, after we decided on this change we realised that there is a version of Cluedo for children [14] that goes along these lines. We decided to model the game and analyse it with some of the most prominent model checking and simulation tools, PRISM [18] and STORM [15], to a great extent courtesy of Joost-Pieter Katoen's impressive work. We use the statistical model checking tool of PRISM for obtaining quick estimates, and the STORM model checker to check the properties on the obtained MDPs.

The game provides an interesting family of models, based on a "board", i.e., an imaginary plan of Joost-Pieter's house. It also shows the limits of what can be achieved, as the state space grows very rapidly. We simplify the board layout, and the game in some other respects, and create a family of models [4] of different complexity based on the "intelligence" of the players. The house layout in our model has four rooms and we have modelled four characters, thus simplifying the original game that has nine rooms and six characters. Initially, our model involved three players and one passive character. Due to the state space explosion, we were forced to limit ourselves to two players. The number of characters does not influence the size of the model and remains four in this case. We have created multiple versions of the model that are parametric in the level a player plays. We identify four levels starting from the simplest one, where a player just randomly guesses and uses no accumulated knowledge at all, to a level where a player uses the knowledge of players having a certain card (positive knowledge) and players not having a certain card (negative knowledge). In this first step, we have not modelled any sophisticated deduction mechanisms. We build the model using the PRISM modelling language. Despite the game being fairly simple, the model is huge and there were many interesting choices to make during the modelling process.

We believe that with this modest birthday present for Joost-Pieter, we have also contributed the following to the community of probabilistic analysis:

– We have created a new interesting case study for probabilistic model checking that involves probability, nondeterminism, different communication means like broadcast and handshaking, and can be scaled–by changing the size and layout of the board, by varying the number of characters and the number of players, etc. This work thus further reduces the lack of benchmarks for probabilistic analysis including both probability and nondeterminism, a lack that we have noticed in previous work [3], together with Joost-Pieter Katoen, and which has improved since then [5, 12]. Our models are freely available [4] and will be added to the QComp and PRISM benchmark sets.
– We explore the limits of probabilistic model checking, and report the huge numbers of states obtained even for the simplified games. We then simplify even further in order to get a model that can be model-checked.

- We verify the intuitively made conjectures that the game is fair, i.e., the probabilities to win are more or less the same for all players, with slight advantage of the player whose turn is first.
- We investigate the expected number of turns needed to win the game. Moreover, we investigate "stupid" vs. "more intelligent" strategies of playing and show that players who play at a more advanced level have higher probability of winning and lower expected number of turns until they win, against players who play at a simpler level. Even a simple setup with no sophisticated deduction mechanisms makes a difference–in the original game (when played by humans) as well as in the simplified one that we model. We do not explore advanced epistemic deduction nor answer set programming approaches, although both could be done for more in-depth analysis.

The rest of the paper reports on: Related work in Sect. 2; The original game Cluedo and the rules, in Sect. 3; The representation of knowledge and the different strategies in Sect. 4; Our simplified version of the game, in Sect. 5; The PRISM model and the logic behind it, in Sect. 6; The PRISM and STORM results on the properties checked, in Sect. 7. We wrap up with conclusions and lessons learned in Sect. 8.

2   Related Work

In a *knowledge* game [21] such as Cluedo, winning requires from each player to gain knowledge about the ownership of the cards. A player can enrich their knowledge by moving to different rooms, by asking the right questions, and by reasoning about the answers of the other players. As such, this game is a natural case study in the field of epistemic reasoning [8,9,16,21,22]. In [21,22], van Ditmarsch was the first to provide a precise formalisation of the player's actions using dynamic epistemic logic for multi-agents with shared knowledge [19]. The use of epistemic logic allows to model the local knowledge of each player and to reason about the consequences of each player's action. Later, Dixon formalised in [9] the change of knowledge over time using temporal epistemic logic. Although these works provide a powerful framework to reason about the game dynamics, they do not consider the uncertainty due to rolling of the dice and they do not address the problem of assessing the effectiveness of different playing strategies.

Cluedo is also a suitable game environment to test artificial intelligent approaches [6,17,20,24] for learning and testing optimal strategies. Examples include expert systems [17], reinforcement learning [6], and entropy-reduction based strategy [24]. In [17], the author developed an *expert system* that can play Cluedo with five different strategies. These were tested on specific "deals" each one representing the "combination of 'guilty' cards". In these tests, all the players adopted the same strategy. Their strategies are partly similar to ours (the simplest - using no knowledge at all - being the same). However, in our work we also consider games where different players are using different strategies.

In [13], the authors analysed the trade-off between costs and benefits for a player adopting a "bluffing" strategy that consists in leading the other players to infer the wrong knowledge from their actions. Their quantitative analysis is based on gathering statistical information over 20000 simulated games with random initial conditions. In contrast with the methods using simulation and testing, our approach based on exact model checking, is exhaustive. The game model we provide in this paper is the first PRISM model of a (simplified) variant of Cluedo. If we consider the state space, our model is the second (largest) Markov Decision Process in terms of size with respect to the ones presented in the quantitative verification competitions[1] [5,12] in the last years.

Last but not least, recent work focused on probabilistic analysis of other games using formal methods techniques. Such is, in particular, the mCRL2-based probabilistic analysis of the Game of the Goose [11] and Slot Machines [10]. We leave the investigation of how mCRL2 compares to PRISM and STORM in the context of Cluedo and related games for future work.

3   The Original Game Cluedo

Our original motivation was to provide a PRISM/STORM model for the game Cluedo [23], a popular logic-based, probabilistic board game. As expected, this turned out to be a very ambitious and computationally challenging task, so we simplified the game. Still, for the sake of completeness and reference to the original game we provide a brief, yet almost complete, description of the Cluedo game and rules here. Later in the paper, we describe our simplified version in more detail.

Fig. 1. The traditional board arrangement. Colored dots denote the initial positions of the characters. "The arrows in the four corner rooms denote secret passages to the opposite corner". Source: [23].

---

[1] https://qcomp.org.

3.1   Brief Description

Cluedo is a board game that involves:

- A **board** with rooms and intermediate positions, that we sometimes refer to as fields, described by a grid, illustrated in Fig. 1.
- Six **character** pieces, each representing a possible suspect. that moves on the board. At any point in time a character is positioned on one of the fields of the board.
- **Weapon** pieces (because in the original game, the players also have to deduce what the murder weapon is).
- A set of **cards** consisting of: one card for each room, one card for each character, one card for each weapon.
- Up to six **players**, each playing a particular character. Thus some characters are not "played", but they are nonetheless potential suspects.
- A pair of **dice**, which are rolled by the active player at each turn in order to determine the next set of possible positions.

The rules for Cluedo are described next.

Initialisation

Prior to the start of the game, one room card, one character card, and one weapon card are selected by a random draw and stored in a safe place. These cards represent the committed **crime**: in which room it happened, who was the culprit, and which weapon was used. All other cards are evenly distributed among the players. As for character figures, they are positioned in their clearly marked positions on the board, according to their color. Weapons do not have a specific position.

Game Progress

The game proceeds in **rounds**. In each round, one of the players, the *active* player, has their[2] **turn**. The players take turns in a standard round-robin way. One round consists of the following steps:

1. The active player rolls the dice and chooses nondeterministically among a set of possible positions, that would bring the corresponding character in or closer to a room. For example, if the dice roll results in the number 10, the player can move their character in any direction for up to 10 steps, where moving to a neighbouring field on the board counts as one step. This is the standard way of moving on a grid in board games. If a room is reachable in, e.g., 7 steps, then the player can decide to move to this room and stay there. However, if a player starts a turn inside a room, they have to leave the room within this turn. We omit the rules pertaining to secret passages as they are not modelled in our version of the game.

---

[2] We use the gender-neutral personal pronoun form "they"/"their" throughout the paper in both singular and plural.

2. If no room was reached, the turn ends here.
3. If a room was reached, the player expresses a—potentially announced as final—**suspicion** which is the room the active player is in, a guess of a character, and a guess of a weapon. This suspicion is broadcasted, i.e., it is communicated to all players. The guessed character is moved to the room if it is not already there. If the suspicion is final, the active player is shown the hidden cards. If they match the suspicion made, this player wins and the game ends. If not, the game ends for this player only, the player loses the game. Final suspicions are not modelled in our version of the game since a simpler way of ending the game is possible.
4. Players respond to a stated non-final suspicion as follows:
   - If a player has one or more of the mentioned cards, they show one of these cards, in a secret (handshaking) way, to the active player.
   - If a player has none of the cards, they simply pass.
5. After the responses, if the game has not ended, everybody updates their knowledge according to the obtained information and the next player, in a round-robin fashion, becomes active and starts their turn.

4   Knowledge Representation, Updates, and Strategies

In this section we present our choices for representing and using the gathered knowledge and we identify and describe the different strategies, in form of different levels, for the players.

The dealing of the cards, which is the essence of the global state, is given by a function c that attributes cards to either a player or to the hidden pile (representing the crime):

$$c\colon \mathrm{Cards} \to \mathrm{Players} \cup \{\texttt{hidden}\},$$

with

$$c(C) = \begin{cases} p & \text{if player } p \text{ has card } C, \\ \texttt{hidden} & \text{if card } C \text{ is part of the crime.} \end{cases}$$

Note that the use of a capital letter for C is to contrast with the lower case c next to it and will be even more justified by further definitions.

The knowledge of players consists of an approximation of this function. We distinguish between positive and negative knowledge.

The **positive knowledge** of player p is a function

$$\mathrm{knows}(p)\colon \mathrm{Cards} \to \mathrm{Players} \cup \{-1\}$$

with

$$\mathrm{knows}(p)(C) = \begin{cases} p' & \text{if player } p \text{ knows that } p' \text{ has the card } C, \\ -1 & \text{otherwise.} \end{cases}$$

This local knowledge of player p is updated to a value different than -1 or p, when p is active and when, after having formulated a suspicion, they receive a card C from another player p'. Of course, if a player p has a card C, we have $\text{knows}(p)(C) = p$. Because we consider different levels of strategy, this update will not always be used by the players (in particular it is not used for levels below 2).

The *negative* knowledge is enriched when a player p' declares a "pass" on a guess from player p. This information is the same for all players, as it is broadcasted, and hence, we make it a global function instead of parametrizing it per player. The **global negative knowledge** is a function

$$\text{neg\_know} : \text{Cards} \times \text{Players} \to \{\texttt{true}, \texttt{false}\}$$

with

$$\text{neg\_know}(C, p) = \begin{cases} \texttt{true} & \text{if everybody knows } C \text{ is not in } p\text{'s hand,} \\ \texttt{false} & \text{otherwise.} \end{cases}$$

Clearly, both types of knowledge agree with the true dealing of cards:

$$\text{knows}(p)(C) = p' \Rightarrow \mathsf{c}(C) = p',$$
$$\text{neg\_know}(C, p) = \texttt{true} \Rightarrow \mathsf{c}(C) \neq p.$$

Note that, since the negative knowledge is global, we cannot infer negative knowledge on other players from the fact that $\text{knows}(p)(C) = p'$.

There is more knowledge and deduction involved in playing the original Cluedo game. One could use more epistemic deduction and/or answer set programming methods to design a strategy, see e.g., [8,9,21,22]. The primary interest for us is to produce a probabilistic nondeterministic model, which could be model checked by existing tools. We therefore keep it simple and assume only this limited positive and negative knowledge.

We next identify several meaningful and clearly simplified **strategies** for a player. These are based on the notion of *a card being considered decided for a player*. Such cards will be ignored at the time of guessing. The idea is that a player will only suspect a room and/or character if the corresponding card is *undecided*, i.e., it is of interest to the player. We identify four different levels, described next. The difference between them is in the definition of a decided card.

- Level 0 – no knowledge used: A player just makes a random guess among the available options without using any knowledge, so no card is considered decided.
- Level 1 – own positive knowledge: player p makes a guess only on cards that they do not own, i.e., such that $\text{knows}(p)(C) \neq p$. Hence, a card is considered decided if the active player owns it.
- Level 2 – all positive knowledge used: player p makes a guess only on cards such that $\text{knows}(p)(C) = -1$. Hence, a card is considered decided for the active player if they know who owns this card.

- Level 3 – positive and negative knowledge used: Here, a card C is considered decided and hence will be ignored by player p if p knows who has it or p knows that no (other) player has it. Formally,

$$\mathrm{knows}(p)(C) \neq -1 \vee \forall p' \neq p.\, \mathrm{neg\_know}(C, p') = \texttt{true}.$$

However, there are situations where players have to make a guess even if cards are decided, in order to prevent the game from deadlocking. This is, for example, the case when all character cards are decided, but the game has not ended yet. In such a case, we suspect the room where we are and randomly choose a character card, with probability $\frac{1}{|\mathrm{Characters}|}$, and proceed. Note that this might seem not to be the best strategy for the active player, it might seem as if it would have been better to choose one of the character cards this player owns, if there are such, but it is necessary to prevent deadlock as we nowhere store the (local) knowledge of the hidden card and only make the winning guess more likely as the game proceeds. Hence, this is needed for the current version of the model.

Note that in a two-player game, playing at level 3 is in a sense (that we do not make precise here) equivalent to playing at level 2, as our experiments in Sect. 7 confirm.

These strategies could be seen as memoryless and a player could mix them nondeterministically at each turn. However, we do not expect that mixing would show meaningful results, and therefore investigate the behaviour of *consistent* players only, that is, players that stick to a level throughout the game. We reckon that there are many other possible strategies we could have considered, maybe some clever ones, but these offer simplicity as well as a satisfactory diversity.

We note that in our models the choice of strategy is hardcoded in the formula defining the predicate when a card is considered decided, except the code for level 0 which does not mention decided cards. The rest of the model is unaffected by this choice.

5   Simple Birthday Cluedo

We now briefly discuss the exact layout of the board as well as the choices made in our simple birthday version of Cluedo. Our board consists of eleven positions, shown in Fig. 2. The corner positions of the 3×3 square represent the four rooms: the kitchen at position 0, the living room at position 2, the library at position 6, and the dining room at position 8. Hence, the rooms are near to each other and near to the initial positions of the players, at most a couple of steps away. Moreover, one can imagine the rooms having doors on both sides, e.g., the kitchen is reachable both from position 1 and from position 3 in one step. The additional positions 9 and 10 that stick out of the square are the initial positions of the two players. We originally planned four such position, in order to accommodate up to four players, but as mentioned we limit ourselves to two only. These positions are never visited later in the game, as a player needs to

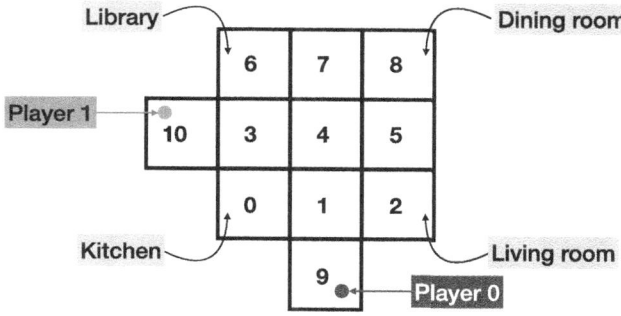

Fig. 2. The board of our simple birthday Cluedo game.

be in a room in order to make a guess and these positions are bringing players further away from the rooms.

There are no weapons (and hence no weapons cards) in the simplified birthday Cluedo. Clearly, this reduces the state space.

Moreover, we do not model the secret passages, as on the small board they would make all rooms easily accessible to the players.

While designing the model, we have noticed that it is of no importance at all where the inactive characters are positioned and hence we do not store and update their positions.

As already mentioned, originally we created a model with three players and one inactive character. The model was never fully built by STORM as we ran out of the approximately 8 TB memory that we had available at a point where the model had 4600 billion states. We therefore reduced the model further to two players and two inactive characters. However, we leave the logic of the game and the representation and use of knowledge as in the case of multiple players, that is, in the deduction we do not take advantage of the fact that there are (only) two players.

Finally, since our board is quite small, we only roll a single die in order to determine where to move next.

6   The PRISM Model

In order to use the STORM model checker, we construct the model [4] using the PRISM language. Reasoning about states is always through values of variables, transitions can be probabilistic, e.g., the dice roll example shown in Listing 1.1, or nondeterministic, if more transitions apply in a state. The language is very simple in its functionality, at times we wished for more expressive features, yet the simplicity also has its merits and the language is very clear and easy to use. Transitions are guarded by Boolean-formula guards that may test all variables in the system. For more information on the PRISM language, please consult [1,18].

```
1  // Module for a simple coin flip
2  module coin
3      // Face of the coin, 0 is tail and 1 is head
4      face : [0..1] init 0;
5
6      // Transition probabilities
7      [flip] true -> 1/2 : (face'=0) + 1/2 : (face'=1);
8  endmodule
```

Listing 1.1. Prism Module of the Coin Example

Logically, on a high level, the model is a parallel composition of several processes:

- A *master* process that takes care of the initialization, the distribution of the cards, and gives the turn to the players in a round-robin fashion.
- The *board* with its movement restrictions and probabilistic information.
- A number of (here only two) *player processes*, one per player. These are different instances of the same PRISM module.

The Dealing

The first step is the assignment of all the cards, that is, who has which card and which cards are hidden as the solution. This information is given by the function c and is stored using a variable cC for each card C. These card variables take values from -1 to n, where n is the number of players, as follows (and assigned in this order):

$$cC = \begin{cases} -1 & \text{if card } C \text{ has not been assigned to a player yet (initial value),} \\ n & \text{if card } C \text{ is hidden (one of the two cards of the solution),} \\ i & \text{if card } C \text{ is in the hand of player } i \in \{0, 1, \ldots, n-1\}. \end{cases}$$

These variables are written as, e.g., cKitchen for the kitchen card, and cChar3 for the card representing character 3.

The Rounds

In each round of the game we have an active player, which we often consider to be player 0 in the sequel. The round consists of the following steps, to be executed sequentially:

1. Dice roll and choice within the set of available rooms;
2. Stating a suspicion;
3. Collecting responses;
4. Updating;
5. End of game or re-initialization for the next round.

In order to ensure sequentiality, and distinguish between the different phases (as well as eliminate needless states), we introduce global Boolean flag variables.

These are: `dice`, `guess`, `response`, `update0`, `update1` as well as some others that guard the corresponding sequential phases in the behaviour of the active player. For example, `dice` is only true in the first phase (dice roll) when it is time to roll the dice and move across the board accordingly, as described next. We will discuss why we need multiple variables in the, e.g., update phase when we detail the corresponding phase below.

In the rules expressed in the sequel we skip writing unnecessary guards. For example, all the mentioned phases happen after the initialisation phase, and hence include a guard that checks that initialisation has been completed, but we do not write that in the rules to keep them a bit shorter and easier to read.

The Suspicion

We use global variables, `roomSusp` and `charSusp`, to express the two suspicions. They take a value between 0 and 7, following the encoding in Table 1. The same type is used for variables `show0` and `show1` which record the card that a player shows upon a guess from another player.

Table 1. Encoding of the cards

Room card	Encoding room card	Character card	Encoding character card
Kitchen	0	Character 0	4
Living room	1	Character 1	5
Library	2	Character 2	6
Dining room	3	Character 3	7

The Knowledge

For representing the knowledge functions, we also use global and local variables. For the local positive knowledge of player $p \in \{0, 1, \ldots, n-1\}$ we use variables of the form

$$\mathsf{c}C\mathsf{p} = \begin{cases} i & \text{if } p \text{ knows that card } C \text{ is owned by player } i \in \{0, 1, \ldots, n-1\}, \\ -1 & \text{otherwise (initial value).} \end{cases}$$

For example, `cKitchen0` $= 1$ denotes that player 0 knows that the kitchen card is owned by player 1; This is close to the notation of Sect. 4, where it is $\text{knows}(0)(\mathsf{cKitchen}) = 1$.

The negative knowledge is a global information as in Sect. 4. Which card is *not* owned by which player is stored in a set of Boolean variables of the shape $\mathsf{n}C\mathsf{Player}p$ where C is a card, and p a player. For example,

$$\mathsf{ncKitchenPlayer0} = \mathsf{true}$$

represents the common knowledge that player 0 does not have the kitchen card.

Dice Roll and Move to the Next Position

Given that the active player is at a position of the board, we precompute the probabilities of moving to a set of new positions, see Table 2. This is the main source of probabilistic information in the model.

Table 2. Probabilistic moves from any position to a set of reachable positions after rolling the dice.

$0 \rightarrow \frac{1}{6}: (1 \vee 3) + \frac{1}{6}: (2 \vee 4 \vee 6) + \frac{1}{6}: (2 \vee 5 \vee 6 \vee 7) + \frac{1}{2}: (2 \vee 6 \vee 8)$
$1 \rightarrow \frac{1}{6}: (0 \vee 2 \vee 4) + \frac{1}{6}: (0 \vee 2 \vee 3 \vee 5 \vee 7) + \frac{2}{3}: (0 \vee 2 \vee 6 \vee 8)$
$2 \rightarrow \frac{1}{6}: (1 \vee 5) + \frac{1}{6}: (0 \vee 4 \vee 8) + \frac{1}{6}: (0 \vee 3 \vee 7 \vee 8) + \frac{1}{2}: (0 \vee 6 \vee 8)$
$3 \rightarrow \frac{1}{6}: (0 \vee 4 \vee 6) + \frac{1}{6}: (0 \vee 1 \vee 5 \vee 6 \vee 7) + \frac{2}{3}: (0 \vee 2 \vee 6 \vee 8)$
$4 \rightarrow \frac{1}{6}: (1 \vee 3 \vee 5 \vee 7) + \frac{5}{6}: (0 \vee 2 \vee 6 \vee 8)$
$5 \rightarrow \frac{1}{6}: (2 \vee 4 \vee 8) + \frac{1}{6}: (1 \vee 2 \vee 3 \vee 7 \vee 8) + \frac{2}{3}: (0 \vee 2 \vee 6 \vee 8)$
$6 \rightarrow \frac{1}{6}: (3 \vee 7) + \frac{1}{6}: (0 \vee 4 \vee 8) + \frac{1}{6}: (0 \vee 1 \vee 5 \vee 8) + \frac{1}{2}: (0 \vee 2 \vee 8)$
$7 \rightarrow \frac{1}{6}: (4 \vee 6 \vee 8) + \frac{1}{6}: (1 \vee 3 \vee 5 \vee 6 \vee 8) + \frac{2}{3}: (0 \vee 2 \vee 6 \vee 8)$
$8 \rightarrow \frac{1}{6}: (5 \vee 7) + \frac{1}{6}: (2 \vee 4 \vee 6) + \frac{1}{6}: (1 \vee 2 \vee 3 \vee 6) + \frac{1}{2}: (0 \vee 2 \vee 6)$
$9 \rightarrow \frac{1}{6}: (1) + \frac{1}{6}: (0 \vee 2 \vee 4) + \frac{1}{6}: (0 \vee 2 \vee 3 \vee 5 \vee 7) + \frac{1}{2}: (0 \vee 2 \vee 6 \vee 8)$
$10 \rightarrow \frac{1}{6}: (3) + \frac{1}{6}: (0 \vee 4 \vee 6) + \frac{1}{6}: (0 \vee 1 \vee 5 \vee 6 \vee 7) + \frac{1}{2}: (0 \vee 2 \vee 6 \vee 8)$

For example, the line for position 0 states that with probability $\frac{1}{6}$, which is the probability of outcome 1 after rolling the dice, the player can move to position 1 or 3, as these are one step away from the position 0. In two steps, with probability $\frac{1}{6}$ the player can reach positions 2, 4, or 6. In three steps, again with probability $\frac{1}{6}$ it could reach 2, 5, 6, or 7. Here, 2 is still there, as the player may decide to go to this room (living room) next, no matter that it could go further away. Moreover positions 5 and 7 are also legal, as they bring the player closer to a room that is not reachable yet. Finally, with the remaining probability of $\frac{1}{2}$ corresponding to the dice outcome being 4, 5, or 6, the player can reach all other rooms and has therefore the choice between positions 2, 6, and 8.

Clearly, the data from the table can be pre-computed in an automated way for larger boards. Note that just like in the original Cluedo game, we do not allow the active player to remain at their old position.

We originally modelled the move to a room as a nondeterministic choice, indicated in the table by using the disjunction symbol. However, this gave the model-checker the possibility to use information unavailable to players, as we will discuss in the next section. Moreover, the model was huge and impossible to check, see Sect. 7. Hence, we convinced ourselves that it makes sense to choose randomly within the rooms of interest after ignoring decided ones (according to the level played) – and this is exactly what we model now. In our current models, we now have a probabilistic choice, influenced by the level of the active player, i.e., by cards being decided.

For example, if the active player 0 is at position 0 and the cards for library and dining room are decided, then the player can move to the living room (encoded by 1) and suspect it or to the other available positions and end their turn without making a suspicion, according to the following probabilistic transition rule:

```
dice & (turn = 0) & (pos0 = 0)
      & (!cKitchenDecided0)
      & (!cLivingRoomDecided0)
      & (cLibraryDecided0)
      & (cDiningRoomDecided0) ->
              1/12:   (pos0' = 1) & (dice' = false)
                      & (endTurn' = true)                     +
              23/36:  (pos0' = 2) & (dice' = false)
                      & (guess' = true) & (roomSusp' = 1) +
              1/12:   (pos0' = 3) & (dice' = false)
                      & (endTurn' = true)                     +
              1/12:   (pos0' = 4) & (dice' = false)
                      & (endTurn' = true)                     +
              1/18:   (pos0' = 5) & (dice' = false)
                      & (endTurn' = true)                     +
              1/18:   (pos0' = 7) & (dice' = false)
                      & (endTurn' = true).
```

The probabilities are calculated by replacing the nondeterministic disjunction with a uniform probability distribution in each parenthesis, after ignoring the rooms of the decided cards.

It suffices to have 8 rules (testing whether the dining room, the living room, and the library cards are decided) of this kind for position 0. Note that we need not test the kitchen card at position 0 as the player is in the kitchen and has to change their position. At positions that are not rooms, we need to have 16 rules per line in the table, testing which room cards are decided. We precompute the rules using a Python script. This is one of the main sources of complexity in the model. However, our current Python script actually creates 16 rules for each position, hence in the model we are also (unnecessarily) testing for the kitchen card in the above situation.

The Guess

As we saw in the rule above, changing the position upon throwing a dice immediately determines the guess for the "suspected room". It is now time to make the guess for the "suspected character" in the current turn.

This is again a point where the level information is used in order to express a guess. However, thanks to the notion of a decided card, the rules are the same in all levels. We have 16 rules, each testing which of the 4 character cards have been decided and normalizing the probabilities accordingly. If none of the cards is decided, then the rule (for player 0 being the active player) is:

```
guess & (turn = 0)
      & (!cChar0Decided0)
      & (!cChar1Decided0)
      & (!cChar2Decided0)
      & (!cChar3Decided0) ->
            1/4: (charSusp' = 4) & (guess' = false)
                 & (response' = true) & (update0' = true) +
            1/4: (charSusp' = 5) & (guess' = false)
                 & (response' = true) & (update0' = true) +
            1/4: (charSusp' = 6) & (guess' = false)
                 & (response' = true) & (update0' = true) +
            1/4: (charSusp' = 7) & (guess' = false)
                 & (response' = true) & (update0' = true).
```

The reason why we set the update-flag for player 0 to true will be discussed below in the update subsection.

Here, again, we decided for a uniform distribution instead of nondeterminism. This is not only to make the model smaller, but also to comply with reality. Nondeterminism is not the right modelling choice for this situation in the game, as it could lead the model to use global information that a single player does not have. If the choice was nondeterministic here, the maximum probability would be obtained by guessing the right character from the start, which is a piece of global information stored in the model that a single player does not have.

The rule when all cards are decided has exactly the same conclusion, due to our choice to then select randomly between any of the four cards, as mentioned above in the discussion of the levels.

Another example, where we do not have all possible options is expressed by the following rule:

```
guess & (turn = 0)
      & (cChar0Decided0)
      & (!cChar1Decided0)
      & (cChar2Decided0)
      & (!cChar3Decided0) ->
            1/2: (charSusp' = 5) & (guess' = false)
                 & (response' = true) & (update0' = true) +
            1/2: (charSusp' = 7) & (guess' = false)
                 & (response' = true) & (update0' = true).
```

The Response

The response of the players in the current round is recorded in the variables show0, show1 which can contain one card—the number encoding the card, or −1 for "pass", or for the case when the player is the active player who does not show anything.

When a player, say player 1, shows a card, we change the value of the equally numbered variable `update1` to true. This is sort of a way to count how many of the players are done with showing cards. Only when all are done, the update step can start. This is also the reason why the active player, player 0, sets `update0` to true immediately after making the guess.[3] The rules for the response are, for example, as follows:

```
response & (turn != 1) & (update1 = false)
         & (roomSusp = 2) & (charSusp = 7)
         & (cLibrary = 1) & (cChar3 = 1) ->
             (show1' = 7) & (update1' = true).
```

This rule refers to an action of player 1, who is not the active one - not their turn now, but who owns both of the suspected cards. Note that with the encoding, the suspect room is the library and the suspect character is character 3. In this case, player 1 decides nondeterministically to show the card character 3. The other (nondeterministic) option for this player is:

```
response & (turn != 1) & (update1 = false)
         & (roomSusp = 2) & (charSusp = 7)
         & (cLibrary = 1) & (cChar3 = 1) ->
             (show1' = 2) & (update1' = true).
```

In our view, the nondeterministic response is adequate in the model and it reflects the nature of the game, as there is little to use in the global state. Moreover, it makes the model amenable to the addition of more sophisticated strategies in the future.

If player 1 (who is not the active player) has only one of the two cards, then this is the card they have to show. The corresponding rules are then as follows:

```
response & (turn != 1) & (update1 = false)
         & (roomSusp = 2) & (charSusp = 7)
         & (cLibrary = 1) & (cChar3 != 1) ->
             (show1' = 2) & (update1' = true).
```

```
response & (turn != 1) & (update1 = false)
         & (roomSusp = 2) & (charSusp = 7)
         & (cLibrary != 1) & (cChar3 = 1) ->
             (show1' = 7) & (update1' = true).
```

as well as the last possibility, when the player has none of the cards and broadcasts "pass":

---

[3] Note that having a show-flag and an update-flag per player is not necessary in the case of two players only, but we have designed the model to work for multiple players too, and only reduced to two due to the limits of computational resources.

```
response & (turn != 1) & (update1 = false)
         & (roomSusp = 2) & (charSusp = 7)
         & (cLibrary != 1) & (cChar3 != 1) ->
             (show1' = -1) & (update1' = true).
```

We could have saved two of the four rules that refer to showing a card that a player has. We keep the presentation here faithful to the model, which cannot easily be changed due to the need to rerun experiments that take many hours. This only influences the number of lines of code in the model.

The Update

Given our setup, in particular the negative knowledge being global, most of the updates are made by the active player, player 0.

This player needs to update their local positive knowledge based on the cards shown to them and to update the global negative knowledge based on players not showing cards.

Due to the design of the language and the nondeterminism involved, we need a way to record that all this has been done. We achieve this with two more Boolean flags, updateShow0 and updateShow1, one per player. Initially, their value is false, and it becomes true if the knowledge gained from show0, show1 has been updated, respectively. An example rule is:

```
(turn = 0) & (update0 = true) & (update1 = true)
         & (updateShow1 = false) & (show1 = 0) ->
             (cKitchen' = 1) & (updateShow1' = true).
```

Here, show1 = 0 means that the card shown by player 1 was the kitchen card, as 0 encodes this card. We have such a rule for each possible card (room and character). Furthermore, we need all of these rules also checking show0 and updateShow0. Finally, we need checks for a "pass" that updates the global knowledge:

```
(turn = 0) & (update0 = true) & (update1 = true)
         & (updateShow1 = false) & (show1 = -1)
         & (roomSusp = 0) & (charSusp = 4) ->
             (ncKitchenPlayer1' = true)
             & (ncChar0Player1' = true)
             & (updateShow1' = true).
```

Such a rule is needed for each possible combination of room and character cards, as suspects, to update the global knowledge (for player 1 here, as player 1 responds with a "pass").

Now, it only remains to move the suspect into the suspected room. Note that we do not store the position of characters that are passive, and hence we only move the suspect character if it is a player. This is given by the rule (here we also assume the affected player is player 0):

```
(turn = 0) & (update0 = true) & (update1 = true)
           & (updateShow0 = true) & (updateShow1 = true)
           & (charSusp = 4) & (roomSusp = 0) ->
                (pos0' = 0) & (response' = false)
                    & (checkWinner' = true).
```

This completes the update of the current round. We need such a rule for every possible value of `roomSusp`. Note that `checkWinner` is another flag that takes us to the last phase of the round, described next.

The Final Step before a New Round, or Game Over

At this point, we may have reached the end of the game. This is the case if none of the players has shown anything, and the active player 0 has none of the cards they asked for. We encode the end of the game as value n (here 2) of the global variable `turn` which normally takes a value i with $0 \leq i \leq n - 1$ if player i is supposed to take the next turn, respectively. One can see this as the master getting the last turn. At the same time we also declare the winner, by assigning the identity of the active player to the global variable `winner`. To achieve this, we have rules of the kind:

```
(turn = 0) & (checkWinner = true) & (show1 = -1)
           & (update0 = true) & (update1 = true)
           & (updateShow0 = true) & (updateShow1 = true)
           & (roomSusp = 0) & (charSusp = 4)
           & (cKitchen != 0) & (cChar0 != 0) ->
                (winner' = 0) & (turn' = n).
```

We have such a rule for every possible room and character suspect, and every player in place of the active player.

In order to proceed in case there is no winner yet, we add a set of rules like the following rule:

```
(turn = 0) & (checkWinner = true)
           & (update0 = true) & (update1 = true)
           & (updateShow0 = true) & (updateShow1 = true)
           & ((show1 != -1) | (cKitchen = 0) | (cChar0 = 0))
           & (roomSusp = 0) & (charSusp = 4) ->
                (checkWinner' = false) & (endTurn' = true),
```

where | denotes disjunction, as in the PRISM language and `endTurn` is another Boolean flag used to signal that a new turn should start. One such rule per suspect pair and non-active player (testing that the player passed) is added to the model.

This completes the turn. We can then give the turn to the next player by:

```
endTurn & (checkWinner = false) ->
            (turn' = (turn + 1) mod n)
            & (dice' = true) & (endTurn' = false)
            & (update0' = false) & (update1' = false)
            & (show0' = -1) & (show1' = -1)
            & (updateShow0' = false)
            & (updateShow1' = false)
            & (guess' = false) & (response' = false).
```

7 Verification with PRISM and STORM

For our experiments, we first used the statistical model checking feature of PRISM `4.8.1` to obtain some early results on our model. Afterwards, we performed precise model checking using a development build of STORM `1.8.2`. We present the results of the runs in the subsequent sections.

In a nutshell, our results confirm that the game is well-designed, i.e., the individual players have almost the same winning probabilities. Moreover, the more advanced the strategy the players used, the shorter the game.

7.1 Hardware and Technical Setup

We ran PRISM on an Intel-based consumer-grade machine running Ubuntu 22.04.3 LTS, equipped with an Intel i7-13700H processor featuring 20 cores at 3.7–5.0 GHz (24 MB L3 cache) with 32 GB of memory. The results are briefly discussed in the following subsection.

Afterwards, we performed precise model checking using a development build of STORM `1.8.2` on the Mach-2, which "is the largest shared-memory machine in Austria" [2]. The Mach-2 is operating on SuSE Linux Enterprise Server 12 with a total amount of 1728 processor cores and approximately 20 TB of global shared memory. These 1728 cores are allocated across 72 blades, each holding "two 12-core processors of type Intel Xeon E5-4650V3 operating at 2.1–2.8 GHz with 30 MB L3 cache" [2]. To execute STORM, we had access to 18 of these blades, totalling 432 cores, and approximately 8 TB memory. Due to the size of our model, we enabled the `TRACE` logs to gain more insight into running computations and set the precision of the solvers used by STORM to 0.01. This allowed us to obtain results within an acceptable timeframe, at the cost of slightly reduced precision.

Note that using Mach-2 was not an overkill: we previously tried (and failed) using the Intel-based consumer-grade machine mentioned above, as well as two local servers (bigiron8 and bigiron9) of which the larger (bigiron9) has 64 processors of type AMD Opteron 6376 at 2.3–3.2 GHz (12 MB L3 cache), and 528354580 kiB, i.e., approximately 504 GiB of memory.

7.2 Statistical Model Checking Using PRISM

Table 3 shows the results of statistical model checking with PRISM, which we used for obtaining quick results and estimates. We used the CI (confidence interval) simulation method, unknown width, 0.01 confidence, 50000 simulation samples, and maximal path length of 10000. Increasing the number of simulation samples resulted in only insignificant changes.

Recall that the higher the level, the better a player in this level is supposed to perform. Indeed, this is confirmed by our results. In particular, we see that if player 0 plays at level 3, their probability of winning against a dumb adversary (with level 0) is very high, around 0.86. If both players follow the dumb strategy and play at level 0, then the expected number of rounds for the game is the highest, at more than 21. Moreover, also as expected, the chances of winning for the player who starts the game, player 0 in our experiments, are slightly higher than for the other player independent of the configuration, i.e., their levels.

Table 3. Results of statistical model checking using PRISM, with properties: P(Player0 wins) = P=? [F(turn=2)&(winner=0)], P(Player1 wins) = P=? [F(turn=2)&(winner= 1)], R(rounds) = R{''rounds''}=? [F(turn=2)].

Levels		Properties		
Player0	Player1	P(Player0 wins)	P(Player1 wins)	R(rounds)
0	0	0.5126	0.4874	21.26188
0	1	0.27598	0.72402	11.64354
0	2	0.18804	0.81196	8.1258
0	3	0.19398	0.80602	8.09902
1	0	0.7668	0.2332	11.12688
1	1	0.54422	0.45578	7.90266
1	2	0.446	0.554	6.48912
1	3	0.44302	0.55698	6.48658
2	0	0.86494	0.13506	6.94006
2	1	0.6704	0.3296	5.89656
2	2	0.56972	0.43028	5.52136
2	3	0.56478	0.43522	5.54222
3	0	0.86226	0.13774	6.95394
3	1	0.67554	0.32446	5.92966
3	2	0.56586	0.43414	5.49614
3	3	0.56682	0.43318	5.51918

We note that the PRISM statistical engine resolves nondeterministic choices by first uniformly sampling one of the enabled nondeterministic transitions, and then choosing the next state according to the probability distribution of the chosen transition. Hence, it considers only one randomised scheduler, turning an MDP into an MC, in contrast to STORM that computes the min/max probability of a property over all possible schedulers.

7.3 Probabilistic Model Checking Using STORM

Using STORM, we checked for the minimum expected number of rounds ($R_{\min}$) for the game to end. It would also be interesting to investigate the minimum and maximum probabilities of winning in the future, as the model still contains a small amount of nondeterminism. It is worth mentioning that we initially started with a model that had a high degree of nondeterminism. Specifically, the choice of a position on the board after the dice roll was nondeterministic, and in addition, we had three players. Even Mach-2, with approximately 8 TB of RAM, ran out of memory while building that model. The machine entered an endless loop of garbage collection by the Sylvan [7] library, which is used to represent the model symbolically. The number of states in the model was 4,628,706,795,793, hence 4600 billion, at the time STORM stopped making progress.

We also experimented with different STORM engines. In the beginning, we tried the Sparse engine on the initial large model, but later switched to the symbolic DD engine, which provides the results reported here. We also attempted to use the abstraction-refinement engine, but it does not support checking expected rewards, which was our focus. It is worth noting that prior to reducing the model to the stage described here, we experimented with intermediate models, particularly those with high nondeterminism. For these models, we used the abstraction-refinement engine to check the minimum and maximum probability for a certain player to win. However, the results were trivial: The minimal probability was 0 and the maximum was 1. As we mentioned earlier, this outcome is due to the "trivial schedulers" that just guess the right answer immediately for one player or the other.

In Table 4, we present the results of our experiments with STORM on the family of models described in the paper. In the discussion of the results, we refer to the experiment runs using two-digit numbers, the first one representing the strategy level of player 0 and the second one the level of player 1. So 00 stands for: both players follow the strategy of level 0. When STORM checks the expected number of rounds, that we report in the table, it chooses a scheduler in a way that the cards the players show each other will be optimal, in order to minimize the expected number of rounds, i.e., turns. We implemented this by defining a reward `rounds` inside our model, which just counts the number of turns. The results that we obtain for the expected number of rounds are similar, slightly smaller, to the ones computed with PRISM and statistical model checking.

We monitored the memory consumption of each configuration using the GNU `time` command, which gives statistics about a specified program. These statistics also include the maximum resident set size which we report on in Table 4. The most memory intensive task, as expected, concerns the game in which both players play at level 0. For this configuration and all others marked with a star, garbage collection was initiated.

Table 4. Results of probabilistic model checking using STORM where M abbreviates million, and B abbreviates billion.

Levels		Results					
Player0	Player1	R_{min} (rounds)	Execution time	Memory (Peak)	States	Transitions	
0	0	20.81023631	12:05:53	7.591 TiB*	14.780 B	47.271 B	
0	1	11.60163129	17:04:42	7.452 TiB*	637 M	1.952 B	
0	2	7.451742675	41:11:13	7.451 TiB*	620 M	2.429 B	
0	3	7.451742675	24:57:51	7.454 TiB*	620 M	2.429 B	
1	0	11.11053715	26:36:12	7.459 TiB*	641 M	1.964 B	
1	1	7.905685058	22:46:12	7.138 TiB	23 M	66.200 M	
1	2	6.064613559	15:32:07	6.806 TiB	23 M	85.421 M	
1	3	6.064613559	08:38:40	6.806 TiB	23 M	85.421 M	
2	0	6.730102023	06:01:02	6.603 TiB	594 M	1.784 B	
2	1	5.764917719	08:31:56	6.149 TiB	20 M	56.541 M	
2	2	5.33706423	07:34:15	5.844 TiB	18 M	47.481 M	
2	3	5.33706423	05:31:12	5.844 TiB	18 M	47.481 M	
3	0	6.730102023	22:28:10	6.603 TiB	594 M	1.784 B	
3	1	5.764917719	10:03:21	6.149 TiB	20 M	56.541 M	
3	2	5.33706423	06:42:59	5.844 TiB	18 M	47.481 M	
3	3	5.33706423	06:49:06	5.844 TiB	18 M	47.481 M	

Somewhat surprising, the runtimes of our experiments in different configurations vary significantly: the span is between approximately 6 and 26 h per configuration. In particular, we sometimes get very different runtimes even for configuration models that are of comparable size, see e.g., the results for the 20 and 30 runs, where player 0 plays at level 2 and 3, respectively, and player 1 plays at level 0. Another curious fact about the runs 20 and 30 is that the obtained results are identical. This simply demonstrates that for two players only, the use of the global negative knowledge makes no difference. This observation is strengthened by all runs where one player plays at level 2 and at level 3, for which we obtained the same expected number of rounds. The complete list of experiments is also available via [4].

8   Conclusions

We investigated a family of probabilistic models implemented in the PRISM language to reason about different playing strategies in a simplified version of the Cluedo game. In our variant, we considered two players on a board with four rooms located at the four different corners of a 3×3 grid where one of four possible characters is suspected to have eaten the birthday cake. We formalised the global knowledge of the ownership of each card and the local knowledge of each player encoding it also in our PRISM models.

We considered different scenarios where each player uses different levels of knowledge and compared the effectiveness of different combinations of these levels for both players. We then employed both statistical and exact model checking to check different properties on all the models: the probability for each player to win (in the statistical case) and the expected minimum number of turns to win the game. Encoding these models in the PRISM language and verifying such properties using exact model checking tools such as STORM was interesting and challenging. Each model has almost a thousand of lines of code. We believe that this effort could be relieved with new probabilistic programming language primitives that could support the definition of more complex model patterns at a higher level. Another option would be to define an independent higher-level probabilistic language that compiles to PRISM code. We are interested in working on this, possibly in collaboration with Joost-Pieter, in the future.

Recall that the largest generated state space of almost 15 billion states required about 8 TB of memory, while each verification task required multiple hours. To the best of our knowledge, compared with the quantitative verification competition reports [5,12], this is the second largest MDP benchmark for STORM. We hope that the proposed benchmark will stimulate further improvement of the STORM model checker, but first of all we wish you a happy birthday, Joost-Pieter!

References

1. The probabilistic model checker PRISM (2024). https://www.prismmodelchecker.org/
2. The supercomputer MACH-2 (2024). https://www3.risc.jku.at/projects/mach2/
3. Arming, S., Bartocci, E., Chatterjee, K., Katoen, J.-P., Sokolova, A.: Parameter-independent strategies for pMDPs via POMDPs. In: McIver, A., Horvath, A. (eds.) QEST 2018. LNCS, vol. 11024, pp. 53–70. Springer, Cham (2018). https://doi.org/10.1007/978-3-319-99154-2_4
4. Bartocci, E., Desharnais, J., Lindner, P., Sokolova, A.: Birthday cake cluedo: models and additional data (2024). https://github.com/plindnercs/birthday-cluedo
5. Budde, C.E., et al.: On correctness, precision, and performance in quantitative verification. In: Margaria, T., Steffen, B. (eds.) ISoLA 2020. LNCS, vol. 12479, pp. 216–241. Springer, Cham (2021). https://doi.org/10.1007/978-3-030-83723-5_15
6. Cai, C., Ferrari, S.: A Q-learning approach to developing an automated neural computer player for the board game of CLUE®. In: Proceedings of IJCNN 2008, pp. 2346–2352. IEEE (2008). https://doi.org/10.1109/IJCNN.2008.4634123
7. van Dijk, T., van de Pol, J.: Sylvan: multi-core decision diagrams. In: Baier, C., Tinelli, C. (eds.) TACAS 2015. LNCS, vol. 9035, pp. 677–691. Springer, Heidelberg (2015). https://doi.org/10.1007/978-3-662-46681-0_60
8. van Ditmarsch, H.P., van der Hoek, W., Kooi, B.P.: Concurrent dynamic epistemic logic for MAS. In: Proceedings of AAMAS 2003, pp. 201–208. ACM (2003). https://doi.org/10.1145/860575.860608
9. Dixon, C.: Using temporal logics of knowledge for specification and verification - a case study. J. Appl. Log. 4(1), 50–78 (2006). https://doi.org/10.1016/J.JAL.2005.08.003

10. Groote, J.F., van Heesch, S., Volk, M.: Formal modelling and analysis of slot machines (2024). arXiv:2407.06809
11. Groote, J.F., Wiedijk, F., Zantema, H.: A probabilistic analysis of the game of the goose. SIAM Rev. **58**(1), 143–155 (2016). https://doi.org/10.1137/140983781
12. Hahn, E.M., et al.: The 2019 comparison of tools for the analysis of quantitative formal models. In: Beyer, D., Huisman, M., Kordon, F., Steffen, B. (eds.) TACAS 2019. LNCS, vol. 11429, pp. 69–92. Springer, Cham (2019). https://doi.org/10.1007/978-3-030-17502-3_5
13. Hansen, D.M., Hansen, K.D.: Clues about bluffing in clue: is conventional wisdom wise? IEEE Trans. Games **13**(3), 310–314 (2021). https://doi.org/10.1109/TG.2019.2957353
14. Hasbro: Clue Jr, The Case of the Missing Chocolate Cake (2003). http://www.hasbro.com/common/instruct/Clue_Jr.,The_Case_of_the_Missing_Chocolate_Cake_(2003).pdf
15. Hensel, C., Junges, S., Katoen, J., Quatmann, T., Volk, M.: The probabilistic model checker Storm. Int. J. Softw. Tools Technol. Transf. **24**(4), 589–610 (2022). https://doi.org/10.1007/S10009-021-00633-Z
16. Iepsma, R.: Preposterior Decision Analysis in the game Cluedo. Bachelor's thesis, Faculty of Science, University of Amsterdam (2012). https://staff.fnwi.uva.nl/b.bredeweg/pdf/BSc/20112012/Iepsma.pdf
17. Kingston, J.: Comparing question answering strategies for Cluedo. In: Proceedings of AISB 2017: Workshop on AI and Games, pp. 332–335. Society for Study of Artificial Intelligence and the Simulation of Behaviour (2017). https://research.brighton.ac.uk/files/452820/conference-edition-proceedings.pdf
18. Kwiatkowska, M., Norman, G., Parker, D.: PRISM 4.0: verification of probabilistic real-time systems. In: Gopalakrishnan, G., Qadeer, S. (eds.) CAV 2011. LNCS, vol. 6806, pp. 585–591. Springer, Heidelberg (2011). https://doi.org/10.1007/978-3-642-22110-1_47
19. Meyer, J.C., van der Hoek, W.: Epistemic logic for AI and computer science, Cambridge tracts in theoretical computer science, vol. 41. Cambridge University Press, Cambridge (1995). https://doi.org/10.1017/CBO9780511569852
20. Mitchell, K.: Investigating Artificial Intelligence for Playing 'Speed Clue', a Stochastic Game involving Logical Inference. Bachelor's thesis, school of Computing, University of Leeds (2020). https://info.bb-ai.net/student_projects/project_reports/Games/Katie-Mitchel-Cluedo-project-report.pdf
21. van Ditmarsch, H.: Killing Cluedo. Natuur en Techniek **11**, 32–40 (2001)
22. van Ditmarsch, H.: The description of game actions in Cluedo. In: Game theory and Applications, vol. 8, pp. 1–28 (2002). https://personal.us.es/hvd/oldpubs/gta8.pdf
23. Wikipedia: Cluedo (2024). https://en.wikipedia.org/wiki/Cluedo. Fig. 1 by cmglee, Google, Twitter, emojione contributors, Construct, Zeus, Patrick Yavitz, La Mula Francis - This file was derived from: Cluedo board.svg, CC BY-SA 4.0. https://commons.wikimedia.org/w/index.php?curid=127937647
24. Xu, J.: Playing clue: an entropy-based computer AI for the classic board game. Bachelor's thesis, Computer Science, Princeton University Senior Theses (2013). http://arks.princeton.edu/ark:/88435/dsp01hx11xf36z

Riding the Storm in a Probabilistic Model Checking Landscape

Christian Hensel[2], Sebastian Junges[1]($\boxtimes$)(ID), Tim Quatmann[2](ID),
and Matthias Volk[3](ID)

[1] Radboud University, Nijmegen, The Netherlands
`sebastian.junges@ru.nl`
[2] RWTH Aachen University, Aachen, Germany
[3] Eindhoven University of Technology, Eindhoven, The Netherlands

Abstract. Probabilistic model checking is a formal verification technique to check whether stochastic models satisfy properties of interest. Along with a rich theory, the community has developed mature tool support, which in turn has been applied to a set of industrial case studies. This paper demonstrates various abilities of the probabilistic model checker Storm by a set of simple and more accessible examples.

1 Introduction

"Randomization is a key element in sequential and distributed computing. Reasoning about randomized algorithms is highly non-trivial. (...) The field of probabilistic verification has developed considerably since the 1980s", according to the paper *The Probabilistic Model Checking Landscape*, written by Joost-Pieter Katoen as an accompanying paper for his LICS 2016 keynote [27]. While that paper surveyed probabilistic model checking as an algorithmic technique for probabilistic verification, this paper takes a more practical stance. It takes the state-of-the-art probabilistic model checker Storm [23][1] and showcases the progress in the last decades *by example*. While the use of probabilistic model checking in applications in aerospace, systems biology, robotics, reliability engineering, etc. is well documented, this paper asks the question: *How can Storm help in important decisions in the life of a (perhaps quite specific) professor?* By answering that question, we hope to inspire novel applications of probabilistic model checking.

This paper is part of a Festschrift in honor of Joost-Pieter Katoen's 60th birthday.

This work was partially funded by NWO Veni grant ProMiSe (222.147), NWO Open Science Fund StormAE (OSF23.2.093), and a KI-Starter grant from the Ministerium für Kultur und Wissenschaft NRW.

[1] In 2016, Storm was available as an alpha-version under heavy development by Joost-Pieter Katoen and the authors of this paper.

© The Author(s), under exclusive license to Springer Nature Switzerland AG 2025
N. Jansen et al. (Eds.): Principles of Verification: Cycling the Probabilistic Landscape,
LNCS 15261, pp. 98–114, 2025.
https://doi.org/10.1007/978-3-031-75775-4_5

	Discrete-time	Continuous-time
Deterministic i.e., purely probabilistic	DTMC	CTMC
(Properly) **Nondeterministic**	MDP	MA (or CTMDP)

Fig. 1. The four main models in the probabilistic model checking landscape.

What Are Markov Models? Probabilistic model checking typically describes systems using an operational model compromising states and transitions between them. We specifically study *Markov* models, i.e., models that possess the *Markov property*. The dynamics of these models from some state onward do not depend on how that state was reached. In the context of probabilistic model checking, the following four standard Markov models are: *discrete-time Markov chains* (DTMCs) and *Markov decision processes* (MDPs) as well as *continuous-time Markov chains* (CTMCs) and *Markov automata* (MAs), which [27] classifies as in Fig. 1:

- In *discrete-time* models, time progresses in steps and exclusively by taking a transition, while in *continuous-time* models, time progresses while residing in a state and the time that one resides in a state is exponentially distributed.
- In *(purely) probabilistic* models, the models describe a stochastic process that generates runs through these models. In models with *(proper) nondeterminism*, a policy[2] may arbitrarily choose how to resolve choices[3].

We illustrate some of these models by example in the sections below. We also note that in the literature, there are more variations, such as probabilistic timed automata and stochastic timed automata, see e.g., [9]. The probabilities in the models above are not always known precisely. This has lead to research on robust and in particular parametric models, also illustrated below.

Furthermore, an important aspect for nondeterministic models is how powerful the policies are and who controls them. Some relevant characterizations regarding these policies include:

- whether they have access to the precise state or only observe statistics of those states, which is prominently captured by *partially-observable MDPs*,
- whether they depend on the complete history, only on the last state, or whether they can use some (bounded) amount of memory, and
- whether the policy is controlled by a single agent or by multiple agents (centralized or decentralized), and whether these work together or whether they compete in a *stochastic game*.

What Is Probabilistic Model Checking? Probabilistic model checking extends classical (non-probabilistic) model checking [8], which deals with

---

[2] also: scheduler or strategy.
[3] also: actions.

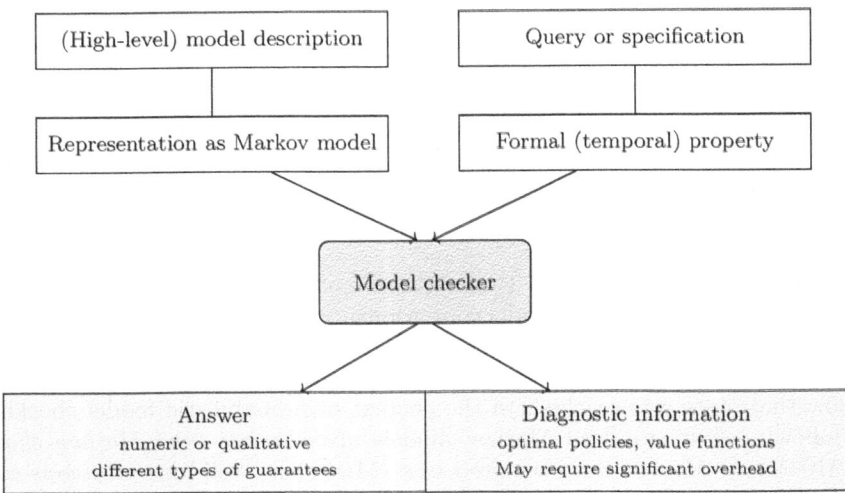

Fig. 2. A graphical description of (probabilistic) model checking, extended from [8].

discrete-time models including non-determinism, but where all probabilities in the system are one or zero. Strictly (logically) speaking, probabilistic model checking (PMC) checks whether a given Markov model satisfies a given property. Figure 2 makes this precise: PMC takes as an input a representation of a Markov model and a (textual representation of a) logical specification and checks whether the Markov model satisfies the specification. While classically, the answer to such a question is either yes or no, PMC methods take a more liberal stance and allow to compute quantitative results with user-configurable guarantees. Specifications are then of the form: *What is the probability to randomly walk through town and not find a coffee store within ten blocks?* or *What is the expected time to reach work among all policies that ensure that we reach work by the start of the lecture with 99% probability?*. We exemplify these and other specifications later in this paper and refer to [8,27] for a formal treatment of the satisfaction relations. The model checker computes *answers* which may come with method-dependent guarantees along with *diagnostic information* such as the policy that maximises some probability or witnesses that explain why a specification is satisfied. We remark that for nondeterministic models, it is essential to also specify the type of policies that should be considered.

What is a Probabilistic Model Checker? The use of probabilistic model checking typically refers to the application of a set of push-button algorithmic approaches that execute probabilistic model checking. Tools that implement these approaches are commonly referred to as *probabilistic model checkers*. Historically, there has been a variety of probabilistic model checkers, including E-(MC)^2 [24], MRMC [28], Modest-mcsta [19], Prism [31], EPMC/iscasMC [18], Storm [23], UPPAAL [32], and PET [34]. Textbook application of probabilistic model checking typically consists of four main procedures followed in a linear order:

1. *Model building.* The model is typically given in a formal language, such as the Modest language [9], the Prism language [31] or JANI [11]. From a high-level representation of the model, we extract a representation of the underlying transition matrices, state labels, etc. The representation of these (typically sparse) matrices can be explicit or condensed (i.e., symbolic).
2. *Reduction.* Using preprocessing steps such as qualitative reachability analysis [8,16], bisimulation minimisation [33], and end-component elimination [1,10], this model and the property is translated into a kind of normal form. What preprocessings are optional and what preprocessings are mandatory depends on the type of property.
3. *Solving.* From the model in normal form, a set of equations are derived, which depending on the model are e.g., linear equations, ODEs, Bellman equations, etc. Solving these equations typically translates into an answer of the original query on the original model.
4. *Diagnostic information.* When the type of query requires more than a simple numeric or qualitative answer, the result must be translated back. This back-translation from results on the normal form to the original input requires a lot of book-keeping and is not always supported.

We remark that for many standard benchmarks, model building is the most expensive step. Furthermore, while there are combinations of models and properties with trillions of states, there are also models with only a few hundred states that are hard to model check, even for simple properties [21].

Model Checking in a Loop. In recent years, the model checking steps above are more and more intertwined in an effort to improve scalability or to tackle some complex specifications. In particular, we see that probabilistic model checkers are embedded in a variety of loops. We observe at least three categories (with hybrid versions possible):

1. *Model-level abstraction-refinement* (Fig. 3a), e.g., (game-based) predicate-abstraction [4,29] or partial exploration [10,36] of a given model or of its normal form. Instead of passing a complete, potentially infinite, Markov model, an abstraction is applied and based on the answer and the diagnostic information, the abstraction is refined.
2. *Guess-and-verify* (Fig. 3b), in particular inductive synthesis approaches within parameter synthesis [12,13] or multi-objective model checking [17,35]. In these cases, the result or some diagnostic information is guessed and then verified, and
3. *Divide-and-conquer* (Fig. 3c), in particular topological and compositional approaches to model checking [14,20,37] and parameter lifting [26]. The analysis of many Markov models jointly yields a result of the original query. Which Markov chains are analysed may be decided on-the-fly.

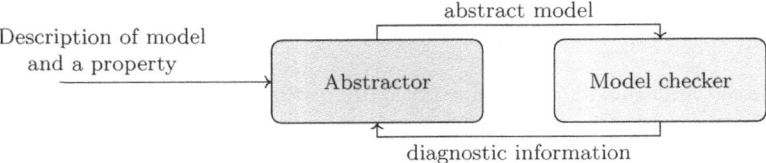

(a) Model-level Abstraction-Refinement: The original model cannot be successfully analysed. The hope is to find an abstraction that can be analysed instead.

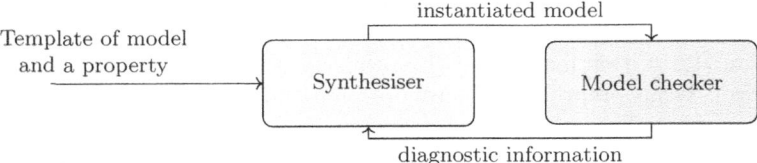

(b) Guess-and-verify: The goal is to synthesise some model or property. The synthesis loop iteratively guesses a model and property and the model checker may verify whether these guesses are correct.

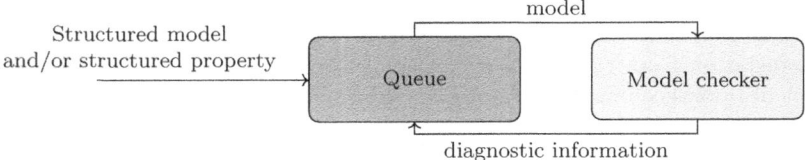

(c) Divide-and-conquer: The verification of a structured model or property can be reformulated by the verification of many smaller models (and some postprocessing). Which smaller models/properties are to be verified depends on the outcome of earlier verification calls.

Fig. 3. Three times model-checking-in-the-loop. While the generic layout is often similar, the relation between the subsequent invocations can be quite different.

The use of model checkers in the loop means that diagnostic information is more often used by tools rather than humans, that some expensive preprocessing options may pay off, and that the configuration of error-tolerances needs to be sufficiently flexible. These challenges are partially relating to research questions, but also largely increase the complexity of efficient model checking tools.

The Probabilistic Model Checker Storm in a Nutshell. Storm is a probabilistic model checker whose development started at Joost-Pieter Katoen's MOVES group at the RWTH Aachen University in 2012[4]. The first public release was in 2017 [15]. Storm's main focus is to provide an open platform that contains fast implementations of the fastest available algorithms in probabilistic model checking under one roof: We believe that such high-speed implementations are important reference points for further research and we believe that the

---

[4] https://github.com/moves-rwth/storm/commit/9da2eaf.

ability to plug-and-play different algorithms within one tool allows to push the state-of-the-art considerably. Storm therefore provides various algorithms and data structures for the main procedures outlined above and has been used to (re)implement many approaches with a model-checker-in-the-loop. To support users to exploit the algorithms and the modular structure, Storm provides a Python interface that allows to plug different parts together and create simple model-checking-in-a-loop scenarios. After 12 years, Storm has been a successful project along different measures [23]: Its speed was testified in tool competitions, the extensibility has been exploited by various researchers that (sometimes independently of the Storm-developers) built upon the tool, Storm has been used in a variety of domains, and Storm is increasingly used in teaching probabilistic model checking[5].

Further Reading. Since *The Probabilistic Model Checking Landscape*, additional surveys and overviews have been appeared that discuss this landscape from different angles and at different levels of detail, including but not limited to the papers [3,5,7,30].

2   The Random Chili Peppers

Around the world, music can be relaxing, prevent being stressed out, help focus, and allow socializing.[6] Finding the right music in a sea of random music can be a challenge though. In this first example[7], we assume we have a music player containing $N = 100$ songs. We can switch songs through two buttons: either going to the *next* or a *random* song. Starting at any song, we want to reach our favourite song at position 42 as fast as possible and we *can't stop* before.

The MDP. We model the music player by an MDP as depicted in Fig. 4. A state k represents the song which currently plays. From each state, two choices are possible. Choice **n** leads to the next song $k + 1$ with probability 1. Choice **r** randomly chooses a next song with a uniform probability distribution of $1/N$.

Playing the Favourite Song. We want to compute the minimal expected number of button presses to reach our favourite song at position 42 from any possible starting position. Using Storm, we compute the minimal expected number of steps to reach state 42 from any state. The result is visualized in Fig. 5.

For most starting positions, we need 13.64 steps to reach our favourite song. For the starting positions 29–42, a lower number of steps can be achieved. By extracting the optimal policy via Storm, we can *give it away* and see the reason for this behaviour. For songs 29–41, the optimal policy is to press the next button **n**, for song 42 we have reached the goal, and for all other songs it is best to randomly choose the next song (choice **r**).

---

[5] In a reaction to a long standing series of jokes, we are especially proud that Storm can be compiled within a few minutes.

[6] See, e.g., the "Nacht der Professoren".

[7] The example is based on a puzzle of FiveThirtyEight.

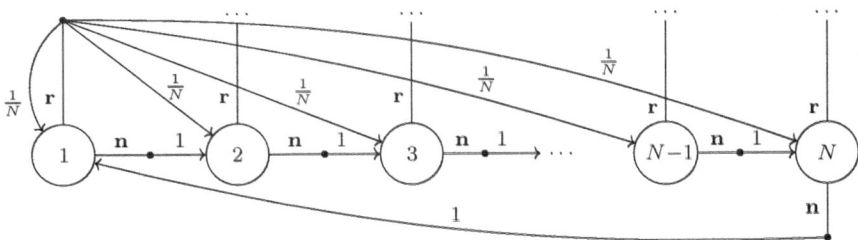

Fig. 4. The MDP model for the music shuffle problem.

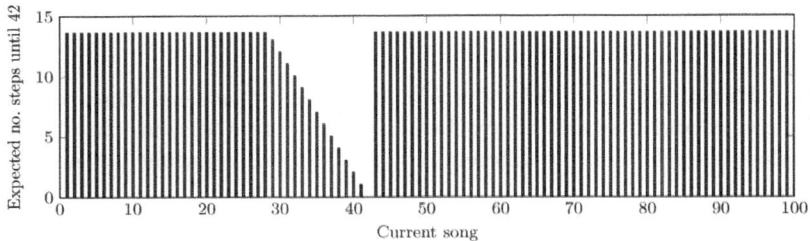

Fig. 5. Expected number of steps to reach song 42 from any song.

3   Enjoyable Road Biking

Road biking is a healthy[8], sustainable and enjoyable activity that can be combined with a daily commute. We therefore adapt a famous MDP model checking example, originally by M. Randour, which went viral due to an appearance on YouTube[9]. Our adaption focuses on the road biking aspect of a commute between Maastricht and Aachen[10].

The MDP. We model the system dynamics of an agent (which we call JPK): In particular, we describe the state of JPK based on its location, the actions reflect the decision to travel towards a next location, and the outcome of this action is arriving at the new location with a high probability, whereas with a lower probability[11] JPK arrives at a different location. We annotate the pairs of cities with travel time, elevation gain, and boredom. In this paper, we use a simple model as in Fig. 6, with the cities and actions outlined in Fig. 6a, the transition probabilities in Fig. 6b and the rewards in Fig. 6c.

The Expected Travel Time. The reward of a path is the sum of the rewards along each transition. For any given policy, we can weight the reward along a

---

[8] Unless accidents occur.

[9] Markov Decision Processes - Computerphile, youtube.com/watch?v=2iF9PRriA7w.

[10] The model checker Uppaal has been used in 2017 to retroactively plan commutes of Kim G. Larsen between the towns of Danmark and Uppsala in 1995.

[11] Abstracting good reasons: road blocks, coffee-deprivation, following famous cyclists.

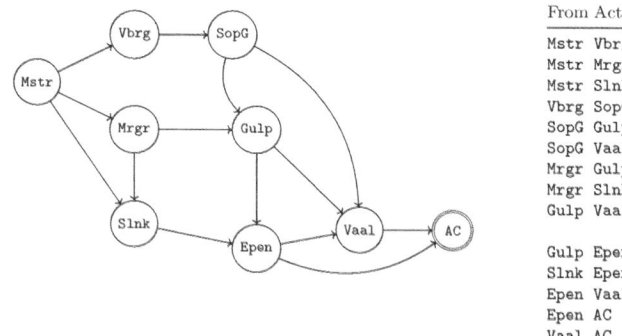

(a) The Bike Riding MDP: Actions

From	Action	Destination
Mstr	Vbrg	0.8: Vbrg, 0.2: Mrgr
Mstr	Mrgr	0.9: Mrgr, 0.1: Vbrg
Mstr	Slnk	1: Slnk
Vbrg	SopG	1: SopG
SopG	Gulp	0.95: Gulp, 0.05: Mrgr
SopG	Vaal	0.8: Vaal, 0.2: Gulp
Mrgr	Gulp	0.6: Gulp, 0.4: SopG
Mrgr	Slnk	0.95: Slnk, 0.05: Gulp
Gulp	Vaal	0.4: Vaal, 0.4: AC, 0.2: SopG
Gulp	Epen	0.9: Slnk, 0.1: Slnk
Slnk	Epen	0.9: Epen, 0.1: Gulp
Epen	Vaal	0.8: Vaal, 0.2: AC
Epen	AC	0.9: AC, 0.1: Vaal
Vaal	AC	0.995: AC, 0.005: Epen

(b) Transition relation

| From | Mstr | | | Mrgr | | | Vbrg | SopG | | | Epen | | Gulp | | | | | Slnk | | Vaal | |
To	Vbrg	Mrgr	Slnk	Gulp	Slnk	SopG	SopG	Gulp	Marg	Vaal	AC	Vaal	Vaal	AC	Epen	Slnk	SopG	Epen	Gulp	AC	Epen
Time	30	24	44	10	16	10	6	23	15	48	52	19	16	23	12	13	5	8	12	7	28
Elev.	99	130	160	0	25	14	6	123	123	250	266	149	109	208	60	50	5	0	80	45	28
Bore.	20	100	20	100	0	0	5	0	0	0	0	0	500	0	0	0	5	0	0	0	0

(c) The reward models

Fig. 6. The Bike Riding MDP

path by the probability that we take this path. This yields the average or *expected* reward. The classical perspective on MDPs then allows us to find a policy that minimises the expected travel time. Indeed, the optimal policy aims to follow the main road

Maastricht − Margraten − Gulpen − Vaals − Aachen,

and if diverted, follow Valkenburg − Schin op Geul − Gulpen as well as Slenaken − Epen − Vaals. With this policy, one arrives in Aachen after roughly 75.3 min.

The Probability of Being on Time. Above, we used the expected travel time. However, when giving a lecture, it does not matter whether the *expected* arrival time is before the lecture, but with what probability one arrives at the lecture on time. In Fig. 7, we display the probability to arrive within T minutes using the policy that optimizes the overall expected travel time (the lower, blue curve). We also plot the maximal probability that (using any policy) we can achieve (the upper, orange curve). These probabilities are *reward-bounded reachability* [2] properties, using the implementation from [20].

Trading Objectives! Above, we consider a single, clear objective. However, we can also ask for a trade-off: Some policies may be marginally better in terms of the probability to arrive on time, but have an expected travel time that is much lower. Indeed, Fig. 8a shows how the expected time to travel to Aachen can be

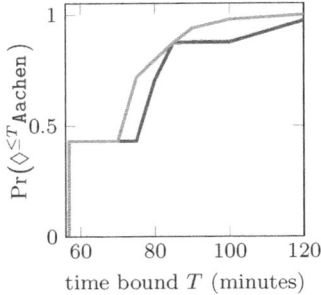

Fig. 7. Probability of reaching Aachen in T time (──── fixed ──── optimal).

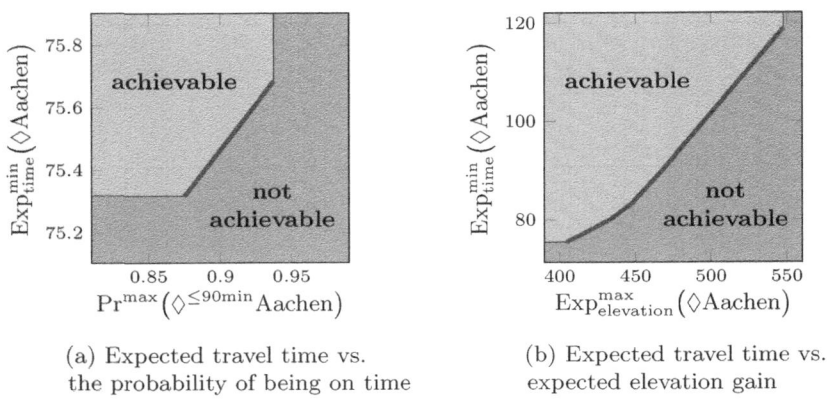

(a) Expected travel time vs. the probability of being on time

(b) Expected travel time vs. expected elevation gain

Fig. 8. Pareto fronts for different objectives for the bike riding MDP.

traded for the probability to reach Aachen within 90 min. It shows that there exist Pareto-optimal policies that reach Aachen in an expected 75.3 min and in 75.65 min respectively, but while the former reaches Aachen on time in only 88% of the cases, the latter reaches Aachen within 90 min in 94% of the cases. Closer inspection of the latter policy shows that this policy takes a more southern route that avoids the temptation in Gulpen to circle via Schin op Geul to climb the *Keutenberg* (back to Gulpen).

We can also analyze trade-offs between different reward assignments, e.g., to simultaneously optimize the expected travel time and the expected elevation gain as shown in Fig. 8b. Here, we see that when minimizing the expected travel time, JPK can only achieve an expected elevation gain of approximately 405 m. To increase this gain, more time needs to be invested. For example, a Pareto optimal policy that achieves an expected elevation gain of 500 m induces an expected travel time of approximately 100 min.

Efficient and Enjoyable, Together. Multi-reward bounded quantiles [20] are a more advanced property to illustrate trade-offs between resource constraints.

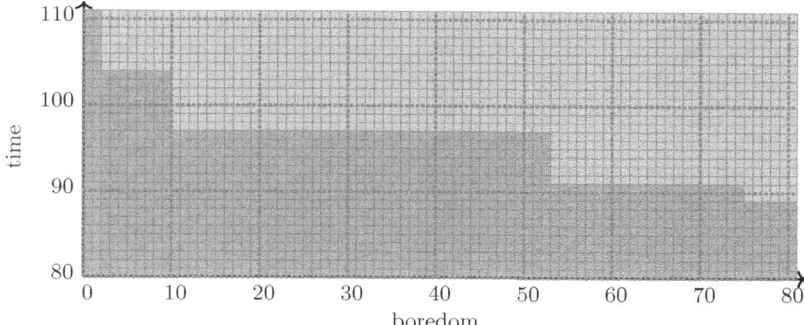

Fig. 9. Two-dimensional quantile: boredom experienced and time required to reach Aachen with more than 90% probability.

Intuitively, such queries fix a threshold on a reward-bounded reachability probability and ask, for which reward-limits the probability threshold is satisfiable. For the road biking scenario, our goal is to reach Aachen in more than 90% of the cases while only taking a certain time t and while limiting the boredom during the trip to some value b. The green cells in the upper right of Fig. 9 illustrate for which time and boredom values this goal is achievable by some policy. We see that JPK can reach Aachen with sufficient probability in 89 min. However, this requires to take a rather boring route with a boredom value of 75. By only taking an additional 2 min, the boredom can already be reduced to a value of 53. Further relaxing the time limit to 97 min yields a quite enjoyable road trip with a boredom value of only 10.

4   Scouting for Coffee Supply

A fine challenge for many researchers is to find coffee of a suitable quality level in unknown towns. Members of the *Random Walk Circle* may approximate a city as a two-dimensional grid and argue that randomly moving through town will ensure that they find coffee. Such a policy is also beneficial because one does not need to remember the route and can instead think about research. By using Storm one can make the most out of a conference visit.

4.1   Optimal Bias to Find a Coffee Place

One member of the Random Walk Circle, we call them JPK, is known for his efficiency. While he adores random walks, he wants to use a probabilistic model checker to optimize the bias of the four-side die that he will use for moving through town.

The (parametric) MC. We model JPK as an agent which has a latitude (x) and a longitude (y), and an orientation in a grid-like city with streets in a perfect grid shape and all roads going either north-south or east-west. The town is bordered by four canals that cannot be crossed. At every crossing, JPK decides to go with likelihood p_W west, with likelihood p_E east, with likelihood p_N north and with likelihood p_S south. JPK initially starts at a hotel quietly located far from the conference venue. It is known that there are two coffee places of sufficient quality in town, aptly named *Cotton & Coffee* (CC) and *Katoen & Koffie* (KK). These coffee places must be on one of the main squares and based on prior knowledge, JPK has a distribution over their locations. The result is a parametric MC (pMC), as depicted partially in Fig. 10b[12].

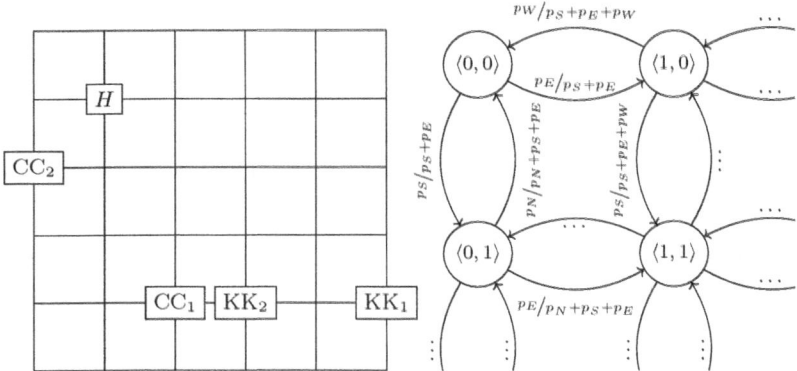

(a) The city with the hotel and the prior over the coffee places: CC is with prob 0.8 at CC_1, KK is with prob 0.3 at KK_1.

(b) Fragment of the parametric MC.

Fig. 10. The Scouting Coffee Model.

Finding the Optimal Bias. The question at hand now is, what is the optimal value for p_W, p_E, p_N, p_S such that the expected time until arriving from the hotel at either CC or KK is lowest? We use parameter synthesis techniques [25]. Computing *the* optimal value is hard and involves solving a system of nonlinear equations. Instead, we use a parameter lifting approach [26] to compute that the values

$$u^* = (p_N \mapsto {}^{281}/_{2560}, p_W \mapsto {}^{49}/_{512}, p_E \mapsto {}^{443}/_{2560}, p_S \mapsto {}^{1487}/_{2560})$$

ensure that JPK may expect to reach coffee after ≈ 15.86 steps. We also obtain a guarantee that it is not possible that, using likelihoods between

---

[12] We want to highlight that pMCs models that use rational functions as transition probabilities are somewhat rare in the literature: The use of polynomials is more standard.

$1/20 \leq p_N, p_W, p_E, p_S \leq 19/20$ to obtain better results than 15.1 steps, in expectation.

Compared with an unbiased random walk, i.e., a walk obtained by

$$u = (p_N, p_W, p_E, p_S \mapsto 1),$$

which requires an expected 41.38 steps, we see the benefits for the agent. We also computed the optimal bias for arriving at a coffee place within 20 steps:

$$u' = (p_N \mapsto 73/1280, p_W \mapsto 217/1280, p_E \mapsto 307/1280, p_S \mapsto 1207/1280)$$

ensures that a coffee place is reached with probability 0.8, together with a guarantee that it is not possible to improve this beyond probability 0.82.

4.2   Getting More Coffee While Avoiding Colleagues

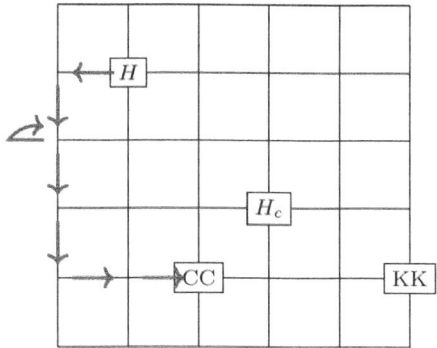

Fig. 11. The Scouting Coffee Model for the partially observable MDP: The city with the hotel, the hotel of the colleague, and the coffee places CC and KK as well as the optimal route to a coffee.

The next day, JPK knows where the coffee spots are. He would like to enjoy his Latte while answering emails and therefore aims to arrive at the coffee spot without bumping in some colleagues that are roaming through town. Under these new circumstances, the optimal parameter values cannot ensure a probability of 0.35 to reach the coffee spot within 20 steps. We are unhappy with this outcome and decide to no longer use a memoryless random walk. Thus, Storm is now used to compute a policy that uses memory. However, this policy cannot depend on the (unknown) location of the colleague: We must analyse a partially observable MDP (POMDP).

The Partially Observable MDP. Similar to above, the agent has a location x, y, as has the colleague. The locations of both coffee places are now fixed and known. The colleague starts in a hotel one block to the south and one block to the east. The colleague moves randomly but fast: They will move uniformly either one or two steps in any cardinal direction. The colleague will spot JPK if they are on the same road (either north-south or east-west) and at most two blocks apart. The goal now is to reach a coffee place without being spotted by this colleague.

The Solution. We obtain a policy that takes a path with 7 steps, which is not the shortest route to the target, but also easy to remember. The path (along with the city map) is drawn in Fig. 11. Following these 7 steps ensures that with at least 72% probability, we achieve our goal. On the other hand, taking at most 6 steps allows for at most 71% probability.

5   The Elfstedentocht Problem

The Elfstedentocht[13] (eleven cities tour) is a Dutch ice skating event hosting thousands of (amateur and professional) participants as well as millions of spectators. The almost 200 km long circular route connects eleven historical Frisian cities via frozen rivers, canals and lakes. The event can only take place when the ice is of sufficient quality. Specifically, the ice needs to be at least 15 centimetres thick along the entire course.

The CTMC. We provide a simple CTMC model for the development of the ice layers in the eleven cities depending on the surrounding temperature. For the latter, a component TEMP is used that lets a variable t oscillate between -20 and $+40\,°C$. A temperature change of $10\,°C$ occurs after an exponentially distributed delay with rate $\lambda_{\text{TEMP}} = 12$. A full cycle thus takes 12 steps and (on expectation) $12 \cdot 1/\lambda_{\text{TEMP}} = 1$ time unit, roughly representing the temperature development in the Netherlands over a year. For the thickness of the ice in the eleven cities, components ICE_i for $1 \leq i \leq 11$ are considered, each managing a variable $c_i \in \{0, \ldots, 15\}$ for the current thickness of the ice in city i. If the temperature t is negative (positive), the thickness c_i increases (decreases) by $5\,cm$ with rate $\lambda_{\text{ICE}}^t = |t|$.[14] Our final CTMC model is given by the parallel composition $\text{TEMP} \parallel \text{ICE}_1 \parallel \cdots \parallel \text{ICE}_{11}$. A label 𝕏 is given to all states in which the ice is thick enough in all eleven cities. The final model has $12 \cdot 4^{11} \approx 50$ million states connected by approximately 400 million transitions.

Damming the State-Space Explosion Problem. Our model grows exponentially in the number of Frisian cities, resulting in a huge state-space that becomes challenging for model checkers. As a countermeasure, we apply a combination of two techniques which are implemented in Storm:

---

[13] https://elfstedentocht.frl/en.

[14] The model is intentionally simple and does not accurately reflect the physical process of freezing or melting ice layers.

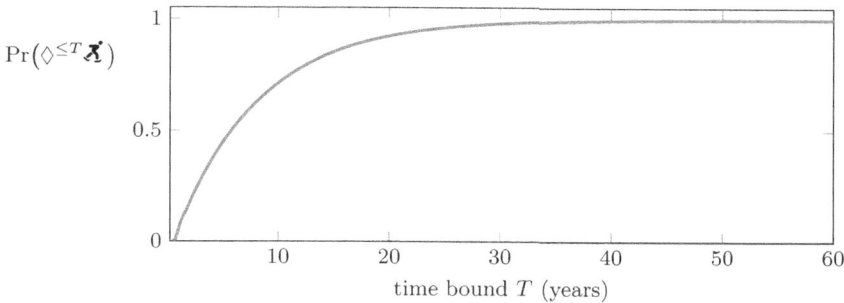

Fig. 12. Probability of experiencing at least one Elfstedentocht within 60 years.

- the original model is represented symbolically using multi-terminal binary decision diagrams (MTBDDs), and
- bisimulation minimisation [33] is applied on the (symbolic) model to merge states with equivalent behaviour into a single state.

The result is an explicitly represented CTMC with 4 368 states and 12 948 transitions which preserves all relevant properties of the original CTMC [6].

Expected Long-Run Frequency of Elfstedentocht. For a given reward assignment, the *long-run average reward* is the average reward accumulated per time unit in the long run. For the Elfstedentocht problem, we assign a reward of 1 to transitions that enter a $\not{\mathcal{X}}$ -state from a state that does not have that label. The corresponding long-run average reward yields the expected number of Elfstedentochts per year. Using Storm, we obtain a value of approx. 0.1218. The reciprocal value 8.21 is the long-run average number of years between two Elfstedentochts, although we note that the last Elfstedentocht was in 1997.

Probability of Elfstedentocht within 60 years. Using algorithms from [6], we compute the probability to reach a $\not{\mathcal{X}}$ -state within T years for various $T \in (0, 60]$. Figure 12 depicts the resulting probabilities. The probability to experience an Elfstedentocht within $T = 60$ years is approximately 99.96%.

6   Conclusion

This paper presents a number of easy-to-explain problems that can be tackled with a probabilistic model checker. While both the motivation behind the models and their structure is quite different from typical benchmarks in quantitative verification [22], the queries can be solved with an off-the-shelf version of Storm. The models are scalable and larger versions of the presented models are surprisingly challenging for the current generation model checkers.

Data Availability. We provide Jupyter notebooks with the Markov models, properties and analysis queries that allow to reproduce the results presented in this paper. The notebooks are available online at stormchecker.org/publications/festschrift.

Acknowledgements. We are grateful to the many contributors to Storm and refer to our Git repository for a complete list. Furthermore, we want to highlight that the research on probabilistic model checking and the development of tool support has been actively pursued by an active and friendly community of researchers whose efforts have also shaped the contents of this paper. Last but not least, the authors would like to thank Joost-Pieter Katoen for his warm leadership and guidance during the last decade. His leadership goes well beyond his impressive and well-recognised academic achievements and includes the need for a healthy work-life balance, good coffee and good music.

References

1. de Alfaro, L.: Formal verification of probabilistic systems. Ph.D. thesis, Stanford University, USA (1997)
2. Andova, S., Hermanns, H., Katoen, J.-P.: Discrete-time rewards model-checked. In: Larsen, K.G., Niebert, P. (eds.) FORMATS 2003. LNCS, vol. 2791, pp. 88–104. Springer, Heidelberg (2004). https://doi.org/10.1007/978-3-540-40903-8_8
3. Andriushchenko, R., et al.: Tools at the frontiers of quantitative verification. CoRR arxiv:2405.13583 (2024). https://doi.org/10.48550/ARXIV.2405.13583
4. Andriushchenko, R., Češka, M., Junges, S., Katoen, J.-P.: Inductive synthesis for probabilistic programs reaches new horizons. In: TACAS 2021. LNCS, vol. 12651, pp. 191–209. Springer, Cham (2021). https://doi.org/10.1007/978-3-030-72016-2_11
5. Baier, C., de Alfaro, L., Forejt, V., Kwiatkowska, M.: Model checking probabilistic systems. In: Handbook of Model Checking, pp. 963–999. Springer, Cham (2018). https://doi.org/10.1007/978-3-319-10575-8_28
6. Baier, C., Haverkort, B.R., Hermanns, H., Katoen, J.P.: Model-checking algorithms for continuous-time Markov chains. IEEE Trans. Softw. Eng. **29**(6), 524–541 (2003). https://doi.org/10.1109/TSE.2003.1205180
7. Baier, C., Hermanns, H., Katoen, J.-P.: The 10,000 facets of MDP model checking. In: Steffen, B., Woeginger, G. (eds.) Computing and Software Science. LNCS, vol. 10000, pp. 420–451. Springer, Cham (2019). https://doi.org/10.1007/978-3-319-91908-9_21
8. Baier, C., Katoen, J.P.: Principles of Model Checking. MIT Press, Cambridge (2008)
9. Bohnenkamp, H.C., D'Argenio, P.R., Hermanns, H., Katoen, J.P.: MODEST: a compositional modeling formalism for hard and softly timed systems. IEEE Trans. Softw. Eng. **32**(10), 812–830 (2006). https://doi.org/10.1109/TSE.2006.104
10. Brázdil, T., et al.: Verification of Markov Decision processes using learning algorithms. In: Cassez, F., Raskin, J.-F. (eds.) ATVA 2014. LNCS, vol. 8837, pp. 98–114. Springer, Cham (2014). https://doi.org/10.1007/978-3-319-11936-6_8
11. Budde, C.E., Dehnert, C., Hahn, E.M., Hartmanns, A., Junges, S., Turrini, A.: JANI: quantitative model and tool interaction. In: Legay, A., Margaria, T. (eds.) TACAS 2017. LNCS, vol. 10206, pp. 151–168. Springer, Heidelberg (2017). https://doi.org/10.1007/978-3-662-54580-5_9

12. Ceska, M., Hensel, C., Junges, S., Katoen, J.P.: Counterexample-guided inductive synthesis for probabilistic systems. Formal Aspects Comput. **33**(4–5), 637–667 (2021). https://doi.org/10.1007/S00165-021-00547-2

13. Cubuktepe, M., Jansen, N., Junges, S., Katoen, J.P., Topcu, U.: Convex optimization for parameter synthesis in MDPs. IEEE Trans. Autom. Control **67**(12), 6333–6348 (2022). https://doi.org/10.1109/TAC.2021.3133265

14. Dai, P., Weld, D.S.M., Goldsmith, J.: Topological value iteration algorithms. J. Artif. Intell. Res. **42**, 181–209 (2011)

15. Dehnert, C., Junges, S., Katoen, J.-P., Volk, M.: A storm is coming: a modern probabilistic model checker. In: Majumdar, R., Kunčak, V. (eds.) CAV 2017. LNCS, vol. 10427, pp. 592–600. Springer, Cham (2017). https://doi.org/10.1007/978-3-319-63390-9_31

16. Forejt, V., Kwiatkowska, M., Norman, G., Parker, D.: Automated verification techniques for probabilistic systems. In: Bernardo, M., Issarny, V. (eds.) SFM 2011. LNCS, vol. 6659, pp. 53–113. Springer, Heidelberg (2011). https://doi.org/10.1007/978-3-642-21455-4_3

17. Forejt, V., Kwiatkowska, M., Parker, D.: Pareto curves for probabilistic model checking. In: Chakraborty, S., Mukund, M. (eds.) ATVA 2012. LNCS, pp. 317–332. Springer, Heidelberg (2012). https://doi.org/10.1007/978-3-642-33386-6_25

18. Hahn, E.M., Li, Y., Schewe, S., Turrini, A., Zhang, L.: ISCASMC: a web-based probabilistic model checker. In: Jones, C., Pihlajasaari, P., Sun, J. (eds.) FM 2014. LNCS, vol. 8442, pp. 312–317. Springer, Cham (2014). https://doi.org/10.1007/978-3-319-06410-9_22

19. Hartmanns, A., Hermanns, H.: The modest toolset: an integrated environment for quantitative modelling and verification. In: Ábrahám, E., Havelund, K. (eds.) TACAS 2014. LNCS, vol. 8413, pp. 593–598. Springer, Heidelberg (2014). https://doi.org/10.1007/978-3-642-54862-8_51

20. Hartmanns, A., Junges, S., Katoen, J.P., Quatmann, T.: Multi-cost bounded trade-off analysis in MDP. J. Autom. Reason. **64**(7), 1483–1522 (2020). https://doi.org/10.1007/S10817-020-09574-9

21. Hartmanns, A., Junges, S., Quatmann, T., Weininger, M.: A practitioner's guide to MDP model checking algorithms. In: TACAS (1). Lecture Notes in Computer Science, vol. 13993, pp. 469–488. Springer, Heidelberg (2023). https://doi.org/10.1007/978-3-031-30823-9_24

22. Hartmanns, A., Klauck, M., Parker, D., Quatmann, T., Ruijters, E.: The quantitative verification benchmark set. In: Vojnar, T., Zhang, L. (eds.) TACAS 2019. LNCS, vol. 11427, pp. 344–350. Springer, Cham (2019). https://doi.org/10.1007/978-3-030-17462-0_20

23. Hensel, C., Junges, S., Katoen, J.P., Quatmann, T., Volk, M.: The probabilistic model checker storm. Int. J. Softw. Tools Technol. Transf. **24**(4), 589–610 (2022). https://doi.org/10.1007/S10009-021-00633-Z

24. Hermanns, H., Katoen, J.-P., Meyer-Kayser, J., Siegle, M.: A Markov chain model checker. In: Graf, S., Schwartzbach, M. (eds.) TACAS 2000. LNCS, vol. 1785, pp. 347–362. Springer, Heidelberg (2000). https://doi.org/10.1007/3-540-46419-0_24

25. Jansen, N., Junges, S., Katoen, J.P.: Parameter synthesis in Markov models: a gentle survey. In: Principles of Systems Design. Lecture Notes in Computer Science, vol. 13660, pp. 407–437. Springer, Heidelberg (2022). https://doi.org/10.1007/978-3-031-22337-2_20

26. Junges, S., et al.: Parameter synthesis for Markov models: covering the parameter space. Formal Methods Syst. Des. **62**(1), 181–259 (2024). https://doi.org/10.1007/S10703-023-00442-X

27. Katoen, J.P.: The probabilistic model checking landscape. In: LICS, pp. 31–45. ACM (2016). https://doi.org/10.1145/2933575.2934574

28. Katoen, J.P., Zapreev, I.S., Hahn, E.M., Hermanns, H., Jansen, D.N.: The ins and outs of the probabilistic model checker MRMC. Perform. Eval. **68**(2), 90–104 (2011). https://doi.org/10.1016/J.PEVA.2010.04.001

29. Kattenbelt, M., Kwiatkowska, M.Z., Norman, G., Parker, D.: A game-based abstraction-refinement framework for Markov decision processes. Formal Methods Syst. Des. **36**(3), 246–280 (2010). https://doi.org/10.1007/S10703-010-0097-6

30. Kwiatkowska, M., Norman, G., Parker, D.: Probabilistic model checking and autonomy. Ann. Rev. Control. Rob. Auton. Syst. **5**, 385–410 (2022). https://doi.org/10.1146/ANNUREV-CONTROL-042820-010947

31. Kwiatkowska, M., Norman, G., Parker, D.: PRISM 4.0: verification of probabilistic real-time systems. In: Gopalakrishnan, G., Qadeer, S. (eds.) CAV 2011. LNCS, vol. 6806, pp. 585–591. Springer, Heidelberg (2011). https://doi.org/10.1007/978-3-642-22110-1_47

32. Larsen, K.G., Pettersson, P., Yi, W.: UPPAAL in a nutshell. Int. J. Softw. Tools Technol. Transf. **1**(1–2), 134–152 (1997). https://doi.org/10.1007/S100090050010

33. Larsen, K.G., Skou, A.: Bisimulation through probabilistic testing. Inf. Comput. **94**(1), 1–28 (1991). https://doi.org/10.1016/0890-5401(91)90030-6

34. Meggendorfer, T.: PET - a partial exploration tool for probabilistic verification. In: ATVA. LNCS, vol. 13505, pp. 320–326. Springer, Heidelberg (2022). https://doi.org/10.1007/978-3-031-19992-9_20

35. Quatmann, T., Katoen, J.-P.: Multi-objective optimization of long-run average and total rewards. In: TACAS 2021. LNCS, vol. 12651, pp. 230–249. Springer, Cham (2021). https://doi.org/10.1007/978-3-030-72016-2_13

36. Volk, M., Junges, S., Katoen, J.P.: Fast dynamic fault tree analysis by model checking techniques. IEEE Trans. Ind. Inf. **14**(1), 370–379 (2018). https://doi.org/10.1109/TII.2017.2710316

37. Watanabe, K., van der Vegt, M., Hasuo, I., Rot, J., Junges, S.: Pareto curves for compositionally model checking string diagrams of MDPs. In: TACAS (2). Lecture Notes in Computer Science, vol. 14571, pp. 279–298. Springer, Heidelberg (2024). https://doi.org/10.1007/978-3-031-57249-4_14

Modest Models and Tools for Real Stochastic Timed Systems

Carlos E. Budde[1] , Pedro R. D'Argenio[2,3] , Juan A. Fraire[3,4] ,
Arnd Hartmanns[5(✉)] , and Zhen Zhang[6]

[1] University of Trento, Trento, Italy
[2] Universidad Nacional de Córdoba, Córdoba, Argentina
[3] CONICET, Córdoba, Argentina
[4] Inria, INSA Lyon, Université de Lyon, Lyon, France
[5] University of Twente, Enschede, The Netherlands
a.hartmanns@utwente.nl
[6] Utah State University, Logan, Utah, USA

Abstract. We depend on the safe, reliable, and timely operation of
cyber-physical systems ranging from smart grids to avionics components. Many of them involve time-dependent behaviours and are subject
to randomness. Modelling languages and verification tools thus need to
support these quantitative aspects. This paper gives an introduction to
quantitative verification using the MODEST modelling language and the
MODEST TOOLSET. It highlights three recent case studies with increasing demands on model expressiveness and tool capabilities: A case of
power supply noise in a network-on-chip modelled as a Markov chain;
a case of message routing in satellite constellations that needs Markov
decision processes with distributed information; and a case of optimising
an attack on Bitcoin via Markov automata model checking. For each, we
explain the particular conceptual and technical challenges in modelling
and verification, and point out open problems for future work.

1 Introduction

Cyber-physical systems consist of discrete (usually digital, often implemented in
software) controllers interacting with a continuous physical environment. Control is often networked, sometimes wirelessly. Many cyber-physical systems are
safety- or performance-critical, or economically vital. We thus need to ensure
that they operate as desired, which includes dependability requirements such as
reliability assurances, availability levels, or response time guarantees. Reliability and availability are stochastic timed properties: the probability of avoiding

This work was supported by Agencia I+D+i grant PICT 2022-09-00580 (CoSMoSS),
the European Union's Horizon 2020 research and innovation programme under MSCA
grant agreements 101008233 (MISSION) and 101067199 (ProSVED), the Interreg North
Sea project STORM_SAFE, the NextGenerationEU projects D53D23008400006 (SMARTI-
TUDE) under the MUR PRIN 2022 and PE00000014 (SERICS) under the MUR PNRR,
NWO VIDI grant VI.Vidi.223.110 (TruSTy), and SeCyT-UNC grant 33620230100384CB
(MECANO).

© The Author(s), under exclusive license to Springer Nature Switzerland AG 2025
N. Jansen et al. (Eds.): Principles of Verification: Cycling the Probabilistic Landscape,
LNCS 15261, pp. 115–142, 2025.
https://doi.org/10.1007/978-3-031-75775-4_6

unsafe behaviour within a certain time horizon, and the expected fraction of time that the system is ready to provide service, respectively. The critical systems themselves are also typically subject to randomisation, for example due to random message loss in wireless communication or due to employing randomised algorithms, and they are timed systems dealing with e.g. transmission delays and timeouts or faults occurring unpredictably over time. Thus, to assure their dependability by way of modelling and verification (ideally at design-time), we need stochastic timed formalisms and modelling languages supported by tools able to check stochastic timed properties.

This paper showcases the MODEST approach to modelling and verification of stochastic timed systems. MODEST, introduced by Bohnenkamp, D'Argenio, Hermanns, and Katoen in 2006 [10], was designed as a modelling language that provides process algebra-inspired modelling in a programming language-like syntax for the highly expressive model of stochastic timed automata (STA) [10], now extended to stochastic hybrid automata (SHA) [46]. Originally supported by the MoTor tool [11], today the MODEST TOOLSET [49]—in continuous development since 2008 and publicly available at modestchecker.net—provides a comprehensive collection of tools supporting the modelling, transformation, and verification of MODEST models. It notably includes the mcsta model checker [50] and the modes simulator [15]. It is part of an ecosystem of quantitative verification tools that support the interchange of models written in various modelling languages via the JSON-based JANI format [16] such as ePMC [47], Momba [61], or Storm [57]. In Sect. 2, we describe MODEST, JANI, and the MODEST TOOLSET.

MODEST and the MODEST TOOLSET have been applied to a multitude of case studies ranging from wireless ad-hoc routing protocols [59] over electricity grid stabilisation mechanisms [52] to the security evaluation of cyber-physical systems [66]. The formal modelling and analysis of any case study requires careful consideration of the modelling requirements—e.g. which kinds of quantities are relevant for the questions that the stakeholders want answered and consequently which type of underlying mathematical formalism is the most appropriate—in connection to the capabilities of the available tools. Finding the right level of abstraction is crucial as analysis techniques for more expressive types of models such as stochastic hybrid automata [36] are practically limited to much smaller model sizes compared to those for simpler models like Markov chains or decision processes [17]. Similarly, analysis techniques that provide stronger results, such as hard guarantees that the answer is within a user-specified ϵ-interval around the true optimal value, tend to be less scalable than those delivering weaker results, such as statistical guarantees or eventual convergence to the optimum only. Probabilistic model checking (PMC) [6,7], for example, is severely limited by the state space explosion problem that statistical model checking (SMC) [1] avoids entirely with its constant memory usage, at the cost of being restricted to estimation problems and delivering statistical guarantees only.

In Sects. 3 to 5 of this paper, we review three different case studies that MODEST and the MODEST TOOLSET have been applied to recently. We point out how the specific requirements of the case study determined the choice of

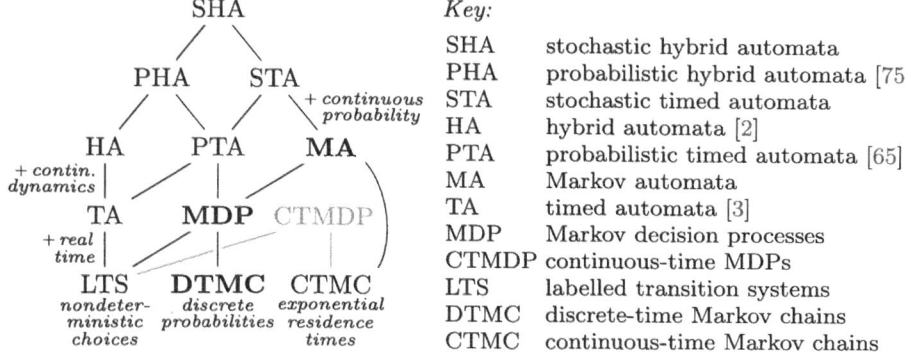

Fig. 1. The family tree of automata-based quantitative formalisms

model type and analysis techniques, showcasing the versatility of the MODEST TOOLSET as well as providing guidance to the modelling and verification practitioner by way of example. Our first case study (in Sect. 3) evaluates aspects of power supply noise in a two-by-two network-on-chip system by way of a discrete-time Markov chain (DTMC) model and a PMC analysis with mcsta; the second one (in Sect. 4) is about finding optimal routes through sparse constellations of nanosatellites using an abstract Markov decision process (MDP) [9,58] model analysed with an SMC-based approach that employs strategy sampling under distributed information as implemented in the modes tool; and finally (in Sect. 5) we optimise an attack on the Bitcoin cryptocurrency system via a Markov automata (MA) [33] model that permits mcsta to synthesise the strategy that minimises the expected time to success or maximises the probability of success within a certain time bound, which we turn into a human-readable decision tree representation via a new connection from mcsta to the dtControl tool [5].

This Extended Version. This paper is an extended version of a long presentation abstract [48] for author A. Hartmanns' invited talk at the MARS workshop at ETAPS 2022. Compared to the presentation abstract, we have expanded our introduction to MODEST and JANI in Sect. 2 along concrete examples; we added more details to the presentations of the three case studies, in particular examples and insights on interesting modelling aspects for all three case studies, new research results on using Q-learning for the satellite routing case study, and results of a newly-implemented connection from mcsta to dtControl to obtain an explainable representation of the optimal attack strategy for the Bitcoin case. Throughout, we added summaries of remaining challenges and open problems.

2   Modest Languages and Tools

A well-defined semantics in terms of a mathematically well-understood object is a cornerstone of formal models. For quantitative models, we use automata-based formalisms—that represent the evolution of a system from state to state via (randomised) transitions—building on labelled transition systems (LTS, or Kripke structures) and discrete- and continuous-time Markov chains (DTMC and CTMC, respectively) [8]. By combining these basic mathematical formalisms in various ways, and extending them with features such as real-time clocks or continuous variables evolving according to differential equations, we obtain further formalisms as depicted in Fig. 1. Since writing real-life models as, say, large Markov chains would be cumbersome, we specify them using a higher-level modelling language that offers at least discrete variables with standard arithmetic and Boolean operators plus a notion of parallel composition for the natural specification of distributed and component- or actor-based systems.

The Modest Language. One such language is MODEST, originally the modelling and description language for stochastic timed systems [10]. Its formal semantics was first defined in terms of STA [10] and later extended to SHA [46]. MODEST is a textual modelling language; its syntax is designed to be similar to widely used programming languages like C or Java to lower the barrier of entry for domain experts. At the same time, it is a process algebra in spirit, based on standard operators such as sequential and parallel composition, allowing the definition of and recursive calls to processes, and emphasising compositionality. In fact, MODEST consists of two largely orthogonal languages: one to define *behaviour*, which is the one based on process-algebraic ideas, and one to manipulate *data* such as the values of discrete variables. The latter provides arrays, recursive datatypes (e.g. allowing the definition of a linked list type via pairs of a head containing a data item and a linked list option tail), and mutually recursive functions. These features allow for concise and natural models of complex real-life systems. The properties of interest to be analysed by tools, such as queries for the maximum probability of reaching a certain goal state or requirements for the expected long-run average reward to remain below a given threshold, are specified within MODEST models as temporal logic formulas.

MODEST is equipped with a two-step semantics: The symbolic semantics maps the textual MODEST model to a network of SHA with discrete variables, where the top-level parallel composition and the values of variables are not made explicit, i.e. the composition and any operations involving variables remain as symbolic expressions. Then, the concrete semantics defines the meaning of parallel composition and variables as well as of the continuous (hybrid or timed) behaviour of the SHA, resulting in a nondeterministic labelled Markov process [30] in the most general case. As many simpler formalisms are special cases of SHA, MODEST models syntactically conforming to the restrictions of any of these sub-models have a semantics that also maps to that sub-model.

Example 1. Listing 1 shows a MODEST PTA model of a simple communication scenario: A `Sender` process transmits some file consisting of N data chunks over an unreliable `Channel` that loses a message with probability 0.5. One instance of the `Sender` and `Channel` processes each run in parallel, communicating by handshaking on the shared `send` and `ack` actions.

```
const int N;
action send, ack;
transient int sent;
bool done;
property ETimeDone = Xmin(T, done);
property PInTwiceN = Pmax(<>[S(sent) <= N * 2] done);
process Channel() {
   clock c;
   send palt {
   :0.5: {= c = 0 =}; when(c >= 2) invariant(c <= 4) ack // transmission success, acknowledge
   :0.5: {==}                                            // the message is lost
   }; Channel()
}
process Sender(int(0..N) i) {
   clock c;
   do {
   :: when(i > 0) send {= c = 0, sent = 1 =}; alt {
      :: ack {= i-- =}                                   // transmission succeeded
      :: when(c >= 5) invariant(c <= 5) tau              // timeout, retry chunk
      }
   :: when(i == 0) invariant(c <= 0) {= done = true =}   // done: all chunks transmitted
   }
}
par { :: Channel() :: Sender(N) }
```

Listing 1. MODEST PTA model of a communication scenario

After receiving a message to `send`, the `Channel`'s probabilistic message loss is implemented via MODEST's `palt` construct. We assume that the `Channel`'s precise transmission delay is unknown, but guaranteed to be between 2 and 4 time units because we, for example, know the message processing times and the minimum and maximum cable length or distance between wireless nodes. The timer `clock c` is used to implement this nondeterministic delay: the `ack` in `Channel` is guarded with the condition `c >= 2` and forced to execute once `c` reaches value 4 by the `invariant` condition, expressing a standard TA pattern in MODEST. The semicolon `;` is MODEST's sequential composition operator.

Nondeterministic choices between multiple behaviours are specified with the `alt` construct. It is used in the `Sender` after handing a chunk to the `Channel`: we either receive an acknowledgment, or determine that the message was lost after a timeout of exactly 5 time units. In this model, we know that, for each attempt to send, exactly one of the two possibilities will occur; in general, multiple of the choices of an `alt` can be available: a nondeterministic choice. Assignments are given in atomically-executed assignment blocks like `{= c = 0, sent = 1 =}`. Here, `sent` is a *transient* variable that is not part of the model's concrete states, but only takes values during the execution of assignment blocks.

Transient variables can also be observed by properties. In this model, we specify that we would like to know the minimum expected time until all chunks have been transmitted in property `ETimeDone`, and the maximum probability of transmitting all chunks in at most 2·N attempts in property `PInTwiceN`. The former is an expected accumulated reachability reward property; the latter queries for a reward-bounded reachability probability. The way rewards are accumulated

```
{ "jani-version": 1,
  "type": "pta",
  "actions": [ { "name": "send" }, { "name": "ack" } ,
  "constants": [ { "name": "N", "type": "int" } ],
  "variables": [ { "name": "sent", "type": "int", "transient": true, "initial-value": 0 },
                 { "name": "done", "type": "bool", "initial-value": false } ],
  "properties": [ ... ],
  "automata": [
  { "name": "Channel",
    "locations": [ { "name": "loc_1" },
                   { "name": "loc_6",
                     "time-progress": { "exp": { "op": "≤", "left": "c", "right": 4 } } } ],
    ...
    "edges": [ { "location": "loc_1", "action": "send",
                 "destinations": [
                 { "location": "loc_6",
                   "probability": { "exp": { "op": "/", "left": 1, "right": 2 } },
                   "assignments": [ { "ref": "c", "value": 0 } ] },
                 ... ] },
               ... ]
  }, ... ],
  "system": { "elements": [ { "automaton": "Channel" }, { "automaton": "Sender" } ],
              "syncs": [ { "synchronise": [ "send", "send" ], "result": "send" },
                         { "synchronise": [ "ack", "ack" ], "result": "ack" } ] }
}
```

Listing 2. JANI translation of the MODEST communication PTA model (excerpt)

is specified within the properties, with T being a shortcut for T(1)—accumulate a reward of 1 per time unit—and S(exp) specifying that a reward of exp is accumulated every time the system transitions from one state to another.

PTA are a good fit for modelling communication protocols and networking scenarios: their real-time features capture transmission delays and timeouts, while probabilistic choices stem from the environment (such as random message loss) and the use of randomised algorithms (like exponential backoff schemes). Consequently, the AODV routing protocol was modelled in MODEST's PTA subset [59].

The JANI Model Interchange Format. While MODEST is a convenient modelling language for end-users, implementing a MODEST parser and its symbolic semantics is a significant effort. The same problem affects many other modelling languages, e.g. Prism's [63], too. To ease tool development and facilitate the exchange of models between different tools, in 2016, the developers of several quantitative verification tools defined the JSON-based JANI [16] format. It is not designed to be human-writable, but rather serve as a model interchange format that is generated by tools from other modelling languages, such as MODEST. Today, JANI is supported by the MODEST TOOLSET (see below), ePMC [47], Storm [57], Momba [61], and several other tools. All models in the quantitative verification benchmark set (QVBS) [54] are available in both their original formats as well as in JANI. The QVBS served as the foundation for the QComp 2019 [45] and QComp 2020 [17] tool competitions.

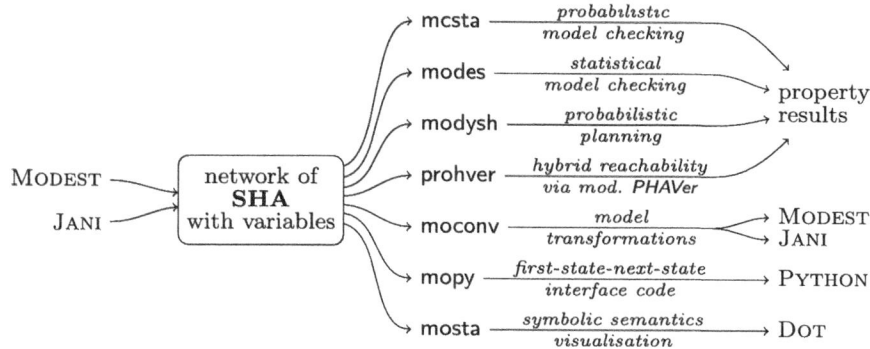

Fig. 2. Schematic overview of the MODEST TOOLSET

Example 2. In Listing 2, we show an excerpt of the JANI translation of the MODEST communication PTA model of Example 1. It is clear that JANI is not suited for human reading and quick understanding, but it is editable and inspectable. The JANI model starts with the same declarations of global items—actions, constants, global variables (discrete and continuous), and properties—as the MODEST model. Then, every element of the top-level **parallel** composition in MODEST is represented as one **automaton** in JANI. These automata correspond to MODEST's symbolic semantics, in which MODEST's textual control flow is turned into a control flow graph representation; its nodes appear as **locations** in JANI. We show some details of the **Channel** process' automaton: **invariant(c <= 4)** appears as location **loc_6**'s **time-progress** condition; every occurrence of an action in the MODEST model generates an edge in the automaton, of which we show the **send**-labelled one. All expressions are represented as syntax trees in JANI, which removes much of the complications of writing a parser. The MODEST model's top-level **par** determines the JANI **system** element: the parallel composition of one instance each of the **Channel** and **Sender** automata. While handshaking on shared actions is implicit in MODEST, JANI uses *synchronisation vectors* (inspired by CADP's exp.open tool [38]) in the **syncs** array to explicitly describe which actions from each parallel component synchronise.

The Modest Toolset. To support the creation of MODEST models, and to compute the values of properties or check requirements specified as part of models, the MODEST TOOLSET [49] provides a collection of visualisation, model transformation, model checking, and simulation tools. The MODEST TOOLSET has been in development since 2008; it is written in C#, and is available as precompiled binaries for common Linux distributions, macOS, and Windows running on x86-64 and ARM-64 platforms at modestchecker.net. An overview of the MODEST TOOLSET's components is shown in Fig. 2.

As input languages, the MODEST TOOLSET supports MODEST and JANI; its moconv tool can convert between the two and apply various transformations, such as converting a suitable PTA model into its digital clocks [64] MDP. The mosta tool visualises a model's symbolic semantics, helping in learning MODEST and in debugging models. The mopy tool converts a model into Python code implementing a first-state-next-state interface [11] that can be used to quickly prototype explicit-state verification algorithms.

The mcsta [50] tool implements PMC in an explicit-state fashion with a unique disk-based approach to mitigate the state space explosion problem. It includes efficient model reductions such as the essential states abstraction [28], and provides state-of-the-art algorithms for model checking MA [20]. A variant of mcsta implements a symblicit approach that can tackle very large models of certain structures by way of binary decision diagram (BDD)-based exploration followed by incremental explicit state elimination [44].

The statistical model checker modes [15] complements mcsta's capabilities for cases where model checking cannot be applied, such as when facing state space explosion or models with non-Markovian probability distributions like STA. SMC is, in essence, Monte Carlo simulation applied to formal models and properties. A constant-memory technique, it however incurs a runtime explosion when faced with rare events (as a prohibitively large number of samples would be needed to obtain an error that is smaller than the low probability of the rare event itself), and does not directly support nondeterministic models such as MDP. The modes tool addresses these shortcomings by providing rare event simulation [74] via a highly automated implementation of importance splitting [13], and by offering lightweight strategy sampling [67] for MDP, PTA [26,55], and (with limitations) stochastic-time models like MA and STA [27].

Finally, modysh [60] provides variants of the probabilistic planning algorithm LRTDP [12] for MDP, and prohver [46] implements an abstraction-based approach to safety verification of SHA that internally employs a modified version of the PHAVer [37] HA model checker for the hybrid reachability analysis.

Example 3. The JANI model of Example 2 was obtained by moconv from Example 1, which we model-check via

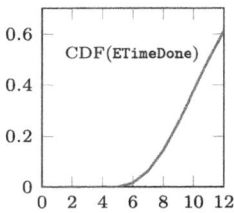

Fig. 3. CDF over N

```
modest mcsta pta.modest -E "N=6"
```

to run mcsta with model parameter N set to 6 and using the value iteration algorithm. As a result, mcsta reports values (that are usually but not always [41] very close to the true value) of 41.99997556955714 for ETimeDone and 0.61279296875 for PInTwiceN. To obtain results with guaranteed error of at most $\pm\ \epsilon$ instead, we can use one of mcsta's sound value iteration algorithms: interval iteration [42], sound value iteration [71], or optimistic value iteration [53]. By adding command-line parameter --alg IntervalIteration, we get ETimeDone = 42.00059918910847 $\pm\ \epsilon$ and PInTwiceN = 0.61279296875 $\pm\ \epsilon$ with mcsta's default $\epsilon = 10^{-3}$. For ETimeDone, mcsta in fact computes the entire cumulative distribution function (CDF) as plotted in Fig. 3, i.e. the reward-bounded probability for all bounds from 0 up to the specified 12 = 2· N, via its sequential interval iteration algorithm [43].

If we run modes on this model with default settings, we get an error message: `pta.modest: error: Encountered temporal nondeterminism for ack`. This is because SMC only solves an *estimation* problem: it samples a large number of model executions (called *simulation runs*) to return the averages of the executions' property values as estimates for the expected value or probability. Yet this model poses an *optimisation* problem: find the resolutions of the nondeterministic choices that deliver the minimum expected reward or maximum probability. The error message points to the nondeterminstic choice that caused modes to abort: the undetermined transmission delay $\in [2, 4]$ time units. If we fix all transmission delays to 2 time units by calling modes with parameter `-S ASAP`, we get `ETimeDone` = 42.00375880801009 with a 95 % confidence interval of $[41.99375880998429, 42.01375880603589]$, and `PInTwiceN` = 0.6092194570135746 with the (a priori) statistical guarantee that obtaining a result within $\pm\,0.01$ of the true value of `PInTwiceN` has probability 0.95.

3   Power Supply Noise in a Network-on-Chip System

As the complexity of distributed many-core systems advances, the *network-on-chip* (NoC) architecture has become the de-facto standard for on-chip communication. A NoC is typically composed of topologically homogeneous routers operating synchronously in a decentralized manner using a predefined routing protocol. *Power supply noise* (PSN) can significantly influence the performance of the transistor devices in a NoC. PSN is created by the simultaneous switching of logic devices, which causes a drop in the effective power supply voltage. PSN is composed of two major components: resistive noise (related to the current drawn and the resistance of the circuit) and inductive noise (which is proportional to the rate of change of current through the inductance of the power grid).

To study PSN in NoC architectures, we first focused on a single central NoC router [68] and later expanded to a 2×2 NoC consisting of four symmetric routers as shown in Fig. 4. We focus on the latter in this section. Each router has three buffers responsible for storing incoming network data packets, called *flits*, and each buffer can store up to four flits.

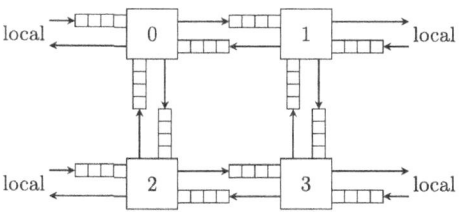

Fig. 4. Architecture of the 2×2 NoC [73]

One of the buffers takes flits generated locally at the router (e.g. at a CPU attached via this router) while the other two buffer flits received from the adjacent routers (which may be destined for this router, e.g. for its attached CPU).

Our goal is to compute the probability for behavioural patterns that are likely to result in resistive resp. inductive noise to occur at least n times within t clock cycles, starting from an initial state where all buffers are empty. We consider two different flit generation patterns: one where each router receives a flit into its local buffer (e.g. from the one core it is connected to) every other cycle, and one

```
// Datatype for unbounded lists of integers to represent queues of flits with destinations
datatype intlist = { int(0..NOCSIZE * NOCSIZE - 1) hd, intlist option tl };
// Datatype for a channel connecting two routers
datatype channel = { int(-1..4) direction,        // direction of buffer (N/S/W/E)
                     bool serviced, int(0..2) priority, // for round−robin protocol
                     intlist option buff };        // queue of flits to transmit
// Datatype for a router, containing incoming channels and some router−specific variables
datatype router = { channel[] channelArray, int(0..3) unserviced, ... };
// The whole NoC consists of 4 router instances with initially empty channels
router[] noc = [ router { unserviced: 0 }, router { unserviced: 0 },
                 router { unserviced: 0 }, router { unserviced: 0 } ];
```

Listing 3. User-defined datatypes in the concrete MODEST 2×2 NoC model

where flits are generated in bursts. We assume the destination of a flit to be one of the other router's local outputs, with the actual router selected uniformly at random for each flit. The routers use X-Y routing, where a flit is first routed in the horizontal direction, and a round-robin-style protocol to handle contention.

A Case for DTMC Model Checking. With all decisions fixed to be either deterministic (flit generation times and routing choices) or random (flit destinations), and the whole NoC running on a discrete clock, this system can naturally be modelled as a DTMC. DTMC are well-suited for SMC due to the absence of nondeterminism, but there are arguments to use PMC with mcsta instead: First, a PMC analysis can deliver guaranteed ϵ-precise results (as in Example 3), whereas SMC only provides weaker statistical guarantees. Second, as we will see below, some of the probabilities we want to compute especially for small numbers of clock cycles t are very low, thus we would need to engage modes' rare event simulation engine whose automation features do not match well with the structure of the NoC model. Finally, and most importantly, we would actually like to obtain the full CDF for resistive and inductive noise events over increasing values of t. The sequential iteration approach implemented in mcsta that we already saw in Example 3 would be able to compute this CDF very efficiently, with hard guarantees on the results. The main challenge for model checking with mcsta is then to deal with the state space explosion problem.

A Sequence of Abstractions. We started by creating a detailed MODEST model of the 2×2 NoC, exploiting the availability of user-defined datatypes in MODEST to represent the state of the network's routers and buffers in full detail. To the best of our knowledge, MODEST and Uppaal's TA modelling interface are the only language for quantitative verification that support the definition of complex datatypes, with mcsta or modes and Uppaal or Uppaal SMC [18,32] being the only probabilistic/timed or statistical model checkers, respectively, supporting models with such datatypes. We show the declarations of the datatypes for the *concrete* 2×2 NoC model in Listing 3. A **router** mainly consists of its incoming **channel**s, which in turn contain a buffer of flits plus the information needed for the router's round-robin algorithm to determine which channel to serve next in case of contention. A flit is simply an integer representing its destination; the buffers are this simple functional-style lists of integers of type `intlist`. The last line of Listing 3 defines the variable representing the state of the full 2×2 NoC as an array of four individual router datatype instances.

`mcsta` runs out of memory during state space exploration on the concrete model. Thus we cannot apply sequential iteration algorithm; however, by making the clock cycle counter a state variable (and thus effectively "unfolding" the state space over the counter's values), we were able to perform model checking for up to $t = 4$ clock cycles. This is because initially, few flits are present throughout the system, and thus the number of combinations of buffer occupancies with different flits remains small over the first few clock cycles. Nevertheless, $t = 4$ is much too low to be useful: with bursty flit generation, we have 3 flit-generating cycles every 10 clock cycles, so we do not even cover one burst cycle.

We then manually applied a series of abstractions to achieve tractability. We first applied predicate abstraction, transforming the model to replace all complex datatype instances by predicate variables that capture the model's critical decision points. For example, the two predicate variables
`bool r0L1; // for noc[0].channel[local].direction == east`
`bool r0L2; // for noc[0].channel[local].direction == south`
capture the two possible forwarding directions of the front flit in the local channel buffer of router 0. This only delayed running out of memory to $t = 7$.

The next step is a novel *probabilistic choice abstraction*: A flit's destination is uniformly randomly selected when it is *put into* the local buffer of a router, but the destination information is not checked until the flit enters the router, to decide the forwarding direction. Thus the random choice of the destination can be delayed until the flit is *taken from* the buffer. In abstract terms, probabilistic choice abstraction delays the resolution of a probabilistic choice until its evaluation point, then removes relevant state variables by replacing them with an explicit probability distribution. We implement this abstraction by modifying the MODEST code accordingly, i.e. manually and on the syntax level.

Finally, as a result of the previous abstraction steps, we can eliminate some buffer priority orders, then observe that the X-Y routing scheme now makes it unnecessary to keep track of each flit's destination, and so replace the buffer queues by bounded integer variables counting the number of waiting flits only.

In Fig. 5, we show the impact of these abstractions on the number of states (in millions) explored in the unfolded model for increasing clock cycle bound t (blue circles: concrete model, red triangles: after predicate abstraction, purple diamonds: probabilistic choice abstraction, green squares: final).

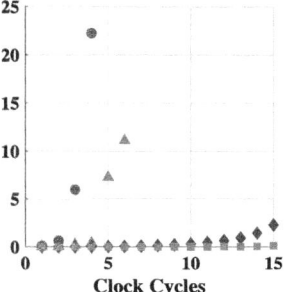

Fig. 5. State count [73]

PMC Results. The final model was still too large to fully explore in non-unfolded form (i.e. treating clock cycles as rewards, like variable `sent` in Example 1) under the every-other-cycle flit generation pattern. By unfolding the clock cycle counter into the state space as described above, PMC became possible for up to 30 clock cycles. With bursty flit generation, however, we could build the non-unfolded state space and thus apply the sequential iteration technique to compute the entire CDF as shown in Fig. 6. The difference between the two patterns is that, with every-other-cycle generation, the buffers slowly fill up with flits to various destinations; the full state space that includes all combinations of buffer occupancies with different flits is too large to handle today. With bursty flit generation, however, all buffers periodically return to an empty state; the period is small enough for the entire state space to fit into memory, i.e. buffers do not fill up far enough for the number of combinations of buffer states to grow too large.

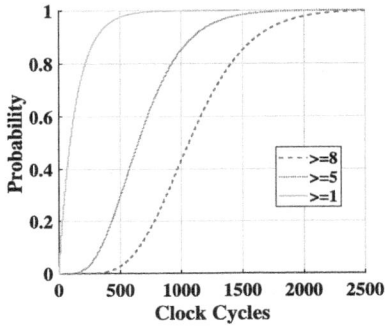

Fig. 6. Inductive noise events [73]

SMC and BDDs. We also applied SMC, which however was limited in the case of every-other-cycle generation by noise events being relatively rare, and in the case of bursty generation by not being able to compete in terms of runtime with the sequential iteration technique. Similarly, our attempts to use Storm's BDD-based state space exploration did not provide scalability improvements, possibly due to the model not being as structured as we think it is, or simply due to a bad variable ordering in the model. For further details on this first case study, we refer the reader to the original FMICS 2021 paper [73].

Open Problems. The probabilistic choice abstraction was manually applied to the NoC model on the MODEST code level; we would like to generalise and automate it. This case study also highlights the need to further improve the scalability of PMC; we need to investigate why the standard approach to handle large models—using BDDs—failed here and what alternatives could be.

Data Availability. The MODEST models described above from [73] are available at github.com/formal-verification-research/Modest-Probabilistic-Models-for-NoC.

4   Routing in Satellite Constellations

Satellite networks in low-Earth orbit are increasingly used to collect and distribute information across the globe, including access to the Internet. Real-time applications like Internet access require very large constellations (such as the

SpaceX's Starlink constellation); even when using low-cost satellites based on off-the-shelf components that are not space-qualified, such constellations are extremely expensive. A different and more sustainable approach is to relax the real-time constraint and leverage the store-carry-and-forward principle where nodes store received messages for later forwarding to other nodes in the network, once a communication window appears. The result is a *delay-tolerant network* (DTN).

In satellite constellations, the orbits are known with sufficient precision to calculate upcoming *contacts*, i.e. communication windows, over the next few days, giving rise to a *contact plan*. However, message transmissions may fail for various reasons such as unreliable (low-cost) components, contact mispredictions, or interference during the wireless communication. If statistical data is available or the error margins of calculations are known, we can assign a success probability to each contact, giving rise to an *uncertain* contact plan. Fig. 7 shows an abstract representation of such a plan. This artificial example comprises four satellites (or ground stations) N_1 to N_4 with contacts over time slots T_1 to T_5. The numbers annotating contacts are the transmission success probabilities. Given a message's source and destination, and a limit n on the number of message copies present in the network to avoid exhausting the satellites' limited resources, we would like to compute the routing strategy that maximises the probability of message delivery within the time window covered by the contact plan.

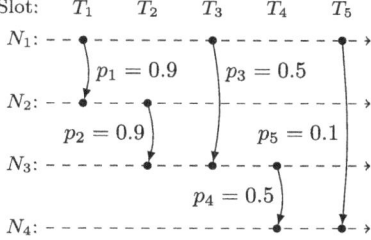

Fig. 7. Uncertain contact plan [23]

A Case for MDP with Distributed Information. Due to the combination of randomness (in transmission failures) with nondeterministic decisions to be optimised (which contacts to use to send how many copies) in a discrete-time setting (a sequence of contacts), MDP are the perfect match among the formalisms of Fig. 1 to model this problem. The goal is to find an optimal (routing) strategy in the MDP. This looks like the perfect job for PMC, which, by computing the maximum message delivery probability, would implicitly also compute the corresponding optimal strategy. By running mcsta with the `--write-scheduler` parameter, it would create a text file mapping every state of the MDP to the strategy's choice among that state's enabled actions.

However, PMC works with complete, global information. Consider the contact plan of Fig. 7 with $n = 2$ copies to send: N_1 will send one copy to N_2 in slot T_1, and if successful, N_2 will forward it in slot T_2. In slot T_3, the best course of action computed by PMC for satellite N_1 is to send its remaining copy to N_3 *if and only if* N_3 did not receive the first copy. Thus the model checker, and the strategy it computes, "sees" the state of all satellites. Yet satellites do not have global information about the state of all other satellites in the constellation, making the optimal strategies found by PMC potentially unimplementable.

In fact, what we need are distributed strategies [39]. Unfortunately, the model checking problem under distributed strategies is undecidable, and even with simplifications such as restricting to memoryless strategies, it remains practically intractable [40]. Recently, L-RUCoP, an approximative model checking-based approach specifically tailored to the uncertain DTNs case, has become available [72], which, however, remains limited by state space explosion as n increases.

Using SMC to Find Distributed Strategies. We instead adapted two methods for finding (near-)optimal strategies with SMC to the distributed-information setting [24]: lightweight strategy sampling (LSS) [67], and the reinforcement learning [76] technique of Q-learning [77]. We implemented both in modes.

LSS. The key idea of LSS is to represent each strategy with a fixed-size (e.g. 32-bit) integer, i.e. in constant memory. LSS with the smart sampling heuristics [29] then randomly samples m strategies (i.e. integers), performs k simulation runs computing the average message delivery probability for each, discards the $\lceil \frac{m}{2} \rceil$ worst-performing strategies, simulates the remaining strategies with $2k$ runs each, and so on until only one "optimal" strategy remains. For this one, the message delivery probability is subsequently estimated in a standard SMC analysis. The result is a best-effort underapproximation of the maximum probability achievable with the unknown optimal strategy. During simulation for strategy i, when the simulator needs to choose between $k > 1$ actions in state s, it concatenates the bitstring representations of s and i, applies a hash function $\mathcal{H}$ mapping this value to a fixed-size integer j, and selects the $((j \bmod k) + 1)$-th action:

$$a := ((\mathcal{H}(\sigma.s) \bmod |\{\text{ actions from } s \}|) + 1)\text{ -th element of } \{\text{ actions from } s \}$$

To perform the same analysis w.r.t. distributed strategies, all we need to change is the input to $\mathcal{H}$: instead of the bitstring for s, we use that for a projection of s to the variables observable by the currently active component (here: satellite). We also introduce a condition of good-for-distribution models that, when satisfied, ensures that no two components may have a decision at the same time instant, making a global arbiter to break such ties unnecessary [23].

Q-learning stores a *Q-table* that maps state-action pairs to values indicating the action's "quality", approximating the goal probability or expected reward via the action. The table is updated during simulation runs called *episodes* as

$$Q(s,a) := (1 - \alpha) \cdot Q(s,a) + \alpha \cdot (r + \gamma \cdot \max_{\text{action } a' \text{ from } s'} Q(s', a'))$$

for each visited state s, where γ is the discount factor that we set to 1, and α is the *learning rate* hyperparameter that determines the impact of the new information gained during the episode over the previous information in the Q-table. Typically, α is high in the first episodes and then gradually decreases. As the number of episodes goes towards infinity, the Q-table entries approach the optimal values, with the corresponding strategy for state s being to choose $\arg\max_{\text{action } a \text{ from } s} Q(s, a)$. After learning, modes performs an independent SMC analysis under this strategy to estimate the message delivery probability.

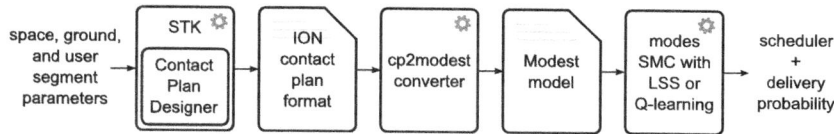

Fig. 8. Satellite routing scheduling toolchain for uncertain DTNs [23]

Q-learning is popular in machine learning and artificial intelligence applications today, where a neural network stores the Q-table approximately. We work with an explicit Q-table stored in memory. The worst-case memory usage of Q-learning is thus in $\mathcal{O}(|S| \cdot |A|)$ for state set S and actions A, which is in stark contrast to the otherwise constant memory usage of SMC. The hope is that, in practice, many states either have no choices or there is a small "core" of states [62] reached during learning that suffices to obtain a good strategy.

We adapt Q-learning to distributed strategies by using the *concurrent learning* approach [70]: each agent (in our case: DTN node) learns on its own, keeping and updating its own Q-table and only observing that part of the current state that contains the agent's local information. While straightforward to implement, concurrent learning no longer guarantees convergence and optimality [22]. Its main advantage is that, instead of storing Q-table entries for states from the product state space of all agents, each node's learner only sees the local component state space, so the number of Q-values stored in concurrent Q-learning grows only linearly instead of exponentially with the number of components.

A Modest Toolchain for Uncertain DTNs. We developed the toolchain outlined in Fig. 8 to convert concrete contact plans (with exact contact timings, obtained from a commercial physics-based modeling environment) into an abstract MODEST MDP model. The generated models follow a simple pattern and are good-for-distribution by construction.

In Listing 4 , we show an excerpt from the MODEST model for the example contact plan of Fig. 7. Whenever a node has a contact, the process that models that node contains an `alt` for the three possibilities of sending 1 or 2 copies if available, or listening for incoming data (which may not arrive because either the other node also chose to listen or the data was randomly lost). The model shown is for unreliable communication; we can also generate a reliably communicating variant that uses acknowledgments. Note that the `snd...` and `rcv...` actions do not synchronise: they exist only to make the model more readable, and to identify the choices that the strategy found by LSS or Q-learning makes. Information is exchanged between the Node*N* processes by value passing through transient variables. Listing 4 shows a first model: [24] then implemented many optimisations to that pattern by graph analysis of the contact plan in the `cp2modest` converter, to make modes execute faster and to remove spurious choices in `alt`s [24, Section 3.2.2]. The latter reduces the space of strategies that LSS samples from,

```
transient int(0..4) dest1, dest2, dest3, dest4; // destX: target of copies sent by node X
transient int(0..2) data1, data2, data3, data4; // dataX: #copies just sent by node X
action sync;                                    // to synchronise time slots
action snd1to2_1, snd1to2_2, rcv1to2, ...;  // only for labelling, no synchronisation
...
process Node2(int(0..2) copies)
{
   alt { // slot 0: contact with 1
   :: when(copies >= 1) snd2to1_1;
      sync palt { :0.9: {= data2 = 1, dest2 = 1, copies -= 1 =} :0.1: {= copies -= 1 =} }
   :: when(copies >= 2) snd2to1_2;
      sync palt { :0.9: {= data2 = 2, dest2 = 1, copies -= 2 =} :0.1: {= copies -= 2 =} }
   :: rcv1to2;
      sync {= 1: copies += dest1 == 2 ? data1 : 0 =}
   };
   alt { // slot 1: contact with 3
   :: when(copies >= 1) snd2to3_1;
      sync palt { :0.9: {= data2 = 1, dest2 = 3, copies -= 1 =} :0.1: {= copies -= 1 =} }
   :: when(copies >= 2) snd2to3_2;
      sync palt { :0.9: {= data2 = 2, dest2 = 3, copies -= 2 =} :0.1: {= copies -= 2 =} }
   :: rcv3to2;
      sync {= 1: copies += dest3 == 2 ? data3 : 0 =}
   };
   sync; // slot 3: no contact
   sync; // slot 4: no contact
   sync  // slot 5: no contact
}
...
par { :: Node1(2) :: Node2(0) :: Node3(0) :: Node4(0) }
```

Listing 4. Excerpt of the MODEST model for the contact plan of Fig. 7

making it more likely to sample good strategies; it also reduces the size of the Q-tables in Q-learning.

SMC Results. We implemented LSS and Q-learning for distributed strategies as described above in modes, and applied this implementation in particular to a realistic LEO Walker constellation of 16 satellites as shown in Fig. 9. In Fig. 10, we show two examples of the results we obtained for this example in [24], comparing LSS and Q-learning

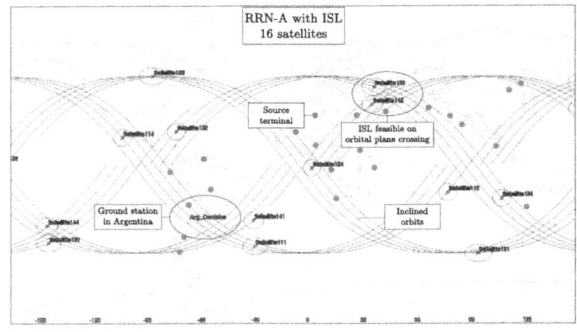

Fig. 9. Walker DTN [24]

(QL) with global and with distributed (local, prefix "L-") information. We show the message delivery probability (SDP) as we vary the message loss probability of all contacts. As a baseline, we used the standard CGR routing algorithm [4,35] that does not take probabilities or multiple message copies into account, and also

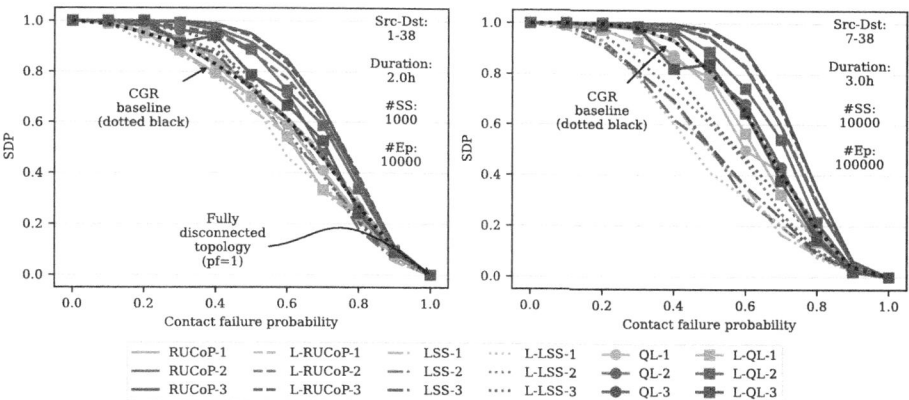

Fig. 10. Message delivery probabilities of best strategies found for the Walker DTN [24]

compared with the model checking-based (L-)RUCoP approach that is implemented in a separate tool using its own input format. In the plots, "Src-Dst" indicates the node numbers of the message source and destination, "Duration" is the real-time length of the contact plan, "#SS" is the number of strategies sampled in LSS, and "#Ep" is the number of episodes in Q-learning.

We found that L-RUCoP is notably superior to L-LSS for failure probabilities between 0.4 and 0.8. Interestingly, the gap is reduced if we raise the number of schedulers to 10000 in LSS, indicating we are right on the boundary of what can effectively be solved via LSS. Nevertheless, the uninformed sampling strategy of LSS may not be fully adequate for realistic DTN topologies. Q-learning appears to perform better. We also observed that LSS and L-LSS are typically close, but we frequently attain a better probability with distributed strategies. This is likely because of the smaller space of strategies to sample from (see above). We also measured memory usage and runtime, showing that RUCoP's better results come at the expense of significantly higher memory usage and runtime. It needed up to ≈ 20 minutes to terminate, while LSS and Q-learning typically delivered a result in less than a minute. While RUCoP needed as much as 600 MB of memory, LSS consistently used about 100 MB, while Q-learning used slightly more as expected. On some of the other examples we considered in [24], L-RUCoP ran out of memory while L-LSS still delivered results quickly.

Open Problems. Both the concrete problem of finding optimal routes for uncertain contact plans as well as the underlying challenge to find practical solutions for distributed-information model checking remain mostly open. LSS and Q-learning are attractive as generic and easy-to-implement approaches that can deliver useful results, but in complex examples, the strategies they find may be far from optimal, and they provide no information about how far these strategies are from the optimum. We would in particular like to investigate modifications to LSS that incorporate more structural information about the current strategy (in contrast to its current opaque integer identifier implementation), and using deep Q-learning methods with neural networks.

Data Availability. The models and tools needed to replicate the DTN evaluation described in this section are archived at DOI 10.5281/zenodo.11214677 [25].

5 Optimally Attacking Bitcoin

The Bitcoin [69] cryptocurrency records its transactions in a blockchain to which blocks are added via the proof-of-work principle: participants need to solve a computationally intensive problem to be able to generate or *mine* a valid block. Generally, the first new valid block mined gets appended to the chain, and a certain number of Bitcoins is awarded to the participant that found the block as a reward. However, as a distributed system spanning the globe via the Internet, Bitcoin has to deal with asynchrony: If multiple participants find new blocks at roughly the same time, there are different alternative forks of the Bitcoin blockchain, and a consensus must be reached on which is the valid one. In Bitcoin, the longest available chain is considered the valid one.

Bitcoin as a CTMC. The problem miners have to solve is finding a number that, together with their new block's content, hashes to a value that is smaller than the network's current *difficulty target* value [69, Section 4]. This is done by trying many randomly selected numbers. A try is successful with probability p; then the time until a new block is mined follows a geometric distribution (assuming a constant time t per try, for computing the hash of number and block together). The geometric distribution for ever smaller p and t converges to an exponential distribution, and in practice p and t for Bitcoin are *very* small.

Thus the mining of blocks can abstractly be modelled by a CTMC in which the transition from a chain with n blocks to one with $n + 1$ blocks occurs with a certain rate. As the total computational power applied to mining blocks by all miners worldwide (the *hash rate*) changes, the Bitcoin network periodically adjusts the hardness of the problem via the difficulty target value such that the average time to find a new block (the confirmation time) is 10 minutes. In practice the actual confirmation time varies; it was about 12 minutes in 2017 [34]. Thus we use a rate of $\frac{1}{12}$ for the n-to-$n+1$-blocks transition in the CTMC.

Attacking Trust in Bitcoin. If a large amount of the hash rate (some fraction $M \in [0,1]_{\mathbb{R}}$) is controlled by a malicious party, they could attack the Bitcoin network by secretly working on their own fork until it becomes longer than the "public" one, and then broadcasting the secret fork. These attacks (to Bitcoin but also blockchain in general) are known as *block withholding attacks* and come in several variants. For example, in the double-spending variant a Bitcoin can be spent twice: once on the public fork in block b_i, and once on the secret fork that branches off from publicly known block b_j that is before b_i in the chain.

This behaviour can be integrated into an abstract CTMC model of Bitcoin to e.g. compute the expected time until the attack succeeds (i.e. the secret fork becomes longer than the public one by a certain margin) for various values of M. We built such a model in MODEST and studied similar properties using mcsta and modes in [51].

A more interesting and somewhat easier block withholding attack attempts to undermine the public trust in Bitcoin by just obtaining a longer secret fork from *any* block and then publishing that fork. If done repeatedly, regular users could no longer rely on the persistence of transactions that initially appeared to have become a part of the valid Bitcoin blockchain. In this attack, every time the public fork is extended, the malicious entity may decide between (a) continuing to work on its current secret fork and (b) restarting its secret fork from the new public block. This is because it is no longer necessary to purge a specific block b_i from the public chain as in the double-spending attack.

A Case for Markov Automata. Due to the presence of the above nondeterministic choice between (a) and (b) to be optimised, this attack can thus no longer be represented in a CTMC model. Our automata formalisms family tree of Fig. 1 contains two direct combinations of CTMCs with the ability to represent nondeterministic choices: CTMDPs and MAs. The latter are a very orthogonal combination of CTMCs and MDPs: They provide two types of transitions—Markovian transitions that execute independently but after a random delay that follows an exponential distribution whose rate is given as part of the transition, and probabilistic transitions that take place immediately, but can synchronise with other probabilistic transitions in parallel composition and lead to a discrete probability distribution over the successor state. This partitioning of the transitions enables parallel composition with action synchronisation without the need to prescribe an ad-hoc operation for combining rates as would be necessary for CTMC or CTMDP. For this reason, MA are preferable for practical modelling, and are supported by MODEST while CTMDPs are not.

Uppaal and Modest Models. The attack on trust in Bitcoin was first formally analysed by Fehnker and Chaudhary [34] using SMC with Uppaal SMC. As a consequence of using SMC, they had to run a separate analysis for every possible strategy determining the conditions for when to continue and when to restart, and their results came with a statistical error. Today, Uppaal Stratego [31] may alleviate the former problem.

We instead modelled the same scenario in the MA subset of MODEST, in order to let mcsta find the best strategy directly via PMC and thus without any statistics or the need to run multiple separate analyses. This model is shown in Listing 5. The `HonestPool` process represents the regular Bitcoin miners, who have $100 \cdot (1 - M)\%$ of the global hash rate at their disposal and therefore mine a new block every $\frac{12}{1-M}$ minutes. They announce every new block via the `sln` action. The malicious entity's behaviour is defined by the `TrustAttacker` process. They mine new blocks every $\frac{12}{M}$ minutes, and also listen for messages

```
const real M;          // fraction of hash rate controlled by malicious pool
const int CD;          // confirmation depth required by victim
const int DB = CD;     // attacker gives up when this far behind
action sln;            // signal that honest pool mined a new block
action rst;            // signal that attacker restarts from public fork
action cnt;            // signal that attacker continues
int(0..CD+1) m_len;    // length of the secret fork
int(-DB..CD+1) m_diff = 0; // length of secret fork minus honest fork
property T_MWinMin = Xmin(T, m_len >= CD && m_diff > 0); // min. exp. time to malicious win
property P_MWinMax = Pmax(<>[T<=2880] (m_len >= CD && m_diff > 0)); // max. prob in 2 days
process HonestPool()
{
   rate(1/12 * (1 - M)) tau; // every 12 / (1 - M) minutes on average:
   sln;                      // honest pool mines a new block
   HonestPool()
}
process TrustAttacker()
{
   do {
   :: rate((1/12) * M)              // every 12 / M minutes on average:
      {= m_len = min(CD, m_len + 1), // malicious pool mines a new block
         m_diff++ =}
   :: sln {= m_diff-- =};           // extension of public fork results in
      alt {                         // strategy choice for malicious fork:
      :: rst {= m_len = 0, m_diff = 0 =} // restart (always possible) or
      :: when(m_diff > -DB) cnt     // continue (if not too far behind)
      }
   }
}
par { :: HonestPool() :: TrustAttacker() }
```

Listing 5. MODEST model for optimising the trust attack on Bitcoin [51]

about new blocks from the regular miners. Whenever those find a new block, the **TrustAttacker** is faced with a nondeterministic choice: (a) **cnt**: continue their secret fork, or (b) **rst**: start over from the block just found by the regular miners. The attacker keeps track of the length of their secret fork since branching off in variable **m_len** and of its length difference compared to the public chain in **m_diff**. The attacker will make its secret fork public once it is (i) longer than the public chain and (ii) at least CD blocks long; this latter *confirmation depth* ensures that the new chain is unlikely to be overtaken by other miners.

Model Checking Results and Strategies. We set M to 0.2—a hash rate that was at several points in the past achieved by some mining pools—and CD to 6, a commonly used value. Our MODEST model specifies two properties of interest: T_MWinMin asks for the minimum expected time until the attacker "wins" by publicising their longer chain, while P_MWinMax asks for the time-bounded probability that the attacker manages to win within two days (i.e. 2880 minutes). mcsta takes under a second to model-check them with sound algorithms, finding that T_MWinMin = $3736.5920429883377 \pm \epsilon$ and P_MWinMax = $0.5351007861781778 \pm \epsilon$ with the default $\epsilon = 10^{-3}$. That is, the shortest possible expected time for the attack to succeed is 2.6 days, while there is a more than

50/50 chance to succeed within just 2 days. It is thus doubtful whether we should trust Bitcoin if any single actor amasses 20 % or more of the global hashrate.

Now, the above values are *best-case* values for the attacker, if they play the optimal strategy in terms of resetting and continuing their fork. We can let mcsta output this strategy for T_MWinMin [51], which results in a file containing 33 state-action decision pairs like

```
+ State: (..., m_len = 5, m_diff = 4)
   Choice: cnt
```

that exhaustively describe the strategy. While 33 textual pairs may still be humanly-interpretable, viz. to understand whether there is some structure or idea to the strategy, this kind of representation is not useful in the general case where models may have millions of states. We thus implemented [14] a connection from mcsta to the dtControl tool [5] that can learn a decision tree from this kind of representation. The resulting tree for this strategy is shown in Fig. 11, and is arguably an explainable and more compact way to present this strategy.

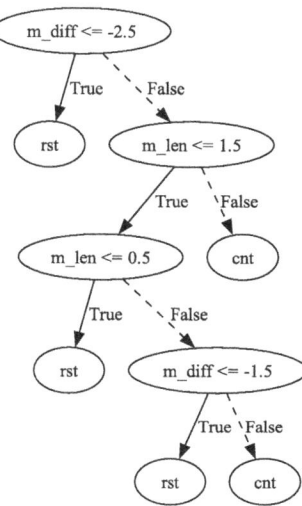

Fig. 11. Decision tree

Open Problems. Model checking MA is easy for untimed properties and unbounded expected rewards by running PMC on the embedded MDP. For timed properties, optimal strategies need to know about the remaining time, so dedicated algorithms are needed. For time-bounded reachability, two decent ones with complementary performance exist [19,21]. While these could be improved further—e.g. by developing one algorithm that performs at least as well as either of them on all models—other interesting properties currently lack scalable model checking algorithms: for example, the only available algorithm for time-bounded expected rewards is based on discretisation [56], which drastically exacerbates the state space explosion problem. On the SMC side, LSS does not work for continuous-time strategies out of the box [27], and new clever solutions are needed to make it work beyond simply considering untimed strategies only.

Data Availability. The bitcoin-attack.modest model presented in this section is part of the QVBS [54], available online at qcomp.org/benchmarks.

6   Conclusion

Different case studies have different needs in terms of conceptual modelling power, modelling language features, and analysis tool capabilities. The MODEST language and the MODEST TOOLSET provide the means to easily model and analyse systems containing various quantitative aspects ranging from discrete probabilistic choices to stochastic hybrid behaviour. We highlighted three examples that were modelled in MODEST and analysed using different tools from the MODEST TOOLSET: First, in the case of **power supply noise in a NoC**, the simple formalism of DTMC was sufficient. For the detailed concrete model, however, the MODEST language feature of declaring and using one's own complex data types was very helpful. PMC via mcsta was the analysis method of choice, however significant effort was needed to abstract the model until it became tractable for PMC due to the state space explosion problem. Second, for **routing in satellite constellations**, nondeterministic choices needed to be modelled, and optimised over by the analysis tool. Here, MDP fit the problem very well with their ability to model decision-making under uncertainty. We auto-generated MODEST models from contact plans computed by domain-specific software. Due to the need to find implementable routing strategies in the distributed-information setting of satellite constellations, we could not use PMC; instead, we adapted the LSS and Q-learning approaches to allow SMC to handle both distributed information and nondeterminism. Finally, to **optimally attack Bitcoin**, we showed that MA fit the problem well due to the combination of the stochastic time-to-next-block with the nondeterministic choices between continuing and restarting the secret fork. Using PMC with mcsta again, we were able to compute an optimal strategy with little computational effort and present it in a compact and explainable manner as a decision tree generated via a new connection to dtControl.

References

1. Agha, G., Palmskog, K.: A survey of statistical model checking. ACM Trans. Model. Comput. Simul. **28**(1), 6:1–6:39 (2018). https://doi.org/10.1145/3158668
2. Alur, R., Courcoubetis, C., Henzinger, T.A., Ho, P.-H.: Hybrid automata: an algorithmic approach to the specification and verification of hybrid systems. In: Grossman, R.L., Nerode, A., Ravn, A.P., Rischel, H. (eds.) HS 1991-1992. LNCS, vol. 736, pp. 209–229. Springer, Heidelberg (1993). https://doi.org/10.1007/3-540-57318-6_30
3. Alur, R., Dill, D.L.: A theory of timed automata. Theor. Comput. Sci. **126**(2), 183–235 (1994). https://doi.org/10.1016/0304-3975(94)90010-8
4. Araniti, G., et al.: Contact graph routing in DTN space networks: overview, enhancements and performance. IEEE Comms. Magazine **53**(3), 38–46 (2015). https://doi.org/10.1109/MCOM.2015.7060480
5. Ashok, P., Jackermeier, M., Křetínský, J., Weinhuber, C., Weininger, M., Yadav, M.: dtControl 2.0: explainable strategy representation via decision tree learning steered by experts. In: TACAS 2021. LNCS, vol. 12652, pp. 326–345. Springer, Cham (2021). https://doi.org/10.1007/978-3-030-72013-1_17
6. Baier, C.: Probabilistic model checking. In: Esparza, J., Grumberg, O., Sickert, S. (eds.) Dependable Software Systems Engineering, NATO Science for Peace and

Security Series – D: Information and Communication Security, vol. 45, pp. 1–23. IOS Press (2016). https://doi.org/10.3233/978-1-61499-627-9-1

7. Baier, C., de Alfaro, L., Forejt, V., Kwiatkowska, M.: Model checking probabilistic systems. In: Handbook of Model Checking, pp. 963–999. Springer, Cham (2018). https://doi.org/10.1007/978-3-319-10575-8_28

8. Baier, C., Katoen, J.P.: Principles of Model Checking. MIT Press, Cambridge (2008)

9. Bellman, R.: A Markovian decision process. J. Math. Mech. **6**(5), 679–684 (1957)

10. Bohnenkamp, H.C., D'Argenio, P.R., Hermanns, H., Katoen, J.P.: MoDeST: a compositional modeling formalism for hard and softly timed systems. IEEE Trans. Software Eng. **32**(10), 812–830 (2006). https://doi.org/10.1109/TSE.2006.104

11. Bohnenkamp, H., Hermanns, H., Katoen, J.-P., Klaren, R.: The MODEST modeling tool and its implementation. In: Kemper, P., Sanders, W.H. (eds.) TOOLS 2003. LNCS, vol. 2794, pp. 116–133. Springer, Heidelberg (2003). https://doi.org/10.1007/978-3-540-45232-4_8

12. Bonet, B., Geffner, H.: Labeled RTDP: improving the convergence of real-time dynamic programming. In: Giunchiglia, E., Muscettola, N., Nau, D.S. (eds.) 13th International Conference on Automated Planning and Scheduling (ICAPS), pp. 12–21. AAAI (2003)

13. Budde, C.E., D'Argenio, P.R., Hartmanns, A.: Automated compositional importance splitting. Sci. Comput. Program. **174**, 90–108 (2019). https://doi.org/10.1016/j.scico.2019.01.006

14. Budde, C.E., D'Argenio, P.R., Hartmanns, A.: Digging for decision trees: a case study in strategy sampling and learning. In: International Symposium on Leveraging Applications of Formal Methods, Verification and Validation (ISoLA) (2024), submitted, under review

15. Budde, C.E., D'Argenio, P.R., Hartmanns, A., Sedwards, S.: An efficient statistical model checker for nondeterminism and rare events. Int. J. Softw. Tools Technol. Transf. **22**(6), 759–780 (2020). https://doi.org/10.1007/s10009-020-00563-2

16. Budde, C.E., Dehnert, C., Hahn, E.M., Hartmanns, A., Junges, S., Turrini, A.: JANI: quantitative model and tool interaction. In: Legay, A., Margaria, T. (eds.) TACAS 2017. LNCS, vol. 10206, pp. 151–168. Springer, Heidelberg (2017). https://doi.org/10.1007/978-3-662-54580-5_9

17. Budde, C.E., et al.: On correctness, precision, and performance in quantitative verification. In: Margaria, T., Steffen, B. (eds.) ISoLA 2020. LNCS, vol. 12479, pp. 216–241. Springer, Cham (2021). https://doi.org/10.1007/978-3-030-83723-5_15

18. Bulychev, P.E., et al.: UPPAAL-SMC: Statistical model checking for priced timed automata. In: Wiklicky, H., Massink, M. (eds.) 10th Workshop on Quantitative Aspects of Programming Languages and Systems (QAPL). EPTCS, vol. 85, pp. 1–16 (2012). https://doi.org/10.4204/EPTCS.85.1

19. Butkova, Y., Fox, G.: Optimal time-bounded reachability analysis for concurrent systems. In: Vojnar, T., Zhang, L. (eds.) TACAS 2019. LNCS, vol. 11428, pp. 191–208. Springer, Cham (2019). https://doi.org/10.1007/978-3-030-17465-1_11

20. Butkova, Y., Hartmanns, A., Hermanns, H.: A Modest approach to Markov automata. ACM Trans. Model. Comput. Simul. **31**(3), 14:1–14:34 (2021). https://doi.org/10.1145/3449355

21. Butkova, Y., Hatefi, H., Hermanns, H., Krčál, J.: Optimal continuous time markov decisions. In: Finkbeiner, B., Pu, G., Zhang, L. (eds.) ATVA 2015. LNCS, vol. 9364, pp. 166–182. Springer, Cham (2015). https://doi.org/10.1007/978-3-319-24953-7_12

22. Claus, C., Boutilier, C.: The dynamics of reinforcement learning in cooperative multiagent systems. In: Mostow, J., Rich, C. (eds.) 15th National Conference on Artificial Intelligence and 10th Innovative Applications of Artificial Intelligence Conference (AAAI, IAAI), pp. 746–752. AAAI Press/The MIT Press (1998)

23. D'Argenio, P.R., Fraire, J.A., Hartmanns, A.: Sampling distributed schedulers for resilient space communication. In: Lee, R., Jha, S., Mavridou, A., Giannakopoulou, D. (eds.) NFM 2020. LNCS, vol. 12229, pp. 291–310. Springer, Cham (2020). https://doi.org/10.1007/978-3-030-55754-6_17

24. D'Argenio, P.R., Fraire, J.A., Hartmanns, A., Raverta, F.: Comparing statistical, analytical, and learning-based routing approaches for delay-tolerant networks. ACM Trans. Model. Comput. Simul. (2024). to appear

25. D'Argenio, P.R., Fraire, J.A., Hartmanns, A., Raverta, F.: Comparing statistical, analytical, and learning-based routing approaches for delay-tolerant networks (artifact). Zenodo (2024). https://doi.org/10.5281/zenodo.11214677. , to appear

26. D'Argenio, P.R., Hartmanns, A., Legay, A., Sedwards, S.: Statistical approximation of optimal schedulers for probabilistic timed automata. In: Ábrahám, E., Huisman, M. (eds.) IFM 2016. LNCS, vol. 9681, pp. 99–114. Springer, Cham (2016). https://doi.org/10.1007/978-3-319-33693-0_7

27. D'Argenio, P.R., Hartmanns, A., Sedwards, S.: Lightweight statistical model checking in nondeterministic continuous time. In: Margaria, T., Steffen, B. (eds.) ISoLA 2018. LNCS, vol. 11245, pp. 336–353. Springer, Cham (2018). https://doi.org/10.1007/978-3-030-03421-4_22

28. D'Argenio, P.R., Jeannet, B., Jensen, H.E., Larsen, K.G.: Reduction and Refinement Strategies for Probabilistic Analysis. In: Hermanns, H., Segala, R. (eds.) PAPM-PROBMIV 2002. LNCS, vol. 2399, pp. 57–76. Springer, Heidelberg (2002). https://doi.org/10.1007/3-540-45605-8_5

29. D'Argenio, P.R., Legay, A., Sedwards, S., Traonouez, L.M.: Smart sampling for lightweight verification of Markov decision processes. Int. J. Softw. Tools Technol. Transf. **17**(4), 469–484 (2015). https://doi.org/10.1007/S10009-015-0383-0

30. D'Argenio, P.R., Wolovick, N., Terraf, P.S., Celayes, P.: Nondeterministic labeled Markov processes: Bisimulations and logical characterization. In: 6th International Conference on Quantitative Evaluation of Systems (QEST). pp. 11–20. IEEE Computer Society (2009). https://doi.org/10.1109/QEST.2009.17

31. David, A., Jensen, P.G., Larsen, K.G., Mikucionis, M., Taankvist, J.H.: Uppaal Stratego. In: Baier, C., Tinelli, C. (eds.) 21st International Conference on Tools and Algorithms for the Construction and Analysis of Systems (TACAS). Lecture Notes in Computer Science, vol. 9035, pp. 206–211. Springer (2015). https://doi.org/10.1007/978-3-662-46681-0_16

32. David, A., Larsen, K.G., Legay, A., Mikucionis, M., Wang, Z.: Time for statistical model checking of real-time systems. In: Gopalakrishnan, G., Qadeer, S. (eds.) 23rd International Conference on Computer Aided Verification (CAV). Lecture Notes in Computer Science, vol. 6806, pp. 349–355. Springer (2011). https://doi.org/10.1007/978-3-642-22110-1_27

33. Eisentraut, C., Hermanns, H., Zhang, L.: On probabilistic automata in continuous time. In: 25th Annual IEEE Symposium on Logic in Computer Science (LICS). pp. 342–351. IEEE Computer Society (2010). https://doi.org/10.1109/LICS.2010.41

34. Fehnker, A., Chaudhary, K.: Twenty percent and a few days – optimising a Bitcoin majority attack. In: Dutle, A., Muñoz, C.A., Narkawicz, A. (eds.) 10th International NASA Formal Methods Symposium (NFM). Lecture Notes in Computer

Science, vol. 10811, pp. 157–163. Springer (2018). https://doi.org/10.1007/978-3-319-77935-5_11

35. Fraire, J.A., De Jonckère, O., Burleigh, S.C.: Routing in the space Internet: A contact graph routing tutorial. Journal of Network and Computer Applications **174**, 102884 (2021). https://doi.org/10.1016/j.jnca.2020.102884

36. Fränzle, M., Hahn, E.M., Hermanns, H., Wolovick, N., Zhang, L.: Measurability and safety verification for stochastic hybrid systems. In: Caccamo, M., Frazzoli, E., Grosu, R. (eds.) 14th ACM International Conference on Hybrid Systems: Computation and Control (HSCC). pp. 43–52. ACM (2011). https://doi.org/10.1145/1967701.1967710

37. Frehse, G.: PHAVer: algorithmic verification of hybrid systems past HyTech. Int. J. Softw. Tools Technol. Transf. **10**(3), 263–279 (2008). https://doi.org/10.1007/S10009-007-0062-X

38. Garavel, H., Lang, F., Mateescu, R., Serwe, W.: CADP 2011: a toolbox for the construction and analysis of distributed processes. Int. J. Softw. Tools Technol. Transf. **15**(2), 89–107 (2013). https://doi.org/10.1007/S10009-012-0244-Z

39. Giro, S., D'Argenio, P.R.: Quantitative model checking revisited: Neither decidable nor approximable. In: Raskin, J.F., Thiagarajan, P.S. (eds.) 5th International Conference on Formal Modeling and Analysis of Timed Systems (FORMATS). Lecture Notes in Computer Science, vol. 4763, pp. 179–194. Springer (2007). https://doi.org/10.1007/978-3-540-75454-1_14

40. Giro, S., D'Argenio, P.R.: On the expressive power of schedulers in distributed probabilistic systems. Electron. Notes Theor. Comput. Sci. **253**(3), 45–71 (2009). https://doi.org/10.1016/j.entcs.2009.10.005

41. Haddad, S., Monmege, B.: Reachability in MDPs: Refining convergence of value iteration. In: Ouaknine, J., Potapov, I., Worrell, J. (eds.) 8th International Workshop on Reachability Problems (RP). Lecture Notes in Computer Science, vol. 8762, pp. 125–137. Springer (2014). https://doi.org/10.1007/978-3-319-11439-2_10

42. Haddad, S., Monmege, B.: Interval iteration algorithm for MDPs and IMDPs. Theor. Comput. Sci. **735**, 111–131 (2018). https://doi.org/10.1016/J.TCS.2016.12.003

43. Hahn, E.M., Hartmanns, A.: A comparison of time- and reward-bounded probabilistic model checking techniques. In: Fränzle, M., Kapur, D., Zhan, N. (eds.) Second International Symposium on Dependable Software Engineering: Theories, Tools, and Applications (SETTA). Lecture Notes in Computer Science, vol. 9984, pp. 85–100 (2016). https://doi.org/10.1007/978-3-319-47677-3_6

44. Hahn, E.M., Hartmanns, A.: Symblicit exploration and elimination for probabilistic model checking. In: Hung, C.C., Hong, J., Bechini, A., Song, E. (eds.) 36th ACM/SIGAPP Symposium on Applied Computing (SAC). pp. 1798–1806. ACM (2021). https://doi.org/10.1145/3412841.3442052

45. Hahn, E.M., Hartmanns, A., Hensel, C., Klauck, M., Klein, J., Kretínský, J., Parker, D., Quatmann, T., Ruijters, E., Steinmetz, M.: The 2019 comparison of tools for the analysis of quantitative formal models (QComp 2019 competition report). In: Beyer, D., Huisman, M., Kordon, F., Steffen, B. (eds.) 25 Years of TACAS: TOOLympics. Lecture Notes in Computer Science, vol. 11429, pp. 69–92. Springer (2019). https://doi.org/10.1007/978-3-030-17502-3_5

46. Hahn, E.M., Hartmanns, A., Hermanns, H., Katoen, J.P.: A compositional modelling and analysis framework for stochastic hybrid systems. Formal Methods Syst. Des. **43**(2), 191–232 (2013). https://doi.org/10.1007/s10703-012-0167-z

47. Hahn, E.M., Li, Y., Schewe, S., Turrini, A., Zhang, L.: iscasMc: A web-based probabilistic model checker. In: Jones, C.B., Pihlajasaari, P., Sun, J. (eds.) 19th International Symposium on Formal Methods (FM). Lecture Notes in Computer Science, vol. 8442, pp. 312–317. Springer (2014). https://doi.org/10.1007/978-3-319-06410-9_22

48. Hartmanns, A.: An overview of Modest models and tools for real stochastic timed systems. In: Dubslaff, C., Luttik, B. (eds.) 5th Workshop on Models for Formal Analysis of Real Systems (MARS@ETAPS). EPTCS, vol. 355, pp. 1–12 (2022). https://doi.org/10.4204/EPTCS.355.1

49. Hartmanns, A., Hermanns, H.: The Modest Toolset: An integrated environment for quantitative modelling and verification. In: Ábrahám, E., Havelund, K. (eds.) 20th International Conference on Tools and Algorithms for the Construction and Analysis of Systems (TACAS). Lecture Notes in Computer Science, vol. 8413, pp. 593–598. Springer (2014). https://doi.org/10.1007/978-3-642-54862-8_51

50. Hartmanns, A., Hermanns, H.: Explicit model checking of very large MDP using partitioning and secondary storage. In: Finkbeiner, B., Pu, G., Zhang, L. (eds.) 13th International Symposium on Automated Technology for Verification and Analysis (ATVA). Lecture Notes in Computer Science, vol. 9364, pp. 131–147. Springer (2015). https://doi.org/10.1007/978-3-319-24953-7_10

51. Hartmanns, A., Hermanns, H.: A Modest Markov automata tutorial. In: Krötzsch, M., Stepanova, D. (eds.) 15th International Reasoning Web Summer School. Lecture Notes in Computer Science, vol. 11810, pp. 250–276. Springer (2019). https://doi.org/10.1007/978-3-030-31423-1_8

52. Hartmanns, A., Hermanns, H., Berrang, P.: A comparative analysis of decentralized power grid stabilization strategies. In: Rose, O., Uhrmacher, A.M. (eds.) Winter Simulation Conference (WSC). pp. 158:1–158:13. WSC (2012). https://doi.org/10.1109/WSC.2012.6465083

53. Hartmanns, A., Kaminski, B.L.: Optimistic value iteration. In: Lahiri, S.K., Wang, C. (eds.) 32nd International Conference on Computer Aided Verification (CAV). Lecture Notes in Computer Science, vol. 12225, pp. 488–511. Springer (2020). https://doi.org/10.1007/978-3-030-53291-8_26

54. Hartmanns, A., Klauck, M., Parker, D., Quatmann, T., Ruijters, E.: The quantitative verification benchmark set. In: Vojnar, T., Zhang, L. (eds.) 25th International Conference on Tools and Algorithms for the Construction and Analysis of Systems (TACAS). Lecture Notes in Computer Science, vol. 11427, pp. 344–350. Springer (2019). https://doi.org/10.1007/978-3-030-17462-0_20

55. Hartmanns, A., Sedwards, S., D'Argenio, P.R.: Efficient simulation-based verification of probabilistic timed automata. In: 2017 Winter Simulation Conference (WSC). pp. 1419–1430. IEEE (2017). https://doi.org/10.1109/WSC.2017.8247885

56. Hatefi-Ardakani, H.: Finite horizon analysis of Markov automata. Ph.D. thesis, Saarland University, Germany (2017), http://scidok.sulb.uni-saarland.de/volltexte/2017/6743/

57. Hensel, C., Junges, S., Katoen, J.P., Quatmann, T., Volk, M.: The probabilistic model checker Storm. Int. J. Softw. Tools Technol. Transf. **24**(4), 589–610 (2022). https://doi.org/10.1007/S10009-021-00633-Z

58. Howard, R.A.: Dynamic Programming and Markov Processes. MIT Press (1960)

59. Kamali, M., Katoen, J.P.: Probabilistic model checking of AODV. In: Gribaudo, M., Jansen, D.N., Remke, A. (eds.) 17th International Conference on Quantitative Evaluation of Systems (QEST). Lecture Notes in Computer Science, vol. 12289, pp. 54–73. Springer (2020). https://doi.org/10.1007/978-3-030-59854-9_6

60. Klauck, M., Hermanns, H.: A Modest approach to dynamic heuristic search in probabilistic model checking. In: Abate, A., Marin, A. (eds.) 18th International Conference on Quantitative Evaluation of Systems (QEST). Lecture Notes in Computer Science, vol. 12846, pp. 15–38. Springer (2021). https://doi.org/10.1007/978-3-030-85172-9_2

61. Köhl, M.A., Klauck, M., Hermanns, H.: Momba: JANI meets Python. In: Groote, J.F., Larsen, K.G. (eds.) 27th International Conference on Tools and Algorithms for the Construction and Analysis of Systems (TACAS). Lecture Notes in Computer Science, vol. 12652, pp. 389–398. Springer (2021). https://doi.org/10.1007/978-3-030-72013-1_23

62. Kretínský, J., Meggendorfer, T.: Of cores: A partial-exploration framework for Markov decision processes. Log. Methods Comput. Sci. **16**(4) (2020), https://lmcs.episciences.org/6833

63. Kwiatkowska, M.Z., Norman, G., Parker, D.: PRISM 4.0: Verification of probabilistic real-time systems. In: Gopalakrishnan, G., Qadeer, S. (eds.) 23rd International Conference on Computer Aided Verification (CAV). Lecture Notes in Computer Science, vol. 6806, pp. 585–591. Springer (2011). https://doi.org/10.1007/978-3-642-22110-1_47

64. Kwiatkowska, M.Z., Norman, G., Parker, D., Sproston, J.: Performance analysis of probabilistic timed automata using digital clocks. Formal Methods Syst. Des. **29**(1), 33–78 (2006). https://doi.org/10.1007/s10703-006-0005-2

65. Kwiatkowska, M.Z., Norman, G., Segala, R., Sproston, J.: Automatic verification of real-time systems with discrete probability distributions. Theor. Comput. Sci. **282**(1), 101–150 (2002). https://doi.org/10.1016/S0304-3975(01)00046-9

66. Lanotte, R., Merro, M., Munteanu, A.: A Modest security analysis of cyber-physical systems: A case study. In: Baier, C., Caires, L. (eds.) 38th IFIP WG 6.1 International Conference on Formal Techniques for Distributed Objects, Components, and Systems (FORTE). Lecture Notes in Computer Science, vol. 10854, pp. 58–78. Springer (2018). https://doi.org/10.1007/978-3-319-92612-4_4

67. Legay, A., Sedwards, S., Traonouez, L.M.: Scalable verification of Markov decision processes. In: Canal, C., Idani, A. (eds.) 4th Workshop on Formal Methods in the Development of Software (WS-FMDS). Lecture Notes in Computer Science, vol. 8938, pp. 350–362. Springer (2014). https://doi.org/10.1007/978-3-319-15201-1_23

68. Lewis, B., Hartmanns, A., Basu, P., Shridevi, R.J., Chakraborty, K., Roy, S., Zhang, Z.: Probabilistic verification for reliable network-on-chip system design. In: Larsen, K.G., Willemse, T.A.C. (eds.) 24th International Conference on Formal Methods for Industrial Critical Systems (FMICS). Lecture Notes in Computer Science, vol. 11687, pp. 110–126. Springer (2019). https://doi.org/10.1007/978-3-030-27008-7_7

69. Nakamoto, S.: Bitcoin: A peer-to-peer electronic cash system (2008), https://bitcoin.org/bitcoin.pdf

70. Panait, L., Luke, S.: Cooperative multi-agent learning: The state of the art. Auton. Agents Multi Agent Syst. **11**(3), 387–434 (2005). https://doi.org/10.1007/s10458-005-2631-2

71. Quatmann, T., Katoen, J.: Sound value iteration. In: Chockler, H., Weissenbacher, G. (eds.) 30th International Conference on Computer Aided Verification (CAV). Lecture Notes in Computer Science, vol. 10981, pp. 643–661. Springer (2018). https://doi.org/10.1007/978-3-319-96145-3_37

72. Raverta, F.D., Fraire, J.A., Madoery, P.G., Demasi, R.A., Finochietto, J.M., D'Argenio, P.R.: Routing in delay-tolerant networks under uncertain contact plans. Ad Hoc Netw. **123**, 102663 (2021). https://doi.org/10.1016/j.adhoc.2021.102663

73. Roberts, R., Lewis, B., Hartmanns, A., Basu, P., Roy, S., Chakraborty, K., Zhang, Z.: Probabilistic verification for reliability of a two-by-two network-on-chip system. In: Lluch-Lafuente, A., Mavridou, A. (eds.) 26th International Conference on Formal Methods for Industrial Critical Systems (FMICS). Lecture Notes in Computer Science, vol. 12863, pp. 232–248. Springer (2021). https://doi.org/10.1007/978-3-030-85248-1_16

74. Rubino, G., Tuffin, B. (eds.): Rare Event Simulation using Monte Carlo Methods. Wiley (2009). https://doi.org/10.1002/9780470745403

75. Sproston, J.: Decidable model checking of probabilistic hybrid automata. In: Joseph, M. (ed.) 6th International Symposium on Formal Techniques in Real-Time and Fault-Tolerant Systems (FTRTFT). Lecture Notes in Computer Science, vol. 1926, pp. 31–45. Springer (2000). https://doi.org/10.1007/3-540-45352-0_5

76. Sutton, R.S., Barto, A.G.: Reinforcement learning - An introduction. MIT Press, Adaptive computation and machine learning (1998)

77. Watkins, C.J.C.H., Dayan, P.: Q-learning. Mach. Learn. **8**, 279–292 (1992). https://doi.org/10.1007/BF00992698

Model Checking Techniques

Analyzing Value Functions of States in Parametric Markov Chains

Kasper Engelen$^{(\boxtimes)}$, Guillermo A. Pérez$^{(\boxtimes)}$, and Shrisha Rao$^{(\boxtimes)}$

University of Antwerp – Flanders Make, Antwerpen, Belgium
{kasper.engelen,guillermo.perez,shrisha.rao}@uantwerpen.be

Abstract. Parametric Markov chains (pMC) are used to model probabilistic systems with unknown or partially known probabilities. Although (universal) pMC verification for reachability properties is known to be coETR-complete, there have been efforts to approach it using potentially easier-to-check properties such as asking whether the pMC is monotonic in certain parameters. In this paper, we first reduce monotonicity to asking whether the reachability probability from a given state is never less than that of another given state. Recent results for the latter property imply an efficient algorithm to collapse same-value equivalence classes, which in turn preserves verification results and monotonicity. We implement our algorithm to collapse "trivial" equivalence classes in the pMC and show empirical evidence for the following: First, the collapse gives reductions in size for some existing benchmarks and significant reductions on some custom benchmarks; Second, the collapse speeds up existing algorithms to check monotonicity and parameter lifting, and hence can be used as a fast pre-processing step in practice.

Keywords: Markov chains · State-space reduction · Parameters

1 Introduction

Finite-state Markovian models are widely used as an operational model for the quantitative analysis of systems with probabilistic behavior. For state reachability in Markov chains, there are well known probabilistic model checkers such as Storm [13] and PRISM [20]. However, in practice, it is not guaranteed that the exact probabilities in the model are known. One way to circumvent this is by modeling unknown probabilities as parameters and known relations between probabilities as functions over shared parameters.

Parametric Markov chains (pMCs, for short) [11] extend classical Markov chains with parameters, i.e. a finite set of real-valued variables, so that transition probabilities are now polynomials over these parameters. Applications of pMCs include model repair [5,8,9,16,25], planning in POMDPs [18], and optimizing randomized distributed algorithms [1]. Analysis of pMCs is supported

---

Work supported by the Flemish (Belgium) inter-university (iBOF) "DESCARTES" and the Belgian F.R.S.-FNRS/FWO SynthEx (G0AH524N) projects.

© The Author(s), under exclusive license to Springer Nature Switzerland AG 2025
N. Jansen et al. (Eds.): Principles of Verification: Cycling the Probabilistic Landscape,
LNCS 15261, pp. 145–165, 2025.
https://doi.org/10.1007/978-3-031-75775-4_7

by established probabilistic model checkers Storm, PRISM, as well as dedicated tools such as PARAM [17] and PROPhESY [12].

The pMC verification problem asks: *Given $\lambda \in [0,1]$, is the probability of reaching the target state from the start state, for all valid parameter valuations, at least λ?* This problem is known to be coETR-complete [15, 28]. Related to the verification problem, the concept of the never-worse relation (NWR) for pMCs has been introduced in [15, 27]. Intuitively, a state is never worse than another if, for all valuations of the parameters, the probability of reaching the target state from the former state is at least as much as that from the latter. Another related notion is that of monotonicity: The (value from a) state is said to be monotonically increasing in a parameter if, for all valuations of the parameters, the probability of reaching the target state from it increases when the value of the parameter increases. Both the NWR and monotonicity turn out to be coETR-complete: Spel et al. [30] give a simple polynomial-time reduction from pMC verification to the monotonicity problem by first reducing it to the NWR problem and then reducing the NWR problem to the monotonicity problem. Since the NWR problem is coNP-hard even when parameterization is trivial (i.e., every transition is labeled with a unique variable) [27], this implies that the monotonicity problem is also coNP-hard when the parameters are trivial.

Despite the discouraging complexity lower bounds recalled above, efficiently-checkable sufficient conditions to establish monotonicity were given in [30]. Similarly, efficiently-checkable sufficient conditions for establishing never-worse relationships were studied in [15]. In particular, an efficient algorithm to compute equivalence classes of trivially parameterized MCs also follows from [15].

Contributions. In this work, we first give a quasi-polynomial-time construction of a pMC whose solution function is the derivative of the solution function of a given pMC. Interestingly, our construction relies on classical results from circuit complexity theory that also allow us to give a polynomial-sized representation of solution functions. Having access to this derivative pMC, we establish a reduction from monotonicity to the NWR problem. Then, we give an algorithm for collapsing some (not necessarily all) equivalence classes of the pMC using the techniques from [15]. We present an implementation in Storm and perform experiments. We evaluate our implementation on several benchmarks from the existing literature and some custom benchmarks, showing that the equivalence-class collapse runs very fast, even for larger benchmarks, and speeds up the monotonicity check in many cases. Finally, we also evaluate our tool as a pre-processing step before parameter lifting (a technique used for near-optimal parameter synthesis) [30] and observe that there too the equivalence-class collapse is sometimes useful.

2   Preliminaries

In this section, we introduce the notation we will be using for polynomials, circuits, and Markov chains with parameters. For the latter, we follow as much as possible the notation used in [2]. Let $x_1, \ldots, x_m$ be *parameters* that can take real values and write $\boldsymbol{x} = (x_1, \ldots, x_m)$.

2.1   Polynomials and Rational Functions

By $\mathbb{Q}[x]$, we denote the *polynomial ring* in x over the rationals; by $\mathbb{Q}(x)$, the analogue *rational field*. For an (exponent) vector $\alpha \in \mathbb{N}^m$, we write x^α to denote the monomial $\prod_{i=1}^m x_i^{\alpha_i}$. Now, every *polynomial* $f \in \mathbb{Q}[x]$ can be written as a sum of products $\sum_{\alpha \in I} c_\alpha x^\alpha$ for I a finite subset of $\mathbb{N}^m$ and where $c_\alpha \in \mathbb{Q}$ for all $\alpha \in I$. The *support* of f is the subset of I with a nonzero coefficient, $\mathrm{supp}(f) = \{\alpha \in \mathbb{N}^m \mid c_\alpha \neq 0\}$. When $\mathrm{supp}(f)$ is empty, we say f is the zero function and write $f \equiv 0$. The *degree* and *maximal coefficient component* of f are $\deg(f) = \max\{\sum_{i=1}^m \alpha_i \mid \alpha \in \mathrm{supp}(f)\}$ and $\mathrm{coeff}(f) = \max\{|a|, |b| \in \mathbb{N} : \alpha \in \mathrm{supp}(f), \frac{a}{b} = c_\alpha$ and is irreducible$\}$, with the convention that $\max \emptyset = 0$.

2.2   Circuits for Polynomials

An *(arithmetic) circuit* over $\mathbb{Q}[x]$ is a labeled directed acyclic graph (DAG) $\mathcal{C} = (V, E, \ell, o)$. Vertices with indegree (a.k.a. *fanin*) 0 are called *input gates* and they are labeled by ℓ with some x_i or a constant from $\{-1, 0, 1\}$. The other vertices all have fanin 2, are called *computation gates*, and are labeled by one of the operations from the ring, i.e. $+$ and $\times$. The *output gate* is $o \in V$. The *size* $|\mathcal{C}|$ of the circuit is $|V|$; its *depth*, noted $\mathrm{depth}(\mathcal{C})$, is the length of a maximal path in $\mathcal{C}$. Every vertex v of the circuit *computes* a polynomial function defined inductively: If v is an input gate, its function is the expression with which it is labeled, i.e. $[\![v]\!] = \ell(v)$; otherwise, $[\![v]\!]$ is the application of the operation $\ell(v)$ to all $[\![u_i]\!]$ such that $(u_i, v) \in E$. Finally, we write $[\![\mathcal{C}]\!] = [\![o]\!]$ for the function computed by the output gate.

Let $f \in \mathbb{Q}[x]$ be a polynomial. If f is given in its sum-of-products representation, one can construct a circuit $\mathcal{C}$ of size $O(|\mathrm{supp}(f)|\deg(f)\log(\mathrm{coeff}(f)))$ such that $[\![\mathcal{C}]\!]$ computes f. Further, if the degree of f is small (e.g. the exponent vectors are given in unary), we can ensure $\mathcal{C}$ has poly-logarithmic depth.

Theorem 1. (From [32, Theorem 2]) *Let $\mathcal{C}$ be a circuit over $\mathbb{Q}[x]$ such that $d = \deg([\![\mathcal{C}]\!])$. Then, we can construct a circuit $\mathcal{C}'$ of size $O((|\mathcal{C}|d^2)^3)$ and depth $O(\log(|\mathcal{C}|d)\log(d))$ that computes the same polynomial.*

2.3   Circuits for Rational Functions

Arithmetic circuits over $\mathbb{Q}(x)$ have also been studied in the literature. Compared to the ones defined above, we would need to further allow for *division gates*. In general, such circuits compute rational functions instead of polynomials. A well-known fact is that one can remove all division gates and replace them by a single division at the output of the circuit: We carry through the gates both the numerator and the denominator of the current function. Multiplication affects both of them the same, but addition results in three extra multiplication gates since we need a common denominator. This pushing of divisions to the top of the circuit is attributed to Strassen [31]. The main result of that same paper is to argue that if a circuit over $\mathbb{Q}(x)$ computes a polynomial, then a polynomial-sized circuit over $\mathbb{Q}[x]$ can compute the same function.

Theorem 2. (From [31]) *Let $\mathcal{C}$ be a circuit over $\mathbb{Q}(\boldsymbol{x})$ computing a polynomial such that $d = \deg(\llbracket \mathcal{C} \rrbracket)$. Then, we can construct a circuit $\mathcal{C}'$ over $\mathbb{Q}[\boldsymbol{x}]$ of size $(|\mathcal{C}|d)^{O(1)}$ that computes the same polynomial.*

2.4 Parametric Markov Chains

A *parametric Markov chain* (pMC, for short) is a tuple $\mathcal{M} = (S, P)$ where S is a finite set of states and $P \colon S \times S \to \mathbb{Q}[\boldsymbol{x}]$ is a (parameterized) probabilistic transition function. For convenience, we write p_{ij} for $P(i,j)$, with the convention $S = \{1, 2, \ldots, n\}$. A valuation $\boldsymbol{v} \in \mathbb{R}^m$ is *graph preserving* if for all $0 \le i, j \le n$ we have $p_{ij} \not\equiv 0 \implies 0 < p_{ij}(\boldsymbol{v}) \le 1$ and $\sum_{k=1}^{n} p_{ik}(\boldsymbol{v}) = 1$. Intuitively, a graph-preserving valuation allows us to instantiate a classical Markov chain (i.e. a nonparametric one) from $\mathcal{M}$. If the set of all graph-preserving valuations is exactly $(0,1)^m$, we say it is a *simple pMC*[1].

For classical Markov chains, several interesting quantities like the probability of eventually reaching a given state, are computable, e.g. via linear programming [26]. When the Markov chain has parameters, instead of a concrete probability, we can compute a rational function f in $\boldsymbol{x}$ which yields the corresponding value $f(\boldsymbol{v})$ given a graph-preserving valuation $\boldsymbol{v}$. In this work, we focus on computing such functions for reachability.

Encoding and Size of a pMC. Let $f \in \mathbb{Q}[\boldsymbol{x}]$ be a polynomial. Henceforth, we write $\|f\|$ for its representation size: $|\mathrm{supp}(f)|\deg(f)\log(\mathrm{coeff}(f))$. Intuitively, we suppose the polynomial is represented as a sum of products with constants and coefficients encoded as numerator-denominator pairs in binary while the exponent vectors are encoded in unary. Then, by $|\mathcal{M}|$, we denote the *size of the pMC*, that is $\sum_{i,j} \|p_{ij}\|$.

3 Reachability Value Functions

For this section, we fix a pMC $\mathcal{M} = (S, P)$ with $S = \{1, \ldots, n\}$ and $p_{ij} \in \mathbb{Q}[\boldsymbol{x}]$ for all $1 \le i, j \le n$. Without loss of generality, we assume that n is the unique target state and that $n - 1$ is the unique state that does not eventually reach n with positive probability. This is no loss of generality since having such extremal reachability probabilities are *qualitative properties* that can be decided in polynomial time based on the graph structure of the pMC only (see, e.g., [2, Thm. 10.29 and Cor. 10.31]) and all states that have the same extremal value can be "merged" while preserving reachability probabilities.

Consider rational functions $\boldsymbol{g} = (g_1, \ldots, g_n)$. We call these *(reachability) value functions* if they are a solution to the following system of linear equations with polynomial coefficients. Intuitively, the ith value function g_i, for $1 \le i \le n$, represents the probability of reaching state n from state i. Below, A is an $n \times n$

---

[1] Our definition of a simple pMC is more general than the one used in the literature (e.g., [19,29]).

matrix whose entries A_{ij} are p_{ij}, for all $1 \leq i < n - 1$ and all $1 \leq j \leq n$, and 0 for $i \in \{n - 1, n\}$ and all $1 \leq j \leq n$.

$$(\mathbb{I}_n - A)\boldsymbol{y} = \begin{bmatrix} \boldsymbol{0} \\ 1 \end{bmatrix} \tag{1}$$

The matrix $\mathbb{I}_n - A$ is guaranteed to be nonsingular for all graph-preserving valuations (see, e.g., [3, Theorem 10.19]) so value functions exist and are even unique, up to extensional equivalence [11]. Furthermore, they are known to be computable, e.g., using Gaussian elimination [2,21].

3.1   Monotonicity and Being Never Worse

We will now formally define two properties of states and their value functions. Namely, when the functions are *monotonic* and when the value of a state is *never worse* than that of another given state. We will continue with our fixed pMC $\mathcal{M} = (S, P)$ having $S = \{1, \ldots, n\}$ and $\boldsymbol{g} = (g_1, \ldots, g_n)$ its value functions.

Monotonicity. Let $i \in S$ be a state and x_j, for $1 \leq j \leq m$, a parameter. We say that $\mathcal{M}$ is *monotonically increasing* [29] from i and in x_j, written $\mathcal{M}\uparrow_i^{x_j}$, if $g_i(\boldsymbol{u}) \leq g_i(\boldsymbol{v})$ for all graph-preserving valuations $\boldsymbol{u}, \boldsymbol{v}$ such that $\boldsymbol{v} - \boldsymbol{u} = \varepsilon \boldsymbol{e}_j$ for some $\varepsilon \in \mathbb{R}_{\geq 0}$, where $\boldsymbol{e}_j$ is the null vector with 1 only in the jth position. Being *monotonically decreasing* can be defined analogously.

The Never-Worse Relation. Let $i, j \in S$ be states. We say that j is *never-worse* than i, denoted $i \trianglelefteq j$, if $g_i(\boldsymbol{v}) \leq g_j(\boldsymbol{v})$ for all graph-preserving valuations $\boldsymbol{v}$. The relation $\trianglelefteq$ is called the *never-worse relation* [15,27], or NWR for short.

The natural decision problems associated with monotonicity and the NWR are coETR complete [15,29]. For monotonicity, the problem asks, given a pMC $\mathcal{M}$, a state i, and a parameter x_j, whether $\mathcal{M}\uparrow_i^{x_j}$ holds. For the NWR, the problem asks, given a pMC $\mathcal{M}$, and two states i and j, whether $i \trianglelefteq j$ holds. A clear relationship between the two problems has been established in one direction.

Theorem 3. (From [29, Lemma 2]) *There is a polynomial-time many-one reduction from the NWR problem to the monotonicity problem.*

Proof (Sketch). Add a new state $n + 1$, a new parameter x_{m+1}, and two new transitions to the states for which we want to check the NWR: with probability x_{m+1} we transition from $n + 1$ to j; with $1 - x_{m+1}$, from $n + 1$ to i. The new pMC is monotonically increasing from $n + 1$ in x_{m+1} if and only if $i \trianglelefteq j$ in the original pMC.   □

Example 1. Fig. 1a shows an example of a (simple) pMC with 6 states where 1 is the target state. It is easy to verify that the value functions $g_s = p^2 + r - rp$ and $g_t = rp + r - r^2$ are monotonically increasing in r and p (respectively), but not in p and r (respectively). In Fig. 1b, we have $v \trianglelefteq u$ since $g_v = p - p^2 < 1 - p = g_u$ for all graph preserving valuations. This relation can be witnessed from the state s by checking monotonicity in r. In this case, $g_s = r(1 - p)^2 + p(1 - p)$ is indeed monotonically increasing in r.

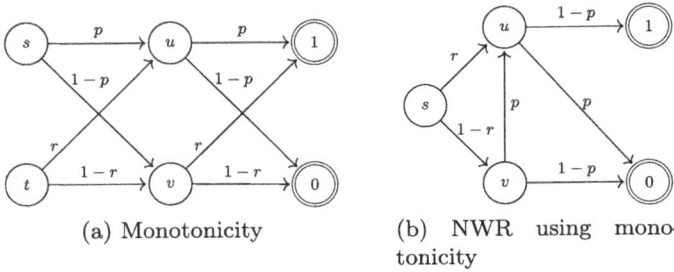

(a) Monotonicity

(b) NWR using mono-
tonicity

Fig. 1. Examples of pMCs with parameters p and r.

The reduction from Theorem 3 is useful because it allows any (approximation) algorithm developed for the monotonicity problem to be translated into one
for the NWR. We would like to establish a relationship in the opposite direction.
Towards that, we present the following reduction which assumes the given pMC
$\mathcal{M}$ is simple and that it is paired with a *partial-derivative pMC*.

Theorem 4. *Consider being given simple pMCs $\mathcal{M} = (S, P), \mathcal{M}'$ over $\boldsymbol{x}$ with
value functions $\boldsymbol{g}, \boldsymbol{g}'$, $i \in S$, and $0 \leq k \leq m$, such that $\frac{\partial g_i}{\partial x_k} = \beta + N g_1'$ where
$N \in \mathbb{N}_{>0}, \beta \in \mathbb{Q}$. Then, there is a polynomial-time (in the size of $\mathcal{M}'$) many-one
reduction from the monotonicity problem for $\mathcal{M}$ to the NWR problem.*

Proof. Since $\mathcal{M}$ is simple, its set of graph-preserving valuations is connected (in
the topological sense). Therefore, $\mathcal{M} \uparrow_{x_k}^i$ holds if and only if $\frac{\partial g_i}{\partial x_k}(\boldsymbol{v}) \geq 0$ for all
graph-preserving valuations $\boldsymbol{v}$ (cf. [29, Def. 1] and [30, Def. 2]). Because $\mathcal{M}'$ is
also simple, the sets of graph-preserving valuations of the two pMCs coincide.
Hence, to check for monotonicity in $\mathcal{M}$ we focus on the value function g_1' of $\mathcal{M}'$.

Now, if $\frac{\beta}{N} \geq 0$ we will have monotonicity and if $\frac{\beta}{N} \leq -1$ we can conclude
the opposite (unless $g_1' = 1$). Since all of the latter can be checked in polynomial
time, we suppose $-1 < \frac{\beta}{N} < 0$, which is the same as $0 < \frac{-\beta}{N} < 1$. In this
case, monotonicity holds if and only if $g_1'(\boldsymbol{v}) \geq \frac{-\beta}{N}$ for all graph-preserving
valuations $\boldsymbol{v} \in (0, 1)^m$. This concludes the reduction because that property is
straightforward to encode as an instance of the NWR problem: we can add a
new state s to $\mathcal{M}'$ that transitions with probability $\frac{-\beta}{N}$ to the target and $1 + \frac{\beta}{N}$
to the sink, and then ask whether $s \trianglelefteq 1$.   □

We observe that the proof of the theorem does not crucially rely on $\mathcal{M}$ being
a simple pMC. The same argument can be used for any pMC whose graph-
preserving valuations form a connected subset of $(0, 1)^m$ if it is definable via
a system of strict polynomial inequalities $\boldsymbol{0} < \boldsymbol{A} < \boldsymbol{1}$. Then, the entries of $\boldsymbol{A}$
could be put as transition probabilities between new "dummy" states in $\mathcal{M}'$ to
constrain its set of graph-preserving valuations.

Unfortunately, we do not know whether we incur in a loss of generality
because of the assumption that the partial-derivative pMC is given. In the sequel,
we do provide a quasi-polynomial construction for a simple partial-derivative

pMC. Together with Theorem 4, this gives us a quasi-polynomial reduction from the monotonicity problem to the NWR problem for simple pMCs.

4   Computing Representations of Value Functions

In this section, we recall the main ideas behind how one can compute the value functions of a given pMC. We argue that a suitable polynomial-size representation of them via circuits can be efficiently computed by symbolically executing the known algorithms. Then, we use this and a connection between circuits and yet another representation of polynomial functions to give a quasi-polynomial construction of partial-derivative pMCs.

4.1   Value Functions via One-Step Division-Free Gaussian Elimination

Using one-step division-free Gaussian elimination [4], as proposed in [2, Section 3.2], Equation (1) can be put into *row echelon form* while guaranteeing all entries are still polynomials. In fact, we obtain the following system of linear equations with a diagonal matrix of polynomial coefficients that is equivalent to Equation (1) (see [2, Algorithm 1]).

$$\begin{bmatrix} a_{11} & \cdots & 0 \\ \vdots & \ddots & \vdots \\ 0 & \cdots & a_{nn} \end{bmatrix} \boldsymbol{y} = \begin{bmatrix} b_1 \\ \vdots \\ b_n \end{bmatrix} \tag{2}$$

Furthermore, the a_{ii} and b_i are all polynomials and their degree is at most $O(nd)$, where $d = \max_{i,j} \deg(p_{ij})$ (see [2, Proof of Lem. 3]). The a_{ii} and b_i are obtained from the p_{ij} polynomials by applying addition, multiplication, subtraction, and division—$O(n^3)$ times, to be precise. Hence, for each a_{ii} or b_i we can construct a circuit $\mathcal{C}$ over $\mathbb{Q}(\boldsymbol{x})$ of polynomial size, in n and d, such that the polynomial is computed by $\mathcal{C}$. Since b_i/a_{ii}, for all $1 \leq i \leq n$, is a solution to the system, appealing to Theorem 2, followed by Theorem 1, we obtain the following.

Theorem 5. *Let $\mathcal{M} = (S, P)$ be a pMC with $S = \{1, \ldots, n\}$ and write $d = \max_{i,j} \deg(p_{ij})$. Then, we can construct two families of circuits $\mathcal{N}_i, \mathcal{D}_i$ over $\mathbb{Q}[\boldsymbol{x}]$ of size $|\mathcal{M}|^{O(1)}$ and depth $O(\log(|\mathcal{M}|) \log(nd))$ such that $[\![\mathcal{N}_i]\!]/[\![\mathcal{D}_i]\!]$ is the i-th value function g_i, for all $1 \leq i \leq n$.*

This means that, while the sum-of-products representation of value functions may be exponential [2, Lemma 2], their circuit representation is always small!

Before we close this subsection, we leverage the previous theorem to establish that also the partial derivatives of the value functions always have a small circuit representation. For this, we abuse our notation for circuits to allow for multiple (ordered) output gates so that a circuit can compute a vector-valued function. We need the following result about partial derivatives of functions as circuits.

Theorem 6. *(From [6,23]) Let $\mathcal{C}$ be a circuit over $\mathbb{Q}(\boldsymbol{x})$ that computes a (scalar) function f. Then, we can construct a circuit $\mathcal{C}'$ over $\mathbb{Q}(\boldsymbol{x})$ of size $O(|\mathcal{C}|)$ and depth $O(\mathrm{depth}(\mathcal{C}))$ that computes $(f, \frac{\partial f}{\partial x_1}, \ldots, \frac{\partial f}{\partial x_m})$.*

Now, we can use the construction from Theorem 6 on the circuits representing the numerator and denominator of the value functions in Theorem 5. Then, using the quotient rule, we obtain the following.

Theorem 7. *Let $\mathcal{M} = (S, P)$ be a pMC with $S = \{1, \ldots, n\}$ and write $d = \max_{ij} \deg(p_{ij})$. Then, we can construct two families of circuits $\mathcal{N}_i, \mathcal{D}_i$ over $\mathbb{Q}[\boldsymbol{x}]$ of size $|\mathcal{M}|^{O(1)}$ and depth $O(\log(|\mathcal{M}|)\log(nd))$ such that $[\![\mathcal{N}_i]\!]/[\![\mathcal{D}_i]\!]$ gives g_i and its partial derivatives $(g_i, \frac{\partial g_i}{\partial x_1}, \ldots, \frac{\partial g_i}{\partial x_m})$, for all $1 \le i \le n$.*

4.2 Quasi-Polynomial Partial-Derivative Chains

In this subsection we aim at an extension of Theorem 7 where we get, for a value function g_i and a given variable x_j, a pMC such that one of its value functions corresponds to $\frac{\partial g_i}{\partial x_j}$ (cf. [18, Section 3.2], where the authors construct parametric weighted automata computing the partial derivatives). To realize this, we use a classical result due to Ben-Or and Cleve [7] to go from the circuit representation of the partial derivative to something closer to pMCs. Namely, we obtain an *algebraic branching program*.

An algebraic branching program (ABP, for short) [24] over $\mathbb{Q}[\boldsymbol{x}]$ is a labeled DAG $\mathcal{A} = (V, E, \ell)$ with $d + 1$ layers of vertices V. This means that V is partitioned into $V_0, \ldots, V_d$ such that $(u, v) \in E$ implies $u \in V_i$ and $v \in V_{i+1}$ for some $0 \le i < d$. The *size* of $\mathcal{A}$ is $|V|$; its *width* is the cardinality of the largest layer, $\max_{i=0}^{d} |V_i|$. We will be interested in the single-source single-sink kind of ABP, meaning the first and last layers have a single vertex. Every edge $e \in E$ is labeled by a linear term $\ell(e)$ over $\boldsymbol{x}$, i.e. $\ell : E \to \mathbb{Q}[\boldsymbol{x}]$ and $\deg(\ell(e)) \le 1$ for all $e \in E$. The linear terms are encoded just like polynomials are in pMCs (as sum of products with binary encoding for coefficients and constants, unary for exponents). Write $P(\mathcal{A})$ for the set of all maximal paths in $\mathcal{A}$. We say that $\mathcal{A}$ computes the polynomial $[\![\mathcal{A}]\!] = \sum_{\pi \in P(\mathcal{A})} \prod_{e \in \pi} \ell(e)$. Just like in circuits, each vertex v computes a polynomial $[\![v]\!]$, i.e. taking them as the single source of the ABP. The result below links circuits and ABPs in the required direction.

Theorem 8. *(From [7, Theorem 1]) Let $\mathcal{C}$ be a circuit over $\mathbb{Q}[\boldsymbol{x}]$. Then, we can construct an ABP $\mathcal{A}$ of size $O(4^{\text{depth}(\mathcal{C})})$ and width 4 that computes the same polynomial.*

Using the result above on Theorem 7, we get an ABP as stated below.

Theorem 9. *Let $\mathcal{M} = (S, P)$ be a pMC with $S = \{1, \ldots, n\}$ and write $d = \max_{ij} \deg(p_{ij})$. Then, we can construct two families of ABPs $\mathcal{N}_i, \mathcal{D}_i$ over $\mathbb{Q}[\boldsymbol{x}]$ of size $|\mathcal{M}|^{O(\log(nd))}$ and width 4 such that $[\![\mathcal{N}_i]\!]/[\![\mathcal{D}_i]\!]$ gives the partial derivatives $(\frac{\partial g_i}{\partial x_1}, \ldots, \frac{\partial g_i}{\partial x_m})$ of g_i, for all $1 \le i \le n$.*

Next, we will give a translation from ABPs to pMCs. The following result will be useful to rewrite polynomials into a form that is easy to encode as probability distributions. For completeness, and because it is a good warm-up for the sequel, we also give a proof of the result.

Lemma 1. *(Chonev's trick [10, Remark 1]) Let $f \in \mathbb{Q}[\boldsymbol{x}]$ be a polynomial. Then, there are $c \in \mathbb{Z}$, $d, N \in \mathbb{N}_{>0}$, and $\boldsymbol{a}, \boldsymbol{b} \in \mathbb{N}_{>0}^T$ with $\frac{|c|}{d} + \sum_{i=1}^T \frac{a_i}{b_i} \leq 1$, such that $f = N(\frac{c}{d} + \sum_{i=1}^T \frac{a_i}{b_i} Q_i(\boldsymbol{x}))$ where the Q_i are products of at most $\deg(f)$ terms from $\bigcup_{i=1}^m \{x_i, 1 - x_i\}$. Moreover,*

- *$T \leq |\mathrm{supp}(f)|\deg(f)$ and*
- *$\log N, \log |c|, \log d, \log a_i, \log b_i$ are all $O(\|f\|)$.*

Proof. Starting from a sum-of-products representation of f, we choose some monomial $t_\alpha \boldsymbol{x}^\alpha$ such that t_α is negative and $\boldsymbol{\alpha} \neq \boldsymbol{0}$, i.e. it is not the constant term. Now, we choose one of the variables x_i and replace it with $1 - x_i$ in the product so that we can flip the sign of t_α. To obtain a sum of terms equivalent to the original monomial, we need to cancel out the new monomial we have introduced. The latter has degree strictly smaller than the original monomial so we can repeat our approach until we get a constant (whose sign does not matter in the claim). The original example by Chonev is quite instructive: If we start with $-2x_1 x_2 x_3$, we can rewrite it as: $2(1 - x_1)x_2 x_3 + 2(1 - x_2)x_3 + 2(1 - x_3) - 2$.

Observe that, in the rewriting process described above, every monomial is transformed into a sum of at most $\deg(f)$ terms. The first bound in the claim follows from this observation. For the second bound, we note that all coefficients $\frac{a_i}{b_i}$ and the constant $\frac{c}{d}$ are sums of rational constants from f whose bitsize is at most $\log(\mathrm{coeff}(f))$. Now we consider, in turn, each of the operations which make the bitsize of the result larger.

To obtain a common denominator for the sums, in the worst case, we need to multiply all denominators. This results in adding $\log(\mathrm{coeff}(f))$ to the bitsize (of both the numerator and denominator) at most T times.

The sums to obtain each numerator a_i may incur in a further blow-up of the bitsize by adding T to it. So far, the bitsize of $|c|, d, a_i, b_i$ is at most:

$$(|\mathrm{supp}(f)|\deg(f) + 1)\log(\mathrm{coeff}(f)) + |\mathrm{supp}(f)|\deg(f)$$
$$\leq (|\mathrm{supp}(f)|\deg(f) + 1)(\log(\mathrm{coeff}(f)) + 1).$$

To get a sum of at most one and to factor out N, we can set N to be the sum of all numerators a_i. Then, all denominators get multiplied by N and we can factor it out as required. Hence, the bitsize of N is at most:

$$(|\mathrm{supp}(f)|\deg(f) + 1)(\log(\mathrm{coeff}(f)) + 1) + |\mathrm{supp}(f)|\deg(f)$$
$$\leq (|\mathrm{supp}(f)|\deg(f) + 1)(\log(\mathrm{coeff}(f)) + 2),$$

while the final bitsize of the b_i is at most double that of N due to their multiplication by N.

The claim thus follows from the definition of $\|f\|$. $\qquad\square$

Now, using Chonev's trick, we can inductively construct an acyclic pMC from any ABP such that one of the value functions of the former and the polynomial computed by the latter have a linear relation.

Lemma 2. *Let $\mathcal{A} = (V, E, \ell)$ be an ABP over $\mathbb{Q}[\boldsymbol{x}]$ of width w and write $s = \max_{e \in E} |\mathrm{supp}(\ell(e))|$. Then, we can compute $N \in \mathbb{N}_{>0}, \beta \in \mathbb{Q}$ and a simple pMC $\mathcal{M} = (S, P)$ with value functions $\boldsymbol{g}$ such that $[\![\mathcal{A}]\!] = \beta + N g_1$, $|S|$ is $O(|V|sw)$ and β, N, and all p_{ij}, have polynomial bitsize in $|V|, w, \max_{e \in E} \|\ell(e)\|$.*

Before we prove the lemma, we observe that together with Theorem 9 it implies that we can construct quasi-polynomial partial-derivative pMCs.

Theorem 10. *Let $\mathcal{M} = (S, P)$ be a pMC with value functions $\boldsymbol{g}$ and $d = \max_{i,j} \deg(p_{ij})$. Then, for any $i \in S$ and $0 \leq k \leq m$, we can compute $N \in \mathbb{N}_{>0}, \beta \in \mathbb{Q}$ and a simple pMC $\mathcal{M}'$ of size $|\mathcal{M}|^{O(\log(|S|d))}$ with value functions $\boldsymbol{g}'$ s.t. $\frac{\partial g_i}{\partial x_k} = \beta + N g_1'$ where β and N have $|\mathcal{M}|^{O(\log(|S|d))}$ bitsize representations.*

Proof (of Lemma 2). Let $\mathcal{A}$ have $L + 1$ layers $V_0, \ldots, V_L \subseteq V$. Then, for all $u \in V_{L-1}$ we have that $[\![u]\!] = \ell(u, t)$, where $t \in V_L$ is the unique sink. Similarly, for all $0 \leq j < L - 1$ and all vertices $u \in V_j$:

$$[\![u]\!] = \sum_{v \in V_{j+1}} \ell(u, v)[\![v]\!]. \tag{3}$$

Based on the equation above, we will give an inductive construction of a pMC $\mathcal{M}$ based on Chonev's trick now.

Our induction is on the layer j and we will argue that for all $u \in V_j$ we have states $\overline{u}, \underline{u}$ in the pMC such that $[\![u]\!]/N_u - \beta_u = g_{\overline{u}} = 1 - g_{\underline{u}}$. First, we add states $\perp$ and $\top$ to $\mathcal{M}$ with the intention of $\top$ being the target state and $\perp$ a state with only itself as successor. For $j = L - 1$ and each vertex $u \in V_j$ we add to $\mathcal{M}$ states $\overline{u}, \underline{u}$. Using Chonev's trick, we then rewrite $\ell(u, t)$ as $N_u(\beta_u + \sum_{k=1}^{T} \alpha_k Q_k(\boldsymbol{x}))$. Note that since $\ell(u, t)$ is a linear function, $T \leq 2s$ and the $Q_k(\boldsymbol{x})$ are also linear. For each $Q_k(\boldsymbol{x})$ we add a state to $\mathcal{M}$ and a transition from it to $\top$ with probability $Q_k(\boldsymbol{x})$ and one to $\perp$ with probability $1 - Q_k(\boldsymbol{x})$. From $\overline{u}$ we add transitions to the states Q_k states with corresponding probability α_k and one to $\perp$ with probability $1 - \sum_{k=1}^{T} \alpha_k$. To conclude, we add another state for each Q_k and transitions from them to $\perp$, instead of $\top$, with probability Q_k and transitions to $\top$ with $1 - Q_k$, as well transitions from $\underline{u}$ to these new copies of Q_k with the α_k as probabilities and to $\top$, not $\perp$, with $1 - \sum_{k=1}^{T} \alpha_k$. It is easy to check all the desired properties hold so the claim holds for some j.

For the inductive step, consider $0 \leq j < L - 1$ and a vertex $u \in V_j$. We again add states $\overline{u}, \underline{u}$ to $\mathcal{M}$ and consider Eq. (3). From the inductive hypothesis,

$$[\![u]\!] = \sum_{v \in V_{j+1}} \ell(u, v) N_v (\beta_v + g_{\overline{v}}) = N_v \sum_{v \in V_{j+1}} \beta_v \ell(u, v) + \ell(u, v) g_{\overline{v}}. \tag{4}$$

Interpreting the $g_{\overline{v}}$ as variables for a moment, we can again use Chonev's trick to rewrite the above as $N_u(\beta_u + \sum_{k=1}^{T} \alpha_k Q_k(\boldsymbol{x}))$. This time we started from a sum of (at most sw) quadratic terms, so $T \leq 3sw$ and the $Q_k(\boldsymbol{x})$ are at most quadratic. For each Q_i we construct a chain of length at most 2 leading to $\top$, $\overline{v}$, or $\underline{v}$ depending on whether it has no term with $g_{\overline{v}}$ as a factor, it has $g_{\overline{v}}$ as a factor, or it has $(1 - g_{\overline{v}})$ as a factor. From $\overline{u}$ we add transitions to the start of the new chains with corresponding probabilities α_k and to $\bot$ with the remaining probability. Similarly, we construct chains of length at most 2 leading to $\bot$, $\underline{v}$, or $\overline{v}$ with the same conditions as before, in the same order. Then, from $\underline{v}$ we add transitions to the new chains and to $\top$ with the remaining probability. Once more the desired properties hold and we thus conclude the description of how to construct the simple pMC.

The bound on the number of states from the pMC is immediate from the construction and the bounds on the number of chains constructed per state per layer (all linear in sw) and their size being constant. For the bounds on the bitsize of the numbers, we revisit the cases considered for the proof of Lemma 1 with special attention to the substitution applied to get Equation (4). Write M for the value $\max_{e \in E} \log(\mathrm{coeff}(\ell(e)))$.

To obtain a common denominator for the sums, we may need to multiply all denominators. However, we can make sure that all β_v (from the same layer) have the same common denominator. This means that it suffices to compute a common denominator for the coefficients of the $\ell(u, v)$ and multiply it by that of the β_v. Hence, in each layer, we add M to the bitsize (of both the numerator and denominator) at most $T \le 3sw$ times.

The sums to obtain each numerator may incur in a further blow-up of the bitsize by adding $T \le 3sw$ to it. This is on top of the M additional bits relative to the representation of the numerator of the β_v.

To get a sum of at most one and to factor out N_u we again need to be careful. Note that we can make sure all the N_v (from the same layer) are equal. Now, since $\beta_v \le 1$, it suffices to add the absolute values of all numerators of coefficients and constants from the $\ell(u, v)$ (for all v in the same layer), call that A, and to set $N_u = AN_v$. Then, all denominators get multiplied by A too and we get an increase in bitsize, for numerators and denominators and for N_u relative to N_v, of at most $3swM$.

From the above analysis we get that every layer results in adding $O(swM)$ to the bitsize of the integers required to write down the polynomials we manipulate. Since the number of layers is at most $|V|$, all the $\|p_{ij}\|$ are bounded by $O(|V|w \max_{e \in E} \|\ell(e)\|)$ as required. □

Unfortunately, it seems difficult to improve Theorem 10 and get a polynomial-time reduction using techniques from arithmetic circuits and branching programs as we have. Indeed, the question of whether the former can be translated into polynomial-sized branching programs (a.k.a. *skewed circuits*) seems to be open (cf. [22, Sec. 3, p. 10]). It is also not clear how to adapt our inductive translation from ABPs to get pMCs from the weighted automata used in [18, Section 3.2] to represent partial derivatives of value functions. Here, the main complication is that the automata may have cycles.

5   NWR Equivalence Classes

In the rest of the paper, we adopt a practical approach in reducing the state space of pMCs by collapsing NWR equivalent states. To keep the algorithm efficient and to avoid the difficulties of ETR-hardness, we focuss on a subclass of pMCs, which we define below. It is important to note that even in a general pMC, if we ignore the parameters to obtain a "trivial" pMC, any equivalence in the new pMC is also one in the original pMC.

A *trivially parametric* Markov chain is a pMC where the polynomial on each transition t is the linear function x_t, so x_t appears uniquely in the label of t. It is known that equivalence classes of trivially parametric Markov chains can be computed in polynomial time [15]. This is due to the fact that every equivalence class has a unique "exit", that is, a unique state that has transitions leaving the equivalence class. This exit is the closest state to the target among all states in the equivalence class. It follows that equivalence classes can be found by doing a reverse breadth-first search (BFS) from the target state to find these exits and then looking for states that almost-surely reach these exits (see Algorithm 1).

One can easily verify that the algorithm runs in $O(n^2)$ time, where n is the number of states of the pMC. The extremal states can certainly be computed and collapsed in $O(n^2)$ [3]. Furthermore, each state $u \in S$ is visited at most once during the reverse BFS from the final state and computing the set of all states which have a path to the final or fail states after removing u takes linear time.

Algorithm 1: Compute and collapse equivalence classes

Inputs : A pMC $\mathcal{M} = (S, P)$, final state ☺ and fail state ☹

Output : The pMC with all equivalence classes collapsed

1 Contract extremal-value states;
2 TODO ← S;
3 EC ← ∅;
4 Order the states in reverse BFS order, starting from the final state;
5 **foreach** $u \in S$ **do**
6   **if** $u \notin TODO$ **then**
7 | **continue**;
8   Determine set U of states that have a path to ☺ or a path to ☹ without going through the state u;
9     $\tilde{u} \leftarrow \{u\} \cup (V \setminus U)$;
10   TODO ← TODO $\setminus \tilde{u}$;
11   EC ← EC $\cup \{u\}$;
12 **foreach** $u \in EC$ **do**
13   Collapse all states in $\tilde{u}$ into u;

The following is immediate from the definitions of NWR and monotonicity.

Remark 1. Collapsing NWR equivalence classes preserves monotonicity.

We implemented our algorithm and tested its performance against a number of benchmarks. These benchmarks can be divided into three categories: those from Spel et al. [30] which focus on the monotonicity analysis module of Storm; those from Heck et al. [18]; and a number of benchmarks we constructed ourselves based on the properties of our algorithm. Our code and experimental data can be found on Zenodo [14].

Our experiments aim to answer the following three questions:

Q1. How much does Algorithm 1 reduce the size of (parametric) Markov chains?
Q2. Does using the algorithm as a pre-processing step cause the monotonicity analysis algorithm from [30] to run more efficiently?
Q3. Does our pre-processing algorithm make parameter lifting [18] more efficient?

5.1 Experimental Set-up

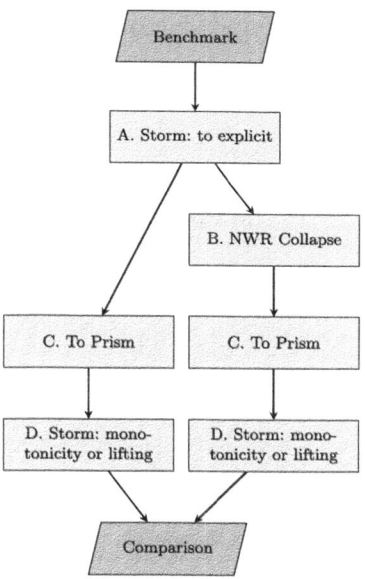

Fig. 2. Overview of the experimental setup.

We implemented Algorithm 1 in Python and set up an experimental pipeline as depicted in Fig. 2. First each model, specified in PRISM format, is read by Storm-pars (v1.8.1) and converted to the JSON explicit format (A). This explicit model is then reduced in size using our algorithm (B). Then, the explicit representations of both the original and collapsed models are converted back into PRISM (C). The latter is done by explicitly hard-coding every transition. Finally, both the original and collapsed models are used as input to either the monotonicity or parameter lifting module of Storm-pars (D).

All experiments were run on a 2021 MacBook M1 Pro. For Storm, this we used the docker image `movesrwth/storm:1.8.1` with 8GB allocated memory. When reproducing the monotonicity experiments from [29], a time-out of 4h was

158   K. Engelen et al.

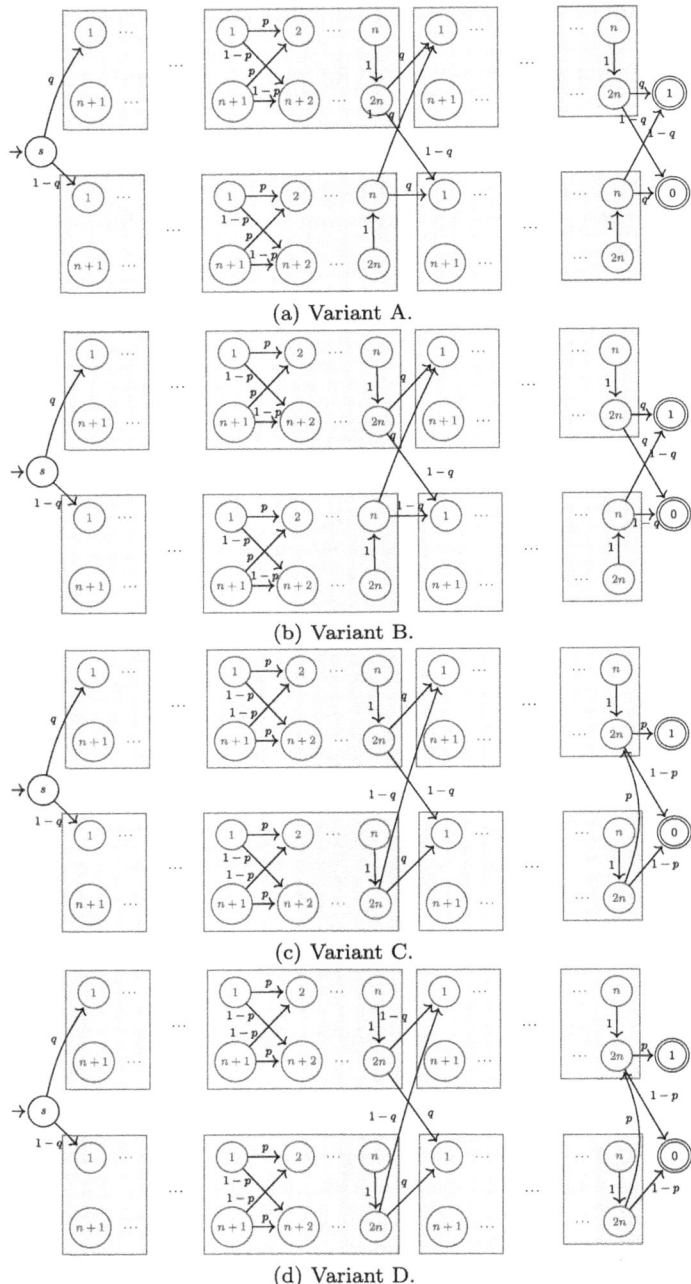

(a) Variant A.

(b) Variant B.

(c) Variant C.

(d) Variant D.

Fig. 3. The 4 variants of our benchmark for a given parameter n which have $4n^2 + 3$ states and $2n + 3$ equivalence classes each. Every red box represents one equivalence class with $2n$ states. (Color figure online)

used; the parameter-lifting experiments from [30] were given a 30min timeout. The bounds were chosen to match the experimental setup of the cited papers.

We should note that we only ran the monotonicy analysis and parameter-lifting modules of Storm on the benchmarks that actually reported a size reduction. Those benchmarks for which there was no size reduction were not considered further. The excluded benchmarks include the Gambler, Zeroconf, and Message authentication benchmarks [30] as well as the Herman benchmark [18].

5.2   Custom Benchmarks

In order to more accurately evaluate the performance of our algorithm we have also constructed our own benchmark with 4 variants. These are depicted in Fig. 3a to 3d. All of these variants consist of a start state s, the final state 1, the fail state 0 and $2n$ red "blocks" with each block depicting an equivalence class containing $2n$ states. Hence, the total number of states in each block is $4n^2 + 3$, although in our implementation the states in the beginning of each block with no incoming edges (for instance, the state $n + 1$ in the blocks in Fig. 3a) are automatically deleted. This leads to the actual number of states in the model being $4n^2 - 2n + 1$. These variants all share the same structure of the states, but differ slightly in the transitions between them. It is shown in Table 1 that these different benchmarks induce different behavior in the monotonicity analysis.

All variants have an equal number of states, and also have two parameters p and q. The size of the model can be adjusted using the variable n. In variants A and B the parameter p is no longer present after applying our algorithm, leaving only q since the only transitions with the parameter p are present within the blocks, and these are collapsed into a single state. The variants C and D retain both parameters p and q after applying our algorithm since p also occurs in the transitions from the last two blocks to the final and fail states.

The monotonicity properties of the four variants also differ. Variants A and C are not monotonic in q while variants B and D are monotonically increasing in q. Moreover, C and D are both monotonically increasing in p.

5.3   Results and Tables

A quantitative summary of the results can be found in Tables 2 and 3. Experiments that were not performed are denoted as N/A. The benchmarks are listed together with the constant values used when instantiating the models.

Table 1 contains the results of applying our algorithm, as well as the monotonicity analysis and parameter lifting modules of Storm. The first column contains the details of the benchmarks. Next is the size of the model before and after applying our algorithm. This is followed by the time our algorithm took to identify and collapse the equivalence classes. The last four columns contain the running times of the Storm-pars modules for monotonicity analysis, and parameter lifting. Times are listed with and without applying our algorithm before the model is passed to Storm. The reported time of the collapse algorithm only includes the time it took to identify and collapse the equivalence classes, and

Table 1. Comparison of sizes and times to check monotonicity and realize parameter lifting with and without our reduction techniques. We write TO to denote time-outs, N/A when the experiment was not executed, and TO (file) when the module ran out of time while parsing the file. (Recall we are using explicitly encoded transitions.)

Benchmark	Size (states)		Collapse time (s)	Mono. time (s)		Lifting time (s)	
	Before	after		before	after	before	after
Custom (A)							
n=2	15	7	<1	<1	<1	<1	<1
n=3	33	9	<1	<1	<1	<1	<1
n=8	243	19	<1	4.38	<1	<1	<1
n=10	383	23	<1	TO	<1	<1	<1
n=15	873	33	<1	TO	<1	<1	<1
n=50	9903	103	3.52	TO	<1	5.781	<1
n=100	39803	203	28.26	N/A	N/A	87.535	<1
n=150	89703	303	88.78	N/A	N/A	TO (file)	<1
Custom (B)							
n=2	15	7	<1	<1	<1	<1	<1
n=25	2453	53	<1	<1	<1	<1	<1
n=50	9903	103	3.29	<1	<1	<1	<1
n=100	39803	203	25.71	N/A	N/A	<1	<1
n=150	89703	303	87.76	N/A	N/A	TO (file)	<1
Custom (C)							
n=2	15	7	<1	<1	<1	<1	<1
n=3	33	9	<1	<1	<1	<1	<1
n=8	243	19	<1	2.24	<1	<1	<1
n=10	383	23	<1	30.28	<1	<1	<1
n=15	873	33	<1	10381.17	<1	<1	<1
n=20	1563	43	<1	TO	<1	<1	<1
n=50	9903	103	3.29	TO	<1	<1	<1
n=100	39803	203	25.60	N/A	N/A	<1	<1
n=150	89703	303	86.36	N/A	N/A	TO (file)	<1
Custom (D)							
n=2	15	7	<1	<1	<1	<1	<1
n=25	2453	53	<1	<1	<1	<1	<1
n=50	9903	103	3.35	<1	<1	<1	<1
n=100	39803	203	25.73	N/A	N/A	1.330	<1
n=150	89703	303	89.31	N/A	N/A	TO (file)	<1

does not include parsing or collapsing of the extremal states; the values for monotonicity-analysis and parameter-lifting times are those reported by Storm as "monotonicity analysis" and "model checking", respectively.

In Table 1, we observe that there is a significant difference in the running time of the monotonicity analysis for those benchmarks that have a non-monotonic parameter (i.e., variants A and C). For parameter lifting, there are differences in running times for bigger models ($n \geq 50$) coming from benchmarks that contain a non-monotonic parameter.

For some values of benchmark constants, we did not run the monotonocity analysis or parameter lifting, since we expected time-outs or memory-outs. We did, however, run our reduction algorithm on those models, with the results visible in Table 2. We observe it is possible to run our algorithm on models of up to a million states in a reasonable amount of time.

Table 2. Comparison of size and reduction times only, for larger instances of our custom benchmarks.

Benchmark	Size (states)		Collapse time (s)
	before	after	
Custom (A)			
n=300	359403	603	721.19
n=400	639203	803	1647.76
n=500	999003	1003	3162.41
Custom (B)			
n=300	359403	603	734.91
n=400	639203	803	1634.48
n=500	999003	1003	3106.48
Custom (C)			
n=300	359403	603	709.35
n=400	639203	803	1630.56
n=500	999003	1003	3095.20
Custom (D)			
n=300	359403	603	699.97
n=400	639203	803	1624.82
n=500	999003	1003	3050.54

Aside from running our algorithm on our custom benchmarks, we also performed experiments on the benchmarks from Spel et al. [30] as well as Heck et al. [18]. The results can be seen in Tables 3 and 4, respectively. The meaning of the columns is the same as in Table 1. For these benchmarks, our algorithm causes no noticeable differences in the running times of the Storm-pars modules. The model size is significantly reduced, however.

Table 3. Comparison of sizes and times to check monotonicity with and without our reduction technique for some benchmarks from the original monotonicity study.

Benchmark	Size (states)		Collapse time (s)	Mono. time (s)	
	before	after		before	after
brp					
MAX=2, N=16	494	192	<1	<1	<1
MAX=2, N=32	990	384	1.02	<1	<1
MAX=4, N=16	906	350	<1	<1	<1
MAX=4, N=32	1818	702	3.47	<1	<1
Crowds					
Size=5, Runs=3	268	182	<1	82.19	71.66
Size=5, Runs=6	6905	3782	79.10	TO	TO

Table 4. Comparison of sizes and times to realize parameter lifting with and without our reduction technique for the NRP benchmark from the original parameter lifting. We write MO when the memory ran out.

Benchmark	Size (states)		Collapse time (s)	Lifting time (s)	
	Before	after		before	after
NRP					
5,1	33	18	<1	33.26	33.58
6,1	45	24	<1	1028.81	1029.974
7,1	59	31	<1	TO	MO
8,1	75	39	<1	TO	TO
9,1	93	48	<1	TO	MO

6   Conclusions

We have established a reduction from the NWR problem to the monotonicity problem. On the way, we used arithmetic circuits to restate and reformulate some known results about the computation of value functions. This new approach allowed us to obtain a pMC representation of the partial derivatives of the value functions of a given pMC. This representation turned out to be quasi-polynomial. The question of whether such a partial-derivative pMC of polynomial size can always be constructed is left unanswered.

In a more practical direction, we took the equivalence-class detection algorithm from [15] and presented it as a pre-processing step for monotonicity analysis and parameter lifting. To evaluate the idea, we implemented the algorithm and realized some experiments on old and new benchmarks. Our results point to the algorithm being useful in reducing the size of (our custom) benchmarks. Unsurprisingly, when our algorithm succeeds in drastically reducing the size of a (custom) benchmark, monotonicity analysis and parameter lifting do benefit from a performance boost by working on a smaller model. Unfortunately, for benchmarks introduced in previous works, while we do see some reduction in size by using our algorithm, neither monotonicity analysis nor parameter lifting seem to run faster in the resulting model. Based on these, we believe it may be a good idea to implement the pre-processing step as an option within the Storm model checker.

Acknowledgements. We thank Michaël Cadilhac and Nikhil Balaji for pointers to the arithmetic-circuit literature. We are also grateful to Linus Heck for helping us with Storm.

References

1. Aflaki, S., Volk, M., Bonakdarpour, B., Katoen, J., Storjohann, A.: Automated fine tuning of probabilistic self-stabilizing algorithms. In: 36th IEEE Symposium on Reliable Distributed Systems, SRDS 2017, Hong Kong, September 26-29, 2017, pp. 94–103. IEEE Computer Society (2017)). https://doi.org/10.1109/SRDS.2017.22
2. Baier, C., Hensel, C., Hutschenreiter, L., Junges, S., Katoen, J., Klein, J.: Parametric Markov chains: PCTL complexity and fraction-free gaussian elimination. Inf. Comput. **272**, 104504 (2020). https://doi.org/10.1016/J.IC.2019.104504
3. Baier, C., Katoen, J.: Principles of Model Checking. MIT Press (2008)
4. Bareiss, E.H.: Computational solutions of matrix problems over an integral domain. IMA J. Appl. Math. **10**(1), 68–104 (1972). https://doi.org/10.1093/imamat/10.1.68
5. Bartocci, E., Grosu, R., Katsaros, P., Ramakrishnan, C.R., Smolka, S.A.: Model repair for probabilistic systems. In: Abdulla, P.A., Leino, K.R.M. (eds.) TACAS 2011. LNCS, vol. 6605, pp. 326–340. Springer, Heidelberg (2011). https://doi.org/10.1007/978-3-642-19835-9_30
6. Baur, W., Strassen, V.: The complexity of partial derivatives. Theor. Comput. Sci. **22**, 317–330 (1983)
7. Ben-Or, M., Cleve, R.: Computing algebraic formulas using a constant number of registers. SIAM J. Comput. **21**(1), 54–58 (1992)
8. Chatzieleftheriou, G., Katsaros, P.: Abstract model repair for probabilistic systems. Inf. Comput. **259**(1), 142–160 (2018). https://doi.org/10.1016/J.IC.2018.02.019
9. Chen, T., Hahn, E.M., Han, T., Kwiatkowska, M.Z., Qu, H., Zhang, L.: Model repair for Markov decision processes. In: Seventh International Symposium on Theoretical Aspects of Software Engineering, TASE 2013, 1-3 July 2013, Birmingham, UK, pp. 85–92. IEEE Computer Society (2013). https://doi.org/10.1109/TASE.2013.20
10. Chonev, V.: Reachability in augmented interval Markov chains. In: Filiot, E., Jungers, R., Potapov, I. (eds.) RP 2019. LNCS, vol. 11674, pp. 79–92. Springer, Cham (2019). https://doi.org/10.1007/978-3-030-30806-3_7
11. Daws, C.: Symbolic and parametric model checking of discrete-time Markov chains. In: Liu, Z., Araki, K. (eds.) ICTAC 2004. LNCS, vol. 3407, pp. 280–294. Springer, Heidelberg (2005). https://doi.org/10.1007/978-3-540-31862-0_21

12. Dehnert, C., et al.: PROPhESY: a PRObabilistic ParamEter SYnthesis tool. In: Kroening, D., Păsăreanu, C.S. (eds.) CAV 2015. LNCS, vol. 9206, pp. 214–231. Springer, Cham (2015). https://doi.org/10.1007/978-3-319-21690-4_13
13. Dehnert, C., Junges, S., Katoen, J.-P., Volk, M.: A storm is coming: a modern probabilistic model checker. In: Majumdar, R., Kunčak, V. (eds.) CAV 2017. LNCS, vol. 10427, pp. 592–600. Springer, Cham (2017). https://doi.org/10.1007/978-3-319-63390-9_31
14. Engelen, K., Perez, G., Rao, S.: Code for: Analyzing value functions of states in parametric Markov chains (2024). https://doi.org/10.5281/zenodo.11474465
15. Engelen, K., Pérez, G.A., Rao, S.: Graph-based reductions for parametric and weighted MDPS. In: André, É., Sun, J. (eds.) Automated Technology for Verification and Analysis. ATVA 2023. LNCS, vol. 14215. Springer, Cham (2023). https://doi.org/10.1007/978-3-031-45329-8_7
16. Gouberman, A., Siegle, M., Tati, B.: Markov chains with perturbed rates to absorption: theory and application to model repair. Perform. Eval. 130, 32–50 (2019). https://doi.org/10.1016/J.PEVA.2018.11.006
17. Hahn, E.M., Hermanns, H., Wachter, B., Zhang, L.: PARAM: a model checker for parametric Markov models. In: Touili, T., Cook, B., Jackson, P. (eds.) CAV 2010. LNCS, vol. 6174, pp. 660–664. Springer, Heidelberg (2010). https://doi.org/10.1007/978-3-642-14295-6_56
18. Heck, L., Spel, J., Junges, S., Moerman, J., Katoen, J.P.: Gradient-descent for randomized controllers under partial observability. In: Finkbeiner, B., Wies, T. (eds.) VMCAI 2022. LNCS, vol. 13182, pp. 127–150. Springer, Cham (2022). https://doi.org/10.1007/978-3-030-94583-1_7
19. Junges, S., Katoen, J., Pérez, G.A., Winkler, T.: The complexity of reachability in parametric Markov decision processes. J. Comput. Syst. Sci. 119, 183–210 (2021). https://doi.org/10.1016/J.JCSS.2021.02.006
20. Kwiatkowska, M., Norman, G., Parker, D.: PRISM 4.0: verification of probabilistic real-time systems. In: Gopalakrishnan, G., Qadeer, S. (eds.) CAV 2011. LNCS, vol. 6806, pp. 585–591. Springer, Heidelberg (2011). https://doi.org/10.1007/978-3-642-22110-1_47
21. Lanotte, R., Maggiolo-Schettini, A., Troina, A.: Parametric probabilistic transition systems for system design and analysis. Formal Aspects Comput. 19(1), 93–109 (2007). https://doi.org/10.1007/S00165-006-0015-2
22. Mahajan, M.: Algebraic complexity classes. arXiv preprint arXiv:1307.3863 (2013)
23. Morgenstern, J.: How to compute fast a function and all its derivatives: a variation on the theorem of Baur-Strassen. SIGACT News 16(4), 60–62 (1985)
24. Nisan, N.: Lower bounds for non-commutative computation (extended abstract). In: STOC, pp. 410–418. ACM (1991)
25. Pathak, S., Ábrahám, E., Jansen, N., Tacchella, A., Katoen, J.P.: A greedy approach for the efficient repair of stochastic models. In: Havelund, K., Holzmann, G., Joshi, R. (eds.) NFM 2015. LNCS, vol. 9058, pp. 295–309. Springer, Cham (2015). https://doi.org/10.1007/978-3-319-17524-9_21
26. Puterman, M.L.: Markov Decision Processes: Discrete Stochastic Dynamic Programming, Wiley Series in Probability and Statistics. Wiley (1994). https://doi.org/10.1002/9780470316887
27. Le Roux, S., Pérez, G.A.: The complexity of graph-based reductions for reachability in Markov decision processes. In: Baier, C., Dal Lago, U. (eds.) FoSSaCS 2018. LNCS, vol. 10803, pp. 367–383. Springer, Cham (2018). https://doi.org/10.1007/978-3-319-89366-2_20

28. Schaefer, M.: Complexity of some geometric and topological problems. In: Eppstein, D., Gansner, E.R. (eds.) GD 2009. LNCS, vol. 5849, pp. 334–344. Springer, Heidelberg (2010). https://doi.org/10.1007/978-3-642-11805-0_32

29. Spel, J., Junges, S., Katoen, J.P.: Are parametric Markov chains monotonic? In: Chen, Y.F., Cheng, C.H., Esparza, J. (eds.) ATVA 2019. LNCS, vol. 11781, pp. 479–496. Springer, Cham (2019). https://doi.org/10.1007/978-3-030-31784-3_28

30. Spel, J., Junges, S., Katoen, J.-P.: Finding provably optimal Markov chains. In: TACAS 2021. LNCS, vol. 12651, pp. 173–190. Springer, Cham (2021). https://doi.org/10.1007/978-3-030-72016-2_10

31. Strassen, V.: Vermeidung von divisionen. J. für die reine und angewandte Math. **264**, 184–202 (1973). http://eudml.org/doc/151394

32. Valiant, L.G., Skyum, S., Berkowitz, S., Rackoff, C.: Fast parallel computation of polynomials using few processors. SIAM J. Comput. **12**(4), 641–644 (1983). https://doi.org/10.1137/0212043

Expectation vs. Reality: Towards Verification of Psychological Games

Marta Kwiatkowska[1] , Gethin Norman[1,2] , David Parker[1] ,
and Gabriel Santos[1(✉)]

[1] Department of Computer Science, University of Oxford, Oxford, UK
{marta.kwiatkowska,david.parker,gabriel.santos}@cs.ox.ac.uk
[2] School of Computing Science, University of Glasgow, Glasgow, UK
gethin.norman@glasgow.ac.uk

Abstract. Game theory provides an effective way to model strategic interactions among rational agents. In the context of formal verification, these ideas can be used to produce guarantees on the correctness of multi-agent systems, with a diverse range of applications from computer security to autonomous driving. Psychological games (PGs) were developed as a way to model and analyse agents with belief-dependent motivations, opening up the possibility to model how human emotions can influence behaviour. In PGs, players' utilities depend not only on what *actually* happens (which strategies players choose to adopt), but also on what the players had *expected* to happen (their belief as to the strategies that would be played). Despite receiving much attention in fields such as economics and psychology, very little consideration has been given to their applicability to problems in computer science, nor to practical algorithms and tool support. In this paper, we start to bridge that gap, proposing methods to solve PGs and implementing them within PRISM-games, a formal verification tool for stochastic games. We discuss how to model these games, highlight specific challenges for their analysis and illustrate the usefulness of our approach on several case studies, including human behaviour in traffic scenarios.

1 Introduction

Probabilistic model checking is a well established technique for formally verifying computerised systems that operate in uncertain or stochastic environments. In order to verify systems comprising multiple autonomous agents and/or those involving human interactions, various models and concepts from game theory have been adapted for probabilistic model checking. Stochastic games, in particular, have shown to be a versatile and useful formalism to model and study situations involving collaboration or competition among agents, successfully applied to, for example human-in-the-loop autonomous systems [12], robot navigation in the presence of humans [18] and attack-defence scenarios [2].

While traditional game theory is often used to model human decision making, it is unable to model situations such as emotional response and social norms,

© The Author(s), under exclusive license to Springer Nature Switzerland AG 2025
N. Jansen et al. (Eds.): Principles of Verification: Cycling the Probabilistic Landscape,
LNCS 15261, pp. 166–191, 2025.
https://doi.org/10.1007/978-3-031-75775-4_8

where the utilities that players aim to maximise can depend on their *beliefs*. This inadequacy has been pointed out in [13], which proposed the seminal model of *psychological games* (PGs). In these games, a player's utility depends not only on what *actually* happens in the game (i.e., which strategies are chosen by the players), but also on what the players had *expected* to happen (i.e., their belief as to the future behaviour of the other players).

This class of models makes it possible to consider different aspects that contribute to human decision-making, such as regret, trust, fear, reciprocity and fairness, and how these may influence player behaviour. Crucially, psychological game predictions have been reproduced in human experiments, thus supporting the notion of belief-dependent motivations [3]. This has been of particular relevance in economics, when trying to predict and understand how people behave regarding non-material payoffs. Naturally, though, as autonomous computerised systems become more commonplace, ensuring that they interact safely and efficiently with humans will also require this kind of reasoning.

In this paper, we make the first steps towards a more practical approach to modelling and analysing PGs, and in applying them to other scenarios. We begin with one-shot (normal form) games, considering the *normal form psychological games* (NFPGs) proposed in [13]. We work with the commonly employed solution concept of *Nash equilibria* (NE), which establishes rational strategies for a game to be those where no player has an incentive to unilaterally deviate from their strategy. Using the psychological extension of NE from [13], we propose an approach to finding optimal equilibria for NFPGs using support enumeration and non-linear programming, and highlight why computing equilibria for such games is more computationally challenging.

We next investigate extensive (multi-stage) games with psychological payoffs, under the assumption that beliefs are *local* and *state*-based. We do so by considering an extension of concurrent stochastic games (CSGs) whose reward functions can depend on both the actions taken and beliefs about those actions, proposing a method to find equilibria for finite-horizon cumulative rewards using backward induction. We develop prototype tool support for psychological games, building on the PRISM-games model checker for stochastic games [23]. Using this, we model and analyse a variety of psychological games, notably studying human behaviour in several different traffic scenarios, and showcase the analysis and insights made possible by our approach.

Related Work. Psychological games were proposed in [13] and shown to admit standard game-theoretic techniques such as backward induction under some restrictions. However, they assume a fixed payoff structure and do not support belief inference or updating. *Dynamic psychological games* [4–6] address some of these limitations by allowing belief update. More specifically, they remove restrictions enforced in [13] that make beliefs endogenous to the games, and propose a *forward induction* algorithm with belief updates which allows for more sophisticated analysis. In [31], *fairness equilibria* are introduced as an extension of the framework established in [13], where the payoff of each player is defined as a combination of a material payoff and a psychological payoff whose value depends on how fairly they think they are being treated.

From an application perspective, conventional game theory has been employed to model a range of road user behaviours [7,10,11,19,29,34], including merging into traffic and speed selection, and has been able to explain how informal norms of behaviour can develop among road users and be sustained even if these informal norms violate the formal regulations of the traffic code. In [19], the authors point out that autonomous agents should have inferable behaviour and model a pedestrian crossing interaction as a repeated bimatrix Stackelberg game in order to measure and establish a bound to inferability loss. A more complex interaction involving vehicles, pedestrians and cyclists at a crossing was investigated as a non-zero sum game in [7], which showed that real life behaviour corresponded to an equilibrium strategy that went against Norwegian traffic laws. This example served as inspiration for [29], which used Bayesian games and examined possible differences in the strategies pedestrians and cyclists would be likely to adopt when considering autonomous and human drivers. Another example is [11], which also considers a game-theoretic stochastic model to analyse interactions among pedestrians, autonomous and regular vehicles and investigates strategies for conflict resolution in uncontrolled traffic environments based on Stackelberg equilibria. However, to the best of our knowledge, psychological games have not been explored in road user scenarios.

The verification community has developed various software tools with support for Nash equilibria, such as PRALINE [8], EAGLE [35] and EVE [17], but we are aware of no tool support for psychological equilibria computation, in either normal or extensive forms. For probabilistic systems, model checkers such as PRISM [22] and Storm [16] support a wide range of probabilistic models, with partially observable Markov decision processes providing an alternative way to reason about belief, over (unobservable) states rather than strategies. PRISM-games [23] provides verification and equilibria synthesis for various types of stochastic games including CSGs, but until now not for psychological variants.

2   Preliminaries

We first recall normal form games (NFGs), over which we define Nash equilibria (NE), and then proceed by defining the psychological equivalents: normal form psychological games (NFPGs) and psychological Nash equilibria (PE).

Classical Games. We will write $Dist(X)$ for the set of probability distributions over a finite set X.

Definition 1 (Normal form game). *A (finite, n-person) normal form game (NFG) is a tuple* $\mathsf{N} = (N, A, u)$ *where:*

- $N = \{1, \ldots, n\}$ *is a finite set of* players;
- $A = A_1 \times \cdots \times A_n$, A_i *is a finite set of* actions *available to player* $i \in N$ *and* $A_i \cap A_j = \varnothing$ *for* $i \neq j \in N$;

– $u = (u_1, \ldots, u_n)$ *and* $u_i \colon A \to \mathbb{Q}$ *is a* utility function *for player* $i \in N$.

In an NFG, each player $i \in N$ simultaneously chooses an action $a_i \in A_i$ from their action set and each player j then receives utility $u_j(a_1, \ldots, a_n)$. Two-player NFGs are often called *bimatrix games* since they can be represented by two matrices $\mathsf{Z}_1, \mathsf{Z}_2 \in \mathbb{Q}^{l \times m}$ where $A_1 = \{a_1, \ldots, a_l\}$, $A_2 = \{b_1, \ldots, b_m\}$, $\mathsf{Z}_1(i, j) = u_1(a_i, b_j)$ and $\mathsf{Z}_2(i, j) = u_2(a_i, b_j)$. Below, we assume a fixed NFG $\mathsf{N} = (N, A, u)$.

Definition 2 (Strategy and strategy profile). *A* (mixed) strategy *for player* i *of NFG* N *is a distribution* $\sigma_i \in Dist(A_i)$, *specifying the probability of choosing each action in its action set. A* strategy profile *of* N *(or just* profile*) is a tuple* $\sigma = (\sigma_1, \ldots, \sigma_n)$ *of strategies for all players.*

The *expected utility* of player i under strategy profile $\sigma = (\sigma_1, \ldots, \sigma_n)$ is:

$$u_i(\sigma) \overset{\text{def}}{=} \sum_{(a_1, \ldots, a_n) \in A} u_i(a_1, \ldots, a_n) \cdot \left(\prod_{j=1}^{n} \sigma_j(a_j) \right).$$

We let $\Sigma_{\mathsf{N}}^i = Dist(A_i)$ denote the set of all player i strategies, $\Sigma_{\mathsf{N}} = \prod_{i \in N} \Sigma_{\mathsf{N}}^i$ the set of all strategy profiles and $\Sigma_{\mathsf{N}}^{-i} = \prod_{j \neq i} \Sigma_{\mathsf{N}}^j$ the set of strategy tuples for all players except i. For strategy profile $\sigma = (\sigma_1, \ldots, \sigma_n)$ and player i strategy σ_i', we define the strategy tuple $\sigma_{-i} = (\sigma_1, \ldots, \sigma_{i-1}, \sigma_{i+1}, \ldots, \sigma_n)$ and strategy profile $\sigma_{-i}[\sigma_i'] = (\sigma_1, \ldots, \sigma_{i-1}, \sigma_i', \sigma_{i+1}, \ldots, \sigma_n)$.

Definition 3 (Support). *The* support $Q_i \subseteq A_i$ *of a strategy* σ_i *for player* i *is the set of actions it chooses with positive probability, i.e.,* $Q_i = \{a_i \in A_i \mid \sigma_i(a_i) > 0\}$. *The support of a profile* σ *is the product of the supports of its individual strategies* σ_i.

We now define the notion of *Nash equilibria* (NE), which are strategy profiles for which there is no incentive for any player to unilaterally change their strategy.

Definition 4 (Best response). *For strategy tuple* $\sigma_{-i} \in \Sigma_{\mathsf{N}}^{-i}$, *a best response to* σ_{-i} *for player* i *is a strategy* $\sigma_i^\star \in \Sigma_{\mathsf{N}}^i$ *such that* $u_i(\sigma_{-i}[\sigma_i^\star]) \geqslant u_i(\sigma_{-i}[\sigma_i])$ *for all* $\sigma_i \in \Sigma_{\mathsf{N}}^i$.

Definition 5 (Nash equilibrium). *A strategy profile* $\sigma^\star$ *is a* Nash equilibrium *(NE) and* $\langle u_i(\sigma^\star) \rangle_{i \in N}$ NE values *if* $\sigma_i^\star$ *is a best response to* $\sigma_{-i}^\star$ *for all* $i \in N$.

Since multiple NE can exist for an NFG, we are also interested in finding the *optimal* equilibrium for a given criterion. In this paper, we focus on *social welfare* NE, which are those that maximise the sum of the players' utilities.

Definition 6 (Social welfare NE). *An NE* $\sigma^\star$ *is a* social welfare optimal NE *(SWNE) and* $\langle u_i(\sigma^\star) \rangle_{i \in N}$ *corresponding* SWNE values *if* $u_1(\sigma^\star) + \cdots + u_n(\sigma^\star) \geqslant u_1(\sigma) + \cdots + u_n(\sigma)$ *for all NE* σ.

We are now ready to discuss *normal form psychological games* (NFPGs) [13], a generalisation of NFGs in which a player's utility can depend not only on the game's outcome (actions taken), but also on the player's *belief* as to the outcome. The notions of actions, strategies and strategy profiles remain the same as for NFGs and, for NFPG N_P, we use the same notation $\Sigma^i_{N_P}$, Σ_{N_P} and $\Sigma^{-i}_{N_P}$.

Beliefs and Coherence. The *first-order beliefs* for player i represent their belief as to the (mixed) strategies that will be taken by the other players. So, the set of all first-order beliefs for player i is defined as $B^1_i = Dist(\Sigma^{-i}_{N_P})$. *Higher-order beliefs* are beliefs about the beliefs of other players. We will denote the kth order beliefs for player i by B^k_i and write $B^k_{-i} = \prod_{j \neq i} B^k_j$ for the set of kth order beliefs for all players other than i. Higher-order beliefs are then defined inductively by:

$$B^{k+1}_i \stackrel{\text{def}}{=} Dist(\Sigma^{-i}_{N_P} \times B^1_{-i} \times \cdots \times B^k_{-i}).$$

Notice that information about beliefs appears multiple times. This allows for correlation between different orders of belief, e.g., second-order beliefs B^2_i assign probabilities to combinations of the strategies $\Sigma^{-i}_{N_P}$ and first-order beliefs B^1_{-i} of the other players. As in [13], we will assume that beliefs are *coherent*, meaning that this information is consistent. For example, the marginal of player i's second-order beliefs with respect to $\Sigma^{-i}_{N_P}$ should coincide with i's first-order beliefs. The same condition is applied inductively to higher-order belief sets.

Furthermore, since players are rational and know that other players are also rational, coherency is assumed to be common knowledge and we will require beliefs to be *collectively coherent*. In other words, each player i only ever believes that another player j's beliefs are coherent, that player j believes other players to be coherent, and so on. We will write B_i for the set for all collectively coherent higher-order beliefs for player i, and define $B = \prod_{i \in N} B_i$ to be the set of collectively coherent *belief profiles*, i.e., the set of beliefs for all players.

Psychological Games. We can now formally define the psychological variant of normal form games, where the key difference is that the utility for player i now also depends on their (collectively coherent) belief $b_i \in B_i$ about the other players, as well as the actions they actually take.

Definition 7 (Normal form psychological game). *A (finite, n-person) normal form psychological game (NFPG) is a tuple* $N_P = (N, A, u)$ *where:*

- $N = \{1, \ldots, n\}$ *is a finite set of players;*
- A_i *is a finite set of* actions *available to player* $i \in N$ *and* $A_i \cap A_j = \varnothing$ *for* $i \neq j \in N$;
- $u = (u_1, \ldots, u_n)$ *and* $u_i \colon (B_i \times A) \to \mathbb{Q}$ *is a utility function for player* $i \in N$.

As for NFGs, we can define the *expected* utility of player i for a given strategy profile σ. However, here we must now also include beliefs. More precisely, for belief $b_i \in B_i$ for player i and strategy profile σ, we write $u_i(b_i, \sigma)$ for the expected utility of player i under b_i and σ.

We can now define the notion of *psychological Nash equilibrium* (PE). While an NE for an NFG N is a strategy profile $\sigma \in \Sigma_N$, a PE for an NFPG N_P is a pair $(b, \sigma) \in B \times \Sigma_{N_P}$ comprising a belief profile b and a strategy profile σ. Crucially, as explained in [13], it is assumed that, in equilibrium, the beliefs b of the players match a commonly held view of reality. In other words, each player i believes, with probability 1, that each other player j follows strategy σ_j, that player j's beliefs match σ_{-j}, and so on. For strategy profile σ, this matching belief profile for all n players is denoted $\beta(\sigma)$.

Definition 8 (Psychological Nash equilibrium). *A pair $(b^\star, \sigma^\star)$ of belief profile $b^\star = (b_1^\star, \ldots, b_n^\star) \in B$ and strategy profile $\sigma^\star = (\sigma_1^\star, \ldots, \sigma_n^\star) \in \Sigma_{N_P}$ for NFPG N_P is a* psychological Nash equilibrium *(PE) if:*

$$b^\star = \beta(\sigma^\star) \tag{1}$$

$$u_i(b_i^\star, \sigma^\star) \geqslant u_i(b_i^\star, \sigma_{-i}[\sigma_i]) \text{ for all } \sigma_i \in \Sigma_{N_P}^i \text{ and } i \in N. \tag{2}$$

The first condition (1) implies that, as discussed above, the players' beliefs match a commonly held view of reality. The second condition (2) matches the corresponding requirements for NEs of NFGs (see Definitions 4 and 5). As for NEs, we will generally aim to find a PE that is *social welfare optimal*, where the sum of the players' utilities is maximised.

Defining Utility Functions. Since we focus on psychological Nash equilibria, condition (1) above, combined with the assumption of collective coherence for higher-order beliefs, allows us to adopt a simpler formulation of an NFPG's utility functions in practice. Although player i's utility function u_i depends on its (collectively coherent, higher-order) beliefs about the other players, since we know that there is a common belief in equilibrium we can simply define u_i in terms of the strategies alone, that is, as a function of the probabilities that each player j takes each of its actions. Additionally, for simplicity, we allow each player's utility to be defined in terms of *all* the player's strategies, including the players' *own* choices of actions.

Example 1. To illustrate NFPGs, let us consider the *confidence* game from [13], which comprises three players. Player 1 submits a proposal, which is randomly assigned with equal probability to player 2 or 3. They can then chose to either *accept* or *reject* this proposal. We abbreviate these actions to a_i and r_i, respectively, for player $i = 2, 3$. Player 1 has no actions to take.

The game has belief-dependent utilities, involving both first-order and second-order beliefs. We will write p_a for the *probability* that a player i chooses action a in their (mixed) strategy, $\overline{p_a}$ for the expectation of another player $j \neq i$ as to the probability p_a, i.e., the first-order belief for player j, and $\overline{\overline{p_a}}$ for the expected value of $\overline{p_a}$ from the perspective of another player, i.e., the second-order belief.

Player 1 wants the proposal to be accepted, but their satisfaction about acceptance is influenced by their belief about how likely this is to happen: being more *optimistic* means they are happier about an acceptance, but also much unhappier in the case of a rejection. Player 2 is influenced by how *confident* player 1 is about acceptance, and is more likely to accept the proposal if they believe player 1 is more confident. Player 3 always prefers rejection.

These notions are encoded in the players' utility functions as follows, where we follow [13] but show extra details of the derivation. Let us denote the probability that player 1's proposal is accepted as p_{acc}. We have $p_{acc} = (1/2) \cdot (p_{a_2} + p_{a_3})$ since players 2 and 3 are assigned the proposal with equal probability. Similarly, $\overline{p_{acc}} = (1/2) \cdot (\overline{p_{a_2}} + \overline{p_{a_3}})$ is player 1's belief as to the likelihood of acceptance, and $\overline{\overline{p_{acc}}} = (1/2) \cdot (\overline{\overline{p_{a_2}}} + \overline{\overline{p_{a_3}}})$ equals player 2's belief about $\overline{p_{acc}}$.

Player 1 has a utility of 1 in case of acceptance, plus a further utility based on their degree of optimism, i.e., in terms of belief of acceptance, of $2 \cdot \overline{p_{acc}}$. Conversely, if rejected, their utility is $-8 \cdot \overline{p_{acc}}$. Player 2 prefers to accept when $\overline{\overline{p_{acc}}} > \frac{1}{6}$ so, when assigned the proposal, receives a utility of $6 \cdot \overline{\overline{p_{acc}}}$ for accepting and 1 for rejecting. Player 3 has a utility of 1 if they are assigned the proposal and reject it, otherwise 0.

Recall from above that, in equilibrium, players' beliefs must match a shared view of reality, so $p_{a_i} = \overline{p_{a_i}} = \overline{\overline{p_{a_i}}}$ for $i = 2, 3$. We therefore express the utility functions for players as expressions in terms of just p_{a_i}. Since player 1 does not choose an action and players 2 and 3 each can choose between two actions, we can write player i's utility function as a 2×2 matrix Z_i. For each pair of actions of players 2 and 3, the value combines the utility arising when each of player 2 and 3 are assigned the proposal, weighted by probability $1/2$:

$$Z_1 = \begin{array}{c} \\ a_2 \\ r_2 \end{array} \begin{array}{cc} a_3 & r_3 \\ \left(\begin{array}{cc} 1 + p_{a_2} + p_{a_3} & 1/2 - (3/2) \cdot (p_{a_2} + p_{a_3}) \\ 1/2 - (3/2) \cdot (p_{a_2} + p_{a_3}) & -4 \cdot (p_{a_2} + p_{a_3}) \end{array} \right) \end{array}$$

$$Z_2 = \begin{array}{c} \\ a_2 \\ r_2 \end{array} \begin{array}{cc} a_3 & r_3 \\ \left(\begin{array}{cc} (3/2) \cdot (p_{a_2} + p_{a_3}) & (3/2) \cdot (p_{a_2} + p_{a_3}) \\ 1/2 & 1/2 \end{array} \right) \end{array} \qquad Z_3 = \begin{array}{c} \\ a_2 \\ r_2 \end{array} \begin{array}{cc} a_3 & r_3 \\ \left(\begin{array}{cc} 0 & 1/2 \\ 0 & 1/2 \end{array} \right) \end{array}$$

When determining PE for the confidence game, we can ignore player 1 since it has no actions. In an equilibrium, suboptimal actions cannot be played with positive probability. We can therefore compute a solution by encoding the problem with the following set of constraints:

$$\left((3/2) \cdot ((p_{a_2} + p_{a_3}) \cdot p_{a_3} + (p_{a_2} + p_{a_3}) \cdot p_{r_3}) \geqslant (1/2) \cdot (p_{a_3} + p_{r_3}) \right) \vee (p_{a_2} = 0) \quad (3)$$

$$\left((1/2) \cdot (p_{a_3} + p_{r_3}) \geqslant (3/2) \cdot ((p_{a_2} + p_{a_3}) \cdot p_{a_3} + (p_{a_2} + p_{a_3}) \cdot p_{r_3}) \right) \vee (p_{r_2} = 0) \quad (4)$$

$$\left(0 \geqslant (1/2) \cdot (p_{a_2} + p_{r_2}) \right) \vee (p_{a_3} = 0) \quad (5)$$

$$\left((1/2) \cdot (p_{a_2} + p_{r_2}) \geqslant 0 \right) \vee (p_{r_3} = 0) \quad (6)$$

For example, (3) must hold because either the action a_2 is optimal for player 2, i.e., the utility obtained by player 2 when action a_2 is chosen is greater than or equal to that when action r_2 is chosen under the optimal strategy of player 3, or the action a_2 is chosen with probability 0. Any assignment that satisfies all four constraints is an equilibrium. Given that $p_{a_2} + p_{r_2} = 1$, the first clause of (5) cannot be satisfied and thus we must have $p_{a_3} = 0$. This is consistent with the fact that a_3 is dominated for player 3, i.e., action r_3 always yields higher utility than a_3. If $p_{a_3} = 0$, we have $p_{r_3} = 1$, which means that the second clause of (6) has to be false. The first clause of (6) is trivially satisfied. Constraints (3) and (4) can then be reduced to:

$$(3{\cdot}p_{a_2} \geqslant 1) \vee (p_{a_2} = 0) \tag{7}$$

$$(1 \geqslant 3{\cdot}p_{a_2}) \vee (p_{r_2} = 0) \tag{8}$$

We then obtain satisfying assignments by setting $p_{a_2} = 1/3$ and $p_{r_2} = 2/3$, $p_{a_2} = 1$ and $p_{r_2} = 0$ or $p_{a_2} = 0$ and $p_{r_2} = 1$ with utility vectors $u = (u_1, u_2, u_3)$ equal to $(-8/9, 1/2, 1/2)$, $(-1, 3/2, 1/2)$ and $(0, 1/2, 1/2)$, respectively. The proposal has the highest chance of being accepted in the second equilibrium, when player 1 is most confident. However, as player 3 is certain to reject, that is also the worst equilibrium for player 1, who is bound to be disappointed. The last two equilibria are social welfare optimal with a combined utility of 1.

3   Equilibria Computation for Psychological Games

We now propose methods for analysing NFPGs in order to determine their PEs and corresponding values. The approach builds upon techniques for the non-psychological setting, i.e., finding NEs for NFGs. For the case of two-player NFGs (bimatrix games), we can use well known approaches such as the Lemke-Howson [28] algorithm or mixed-integer programming based on regret minimisation [32]. For NFGs with more than two players, algorithms include the Govindan-Wilson [14] or Simplicial Subdivision [27], as well as search methods based on *support enumeration* [30].

We take the support enumeration approach for NFPGs, by adapting the method of [24], which has been used to find social welfare optimal NEs for NFGs in a similar fashion. This approach exhaustively inspects sub-regions of the strategy profile space, based on the idea that searching for NEs within a specific *support* (see Definition 3) of a strategy profile is computationally easier. It relies on encoding the computation of a (social welfare optimal) NE as a *non-linear programming* (NLP) problem.

The NLP encoding leverages conditions for a strategy profile to characterise an NE, presented as a lemma in [24], and based on the notion of *feasibility program* introduced in [9,30]. The lemma states that a strategy profile of an NFG is an NE if and only if any player switching to a single action in the support of the profile yields the same utility for the player, and switching to an action outside the support can only decrease its utility. We adapt that lemma here to characterise a PE of an NFPG. This result follows directly from Definition 8 and, in particular, the fact that in equilibrium the belief profile needs to correspond to the strategies being played.

Lemma 1. *A pair (b,σ) comprising a belief profile b and a strategy profile $\sigma = (\sigma_1, \ldots, \sigma_n)$ of $\mathsf{N_P} = (N, A, u)$ is a PE if and only if (1) and the following conditions are satisfied:*

$$\forall i \in N. \forall a_i \in A_i. \ \ \sigma_i(a_i) > 0 \rightarrow u_i(b, \sigma_{-i}[\eta_{a_i}]) = u_i(b, \sigma) \tag{9}$$

$$\forall i \in N. \forall a_i \in A_i. \ \ \sigma_i(a_i) = 0 \rightarrow u_i(b, \sigma_{-i}[\eta_{a_i}]) \leqslant u_i(b, \sigma) \tag{10}$$

where η_{a_i} is the pure strategy that picks action a_i with probability 1.

We now extend the NLP encoding of the computation of an NE presented in [24] to the case of an NFPG $\mathsf{N_P} = (N, A, u)$. Since this encoding uses a support enumeration approach, we need to determine the social welfare optimal PE amongst strategy profiles from a fixed support $Q = Q_1 \times \cdots \times Q_n \subseteq A$, i.e., for a given set of actions of each player. We first choose a *pivot* action $q_i^p \in Q_i$, which can be any action in Q_i, for each player i. The problem is then to maximise:

$$\sum_{i \in N} \left(\sum_{q \in Q} u_i(b^\star, q) \cdot \left(\prod_{j \in N} p_{q_j} \right) \right) \tag{11}$$

subject to:

$$\sum_{c \in Q_{-i}(q_i^p)} u_i(b^\star, c) \cdot \left(\prod_{j \in N_{-i}} p_{c_j} \right) - \sum_{c \in Q_{-i}(q_i)} u_i(b^\star, c) \cdot \left(\prod_{j \in N_{-i}} p_{c_j} \right) = 0 \tag{12}$$

$$\sum_{c \in Q_{-i}(q_i^p)} u_i(b^\star, c) \cdot \left(\prod_{j \in N_{-i}} p_{c_j} \right) - \sum_{c \in Q_{-i}(a_i)} u_i(b^\star, c) \cdot \left(\prod_{j \in N_{-i}} p_{c_j} \right) \geqslant 0 \tag{13}$$

$$\sum_{q_i \in Q_i} p_{q_i} = 1 \quad \text{and} \quad p_{q_i} > 0 \tag{14}$$

for all $i \in N$, $q_i \in Q_i \backslash \{q_i^p\}$ and $a_i \in A_i \backslash Q_i$ where $Q_{-i}(c_i) = Q_1 \times \cdots \times Q_{i-1} \times \{c_i\} \times Q_{i+1} \times \cdots \times Q_n$, $N_{-i} = N \backslash \{i\}$ and $b^\star \in B$.

The variables p_{q_i} represent the probabilities of players choosing different actions, i.e. the probability player i selects action $q_i \in Q_i$. If a satisfying assignment is found, we have a social welfare optimal PE given by the belief and strategy profiles pair $(b^\star, \sigma^\star)$, where, for $a_i \in A_i$, $\sigma_i^\star(a_i) = p_{q_i}$ if $a_i = q_i$ and $q_i \in Q_i$, and 0 otherwise. Following condition (1) of Definition 8, we have $b^\star = \beta(\sigma^\star)$.

Constraints (12) and (13) enforce that the solution corresponds to a PE, encoding constraints (9) and (10), respectively, of Lemma 1 when restricting to pivot actions. This restriction is sufficient as (9) requires all actions in the support to yield the same utility. The objective function in (11) corresponds to the sum of the individual utilities of the players when they play according to the profile corresponding to the solution. By maximising it, we require the solution to be social welfare optimal. As it is possible to have more than one equilibrium for which the sum of utilities is optimal, we specify additional *lower priority* objectives to maximise individual payoffs following an increasing sequence of indices i, and thus output a payoff vector with a consistent ordering.

Example 2. Consider the two-player NFPG whose utility functions are given by the matrices in Fig. 1 (left). Player 1 has no choice (we write $A_1 = \{\bot\}$) and player 2 chooses an action from $A_2 = \{a_2, b_2\}$. Player 2 is indifferent (their utility is always 0), whereas player 1's utility depends on (their expectation about) the probability p_{a_2} of a_2 being played. Therefore, player 1's expected utility (which is also the total expected utility) is a function depending only on p_{a_2}:

$$u_1(p_{a_2}) = -\frac{400}{81}{\cdot}p_{a_2}{}^2 + \frac{40}{9}{\cdot}p_{a_2}$$

Since the only player with a choice is indifferent between their own actions, the constraints in (12) and (13) are trivially satisfied for all supports as long as (14) is also satisfied, and thus any strategy profile (with an accompanying belief profile) is an equilibrium. Figure 1 (right) plots the total expected utility. This shows that, in order to achieve the maximum value of 1, player 2 has to randomise, picking actions a_2 and b_2 with probabilities 0.45 and 0.55, respectively.

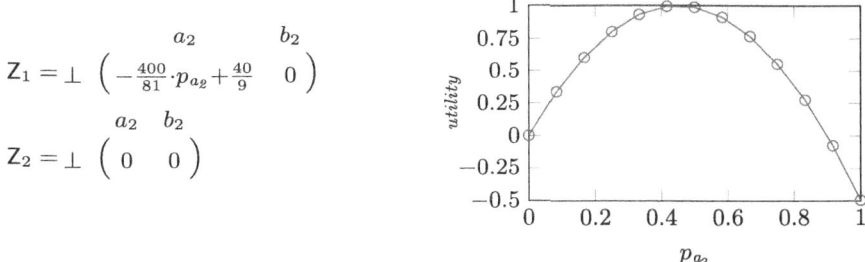

$$Z_1 = \bot \begin{array}{cc} a_2 & b_2 \\ \left(-\frac{400}{81}{\cdot}p_{a_2}+\frac{40}{9}\right. & \left.0\right) \end{array}$$

$$Z_2 = \bot \begin{array}{cc} a_2 & b_2 \\ \left(0\right. & \left.0\right) \end{array}$$

Fig. 1. Player utilities (left) and total expected utility (right) for Example 2.

The above example illustrates a contrast with (non-psychological) NFGs, and gives an indication of why computing optimal equilibria for NFPGs is more computationally challenging. For NFGs, it suffices to consider pure strategies only when finding optimal equilibria with a single active player. This can be exploited [25], avoiding the need to solve an optimisation problem for a given support. For NFPGs, the non-linearity in the function for expected utility means that pure strategies no longer suffice for an indifferent player.

4   Psychological Concurrent Stochastic Games

We next consider concurrent stochastic games (CSGs) [33], which are multi-stage games played over graphs where, at each state, players make simultaneous choices that cause the game's state to be probabilistically updated. We present a *psychological* variant of CSGs, in which, similarly to NFPGs, a player's utility (reward accumulated over a finite horizon) can depend on its *belief* as to the strategies to be played as well as the actions that players select. We outline a procedure to compute equilibria for a class of such games, which restricts the nature of the players' beliefs. As in previous work for CSGs [23], we consider *subgame perfect* equilibria, which are equilibria at every state of a CSG.

Definition 9 (Concurrent stochastic game). *A* concurrent stochastic multi-player game *(CSG) is a tuple* $\mathsf{C} = (N, S, \bar{s}, A, \Delta, \delta)$ *where:*

- $N = \{1, \ldots, n\}$ *is a finite set of players;*
- S *is a finite set of states and* $\bar{s} \in S$ *is the initial state;*
- $A = (A_1 \cup \{\perp\}) \times \cdots \times (A_n \cup \{\perp\})$ *where* A_i *is a finite set of actions available to player* $i \in N$, $A_i \cap A_j = \varnothing$ *for* $i \neq j \in N$ *and* $\perp$ *is an idle action disjoint from the set* $\cup_{i=1}^n A_i$;
- $\Delta \colon S \to 2^{\cup_{i=1}^n A_i}$ *is an action assignment function;*
- $\delta \colon (S \times A) \to Dist(S)$ *is a probabilistic transition function.*

We assume without loss of generality that, for any $i, j \in N$, $i \neq j$, $A_i \cap A_j = \varnothing$. A given CSG C starts in the initial state $\bar{s}$ and, when in state s, each player $i \in N$ selects an action from its available actions $A_i(s) \stackrel{\text{def}}{=} \Delta(s) \cap A_i$ if this set is non-empty, and from $\{\perp\}$ otherwise. Assuming each player i selects action a_i, the next state of the game is determined according to the distribution $\delta(s, (a_1, \ldots, a_n))$. A *path* of C is a sequence $\pi = s_0 \xrightarrow{\alpha_0} s_1 \xrightarrow{\alpha_1} \cdots$ where $s_k \in S$, $\alpha_k = (a_1^k, \ldots, a_n^k) \in A$, $a_i^k \in A_i(s_k)$ for $i \in N$ and $\delta(s_k, \alpha_k)(s_{k+1}) > 0$ for all $k \geqslant 0$. We denote by $\pi(i)$ the $(i{+}1)$th state of π, $\pi[i]$ the action associated with the $(i{+}1)$th transition and, if π is finite, $last(\pi)$ the final state. Let *FPaths* and *IPaths* denote the sets of finite and infinite paths that start in the initial state, respectively.

A *strategy* for a player in C resolves the player's choices in each state. These choices can depend on the execution history and can be randomised, i.e., are of the form $\sigma_i : FPaths \to Dist(A_i)$ such that if $\sigma_i(\pi)(a_i) > 0$, then $a_i \in A_i(last(\pi))$. As for NFGs, a *strategy profile* for C is a tuple $\sigma = (\sigma_1, \ldots, \sigma_n)$ of strategies for all players. For a given strategy profile σ, a probability measure $Prob_{\mathsf{C}}^{\sigma}$ over the infinite paths of C can then be defined in the standard way [20].

Psychological CSGs. In order to introduce a psychological variant of CSGs, we incorporate a notion of beliefs, and then use them to define rewards. Let B_i^A denote, as defined in Sect. 2, the set of (collectively coherent, higher-order) beliefs for player i, where first-order beliefs are over the set of actions A. A *belief* b_i for player is of the form $b_i : S \to B_i^A$. It is *state-based*, in that it provides a separate belief for each state s of the CSG, and *local*, in that these beliefs give the player's expectations regarding the actions to be played in s, not about a more global notion of the player's strategy. A *belief profile* is a tuple $b = (b_1, \ldots, b_n)$.

A *reward structure* for player i takes the form $r_i = (r_i^A, r_i^S)$, where $r_i^A \colon (S \times B_i^A \times A) \to \mathbb{Q}$ is an action reward function (which maps a state, belief and action tuple to a rational value that is accumulated when the action tuple is selected in the state, assuming a given local belief for player i in that state) and $r_i^S \colon S \to \mathbb{Q}$ is a state reward function (which maps each state to a rational value that is accumulated when the state is passed through).

The *utility* (or *objective*) for a player i in CSG C can be defined by a random variable $X_i : IPaths \rightarrow \mathbb{R}$ mapping infinite paths to reals. We denote by $\mathbb{E}_C^\sigma(X_i)$ the expected value of player i's utility under σ, with respect to the probability measure $Prob_C^\sigma$. Given utilities $X_1, \ldots, X_n$ for all the players of C, we can then define (social welfare) psychological Nash equilibria, as for NFPGs. We will restrict our attention to utilities that correspond to *finite-horizon* objectives, which may be used to investigate, for instance, the expected reward accumulated over k steps. Such utilities can be expressed by a finite bound $k \in \mathbb{N}$ and reward structure $r_i = (r_i^A, r_i^S)$, with corresponding random variable:

$$X_i(\pi) = \sum_{j=0}^{k-1} \left(r_i^A(\pi(j), b_i(\pi(j)), \pi[j]) + r_i^S(\pi(j)) \right).$$

Psychological Equilibria Computation. In both [13] and [5], the authors point out the limitations of applying backward induction to computing equilibria for extensive (multi-stage) psychological games and show why that approach cannot be applied to the general case. While a full discussion is outside the scope of this paper, it suffices to imagine a game in which a player's utility in a given state depends on the beliefs they have about actions performed in the *preceding* state. A backward induction algorithm *can*, however, be applied under the assumption that psychological utilities at any given state have to be over *local* strategies, that is, concerning the actions taken at that same state and coherent with an equilibrium solution for the NFPG in that state. We note that a more general approach has been proposed in [5], which we leave as future work.

Using the above restriction, we devise a backward induction algorithm that builds, at each iteration, an NFPG for every state s in C according to the reward structure in s and the values computed for its successors in the previous iteration (initially 0 for all states). We then compute equilibria values and strategies by solving the corresponding NLPs following the definitions in Sect. 3. We compute equilibria which are *locally* social welfare optimal. Other criteria, e.g., *social cost* [25] or *social fair* [26] equilibria, which minimise the overall sum or the difference between the highest and lowest utilities, respectively, could also be applied. In the latter case, however, additional constraints would have to be added to the NLP in Sect. 3, which would significantly increase the complexity of the problem due to the need to numerically encode logical implications. Finding all equilibria for a CSG is generally intractable, as the number may be exponential even with respect to the size of the normal form game at each state.

5   Case Studies and Experimental Results

We have built a prototype implementation to model and solve psychological games, and used it to investigate the applicability and performance of our approach on a selection of normal form and multi-stage psychological games. We first consider two-player instances of the *ultimatum* and *reciprocity* games of [6], which exemplify how psychological games can also be used in the computation of *fairness equilibria*, as well as how psychological utilities can influence the strategies of the players. We then present two- and multi-player normal form games modelling *traffic* interactions between pedestrians, cyclists and vehicles, one of which is then extended to a psychological CSG, used to investigate how information on past decisions can influence players' strategies.

Implementation. We build on top of the PRISM-games model checker [23], extending its existing modelling language for CSGs (in which normal form games can also be encoded as simple instances). The key difference is that in PG models the specification of reward structures needs to incorporate a player's beliefs about the other players' strategies. Since we currently only allow for beliefs in CSGs over local strategies (see Sect. 4), rewards for a state can only make reference to (the probability of) actions played in that state. Figure 2 shows a reward structure definition in our extension of the PRISM-game modelling language for the ultimatum game example (see Sect. 5.1, below). For simplicity, in this syntax, we just use the name of the action to denote the probability of choosing it, e.g., `reject` denotes what we refer to elsewhere as p_{reject}.

As for regular CSGs, our extension of PRISM-games constructs and stores PG models using the tool's Java-based 'explicit' engine. In contrast to CSGs, reward structures for PG models are represented by symbolic expressions over variables representing action choice probabilities and cannot be evaluated prior to model checking. We use Gurobi [15] to solve the NLPs described in Sect. 3 for finding equilibria values of NFPGs at each state.

```
1   // Constants
2   const double theta1; // Player 1's reciprocity sensitivity
3   const double theta2; // Player 2's reciprocity sensitivity
4   // Rewards for player 1
5   rewards "r1"
6           [fair,reject] true : 5+theta1*(-4.5)*(2+0.5*reject);
7           [fair,accept] true : 5+theta1*(4.5)*(2+0.5*reject);
8           [greedy,reject] true : 0+theta1*(-4.5)*(-2-0.5*reject);
9           [greedy,accept] true : 9+theta1*(4.5)*(-2-0.5*reject);
10  endrewards
11  // Rewards for player 2
12  rewards "r2"
13          [fair,reject] true : 5+theta2*(-4.5)*(2+0.5*reject);
14          [fair,accept] true : 5+theta2*(4.5)*(2+0.5*reject);
15          [greedy,reject] true : 0+theta2*(-4.5)*(-2-0.5*reject);
16          [greedy,accept] true : 1+theta2*(4.5)*(-2-0.5*reject);
17  endrewards
```

Fig. 2. Reward structures for the ultimatum game, modelled in PRISM-games.

Efficiency and Scalability. Computing equilibria values and strategies can be a complex task, even for the simpler case of finding an arbitrary (non-optimal) equilibrium of a two-player normal form game. Finding optimal equilibria of multi-player games is considerably harder, given the increased number of supports and the non-linearity of the constraints. The addition of psychological utilities complicates the computation further, as there are no natural restrictions on how these utilities may vary given the players' strategies and beliefs. At the state level, when looking for an optimal equilibrium, we are required to solve an NLP for each support. Given the total number of supports is exponential in the number of actions, i.e., equals $\prod_{i=1}^{n}(2^{|A_i|} - 1)$, computing optimal values via enumeration can only be efficient for small games.

5.1   Reciprocity and Ultimatum Games

We considered instances of the *reciprocity* and *ultimatum* games from [6], which are shown in Fig. 3. In each case, player 1 chooses between making a *fair* (f) or *greedy* (g) proposal, and player 2 decides to *reject* (r) or *accept* (a) it. The rectangular boxes show the corresponding utilities of players 1 and 2, with player 1's utility being above that of player 2. We present the games, as in [6], in extensive form, with the players' decisions taken sequentially, but will treat them as simultaneous moves in a single NFPG. Otherwise, beliefs would no longer be local since player 2's utility would depend on an earlier decision by player 1.

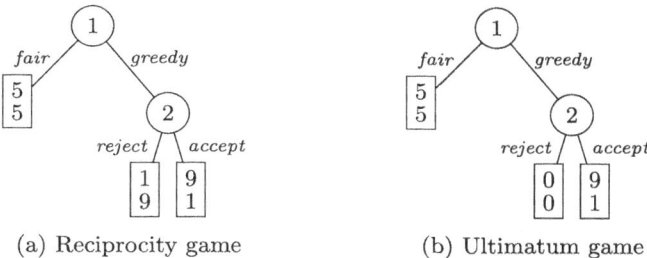

(a) Reciprocity game   (b) Ultimatum game

Fig. 3. Reciprocity and ultimatum games in extensive form. The utilities for players 1 and 2 are given in the top and bottom rows of each leaf node, respectively.

In both games, player i attempts to maximise the expectation of a utility function that depends on the chosen actions (α) and belief (b) and has the form:

$$u_i(\alpha, b) = \lambda_i(\alpha) + \theta_i \cdot \kappa_{ij}(\alpha, b) \cdot \kappa_{ji}(\alpha, b)$$

where λ_i is a *material* utility function (these are the utilities shown in Fig. 3), κ_{ij} reflects player i's *kindness* to player j (expected material payoff, which ranges from negative to positive) and $\theta_i \in \mathbb{R}_{\geq 0}$ is player i's *reciprocity sensitivity*. This type of game was originally studied in the context of *fairness equilibria* [31], in order to model and investigate scenarios in which agents are willing to sacrifice material utility to help or punish others depending on how they think they are being treated.

The concept of kindness was introduced in [31] as a way to measure this type of feeling, and is calculated as the difference between the utility that player i

believes player j will receive (given player i's choice) minus the average of the minimum and maximum utilities player i believes player j could get for i's other choices. For instance, in the reciprocity game, if player 1 chooses *fair*, κ_{12} equals $5-1/2\cdot(5+(9\cdot\overline{p_r}+1\cdot(1-\overline{p_r}))) = 2-4\cdot\overline{p_r}$. As before, we use p_r for the probability of player 2 choosing action r and $\overline{p_r}$ for player 1's belief as to this value.

Reciprocating kindness is expressed by the matching of signs of κ_{ij} and κ_{ji}. Thus, if, by adopting a particular strategy, player i is perceived to be unkind to player j, κ_{ij} will be negative, which will in return motivate player j to be unkind to player i so that the product of κ_{ij} and κ_{ji} is positive. A similar logic applies to when players are perceived to be kind.

As explained earlier in Example 1, when writing the matrices for players' utility values, we can assume that $\overline{p_r} = p_r$ in equilibrium and just express them as functions of the probability p_r. For the reciprocity game we thus have:

$$
Z_1^{\text{reciprocity}} = \begin{matrix} & r & a \\ f & \\ g \end{matrix} \begin{pmatrix} 5+\theta_1\cdot(-4)\cdot(2-4\cdot p_r) & 5+\theta_1\cdot(4)\cdot(2-4\cdot p_r) \\ 1+\theta_1\cdot(-4)\cdot(4\cdot p_r-2) & 9+\theta_1\cdot(4)\cdot(4\cdot p_r-2) \end{pmatrix}
$$

$$
Z_2^{\text{reciprocity}} = \begin{matrix} & r & a \\ f & \\ g \end{matrix} \begin{pmatrix} 5+\theta_2\cdot(-4)\cdot(2-4\cdot p_r) & 5+\theta_2\cdot(4)\cdot(2-4\cdot p_r) \\ 9+\theta_2\cdot(-4)\cdot(4\cdot p_r - 2) & 1+\theta_2\cdot(4)\cdot(4\cdot p_r-2) \end{pmatrix}
$$

and for the ultimatum game:

$$
Z_1^{\text{ultimatum}} = \begin{matrix} & r & a \\ f & \\ g \end{matrix} \begin{pmatrix} 5+\theta_1\cdot(-9/2)\cdot(2+p_r/2) & 5+\theta_1\cdot(9/2)\cdot(2 + p_r/2) \\ 0+\theta_1\cdot(-9/2)\cdot(-2-p_r/2) & 9+\theta_1\cdot(9/2)\cdot(-2-p_r/2) \end{pmatrix}
$$

$$
Z_2^{\text{ultimatum}} = \begin{matrix} & r & a \\ f & \\ g \end{matrix} \begin{pmatrix} 5+\theta_2\cdot(-9/2)\cdot(2+p_r/2) & 5+\theta_2\cdot(9/2)\cdot(2+p_r/2) \\ 0+\theta_2\cdot(-9/2)\cdot(-2-p_r/2) & 1+\theta_2\cdot(9/2)\cdot(-2-p_r/2) \end{pmatrix}
$$

Figure 4 presents the strategies and utility values for SWNEs that we generated for the reciprocity and ultimatum games using different values of θ_1 and θ_2. Although the games are very similar in structure (there is an equal amount of material utility that can be split by the two players in different ways), it is possible to see how the reciprocity sensitivity affects their behaviours and overall utilities. For instance, in the ultimatum game, when $\theta_1 = \theta_2 = 0$ the players are strictly concerned with their material utilities and (*greedy, accept*) is an acceptable SWNE as the sum of utilities is 10. It is possible to see though that, as θ_2 increases, player 1 is less likely to play *greedy* as the split becomes less fair for player 2, who could then retaliate by playing *reject*.

We can also notice that, when $\theta_1 = \theta_2 = 1$, the equilibrium for the reciprocity and ultimatum games is $(fair, accept)$ which, despite leading to material utilities of $(5, 5)$ in both games, accounts for different overall utilities for the players. In the former, the utility for each player is equal to $u_i(fair, accept) = 5 + 1 \cdot 4 \cdot (2 - 4 \cdot p_r) = 13$, and for the latter it corresponds to $u_i(fair, accept) = 5 + 1 \cdot 9/2 \cdot (2 + p_r/2) = 14$.

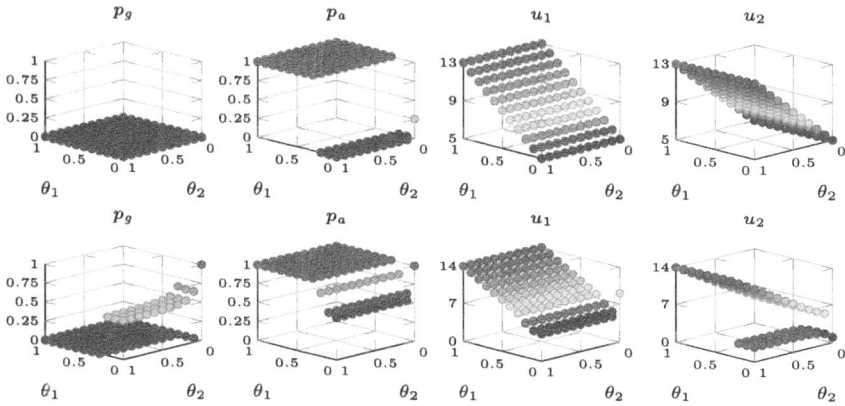

Fig. 4. Possible social welfare PEs for the reciprocity (top) and ultimatum (bottom) games for a range of reciprocity sensitivities θ_1, θ_2. We show the strategy (probabilities p_g, p_a of choosing *greedy*, *accept*) and values (utilities u_1 and u_2).

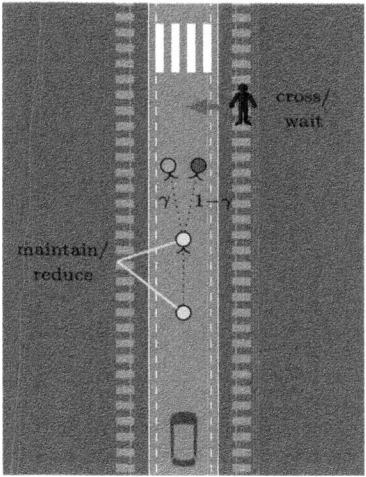

Fig. 5. An illustration for the pedestrian crossing scenario.

5.2   Traffic Games

We now report on a selection of case studies inspired by game-theoretic models of traffic and road user behaviour. We start with a simple one-shot game between a vehicle and a pedestrian in a road crossing scenario, and how their expectations can incentivise safe behaviour. Next we introduce a psychological variant of the Bayesian game presented in [29], which examined how cyclists would interact differently with autonomous and regular vehicles. Finally, we extend the road crossing scenario into a CSG and investigate the impact of combining information on past decisions with local expectations in a multi-stage, probabilistic model.

Pedestrian Crossing. We consider a scenario where a pedestrian is deciding whether to cross a road near oncoming traffic, illustrated in Fig. 5. We assume that the car has a right of way and can *reduce* (r) or *maintain* (m) its speed, while the pedestrian may choose to *cross* (c) or *wait* (w). A psychological game can be constructed by including incentives set to discourage behaviour based on what they expect the other will do. We assume the pedestrian would be (illegally) jaywalking if they decided to cross, and so give them a negative reward proportional to the probability p_c of that action being taken (multiplied by a constant μ), to model the pedestrian's fear of being caught and incurring a penalty. This parameterisation results in the following utility matrices for the vehicle and the pedestrian:

$$
Z_{vehicle} = \begin{matrix} r \\ m \end{matrix}
\begin{pmatrix} 1-p_w & 1+p_c \\ 1+p_w & 1-p_c \end{pmatrix}
\qquad
Z_{pedestrian} = \begin{matrix} r \\ m \end{matrix}
\begin{pmatrix} 1-p_r & 1+p_r-\mu \cdot p_c \\ 1+p_m & 1-p_m-\mu \cdot p_c \end{pmatrix}
$$

with column labels w and c.

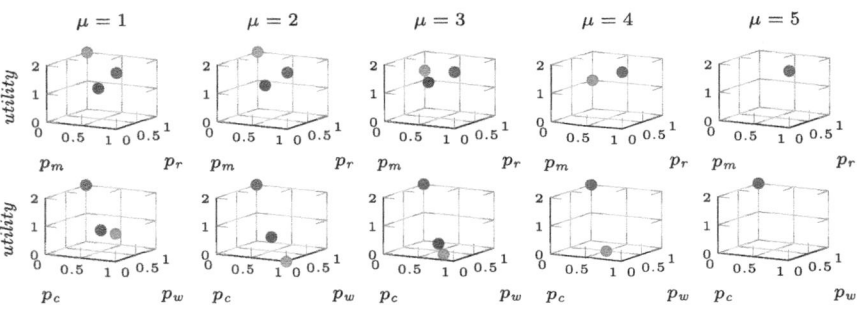

Fig. 6. Equilibria strategies and utilities for the vehicle (top) and pedestrian (bottom) in the pedestrian crossing scenario, for different values of μ.

Figure 6 shows equilibria strategy profiles and utilities of this game for different values of μ (a more detailed version can be found in Fig. 12, Appendix A). The colours for the points in the bottom and top plots for each value of μ serve to match the profiles and utilities of the pedestrian and the vehicle for different equilibria. While it is possible to see that there is always an equilibrium (displayed in red) in which the vehicle maintains its speed and the pedestrian waits, for smaller values of μ we also have an equilibrium strategy profile in which both agents make random choices. For example, in the equilibrium shown in blue for $\mu = 2$, the vehicle randomly chooses between reducing and maintaining its speed with probabilities 3/4 and 1/4 respectively, while the pedestrian crosses or not with probability 1/2, potentially leading to unsafe behaviour. As the pedestrian's uneasiness about crossing grows, i.e., as μ increases, the strategy profiles in which they cross with positive probability disappear, with the only remaining profile for $\mu = 5$ being the one in which they wait.

Cyclist vs. Vehicle. Next, we model a cyclist and a vehicle, where the latter is either autonomous or driven by a human, at a road junction. A similar scenario was considered in [29], but modelled as a Bayesian game to investigate how increasing the share of autonomous vehicles affects the rate of collisions. Figure 7 shows the game in extensive form. The actions for the cyclist are *yield* (y), *walk* (w) and *cycle* (c), and the actions for the vehicle are *go* (g) and *stop* (s).

The utilities of the players reflect preferences over potential collisions, in accordance with traffic rules and an assumption on the part of the cyclist that an autonomous vehicle (AV) would be programmed to be as *risk averse* as possible, while human drivers are often (unintentionally) distracted. So, for example, the

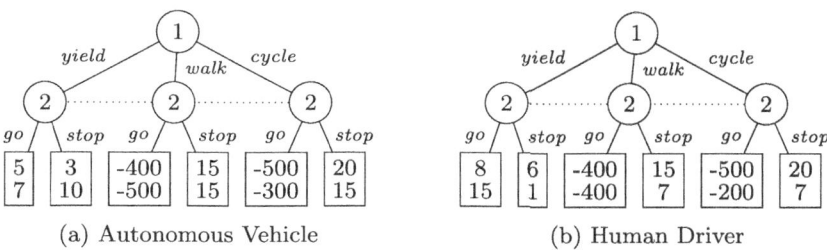

(a) Autonomous Vehicle   (b) Human Driver

Fig. 7. Original cyclist vs. vehicle game. In [29], the left and right games are played with probabilities p and $1 - p$, respectively. The utilities for the cyclist (1) and the vehicle (2) are given in the top and bottom rows of each leaf node.

Table 1. Psychological cyclist vs. vehicle game in normal form. Nature chooses between *autonomous vehicle* (a) or *human driver* (h).

α	u_{nature}	$u_{cyclist}$	$u_{vehicle}$
(a, y, g)	0	$5 \cdot p_a$	7
(a, y, s)	0	$3 \cdot p_a$	10
(a, w, g)	0	$-400 \cdot p_a$	-500
(a, w, s)	0	$15 \cdot p_a$	-15
(a, c, g)	0	$-500 \cdot p_a$	-300
(a, c, s)	0	$20 \cdot p_a$	15

α	u_{nature}	$u_{cyclist}$	$u_{vehicle}$
(h, y, g)	0	$8 \cdot p_h$	15
(h, y, s)	0	$6 \cdot p_h$	1
(h, w, g)	0	$-400 \cdot p_h$	-400
(h, w, s)	0	$15 \cdot p_h$	7
(h, c, g)	0	$-500 \cdot p_h$	-200
(h, c, s)	0	$20 \cdot p_h$	7

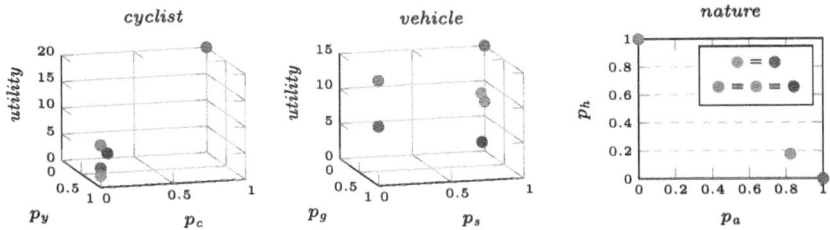

Fig. 8. Strategies and utilities for the cyclist vs. vehicle game.

penalty for an AV not stopping while the cyclist crosses the road is higher than for a human-driven vehicle (300 vs. 200). In the original game, it is assumed that a virtual *nature* player chooses the type of the vehicle according to a prior distribution. Here, we consider *nature* to be an active albeit *indifferent* player picking *autonomous* (a) or *human* (h), and we set the utilities for the cyclist to be the original utilities multiplied by their expectation of the vehicle being driven autonomously (p_a) or by a human (p_h), as detailed in Table 1.

Figure 8 shows results for this variant (a more detailed version is in Fig. 11 of Appendix A). In addition to the equilibria computed in [29] (indicated in blue, orange[1], magenta and brown), two new equilibria (indicated in green and red) are present for the psychological variant, in which *nature* randomly chooses between an autonomous vehicle and one with a human driver with probabilities $p_a = 14/17$ and $p_h = 3/17$. Considering the original model from [29] and combining the utilities of the two original games (Fig. 7(a) and (b)) into one normal form game by multiplying the corresponding utilities by p or $1 - p$, we obtain the bimatrix game as follows:

$$Z_{cyclist} = \begin{matrix} y \\ w \\ c \end{matrix} \begin{pmatrix} -3{\cdot}p+8 & -3{\cdot}p+6 \\ -400 & 15 \\ -500 & 20 \end{pmatrix} \qquad Z_{vehicle} = \begin{matrix} y \\ w \\ c \end{matrix} \begin{pmatrix} -8{\cdot}p+15 & 9{\cdot}p+1 \\ -100{\cdot}p-400 & 14{\cdot}p+7 \\ -100{\cdot}p-200 & 8{\cdot}p+7 \end{pmatrix}$$

We observe that, if the cyclist decides to *yield*, the vehicle would only play *go* with positive probability if $-8{\cdot}p + 15 \geqslant 9{\cdot}p + 1$, which gives $p \leqslant 14/17$. For any value of p above that threshold, the game has only one equilibrium in (*cycle, stop*), with utilities $(20, 8{\cdot}p + 7)$. The analysis in [29] suggests that the number of collisions, i.e., the outcome where the cyclist chooses *cycle* and the vehicle chooses *go*, drops as the proportion of AVs increases. Indeed, if we only have AVs circulating, the only equilibrium (magenta) is (*cycle, stop*). However, by modelling this scenario as a three-player game with nature as an active player, we see in Fig. 8 (and in more detail in Fig. 11 of Appendix A), for a mix of AVs and human-driven vehicles, where AVs correspond to approximately 82% of the fleet, that the equilibrium strategy (green and red) for the cyclist is actually to *yield*. Furthermore, the vehicles can follow two different strategies: one in which they would *go* with probability 1 and another in which they *stop* with probability

---

[1] The utility and strategy for the cyclist are the same as for the one in magenta.

approximately 0.97 (shown in red and green, respectively). Finally, the model in [29] assumes that the cyclists can always differentiate between an AV and a human-driven vehicle, which is not realistic. In contrast, our model allows for the possibility of specifying psychological payoffs, meaning the actions taken by the cyclist can vary according to their beliefs about the type of the vehicle, paving the way for more sophisticated models of similar scenarios.

Multi-stage Pedestrian Crossing. Finally, we consider a probabilistic, multi-stage version of the earlier *pedestrian crossing* game, modelled as a CSG with psychological utilities. The state of the CSG has a variable j counting the number of times the one-shot pedestrian game has been repeated. We also add two discrete integer-valued variables $c_r, c_w \in \{0, 1, \ldots, 10\}$ in order to carry information forward about the actions taken by both agents. The variables c_r and c_w are initialised to 0 and go up (or down) by 1 when the vehicle reduces (or maintains) its speed, and the pedestrian decides to wait (or cross), respectively.

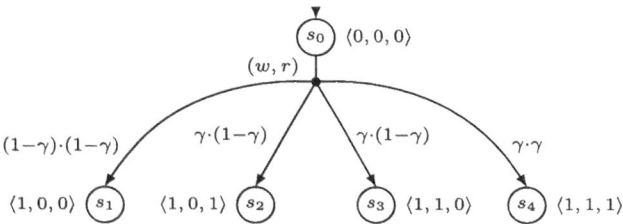

Fig. 9. Transitions for actions (w, r) from the initial state of the CSG for the multi-stage pedestrian crossing example. States are of the form $\langle j, c_r, c_w \rangle$, for step count j and variables c_r, c_w.

To account for the fact that these observations can be imperfectly made by the players, c_r and c_w are updated probabilistically according to an *attention* coefficient $\gamma \in [0, 1]$, and so their values can also remain the same with probability $1 - \gamma$, as illustrated in Fig. 9. The information on past decisions carried by the values of the two variables is then weighted with the local expectations at each state by modifying the reward matrices in following manner:

$$Z_{vehicle} = \begin{array}{c} \\ r \\ m \end{array} \begin{array}{cc} w & c \\ \left(\begin{array}{cc} 1-(1/2)\cdot(p_w+c_w/10) & (3/2)+(1/2)\cdot(p_c-c_w/10) \\ 1+(1/2)\cdot(p_w+c_w/10) & (1/2)-(1/2)\cdot(p_c-c_w/10) \end{array} \right) \end{array}$$

$$Z_{pedestrian} = \begin{array}{c} \\ r \\ m \end{array} \begin{array}{cc} w & c \\ \left(\begin{array}{cc} 1-(1/2)\cdot(p_r+c_r/10) & 1+(1/2)\cdot(p_r+c_r/10)-\mu\cdot p_c \\ (3/2)+(1/2)\cdot(p_m-c_r/10) & (1/2)-(1/2)\cdot(p_m-c_r/10)-\mu\cdot p_c \end{array} \right) \end{array}$$

Figure 10 shows expected utility values and crossing probability averages for different values of γ, paths of length k and $\mu = 1$. In a similar fashion to the one-shot example, we do not focus exclusively on the social welfare solution and there could be multiple equilibria for the NFPGs built at each state. However, for extensive or multi-stage games, it is impractical to compute all possible equilibria unless the number of states is fairly small. This is particularly true when there is probabilistic branching, as the number of equilibria (and hence the number of NLPs to be solved) may grow very rapidly. For this reason, the probability values reported in Fig. 10 (right) are averages over equilibria selected uniformly at random at each state. For each path length and γ, 10 experiments were run and the utility averages for the initial state are displayed in Fig. 10 (left).

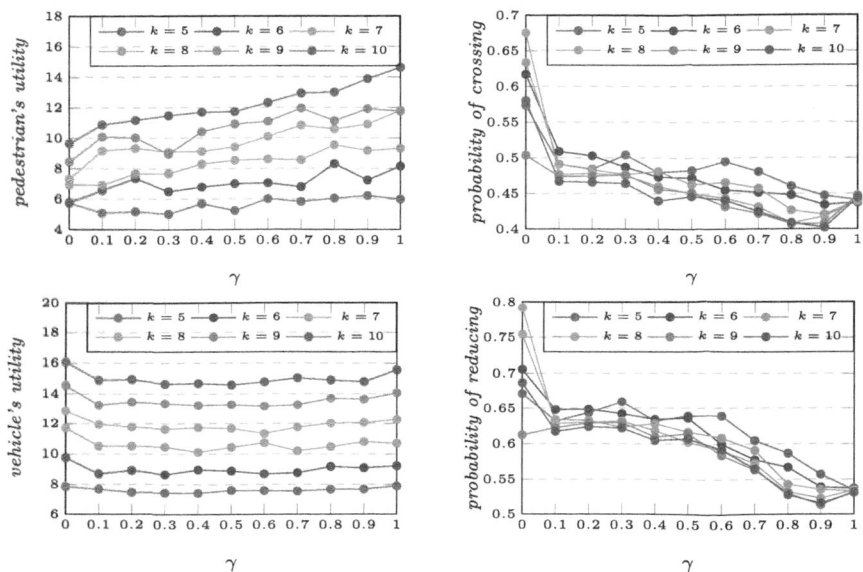

Fig. 10. Utility (left) and probability averages (right) over sampled equilibria for different path lengths in the multi-stage pedestrian crossing example.

As the value of γ grows, it is possible to notice a trend in which the pedestrian's behaviour is safer, with the average probability of a crossing decreasing (top right). This is also reflected in higher utility for the pedestrian (top left), particularly when considering longer paths. For the vehicle, the utility averages (bottom left) remain fairly stable but we can also see that the likelihood of it reducing its speed (bottom right) decreases. This behaviour is desirable, considering it happens in coordination with decreasing probability values of a pedestrian crossing and the fact that the vehicle should have a right of way.

To provide an indication of model sizes that we are able to analyse, Table 2 shows how the number of CSG states and transitions, and the average computation time, vary for different values of k and intervals of γ (note that the number of transitions and states is the same for any value of $\gamma \in (0,1)$, see Fig. 9).

Table 2. Statistics for the (CSG) multi-stage pedestrian crossing case study.

$\gamma \in$	k	States	Transitions	Time(s)	k	States	Transitions	Time(s)
$[0,0]$	5	6	21	0.76	8	9	33	1.33
$(0,1)$		91	701	5.97		285	2,806	25.7
$[1,1]$		91	256	4.82		285	897	23.1
$[0,0]$	6	7	25	0.83	9	10	37	1.73
$(0,1)$		140	1,198	9.12		385	3,981	39.6
$[1,1]$		140	413	8.45		385	1,240	35.1
$[0,0]$	7	8	29	1.06	10	11	41	2.09
$(0,1)$		204	1,889	15.9		506	5,446	58.7
$[1,1]$		204	624	14.5		506	1,661	51.9

6 Conclusions

We have presented techniques that expand the scope of modelling and verification for game-theoretic probabilistic models. Starting with psychological normal form games, we proposed an NLP encoding that allows us to compute optimal equilibria for individual supports and, through support enumeration, an overall optimal equilibrium for a given NFPG. We then considered CSGs whose states can be expressed as NFPGs, and developed an algorithm to compute equilibria for such CSGs under some restrictions on the type of the players' beliefs. Finally, we reported on a prototype implementation and showcased novel automated analysis, made possible through our method, for a range of case studies.

Verification of psychological games is still a largely unexplored topic and there is ample room for expansion in theory, practice and applications to problems in computer science. Equilibria computation is a hard problem in general, and algorithms for psychological equilibria suffer from some of the same computational drawbacks as those for Nash or correlated equilibria, in addition to presenting new challenges of their own. The main current limitation is having to rely on enumeration for computing an optimal solution, which could be somewhat mitigated by parallelisation and filtering supports as a precomputation step. Future work includes investigating dynamic psychological games [5], which have the advantage of allowing belief updates but pose new modelling and computational challenges, and considering aspects of coordination and robustness via correlated [1] and trembling-hand [21] variants.

Acknowledgements. This project was funded by the ERC under the European Union's Horizon 2020 research and innovation programme (FUN2MODEL, grant agreement No. 834115).

A   Appendix

Below, we include larger, more detailed figures for the *cyclist vs. vehicle* and *pedestrian crossing* case studies presented in Sect. 5.2.

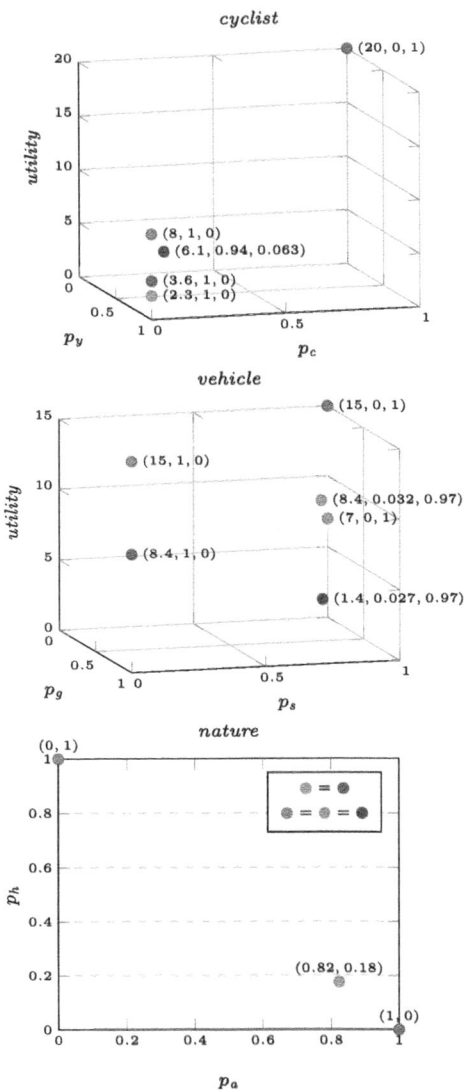

Fig. 11. Equilibria strategies and utilities for the cyclist vs. vehicle game. Coordinates for the *cyclist, vehicle* and *nature* players correspond to (u, p_y, p_c), (u, p_g, p_s) and (p_a, p_h), respectively (where u is the utility). For the cyclist, the utilities and strategies are the same in the orange and magenta equilibria.

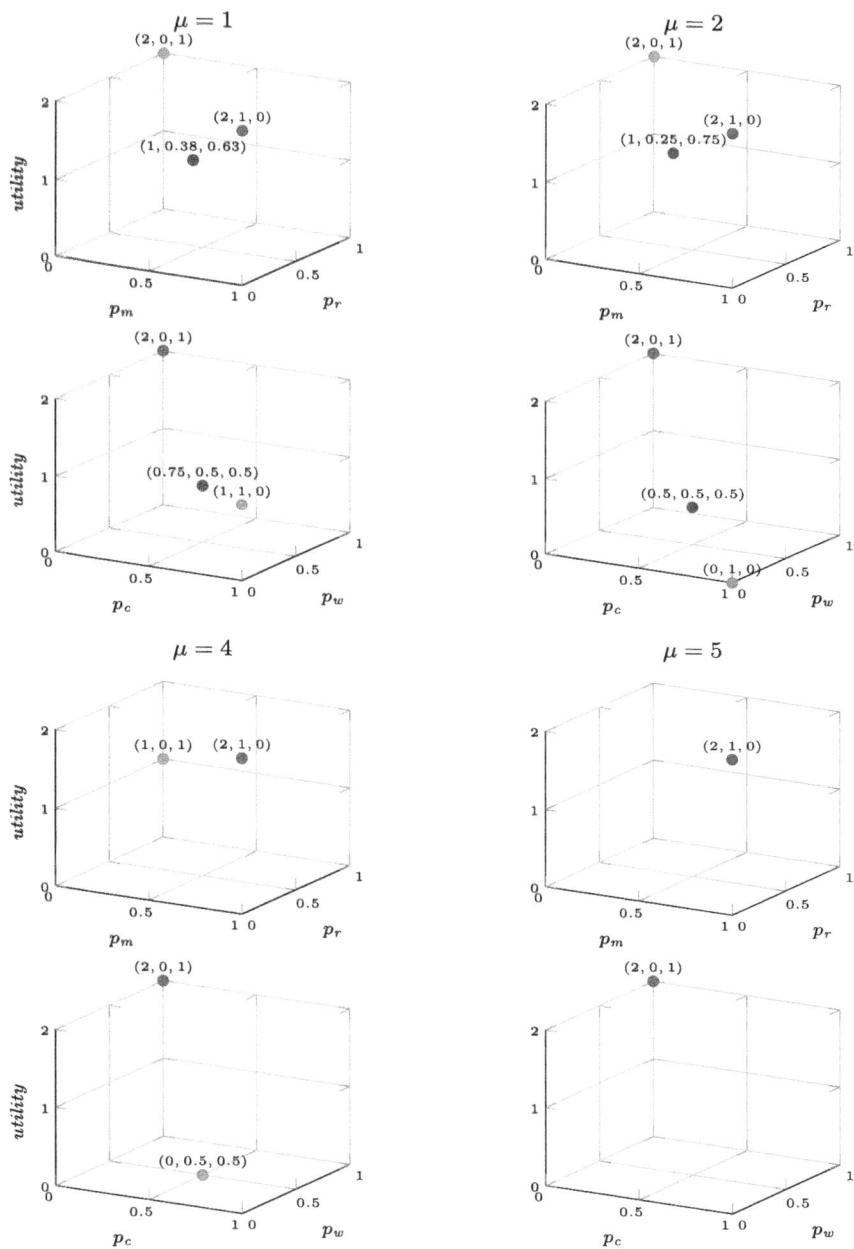

Fig. 12. Equilibria strategies and utilities for the pedestrian crossing game for different values of μ. The top plot for each value of μ corresponds to the pedestrian and the plot below to the vehicle. Point coordinates values are (u, p_m, p_r) for the vehicle and (u, p_c, p_w) for the pedestrian (where u is the utility).

References

1. Andrés, P.: From decision theory to game theory: reasoning about decisions of others (2024). Manuscript in Preparation, Cambridge University Press
2. Aslanyan, Z., Nielson, F., Parker, D.: Quantitative verification and synthesis of attack-defence scenarios. In: Proceedings of CSF 2016, pp. 105–119. IEEE (2016)
3. Attanasi, G., Nagel, R.: A survey of psychological games: theoretical findings and experimental evidence. In: Innocenti, A., Sbriglia, P. (eds.) Games, Rationality and Behavior. Essays on Behavioral Game Theory and Experiments, pp. 204–232 (2008)
4. Battigalli, P., Corrao, R., Dufwenberg, M.: Incorporating belief-dependent motivation in games. J. Econ. Behav. Organ. **167**, 185–218 (2019)
5. Battigalli, P., Dufwenberg, M.: Dynamic psychological games. J. Econ. Theory **144**(1), 1–35 (2009)
6. Battigalli, P., Dufwenberg, M.: Belief-dependent motivations and psychological game theory. J. Econ. Lit. **60**(3), 833–82 (2022)
7. Bjørnskau, T.: The zebra crossing game - using game theory to explain a discrepancy between road user behaviour and traffic rules. Saf. Sci. **92** (2015)
8. Brenguier, R.: PRALINE: a tool for computing nash equilibria in concurrent games. In: Sharygina, N., Veith, H. (eds.) CAV 2013. LNCS, vol. 8044, pp. 890–895. Springer, Heidelberg (2013). https://doi.org/10.1007/978-3-642-39799-8_63
9. Dickhaut, J., Kaplan, T.: A program for finding nash equilibria. In: Varian, H.R. (ed.) Economic and Financial Modeling with Mathematica, pp. 148–166. Springer, New York (1993). https://doi.org/10.1007/978-1-4757-2281-9_7
10. Elvik, R.: A review of game-theoretic models of road user behaviour. Accid. Anal. Prev. **62**, 388–396 (2014)
11. Ezzati Amini, R., Abouelela, M., Dhamaniya, A., Friedrich, B., Antoniou, C.: A game-theoretic approach for modelling pedestrian-vehicle conflict resolutions in uncontrolled traffic environments. Accid. Anal. Prev. **203**, 107604 (2024)
12. Feng, L., Wiltsche, C., Humphrey, L., Topcu, U.: Synthesis of human-in-the-loop control protocols for autonomous systems. IEEE Trans. Autom. Sci. Eng. **13**(2), 450–462 (2016)
13. Geanakoplos, J., Pearce, D., Stacchetti, E.: Psychological games and sequential rationality. Games Econom. Behav. **1**(1), 60–79 (1989)
14. Govindan, S., Wilson, R.: A global Newton method to compute Nash equilibria. J. Econ. Theory **110**(1), 65–86 (2003)
15. Gurobi Optimization, LLC: Gurobi Optimizer Reference Manual (2021). http://gurobi.com/
16. Hensel, C., Junges, S., Katoen, J.P., Quatmann, T., Volk, M.: The probabilistic model checker Storm. Int. J. Softw. Tools Technol. Transfer **24**(4), 589–610 (2022)
17. Gutierrez, J., Najib, M., Perelli, G., Wooldridge, M.: EVE: a tool for temporal equilibrium analysis. In: Lahiri, S.K., Wang, C. (eds.) ATVA 2018. LNCS, vol. 11138, pp. 551–557. Springer, Cham (2018). https://doi.org/10.1007/978-3-030-01090-4_35
18. Junges, S., Jansen, N., Katoen, J.-P., Topcu, U., Zhang, R., Hayhoe, M.: Model checking for safe navigation among humans. In: McIver, A., Horvath, A. (eds.) QEST 2018. LNCS, vol. 11024, pp. 207–222. Springer, Cham (2018). https://doi.org/10.1007/978-3-319-99154-2_13
19. Karabag, M.O., Smith, S., Fridovich-Keil, D., Topcu, U.: Encouraging inferable behavior for autonomy: repeated bimatrix stackelberg games with observations (2023)

20. Kemeny, J., Snell, J., Knapp, A.: Denumerable Markov Chains. Springer, New York (1976). https://doi.org/10.1007/978-1-4684-9455-6
21. Kolpin, V.: Equilibrium refinement in psychological games. Games Econom. Behav. **4**(2), 218–231 (1992)
22. Kwiatkowska, M., Norman, G., Parker, D.: PRISM 4.0: verification of probabilistic real-time systems. In: Gopalakrishnan, G., Qadeer, S. (eds.) CAV 2011. LNCS, vol. 6806, pp. 585–591. Springer, Heidelberg (2011). https://doi.org/10.1007/978-3-642-22110-1_47
23. Kwiatkowska, M., Norman, G., Parker, D., Santos, G.: PRISM-games 3.0: stochastic game verification with concurrency, equilibria and time. In: Lahiri, S.K., Wang, C. (eds.) CAV 2020. LNCS, vol. 12225, pp. 475–487. Springer, Cham (2020). https://doi.org/10.1007/978-3-030-53291-8_25
24. Kwiatkowska, M., Norman, G., Parker, D., Santos, G.: Multi-player equilibria verification for concurrent stochastic games. In: Gribaudo, M., Jansen, D.N., Remke, A. (eds.) QEST 2020. LNCS, vol. 12289, pp. 74–95. Springer, Cham (2020). https://doi.org/10.1007/978-3-030-59854-9_7
25. Kwiatkowska, M., Norman, G., Parker, D., Santos, G.: Automatic verification of concurrent stochastic systems. Formal Methods Syst. Des. **58**, 188–250 (2021)
26. Kwiatkowska, M., Norman, G., Parker, D., Santos, G.: Correlated equilibria and fairness in concurrent stochastic games. In: TACAS 2022. LNCS, vol. 13244, pp. 60–78. Springer, Cham (2022). https://doi.org/10.1007/978-3-030-99527-0_4
27. Laan, G.V.D., Talman, A.J.J., Heyden, L.V.D.: Simplicial variable dimension algorithms for solving the nonlinear complementarity problem on a product of unit simplices using a general labelling. Math. Oper. Res. **12**(3), 377–397 (1987)
28. Lemke, C., Howson, J.: Equilibrium points of bimatrix games. J. Soc. Ind. Appl. Math. **12**(2), 413–423 (1964)
29. Michieli, U., Badia, L.: Game theoretic analysis of road user safety scenarios involving autonomous vehicles. In: Proceedings of PIMRC 2018, pp. 1377–1381 (2018)
30. Porter, R., Nudelman, E., Shoham, Y.: Simple search methods for finding a Nash equilibrium. In: Proceedings of AAAI 2004, pp. 664–669. AAAI Press (2004)
31. Rabin, M.: Incorporating fairness into game theory and economics. Am. Econ. Rev. 1281–1302 (1993)
32. Sandholm, T., Gilpin, A., Conitzer, V.: Mixed-integer programming methods for finding Nash equilibria. In: Proceedings of AAAI 2005, pp. 495–501. AAAI Press (2005)
33. Shapley, L.: Stochastic games. Proc. Natl. Acad. Sci. **39**, 1095–1100 (1953)
34. Shirado, H., Kasahara, S., Christakis, N.A.: Emergence and collapse of reciprocity in semiautomatic driving coordination experiments with humans. Proc. Natl. Acad. Sci. **120**(51) (2023)
35. Toumi, A., Gutierrez, J., Wooldridge, M.: A tool for the automated verification of nash equilibria in concurrent games. In: Leucker, M., Rueda, C., Valencia, F.D. (eds.) ICTAC 2015. LNCS, vol. 9399, pp. 583–594. Springer, Cham (2015). https://doi.org/10.1007/978-3-319-25150-9_34

Process Mining Meets Probabilistic Model Checking via Model and Logical Embeddings

Susmoy Das$^{(\boxtimes)}$ and Arpit Sharma

Department of Electrical Engineering and Computer Science, Indian Institute of
Science Education and Research Bhopal, Bhopal, India
{susmoy18,arpit}@iiserb.ac.in

Abstract. Process mining techniques are widely used to discover, monitor, and improve real processes based on digital traces captured in event logs. This paper proposes an integrated tool framework which allows performance evaluation, and quantitative compliance checking of process models discovered using process mining techniques. Our approach involves learning the process model, i.e., Petri Net from an existing event log by using ProM toolset. We generate its reachability graph, and extract important state and transition related information. We encode this information into mCRL2 formal specification language and use its associated toolset to generate the corresponding Labeled Transition System (LTS). Next, we transform this LTS model into an action-labeled discrete-time Markov chain (ADTMC) by simulating the event log on the LTS model. We use an action-based Probabilistic Computation Tree Logic (APCTL) and APCTL* for specifying interesting performance and compliance related properties. In the final step, we apply probabilistic model and logical embeddings which enable one to efficiently verify probabilistic process algebraic models using PRISM model checker. We validate the efficacy of our approach by applying it on several interesting case studies from different application domains.

Keywords: Process Mining · Probabilistic Verification · Logic · Event · Compliance · Performance

1 Introduction

Process mining involves discovering, monitoring, and improving real processes by extracting knowledge from *event logs* recorded by information systems [3]. It bridges the gap between process science [17] and data mining [24]. An event log contains data related to a single process where each event in the log relates to precisely one process instance, often referred to as *case*. A case is described by a sequence of events, referred to as *trace*, and a multi-set of traces is called an event log. Process mining framework has been successfully applied to industrial case

© The Author(s), under exclusive license to Springer Nature Switzerland AG 2025
N. Jansen et al. (Eds.): Principles of Verification: Cycling the Probabilistic Landscape,
LNCS 15261, pp. 192–218, 2025.
https://doi.org/10.1007/978-3-031-75775-4_9

studies from various application domains like automotive, telecommunication, healthcare, insurance, finance, and aeronautics [47].

Although process mining allows a holistic understanding of complex business processes, it does not provide support for the quantitative temporal compliance checking which involves verifying if the discovered process model satisfies internal or external business rules, e.g., laws, policies, regulatory requirements, and industry standards. For instance consider the following properties: a) less than 25% of the manuscripts should require additional reviewer(s) in a manuscript review process, b) less than 40% of the fines should have added penalties in them for a road traffic fine management process, c) in more than 90% of the applications, fines should be imposed when the second event was failure of payment and the subsequent events were reminder sent and failure of payment, d) if raising an invoice resulted in delay of payment, the customer is contacted in at least 85% of the cases, and e) in 75% of the loan applications, the capacity calculation must be performed only after all the other checks. These types of compliance properties based on probabilistic temporal analysis cannot be checked directly on the models learnt using process mining framework. Moreover, process mining does not provide support for the evaluation of performance, and reliability of discovered process models. For example, it is not clear how to verify the following probabilistic properties on process models learnt using process mining algorithms: a) probability that the event a is always succeeded by event f is higher than 25%, and b) the probability that more than 5 errors occur within the first 100 time units is less than 10%. Finally, process mining can also not be used for filtering the event log by identifying thresholds based on probabilistic analysis of temporal dependencies. For example, we may want to compute the probability of all the traces in which the activity a was followed by b but b was not followed by c, and remove all such traces from the event log only if the probability of their occurrence is less than 0.1. Note that these properties cannot also be checked or evaluated directly on the event logs due to the presence of complex temporal dependencies.

Joost-Pieter Katoen is a highly respected scientist in the field of formal methods, known for his pioneering contributions to model checking, concurrency theory, and probabilistic reasoning. The second author, having worked under the supervision of professor Katoen [51] was inspired by their numerous discussions on the extensive potential of probabilistic and stochastic model checking across various domains. In this article, we investigate the applications of probabilistic model checking for the quantitative analysis of process models extracted from event logs.

More specifically, this paper proposes an integrated tool framework which allows performance evaluation, and quantitative temporal compliance checking of process models discovered using process mining algorithms. Additionally, our approach can also be used for filtering the event log. We deploy probabilistic model checking [8], and probabilistic model and logical embeddings [13–15] which enable one to verify process behavior against interesting compliance and performance-related properties. More specifically, first, we learn the process model, i.e., Petri Net [48] from an existing event log and generate its reachability graph, i.e., labeled transition system (LTS) [8] by using ProM: The Process Mining Toolkit[1] [4,52]. ProM is an extensible framework that supports a wide variety of process mining techniques in the form of plug-ins. Next, we pre-process this reachability graph and extract important information, e.g., the set of states, the set of actions, the initial state and the transition relation. This information is then encoded into the mCRL2 formal specification language [22] which supports modeling and verification of concurrent systems via its associated toolset[2] [10].

Next, we transform the LTS model of mCRL2 into an action-labeled discrete-time Markov chain (ADTMC) by extracting the probability of executing each individual activity from the event log. This is achieved by first simulating each trace from the event log on the LTS to check if it is a valid trace or not, followed by computing the transition probability function using the set of valid traces. Since the process behavior may change over time, we also provide the option to simulate the learnt LTS model to generate new traces (event log), which can subsequently be used to calculate the transition probability function. Next, we specify interesting temporal compliance and performance related properties using APCTL and APCTL* [14] formulae. Since the mCRL2 toolset allows modeling and minimization of probabilistic systems but does not provide support for the verification of probabilistic behavior, we apply the model and logical embeddings proposed in [14] to obtain a corresponding state-labeled discrete-time Markov chain (SDTMC), and Probabilistic Computation Tree Logic (PCTL) (PCTL*, respectively) formulae. In the last step, the SDTMC model can be verified against the PCTL/PCTL* formulae using the PRISM toolset[3] [32] which is a state-of-the-art probabilistic model checker. It supports formal modeling and analysis of systems that exhibit randomized or probabilistic behaviour. Note that recently, in [23], authors have presented a framework for verifying quantitative modal formulas with alternating fixed-point operators, interpreted over probabilistic labeled transition systems. This suggests that in the near future mCRL2 may provide support for the probabilistic model checking of process algebraic models.

In order to validate the efficacy and usefulness of our integrated tool framework, we have applied it to several interesting case studies from different application domains, e.g., loan application process, manuscript review process, telephone repair process, and claim insurance process. The results of our experiments demonstrate that this approach is very useful for verifying temporal compliance and performance-related properties as APCTL/APCTL* formulae can be intuitively used for specifying these properties, followed by the application of model and logical embeddings which enable one to efficiently model check the process behavior using the PRISM toolset. Additionally, this technique can also be used for filtering the event log. In order to support transparency and replicability, we provide all the code files, model files, property files, and readme file.

---

[1] https://promtools.org/.

[2] https://www.mcrl2.org/.

[3] https://www.prismmodelchecker.org/.

Organisation of the Paper. The rest of the paper is organized as follows. Section 2 discusses the basic concepts related to state and action-labeled probabilistic models and logics followed by Sect. 3, which presents the integrated tool approach. Section 4 discusses several interesting case studies. Section 5 presents the related work. Finally, Sect. 6 concludes the paper and provides pointers for future research.

2   Preliminaries

This section presents the necessary definitions and basic concepts related to probabilistic models and logics that are needed to understand the rest of this paper.

2.1   Probabilistic Models

Definition 1 (SDTMC). *An SDTMC is a tuple $\mathcal{D} = (S, AP, \mathcal{P}, s_0, L)$ where: (a) S is a finite, nonempty set of states; (b) AP is a finite set of atomic propositions; (c) $\mathcal{P}$ is the transition probability function satisfying $\mathcal{P} : S \times S \to [0, 1]$ s.t. $\forall s \in S$: $\sum_{s' \in S} \mathcal{P}(s, s') = 1$; (d) s_0 is the initial state; and (e) $L : S \to 2^{AP}$ is a labeling function.*

Let $\to = \{(s, p, s') \mid \mathcal{P}(s, s') = p > 0\}$ denote the set of all transitions for an SDTMC $\mathcal{D}$. We denote $s \xrightarrow{p} s'$ if $(s, p, s') \in \to$. A sequence of states $s_0, s_1, s_2, \ldots$ where $\mathcal{P}(s_i, s_{i+1}) > 0$ forall i is an infinite path in an SDTMC. We denote a path by π. A finite path is of the form : $s_0, s_1, s_2, \ldots, s_n$ where $\mathcal{P}(s_i, s_{i+1}) > 0$ for $0 \le i < n$. The length of a finite path, denoted by $len(\pi)$ is given by the number of transitions along that path. The length of the finite path given above is $len(\pi) = n$. For an infinite path π, we have, $len(\pi) = \infty$. We denote the n-th state along a path π by $\pi[n-1]$ ($\pi[0]$ denotes the first state from which the path starts). Let $Paths(s)$ denote the set of all infinite paths starting in s.

Definition 2 (ADTMC). *An ADTMC is a tuple $\mathcal{D} = (S, Act, \mathcal{P}, s_0)$ where: (a) S is a finite, nonempty set of states; (b) Act is a finite set of actions that contains the special action τ; (c) $\mathcal{P} : S \times Act \times S \to [0, 1]$ is the transition probability function satisfying $\sum_{s' \in S, a \in Act} \mathcal{P}(s, a, s') = 1$ $\forall s \in S$; and (d) s_0 is the initial state.*

τ is a special action used to denote an invisible computation. Let $\to = \{(s, a; p, s') \mid \mathcal{P}(s, a, s') = p > 0\}$ denote the set of all the transitions for an ADTMC $\mathcal{D}$. We denote $s \xrightarrow{a, p} s'$ if $(s, a; p, s') \in \to$. An alternating sequence of states and actions $s_0 \alpha_1, s_1 \alpha_2, s_2 \alpha_3, \ldots$ s.t. $\mathcal{P}(s_i, \alpha_{i+1}, s_{i+1}) > 0$ for all i is an infinite run in an ADTMC. We denote a run by ρ. A finite run is of the form : $s_0 \alpha_1, s_1 \alpha_2, s_2 \alpha_3, \ldots, s_{n-1} \alpha_n, s_n$ where $\mathcal{P}(s_i, \alpha_{i+1}, s_{i+1}) > 0$ for $0 \le i < n$. The length of a finite run, denoted by $len(\rho)$ is given by the number of transitions along that run. The length of the finite run given above is $len(\rho) = n$. For an infinite run ρ, we have $len(\rho) = \infty$. We denote the n-th state along a run ρ by

$\rho[n-1]$ ($\rho[0]$ denotes the first state from which the run starts), and the n-th action along the run by $\rho_\alpha[n]$ ($\rho_\alpha[1]$ denotes the first transition label of the run). Let $Runs(s)$ denote the set of all infinite runs starting in s.

2.2   Probabilistic Logics

State-Based Logics. We briefly recall the syntax and semantics of Probabilistic Computation Tree Logic (PCTL) [8,25] which is interpreted over SDTMCs. PCTL is a probabilistic branching-time temporal logic that allows one to express the probability measures of satisfaction for a temporal property by a state in an SDTMC. The syntax is given by the following grammar where $\Phi, \Phi', \dots$ range over PCTL state formulae and $\Psi, \Psi', \dots$ range over path formulae :

1. State Formulae: $\Phi:: = \textbf{true} \mid a \mid \neg\, \Phi \mid \Phi \wedge \Phi' \mid \mathcal{P}_J(\Psi)$
2. Path Formulae: $\Psi:: = \mathbf{X}\Phi \mid \Phi\mathbf{U}\Phi'$

where $a \in$ AP and $J \subseteq [0,1] \subset \mathbb{R}$ is an interval. The operators $\mathbf{X}$ and $\mathbf{U}$ are called the ne**X**t and the **U**ntil operators, respectively. The satisfaction relation for PCTL can be given as follows. Let $\mathcal{D}$ be an SDTMC. Satisfaction of a PCTL state formula Φ by a state s or a path formula Ψ by a path π, denoted as, $s \models_S \Phi$ or $\pi \models_S \Psi$, respectively, is defined inductively by :

$$
\begin{aligned}
&s \models_S \textbf{true} && \text{always;} \\
&s \models_S a && \text{iff } a \in L(s); \\
&s \models_S \neg\Phi && \text{iff } s \not\models_S \Phi; \\
&s \models_S \Phi \wedge \Phi' && \text{iff } s \models_S \Phi \text{ and } s \models_S \Phi'; \\
&s \models_S \mathcal{P}_J(\Psi) && \text{iff } Pr(s \models_S \Psi) \in J; \\
&\pi \models_S \mathbf{X}\Phi && \text{iff } \pi[1] \models_S \Phi; \text{ and} \\
&\pi \models_S \Phi\mathbf{U}\Phi' && \text{iff } \exists k \geq 0, \text{ s.t. } \pi[k] \models_S \Phi' \,\&\, \forall 0 \leq i < k, \pi[i] \models_S \Phi.
\end{aligned}
$$

where $Pr(s \models_S \Psi) = Pr\{\pi \in Paths(s) \mid \pi \models_S \Psi\}$ and Pr is the unique probability measure defined on the smallest σ-algebra on $Paths(s)$ [8].

Action-Based Logics. Next, we recall the definition of an auxiliary logic of actions ActFor [14,45] which has been subsequently used for defining APCTL. The collection $ActFor$ of action formulae is defined as: $\chi:: = a \mid \neg\chi \mid \chi_1 \vee \chi_2$, where $a \in Act \setminus \{\tau\}$ and χ, χ_1, χ_2 range over action formulae. We write **true** as $a \vee \neg a$, where a is some arbitrarily chosen action, and **false** as $\neg\textbf{true}$. An action formula allows us to express constraints on actions that are visible (along a run or after the next step), e.g. $a \vee b$ implies that only actions a or b are allowed in the run. Here, **true** stands for 'all the visible actions are allowed'. The satisfaction relation for $ActFor$ is given by : (a) $a \models_A b \Leftrightarrow a = b$; (b) $a \models_A \neg\chi \Leftrightarrow a \not\models_A \chi$; and (c) $a \models_A \chi_1 \vee \chi_2 \Leftrightarrow a \models_A \chi_1$ or $a \models_A \chi_2$. The syntax of APCTL is defined by the state formulae generated by the following grammar, where $\Phi, \Phi', \dots$ range over state formulae, Ψ over run formulae, and χ and χ' are action formulae (generated by $ActFor$) :

1. State Formulae: $\Phi ::= \mathbf{true} \mid \neg\Phi \mid \Phi \wedge \Phi' \mid \mathcal{P}_J(\Psi)$
2. Run Formulae: $\Psi ::= \mathbf{X}_\chi \Phi \mid \mathbf{X}_\tau \Phi \mid \Phi_\chi \mathbf{U} \Phi' \mid \Phi_\chi \mathbf{U}_{\chi'} \Phi'$

where $J \subseteq [0,1] \subset \mathbb{R}$ is an interval. Satisfaction of a APCTL state formula Φ by a state s or a run formula Ψ by a run ρ, denoted as $s \models_A \Phi$ ($\rho \models_A \Psi$, resp.) is defined inductively by :

$$
\begin{aligned}
&s \models_A \mathbf{true} &&\text{always;}\\
&s \models_A \neg\Phi &&\text{iff } s \not\models_A \Phi;\\
&s \models_A \Phi \wedge \Phi' &&\text{iff } s \models_A \Phi \text{ and } s \models_A \Phi';\\
&s \models_A \mathcal{P}_J(\Psi) &&\text{iff } Pr(s \models_A \Psi) \in J;\\
&\rho \models_A \mathbf{X}_\chi \Phi &&\text{iff } \rho_\alpha[1] \models_A \chi \text{ and } \rho[1] \models_A \Phi;\\
&\rho \models_A \mathbf{X}_\tau \Phi &&\text{iff } \rho_\alpha[1] = \tau \text{ and } \rho[1] \models_A \Phi;\\
&\rho \models_A \Phi_\chi \mathbf{U} \Phi' &&\text{iff } \exists k \geq 0, \text{ s.t. } \rho[k] \models_A \Phi' \text{ and } \forall 0 \leq i < k,\\
& && \qquad \rho[i] \models_A \Phi \text{ and } \forall 1 \leq j \leq k, \rho_\alpha[j] \models_A \chi \text{ or}\\
& && \qquad \rho_\alpha[j] = \tau; \text{ and}\\
&\rho \models_A \Phi_\chi \mathbf{U}_{\chi'} \Phi' &&\text{iff } \exists k > 0, \text{ s.t. } \rho[k] \models_A \Phi' \text{ and } \rho_\alpha[k] \models_A \chi', \text{ and}\\
& && \qquad \forall 0 \leq i < k, \rho[i] \models_A \Phi \text{ and } \forall 1 \leq j < k,\\
& && \qquad \text{or } \rho_\alpha[j] \models_A \chi \text{ or } \rho_\alpha[j] = \tau.
\end{aligned}
$$

where $Pr(s \models_A \Psi) = Pr\{\rho \in Runs(s) \mid \rho \models_A \Psi\}$ and Pr is the unique probability measure defined on the smallest σ-algebra on $Runs(s)$ [14]. Due to space limitations, we do not provide the syntax and semantics of PCTL* and APCTL*. Interested readers are referred to [7,8,14] for more details.

3   Approach

Figure 1 shows the overall architecture of our integrated tool framework. Our approach involves mining the process model, i.e., Petri net from the (old) event log, transforming this model into an LTS, simulating each trace from the event log on the LTS to identify the set of valid traces, and using this set to compute the probability transition function of the ADTMC. Since the process behavior may change over time, we also provide the option of simulating the LTS to generate a new (event) log which can then be used to obtain the corresponding ADTMC. Next, we specify the properties of interest using APCTL/APCTL*, which will be interpreted over the ADTMC model learnt in the previous step. We use the formal framework of probabilistic model and logical embeddings to transform the ADTMC model into a corresponding SDTMC, and APCTL/APCTL* properties into PCTL/PCTL* properties, respectively. Finally, the process behavior can be verified using the PRISM model checker.

We have used state-of-the-art toolsets from the process mining domain, process algebra, and model checking domain for developing our integrated tool framework. More specifically, The ProM toolset has been used for learning the process models from the event logs, mCRL2 toolset has been used to simulate LTSs to construct a simulated event log and also to generate the ADTMC models, and the PRISM model checker has been used for the verification of SDTMCs.

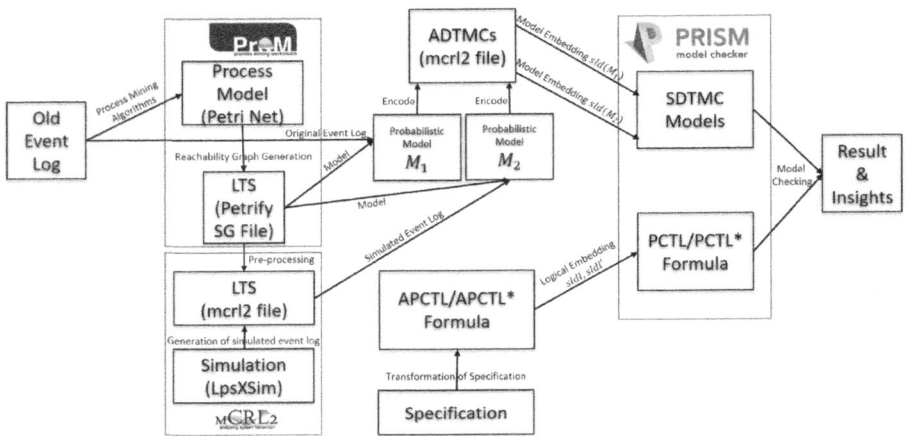

Fig. 1. Framework Overview

3.1   From Original Event Log to Process Models

Process discovery involves the challenge of identifying a process model that best describes the observed behavior based on a given event log. For mining process models from the event logs, we have used 'ProM: The Process Mining Toolkit' [4,52]. We have considered the following two process mining techniques: the Alpha Miner and the Inductive mining approach.

Alpha algorithm [5] stands as the pioneering process discovery method capable of building process models based on the event logs by understanding the relations and causalities between the steps of the processes. This algorithm has several limitations, e.g., the process models may not be sound and may suffer from fitness-related issues. This has led to the quest to propose and develop new techniques that can guarantee fitness and produce sound process models. Inductive Miner [35,36] is a flexible framework that can discover a set of block-structured process models from the event log. These models are both sound (Def. 2.9 [5]) and capable of accurately representing the observed behavior. We have used the default Alpha Miner and Inductive Miner to discover process behavior. For those cases where the models learnt via Alpha Miner did not capture the behavior properly, i.e., at least 75% of the event log cannot be captured by the reachability graph, we have used its variants like 'Alpha++' [53] and 'Alpha#'

[54]. Alpha++ [53] effectively identifies non-free choice processes, characterized by a blend of synchronization and choice leading to potential implicit dependencies. In contrast, Alpha# [54] enhances the mining capabilities of the conventional Alpha mining algorithm by enabling the detection of key invisible tasks within event logs. Both algorithms contribute to the enhancement and optimization of the fitness of the traditional Alpha algorithm in the field of process mining. In the case of Inductive Miner which assures a 100% log fitness, we also use the 'infrequent (IMf)' variant, where the user must provide the 'noise threshold'. As in the case of Alpha algorithm, we have also considered learning process models via the IMf 'variant' with a noise threshold such that at least 75% of the event log is captured by the reachability graph.

3.2 From Process Models to LTSs

ProM provides a plugin that constructs the reachability graph of a Petri Net. We choose the option to augment it with an 'initial marking'. This results in constructing a reachability graph with a set of states where the initial state is marked and stored separately. Transitions are labeled with events that can be considered as actions; hence, the graph can be viewed as a Labeled Transition System (LTS). Using this plugin, we can convert the learnt process models (Petri Nets) to their corresponding reachability graphs or LTSs. This plugin has a restriction, viz., it auto aborts the construction of reachability graph if the state-space exceeds 25000 states. Therefore, for such cases, we have used 'Alpha++' and 'Alpha#' for the process discovery as it allows the ProM plugin to generate the state-space. The reachability graph is then exported from the ProM tool as a 'Petrify sg file'. We have written a script that takes this file as an input, pre-processes it to extract important information like the set of states, the set of actions, the initial state, and the transition relation. This information is then encoded into the mCRL2 formal specification language [22], which comes with an associated toolset [10] to generate the corresponding LTS model.

3.3 From LTSs to ADTMCs

In order to obtain an ADTMC from a LTS, we need to define the transition probability function. This would associate a probability for each transition in the model such that the sum of all the probabilities across all the outgoing transitions from every state is 1 in lieu of Definition 2.

First, to establish the correctness of our methodology in case of the Inductive Miner, we have used the same (original) event log to populate these probabilities. As mentioned earlier, we also provide the option to generate a new event log which represents the process behavior from a different time frame by simulating the learnt LTS model to generate new traces. This new event log can subsequently be used to calculate the probabilities, and obtain an ADTMC. This feature allows us to compare the behavior of a process from different time frames with respect to the performance and compliance related properties. Additionally, it also overcomes the issue of unavailability of event logs for the same process from different time frames. For instance, a negative trend identified in a particular year which is harming the overall productivity of a process can be rechecked at a later point of time to see if it has been properly addressed, i.e., the probability of finding such trends should significantly decrease. In short, the main motivation for generating simulated event logs is to demonstrate that the process behavior may change over time, and therefore, the corresponding ADTMC may or may not satisfy the probabilistic properties that were true in the original setting. Thus, we obtain two ADTMCs, where the first one is obtained by simulating the original event log on the LTS, and the second one is obtained from the simulations of the LTS model. The LTS model originally obtained from the ProM toolset is taken as an input by our code which then pre-processes the file and transforms it to a new LTS file which is compatible with the mCRL2 [10] toolset. Note that mCRL2 comes with a tool 'lpsxsim'[4] that can simulate the LTS model to generate traces randomly. We have saved the output of these simulations, which forms the simulated event log. We have considered 'random play' of at least 50000 events to generate simulated event logs. Next, we apply some pre-processing steps on these traces, and then use them to calculate the probabilities, i.e., ADTMC.

We first check whether a given trace can be modeled by the LTS before using it for computing the transition probability function. We create a subset of the log known as the workflow log. This is because incomplete traces, i.e., traces which do not start (end, respectively) with start (end, respectively) activities, or incorrect traces, i.e., traces with a sequence of action(s) which the process model cannot capture, need to be segregated as they will adversely impact the computation of probabilities. They can only be separated from the good traces once they have been completely simulated on the LTS model. Hence, we cannot achieve this on the fly (simulate and use it for computing probabilities), and need to go through two passes. In the first pass, we identify the set of good traces, and then in the second pass we use this set to calculate the transition probability function. The details of these two passes are as follows. In the first pass, we start from the initial state, and follow the sequence of actions given in the trace to determine if we can successfully reach the final state. This may not always be possible, as two scenarios may arise: 1) when we reach a state, an action is encountered that is not enabled from that state (no outgoing transition exists from the state with that action label), 2) a trace may end without the model reaching the final state. All those traces that are simulated correctly are considered for the second pass, and the rest of the traces are discarded. Additionally, we create a file where the following details are encoded: total number of traces considered, number (percentage) of traces simulated correctly/incorrectly, number of unique traces simulated incorrectly, and a list of these incorrect traces along with their frequencies.

This file can be used to understand and analyze how correctly the learnt model captures the event log. Based on this analysis, the user can fine-tune the

---

[4] The details about this tool can be found at https://www.mcrl2.org/web/user_manual/tools/release/lpsxsim.html.

parameters of the process discovery algorithm, e.g., if the percentage of traces simulated correctly is not to his/her liking or if the user feels that a trace is missing which represents an important behavior. In case the model is able to simulate all the traces, i.e., the log fitness is 100%, the above-mentioned file would not be generated.

As mentioned earlier, we only consider those traces that were simulated correctly by the LTS for calculating the transition probability function. We maintain two counters, one for each time a state is visited in the LTS and one for each transition taken whilst simulating. In this way, at the end, for any state s, we have the number of times it has been visited, say s_n, and the transition counts for each of its outgoing transitions, say $s_{t_1}, s_{t_2} \ldots s_{t_k}$ (where k denotes the number of outgoing transitions from s). Next, the probability associated with each of these transitions is defined as $\frac{s_{t_i}}{s_n}$ ($1 \leq i \leq k$). Note that as $\sum_{j=1}^{k} s_{t_j} = s_n$, the sum of all the outgoing probabilities from each state is 1. Finally, we add a self-loop with probability 1 and action label τ (invisible/internal transition) for the final state.

Models learnt via the Inductive Miner may have τ-labeled transitions in them. Therefore, we need to slightly modify our technique for this case. For instance, consider the trace a, b, c, which can be simulated on an LTS that has the following sequence of activities: $a, \tau, \tau, b, \tau, c$. Here, the state reached after executing action a may not have a b-labeled transition enabled from it, but this does not imply that the trace cannot be simulated correctly. Hence, for such a scenario, we search all possible states that can be reached after performing one or more τ-labeled actions, and check if a b-labeled action is enabled from these states. We recursively check if the trace can be simulated or not in a similar way as discussed above. We deploy the depth-first search (DFS) on the graph generated from the LTS, which is then stored in a separate file (to save the time spent on repeated searches for each log). The DFS may return multiple τ-labeled runs between two states. Therefore, for such cases, we consider the run with the minimum length, and in case if multiple runs of minimum length exist, we consider any one of them. The transition probability function is then computed as discussed in the preceding paragraph.

Next, we can construct the Markovian model where the set of states and actions are the same as that of the LTS. The initial state is also the same as that of the LTS. All this information is encoded into the mCRL2 language such that its associated toolset can be used to generate the corresponding ADTMC model. Note that mCRL2 supports model reduction modulo probabilistic bisimulation which can be used to minimize the size of ADTMC models enabling faster analysis.

3.4   Property Specification Using APCTL/APCTL*

Probabilistic logics for process algebraic systems are either not very expressive, e.g., Hennessy-Milner logic [29, 46] or cannot be intuitively used for specifying interesting compliance, performance and reliability properties due to the presence of fixed-point operators, e.g., probabilistic variants of modal μ-calculus

[33, 40, 43, 44]. Additionally, the tool support for these logics is very limited and is not as efficient as their state-based counterparts. For instance, mCRL2 [10, 21] does not provide support for the model checking of probabilistic and stochastic systems. Similarly, PEPA [20] cannot be used to model check and verify action-based probabilistic logics. In contrast, state-of-the-art tools like PRISM [32] and Storm [16, 26] can be deployed for the efficient verification of probabilistic behavior.

Due to these limitations, we have used APCTL and APCTL* for specifying probabilistic properties. These properties can be transformed into corresponding PCTL and PCTL* formulae, respectively by applying logical embeddings [14, 15], and as a result, can be model checked using PRISM.

3.5   Conversion of Model & Probabilistic Properties to the State-Labeled Domain

We recall the model embedding defined in [13–15], which can be used to construct an SDTMC from an ADTMC. Next, we also present the logical embeddings that allow one to construct an equivalent PCTL property from an APCTL formula [14, 15].

Definition 3 (sld [13, 14]). *Let* $\mathcal{D} = (S, Act, \mathcal{P}, s_0)$ *be an ADTMC. The embedding* sld : $ADTMC \rightarrow SDTMC$ *is formally defined as* $sld(\mathcal{D}) = (S', AP', \mathcal{P}', s_0', L')$ *s.t.*

1. $S' = S \cup \{(a, t) \mid \mathcal{P}(s, a, t) > 0 \text{ for some } s, t \in S \text{ and } a \neq \tau\}$,
2. $AP' = (Act \setminus \{\tau\}) \cup \{\bot\}$ *where* $\bot \notin Act$,
3. *The rate function* $\mathcal{P}'$ *is defined by:*

$$
\begin{aligned}
\mathcal{P}'(s, (a, t)) &= \mathcal{P}(s, a, t) && \text{for all } s, t \in S \text{ s.t. } \mathcal{P}(s, a, t) > 0 \text{ and } a \neq \tau, \\
\mathcal{P}'(s, t) &= \mathcal{P}(s, \tau, t) && \text{for all } s, t \in S \text{ s.t. } \mathcal{P}(s, \tau, t) > 0, \text{ and} \\
\mathcal{P}'((a, t), t) &= 1 && \text{for all } (a, t) \in S' \setminus S,
\end{aligned}
$$

4. $s_0' = s_0$, *and*
5. $L'(s) = \{\bot\} \ \forall s \in S \text{ and } L'((a, t)) = \{a\}$.

The upper bounds on the number of states and transitions in the embedded model as compared to the original model have been discussed in [13].

Given an ADTMC $\mathcal{D}$ and an APCTL formula Φ, the logical embedding $sldl'$ constructs an equivalent PCTL property which can be interpreted over the embedded SDTMC, i.e. $sld(\mathcal{D})$. We define the embedding $sldl' : APCTL \rightarrow PCTL$ inductively as follows :

$$sldl'(\mathbf{true}) \qquad\qquad =\mathbf{true};$$
$$sldl'(\neg\Phi) \qquad\qquad =\neg sldl'(\Phi);$$
$$sldl'(\Phi \wedge \Phi') \qquad\qquad =sldl'(\Phi) \wedge sldl'(\Phi');$$
$$sldl'(\mathcal{P}_J(\mathbf{X}_\chi\Phi)) \qquad =\mathcal{P}_J(\mathbf{X}(\neg\bot \wedge \chi \wedge \mathcal{P}_{[1,1]}(\mathbf{X}(\bot \wedge sldl'(\Phi)))));$$
$$sldl'(\mathcal{P}_J(\mathbf{X}_\tau\Phi)) \qquad =(\bot \wedge \mathcal{P}_J(\mathbf{X}(\bot \wedge sldl'(\Phi))));$$
$$sldl'(\mathcal{P}_J(\Phi_\chi\mathbf{U}\Phi')) \quad =\mathcal{P}_J(((\bot \wedge sldl'(\Phi)) \vee (\neg\bot \wedge \chi))\mathbf{U}(\bot \wedge sldl'(\Phi'))); \text{ and}$$
$$sldl'(\mathcal{P}_J(\Phi_\chi\mathbf{U}_{\chi'}\Phi')) \quad =\mathcal{P}_J(((\bot \wedge sldl'(\Phi)) \vee (\neg\bot \wedge \chi))\mathbf{U}((\neg\bot \wedge \chi')\wedge$$
$$\mathcal{P}_{[1,1]}(\mathbf{X}(\bot \wedge sldl'(\Phi'))))).$$

A similar logical embedding, i.e., $sldl$ can be found in [14] for transforming an APCTL* formula to a PCTL* formula.

3.6 Model Checking SDTMCs

We have automated the process of converting an ADTMC model encoded in mCRL2 to its corresponding SDTMC using the definition of sld (from Definition 3). The output SDTMC is obtained in two formats which are both compatible with the PRISM model checker [32]. We translate the original properties specified using APCTL/APCTL* to PCTL/PCTL* by hand using the logical embeddings, and then model check these properties on the PRISM toolset.

Note that the result computed by the PRISM model checker reflects the probability of a pattern or trend occurring in an event log. In case there is no repetition of events in the event log, this probability will exactly match the proportion of traces where such a trend occurs.

Implementation Details: The event log is assumed to be in the XES format [1]. This is not a limitation, as there are plugins in the ProM toolset that can be used to convert event logs given in other formats to XES. The reachability graph is exported from the ProM toolset as a 'Petrify SG file'. It is also assumed that the start and end event(s) are known for the event logs. The event log in XES format, the reachability graph from ProM, and the information regarding the start and end events are given as input to our code. The code is written in the Python programming language implemented in the Jupyter Notebook. There are two variants of the code, one for the Alpha Miner and the other for the Inductive Miner. Each variant has three modules:

1. The first module converts the reachability graph obtained from the ProM toolset to an LTS file that is compatible with the mCRL2 toolset. For the case of Inductive Miner, this module also stores the DFS traversal of all the states that can perform one or more τ-transitions.
2. The second module pre-processes the event log file to infer the traces. For the case where simulated event logs need to be used, the output of the simulation of the LTSs obtained at the end of the previous step on the mCRL2 toolset is considered. These traces are then simulated on the model to classify them

204 S. Das and A. Sharma

as either correct or incorrect. The ones simulated correctly are then used to calculate the probabilities of the transitions. Information regarding the incorrectly simulated traces is saved in a new file.

3. The third and final module of the code saves the ADTMC model as an mCRL2 file, converts the ADTMC to an SDTMC using the model embeddings, and outputs the SDTMC model compatible with the PRISM model checker.

4 Case Studies

This section focuses on validating the efficacy of our approach by applying it to several interesting case studies from different application domains. The detailed report of our experiments, including the replication package can be found in this repository[5]. Additional details regarding the code and the probabilistic properties for every case study can be found in the appendix. Note that we have considered the activity names while learning the process models, and therefore, in all the formulas, every activity name, say α, should be interpreted as $\alpha_{complete}$, which denotes the completion of the life-cycle of the event. Accordingly, the event log for the last three case studies was filtered to retain only those activities that denote that the corresponding events have been completed.

4.1 Small Process

In order to manually check the correctness of our approach, we first consider a very small event log with only 6 traces. The traces of this log are as follows: 1) a, b, d, c, f, 2) a, c, b, d, f, 3) a, c, d, b, f, 4) a, d, e, f, 5) a, b, c, d, f, and 6) a, e, d, f. The start event is a, and the end event is f. As discussed earlier, two sets of models were generated, one for the original event log from which the process was mined, and the other one for the simulated event log generated by simulating the LTS in the mCRL2 toolset. Each set had three models corresponding to the Alpha and Inductive Miner with 0 and 0.2 (IMf variant) as noise thresholds, respectively. We have model checked the following properties:

1. What is the probability of reaching a state via activity f? This property can be encoded in APCTL as follows:

$$\mathcal{P}_{=?}(\mathbf{true_{true}U}_f\mathbf{true})$$

This APCTL formula can be transformed into a corresponding PCTL formula by applying the logical embeddings $sldl'$:

$$\mathcal{P}_{=?}(((\bot \wedge \mathbf{true}) \vee (\neg\bot \wedge \mathbf{true}))\mathbf{U}((\neg\bot \wedge f) \wedge \mathcal{P}_{[1,1]}(\mathbf{X}(\bot \wedge \mathbf{true}))))$$
$$\equiv \mathcal{P}_{=?}((\mathbf{true})\mathbf{U}((\neg\bot \wedge f) \wedge \mathcal{P}_{[1,1]}(\mathbf{X}(\bot))))$$

---

[5] https://github.com/susmoyd21/Probabilistic_Verification_Process_Models/.

Here, $\equiv$ denote that the formula on the left and the right side evaluate to the same value for all the scenarios. The above formula must always evaluate to 1 across all the models as f is the final event in the event log. This was verified on the PRISM model checker for all the models.

2. What is the probability that activity b is not present in the trace? The specification can be encoded in APCTL as follows:

$$\mathcal{P}_{=?}(\mathbf{true}_{\neg b}\mathbf{U}_f\mathbf{true})$$

Due to space limitations, we do not show the transformation of action-based properties to state-based properties via embeddings $sldl$ and $sldl'$. For the models learnt via the original event log, if the model allows both the traces which satisfy this behavior from a total of six traces, the probability must be evaluated to 0.33. PRISM verified this for all the models learnt via the original event log. The values for the models learnt via simulating LTS, i.e., simulated event log were 0.3 for the Alpha Miner and 0.5 for both the Inductive Miners.

3. What is the probability that activity b (if it occurs) is always succeeded by d? The property can be specified in APCTL* as follows:

$$\mathcal{P}_{=?}((\mathbf{X}_b\mathbf{true} \rightarrow \mathbf{X}_b(\mathbf{true}_{\mathrm{false}}\mathbf{U}_d\mathbf{true}))_{\mathrm{true}}\mathbf{U}_f\mathbf{true})$$

Note that, the clause $(\mathbf{true}_{\mathrm{false}}\mathbf{U}_d\mathbf{true})$ can be simplified to $\mathbf{X}_d\mathbf{true}$ for LTSs which do not have any τ-transitions. Since such transitions may be present, the above-mentioned formula rightly captures the scenario where b is followed by zero or more τ transitions before executing activity d. For example, we should be able to capture not only those traces that have the following pattern b, d, but also traces like b, τ, d, and b, τ, τ, d etc. Note that only four traces (two in which b never occurs and two in which b is followed by d) in the original event log follow the above-mentioned pattern, and hence this should return 0.67. This was verified using the PRISM model checker.

4. What is the probability that the event b occurs (certainly) and is always succeeded by d? The property can be specified in APCTL* as follows:

$$\mathcal{P}_{=?}(\mathbf{true}_{\mathrm{true}}\mathbf{U}_b(\mathbf{true}_{\mathrm{false}}\mathbf{U}_d(\mathbf{true}_{\mathrm{true}}\mathbf{U}_f\mathbf{true})))$$

This is different from the previous query as we now consider only those run(s) in which the event b occurs. Since there are only 2 traces which satisfy this property, the answer should be 0.33. This was verified using the PRISM model checker for all the models learnt via the original event log.

5. From any point in the model reached after the event d, what is the average probability that the final event f occurs in the next state? The APCTL formula corresponding to the above specification is as follows:

$$\mathcal{P}_{=?}(\mathbf{true}_{\mathrm{false}}\mathbf{U}_f\mathbf{true})$$

We use the 'filter' functionality of the PRISM model checker to evaluate this query. The terms, i.e., average, maximum, and minimum probabilities used in the context of probabilistic properties refer to the average, the maximum, and the minimum, respectively calculated over all the probability value(s) obtained across all the state(s) that satisfy the condition, e.g., in this case, all states reached after the event d. The values are 0.25 for the model corresponding to Alpha Miner and 0.4 for the Inductive Miners, respectively (for both the old and the simulated event logs).

4.2 Loan Application Process

The loan application process [9] is a structured framework that outlines the step-by-step sequence of activities and interactions involved in processing a loan application. It visualizes the entire loan application journey, depicting each stage from the initial customer inquiry to the final loan approval or rejection, followed by notification of the decision. It enhances transparency and clarity by providing a clear road map for the applicants and the staff, and reduces ambiguity and potential misunderstandings. It also helps in optimizing and streamlining the process by identifying bottlenecks, redundancies, or unnecessary delays, thus improving efficiency and reducing the processing time. It facilitates effective communication among various stakeholders, such as applicants, loan officers, underwriters, and compliance teams, and ensures that everyone is aligned and informed. Hence, analysing such a process model is pivotal in maintaining consistency, minimizing errors, and enhancing customer satisfaction. We considered two (old) event logs, one with fewer traces, i.e., 62 (Log 1), and the other one with 100 traces (Log 2), for learning the process models. All the event logs start with registering the application and end with the decision on the application being emailed to the customers. The Petri Nets learned via Log 1 corresponding to the Alpha Miner and the Inductive Miner are shown in Fig. 2 and Fig. 3 respectively. We have analysed the following properties:

1. The decision on the application is always intimated.
2. Was a decision on the application made without checking the credit? If yes, what is the probability that this occurs?
3. Was a decision on the application made without checking the system? If yes, what is the probability that this occurs?
4. What is the probability that check credit (if it occurred) is immediately followed by capacity calculation?
5. What is the probability that capacity calculation immediately follows check credit?
6. What is the probability that capacity is calculated before making either of the checks?
7. What is the probability that a loan application is accepted or rejected?
8. What is the probability that a loan application was accepted or rejected, given that the capacity calculation was performed before the checks?

The results of these properties/queries for Log 1 and Log 2 have been shown in Table 1, and Table 2, respectively. Here, 'Inductive 1' refers to the process

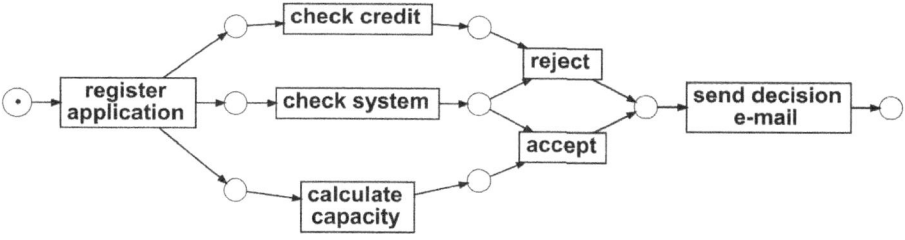

Fig. 2. Process Model learnt via Alpha Miner for the Loan Application Process Event Log (Log 1).

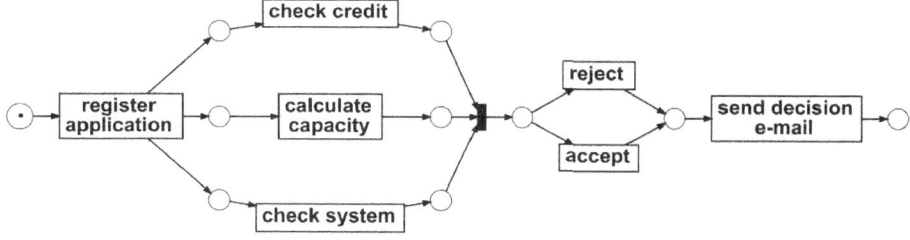

Fig. 3. Process Model learnt via Inductive Miner for the Loan Application Process Event Log (Log 1).

model learnt via the Inductive Miner, and 'Inductive 2' refers to the process model learnt using the 'IMf' variant of the Inductive Miner with a noise threshold of 0.2.

For Prop. 2, and the model learnt via the Alpha Miner (see Table 1), the simulated event log has a non-zero value (0.04). This essentially means that the behavior where the decision on the loan application was made without checking the credit was also present in the simulated event log. Note that this type of behavior did not exist in the original event log. From Table 2, we can observe that the process models learnt with 0 noise threshold, i.e., Inductive 1 allow the behavior where the decision on an application could be taken without checking the system (Prop. 3). Additionally, for the Inductive 1 model learnt via the original event log, 100% of the logs could be simulated on the model compared to 90% for the other two, i.e., Alpha and Inductive 2. This also demonstrates that improving the fitness may result in the introduction of outlier/bad behavior in the model. Note that the sum of the probability values corresponding to an acceptance and the rejection for Prop. 8 should match the value obtained in Prop. 6. This is indeed the case for all the models shown in Table 1 and Table 2.

Table 1. Loan Application Process (Log 1)

Prop.	Original Event Log			Simulated Event Log		
	Alpha	Inductive 1	Inductive 2	Alpha	Inductive 1	Inductive 2
1	1.0	1.0	1.0	1.0	1.0	1.0
2	0.0	0.0	0.0	**0.04**	0.0	0.0
3	0.0	0.0	0.0	0.0	0.0	0.0
4	0.71	0.71	0.71	0.32	0.33	0.33
5	0.71	0.71	0.71	0.28	0.33	0.33
6	0.03	0.03	0.03	0.33	0.33	0.33
7	0.29/0.71	0.29/0.71	0.29/0.71	0.49/0.51	0.5/0.5	0.5/0.5
8	0.01/0.02	0.01/0.02	0.01/0.02	0.2/0.13	0.17/0.16	0.16/0.17

Table 2. Loan Application Process (Log 2)

Prop.	Original Event Log			Simulated Event Log		
	Alpha	Inductive 1	Inductive 2	Alpha	Inductive 1	Inductive 2
1	1.0	1.0	1.0	1.0	1.0	1.0
2	0.0	0.0	0.0	0.0	0.0	0.0
3	0.0	**0.01**	0.0	0.0	**0.5**	0.0
4	0.51	0.54	0.51	0.34	0.42	0.33
5	0.51	0.54	0.51	0.34	0.42	0.33
6	0.02	0.04	0.02	0.33	0.37	0.33
7	0.21/0.79	0.2/0.8	0.21/0.79	0.5/0.5	0.51/0.49	0.5/0.5
8	0.0/0.02	0.01/0.03	0.0/0.02	0.16/0.17	0.19/0.18	0.16/0.17

4.3   Manuscript Review Process

The case study for the manuscript review [2] aims to discover a structured and systematic approach to evaluate the academic and scientific papers submitted for publication[6]. The process model should learn to encompass a series of well-defined stages that manuscripts undergo before being accepted for publication in journals or conferences. With a focus on optimizing efficiency and maintaining rigorous quality standards, the learnt process model must also offer several distinct advantages that contribute to advancing knowledge and disseminating valuable research.

The event logs include activities like inviting the reviewers, following which, if a reviewer does not respond within a stipulated time, it is denoted as a time-

---

[6] https://processmining.org/old-version/event-book.html.

out. Similarly, if the review is received, it is denoted as get-review. This is succeeded by the decision phase, where additional reviewer(s) may be invited, or the manuscript may be accepted or rejected. The additional reviewer functions analogous to other reviewers, i.e., can either submit the review or time-out. We learnt process models from an event log with 10000 traces. All the traces start with inviting reviewers and end with accepting or rejecting the manuscript. We would like to analyse the following properties of the model:

1. A decision (accept/reject) on the manuscript is always made.
2. What is the probability that none of the original reviewers timed out while submitting the reviews?
3. What is the probability that the decision phase is reached without a single review from the original reviewers?
4. What is the probability that an additional reviewer will be invited to decide on the paper?
5. What is the probability that a manuscript will be accepted or rejected?
6. What is the probability that manuscripts that did not require an additional reviewer were accepted or rejected?

The results of the above queries have been shown in Table 3. We have used the 'Alpha++' miner to discover the model as the reachability graph corresponding to the Alpha Miner exceeded 25000 states. The variant of Inductive miner, i.e., IMf has learnt the model with a noise threshold of 0.15. We observe that the manuscripts were accepted or rejected with nearly the same probability (Prop. 5). In around 9–12% of the instances across all the models, all the original reviewers submitted their reviews without being timed out (Prop. 2). Similarly, in around 11–13% of the instances across all the models, the decision phase of an article was reached where no reviews were submitted (Prop. 3). Additional reviewers were always required for the Inductive 2 model; they were not required for very few cases (less than 20% of the cases) in the models learnt via the original event logs (Prop. 4) using Alpha++ and Inductive 1. In contrast, for models learnt via the simulated event log, more than half of the instances showed no requirement for an additional reviewer (67% and 50%, respectively) for the models learnt via Alpha++ and Inductive 1. Finally, the last query informs us that the invitation to an additional reviewer does not affect the acceptance-to-rejection ratio, which remains nearly 50–50 (Prop. 6).

Note that, in this case study, events may repeat during the course of a trace, like inviting an additional reviewer, which may occur multiple times during the review process of a submission. In our methodology, the probability that an event follows another event denotes the number of times this sequence takes place divided by the total number of times the first event occurs. This value will reflect the proportion of traces where such a scenario happens only if events occur exactly once during a trace. Whereas, for event logs in which events are allowed to repeat themselves, this probability value reflects the number of times such a pattern occurs divided by the total number of times the first event occurs in the entire event log, which may not be equal to the number of traces, as in this case study.

Table 3. Manuscript Review Process

Prop.	Original Event Log			Simulated Event Log		
	Alpha++	Inductive 1	Inductive 2	Alpha++	Inductive 1	Inductive 2
1	1.0	1.0	1.0	1.0	1.0	1.0
2	0.11	0.11	0.09	0.12	0.12	0.12
3	0.11	0.11	0.13	0.13	0.13	0.12
4	0.81	0.94	1.0	0.33	0.50	1.0
5	0.51/0.49	0.51/0.49	0.51/0.49	0.5/0.5	0.48/0.52	0.5/0.5
6	0.1/0.09	0.03/0.03	0.0/0.0	0.33/0.33	0.25/0.26	0.0/0.0

Reward Based Analysis: In SDTMCs, one can also assign the reward structures [6,8]. This allows us to calculate the expected rewards collected while reaching a set of goal states from the initial state. For example, using rewards we can calculate the expected number of 'time-outs' during a review process. This would allow us to know the following: on an average how much time gets wasted due to time-outs-related delays? We have manually assigned a reward of 1 to all the states labeled as 'time-out', and calculated the expected value of this reward while reaching the final state, i.e., either the accept state or the reject state in the model. The query was R{"TIMEOUT"}=?[F ("accept"|"reject"))]. The results of this query for the models learnt via the original event log and the Alpha, Inductive 1, and Inductive 2 were 3.59, 3.59, and 3.67, respectively.

4.4   Telephone Repair Process

In this process, a telephone repair company addresses phone defects through a systematic process[7]. It commences with the customer registering their faulty phone, after which the device undergoes the problem detection and analysis phases. The defect is then categorized, and the phone is routed to the Repair department. A notification letter is also dispatched to the customer, providing the details about the issue with the phone. Two specialized teams are deployed within the Repair department: one handles all the simple defects, while the other one deals with the complex defects. Some defects may fall within the purview of both these teams. Once a repair technician completes his/her work of repairing the phone, it undergoes a thorough quality assurance assessment. A dedicated employee examines the device to confirm the successful resolution of the defect. If the issue remains unresolved, the phone is returned for further repair attempts. On the other hand, if the repair is successful, the case is archived, and the phone is promptly returned to the customer.

To optimize the efficiency and reduce the turnaround time, the repair company restricts the number of repair attempts for a given defect. If the defect still persists after these attempts are over, the case is archived, and a brand-new

---

[7] https://www.xes-standard.org/certification:logs:artificial.

device is dispatched to the customer. There are 1000 traces in the original event log, starting with registering the device and ending with archiving the repair. We have model checked the following properties:

1. What is the probability that a telephone only went for a simple/complex repair or no repair at all?
2. What is the probability that the user is informed before testing any repairs on the telephone?
3. What is the probability that a repair must be restarted along its journey from the start to finish?
4. After a complex repair is done, what is the maximum probability that it is tested and the repair is archived subsequently?
5. After a repair is tested, what is the average probability that the order is immediately archived?

The construction of the reachability graph by the ProM toolset on the Petri Net learnt via the Alpha algorithm was aborted automatically when it exceeded $25,000$ states. Therefore, in Table 4, we present the results for those models that were learnt via the 'Alpha#' algorithm, the Inductive Miner and its IMf variant with a noise threshold of 0.2. The last two properties are different from the other properties as they do not reason over the whole system starting from the initial state. Instead, the results are computed from specific states in the model that can be uniquely identified.

Table 4. Telephone Repair Process

Prop.	Original Event Log			Simulated Event Log		
	Alpha#	Inductive 1	Inductive 2	Alpha#	Inductive 1	Inductive 2
1	0.43/0.41	0.38/0.45	0.43/0.41	0.45/0.45	0.22/0.23	0.31/0.3
2	0.66	0.64	0.66	0.67	0.45	0.66
3	0.28	0.28	0.28	0.38	0.71	0.58
4	0.79	0.61	0.79	0.26	0.06	0.5
5	0.39	0.31	0.39	0.26	0.12	0.25

For Prop. 1, one can check that in the case of Inductive 1 with the original event log, more telephones were only sent for the complex repairs (0.38/0.45), as compared to all the other models learnt via original event log where a reverse trend can be observed. Note that the results for the simple and complex repair are very similar for all the models learnt via the simulated event log. In nearly 64–66% of the cases learnt using the original event log, the user was intimated before testing of any of the repairs was started (Prop. 2). The trend is similar in the simulated event log as well with one exception, i.e., Inductive 1 model where the value is 0.45. Restarting the repair work (Prop. 3) is required for fewer instances in the original event log (0.28), as compared to the simulated event log. This may be alarming and needs to addressed. After a complex repair, it would be likely that a test follows, and then it is archived either as fixed or as not fixable. Models learnt from original event logs show higher maximum probability (at least 60% for Prop. 4). After testing the repair, one of the following three actions can be taken in the LTSs: 1) informing the user or 2) restarting the repair or 3) archiving the repair. We see a higher average probability (31–39%) for the models learnt via original event log as compared to the models learnt via simulated event logs (12–26%) (Prop. 5).

4.5   Claim Settlement Process

The claim settlement process is a meticulously structured series of steps designed to ensure a fair and efficient resolution of claims, with the goal to provide rightful compensation while maintaining the integrity of the insurance system. The process begins with a thorough review of the information submitted by the claimant. This information includes details about the incident, supporting documentation, and any other pertinent data. Insurer carefully examines whether the provided information is complete, and meets the initial requirements for the claim consideration. Once the initial information has been checked, the claim is officially registered in the insurer's system. In the next stage, insurer assesses the validity of the claim based on the terms and conditions of the insurance policy. Insurer examines the policy type, coverage limits, and any exclusions that might apply to the specific circumstances of the claim. Claims are then subjected to a detailed assessment to ascertain their authenticity and accuracy. Insurance professionals investigate the incident further, and if required may recommend conducting interviews, inspections, or consultations with the domain experts. The aim is to comprehensively understand the event, and its impact to arrive at a fair and justified compensation amount. Once the validity of the claim has been established, and the assessment is complete, the insurance company calculates the appropriate compensation amount. The claim is officially closed after the compensation amount has been processed and disbursed to the claimant. The original event log has 132 traces. We have model checked the following properties:

1. What is the probability that sufficient information is unavailable in a case?
2. What is the probability that the claim is not assessed?
3. What is the probability that the claim was not assessed, given it was already registered?
4. What is the probability that the payment was initiated on a claim?
5. What is the probability that the claimant was not notified of the reimbursement after initiating the payment?
6. What is the probability that the claimant is notified of the reimbursement before the payment was initiated?

The results of all the queries have been presented in Table 5. The reachability graphs of process models learnt via the Alpha Miner and its variants were not able to capture enough traces for the analysis. Hence, we present the results

Table 5. Claim Settlement Process

Prop.	Original Event Log		Simulated Event Log	
	Inductive 1	Inductive 2	Inductive 1	Inductive 2
1	0.13	0.0	0.5	0.0
2	0.25	0.0	0.76	0.0
3	0.12	0.0	0.26	0.0
4	0.42	0.23	0.75	0.5
5	0.36	0.48	0.12	0.26
6	0.36	0.48	0.12	0.26

only for the Inductive Miner and its variants; all the parameters remain the same as in the previous case study. Note that the Inductive 2 model does not allow the claimants to submit the forms containing insufficient information, but Inductive 1 does allow this behavior (Prop. 1). Inductive 2 also does not allow the claims to go unassessed. In contrast, Inductive 1 does allow this behavior for the original event log (Prop. 2). This may be alarming as it happens in 25% of the cases in the original event log. The probability to initiate the payment is almost twice in the simulated event log as compared to the original event log (Prop. 4). We wish to compute the probability that the claimant was not notified of the reimbursement after initiating the payment (Prop. 5). The results can be seen in Table 5. Next, we wish to examine the probability that it was done before the payment was initiated (Prop. 6). We found out that this query returns the same value as that of Prop. 5 for the original event log, i.e., 0.36 and 0.48. The same pattern is observed for the simulated event log, i.e., 0.12 and 0.26. This implies that the notification was sent before initiating the payment in all those cases where the claimant was not notified after the payment. This behavior should be discouraged and ideally the result of Prop. 5, and Prop. 6 should be 0, i.e., claimants should always be notified after the payment was initiated. We also see a decrease in these probability values for the models learnt using the simulated event log, i.e., 0.12 and 0.26. These values can be plotted over the years to identify the hidden trends/patterns, and accordingly the corrective measures should be taken.

5   Related Work

In the qualitative setting, a formal approach for automated compliance checking using model checking has been proposed in [30,31]. Authors have proposed a translation scheme from BPMN process models to Kripke structures (KSs), and have formalized compliance rules using Linear Temporal Logic (LTL) formulae. In the last step, model checking has been deployed to check if the process model satisfies the compliance rule. In the quantitative setting, a model checking based approach for the analysis of IEC 61499 application has been proposed in [19]. This work involves transforming IEC 61499 to LTS which in turn has been transformed into a Probabilistic Transition System (PTS) using the set of traces collected by monitoring the application. The authors have used the CADP model checker for the verification of quantitative properties. A similar approach for the probabilistic model checking of BPMN processes at runtime has been proposed in [18]. This approach also involves transforming BPMN to LTS, and LTS into PTS by using the set of execution traces obtained by applying the monitoring techniques. In [50], authors utilize process mining techniques along with simulations to learn colored Petri nets which are then used for further analysis. Another approach for modeling and analysis of real-world business workflows using stochastic model checking has been proposed in [27,28].

Unlike the above-mentioned works which mainly focus on the qualitative/qua-ntitative verification of BPMN processes, we focus on the problem of quantitative compliance checking and reliability evaluation of process models learnt by applying process mining on the event logs. We have proposed an integrated tool framework based on the probabilistic model and logical embeddings, and validated our approach on several interesting case studies. The only other work which comes close to our research is [42], where a model checking based approach for the qualitative compliance checking of process models (LTSs) learnt via process mining has been proposed. In order to tackle the state space explosion problem, authors have also applied abstraction techniques based on the set of temporal logic formulae, which has been subsequently used to describe the system behavior in LOTOS.

Besides these, there have been numerous attempts to incorporate time and stochastic aspects of event logs in both the process model discovery and conformance checking measures. In [49], authors present and evaluate process discovery algorithms based on the notion of alignments using raw event execution data to discover various classes of Stochastic Petri nets. Several process mining techniques focus on extracting stochastic process models from event logs [11,12,41]. Stochastic conformance checking techniques can assess how well the discovered models describe the relative likelihood of traces recorded in the log or how well they represent the likelihood of future traces generated by the same system. Additionally, stochastic information can be used by researchers to obtain actionable insights on conformance related issues that are rare. Therefore, various stochastic conformance checking techniques have been proposed in the literature [34,37–39].

6   Conclusion

This paper proposed an integrated tool framework that enables one to verify the performance related properties, and execute quantitative temporal compliance checking of process models discovered using process mining algorithms. Our approach can also be used for event log filtering by identifying important threshold values. We have used probabilistic model checking, combined with model and logical embeddings to verify the process behavior. We have demonstrated the usefulness of our approach by applying it to several interesting case studies from different application domains. This research work can be extended in several interesting directions which are as follows:

- Since the probabilities may vary across models generated by different process mining algorithms, it is important to simulate existing probabilistic models for generating event logs which can then be used as an input for process mining algorithms. This would enable us to evaluate the same set of probabilistic properties on both the original model and the probabilistic process models extracted from different process mining algorithms using our framework. Additionally, this would allow us to recommend process mining algorithms for the performance evaluation, and quantitative compliance checking of process models based on the application domain;
- Investigate the possibility of extending this framework such that step-bounded and reward-based properties can be directly verified, e.g., a pattern of events emerge within k steps or the expected cumulative cost;
- The application of probabilistic model checking for event log filtering and its impact on reducing the size of the LTS model learnt by applying process mining needs to be studied in detail; and
- Extend this framework to those classes of models that support stochastic behavior.

Acknowledgment. The authors would like to acknowledge support from the Science and Education Research Board (SERB), Department of Science and Technology (DST), India, under Grant No: CRG/2023/001847.

References

1. IEEE standard for eXtensible Event Stream (XES) for Achieving Interoperability in Event Logs and Event Streams. IEEE STD 1849-2016, pp. 1–50 (2016)
2. van der Aalst, W.: Synthetic event logs - review example large.xes.gz (2010). https://doi.org/10.4121/UUID:DA6AAFEF-5A86-4769-ACF3-04E8AE5AB4FE. https://data.4tu.nl/articles/_/12716609/1
3. van der Aalst, W.M.P.: Process Mining - Data Science in Action, 2nd edn. Springer, Heidelberg (2016). https://doi.org/10.1007/978-3-662-49851-4
4. van der Aalst, W.M.P., van Dongen, B.F., Günther, C.W., Rozinat, A., Verbeek, E., Weijters, T.: Prom: the process mining toolkit. In: Proceedings of the Business Process Management Demonstration Track (BPMDemos 2009), Ulm, Germany, 8 September 2009 (2009)
5. van der Aalst, W.M.P., Weijters, T., Maruster, L.: Workflow mining: discovering process models from event logs. IEEE Trans. Knowl. Data Eng. **16**(9), 1128–1142 (2004)
6. Andova, S., Hermanns, H., Katoen, J.-P.: Discrete-time rewards model-checked. In: Larsen, K.G., Niebert, P. (eds.) FORMATS 2003. LNCS, vol. 2791, pp. 88–104. Springer, Heidelberg (2004). https://doi.org/10.1007/978-3-540-40903-8_8
7. Aziz, A., Singhal, V., Balarin, F., Brayton, R.K., Sangiovanni-Vincentelli, A.L.: It usually works: the temporal logic of stochastic systems. In: Wolper, P. (ed.) CAV 1995. LNCS, vol. 939, pp. 155–165. Springer, Heidelberg (1995). https://doi.org/10.1007/3-540-60045-0_48

8. Baier, C., Katoen, J.P.: Principles of Model Checking. MIT Press, Cambridge (2008)

9. Buijs, J.: Loan application example, configuration 1 (2013). https://doi.org/10.4121/UUID:CDF3BA31-291D-468D-9712-3A58AC6DA3FC. https://data.4tu.nl/articles/_/12715685/1

10. Bunte, O., et al.: The mCRL2 toolset for analysing concurrent systems. In: Vojnar, T., Zhang, L. (eds.) TACAS 2019. LNCS, vol. 11428, pp. 21–39. Springer, Cham (2019). https://doi.org/10.1007/978-3-030-17465-1_2

11. Burke, A., Leemans, S.J.J., Wynn, M.T.: Stochastic process discovery by weight estimation. In: Leemans, S., Leopold, H. (eds.) ICPM 2020. LNBIP, vol. 406, pp. 260–272. Springer, Cham (2021). https://doi.org/10.1007/978-3-030-72693-5_20

12. Burke, A., Leemans, S.J.J., Wynn, M.T.: Discovering stochastic process models by reduction and abstraction. In: Buchs, D., Carmona, J. (eds.) PETRI NETS 2021. LNCS, vol. 12734, pp. 312–336. Springer, Cham (2021). https://doi.org/10.1007/978-3-030-76983-3_16

13. Das, S., Sharma, A.: Embeddings between state and action labeled probabilistic systems. In: SAC 2021: The 36th ACM/SIGAPP Symposium on Applied Computing, Virtual Event, Republic of Korea, 22–26 March 2021, pp. 1759–1767 (2021)

14. Das, S., Sharma, A.: Embeddings between state and action based probabilistic logics. In: Tapia Tarifa, S.L., Proença, J. (eds.) FACS 2022. LNCS, vol. 13712, pp. 121–140. Springer, Cham (2022). https://doi.org/10.1007/978-3-031-20872-0_8

15. Das, S., Sharma, A.: On the use of model and logical embeddings for model checking of probabilistic systems. In: Huisman, M., Ravara, A. (eds.) FORTE 2023. LNCS, vol. 13910, pp. 115–131. Springer, Cham (2023). https://doi.org/10.1007/978-3-031-35355-0_8

16. Dehnert, C., Junges, S., Katoen, J.-P., Volk, M.: A storm is coming: a modern probabilistic model checker. In: Majumdar, R., Kunčak, V. (eds.) CAV 2017. LNCS, vol. 10427, pp. 592–600. Springer, Cham (2017). https://doi.org/10.1007/978-3-319-63390-9_31

17. Dumas, M., Rosa, M.L., Mendling, J., Reijers, H.A.: Fundamentals of Business Process Management, 2nd edn. Springer, Heidelberg (2018). https://doi.org/10.1007/978-3-662-56509-4

18. Falcone, Y., Salaün, G., Zuo, A.: Probabilistic model checking of BPMN processes at runtime. In: ter Beek, M.H., Monahan, R. (eds.) IFM 2022. LNCS, vol. 13274, pp. 191–208. Springer, Cham (2022). https://doi.org/10.1007/978-3-031-07727-2_11

19. Faqrizal, I., Salaün, G., Falcone, Y.: Probabilistic analysis of industrial IoT applications. In: Proceedings of the 12th International Conference on the Internet of Things, IoT 2022, Delft, The Netherlands, 7–10 November 2022, pp. 41–48 (2022)

20. Gilmore, S., Hillston, J.: The PEPA workbench: a tool to support a process algebra-based approach to performance modelling. In: Haring, G., Kotsis, G. (eds.) TOOLS 1994. LNCS, vol. 794, pp. 353–368. Springer, Heidelberg (1994). https://doi.org/10.1007/3-540-58021-2_20

21. Groote, J.F., Keiren, J.J.A., Luttik, B., de Vink, E.P., Willemse, T.A.C.: Modelling and analysing software in mCRL2. In: Arbab, F., Jongmans, S.-S. (eds.) FACS 2019. LNCS, vol. 12018, pp. 25–48. Springer, Cham (2020). https://doi.org/10.1007/978-3-030-40914-2_2

22. Groote, J.F., Mousavi, M.R.: Modeling and Analysis of Communicating Systems. MIT Press, Cambridge (2014)

23. Groote, J.F., Willemse, T.A.C.: Real equation systems with alternating fixed-points. In: Pérez, G.A., Raskin, J.F. (eds.) 34th International Conference on Concurrency Theory (CONCUR 2023). Leibniz International Proceedings in Informatics (LIPIcs), vol. 279, pp. 28:1–28:17. Schloss Dagstuhl – Leibniz-Zentrum für Informatik, Dagstuhl, Germany (2023)

24. Hand, D.J., Smyth, P., Mannila, H.: Principles of Data Mining. MIT Press, Cambridge (2001)

25. Hansson, H., Jonsson, B.: A logic for reasoning about time and reliability. Formal Asp. Comput. **6**(5), 512–535 (1994)

26. Hensel, C., Junges, S., Katoen, J., Quatmann, T., Volk, M.: The probabilistic model checker storm. Int. J. Softw. Tools Technol. Transf. **24**(4), 589–610 (2022)

27. Herbert, L., Sharp, R.: Using stochastic model checking to provision complex business services. In: 14th International IEEE Symposium on High-Assurance Systems Engineering, HASE 2012, Omaha, NE, USA, 25–27 October 2012, pp. 98–105. IEEE Computer Society (2012)

28. Herbert, L., Sharp, R.: Precise quantitative analysis of probabilistic business process model and notation workflows. J. Comput. Inf. Sci. Eng. **13**(1) (2013)

29. Hermanns, H., Parma, A., Segala, R., Wachter, B., Zhang, L.: Probabilistic logical characterization. Inf. Comput. **209**(2), 154–172 (2011)

30. Kherbouche, O.M., Ahmad, A., Basson, H.: Formal approach for compliance rules checking in business process models. In: 2013 IEEE 9th International Conference on Emerging Technologies (ICET), pp. 1–6 (2013)

31. Kherbouche, O.M., Ahmad, A., Basson, H.: Using model checking to control the structural errors in BPMN models. In: Wieringa, R.J., Nurcan, S., Rolland, C., Cavarero, J. (eds.) IEEE 7th International Conference on Research Challenges in Information Science, RCIS 2013, Paris, France, 29–31 May 2013, pp. 1–12. IEEE (2013)

32. Kwiatkowska, M., Norman, G., Parker, D.: PRISM 4.0: verification of probabilistic real-time systems. In: Gopalakrishnan, G., Qadeer, S. (eds.) CAV 2011. LNCS, vol. 6806, pp. 585–591. Springer, Heidelberg (2011). https://doi.org/10.1007/978-3-642-22110-1_47

33. Larsen, K.G., Mardare, R., Xue, B.: Probabilistic mu-calculus: decidability and complete axiomatization. In: 36th IARCS Annual Conference on Foundations of Software Technology and Theoretical Computer Science, FSTTCS 2016, 13–15 December 2016, Chennai, India. LIPIcs, vol. 65, pp. 25:1–25:18. Schloss Dagstuhl - Leibniz-Zentrum für Informatik (2016)

34. Leemans, S.J.J., van der Aalst, W.M.P., Brockhoff, T., Polyvyanyy, A.: Stochastic process mining: earth movers' stochastic conformance. Inf. Syst. **102**, 101724 (2021)

35. Leemans, S.J.J., Fahland, D., van der Aalst, W.M.P.: Discovering block-structured process models from event logs - a constructive approach. In: Colom, J.-M., Desel, J. (eds.) PETRI NETS 2013. LNCS, vol. 7927, pp. 311–329. Springer, Heidelberg (2013). https://doi.org/10.1007/978-3-642-38697-8_17

36. Leemans, S.J.J., Fahland, D., van der Aalst, W.M.P.: Discovering block-structured process models from event logs containing infrequent behaviour. In: Lohmann, N., Song, M., Wohed, P. (eds.) BPM 2013. LNBIP, vol. 171, pp. 66–78. Springer, Cham (2014). https://doi.org/10.1007/978-3-319-06257-0_6

37. Leemans, S.J.J., Maggi, F.M., Montali, M.: Reasoning on labelled petri nets and their dynamics in a stochastic setting. In: Ciccio, C.D., Dijkman, R.M., del-Río-Ortega, A., Rinderle-Ma, S. (eds.) BPM 2022. LNCS, vol. 13420, pp. 324–342. Springer, Cham (2022). https://doi.org/10.1007/978-3-031-16103-2_22

38. Leemans, S.J.J., Polyvyanyy, A.: Stochastic-aware conformance checking: an entropy-based approach. In: Dustdar, S., Yu, E., Salinesi, C., Rieu, D., Pant, V. (eds.) CAiSE 2020. LNCS, vol. 12127, pp. 217–233. Springer, Cham (2020). https://doi.org/10.1007/978-3-030-49435-3_14

39. Leemans, S.J.J., Polyvyanyy, A.: Stochastic-aware precision and recall measures for conformance checking in process mining. Inf. Syst. **115**, 102197 (2023)

40. Liu, W., Song, L., Wang, J., Zhang, L.: A simple probabilistic extension of modal mu-calculus. In: Proceedings of the Twenty-Fourth International Joint Conference on Artificial Intelligence, IJCAI 2015, Buenos Aires, Argentina, 25–31 July 2015, pp. 882–888 (2015)

41. Mannhardt, F., Leemans, S.J.J., Schwanen, C.T., de Leoni, M.: Modelling data-aware stochastic processes - discovery and conformance checking. In: Gomes, L., Lorenz, R. (eds.) PETRI NETS 2023. LNCS, vol. 13929, pp. 77–98. Springer, Cham (2023). https://doi.org/10.1007/978-3-031-33620-1_5

42. Martinelli, F., Mercaldo, F., Nardone, V., Orlando, A., Santone, A., Vaglini, G.: Model checking based approach for compliance checking. Inf. Technol. Control. **48**(2), 278–298 (2019)

43. Mio, M.: Game semantics for probabilistic modal μ-calculi. The University of Edinburgh (2012)

44. Mio, M.: Probabilistic modal mu-calculus with independent product. Log. Methods Comput. Sci. **8**(4) (2012)

45. De Nicola, R., Vaandrager, F.: Action versus state based logics for transition systems. In: Guessarian, I. (ed.) LITP 1990. LNCS, vol. 469, pp. 407–419. Springer, Heidelberg (1990). https://doi.org/10.1007/3-540-53479-2_17

46. Parma, A., Segala, R.: Logical characterizations of bisimulations for discrete probabilistic systems. In: Seidl, H. (ed.) FoSSaCS 2007. LNCS, vol. 4423, pp. 287–301. Springer, Heidelberg (2007). https://doi.org/10.1007/978-3-540-71389-0_21

47. Reinkemeyer, L.: Process Mining in Action - Principles, Use Cases and Outlook. Springer, Cham (2021). https://doi.org/10.1007/978-3-030-40172-6

48. Reisig, W.: Understanding Petri Nets - Modeling Techniques, Analysis Methods, Case Studies. Springer, Heidelberg (2013). https://doi.org/10.1007/978-3-642-33278-4

49. Rogge-Solti, A., van der Aalst, W.M.P., Weske, M.: Discovering stochastic petri nets with arbitrary delay distributions from event logs. In: Lohmann, N., Song, M., Wohed, P. (eds.) BPM 2013. LNBIP, vol. 171, pp. 15–27. Springer, Cham (2014). https://doi.org/10.1007/978-3-319-06257-0_2

50. Rozinat, A., Mans, R.S., Song, M., van der Aalst, W.M.P.: Discovering simulation models. Inf. Syst. **34**(3), 305–327 (2009)

51. Sharma, A.: Reduction techniques for nondeterministic and probabilistic systems. Ph.D. thesis, RWTH Aachen University, Germany (2015). http://publications.rwth-aachen.de/record/462319

52. Verbeek, E., Buijs, J.C.A.M., van Dongen, B.F., van der Aalst, W.M.P.: Prom 6: the process mining toolkit. In: Proceedings of the Business Process Management 2010 Demonstration Track, Hoboken, NJ, USA, 14–16 September 2010 (2010)

53. Wen, L., van der Aalst, W.M.P., Wang, J., Sun, J.: Mining process models with non-free-choice constructs. Data Min. Knowl. Discov. **15**(2), 145–180 (2007)

54. Wen, L., Wang, J., van der Aalst, W.M.P., Huang, B., Sun, J.: Mining process models with prime invisible tasks. Data Knowl. Eng. **69**(10), 999–1021 (2010)

Robustness Analysis of Probabilistic Models with Adversaries or Strategic Entities

Sotirios Gyftopoulos[1,2]([✉]), Stylianos Basagiannis[3], and Panagiotis Katsaros[1]

[1] Aristotle University of Thessaloniki, Thessaloniki, Greece
{sgyftop,katsaros}@csd.auth.gr
[2] Athena Research Center, Xanthi, Greece
sotiris.gyftopoulos@athenarc.gr
[3] International Hellenic University, Thessaloniki, Greece
basagiannis@ihu.gr

Abstract. The robustness analysis of probabilistic models has been recently the research focus towards verifying the extent to which a system is robust against adversaries, as well as for synthesizing worst-case attacks. In addition to the progress achieved in this direction, a system also needs to exhibit resilience against behaviors that undermine its balance in terms of properties referring to quantitative rewards, such as power consumption, work load or other measurable characteristics. In this paper, we introduce a robustness analysis framework for reward properties over Markov decision processes (MDPs). Apart from the problem of adversarial robustness, we also consider the case of strategic entities who seek to maximize their influence in the convergence of network-based systems. To this end, our robustness framework features an infinite horizon analysis for irreducible MDPs.

Keywords: adversarial robustness · parametric model checking · multi-agent systems · reward properties

1 Introduction

In probabilistic models, parameter uncertainty concerns with the assignment of state transition probabilities based on assumptions, which may not be sufficiently realistic or accurate. If the model is of questionable credibility, it is not feasible to perform a faithful analysis of the real system behavior. However, recent advances in parametric analysis techniques [11] open prospects for a more systematic treatment of parameter uncertainty.

Parametric analysis may be also needed when the model includes entities whose interactions are not subject to the control of the system under study. For example, Oakley et al. [17] consider various kinds of possible adversarial behavior based on their impact on the structure of the probabilistic model. They use parameters to model the adversaries' impact on the system's behavior rather

ⓒ The Author(s), under exclusive license to Springer Nature Switzerland AG 2025
N. Jansen et al. (Eds.): Principles of Verification: Cycling the Probabilistic Landscape,
LNCS 15261, pp. 219–233, 2025.
https://doi.org/10.1007/978-3-031-75775-4_10

than to provide exact - and possibly incorrect - valuations of their intervention, a technique that allows for a more credible analysis.

In this work we propose parametric analysis techniques for Markov decision processes (MDPs), towards evaluation of strategies that might be exercised by an adversary or by parties in network-based systems that have diverse objectives.

We analyze the *robustness of reward properties* with respect to perturbations in transition probabilities introduced in the form of parameters, which are subject to certain constraints. Rewards are usually used to attach quantitative information such as power consumption, work load, as well as other quantifiable characteristics such as trust level and numerically encoded opinion/belief. Our robustness analysis aims to assess the resilience of the reward balance in a system against all (parameterized) strategies that introduce perturbations in the system's behavior.

The framework of model robustness analysis, introduced here, consists of the following contributions:

1. we pose the problem of model robustness with respect to reward properties;
2. the robustness analysis of reward properties over MDPs is developed in two different settings, namely, robustness for rewards in reducible MDPs and robustness of rewards in the long run for irreducible MDPs, and
3. we present probabilistic models and their robustness analysis for two relevant applications (navigation interference in grid worlds and opinion influence in social networks) that demonstrate the utility of robustness analysis for rewards in diverse domains.

Our approach can be supported by widely used probabilistic model checking tools, which now offer an extensive range of parametric analysis capabilities.

There are previous works that address the problem of uncertainty in the transition matrices of MDPs like Nilim and El Ghaoui [16], Iyengar [10], Wiesemann et al. [21], and Goyal and Grand-Clément [8]. However, these analyses are based on certain restrictions for representing uncertainty that narrow down the expressiveness of parametric MDPs used in our approach. We refer to these related works in more detail in Sect. 2.

2   Related Work

Parametric analysis of probabilistic models with adversaries, whose interactions are not controlled by the system under attack, has been previously used by Bartocci et al. [3] within the context of the model repair problem. The model that was repaired in one of the applications was a continuous-time Markov chain (CTMC) for the Kaminsky DNS Cache-Poisoning Attack [1] and the parameters were introduced in *controllable* transitions, which adjust the intensity of a countermeasure, such that the structure of the model is preserved.

In Oakley et al. [17], the authors expanded the possible perturbations in transition probabilities, grouped the perturbed matrices into *perturbation sets* based on their structural characteristics and classified accordingly the adversarial behavior to threat models (i.e., structure preserving and non structure preserving threats). Adversarial robustness was defined with respect to PCTL* path formulae [2] over discrete-time Markov chains (DTMCs), i.e., no reward properties were considered. The authors also provided a solution to the quest of adversarially robust strategies (policies) in MDP models, which is different than the robustness analysis for reward properties in MDPs that is presented here.

In [16], a work by Nilim and El Ghaoui and in [10] by Iyengar, the authors formulate uncertainty via classes of transition matrices for MDPs and assume that each class consists of a group of alternatives. They use a parameter to control the size of the classes thus representing the *uncertainty level*. Central in their analysis is the notion of *rectangularity*: (s, a)-rectangulatiry assumes that the state-action pairs of the MDP are not correlated implying that the parameters in a state-action pair, that are reflected in the corresponding probability distribution, may not appear anywhere else in the model. Wiesemann et al. [21] defined *robust MDPs* and analyze them under the assumption of (s, a)-rectangularity and s-rectangularity, which only requires independence between the MDP states. Recently Goyal and Grand-Clément [8] introduced the factor matrix uncertainty set that allows the connection between states to some extent, providing a more expressive representation method. However, none of the aforementioned mathematical tools is characterized by the expressiveness of parametric MDPs that are used in our analysis.

The probabilistic models that we introduced in a previous work [9], for networks of participants that interact with each other, did not include the adversarial actions (as in [3] and [17]) in the model, but implicitly assumed one or more strategic entities who seek to maximize their influence in the convergence of the network. Our analysis, based on MDPs and stochastic games, was focused on reward properties in the long run. Though our models were the main source of inspiration for the robustness analysis of reward properties reported here, in that article we did not provide any parametric analysis results. From a more general perspective, this type of analysis is different but complementary to other probabilistic verification analyses for multi-agent systems [7,18], where the objectives of one agent can be influenced by the actions of other agents [19].

3   Background

In this section, we compile the necessary theoretical underpinnings for our analysis.

Definition 1 (DTMC [17]). *A Discrete-time Markov chain (DTMC) is a 5-tuple*

$$\mathcal{C} = (\mathcal{S}, s_0, \mathbf{P}, AP, L)$$

where $\mathcal{S}$ is a finite set of states with $s_0 \in \mathcal{S}$ the initial state, AP a set of atomic propositions, and $L : \mathcal{S} \to 2^{AP}$ a labeling function. $\mathbf{P}$ is an $|S| \times |S|$ matrix where $0 \leq \mathbf{P}_{s,s'} \leq 1$ indicates the probability that the system transitions from state s to s'. Moreover, $\forall s \in \mathcal{S}, \sum_{s' \in \mathcal{S}} \mathbf{P}_{s,s'} = 1$, i.e., all rows in $\mathbf{P}$ sum to 1.

By incorporating *reward structures* in DTMCs, we represent additional information about the system and analyze extended scenarios that focus on the expected payoffs or costs of a system's behavior. We restrict our analysis to rewards that represent the gain or loss that occurs when the system reaches a state (i.e., *state rewards*).

Definition 2 (Reward Structure for DTMC). *A reward structure of a DTMC $C = (S, s_0, \mathbf{P}, AP, L)$ consists of a reward function $r_{state} : S \to \mathbb{R}_{\geqslant 0}$.*

We use $r = r_{state}$ throughout the rest of the paper for simplicity purposes. The introduction of non-determinism in the transition between states transforms a DTMC to a *Markov decision process (MDP)*.

Definition 3 (MDP). *A Markov decision process (MDP) is a 6-tuple*

$$\mathcal{M} = (S, s_0, \mathcal{A}, T, AP, L)$$

where $S, \mathcal{A}$ are respectively finite sets of states and actions, $s_0 \in S$ is the initial state, AP a set of atomic propositions, and $L : S \to 2^{AP}$ is a labeling function; $T : S \times \mathcal{A} \times S \to [0,1]$ is a probabilistic transition function where $T(s, a, s')$ represents the probability that the system transitions from s to s', given action a. Moreover, $\forall (s, a) \in S \times \mathcal{A}, \sum_{s' \in S} T(s, a, s') = 1$.

Similarly to DTMCs, state rewards allow us to model additional information about MDPs. Thus, the definition of reward structures can be easily extended from DTMCs to MDPs accordingly.

A *stationary strategy* or *policy* $\sigma : S \to \mathcal{A}$ is a function that indicates the action for every state of the model and is independent of the time variable. We restrict our analysis to memoryless strategies, i.e., strategies that depend solely on the current state of the system regardless of the previous visited states. We assume that the construction of a strategy is the responsibility of a *strategic entity* $\mathcal{E}$ which resolves the non-determinism between alternative actions thus representing the interference of adversarial behavior such that a reward quantity is maximized/minimized. The application of a strategy on an MDP induces the model to a corresponding DTMC.

Definition 4 (Induced DTMC of an MDP [17]). *The DTMC of an MDP, $\mathcal{M} = (S, s_0, \mathcal{A}, T, AP, L)$, induced by a memoryless (deterministic) policy $\sigma : S \to \mathcal{A}$ is:*

$$\mathcal{M}_\sigma = (S, s_0, \mathbf{P}, AP, L)$$

where $\forall s, s' \in S, \mathbf{P}_{s,s'} = T(s, \sigma(s), s')$.

Property Specification. We utilize properties expressed in an extension of PCTL that incorporates reward structures [6], and is implemented in PRISM [14], an established probabilistic model checker.

Definition 5 (Syntax of PCTL with Rewards [14]). *The syntax for state formulas of PCTL with reward structures over a set of atomic propositions AP is as follows:*

$$\phi ::= \texttt{true} \mid c \mid \phi \wedge \phi \mid \neg \phi \mid P_{\bowtie p}[\psi] \mid R^r_{\bowtie x}[\mathrm{I}^{=k}] \mid R^r_{\bowtie x}[\mathtt{C}^{\leqslant k}] \mid R^r_{\bowtie x}[\mathrm{F}\,\phi]$$

where $c \in AP$, $\bowtie \in \{\leqslant, <, \geqslant, >\}$, $p \in [0,1]$, r *is a reward structure with* $r \in \mathbb{R}_{\geqslant 0}$, $x \in \mathbb{R}$, $k \in \mathbb{N}$, *and* ψ *is a path formula of the form:*

$$\psi ::= \mathtt{X}\,\phi \mid \phi\,\mathtt{U}^{\leqslant k}\,\phi \mid \phi\,\mathtt{U}\,\phi$$

Semantically, given a state s of an MDP $\mathcal{M}$ and the set of all memoryless (deterministic) policies $\mathfrak{S}$, the formulas of the syntax correspond to the following:

$$s \models_{\mathfrak{S}} P_{\bowtie p}[\psi] \iff \forall \sigma \in \mathfrak{S}, Pr^\sigma_{\mathcal{M},s}(s \models \psi) \bowtie p$$

$$s \models_{\mathfrak{S}} R^r_{\bowtie x}[\mathrm{I}^{=k}] \iff \forall \sigma \in \mathfrak{S}, \mathbb{E}^\sigma_{\mathcal{M},s}(\mathrm{I}^{=k}_r) \bowtie x$$

$$s \models_{\mathfrak{S}} R^r_{\bowtie x}[\mathtt{C}^{\leqslant k}] \iff \forall \sigma \in \mathfrak{S}, \mathbb{E}^\sigma_{\mathcal{M},s}(\mathtt{C}^{\leqslant k}_r) \bowtie x$$

$$s \models_{\mathfrak{S}} R^r_{\bowtie x}[\mathrm{F}\,\phi] \iff \forall \sigma \in \mathfrak{S}, \mathbb{E}^\sigma_{\mathcal{M},s}(\mathrm{F}^{Sat_{\mathfrak{S}}(\phi)}_r) \bowtie x$$

where $Pr^\sigma_{\mathcal{M},s}(s \models \psi)$ denotes the probability of satisfying $\bowtie p$ in s for strategy $\sigma \in \mathfrak{S}$, $\mathbb{E}^\sigma_{\mathcal{M},s}(\mathrm{I}^{=k}_{r_{state}})$ expresses if the expected instantaneous rewards at the kth step of a path in $\mathcal{M}$ satisfy $\bowtie x$ under strategy $\sigma \in \mathfrak{S}$, $\mathbb{E}^\sigma_{\mathcal{M},s}(\mathtt{C}^{\leqslant k}_r)$ is the expected cumulative reward of paths with up to k steps under strategy $\sigma \in \mathfrak{S}$, and $\mathbb{E}^\sigma_{\mathcal{M},s}(\mathrm{F}^{Sat_{\mathfrak{S}}(\phi)}_r)$ is the expected cumulative reward along all paths reaching a state that satisfies ϕ under strategy $\sigma \in \mathfrak{S}$. When a model checker is asked to evaluate these formulas, the upper and lower bounds of the properties are estimated depending on the formula [14], i.e., $P_{\texttt{min}=?}[\psi]$, $P_{\texttt{max}=?}[\psi]$, $R^r_{\texttt{min}=?}[\cdot]$ and $R^r_{\texttt{max}=?}[\cdot]$. Consequently, we can express *quantitative* properties for the models and ask questions of the type *"what is the minimum/maximum probability or expected reward of ψ holding?"*.

3.1   Infinite Horizon Analysis of MDP Rewards

In many cases, we are interested in the long run behavior of a model for paths over the infinite planning horizon, a notion parallel to the steady state behavior of DTMCs. PCTL allows the formulation of steady state reward properties for DTMCs through formulas of the type $R^r_{\bowtie x}[\mathtt{S}]$ that check whether the average expected reward in the long run (i.e., in the steady state $\mathtt{S}$) satisfies $\bowtie x$ [13]. However, this type of formulas is currently not available for MDPs since the steady state behavior cannot be defined due to the non-determinism present in the models. The non-determinism can be eliminated by a strategy, in which case the steady state of the MDP corresponds to the induced DTMC. Under this rationale, we state an objective in PCTL that aligns with the strategic entity's intention to construct an optimal strategy and examine the behavior of the system for paths of sufficient length which converge to the long run of the induced DTMC, as stated and proved originally in Proposition 1 of [9] and generalized here:

Proposition 1. *Assume an MDP $\mathcal{M}$, a reward structure r, and the set of stationary strategies $\mathfrak{S}$. There exists a $t_L \in \mathbb{N}$ such that, for all paths with length $t > t_L$, if strategy $\sigma^* \in \mathfrak{S}$ minimizes or maximizes the cumulative expected reward of the MDP over finite planning horizons with length greater than t_L, then σ^* minimizes or maximizes the average reward of the MDP over the infinite planning horizon.*

The intuition for Proposition 1 is that, if σ^* is the optimal strategy that minimizes/maximizes the average reward of an MDP over the infinite planning horizon, then there exists a sufficiently large t_L such that, for all finite paths with length greater than t_L, σ^* is the strategy that minimizes/maximizes the average reward. In other words, the optimal strategies for the infinite planning horizon and the finite planning horizon for sufficiently large paths (with length greater than t_L) are identical.

On the basis of Proposition 1, we are able to construct optimal strategies based on cumulative reward properties and estimate the corresponding average expected reward for MDPs in the long run by utilizing formulas of the type $R^r_{\bowtie x}[C^{\leq t}]/t$ for sufficiently large t, as a means to converge to $R^r_{\bowtie x}[S]$.

3.2 Parametric Processes

In real world cases, it is unrealistic to evaluate accurately all probabilities in the transition matrix of a system. We introduce a set of parameters X and express the transition probabilities of the system as rational functions of $\mathbb{Q}(X)$ allowing them, thus, to fluctuate within bounded intervals. This leads to the parametric version of the models.

Definition 6 (Parametric DTMC [17]). *A labeled parametric DTMC (pDTMC) with formal parameter set X can be described as a 5-tuple*

$$\mathcal{C}_X = (\mathcal{S}, s_0, \mathbf{P}^X, AP, L)$$

where $\mathcal{S}$ is a set of states, s_0 an initial state, AP a set of atomic propositions, $L : \mathcal{S} \to 2^{AP}$ a labeling function, and $\mathbf{P}^X$ a parametric probability matrix such that $\mathbf{P}^X_{s,s'}$ indicates the probability that the system transitions from state s to s' in the form of a rational function over X.

The ranges of parameters in X should be properly defined to ensure that $\mathbf{P}^X$ remains a stochastic matrix. We can define the parametric MDP accordingly.

Definition 7 (Parametric MDP). *A labeled parametric MDP (pMDP) with formal parameter set X is a 6-tuple*

$$\mathcal{M}_X = (\mathcal{S}, s_0, \mathcal{A}, T^X, AP, L)$$

where $\mathcal{S}$ is a set of states, s_0 an initial state, $\mathcal{A}$ is a finite set of actions, $T^X : \mathcal{S} \times \mathcal{A} \times \mathcal{S} \to \mathbb{Q}(X)$ is a parametric probabilistic transition function, AP a set of atomic propositions, and $L : \mathcal{S} \to 2^{AP}$ a labeling function.

Similarly to MDPs, a strategy that eliminates non-determinism in a pMDP reduces the model to a pDTMC.

4   Model Robustness with Respect to Reward Properties

The problem of adversarial robustness was tackled by Oakley et al. [17] through the prism of perturbed transition matrices. The authors introduced the *perturbation space* $\mathcal{PS}^{\mathcal{C}}$ of a DTMC $\mathcal{C} = (\mathcal{S}, s_0, \mathbf{P}, AP, L)$ as the set of all DTMCs of the form $\mathcal{C} = (\mathcal{S}, s_0, \mathbf{P}', AP, L)$ that have the same set of states, initial state, atomic propositions, and labeling set as $\mathcal{C}$ but different transition matrices. Any subset of $\mathcal{PS}^{\mathcal{C}}$ is a *perturbation set* $PS^{\mathcal{C}}$. Since a pDTMC $\mathcal{C}_X$ can be instantiated for discrete values of the parameters in X to DTMCs that differ only in their transition probability matrix, the parametric $\mathcal{C}_X$ corresponds to a perturbation set $PS^{\mathcal{C}_X}$ containing only the instantiations of $\mathcal{C}_X$.

The notion of perturbation can be extended to MDPs: the perturbation space $\mathcal{PS}^{\mathcal{M}}$ of an MDP $\mathcal{M} = (\mathcal{S}, s_0, \mathcal{A}, T, AP, L)$ is the set of all MDPs of the form $(\mathcal{S}, s_0, \mathcal{A}, T', AP, L)$, i.e., models that differ only in their transition function. The application of a strategy σ on a pMDP $\mathcal{M}_X$ reduces the model to a pDTMC $\mathcal{M}_X^{\sigma}$ and, consequently, each strategy corresponds to a perturbation set $PS^{\mathcal{M}_X^{\sigma}}$ containing all instances of $\mathcal{M}_X^{\sigma}$ for the discrete values of the parameters in X.

To demonstrate our approach, we present two illustrative examples of perturbed MDPs, namely $\mathcal{M}_{ex1}$ and $\mathcal{M}_{ex2}$ in Fig. 1. Each model consists of four states (S_0-S_3) and the transition probabilities are indicated by the values attached to the arrows. A strategic entity $\mathcal{E}$ is responsible for the construction of a policy using actions from the set $\mathsf{Act} = \{\mathsf{m}_1, \mathsf{m}_2\}$ that affect transition probabilities from S_0 to S_1 and S_2 respectively. Since Act includes two actions for the same set of transitions, $\mathcal{E}$ may construct two different policies, one for each action. The actions define the transition probabilities as functions of $\mathsf{p}, \mathsf{q} \in X$ incorporating the parametric nature of the models. The parameters range in the interval $(0, 0.5)$ since any value in this interval guarantees the stochasticity of the transition matrix and preserves the transitions from S_0 to S_1 and S_2. Hence, $\mathcal{M}_{ex1}$ is, according to Kallenberg [12], a reducible MDP (i.e., unichain) with transient states $\{\mathsf{S}_0, \mathsf{S}_1, \mathsf{S}_2\}$ and exactly one ergodic class $\{\mathsf{S}_3\}$, whereas $\mathcal{M}_{ex2}$ is irreducible.

$\mathcal{M}_{ex1}$ and $\mathcal{M}_{ex2}$ incorporate a reward structure r that assigns the value 1 to S_2. Using the reward structure, we can formulate properties that express incentives to aim for or avoid S_2 when traversing the states of the models. The operators used for the properties depend on the type of the model: for the reducible $\mathcal{M}_{ex1}$, we use the until operator F to evaluate paths that originate from S_0 and end at the absorbing state S_3 while, in the case of irreducible $\mathcal{M}_{ex2}$, we evaluate indirectly the average expected reward in the long run through the cumulative operator C based on the rationale of Proposition 1. The properties of Listing 1 evaluate the lower and upper bounds of S_2's visitation.

Since $\mathcal{E}$ can wield its influence on the models via the two available policies, these properties offer the means to examine the models' robustness against the non-deterministic behaviour of $\mathcal{E}$. Oakley et al. [17] defined *DTMC Adversarial Robustness* focusing on the lower bound of a probability, that satisfies a path formula, from a perturbation set of DTMCs to model scenarios of adversarial

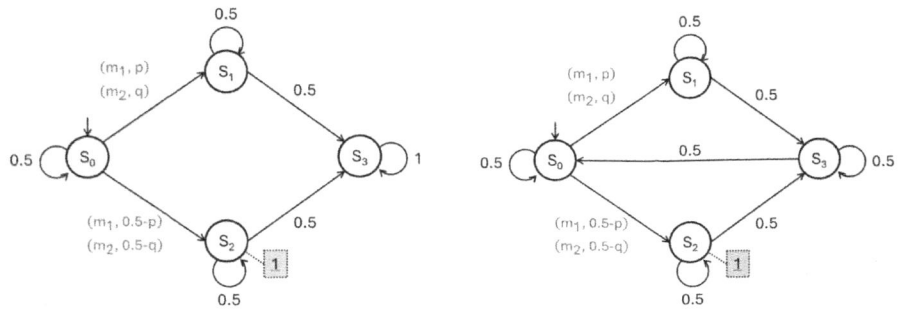

(a) Reducible MDP $\mathcal{M}_{ex1}$ (b) Irreducible MDP $\mathcal{M}_{ex2}$

Fig. 1: Illustrative examples of perturbed MDPs

$$\mathtt{R}^r_{\max=?}[\mathtt{F}\ \mathtt{S}_3]$$
$$\mathtt{R}^r_{\min=?}[\mathtt{F}\ \mathtt{S}_3]$$

$$\mathtt{R}^r_{\max=?}[\mathtt{C}^{\leq t}]/t$$
$$\mathtt{R}^r_{\min=?}[\mathtt{C}^{\leq t}]/t$$

(a) Reducible MDP $\mathcal{M}_{ex1}$ (b) Irreducible MDP $\mathcal{M}_{ex2}$

Listing 1: Properties for robustness analysis

events. In this work, we extend the definition of model robustness to MDPs that incorporate reward structures.

Definition 8 (Model Robustness for Rewards in the Long Run). *Given* $0 \leq \delta_1 \leq \delta_2$, *an irreducible MDP* $\mathcal{M} = (\mathcal{S}, s_0, \mathcal{A}, T, AP, L)$, *a reward structure* r, *the set of all stationary strategies* $\mathfrak{S}$, *and the perturbation set* $PS \subseteq \mathcal{PS}^{\mathcal{M}}$, $\mathcal{M}$ *is robust with respect to* PS, δ_1, δ_2, *if*

$$\delta_1 \leq \frac{\mathbb{E}^\sigma_{\mathcal{M}',s_0}(\mathtt{C}^{\leq t}_r)}{t} \leq \delta_2$$

for all $\mathcal{M}' \in PS$, $\sigma \in \mathfrak{S}$, *and* $max_{\mathcal{M}'}(t_l) \leqslant t$, *where* t_l *is the length of paths in the MDPs of* $\mathcal{M}'$ *that suffices for the construction of optimal strategies over the infinite planning horizon (cf. Proposition 1).*

In this definition, the criterion for an MDP's robustness is the average expected reward in the long run under all possible strategies. The intuition is that the average expected reward in the steady state of an MDP under every possible strategy should be bounded. The convergence to the lower and upper bounds can be achieved by two different strategies that are optimal for two contradicting incentives: to minimize and maximize the average expected reward. Under this rationale, we define robustness as the range of average rewards under every possible strategy.

The definition refers to the overall model robustness and allows us to apply the notion to a wider range of models. We can describe more accurately desirable properties of systems compared to the definition of Oakley et al. [17] which considers only reachability properties of the models for a given strategy and refers to policy robustness. Since reward structures are used to model additional quantifiable information of the system (e.g., power consumption, opinion, work load, trust) we are able to cover a wider range of aspects regarding the resilience of a network-based system against all possible strategies that aim to perturb it. For instance, we can formally define and examine the robustness of a network of devices against a malicious user who aims to disable nodes by employing actions that unnecessarily increase their power consumption and work load, or to investigate the resilience of a social network against the intentional diffusion of extreme opinions by manipulative users.

Model robustness, as defined in Definition 8, is applicable to irreducible MDPs that can be induced to ergodic DTMCs when a strategy is applied, such as $\mathcal{M}_{ex2}$. However, when the induced DTMCs are not ergodic, Definition 8 is insufficient to describe the behavior of the system since the contribution of transient states in the average expected reward is diminished as the paths are confined in the states of the ergodic classes. For example, in $\mathcal{M}_{ex1}$ the traversal in the model is trapped in S_3 (the state in the single ergodic class), and any contribution of state S_2 in the average expected reward is faded out in the long run. An alternative definition of model robustness for rewards based on the reachability of states is appropriate.

Definition 9 (Model Robustness for Rewards in Reducible MDPs). *Given* $0 \leq \delta_1 \leq \delta_2$, *a reducible MDP* $\mathcal{M} = (\mathcal{S}, s_0, \mathcal{A}, T, AP, L)$, *a reward structure* r, *the set of all stationary strategies* $\mathfrak{S}$, *a PCTL state formula* ϕ, *and the perturbation set* $PS \subseteq \mathcal{PS}^\mathcal{M}$, $\mathcal{M}$ *is robust with respect to* PS, δ_1, δ_2, *if*

$$\delta_1 \leq \mathbb{E}_{\mathcal{M},s_0}^\sigma (\mathrm{F}_r^{Sat_\mathfrak{S}(\phi)}) \leq \delta_2$$

for all $\mathcal{M}' \in PS$, $\sigma \in \mathfrak{S}$.

5   Applications of Probabilistic Model Robustness

We explore the notion of model robustness, as defined in this work, in two illustrative examples: a) the navigation interference problem in the Grid World, and b) the opinion influence problem in social networks. The former demonstrates the applicability of robustness on a reducible MDP while the latter considers an irreducible MDP.

5.1   Navigation Interference Problem in the Grid World

The grid world class of problems considers abstract navigation scenarios for autonomous devices in worlds that are represented as grids of cells [4,15]. A device is placed in a starting cell and moves to the neighboring cells according to a set of available moves. The world contains cells that are considered as targets and the device aims to reach them while avoiding potential obstacles/threats.

We consider a world containing a 3×3 grid of cells (Fig. 2), similar to the example presented and analyzed by Oakley et al. [17]. The states in the grid are indexed from left to right and bottom to top, and an autonomous device (robot) starts from S_0. The available moves for the robot are north, south, east, and west, depending on the current state, and the goal is to reach S_8 (the top right state) while avoiding S_2 and S_6 (the bottom right and top left states) that are considered hazardous (e.g., traps).

The device is equipped with navigation guidelines that define the probability distribution of next moves in each state, as depicted in Fig. 2a. The guidelines do not allow the transition from state S_7 to S_6 and to S_2 from any other state since these states are hazardous. The navigation in the world is equivalent to a DTMC model where the cells of the world correspond to states of a Markov chain and the distributions of next moves to transition probabilities.

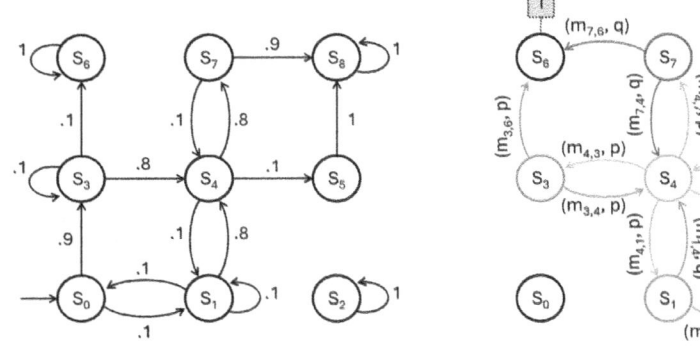

(a) Probability distribution of next moves.

(b) Available moves at each state and costs.

Fig. 2: Illustrative example of a 3×3 Grid World. An autonomous device starts its navigation from S_0 and aims to reach S_8. S_2 and S_6 are hazardous states (traps).

We introduce a strategic entity $\mathcal{E}$ to the grid world which interferes with the navigation guidelines of the robot and aims to increase the possibility of reaching a hazardous state. The entity tampers with the probability distribution of next moves in S_1, S_3, S_4, S_5 and S_7: at each vulnerable state the entity selects an action of the form $(m_{i,j}, p$ or $q)$ that increases the probability of reaching state j from i by a factor p or q, and the transition probabilities of all moves are normalized to maintain the stochasticity. By selecting an action for each vulnerable state, the entity compiles a strategy that interferes with the navigation of the robot.

The set of vulnerable states and the number of available factors to the entity may vary across different settings of the world. In our version of grid world, we assume that $\mathcal{E}$ tampers with all states except the starting, the hazardous and the goal state. Moreover, the available actions allow the creation of transitions that did not exist in the initial setting of the world (from S_1 and S_5 to S_2, and from S_7 to S_6) allowing, thus, changes in the structure of the model.

States S_2 and S_6 are assigned with costs of a unit to model their hazardous nature. Figure 2b depicts the available actions, coloured distinctively for each state, and the cost structure for S_2 and S_6. The enriched setting transforms the navigation to a reducible MDP, since the set of transient states is non-empty, and we examine the model's robustness on the grounds of Definition 9.

We utilized PRISM to model the MDP that incorporates the actions of the strategic entity $\mathcal{E}$ and the costs of S_2 and S_6 in the form of a reward structure. The properties of Listing 1a were properly adapted to the grid world model and the parameters p and q ranged in two possible intervals ($[0.2, 0.4]$ and $[0.6, 0.8]$) resulting, thus, in four scenarios of parametric analysis, based on the combinations of intervals for p and q. PRISM allows the extraction of the properties as parametric rational functions and, hence, we optimized the extracted functions using the Sequential Least SQuares Programming (SLSQP) algorithm provided by SciPy [20] to estimate the values of p and q that achieve the maxima and minima of the properties.

Table 1: Evaluation of robustness for the 3×3 grid world example.

Scenario	p ∈	q ∈	$R^r_{min=?}[F\ S_8]$	$R^r_{max=?}[F\ S_8]$
#1	$[0.2, 0.4]$	$[0.2, 0.4]$	0.070340	0.647480
#2	$[0.2, 0.4]$	$[0.6, 0.8]$	0.053710	0.785906
#3	$[0.6, 0.8]$	$[0.2, 0.4]$	0.070144	0.741528
#4	$[0.6, 0.8]$	$[0.6, 0.8]$	0.053584	0.837766

The results of our analysis, presented in Table 1, indicate that the maxima and minima of the properties were achieved for the upper bounds of the parameters p and q in each scenario, a result that confirms the incentive that the extrema are achieved when the entity wields the strongest influence. As a result, the lowest and the highest values of the properties - that define the bounds of robustness for the model - are detected in scenario #4 where that parameters p and q have their greatest values. Furthermore, using PRISM we are able to extract the strategy of the entity that wields the maximum and minimum impact and determine the corresponding instantiations of the induced DTMC in the perturbation space.

5.2 Opinion Influence Problem in Social Networks

The DeGroot model is a well studied model of opinion dynamics [5]. Its core idea is that individuals update their beliefs to a weighted average of their friends' opinions. In a previous work [9], we utilized the common mathematical underpinnings of the model with stochastic processes, and examined it using probabilistic model checking techniques. The individuals of a social network were represented as states of a Markov chain and their trust to their friends' opinions was reflected on the transition probabilities between the states. The opinions were expressed as numerical values in reward structures that assigned a value (opinion) to each state (individual). Under this modelling approach, the diffusion of opinions in the social network corresponds to the average reward of a random walk and the consensus equals to the average expected reward of an infinite traversal. The model was encoded in PRISM language and we examined the performance of PRISM in evaluating the consensus in a set of experimental settings.

In order to examine the impact of external influence, we developed scenarios where strategic entities aimed to tamper with the transition probabilities (i.e., trust factors) between states (individuals) to promote their favored opinion. The process was defined as *DeGroot Influence Problem (DIP)* and was analyzed using model checking techniques.

In this work, we present an illustrative example of a DIP scenario and examine the network's robustness to the influence wielded by an external entity. Figure 3a presents a social network consisting of four members where the strategic entity aims to tamper with the consensus formation. Based on our modelling technique, the opinions of the members are represented as numerical values of a reward structure r where states (individuals) S_0 and S_3 host the two extreme values (0 and 1 respectively) while S_1 and S_2 are neutral (opinion of 0.5).

The entity applies its influence through actions of $\mathcal{A} = \{m_{1,0}, m_{1,2}, m_{1,3}, m_{2,0}, m_{2,1}, m_{2,3}\}$ at S_1 and S_2 indicated as tuples of the form $(m_{i,j}, \mathsf{p} \text{ or } \mathsf{q})$ in Fig. 3a: each action $m_{i,j}$ alters the weight (trust) of node i to the opinion of the targeting friend j by increasing it with a factor p or q respectively. Once the extra weight is added, the weights of all outgoing transition probabilities are normalized to maintain the stochasticity of the model, as illustrated in Fig. 3b. The values of p or q are represented as parameters and, hence, the example is a *parametric DeGroot Influence Problem (pDIP)*.

Since the consensus of the social group corresponds to the average expected reward of an infinite random walk, the entity can bias the consensus through the manipulation of the transition probabilities between the states. In order to evaluate the network's robustness, it suffices to examine the minimum and maximum impact applied on the average expected reward in the long run, as defined in Definition 8.

We evaluated the minimum and the maximum values of the consensus for all possible strategies of the entity using the properties in Listing 1b. For our analysis, we used two alternatives for the intervals of the parameters p and q, $[0.2, 0.4]$ and $[0.6, 0.8]$, resulting to four different parametric scenarios, based on the number of possible combinations of the intervals. PRISM was utilized for the modelling of the network and the evaluation of its properties. Since the software does not allow the extraction of cumulative properties as parametric rational functions, we resorted to experiments that exhaustively verify their values to

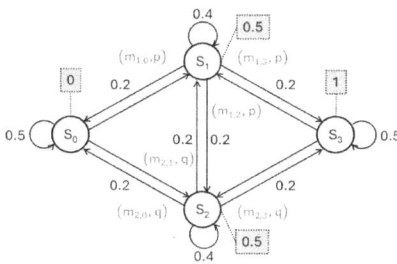

(a) Social network of four individuals where an entity constructs its strategy using $\mathcal{A} = \{m_{1,0}, m_{1,2}, m_{1,3}, m_{2,0}, m_{2,1}, m_{2,3}\}$

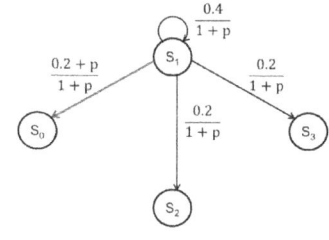

(b) Impact of $m_{1,0}$ on the network due to the normalization process.

Fig. 3: Illustrative example of a parametric DeGroot Influence Problem (pDIP) consisting of four members.

approximate p and q that achieve maxima and minima. The step of the parameters for each instance of the exhaustive analysis was set to 10^{-3}. We empirically verified that a length of the random walk $t > 10^6$ suffices for an accuracy of at least 10^{-5}.

The results of our analysis are presented in Table 2. A prominent conclusion is that the minima and maxima in each scenario are symmetrical to the neutral opinion (0.5), which reflects the symmetry of the network, the opinions and the available actions for the strategic entity. The symmetry is also present in scenarios #2 and #3 where the intervals of the parameters are swapped. As anticipated, the extreme values for both properties where achieved for the upper bounds of the parameters' intervals (0.4 and 0.8) since these values allow the maximum influence to the entity in each scenario. Finally, the greatest impact - and consequently the lowest bound of robustness for the network - occurs in the last scenario were the parameters allow the maximum impact of the entities' actions.

Table 2: Evaluation of robustness for the social network with four members.

Scenario	p $\in$	q $\in$	$R^r_{\min=?}[C^{\leqslant t}]/t$	$R^r_{\max=?}[C^{\leqslant t}]/t$
#1	$[0.2, 0.4]$	$[0.2, 0.4]$	0.366667	0.633333
#2	$[0.2, 0.4]$	$[0.6, 0.8]$	0.337399	0.662601
#3	$[0.6, 0.8]$	$[0.2, 0.4]$	0.337399	0.662601
#4	$[0.6, 0.8]$	$[0.6, 0.8]$	0.309524	0.690476

6   Conclusions

Adversarial robustness has been recently the focus of research works that investigate the resilience of systems against influence wielded by external entities. These works aim to examine the impact of adversarial strategies on properties of single or multi-partite systems and to estimate their credibility under scenarios of attack. In this work, we considered models represented as parametric MDPs where strategic entities aim to manipulate their behavior. We defined model robustness with respect to reward properties that allow us to describe advanced features of their operation. For example, we are able to represent energy consumption, opinion, or trust in a model, and examine its resilience with respect to these features towards manipulative entities.

We examined the soundness of our approach by investigating the robustness of two models from diverse domains: the navigation interference problem in the grid world, and the opinion influence problem in a social network. The former demonstrated the methodological pathway in the case of reducible MDPs while the latter examined the model's robustness of irreducible MDPs in the long run. In both cases, the applicability of our approach was verified and challenges were highlighted. Previous works focused on models that were fully deterministic (DTMCs); in this work we extended robustness to single entity models with non-deterministic behavior (MDPs). The introduction of more strategic entities would elevate the models to stochastic games and provide solid ground for research in future work.

References

1. Alexiou, N., Basagiannis, S., Katsaros, P., Dashpande, T., Smolka, S.A.: Formal analysis of the Kaminsky DNS cache-poisoning attack using probabilistic model checking. In: 2010 IEEE 12th International Symposium on High Assurance Systems Engineering, pp. 94–103 (2010). https://doi.org/10.1109/HASE.2010.25
2. Baier, C., Katoen, J.P.: Principles of Model Checking (Representation and Mind Series). The MIT Press (2008)
3. Bartocci, E., Grosu, R., Katsaros, P., Ramakrishnan, C.R., Smolka, S.A.: Model repair for probabilistic systems. In: Abdulla, P.A., Leino, K.R.M. (eds.) TACAS 2011. LNCS, vol. 6605, pp. 326–340. Springer, Heidelberg (2011). https://doi.org/10.1007/978-3-642-19835-9_30
4. Cassandra, A.R., Kaelbling, L.P., Littman, M.L.: Acting optimally in partially observable stochastic domains. In: Proceedings of the Twelfth National Conference on Artificial Intelligence (AAAI 1994), vol. 2, pp. 1023–1028. American Association for Artificial Intelligence (1994)
5. Degroot, M.H.: Reaching a consensus. J. Am. Stat. Assoc. **69**(345), 118–121 (1974). https://doi.org/10.1080/01621459.1974.10480137
6. Forejt, V., Kwiatkowska, M., Norman, G., Parker, D.: Automated verification techniques for probabilistic systems. In: Bernardo, M., Issarny, V. (eds.) SFM 2011. LNCS, vol. 6659, pp. 53–113. Springer, Heidelberg (2011). https://doi.org/10.1007/978-3-642-21455-4_3

7. Fu, C., et al.: EPMC gets knowledge in multi-agent systems. In: Finkbeiner, B., Wies, T. (eds.) VMCAI 2022. LNCS, vol. 13182, pp. 93–107. Springer, Cham (2022). https://doi.org/10.1007/978-3-030-94583-1_5

8. Goyal, V., Grand-Clement, J.: Robust Markov decision processes: beyond rectangularity. Math. Oper. Res. **48**(1), 203–226 (2022). https://doi.org/10.1287/moor.2022.1259

9. Gyftopoulos, S., Efraimidis, P.S., Katsaros, P.: Formal analysis of degroot influence problems using probabilistic model checking. Simul. Model. Pract. Theory **89**, 144–159 (2018). https://doi.org/10.1016/j.simpat.2018.09.009

10. Iyengar, G.N.: Robust dynamic programming. Math. Oper. Res. **30**(2), 257–280 (2005). https://doi.org/10.1287/moor.1040.0129

11. Junges, S., et al.: Parameter synthesis for Markov models: covering the parameter space. In: Formal Methods in System Design (2024). https://doi.org/10.1007/s10703-023-00442-x

12. Kallenberg, L.: Markov decision processes. In: Lecture Notes (2016). https://www.math.leidenuniv.nl/7Ekallenberg/Lecture-notes-MDP.pdf

13. Kwiatkowska, M., Norman, G., Parker, D.: Stochastic model checking. In: Bernardo, M., Hillston, J. (eds.) SFM 2007. LNCS, vol. 4486, pp. 220–270. Springer, Heidelberg (2007). https://doi.org/10.1007/978-3-540-72522-0_6

14. Kwiatkowska, M., Norman, G., Parker, D.: PRISM 4.0: verification of probabilistic real-time systems. In: Gopalakrishnan, G., Qadeer, S. (eds.) CAV 2011. LNCS, vol. 6806, pp. 585–591. Springer, Heidelberg (2011). https://doi.org/10.1007/978-3-642-22110-1_47

15. Littman, M.L., Cassandra, A.R., Kaelbling, L.P.: Learning policies for partially observable environments: scaling up. In: Machine Learning Proceedings 1995. Morgan Kaufmann (1995). https://doi.org/10.1016/B978-1-55860-377-6.50052-9

16. Nilim, A., El Ghaoui, L.: Robust control of Markov decision processes with uncertain transition matrices. Oper. Res. **53**(5), 780–798 (2005). https://doi.org/10.1287/opre.1050.0216

17. Oakley, L., Oprea, A., Tripakis, S.: Adversarial robustness verification and attack synthesis in stochastic systems. In: 2022 IEEE 35th Computer Security Foundations Symposium (CSF), pp. 380–395 (2022). https://doi.org/10.1109/CSF54842.2022.9919660

18. Parker, D.: Multi-agent verification and control with probabilistic model checking. In: Jansen, N., Tribastone, M. (eds.) QEST 2023, pp. 1–9. Springer, Cham (2023). https://doi.org/10.1007/978-3-031-43835-6_1

19. Tolstaya, E., Gama, F., Paulos, J., Pappas, G., Kumar, V., Ribeiro, A.: Learning decentralized controllers for robot swarms with graph neural networks. In: Proceedings of the Conference on Robot Learning. Proceedings of Machine Learning Research, vol. 100, pp. 671–682. PMLR (020)

20. Virtanen, P., et al.: SciPy 1.0 Contributors: SciPy 1.0: Fundamental algorithms for scientific computing in python. Nat. Methods **17**, 261–272 (2020). https://doi.org/10.1038/s41592-019-0686-2

21. Wiesemann, W., Kuhn, D., Rustem, B.: Robust Markov decision processes. Math. Oper. Res. **38**(1), 153–183 (2012). https://doi.org/10.1287/moor.1120.0566

A Scenario Approach for Parametric Markov Decision Processes

Zhiming Chi[1,2], Ying Liu[3], Andrea Turrini[1,4], Lijun Zhang[1,2,4(✉)],
and David N. Jansen[1,2,4]

[1] Key Laboratory of System Software (Chinese Academy of Sciences) and State Key
Laboratory of Computer Science, Institute of Software, Chinese Academy of Sciences,
Beijing, China
zhanglj@ios.ac.cn
[2] University of Chinese Academy of Sciences, Beijing, China
[3] Institute of Optics and Electronics, Chinese Academy of Sciences, Chengdu, China
[4] Institute of Intelligent Software Guangzhou, Guangzhou, China

Abstract. In this paper, we consider the parameter synthesis problem
for parametric Markov decision processes (MDP). Computing the maximal expected value of satisfaction of a logical formula in parametric MDP
is a challenging task. Thus, we adopt the *scenario approach*: instead of
computing the precise rational function f_φ representing e.g. the maximal expected value, we aim at the approximation function $\tilde{f}_{\varphi,\lambda}$ that is
λ-probably approximately correct with respect to the desired statistical
guarantees. The approximation function is based on a template chosen by
the user, for instance a polynomial with fixed degree. By means of several
theoretical results, we discuss the relation of $\tilde{f}_{\varphi,\lambda}$ and f_φ, and propose a
framework for checking properties of the Markov model using $\tilde{f}_{\varphi,\lambda}$. An
extensive empirical evaluation show the effectiveness of our framework.

1 Introduction

When dealing with systems exhibiting both probabilistic and nondeterministic
behaviors, Markov models (see, e.g., [39]) are the main framework of choice, given
their elegant and clean formalism. In literature, we can find them often used to
model such as biological systems, distributed systems, networked systems, and
reinforcement learning. Depending on whether nondeterminism is present, we
have discrete-time Markov chains (MCs) or Markov decision processes (MDPs),
where the former have only one transition leaving each state with a single probability distribution over successor states, while the latter each state allows a non-
deterministic choice between multiple transitions with each of them (potentially)
distinct probability distributions. Properties of interest on a Markov model are
usually expressed by means of formulas belonging in a probabilistic logic like
PCTL [9,26] and its reward extension PRCTL [1]; typical properties expressed
in these logics have the form $\varphi = \text{Pmax}_{=?}[safe\ \mathbf{U}\ \checkmark]$ or $\varphi = \text{Rmin}_{=?}[\mathbf{F}\,goal]$.
The first formula asks for the maximum probability of eventual success, i.e., to

© The Author(s), under exclusive license to Springer Nature Switzerland AG 2025
N. Jansen et al. (Eds.): Principles of Verification: Cycling the Probabilistic Landscape,
LNCS 15261, pp. 234–266, 2025.
https://doi.org/10.1007/978-3-031-75775-4_11

reach a state marked with ✓ while staying *safe*; the second asks for the minimum expected reward accumulated before visiting a *goal* state. Various tools have been implemented to support the automatic verification of Markov models against formulas in PRCTL and PCTL*, the combination of PCTL and the linear-time temporal logic LTL, such as PRISM [33], MRMC [32], CADP [20], IscasMc [25], PROPhESY [16], and STORM [27].

One issue one faces when abstracting a real-world system as a Markov model, being it a Markov chain or a Markov decision process, is the choice of the probability values governing the transitions of the model. Precise probability values are difficult to get, so Markov models have been extended by adding parameters and by expressing the transition probabilities in terms of such parameters. Thus as parametric Markov models we have for instance interval MDPs [22], where transition probabilities simply lie in the given intervals, and the more general parametric MDPs (pMDPs) [15,24], where transition probabilities can be expressed as a (rational) function of the parameters; the latter are the model we consider in this paper.

When computing the satisfaction value for a PRCTL formula φ against a parametric Markov model, we obtain a function f_φ over the parameters, instead of a single value as happens for ordinary Markov models. The function f_φ is in general a rational function, that is, a fraction between two polynomials. Already for parametric Markov chains (pMCs), computing such a rational function is a challenging task, since it requires to work with polynomials with very high degree [3,31], which need to be factorized and simplified during the computation. In the context of pMDPs, nondeterminism needs to be taken into account when computing the rational function f_φ, since for different values of the parameters the optimal policy might change; this means that f_φ is likely to be a piece-wise defined function, where each piece is defined on a subspace of the domain of the parameters where the same policy is the optimal one. This means that multiple rational functions need to be computed, instead of just one as for pMCs, further increasing the amount of work that needs to be done to complete the model checking task, together with identifying the different subspaces of the domain of the parameters. However, in practice, it is often sufficient to have a simpler approximation of the actual rational function to establish whether the parametric Markov model satisfies the desired properties, provided that the approximation comes with enough guarantees about its error level.

Contribution of the Paper. In our previous work [37], we exploited the *scenario approach* [12,14] to synthesize an approximation function $\tilde{f}_{\varphi,\lambda}$ with PAC (probably approximately correct) guarantees in the context of pMCs. In this paper we extend the framework to pMDPs decorated with rewards. To deal with the fact that for different choices of the parameters the policy optimizing the value of the PRCTL formula $\varphi = \text{Qopt}_{=?}[\psi]$ might change, we treat the MDP policy as in [2], that is, we allow the policy to be different for each of the instantiated MDPs and we synthesize a common approximating function $\tilde{f}_{\varphi,\lambda}$ for all subspaces of the parameter domain space corresponding to the different policies. When enough samples of the parameters are considered, the synthesized function $\tilde{f}_{\varphi,\lambda}$ is guaranteed by construction to approximate the actual function f_φ with λ-PAC guarantee, that is, with confidence $1 - \eta$, the probability that the error due to the approximation is within the margin λ (obtained as a byproduct while synthesizing $\tilde{f}_{\varphi,\lambda}$) is at least $1 - \varepsilon$. As in [37], the coefficients of $\tilde{f}_{\varphi,\lambda}$ and the margin λ are computed by solving a Linear Programming (LP) problem, whose number of constraints is linearly related to the number ℓ of samples that is computed with respect to the desired (ε, η)-statistical guarantee, the number of parameters in the pMDP, and the degree of the polynomial template used for synthesizing $\tilde{f}_{\varphi,\lambda}$. We then extend the set of properties of the rational function f_φ we can analyze by working with $\tilde{f}_{\varphi,\lambda}$ to the pMDP/pMDRM models, as well as by introducing new results specific for nondeterministic Markov models, where we compare the effect of applying different policies π on the induced rational functions f_φ^π and the corresponding approximations $\tilde{f}_{\varphi,\lambda}^\pi$. Lastly, we show how scenario-based model checking for parametric Markov models can be combined with statistical model checking, so to combine the advantages of both approaches while preserving statistical guarantees for the computed functions. We implemented our framework in our tool PacPMA[1] and performed an extensive experimental evaluation that shows that our approach outperforms PRISM in the number of solved cases, with the computed margins being usually reasonably small even when approximating multiple rational functions with a single polynomial.

Related Work. In literature, several works focus on how to compute efficiently the rational function f_φ relative to the PRCTL property φ. The approach proposed by Daws in [15] focuses on reachability analysis for pMCs. It is based on considering the pMC as a finite automaton whose language, represented as a regular expression, allows the rational function f_φ to be computed. Daws' approach has been extended by Hahn et al. [24] to bounded reachability and expected reward in the PARAM tool, by optimizing the steps of the state elimination [28] used by Daws and of the rational function computation. Further improvements have been proposed by e.g. Jansen et al. [29], who optimize the order of the elimination of the state to shorten the running time; by Gainer et al. [19], who encode rational functions as arithmetic circuits to accelerate model checking; by Baier et al. [3], who adopt a fraction-free Gaussian elimination to speed up the operations on the rational functions; by Spel et al. [42], who use parameter lifting and check for monotonicity to efficiently compute ε-close upper bounds for the maximum reachability probability; and by Fang et al. [17], who split the pMC into multiple fragments, analyze each of them independently, and then combine the results to improve the computation of f_φ for pMCs with several parameters and complex behavior.

Works in literature on model checking parametric Markov models with nondeterminism are, for instance, the ones by Hahn et al. [23] for nested PRCTL formulas, who split the domain of parameters in hyperrectangles so that the

---

optimal policy is the same for each choice of parameters in a single hyperrectangle; and by Quatmann et al. [40], who establish the first sound and feasible approach for parameter synthesis in pMDPs. The above works lack statistical guarantees about being close to the actual rational function. The approach we propose in this paper for pMDPs, based on the one we developed for pMCs in [37], provides statistical guarantees for the efficiently synthesized approximation function. The reader interested in a more comprehensive survey on model checking for parametric Markov models is referred to the recent work by Jansen et al. [30].

The most closely related work to ours is the work by Badings et al. [2], as both make use of the scenario approach, which we briefly introduce now. The scenario-based approach was introduced in [11] to manage uncertainty in optimization problems. One relaxes and simplifies the given problem by sampling a set of constraints to be satisfied and by dropping all remaining ones; if the number of sampled constraints is large enough, then the optimal solution computed for the relaxed problem satisfies the constraints of the original problem with statistical guarantees. The scenario approach has been applied in multiple contexts by e.g. [12,14] for solving robust properties, by [44] for safety properties in black-box continuous-time dynamical systems, and by [36] for robustness of neural networks. The main difference between the work of Badings et al. [2] and ours is about what kind of problems the scenario approach is used for in the analysis of parametric Markov models. They use the scenario approach to compute the probability that the different instances of the pMDP satisfy the given PRCTL formula φ, by solving an ordinary model checking problem for the instantiated pMDP, comparing the obtained value with the desired target value β, and then computing the probability of a successful comparison. In our work, we instead compute a low-degree polynomial approximation $\tilde{f}_{\varphi,\lambda}$ for f_φ and then we use this approximation to evaluate whether the instances of the pMDP satisfy the property φ by comparing the value of $\tilde{f}_{\varphi,\lambda}(\mathbf{v})$ with β for the choice of the parameters $\mathbf{v}$. Moreover, we can use the simpler computed approximation $\tilde{f}_{\varphi,\lambda}(\mathbf{v})$ for further analysis, like plotting it, finding its maxima and minima, whether it remains close to a given target value, etc. with statistical guarantees on the answer while reducing the risk of incurring numerical errors.

Statistical model checking (SMC) is a technique that combines statistical methods with model checking to verify properties of systems with large, potentially infinite, state spaces; see [35] for an overview. In SMC, like in ordinary model checking, the properties of interest are expressed in temporal logics, but the verification is performed by simulating the system and estimating the probability of the property being satisfied. SMC has been applied to various domains, such as cyber-physical systems [43] and autonomous driving systems [5,38]. In our work, we combine the scenario approach with SMC to estimate the real function value of the property of interest, and provide statistical guarantees on the result.

Organization of the Paper. After giving in Sect. 2 some preliminaries, models, and logic we use in this paper, in Sect. 3 we recall the PAC-based model checking approach developed in [37] for Markov chains and we extend it to Markov decision processes; then we present in Sect. 4 how to combine statistical model checking and PAC-based model checking. We evaluate our framework empirically in Sect. 5 before concluding the paper in Sect. 6 with a discussion on possible extensions and some final remarks.

2   Preliminaries

In this section, after introducing some probability theory notions, we briefly recall the definition of MDPs (see, e.g., [4,39]) and related reward structures as well as the probabilistic logic PRCTL we use to express properties on them; then we consider their extension with parameters.

A *σ-field* over a set X is a set $\mathcal{F} \subseteq 2^X$ that includes X and is closed under complement and countable union. A *measurable space* is a pair $(X, \mathcal{F})$ where X is a set, also called the *sample space*, and $\mathcal{F}$ is a σ-field over X. A measurable space $(X, \mathcal{F})$ is called *discrete* if $\mathcal{F} = 2^X$. A *measure* over a measurable space $(X, \mathcal{F})$ is a function $\mu \colon \mathcal{F} \to \mathbb{R}_{\geq 0}$ such that, for each countable collection $\{X_i\}_{i \in I}$ of pairwise disjoint elements of $\mathcal{F}$, $\mu(\cup_{i \in I} X_i) = \sum_{i \in I} \mu(X_i)$. A *probability measure* over a measurable space $(X, \mathcal{F})$ is a measure μ over $(X, \mathcal{F})$ such that $\mu(X) = 1$. A measure over a discrete measurable space $(X, 2^X)$ is called a *discrete measure* over X. The *support* of a discrete measure μ over $(X, \mathcal{F})$, denoted by $Supp(\mu)$, is the set $\{x \in X \mid \mu(x) > 0\}$. When X is finite, we usually call the discrete measure μ over $(X, 2^X)$ a probability distribution and we denote by $Dist(X)$ the set of all probability distributions over X.

2.1   Probabilistic Models

Definition 1. *Given a finite set of atomic propositions AP, a* (labelled) *Markov decision process (MDP) $\mathcal{M}$ is a tuple $\mathcal{M} = (S, \bar{s}, Act, \mathbf{P}, L)$, where S is a finite set of* states; $\bar{s} \in S$ *is the* initial state; *Act is a finite set of* actions; *$\mathbf{P} \colon S \times Act \times S \to \mathbb{R}_{\geq 0}$ is a transition function such that for each $s \in S$ and $a \in Act$, $\sum_{s' \in S} \mathbf{P}(s, a, s') \in \{0, 1\}$; and $L \colon S \to 2^{AP}$ is a labelling function.*

We denote by $Act(s) = \{a \in Act \mid \sum_{s' \in S} \mathbf{P}(s, a, s') = 1\}$ the set of actions enabled by the state s; we require that $|Act(s)| \geq 1$ for all states $s \in S$.

A discrete-time Markov chain can be seen as an MDP where $|Act(s)| = 1$ for all states $s \in S$; thus Act can be omitted and we get the usual definition of Markov chain:

Definition 2. *Given a finite set of atomic propositions AP, a* (labelled) *discrete-time Markov chain (MC) $\mathcal{D}$ is a tuple $\mathcal{D} = (S, \bar{s}, \mathbf{P}, L)$ where S is a finite set of* states; $\bar{s} \in S$ *is the* initial state; *$\mathbf{P} \colon S \times S \to \mathbb{R}_{\geq 0}$ is a transition function such that for each $s \in S$, $\sum_{s' \in S} \mathbf{P}(s, s') = 1$; and $L \colon S \to 2^{AP}$ is a labelling function.*

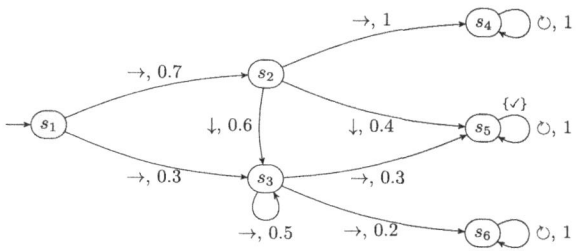

Fig. 1. An example of Markov decision process

The *underlying graph* of an MDP $\mathcal{M} = (S, \bar{s}, Act, \mathbf{P}, L)$ is a directed graph $\langle V, E \rangle$ with $V = S$ as vertices and $E = \{ (s, s') \in S \times S \mid \exists a \in Act.\mathbf{P}(s, a, s') > 0 \}$ as edges.

As an example of MDP, consider the one shown in Fig. 1. It has six states, from s_1 to s_6, with s_1 as initial state (indicated by the gray background and the small incoming arrow). The set of actions is $\{\rightarrow, \downarrow, \circlearrowleft\}$ and the non-zero probability values of the transitions are depicted on the directed arcs connecting the states, together with the action enabling them. As labelling function L, all states are mapped to $\emptyset$ except for s_5 where $L(s_5) = \{\checkmark\}$. Figure 1 also depicts its underlying graph, once we consider only the states and the arcs between them.

Let $\mathcal{M}$ be an MDP; a *path* σ of $\mathcal{M}$ is a (possibly infinite) sequence alternating between states and actions $\sigma = s_0 a_0 s_1 a_1 s_2 \cdots$ such that for each meaningful $i \in \mathbb{N}$, we have $\mathbf{P}(s_i, a_i, s_{i+1}) > 0$; we write $\sigma[i]$ to indicate the state s_i and $\sigma(i)$ to indicate the action a_i. We let $Paths^*(\mathcal{M})$ ($Paths(\mathcal{M})$, resp.) denote the sets of all finite (infinite, resp.) paths of $\mathcal{M}$. Given a finite path $\sigma = s_0 a_1 s_1 a_1 s_2 \cdots s_n$, we denote by $|\sigma| = n + 1$ its number of states and by $last(\sigma) = s_n$ its last state.

Nondeterminism in MDPs is resolved by policies, which decide the next transition to perform by choosing an action enabled by state the MDP is currently in. Formally, a *policy* π for an MDP $\mathcal{M}$ is a total function $\pi \colon Paths^*(\mathcal{M}) \rightarrow Dist(Act)$ such that $Supp(\pi(\sigma)) \subseteq Act(last(\sigma))$ for each $\sigma \in Paths^*(\mathcal{M})$; we denote by $Pol(\mathcal{M})$ the set of all policies for $\mathcal{M}$ and we just write Pol for $Pol(\mathcal{M})$ when $\mathcal{M}$ is clear from the context. We call $\pi \in Pol$ *memoryless* if $\pi(\sigma) = \pi(\sigma')$ for each $\sigma, \sigma' \in Paths^*(\mathcal{M})$ such that $last(\sigma) = last(\sigma')$ and we call π *deterministic* if $|Supp(\pi(\sigma))| = 1$ for each $\sigma \in Paths^*(\mathcal{M})$.

Given an MDP $\mathcal{M}$, a policy $\pi \in Pol$, and a state s, π induces a probability measure over the paths of $\mathcal{M}$ from the state s as follows: the basic measurable events are the cylinder sets of finite paths, where the *cylinder set* of a finite path σ is the set $Cyl(\sigma) = \{ \sigma' \in Paths(\mathcal{M}) \mid \sigma \text{ is a prefix of } \sigma' \}$. The probability $Pr_{s,\pi}$ of a cylinder set $Cyl(\sigma)$ is defined inductively as follows:

$$Pr_{s,\pi}(Cyl(\sigma)) = \begin{cases} 1 & \text{if } \sigma = s, \\ 0 & \text{if } \sigma = t \neq s, \\ Pr_{s,\pi}(Cyl(\sigma')) \cdot \pi(\sigma')(a) \cdot \mathbf{P}(last(\sigma'), a, t) & \text{if } \sigma = \sigma' at. \end{cases}$$

Standard measure-theoretical arguments ensure that $Pr_{s,\pi}$ extends uniquely to the σ-field generated by cylinder sets (see, e.g., [10]).

Similarly to MCs, MDPs can be decorated with reward structures that assign values to states and transitions; such reward structures can be used to model e.g. the power consumption caused by the different actions, or the number of times specific states have been visited.

Definition 3. *A Markov decision reward model (MDRM) $\mathcal{R}$ is a pair $\mathcal{R} = (\mathcal{M}, \mathfrak{r})$ where $\mathcal{M}$ is an MDP and $\mathfrak{r} = \mathfrak{r}_S \cup \mathfrak{r}_{Act}$ where $\mathfrak{r}_S \colon S \to \mathbb{R}_{\geq 0}$ and $\mathfrak{r}_{Act} \colon S \times Act \to \mathbb{R}_{\geq 0}$ is a reward function.*

In our autonomous car example, we can establish a reward function that monitors the number of collisions the vehicle experiences. Specifically, a penalty reward $\mathfrak{r} = 1$ is applied whenever it collides with an obstacle, reflecting the detrimental consequences of striking a wall or another object.

Given an MDRM $\mathcal{R} = (\mathcal{M}, \mathfrak{r})$, a state s, and a policy π, we can define $ExpRew_{s,\pi}^{\mathcal{R}}$, the *expected cumulative reward under* π, as follows (cf. [4]): given a set $T \subseteq S$ of states, $ExpRew_{s,\pi}^{\mathcal{R}}(T)$ is the expectation with respect to the probability $Pr_{s,\pi}$ of the random variable $X^T \colon Paths(\mathcal{M}) \to \mathbb{R}_{\geq 0}$ defined as follows:

$$X^T(\sigma) = \begin{cases} 0 & \text{if } \sigma_0 \in T, \\ \infty & \text{if } \sigma_i \notin T \text{ for each } i \in \mathbb{N}, \\ \displaystyle\sum_{i=0}^{\min\{\, n \in \mathbb{N} \,\mid\, \sigma[n] \in T \,\} - 1} \mathfrak{r}(\sigma[i]) + \mathfrak{r}(\sigma i, \sigma i) & \text{otherwise.} \end{cases}$$

We recall that if the policy π does not make reaching T almost sure, that is, $Pr_{s,\pi}(\{\, \sigma \in Paths^*(\mathcal{M}) \mid last(\sigma) \in T \,\}) < 1$, then $ExpRew_{s,\pi}^{\mathcal{R}}(T) = \infty$ (cf. [4, Definition 10.71]).

2.2   Probabilistic Reward Logic PRCTL

In this paper, we use formulas from PRCTL, the Probabilistic Reward CTL logic [1], that extends PCTL [26] with rewards, to formalize properties about MDRMs. Such formulas are constructed according to the following grammar, where φ is called a *state formula* and ψ is called a *path formula*:

$$\varphi ::= a \mid \neg\varphi \mid \varphi \wedge \varphi \mid \text{Popt}_{\bowtie p}(\psi) \mid \text{Ropt}_{\bowtie r}(\mathbf{F}\varphi)$$
$$\psi ::= \mathbf{X}\varphi \mid \varphi \, \mathbf{U} \, \varphi \mid \varphi \, \mathbf{U}^{\leq k} \, \varphi$$

where $a \in AP$, $opt \in \{\min, \max\}$, $\bowtie \in \{<, \leq, \geq, >\}$, $p \in [0,1]$, $r \in \mathbb{R}_{\geq 0}$, and $k \in \mathbb{N}$. We use freely the usually derived operators, like $\varphi_1 \vee \varphi_2 = \neg(\neg\varphi_1 \wedge \neg\varphi_2)$, $\text{tt} = a \vee \neg a$, and $\mathbf{F}\varphi = \text{tt} \, \mathbf{U} \, \varphi$. If we omit the $\text{Ropt}_{\bowtie r}(\mathbf{F}\varphi)$ operator from PRCTL, we get the standard PCTL logic for MDPs.

The semantics of a state formula φ and of a path formula ψ is given with respect to a state s and a path σ of a DMRM $\mathcal{R} = (\mathcal{M}, \mathfrak{r})$, respectively. The semantics is standard for all Boolean and temporal operators; for the $\mathrm{Popt}_{\bowtie p}$ operator, it is defined as

$$s \models \mathrm{Popt}_{\bowtie p}(\psi) \text{ iff } \mathrm{opt}_{\pi \in \mathrm{Pol}}\{Pr_{s,\pi}(\{\,\sigma \in Paths(\mathcal{M})\,|\,\sigma \models \psi\,\})\} \bowtie p$$

and, similarly,

$$s \models \mathrm{Ropt}_{\bowtie r}(\mathbf{F}\varphi) \text{ iff } \mathrm{opt}_{\pi \in \mathrm{Pol}}\{ExpRew_{s,\pi}(\{\,t \in S\,|\,t \models \varphi\,\})\} \bowtie r.$$

With some abuse of notation, we write $\mathcal{R} \models \varphi$ if $\bar{s} \models \varphi$; we also consider $\mathrm{Popt}_{=?}(\psi)$ and $\mathrm{Ropt}_{=?}(\mathbf{F}\varphi)$ as PRCTL formulas, asking to compute the probability (resp. expected reward) of satisfying ψ (resp. $\mathbf{F}\varphi$) in the initial state $\bar{s}$ of $\mathcal{R}$, i.e., to compute the value $\mathrm{opt}_{\pi \in \mathrm{Pol}}\{Pr_{\bar{s},\pi}(\{\,\sigma \in Paths(\mathcal{M})\,|\,\sigma \models \psi\,\})\}$ (resp. $\mathrm{opt}_{\pi \in \mathrm{Pol}}\{ExpRew_{\bar{s},\pi}(\{\,t \in S\,|\,t \models \varphi\,\})\})$. We just write $\mathrm{Qopt}_{=?}$ to denote either $\mathrm{Popt}_{=?}(\psi)$ or $\mathrm{Ropt}_{=?}(\mathbf{F}\varphi)$, i.e., when we are just interested in computing an expected value about the MDP.

As examples of PRCTL formulas, consider the simple MDP shown in Fig. 1. It is easy to observe that the minimum probability of eventually reaching s_5 is 0.18, which can be formalized as $\mathrm{Pmin}_{=?}(\mathbf{F}\checkmark) = 0.18$, by the memoryless policy $\pi^{\dagger}$ choosing $\to$ in s_2; the maximum probability is instead 0.712, as induced by the memoryless policy $\pi^{\ddagger}$ choosing $\downarrow$ in s_2. On the other hand, both the min and max expected reward accumulated before eventually reaching s_5 are infinite, since s_5 cannot be reached with probability 1.

It is well known that deterministic memoryless policies suffice to compute $\mathrm{Qopt}_{=?}$ and that applying a policy π to a MDRM $\mathcal{R} = (\mathcal{M}, \mathfrak{r})$ induces a MC $\mathcal{M}^{\pi}$ and the corresponding reward structure $\mathfrak{r}^{\pi}$, where for instance the probability of going from state s to state s' in the MC $\mathcal{M}^{\pi}$ induced by a memoryless policy π is $\sum_{a \in Act(s)} \pi(s)(a) \cdot \mathbf{P}(s, a, s')$. For more details, we refer the interested reader to, e.g., [4, 18].

2.3 Parametric Models

We now recall the definition of parametric models from [23, 24, 37]. Let $\mathrm{V} = \{v_1, \ldots, v_n\}$ denote a finite set of *variables*, or *parameters*, each one associated by range: $\mathrm{V} \to \mathbb{R}$ with its closed interval of valid values $\mathrm{range}(v) = [L_v, U_v] \subseteq \mathbb{R}$. To simplify the notation, we consider the parameters given in a predefined order, so we can write them as a vector $\mathbf{v} = (v_1, \ldots, v_n)$. Let $\mathcal{P}_{\mathrm{V}}$ denote the ring of the polynomials with variables V over the field $\mathbb{R}$ of real numbers; a *rational function* f is the ratio between two polynomials $g_1, g_2 \in \mathcal{P}_{\mathrm{V}}$, that is, $f(\mathbf{v}) = \frac{g_1(\mathbf{v})}{g_2(\mathbf{v})}$; let $\mathcal{F}_{\mathrm{V}}$ be the set of all rational functions. An *evaluation* ν is a function $\nu \colon \mathrm{V} \to \mathbb{R}$ assigning to each parameter one specific value in its range, i.e., for each $v \in \mathrm{V}$, $\nu(v) \in \mathrm{range}(v)$; we write $\nu(\mathbf{v})$ to denote the vector of real numbers induced by ν on $\mathbf{v}$, i.e., $\nu(\mathbf{v}) = (\nu(v_1), \cdots, \nu(v_n))$. Given $f = \frac{g_1}{g_2} \in \mathcal{F}_{\mathrm{V}}$ and an evaluation ν, we denote by $f\langle\nu\rangle$ the rational number $f(\nu(\mathbf{v}))$; we assume that $f\langle\nu\rangle$ is well defined for each evaluation ν, that is, we assume that $g_2\langle\nu\rangle \neq 0$ for each evaluation ν.

Definition 4. *Given a finite set of parameters* V, *a parametric Markov decision process (pMDP)* $\mathcal{M}_V$ *with parameters* V *is a tuple* $\mathcal{M}_V = (S, \bar{s}, Act, \mathbf{P}, L)$ *where* $S, \bar{s}, Act$ *and* L *are as in Definition 1, while* $\mathbf{P} \colon S \times Act \times S \to \mathcal{F}_V$.

Definition 5. *Given a pMDP* $\mathcal{M}_V = (S, \bar{s}, Act, \mathbf{P}, L)$, *an evaluation* ν *induces the MDP* $\mathcal{M}\langle\nu\rangle = (S, \bar{s}, Act, \mathbf{P}_\nu, L)$, *provided that* $\mathbf{P}_\nu(s, a, s') = \mathbf{P}(s, a, s')\langle\nu\rangle$ *for each* $s, s' \in S$ *and* $a \in Act$ *satisfies the conditions given in Definition 1.*

Extending MDRMs to parametric MDRMs (pMDRMs) is natural: a pMDRM $\mathcal{R}_V$ is just a pair $\mathcal{R}_V = (\mathcal{M}_V, \mathfrak{r})$ where $\mathcal{M}_V$ is a pMDP and $\mathfrak{r}$ is a reward function.

To simplify the presentation and ensure that the underlying graph of $\mathcal{M}_V$ does not depend on the actual evaluation, we make the following assumption:

Assumption 1 (cf. [23]). *Given a pMDP* $\mathcal{M}_V$ *and any pair of evaluations* ν_1 *and* ν_2, *for the induced MDPs* $\mathcal{M}_V\langle\nu_1\rangle$ *and* $\mathcal{M}_V\langle\nu_2\rangle$ *we have that for each* $s, s' \in S$ *and* $a \in Act$, *it holds that* $\mathbf{P}_{\nu_1}(s, a, s') = 0$ *if and only if* $\mathbf{P}_{\nu_2}(s, a, s') = 0$.

By this assumption, different evaluations can only change the strictly positive probability value of the transition from s to s' by action a, not whether the probability of the transition from s to s' by action a is 0.

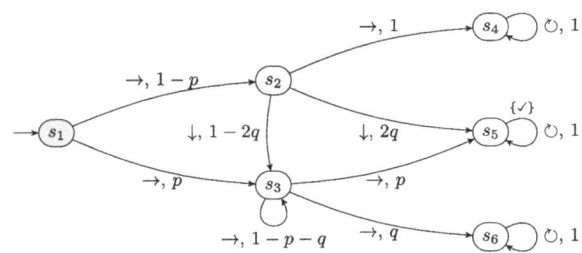

Fig. 2. An example of parametric Markov decision process

As an example of pMDP, consider the one shown in Fig. 2: it is the parametric counterpart of the MDP shown in Fig. 1, where p and q are the parameters. As their ranges, we can take e.g. range$(p) = [0.1, 0.5]$ and range$(q) = [0.1, 0.3]$. One possible evaluation is $\nu(p) = 0.3, \nu(q) = 0.2$, which gives us the MDP shown in Fig. 1. The rational function corresponding to the PRCTL formula Pmax$_{=?}(\mathbf{F}\checkmark)$ is $\frac{p+2q^2-2pq^2}{p+q} = 0.712$ when evaluated on ν, as one would expect; similarly, the rational function for Pmin$_{=?}(\mathbf{F}\checkmark)$ is $\frac{p^2}{p+q}$ that has value 0.18 on ν.

3   Probably Approximately Correct Function Synthesis

In this section, we briefly recall from [37] how to get low-degree polynomials that approximate the exact rational functions corresponding to the PRCTL properties of a discrete-time Markov chain, while providing a statistical PAC guarantee on the closeness of the approximating polynomial with the approximated function. We then extend these constructions to the pMDP setting before presenting new results specific to pMDPs.

3.1   Probably Approximately Correct Models

As mentioned in the introduction and as shown in [37], a polynomial for the rational function relative to a PRCTL property against a pMC can be synthesized by sampling values for the parameters, evaluate the value of the property in the instantiated MC, and then finding the coefficients of the polynomial that minimize the error between the polynomial and the computed property value on the sampled parameters. The synthesized polynomial comes with a probably approximately correctness guarantee with respect to the given significance level η and error rate ε, provided that a sufficiently large number of samples is used.

The synthesis of the approximating polynomial is based on the scenario approach [12,14] that was originally applied in the context of robust convex programming problems [6,7,21]. These problems are in general described by the following uncertain convex optimization problem

$$
\begin{aligned}
\min \quad & \mathbf{a}^T \theta \\
\text{s.t.} \quad & f_\omega(\theta) \leq 0 \qquad \forall \omega \in \Omega \\
& \theta \in \Theta
\end{aligned}
\tag{1}
$$

In the problem above, $\Theta \subseteq \mathbb{R}^m$ is a convex and closed domain of the optimization variables θ so that the objective function $\mathbf{a}^T \theta$ is minimized. Ω is the domain of the uncertain parameters ω and for each of these parameters ω, the constraint $f_\omega(\theta) \leq 0$ is based on the function $f_\omega : \Theta \to \mathbb{R}$ that is assumed to be a convex function of $\theta \in \Theta$.

In general, the size of the set of parameters Ω is infinite, and this makes the optimization problem (1) have infinitely many constraints, thus making it difficult to be solved. To make (1) solvable, Calafiore and Campi [12] proposed to transform (1) into a scenario optimization problem, by relying on the Helly theorem [41]. In the scenario optimization problem, formalized below in Definition 6, only finitely many constraints are used, with their number being chosen so to provide statistical guarantees on the error rate made with respect to the exact solution of (1).

Definition 6. *Given the set Ω, let $\Omega_\ell = \{\omega_1, \ldots, \omega_\ell\}$ be ℓ independent identically distributed samples taken from Ω according to a given probability measure P over Ω. The* scenario optimization problem *corresponding to the problem* (1) *is defined as*

$$
\begin{aligned}
\min \quad & \mathbf{a}^T \theta \\
\text{s.t.} \quad & f_{\omega_i}(\theta) \leq 0 \qquad \forall \omega_i \in \Omega_\ell \\
& \theta \in \Theta
\end{aligned}
\tag{2}
$$

It is easy to observe that the optimization problem (2) is in practice a relaxation of the problem (1), since we consider fewer constraints for the optimization variables θ, so the optimal solution θ_ℓ^* of the problem (2) satisfies all constraints $f_{\omega_i}(\theta_\ell^*) \leq 0$ for each sample $\omega_i \in \Omega_\ell$, but no requirement is imposed on θ_ℓ^* regarding the constraints $f_\omega(\theta_\ell^*) \leq 0$ for $\omega \in \Omega \setminus \Omega_\ell$. The issue now is how to provide a strong enough guarantee that the optimal solution θ_ℓ^* of (2) also satisfies the other constraints $f_\omega(\theta) \leq 0$ with $\omega \in \Omega \setminus \Omega_\ell$ we have not considered.

Statistics theory ensures that if enough samples ℓ are taken, then the probability of θ_ℓ^* violating the omitted constraints is smaller than a given threshold: the following theorem establishes how many samples need to be taken according to P to format $\Omega_\ell = \{\omega_1, \ldots, \omega_\ell\}$ at least to ensure that θ_ℓ^* "works well" also for the constraints $f_\omega(\theta) \leq 0$ with $\omega \in \Omega \setminus \Omega_\ell$ of the problem (1) we have not considered. The fact that θ_ℓ^* "works well" is formalized by using an *error rate* ε to bound the probability that the solution θ_ℓ^* violates the constraints of problem (1) and by a *significance level* η with respect to the random sampling solution algorithm. The minimal number of sampled points ℓ is related to the error rate $\varepsilon \in (0, 1]$ and significance level $\eta \in (0, 1]$ by:

Theorem 1 ([14]). *If the optimization problem (2) is feasible and has a unique optimal solution θ_ℓ^*, then $P(f_\omega(\theta_\ell^*) > 0) < \varepsilon$, with confidence at least $1 - \eta$, provided that the number of constraints ℓ satisfies*

$$\ell \geq \frac{2}{\varepsilon} \cdot \left(\ln \frac{1}{\eta} + m \right),$$

where m is the dimension of θ, that is, $\theta \in \Theta \subseteq \mathbb{R}^m$, ε and η are the given error rate and significance level, respectively.

The uniqueness assumption about θ_ℓ^* in the theorem above is not restrictive, since for multiple optimal solutions we can just use the Tie-break rule [12] to get a unique optimal solution.

Statistical guarantees like the ones established in Theorem 1 can be obtained also when comparing how close two functions are on their common domain. This, together with the results of Theorem 1 applied to the optimization problem (2), will be used later for the synthesis of approximation functions in model checking parametric MDPs.

Definition 7. *Given a set of n variables $V = \{v_1, \ldots, v_n\}$, their domain $\mathcal{V} = \prod_{i=1}^n \text{range}(v_i)$, and a function $f \colon X \to \mathbb{R}$, let P be a probability measure over $\mathcal{V}$ and $\varepsilon, \eta \in (0, 1]$ be an error rate and a significance level, respectively.*

We say that the polynomial $\tilde{f}_\lambda \in \mathcal{P}_V$ is a λ-PAC approximation of f with (ε, η)-guarantee if, with confidence $1 - \eta$, the following condition holds:

$$P(|\tilde{f}_\lambda(\mathbf{v}) - f(\mathbf{v})| \leq \lambda) \geq 1 - \varepsilon,$$

where $\lambda \in \mathbb{R}_{\geq 0}$ is used as a margin to bound the PAC approximation error.

As an example for the above definition, for the pMDP shown in Fig. 2 and the PRCTL property $\varphi = \text{Pmax}_{=?}(\mathbf{F}\checkmark)$, the function f_φ representing φ is the exact rational function $f_\varphi = \frac{p+2q^2-2pq^2}{p+q}$, while a possible polynomial approximation $\tilde{f}_{\varphi,\lambda}$ is the linear function $\tilde{f}_{\varphi,\lambda} = 0.61 + 0.48p - 0.18q$ (where for ease of notation we write the coefficients approximated to the second digit); we obtain such a linear function by applying the method we present in Sect. 3.2, which gives us the corresponding margin $\lambda = 0.05$ when we assign ε and η to be $\varepsilon = \eta = 0.05$. We can check that the approximation function $\tilde{f}_{\varphi,\lambda}$ satisfies the condition of Definition 7 when we consider $\lambda = 0.05$, that is, $\tilde{f}_{\varphi,\lambda}$ is a 0.05-PAC approximation of f_φ with $(0.05, 0.05)$-guarantee.

In Definition 7, for f_φ and $\tilde{f}_{\varphi,\lambda}$ the margin λ can be chosen freely in $\mathbb{R}_{\geq 0}$, as long as $\lambda \geq 0.05$: it is immediate to note that, if $P(|\tilde{f}_{\varphi,\lambda}(\mathbf{v}) - f_\varphi(\mathbf{v})| \leq \lambda) \geq 1 - \varepsilon$ holds with confidence $1 - \eta$ for $\lambda = 0.05$, then the same holds for all values of λ larger than 0.05. This means, for instance, that for the same choice of ε and η, we can have that $\tilde{f}_{\varphi,\lambda}$ is e.g. a 0.1-PAC approximation of f_φ with (ε, η)-guarantee while it may not be a 0.01-PAC approximation of f_φ with (ε, η)-guarantee; this can happen because $\tilde{f}_{\varphi,\lambda}$ can make $P(|\tilde{f}_{\varphi,\lambda}(\mathbf{v}) - f_\varphi(\mathbf{v})| \leq 0.01) \geq 1 - \varepsilon$ fail, with confidence $1 - \eta$. So this means that for the same f_φ, $\tilde{f}_{\varphi,\lambda}$, ε, and η, Definition 7 can be satisfied or not depending on the value of λ we are interested in. As we will see below in Sect. 3.2, when we synthesize the approximation polynomial for the given function f_φ, we obtain a polynomial $\tilde{f}_{\varphi,\lambda}$ together with a value for the margin λ; both of them are the result of solving an optimization problem (cf. problem (3)) determined by the parameters ε and η, and a set of points randomly sampled in $\mathcal{V}$. Therefore, the actual value of λ can be different for different sets of sampled points, as does $\tilde{f}_{\varphi,\lambda}$; still, we can ensure by construction that the obtained polynomial $\tilde{f}_{\varphi,\lambda}$ and the associated margin λ satisfy Definition 7, that is, the approximation function $\tilde{f}_{\varphi,\lambda}$ obtained by solving problem (3) is a λ-PAC approximation of f_φ with (ε, η)-guarantee.

As usual in the PAC approach, we assume that P is the uniform distribution on the domain $\mathcal{V} = \prod_{i=1}^n \text{range}(v_i)$ unless otherwise specified. The intuition underlying Definition 7 is that we want to have statistical guarantees about the fact that the λ-PAC approximation $\tilde{f}_\lambda$ is closer to f than the margin λ, on $\mathcal{V}$. Thus the two statistical parameters η and ε are introduced to quantify how often the difference between $\tilde{f}_\lambda$ and f respects the threshold λ. Specifically, the error rate ε describes the probability that the difference between the value $f(\mathbf{v})$ and $\tilde{f}_\lambda(\mathbf{v})$ is larger than λ on the sampled points, while the significance level η bounds the risk of wrongly accepting this event; these two parameters can be changed to improve the quality of the approximation, that is, to get $\tilde{f}_\lambda$ closer to f.

3.2   Synthesizing Parametric Functions

We now recall and adapt the scenario approach for the synthesis of parametric functions to parametric Markov decision processes, that has been presented in [37] for parametric discrete-time Markov chains.

Let $\mathcal{R}_V = (\mathcal{M}_V, \mathfrak{r})$ be a pMDRM where the underlying pMDP $\mathcal{M}_V$ has components $\mathcal{M}_V = (S, \bar{s}, \mathbf{P}, L)$; let $\mathbf{v}$ denote the vector of parameters $(v_1, \ldots, v_n)$ of $\mathcal{M}_V$. Given the PRCTL state formula $\varphi = \mathtt{Qopt}_{=?}(\psi)$, the analytic function $f_\varphi(\mathbf{v})$, representing the optimal value of satisfying ψ in the pMDRM $\mathcal{R}_V$, can be a rational function with a very complicated form already in the context of parametric MCs [24] since the polynomials in these rational functions may have exponentially many terms. This means that analyzing them can be time consuming and subject to numerical errors; thus, as suggested by [37], we approximate them with some low degree polynomials while giving statistical guarantees on the approximation error we make.

Consider the λ-PAC approximation given in Definition 7. The approximation procedure developed in [37] that we extend to pMDPs computes the coefficients $\mathbf{c}$ of the polynomial $\tilde{f}_{\varphi, \lambda}(\mathbf{v})$ by solving a scenario optimization problem as defined in Definition 6. The scenario problem (2) is obtained by first taking ℓ samples of the parameters to form the set $\tilde{\mathcal{V}}$, which correspond to ℓ evaluations ν_i for $i = 1$ to ℓ; then the value $f_\varphi \langle \nu_i \rangle$ is obtained by solving a standard model checking problem for φ on the instance $\mathcal{M}_V \langle \nu_i \rangle$. Lastly, the corresponding constrains are produced, with the form

$$ |f_\varphi \langle \nu_i \rangle - \mathbf{c} \cdot (1, \mathbf{v}, \ldots, \mathbf{v}^d)^T \langle \nu_i \rangle| \leq \lambda, $$

where $\mathbf{v}^j$ denotes the monomials of degree j of the polynomial with variables $\mathbf{v}$, and then the optimization problem is solved with respect to the variables $\mathbf{c}$ and λ with the aim of minimizing λ. With this approach, it does not matter how complicated the function f_φ is: in order to construct the approximating polynomial $\tilde{f}_{\varphi, \lambda}$ of f_φ by solving an optimization problem, we do not need the analytical form of f_φ to compute $f_\varphi \langle \nu_i \rangle$; we get such values by standard model checking techniques on the instance $\mathcal{M}_V \langle \nu_i \rangle$. Since $\tilde{f}_{\varphi, \lambda}$ comes with statistical guarantees, provided that the number of samples ℓ is large enough, we can use it to analyze various properties the original function f_φ may satisfy. For self-containment of the paper, we now recall the notation and the formulation of the scenario problem sketched above as presented in [37], adapted to the pMDP setting.

Given the vector of parameters $\mathbf{v}$ and a degree $d \in \mathbb{N}$, we denote by $\mathbf{v}^d$ the vector of monomials $\mathbf{v}^d = (\mathbf{v}^\alpha)_{\|\alpha\|_1 = d}$, where each monomial $\mathbf{v}^\alpha$ is defined as $\mathbf{v}^\alpha = v_1^{\alpha_1} v_2^{\alpha_2} \cdots v_n^{\alpha_n}$, with $\alpha = (\alpha_1, \ldots, \alpha_n) \in \mathbb{N}^n$ and $\|\alpha\|_1 = \sum_{i=1}^n \alpha_i$. Then, we associate a vector $\mathbf{c}_i$ of coefficients to each of the monomials in the vector $(\mathbf{v}^i)_{i=0}^d$, obtaining the PAC approximation schema $\tilde{f}_\lambda(\mathbf{v}) = \sum_{i=0}^d \mathbf{c}_i \cdot \mathbf{v}^i$. For example, the pMDP shown in Fig. 2 has two parameters p and q; if we consider as degree $d = 2$, we get the quadratic polynomial $\tilde{f}_\lambda(p, q) = \mathbf{c}_0 \cdot 1 + \mathbf{c}_1 \cdot (p, q) + \mathbf{c}_2 \cdot (p, q)^2 = c_0 \cdot 1 + (c_{11} \cdot p + c_{12} \cdot q) + (c_{21} \cdot p^2 + c_{22} \cdot p \cdot q + c_{23} \cdot q^2)$. In general, for n parameters and a polynomial of degree d, we need $\binom{n+d}{n}$ coefficients.

Given the error rate ε and the significance level η, by Theorem 1 we need only to independently and identically sample at least $\ell \geq \frac{2}{\varepsilon} \left(\ln \frac{1}{\eta} + \binom{n+d}{n} + 1 \right)$ points $\tilde{\mathcal{V}} = \{\mathbf{v}_i\}_{i=1}^\ell$ to form the constraints used in the following relaxed LP problem, which corresponds to the problem (2).

$$\min_{\mathbf{c},\lambda} \quad 1 \cdot \lambda + 0 \cdot \mathbf{c}$$

$$\text{s.t.} \quad -\lambda \leq f_\varphi(\mathbf{v}_i) - \mathbf{c} \cdot (1, \mathbf{v}_i, \dots, \mathbf{v}_i^d)^T \leq \lambda \quad \forall \mathbf{v}_i \in \tilde{\mathcal{V}} \qquad (3)$$

$$\lambda \geq 0$$

where $\mathbf{c} \in \mathbb{R}^{\binom{n+d}{d}}$. We then solve the optimization problem (3) to get the coefficients $\mathbf{c}$ that allow λ to be minimal with respect to the constrains given by the sampled points $\tilde{\mathcal{V}}$, hence the λ-PAC approximation $\tilde{f}_{\varphi,\lambda}$ of the original function f_φ, with the statistical guarantees given by Definition 7.

For example, for the pMDP shown in Fig. 2, $\varphi = \text{Pmax}_{=?}[\mathbf{F}\checkmark]$, and the quadratic polynomial considered above, if we get as sampled point $(p = 0.3, q = 0.2)$, then the corresponding constraint

$$-\lambda \leq f_\varphi(\mathbf{v}_i) - \mathbf{c} \cdot (1, \mathbf{v}_i, \dots, \mathbf{v}_i^d)^T \leq \lambda$$

is instantiated as

$$-\lambda \leq 0.712 - 1 \cdot c_0 + 0.3 \cdot c_{11} + 0.2 \cdot c_{12} + 0.09 \cdot c_{21} + 0.06 \cdot c_{22} + 0.04 \cdot c_{23} \leq \lambda.$$

Discussion on λ and $\tilde{f}_{\varphi,\lambda}$ as Solution of the Problem (3). When we instantiate the problem (3) by sampling randomly ℓ points from $\mathcal{V}$ and then solve it, we get as solution a pair $(\lambda, \mathbf{c})$, so we can synthesize the approximation function $\tilde{f}_{\varphi,\lambda}$ by instantiating the chosen template with $\mathbf{c}$. If we instantiate another time the problem (3) by sampling randomly again ℓ points, we get another pair $(\lambda', \mathbf{c}')$ that is likely different from $(\lambda, \mathbf{c})$, and so the corresponding function $\tilde{f}'_{\varphi,\lambda'}$ is also different from $\tilde{f}_{\varphi,\lambda}$. This means that by instantiating and solving the problem (3) multiple times, we get different outcomes and one may wonder whether this may cause some problem and whether there are differences in the properties one can derive by using e.g. $\tilde{f}'_{\varphi,\lambda'}$ instead of $\tilde{f}_{\varphi,\lambda}$. As stated in [13,14], the margin λ is actually a random variable, since its value depends on the actual points that have been sampled to construct the problem (3); by a similar reasoning, also $\tilde{f}_{\varphi,\lambda}$ can be seen as a random variable. This means that, for λ and $\tilde{f}_{\varphi,\lambda}$ as computed in the first instance of the problem (3), for a point $\mathbf{v} \in \mathcal{V} \setminus \tilde{\mathcal{V}}$, we can have that $|f_\varphi(\mathbf{v}) - \tilde{f}_{\varphi,\lambda}(\mathbf{v})| \leq \lambda$ holds, but we can also have the opposite, that is, $|f_\varphi(\mathbf{v}) - \tilde{f}_{\varphi,\lambda}(\mathbf{v})| > \lambda$. However, Theorem 1 ensures that, if the number of samples ℓ is large enough, so to respect $\ell \geq \frac{2}{\varepsilon}\left(\ln\frac{1}{\eta} + \binom{n+d}{n} + 1\right)$, then the latter situation occurs with probability at most ε, with confidence $1 - \eta$. The same happens when we consider λ' and $\tilde{f}'_{\varphi,\lambda'}$ from the second instance of the problem (3). As suggested in [14], we can take a very small value for η, like 10^{-10} or 10^{-20}: this makes the probability of violating $|f_\varphi(\mathbf{v}) - \tilde{f}_{\varphi,\lambda}(\mathbf{v})| \leq \lambda$ by an ε-fraction of $\mathcal{V}$ negligible while only slightly increasing ℓ, since by Theorem 1 the significance η only provides a logarithmic contribute to the growth of ℓ.

3.3 Extending PRCTL Property Analysis from pMRMs to pMDRMs

Several results were established in [37] about the synthesized approximate function $\tilde{f}_{\varphi,\lambda}$ with respect to the rational function f_φ, in the context of a given pMRM $\mathcal{R}_V$, such as whether the parameters' domain $\mathcal{V}$ of $\mathcal{R}_V$ for the probabilistic formula $\varphi = P_{=?}(\psi)$ is safe, whether f_φ is near a given value ζ on the whole $\mathcal{V}$, or whether f_φ exceeds some given threshold τ for a reward property $\varphi = R_{=?}(F\varphi')$. Since these results depend only on the values assumed by f_φ on $\mathcal{V}$, they naturally extend to the context of parametric Markov decision reward models.

Safe Region. The first result from [37] we extend to pMDRMs is about how to efficiently check whether f_φ or, in general, a function f, is safe over $\mathcal{V}$.

Definition 8. *Let $\mathcal{V} = \prod_{i=1}^n \mathrm{range}(v_i)$ be the domain of a set of n parameters V. Given a function $f: \mathcal{V} \to \mathbb{R}_{\geq 0}$, a safety level $\zeta \in \mathbb{R}_{\geq 0}$, and a comparison $\bowtie \in \{<, >\}$, we say that the point $\mathbf{v} \in V$ is safe if and only if $f(\mathbf{v}) \bowtie \zeta$; we call $\mathcal{V}$ safe if and only if each $\mathbf{v} \in V$ is safe.*

If we want to analyze whether a pMDRM $\mathcal{R}_V$ is safe, i.e., whether it can never make a state property $\varphi = \mathrm{Qopt}_{=?}$ exceed a given safety level ζ, we can either compute f_φ and then compare it with ζ on $\mathcal{V}$, or we can use the following optimization problem that gives us the answer with a (ε, η)-statistical guarantee, provided that we take at least $\ell \geq \left\lceil \frac{2}{\varepsilon} \cdot (\ln \frac{1}{\eta} + 1) \right\rceil$ samples to form $\tilde{\mathcal{V}} \subseteq \mathcal{V}$:

$$
\begin{aligned}
\mathrm{opt}_{\bowtie} \quad & \lambda \\
\text{s.t.} \quad & f_\varphi(\mathbf{v}) \bowtie \lambda \qquad \forall \mathbf{v} \in \tilde{\mathcal{V}},
\end{aligned}
\tag{4}
$$

where $\mathrm{opt}_{\bowtie} = \min$ and $\bowtie = \;<\;$ if $\varphi = \mathrm{Qmax}_{=?}$ and $\mathrm{opt}_{\bowtie} = \max$ and $\bowtie = \;>\;$ if $\varphi = \mathrm{Qmin}_{=?}$. Here, the idea is that $\mathcal{R}_V$ is considered safe if, for instance, its maximum probability of reaching some bad state is at most λ, or the minimum expected reward before reaching failure is at least λ. Since we use polynomials of degree 0 in (4), the term $\binom{n+d}{n}$ occurring in the expression of ℓ reduces to $\binom{n+0}{n} = 1$ (cf. Theorem 1 and problem (3)).

Linear Approximation. By using a linear approximation $\tilde{f}_{\varphi,\lambda}$ instead of a constant one, as done above, by taking $\ell \geq \left\lceil \frac{2}{\varepsilon} \cdot (\ln \frac{1}{\eta} + n + 1) \right\rceil$ samples, we can verify with (ε, η)-statistical guarantee whether the function f_φ is respecting the safety level ζ on the whole domain $\mathcal{V}$, with additional information about where possible counterexamples can be found. More precisely, since it is easy to find the extreme values for a linear function, by e.g. solving a linear programming problem, we can inspect them to evaluate whether the function f exceeds ζ, by computing the value $f_\varphi(\mathbf{v}^*)$ on the parameters $\mathbf{v}^*$ corresponding to the extreme values. Then, we know whether $\mathbf{v}^*$ is a real or a spurious counterexample; in the latter case, we can just add it to the set $\tilde{\mathcal{V}}$ and improve the computation of $\tilde{f}_{\varphi,\lambda}$. This approach gives us the following result:

Lemma 1. *Given a pMDRM $\mathcal{R}_V$ and a PRCTL property $\varphi = \mathtt{Qopt}_{=?}$, let P be a probability measure over $\mathcal{V}$ and $\tilde{f}_{\varphi,\lambda}$ be a linear λ-PAC approximation of f_φ with (ε, η)-guarantee. Let $\pm = +$ and $\lessgtr\; = \;<$ if $\varphi = \mathtt{Qmax}_{=?}$ and symmetrically $\pm = -$ and $\lessgtr\; = \;>$ if $\varphi = \mathtt{Qmin}_{=?}$; let $\mp$ and $\gtrless$ denote the opposite of $\pm$ and $\lessgtr$, respectively.*

Given the safety level $\zeta \in \mathbb{R}_{\geq 0}$, if for each $\mathbf{v} \in \mathcal{V}$ we have $\tilde{f}_{\varphi,\lambda}(\mathbf{v}) \pm \lambda \lessgtr \zeta$, then $P(f_\varphi(\mathbf{v}) \lessgtr \zeta) \geq 1 - \varepsilon$ holds with confidence $1 - \eta$. On the other hand, if $P(\tilde{f}_{\varphi,\lambda}(\mathbf{v}) \mp \lambda \gtrless \zeta) > \varepsilon$, then there exists $\mathbf{v} \in \mathcal{V}$ such that $f_\varphi(\mathbf{v}) \gtrless \zeta$ holds with confidence $1 - \eta$.

Polynomial Approximation. So far, we have seen how to use an approximate polynomial $\tilde{f}_{\varphi,\lambda}$ of degree 0 and 1 in analyzing properties of the rational function f_φ for a pMDRM with respect to a state property $\varphi = \mathtt{Qopt}_{=?}$. We can use higher degree polynomials to better approximate f_φ and get more information about its behavior. For instance, we can check whether f_φ is within distance ζ from a desired target value β with respect to a given norm $\|\cdot\|_p$. This can be done, for instance, by applying the following lemma, first introduced in [37] for pMCs and that extends naturally to pMDRMs since it is not linked to the underlying model.

Lemma 2. *Given the domain $\mathcal{V}$ of a set of parameters, a function $f_\varphi \colon \mathcal{V} \to \mathbb{R}_{\geq 0}$, a safety level ζ, and a target value $\beta \in \mathbb{R}_{\geq 0}$, let M be an upper bound of $f_\varphi(\mathcal{V})$ and $\tilde{f}_{\varphi,\lambda}$ be a λ-PAC approximation of f_φ with (ε, η)-guarantee; let $|\mathcal{V}| = \int_{\mathcal{V}} 1 \, d\mathbf{v}$. For each $p \geq 1$, if $\tilde{f}_{\varphi,\lambda}$ satisfies the condition*

$$\sqrt[p]{\left(\lambda \sqrt[p]{(1-\varepsilon) \cdot |\mathcal{V}|} + \|\tilde{f}_{\varphi,\lambda} - \beta\|_p \right)^p + \varepsilon \cdot |\mathcal{V}| \cdot \max(|M - \beta|^p, \beta^p)} < \zeta \quad (5)$$

then $\|f_\varphi - \beta\|_p < \zeta$ holds with confidence $1 - \eta$.

The condition about M in the statement of Lemma 2 makes the lemma always applicable to the rational function f_φ for the property $\varphi = \mathtt{Popt}_{=?}[\psi]$, since such a function represents the probability of satisfying ψ, so $M = 1$ is an upperbound for f_φ. Instead, when we consider the property $\varphi = \mathtt{Ropt}_{=?}[\mathbf{F}\varphi']$, we have no suitable value for the upperbound M that we can use in all cases. In fact, by definition $\mathtt{Ropt}_{=?}[\mathbf{F}\varphi'] = \infty$ if φ' cannot be satisfied almost surely under the optimizing policy.

Lower Bound for Properties. To overcome this problem, we can rely on the following result, that allows us to check whether average value of e.g. the expected reward over all choices of the parameters exceeds a given threshold:

Lemma 3. *Given the domain $\mathcal{V}$ of a set of parameters, a probability measure P over $\mathcal{V}$, a function $f_\varphi \colon \mathcal{V} \to \mathbb{R}_{\geq 0}$, and a threshold τ, let $\tilde{f}_{\varphi,\lambda}$ be a λ-PAC approximation of f with (ε, η)-guarantee. If $\tilde{f}_{\varphi,\lambda}$ satisfies the condition*

$$\int_{\mathcal{V}} (\tilde{f}_{\varphi,\lambda}(\mathbf{v}) - \lambda) \, dP(\mathbf{v}) - \varepsilon \cdot |\mathcal{V}| \cdot \max_{\mathbf{v} \in \mathcal{V}} (\tilde{f}_{\varphi,\lambda}(\mathbf{v}) - \lambda) > \tau, \tag{6}$$

then $\int_{\mathcal{V}} f_\varphi(\mathbf{v}) \, dP(\mathbf{v}) > \tau$ holds with confidence $1 - \eta$.

3.4   pMDRM Specific PRCTL Analysis

One main difference between pMCs and pMDRMs is that for a given PRCTL property $\varphi = \text{Qopt}_{=?}$, for the former the function f_φ has a single expression while for the latter the function f_φ can be defined piece-wise, since for different subregions of $\mathcal{V}$ the policy optimizing $\text{Qopt}_{=?}$ can be different, so is the corresponding expression of f_φ. This means, for a given pMDRM, that the function f_φ associated with $\varphi = \text{Qopt}_{=?}$ may not be smooth, unlike the rational functions presented in the case of pMRMs. So an interesting question to consider is how to choose the better policy for a pair of given parameters' values or ranges of them.

Locally Better Policy. Since that once a specific policy is determined, the pMDP can degenerate into a pMC, then we can easily calculate the PAC approximation of the rational function, which represents the properties of interest, here we analyze the reachability properties. Specifically, for a pMDP, we want to choose the one with the higher reachability probability from the two policies under some parameter conditions, and we can achieve this goal by the following lemma:

Lemma 4. *Given a pMDRM $\mathcal{R}_V$, let $\mathcal{V} = \prod_{i=1}^{n} \text{range}(v_i)$ be the domain of its parameters and P be a probability measure over $\mathcal{V}$. Given a PRCTL state formula φ and two policies π and π', let f_φ and f'_φ be the two rationals functions corresponding to φ when computed on the induced pMRMs $\mathcal{R}_V^\pi$ and $\mathcal{R}_V^{\pi'}$, respectively. Let $\tilde{g}_{\varphi,\lambda}$ be a λ-PAC approximation of $f_\varphi - f'_\varphi$ with (ε, η)-guarantee.*

1. *If for each parameter $\mathbf{v} \in \mathcal{V}$, we have that*

$$\tilde{g}_{\varphi,\lambda}(\mathbf{v}) - \lambda > 0 \tag{7}$$

   holds, then the functions f and f' satisfy the condition $f_\varphi(\mathbf{v}) > f'_\varphi(\mathbf{v})$ with (ε, η)-guarantee, that is, $P(f_\varphi(\mathbf{v}) > f'_\varphi(\mathbf{v})) \geq 1 - \varepsilon$ holds with confidence $1 - \eta$.
2. *In turn, if $P(\tilde{g}_{\varphi,\lambda}(\mathbf{v}) + \lambda \leq 0) > \varepsilon$, then there exists at least a choice of parameters $\mathbf{v}^*$ in the parameter space such that $f(\mathbf{v}^*) \leq f'(\mathbf{v}^*)$ with confidence $1 - \eta$, that is, the policy π' is better than policy π at the parameter $\mathbf{v}^*$ with confidence $1 - \eta$.*

Proof. We prove the first statement of the lemma as follows. Since $\tilde{g}_{\varphi,\lambda}$ is a λ-PAC approximations of $f_\varphi - f'_\varphi$ with (ε, η)-guarantee, namely,

$$P(\tilde{g}_{\varphi,\lambda}(\mathbf{v}) - \lambda \leq f_\varphi(\mathbf{v}) - f'_\varphi(\mathbf{v}) \leq \tilde{g}_{\varphi,\lambda}(\mathbf{v}) + \lambda) \geq 1 - \varepsilon$$

holds with confidence $1 - \eta$, so it can be easily deduced that

$$P(f_\varphi(\mathbf{v}) - f'_\varphi(\mathbf{v}) \geq \tilde{g}_{\varphi,\lambda}(\mathbf{v}) - \lambda) \geq 1 - \varepsilon.$$

Since the condition $\tilde{g}_{\varphi,\lambda}(\mathbf{v}) - \lambda > 0$ is satisfied, the following inequality can be easily derived:

$$P(f_\varphi(\mathbf{v}) - f'_\varphi(\mathbf{v}) > 0) \geq P(f_\varphi(\mathbf{v}) - f'_\varphi(\mathbf{v}) \geq \tilde{g}_{\varphi,\lambda}(\mathbf{v}) - \lambda) \geq 1 - \varepsilon$$

with confidence $1 - \eta$.

Consider now the second statement of the lemma; we prove it by contradiction: under the hypothesis that $P(\tilde{g}_{\varphi,\lambda}(\mathbf{v}) + \lambda \leq 0) > \varepsilon$, suppose that for all parameters $\mathbf{v} \in \mathcal{V}$, we have that $f(\mathbf{v}) > f'(\mathbf{v})$ holds with the confidence $1 - \eta$. Since $\tilde{g}_{\varphi,\lambda}$ is a λ-PAC approximation of $f_\varphi - f'_\varphi$ with (ε, η)-guarantee, we have that

$$P(|f_\varphi(\mathbf{v}) - f'_\varphi(\mathbf{v}) - \tilde{g}_{\varphi,\lambda}(\mathbf{v})| \leq \lambda) \geq 1 - \varepsilon$$

holds; this implies that

$$P(f_\varphi(\mathbf{v}) - f'_\varphi(\mathbf{v}) - \lambda \leq \tilde{g}_{\varphi,\lambda}(\mathbf{v}) \leq f_\varphi(\mathbf{v}) - f'_\varphi(\mathbf{v}) + \lambda) \geq 1 - \varepsilon,$$

hence

$$P(\tilde{g}_{\varphi,\lambda}(\mathbf{v}) + \lambda \geq f_\varphi(\mathbf{v}) - f'_\varphi(\mathbf{v})) \geq 1 - \varepsilon$$

holds as well. Since by assumption for all parameters $\mathbf{v} \in \mathcal{V}$, $f_\varphi(\mathbf{v}) > f'_\varphi(\mathbf{v})$ holds with confidence $1 - \eta$, we have that

$$P(\tilde{g}_{\varphi,\lambda}(\mathbf{v}) + \lambda > 0) > P(\tilde{g}_{\varphi,\lambda}(\mathbf{v}) + \lambda > f_\varphi(\mathbf{v}) - f'_\varphi(\mathbf{v})) \geq 1 - \varepsilon,$$

which is equal to

$$P(\tilde{g}_{\varphi,\lambda}(\mathbf{v}) + \lambda \leq 0) \leq \varepsilon;$$

this however contradicts the hypothesis that "$P(\tilde{g}_{\varphi,\lambda}(\mathbf{v}) + \lambda \leq 0) > \varepsilon$", so the assumption "for all parameters $\mathbf{v} \in \mathcal{V}$, we have that $f(\mathbf{v}) > f'(\mathbf{v})$ holds with the confidence $1 - \eta$" is false, thus there exists at least a choice of parameters $\mathbf{v}^*$ in the parameter space such that $f(\mathbf{v}^*) \leq f'(\mathbf{v}^*)$ with confidence $1 - \eta$, as desired. □

From Lemma 4, we can know with a high confidence and low error rate that if the inequality (7) is satisfied, then the policy π gives a higher value for the satisfaction of φ than the policy π'. As an application of the lemma, consider a variation of the pMDP shown in Fig. 2, where the transition from s_2 with action a instead of reaching s_4 with probability 1, now it leads to s_4 with probability p and

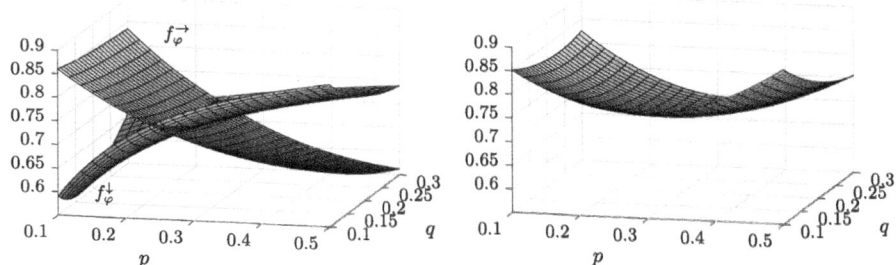

Fig. 3. The rational functions $f_\varphi^\rightarrow$ and $f_\varphi^\downarrow$ (on the left) and the quadratic approximation of $\max\{f_\varphi^\rightarrow, f_\varphi^\downarrow\}$ (on the right)

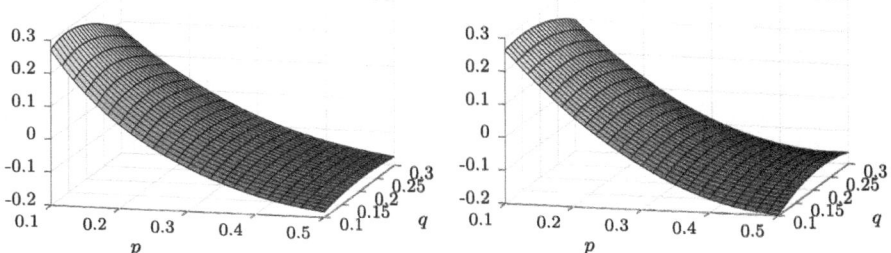

Fig. 4. The difference $f_\varphi^\rightarrow - f_\varphi^\downarrow$ (on the left) and its quadratic approximation (on the right)

to s_5 with probability $1 - p$. On the domain of parameters range$(p) = [0.1, 0.5]$ and range$(q) = [0.1, 0.3]$, we have two rational functions for $\varphi = \text{Pmax}_{=?}(\mathbf{F}\checkmark)$:

$$f_\varphi^\downarrow = \frac{p + 2q^2 - 2pq^2}{p + q} \qquad f_\varphi^\rightarrow = \frac{p + q - p^2 - 2pq + p^3 + p^2q}{p + q}$$

corresponding to the policies $\pi^\downarrow$ and $\pi^\rightarrow$ choosing $\downarrow$ and $\rightarrow$ in s_2, respectively; the rational functions are shown in Fig. 3, as well as the approximation of their maximum values. As we can see from the figure, the maximum probability of reaching s_5, the only state marked with $\checkmark$, heavily depends on the value assumed by p, while q has a minor influence on the total probability, as one would expect. If we take $f_\varphi^\rightarrow - f_\varphi^\downarrow$ and compute its approximation $\tilde{g}_{\varphi,\lambda}$ (both shown in Fig. 4), we can easily see for the computed margin $\lambda \approx 0.016$ that the condition (7) is satisfied for instance at the point $(p, q) = (0.1, 0.2)$, for which we have $\tilde{g}_{\varphi,\lambda}(0.1, 0.2) - 0.016 = 0.247$. On the other hand, the condition is violated for e.g. the point $(p, q) = (0.4, 0.2)$, for which we have $\tilde{g}_{\varphi,\lambda}(0.4, 0.2) - 0.016 = -0.139$. If we consider instead the condition $P(\tilde{g}_{\varphi,\lambda}(\mathbf{v}) + \lambda \leq 0) > \varepsilon$ in the second point of the lemma, then we get that $P(\tilde{g}_{\varphi,\lambda}(\mathbf{v}) + 0.016 \leq 0) \approx 0.59 > 0.05$, so there exists at least a choice of parameters $\mathbf{v}^*$ such that $f_\varphi^\rightarrow(\mathbf{v}^*) \leq f_\varphi^\downarrow(\mathbf{v}^*)$ with confidence $1 - \eta$: this happens for instance for all choices of the parameters (p, q) with $p \geq 0.3$, as it can be seen by inspecting Figs. 3 and 4.

Overall Better Policy. As we have seen from the previous example, different policies can give very different outcomes on the behavior of the pMDP. If we have to choose only one policy to be applied to the pMDP to solve nondeterminism independently on the actual value of the parameters, we need to understand the overall performance of different policies over the entire parameter space to help us choose the policy that performs better overall. Consider again the previous example, where for the pMDP shown in Fig. 2 and the modified $\rightarrow$ transition from s_2, there are two possible policies $\pi^{\rightarrow}$ and $\pi^{\downarrow}$, whose corresponding reachability probability functions of the goal state are $f_{\varphi}^{\rightarrow}$ and $f_{\varphi}^{\downarrow}$, respectively. We say that the policy $\pi^{\rightarrow}$ is better than $\pi^{\downarrow}$ with respect to a given probability measure P over $\mathcal{V}$, the inequality $\int_{\mathcal{V}} f_{\varphi}^{\rightarrow}(\mathbf{v}) \, dP(\mathbf{v}) \geq \int_{\mathcal{V}} f_{\varphi}^{\downarrow}(\mathbf{v}) \, dP(\mathbf{v})$ holds. After calculating the approximate functions of $f_{\varphi}^{\rightarrow}$ and $f_{\varphi}^{\downarrow}$, namely, $\tilde{f}_{\varphi,\lambda}^{\rightarrow}$ and $\tilde{f}_{\varphi,\lambda}^{\downarrow}$, we can use the following lemma to determine the better policy over the whole parameter space.

Lemma 5. *Given a pMDRM with domain of parameters $\mathcal{V}$, a PRCTL property $\varphi = \mathrm{Qopt}_{=?}$, two policies π and π', and their corresponding functions $f_{\varphi} \colon \mathcal{V} \to \mathbb{R}_{\geq 0}$ and $f'_{\varphi} \colon \mathcal{V} \to \mathbb{R}_{\geq 0}$, let $\tilde{g}_{\varphi,\lambda}$ be a λ-PAC approximation of $g_{\varphi} = f_{\varphi} - f'_{\varphi}$ with (ε, η)-guarantee. If for the approximation function $\tilde{g}_{\varphi,\lambda}$, the inequality*

$$\int_{\mathcal{V}} \tilde{g}_{\varphi,\lambda}(\mathbf{v}) \, dP(\mathbf{v}) \geq (\max_{\mathbf{v} \in \mathcal{V}} \tilde{g}_{\varphi,\lambda}(\mathbf{v}) - \inf_{\mathbf{v} \in \mathcal{V}} g_{\varphi}(\mathbf{v})) \cdot \varepsilon \cdot |\mathcal{V}| + \lambda \cdot |\mathcal{V}| \qquad (8)$$

holds, where $|\mathcal{V}| = \int_{\mathcal{V}} 1 \, d\mathbf{v}$, which is the same as in Lemma 2, then the inequality

$$\int_{\mathcal{V}} f_{\varphi}(\mathbf{v}) \, dP(\mathbf{v}) \geq \int_{\mathcal{V}} f'_{\varphi}(\mathbf{v}) \, dP(\mathbf{v})$$

holds with confidence $1 - \eta$.

Proof. We partition the parameter space $\mathcal{V}$ into two disjoint parts $\mathcal{V} = \mathcal{V}_{\leq \lambda} \cup \mathcal{V}_{> \lambda}$ where $\mathcal{V}_{\leq \lambda} = \{ \mathbf{v} \in \mathcal{V} \mid |g_{\varphi}(\mathbf{v}) - \tilde{g}_{\varphi,\lambda}(\mathbf{v})| \leq \lambda \}$ and $\mathcal{V}_{> \lambda} = \{ \mathbf{v} \in \mathcal{V} \mid |g_{\varphi}(\mathbf{v}) - \tilde{g}_{\varphi,\lambda}(\mathbf{v})| > \lambda \}$, which satisfies $P(\mathcal{V}_{\leq \lambda}) \geq 1 - \varepsilon$ and $P(\mathcal{V}_{> \lambda}) < \varepsilon$ with confidence $1 - \eta$. Then we have that

$$\int_{\mathcal{V}_{\leq \lambda}} g_{\varphi}(\mathbf{v}) \, dP(\mathbf{v}) = \int_{\mathcal{V}} g_{\varphi}(\mathbf{v}) \, dP(\mathbf{v}) - \int_{\mathcal{V}_{> \lambda}} g_{\varphi}(\mathbf{v}) \, dP(\mathbf{v});$$

a similar equality holds when $\tilde{g}_{\varphi,\lambda}$ is used instead of g_φ. This implies that

$$\int_{\mathcal{V}_{\leq\lambda}} g_\varphi(\mathbf{v})\,dP(\mathbf{v}) \geq \int_{\mathcal{V}_{\leq\lambda}} (\tilde{g}_{\varphi,\lambda}(\mathbf{v}) - \lambda)\,dP(\mathbf{v})$$

$$= \int_{\mathcal{V}_{\leq\lambda}} \tilde{g}_{\varphi,\lambda}(\mathbf{v})\,dP(\mathbf{v}) - \int_{\mathcal{V}_{\leq\lambda}} \lambda\,dP(\mathbf{v})$$

$$= \int_{\mathcal{V}_{\leq\lambda}} \tilde{g}_{\varphi,\lambda}(\mathbf{v})\,dP(\mathbf{v}) - \lambda \cdot |\mathcal{V}_{\leq\lambda}|$$

$$\geq \int_{\mathcal{V}_{\leq\lambda}} \tilde{g}_{\varphi,\lambda}(\mathbf{v})\,dP(\mathbf{v}) - \lambda \cdot |\mathcal{V}|$$

$$= \int_{\mathcal{V}} \tilde{g}_{\varphi,\lambda}(\mathbf{v})\,dP(\mathbf{v}) - \int_{\mathcal{V}_{>\lambda}} \tilde{g}_{\varphi,\lambda}(\mathbf{v})\,dP(\mathbf{v}) - \lambda \cdot |\mathcal{V}|$$

$$\geq \int_{\mathcal{V}} \tilde{g}_{\varphi,\lambda}(\mathbf{v})\,dP(\mathbf{v}) - (\max_{\mathbf{v}\in\mathcal{V}} \tilde{g}_{\varphi,\lambda}(\mathbf{v})) \cdot \varepsilon \cdot |\mathcal{V}| - \lambda \cdot |\mathcal{V}|.$$

with confidence $1 - \eta$. Moreover, we have that

$$\int_{\mathcal{V}_{>\lambda}} g_\varphi(\mathbf{v})\,dP(\mathbf{v}) \geq (\inf_{\mathbf{v}\in\mathcal{V}} g_\varphi(\mathbf{v})) \cdot \varepsilon \cdot |\mathcal{V}|$$

holds with confidence $1 - \eta$. By combining all inequalities together, we have that

$$\int_{\mathcal{V}} g_\varphi(\mathbf{v})\,dP(\mathbf{v}) \geq \int_{\mathcal{V}} \tilde{g}_{\varphi,\lambda}(\mathbf{v})\,dP(\mathbf{v}) - \lambda \cdot |\mathcal{V}|$$

$$- (\max_{\mathbf{v}\in\mathcal{V}} \tilde{g}_{\varphi,\lambda}(\mathbf{v})) \cdot \varepsilon \cdot |\mathcal{V}| + (\inf_{\mathbf{v}\in\mathcal{V}} g_\varphi(\mathbf{v}) \cdot \varepsilon \cdot |\mathcal{V}|$$

$$= \int_{\mathcal{V}} \tilde{g}_{\varphi,\lambda}(\mathbf{v})\,dP(\mathbf{v}) - \lambda \cdot |\mathcal{V}|$$

$$- (\max_{\mathbf{v}\in\mathcal{V}} \tilde{g}_{\varphi,\lambda}(\mathbf{v}) - \inf_{\mathbf{v}\in\mathcal{V}} g_\varphi(\mathbf{v})) \cdot \varepsilon \cdot |\mathcal{V}|.$$

Therefore, under the condition (8), the inequality

$$\int_{\mathcal{V}} f_\varphi(\mathbf{v})\,dP(\mathbf{v}) \geq \int_{\mathcal{V}} f'_\varphi(\mathbf{v})\,dP(\mathbf{v})$$

holds with confidence $1 - \eta$.   □

Here we focus on the property about the reachability probability, we claim that the value of $\inf_{\mathbf{v}\in\mathcal{V}} g_\varphi(\mathbf{v})$ is at least -1 since the upper bounds and lower bounds of $f_\varphi(\mathbf{v})$ and $f'_\varphi(\mathbf{v})$ are 1 and 0, respectively in this case.

4   Combining PAC Approximations with Statistical Model Checking

When solving the optimization problem (3), computing $f_\varphi(\mathbf{v}_i)$ usually requires the use of model checking software such as STORM or PRISM, which can be very costly for larger models. Therefore, attempting to estimate $f_\varphi(\mathbf{v}_i)$ using Statistical Model Checking (SMC) methods [35] is highly valuable. Furthermore, we will provide probabilistic guarantees of our method after incorporating SMC.

Definition 9 ([35]). *Given a domain of parameters $\mathcal{V}$, a probability measure P over $\mathcal{V}$, a function $f_\varphi \colon \mathcal{V} \to \mathbb{R}_{\geq 0}$, let $\lambda \in \mathbb{R}_{\geq 0}$ be a margin to measure the estimation error and $\varepsilon \in \mathbb{R}_{\geq 0}$ be an error rate.*

We say that the SMC estimation $\hat{f}_\varphi \colon \mathcal{V} \to \mathbb{R}_{\geq 0}$ of f_φ with respect to probability measure P is a (ε, λ)-estimation if we have

$$P(|f_\varphi(\mathbf{v}) - \hat{f}_\varphi(\mathbf{v})| \leq \lambda) \geq 1 - \varepsilon.$$

ε is related to the number of simulations $\mathfrak{N}$ used in the SMC algorithm by

$$\mathfrak{N} \geq \frac{\ln 2 - \ln \varepsilon}{2\lambda^2}.$$

The guarantees provided by SMC can be combined with the PAC guarantees from the scenario approach by means of the following result.

Theorem 2. *Given a domain of parameters $\mathcal{V}$, a probability measure P over $\mathcal{V}$, and a function $f_\varphi \colon \mathcal{V} \to \mathbb{R}_{\geq 0}$, let $\hat{f}_\varphi \colon \mathcal{V} \to \mathbb{R}_{\geq 0}$ be an SMC $(\varepsilon_s, \lambda_s)$-estimation of f_φ and $\tilde{f}_{\varphi,\lambda_p}$ be a λ_p-PAC approximation of $\hat{f}_\varphi$ with (ε_p, η_p)-guarantee. Then $\tilde{f}_{\varphi,\lambda_p}$ is a $(\lambda_s + \lambda_p)$-PAC approximation of f_φ with (ε, η_p)-guarantee, that is,*

$$P(|f_\varphi(\mathbf{v}) - \tilde{f}_{\varphi,\lambda_p}(\mathbf{v})| \leq \lambda_s + \lambda_p) \geq 1 - \varepsilon$$

holds with confidence $1 - \eta_p$, where ε is related to ε_s and ε_p by $\varepsilon = \varepsilon_s + \varepsilon_p - \varepsilon_s \cdot \varepsilon_p$.

The number of simulations $\mathfrak{N}$ used in the SMC algorithm and the number of sampling points ℓ used in the PAC algorithm are related to the error rates ε_s and ε_p, significance level η_p, and margin λ_s by

$$\mathfrak{N} \geq \frac{\ln 2 - \ln \varepsilon_s}{2\lambda_s^2}, \qquad \ell \geq \frac{2}{\varepsilon_p} \cdot \left(\ln \frac{1}{\eta_p} + m \right).$$

Proof. For any parameter $\mathbf{v} \in \mathcal{V}$, we have that

$$|f_\varphi(\mathbf{v}) - \tilde{f}_{\varphi,\lambda_p}(\mathbf{v})| \leq |f_\varphi(\mathbf{v}) - \hat{f}_\varphi(\mathbf{v})| + |\hat{f}_\varphi(\mathbf{v}) - \tilde{f}_{\varphi,\lambda_p}(\mathbf{v})|.$$

This implies the following set inclusion relation on the parameter space $\mathcal{V}$:

$$\{\, \mathbf{v} \in \mathcal{V} \mid |f_\varphi(\mathbf{v}) - \tilde{f}_{\varphi,\lambda_p}(\mathbf{v})| \leq \lambda_s + \lambda_p \,\}$$
$$\supseteq \{\, \mathbf{v} \in \mathcal{V} \mid |f_\varphi(\mathbf{v}) - \hat{f}_\varphi(\mathbf{v})| + |\hat{f}_\varphi(\mathbf{v}) - \tilde{f}_{\varphi,\lambda_p}(\mathbf{v})| \leq \lambda_s + \lambda_p \,\}$$
$$\supseteq \{\, \mathbf{v} \in \mathcal{V} \mid |f_\varphi(\mathbf{v}) - \hat{f}_\varphi(\mathbf{v})| \leq \lambda_s \text{ and } |\hat{f}_\varphi(\mathbf{v}) - \tilde{f}_{\varphi,\lambda_p}(\mathbf{v})| \leq \lambda_p \,\}.$$

Therefore, under the probability measure P, we have

$$P(|f_\varphi(\mathbf{v}) - \tilde{f}_{\varphi,\lambda_p}(\mathbf{v})| \leq \lambda_s + \lambda_p)$$
$$\geq P(|f_\varphi(\mathbf{v}) - \hat{f}_\varphi(\mathbf{v})| + |\hat{f}_\varphi(\mathbf{v}) - \tilde{f}_{\varphi,\lambda_p}(\mathbf{v})| \leq \lambda_s + \lambda_p)$$
$$\geq P(|f_\varphi(\mathbf{v}) - \hat{f}_\varphi(\mathbf{v})| \leq \lambda_s \text{ and } |\hat{f}_\varphi(\mathbf{v}) - \tilde{f}_{\varphi,\lambda_p}(\mathbf{v})| \leq \lambda_p)$$
$$= P(|f_\varphi(\mathbf{v}) - \hat{f}_\varphi(\mathbf{v})| \leq \lambda_s) \cdot P(|\hat{f}_\varphi(\mathbf{v}) - \tilde{f}_{\varphi,\lambda_p}(\mathbf{v})| \leq \lambda_p)$$
$$\overset{*}{\geq} (1 - \varepsilon_s) \cdot (1 - \varepsilon_p)$$
$$= 1 - \varepsilon_s - \varepsilon_p + \varepsilon_s \cdot \varepsilon_p.$$

The inequality $\overset{*}{\geq}$ is justified for the left factor by the conclusion of Definition 9, while for the right factor by the λ_p-PAC (ε_p, η_p)-guarantee on $\tilde{f}_{\varphi,\lambda_p}$. Thus we have that if the number of simulations $\mathfrak{N}$ and the number of sampled points ℓ satisfy the requirements of the SMC and PAC algorithms, respectively:

$$\mathfrak{N} \geq \frac{\ln 2 - \ln \varepsilon_s}{2\lambda_s^2}, \qquad \ell \geq \frac{2}{\varepsilon_p} \cdot \left(\ln \frac{1}{\eta_p} + m \right),$$

then we have that

$$P(|f_\varphi(\mathbf{v}) - \tilde{f}_{\varphi,\lambda_p}(\mathbf{v})| \leq \lambda_s + \lambda_p) \geq 1 - \varepsilon$$

holds with confidence $1 - \eta_p$, where $\varepsilon = \varepsilon_s + \varepsilon_p - \varepsilon_s \cdot \varepsilon_p$. $\qquad \square$

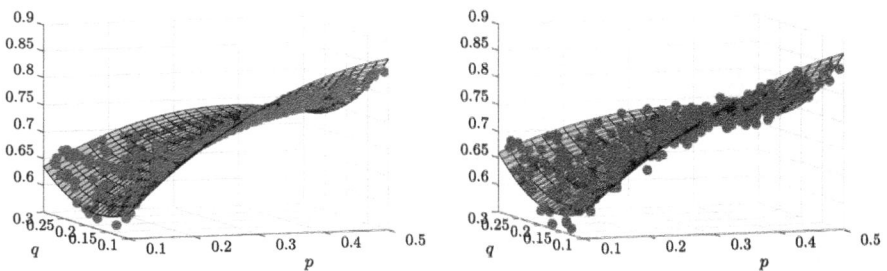

Fig. 5. PAC approximation on exact values (on the left) vs. SMC (on the right)

As an example of combining statistical model checking with approximation based on PAC scenarios, consider again the pMDP shown in Fig. 2. If we synthesize the rational function corresponding to $\varphi = \text{Pmax}_{=?}(\mathbf{F}\checkmark)$, we get the function $f_\varphi = \frac{p + 2q^2 - 2pq^2}{p+q}$ plotted in Fig. 3 as $f_\varphi^\downarrow$. In Fig. 5 we show on the left the quadratic polynomial $\tilde{f}_{\varphi,\lambda}$ superimposed with the blue cloud of 400 points computed by the ordinary model checker and used by the PAC scenario to synthesize it; on the right of the figure we show the quadratic polynomial $\hat{f}_\varphi$ and in purple the cloud of points for the same choice of sampled parameters computed by a statistical model checker. As we can see from the plots, the blue cloud whose z coordinates lie in $[0.568, 0.843]$ is closer to the synthesized function than the purple cloud whose z coordinates lie in $[0.558, 0.851]$; this is reflected by the computed margins, that are $\tilde{\lambda} = 0.017$ for $\tilde{f}_{\varphi,\lambda}$ and $\hat{\lambda} = 0.041$ for $\hat{f}_\varphi$. This is in line with the statement of Theorem 2, where using SMC with PAC scenario is affected by an increase of the margin $\lambda_s + \lambda_p$ and of the error rate ε.

Table 1. Overview of the outcomes of the experiments

Outcome		PRISM	PACPMA^d (1 thread/8 threads)					
			$d=1$	$d=2$	$d=3$	$d=4$	$d=5$	single
Popt$_{=?}$	Success	273	529/530	511/528	500/527	495/514	492/514	575/530
	Memoryout	23	31/191	28/191	27/191	23/191	31/191	17/190
	Timeout	391	163/2	184/4	196/5	205/8	200/18	131/3
	Other failures	36	0/0	0/0	0/0	0/0	0/0	0/0
Ropt$_{=?}$	Success	134	338/364	335/363	330/360	329/356	329/352	419/370
	Memoryout	6	16/154	17/154	15/154	24/154	26/154	16/154
	Timeout	386	172/8	174/9	181/12	173/16	171/20	91/2

5 Experimental Evaluation

We have implemented the PAC-based analysis approach proposed in Sect. 3 in our tool PACPMA[2], the PAC-based Parametric Model Analyzer [37], and evaluated it on several benchmarks: we considered the MDPs available from the PRISM benchmark suite [34] and we replaced the probabilistic choices in them with parameters, similarly to what we have done in [37]. When the MDP is the result of composing multiple PRISM modules, we either use a different parameter for each transition, but the parameter is shared by all modules, or use a different parameter for each module to control its probabilistic choices. By considering the reachability properties available for each MDP and the choice of the constants controlling the size of the model, we get a total of 723 benchmarks for our evaluation for probabilistic properties and 526 benchmarks for expected rewards. We performed our experiments on a desktop machine with an i7-4790 CPU and 16 GB of memory running Ubuntu Server 20.04.6; we used BENCHEXEC [8] to trace and constrain the tools' executions: we allowed each benchmark to use 15 GB of memory and imposed a time limit of 10 min of wall-clock time. Besides using PACPMA for our experiments, we also ran PRISM [33] v4.8 to compute the actual rational functions for the benchmarks, to check how well our PAC approximation works in practice. We also experimented with STORM [27] v1.8.1;

---

[2] https://github.com/iscas-tis/PacPMA/.

however it has failed to computed a rational function for each of the benchmark, so we do not consider it in the following analysis.

5.1   Overall Evaluation

In Table 1 we show the outcome of the different tools on the 723 probabilistic (marked with $\text{Popt}_{=?}[\psi]$) and 526 reward (marked with $\text{Ropt}_{=?}[\psi]$) benchmarks, namely whether they successfully produced a rational function or whether they failed by timeout, by running out of memory, or by some other reason. Besides the results for PRISM computing the actual rational function, we report two values for each outcome of PACPMA^d, where the superscript d indicates the degree of the polynomial used as template: in e.g. the pair 529/530, the first value 529 is relative to the single-threaded PACPMA^1, while the value 530 is for the 8-threaded PACPMA^1, i.e., PACPMA with 8 instances of the STORM wrapper running in parallel. We also report in the "single" column the outcome of PACPMA when limiting the number of samples to be only 1. This allows us to identify the cases where the MDP benchmark is exceeding the model checking capabilities of the tools even as an ordinary, non-parametric MDP. As parameters for PACPMA, we set $\varepsilon = \eta = 0.05$; for the benchmarks with two parameters, this results in sampling between 280 and 1000 points, for $d = 1$ to $d = 5$, respectively. To make the comparison between the different templates fairer, we set the same random seed for each run of PACPMA; this ensures that all samples used by e.g. PACPMA^2 are also used by PACPMA^5.

By looking at the numbers in the "single" column of Table 1, we have that for the 723 probabilistic (526 reward, resp.) benchmarks, only 575 (419, resp.) of them can hopefully be analyzed successfully by PACPMA or PRISM, given that for the remaining 148 (107, resp.) cases, already the less demanding non-parametric probabilistic model checking problem fails to complete their verification. By inspecting carefully the single thread values in the "single" column of Table 1, we can note that there are 16 failures by memory exhaustion when analyzing reward properties, while only 15 of them occur for PACPMA^3. The motivation for this is that there are few failed benchmarks where the failure is caused in one case by the time limit and in the other case by the memory limit; however, the other failure case is just due to happen in few seconds or MB, so minor variations in the memory usage by e.g. the JVM could cause a change in the failure mode.

As we can see from Table 1, PACPMA is able to compute polynomials with different degrees for many more benchmarks than PRISM, in particular for the expected reward properties. This means that PACPMA is able to complete the verification of the large majority of the benchmarks, while PRISM fails on a large part of them. In particular, we have that PRISM goes timeout in more than half of the benchmarks, showing how demanding is the symbolic computation of the analytic function for the analyzed property. Moreover, there are 36 cases (the ones in the "Other failures" row) where PRISM fails since the original benchmarks from the PRISM benchmark suite contain expressions that are only supported by PRISM when analyzing ordinary MDPs. This means that our scenario approach allows us to analyze a wider set of benchmarks without having to explicitly support parametric operations in the input models.

5.2 Relation of the Polynomial Degree d and the Number of Samples with the Margin λ and the Distance $\|f_\varphi - \tilde{f}_{\varphi,\lambda}\|_2$

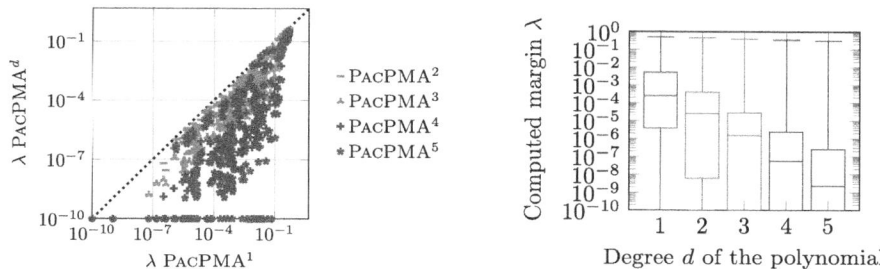

Fig. 6. Scatter plot for the margin λ for different PACPMA^d and box plots for the margin λ

In Fig. 6 we compare the behavior of PACPMA using polynomial templates with different degrees and how the corresponding computed λ changes, when we restrict ourselves to the experiments on probabilistic properties. As we can see from the plots, and as one would expect, the higher the degree of the polynomial is, the lower the margin λ is, since polynomials with higher degree can approximate better the shape of the actual rational function; this is confirmed by the box plots on the right side of the figure, where we can see that the values we get for λ tend to get closer to 0. In particular, in drawing these box plots we use a logarithmic y-axis, thus we substitute the value 0 with 10^{-10} for the lower whisker for all degrees as well as for the lower quartile for the degree $d = 5$. The scatter plot shown on the left side of Fig. 6, where we compare the values of λ produced by PACPMA^1 with those by PACPMA^d, for $d = 2, 3, 4, 5$; since all marks relative to the same benchmark share the same x-coordinate, by looking at the relative y-position of the marks of the higher degrees, we can note again how increasing the degree makes the computed value of λ smaller.

In Fig. 7 we show the value of $\|f_\varphi - \tilde{f}_{\varphi,\lambda}\|_2$ relative to the rational function f_φ computed by PRISM (plotted in Fig. 8) and the approximation function $\tilde{f}_{\varphi,\lambda}$ computed by PACPMA when the latter is set to use different degrees of the polynomial and a fixed number of samples (instead of using ℓ samples as computed according to Theorem 1), as well as the corresponding values of the computed λ. The plots are relative to one expected reward benchmark; we have selected such a benchmark by taking the one that has been successfully computed by PRISM and for which PACPMA^2 computed the largest λ value ($\lambda \approx 1.36$). The rational function f_φ computed by PRISM is rather simple, since it is just a fraction

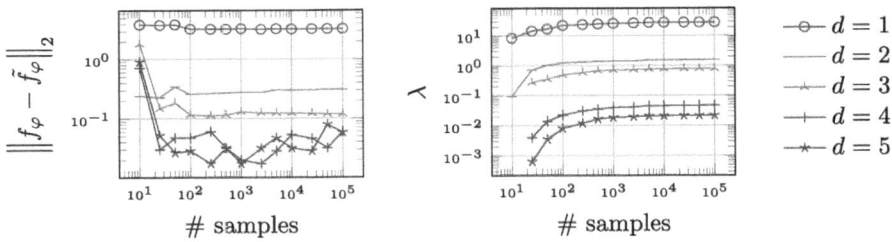

Fig. 7. Value of $\|f_\varphi - \tilde{f}_{\varphi,\lambda}\|_2$ and of λ vs. degree of polynomials and number of samples

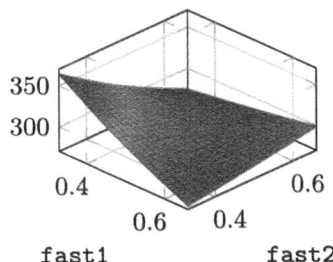

Fig. 8. The rational function $f_\varphi = \dfrac{82 \cdot \mathtt{fast1} \cdot \mathtt{fast2} - 170}{2 \cdot \mathtt{fast1} \cdot \mathtt{fast2} - \mathtt{fast1} - \mathtt{fast2}}$

between two quadratic polynomials $f_\varphi = \dfrac{82 \cdot \mathtt{fast1} \cdot \mathtt{fast2} - 170}{2 \cdot \mathtt{fast1} \cdot \mathtt{fast2} - \mathtt{fast1} - \mathtt{fast2}}$; still, the values of the fraction range over $[275, 360]$, according to the values of $f_\varphi(\mathbf{v}_i)$ in the problem (3) as computed by PacPMA[5] and as it can be seen from the plot of f_φ shown in Fig. 8.

From the plots given in Fig. 7, we can see that very few samples (100 for PacPMA[1] and 25 for the higher degrees) are usually sufficient to synthesize a polynomial that provides a good approximation of the actual rational function. This can be seen from the initial drop of the value of $\|f_\varphi - \tilde{f}_{\varphi,\lambda}\|_2$ in the left plot of Fig. 7; afterwards, the value of $\|f_\varphi - \tilde{f}_{\varphi,\lambda}\|_2$ changes slightly as caused by the increase in the number of samples, which require the approximating polynomial to fit many more values. This is reflected on the computed value of the margin λ (cf. the right plot of Fig. 7): as more points are added, it is more difficult for the polynomial to be as close to them as for fewer samples. This is in particular evident for the case of 10 samples for PacPMA[d] with $d \geq 3$: the computed value of λ is 0 (as indicated by the missing mark at 10^1, since we use logarithmic axes for the plot), so the approximate polynomial perfectly fix the value of f_φ for the 10 samples; still the resulting polynomial $\tilde{f}_{\varphi,\lambda}$ causes a higher value for $\|f_\varphi - \tilde{f}_{\varphi,\lambda}\|_2$ than the one computed by PacPMA[2] simply because there are not enough points to ensure a good approximation with PAC guarantees.

5.3 PAC Scenario Combined with SMC

Table 2. Overview of the outcomes of the experiments with and without SMC

		Outcome	PRISM	PacPMA^d (1 thread/8 threads)					
				$d=1$	$d=2$	$d=3$	$d=4$	$d=5$	single
$P_{=?}$	SMC	Success	—	75/104	62/98	38/87	12/55	0/41	104/104
		Timeout	—	29/0	42/6	66/17	92/49	104/63	0/0
	OMC	Success	58	66/69	65/69	64/69	62/68	62/67	74/70
		Memoryout	33	0/34	0/34	0/34	0/34	0/34	0/34
		Timeout	13	38/1	39/1	40/1	42/2	42/3	30/0
		Common success	—	63/69	57/69	38/69	12/49	0/40	74/70
$R_{=?}$	SMC	Success	—	38/74	17/55	3/33	2/19	2/6	86/84
		Memoryout	—	0/0	0/0	1/3	3/4	4/5	0/0
		Timeout	—	50/14	71/33	84/52	83/65	82/77	2/4
	OMC	Success	25	48/48	45/47	43/44	40/41	31/32	50/48
		Memoryout	30	0/40	0/40	3/40	5/42	8/39	0/40
		Timeout	33	40/0	43/1	42/4	43/5	48/16	38/0
		Other failures	0	0/0	0/0	0/0	0/0	1/1	0/0
		Common success	—	34/44	17/31	3/21	2/15	2/6	50/48

We now consider experiments on a set of 104 probabilistic properties and 88 reward properties on parametric discrete-time Markov chains about combining statistical model checking with the PAC scenario; the results are shown in Table 2, where the rows marked with SMC correspond to experiments using the SMC engine of PRISM as solver for computing f_φ, while the rows marked with OMC use STORM as ordinary model checker back-end tool. As we can see from the table, the higher the polynomial degree is, the more timeout failures we get. This is caused by the fact that SMC needs to sample several paths in the model, according to the number of simulations $\mathfrak{N}$ given in Definition 9; despite each of them taking a small amount of time, the call to the SMC solver to get the value of $f_\varphi(\mathbf{v})$ for a single constraint of the problem (3) takes between 3 and 10 s, depending on the size of the PRISM model and thus the length of the path to be sampled before evaluating whether it satisfies the path formula ψ in $\varphi = P_{=?}[\psi]$. Since the number of constraints grows linearly with $\binom{n+d}{n}$, the calls to the SMC engine of PRISM quickly hit the 10 min time limit assigned to each benchmark. Despite this, we have that as backend solver, SMC is complementary to OMC: by comparing the "Success" rows for SMC and OMC with the rows marked with "Common success", reporting the number of cases solved by both tools, we have several cases where one tool was successful while the other failed; moreover, SMC is less prone than OMC to exhaust the assigned memory, so it is better suited than OMC for computing the approximating function $\tilde{f}_{\varphi,\lambda}$ with PAC guarantees for large parametric models.

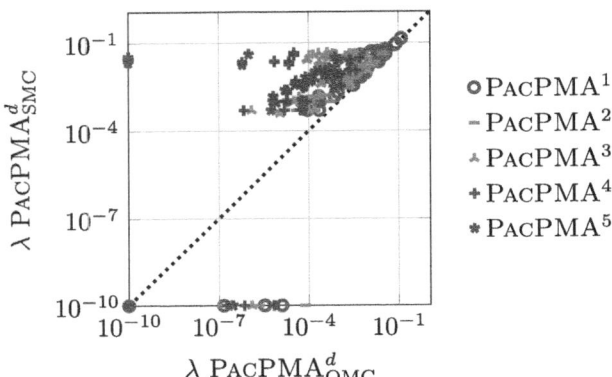

Fig. 9. Scatter plot for the margin λ for different $\textsc{PacPMA}^d$ with and without SMC

In Fig. 9 we compare the reported λ when solving the same pDTMC benchmarks with a model checker ($\textsc{PacPMA}_{\text{OMC}}$) or a statistical model checker ($\textsc{PacPMA}_{\text{SMC}}$) as back-end tool. As we can see, using a statistical model checker as a back-end causes the computed margin λ to be larger than using an ordinary model checker. This is justified by the fact that SMC returns a value $\hat{f}_{\varphi}(\mathbf{v})$ that is near to the exact one $f_{\varphi}(\mathbf{v})$ returned by OMC, according to Definition 9; this means that when we use $\hat{f}_{\varphi}(\mathbf{v}_i)$ instead of $f_{\varphi}(\mathbf{v}_i)$ in problem (3), the constraints generated for the same sample $\mathbf{v}_i$ are different and neighboring samples $\mathbf{v}_i$ and $\mathbf{v}_j$ can have $|\hat{f}_{\varphi}(\mathbf{v}_i) - \hat{f}_{\varphi}(\mathbf{v}_j)| > |f_{\varphi}(\mathbf{v}_i) - f_{\varphi}(\mathbf{v}_j)|$, and this is likely to require a larger λ in order to satisfy all constraints in problem (3).

6 Discussion and Conclusion

In this paper, we presented how the PAC-based approximation framework developed for parametric discrete-time Markov chains in [37] can be extended to study several properties of parametric Markov decision processes. We also showed how it can be combined with statistical model checking, allowing us to analyze properties of black-box parametric Markov models and synthesize the output profiles with the desired PAC-guarantees. The experimental results confirm the effectiveness of our PAC-based framework.

The PAC-based approximation framework we have developed can be extended into multiple directions.

Other Approximation Templates. When formulating the LP problem (3) for the PAC approximation, we used a (low-degree) polynomial template to get the approximation. As such, a template allows us to easily compute properties of the resulting approximation function, such as finding its minimum and maximum values or plotting it. We can easily change the formulation of the LP problem (3) to use non-polynomial templates, involving e.g. trigonometric and transcendental operators: in fact, these functions would not appear explicitly in the constraints of the LP problem (3), since only their value on the sampled parameters is used. Recall from the example just below the LP problem (3) that for the pMDP shown in Fig. 2, the quadratic polynomial template, and the sampled point ($p = 0.3, q = 0.2$), the corresponding constraint

$$-\lambda \leq f_\varphi(\mathbf{v}_i) - \mathbf{c} \cdot (1, \mathbf{v}_i, \ldots, \mathbf{v}_i^d)^T \leq \lambda$$

is instantiated as

$$-\lambda \leq 0.712 - 1 \cdot c_0 + 0.3 \cdot c_{11} + 0.2 \cdot c_{12} + 0.09 \cdot c_{21} + 0.06 \cdot c_{22} + 0.04 \cdot c_{23} \leq \lambda.$$

If we would use as template $c_0 \cdot q \cdot e^p + c_1 \cdot \sin(p \cdot \pi)$, then the corresponding constraint would be instantiated as

$$-\lambda \leq 0.712 - c_0 \cdot 0.2 \cdot e^{0.3} + c_1 \cdot \sin(0.3 \cdot \pi) \leq \lambda,$$

which is a linear constraint as intended.

Synthesizing Multiple Functions. As we have seen in Sect. 3.4, when dealing with pMDPs the domain of the parameters can be partitioned into multiple subspaces, each one associated with a different optimizing policy π and function f_φ^π. The current formulation of the approximation problem (3) does not take into consideration this event, since it aims to synthesize a single (polynomial) function corresponding to the optimal values for satisfying φ on the whole domain of the parameters where samples are taken. Clearly, by synthesizing a single function, the computed margin λ might be larger than by synthesizing multiple functions, one for each subregion.

Extending our approach to work with multiple regions and functions is rather easy: we could just apply our framework and synthesize a PAC-guaranteed approximation function for each subregion independently. The theoretical framework would remain essentially unchanged, except for the fact that the PAC-guarantees would be given for each subregion instead of for the whole domain of the parameters; new results could be provided, to combine together the PAC-guarantees obtained for the subregions and infer appropriate PAC-guarantees for the whole domain of the parameters. The implementation could take advantage of different strategies: the parameters can be sampled, the corresponding instantiated MDPs are evaluated, and, according to the corresponding computed policy, the subregions are determined; or the subregions are first determined by e.g. a bisection procedure and then the current implementation is applied to each subregion. In both cases, the overall number of samples needs to be increased, so that in each subregion there are enough samples to ensure the statistical guarantees according to Theorem 1; the parameters used to obtain the boundaries of the subregions should not contribute to reach ℓ (since they are not randomly sampled), but they can still be used in the problem (3) to provide additional constraints.

Acknowledgements. We thank Jianting Yang (CNRS@CREATE, 1 Create Way, #08-01 CREATE Tower, Singapore 138602) for improving a proof of the paper. Work supported in part by the CAS Project for Young Scientists in Basic Research under grant No. YSBR-040, NSFC under grant No. 61836005, the CAS Pioneer Hundred Talents Program, and the ISCAS New Cultivation Project ISCAS-PYFX-202201. This project is part of the European Union's Horizon 2020 research and innovation programme under the Marie Skłodowska-Curie grant no. 101008233.

References

1. Andova, S., Hermanns, H., Katoen, J.-P.: Discrete-time rewards model-checked. In: Larsen, K.G., Niebert, P. (eds.) FORMATS 2003. LNCS, vol. 2791, pp. 88–104. Springer, Heidelberg (2004). https://doi.org/10.1007/978-3-540-40903-8_8

2. Badings, T.S., Cubuktepe, M., Jansen, N., Junges, S., Katoen, J.-P., Topcu, U.: Scenario-based verification of uncertain parametric MDPs. Int. J. Softw. Tools Technol. Transf. **24**(5), 803–819 (2022). https://doi.org/10.1007/s10009-022-00673-z

3. Baier, C., Hensel, C., Hutschenreiter, L., Junges, S., Katoen, J.-P., Klein, J.: Parametric Markov chains: PCTL complexity and fraction-free Gaussian elimination. Inf. Comput. **272**, 104504 (2020). https://doi.org/10.1016/j.ic.2019.104504

4. Baier, C., Katoen, J.-P.: Principles of Model Checking. MIT Press (2008)

5. Barbier, M., et al.: Validation of perception and decision-making systems for autonomous driving via statistical model checking. In: 2019 IEEE Intelligent Vehicles Symposium, pp. 252–259. IEEE (2019). https://doi.org/10.1109/IVS.2019.8813793

6. Ben-Tal, A., Nemirovski, A.: Robust convex optimization. Math. Oper. Res. **23**(4), 769–805 (1998). https://doi.org/10.1287/moor.23.4.769

7. Ben-Tal, A., Nemirovski, A.: Robust solutions of uncertain linear programs. Oper. Res. Lett. **25**(1), 1–13 (1999). https://doi.org/10.1016/S0167-6377(99)00016-4

8. Beyer, D., Löwe, S., Wendler, P.: Reliable benchmarking: requirements and solutions. Int. J. Softw. Tools Technol. Transf. **21**(1), 1–29 (2019). https://doi.org/10.1007/s10009-017-0469-y

9. Bianco, A., de Alfaro, L.: Model checking of probabilistic and nondeterministic systems. In: Thiagarajan, P.S. (ed.) FSTTCS 1995. LNCS, vol. 1026, pp. 499–513. Springer, Heidelberg (1995). https://doi.org/10.1007/3-540-60692-0_70

10. Billingsley, P.: Probability and Measure. Wiley (1995)

11. Calafiore, G.C., Campi, M.C.: Uncertain convex programs: randomized solutions and confidence levels. Math. Program. **102**(1), 25–46 (2005). https://doi.org/10.1007/s10107-003-0499-y

12. Calafiore, G.C., Campi, M.C.: The scenario approach to robust control design. IEEE Trans. Autom. Control **51**(5), 742–753 (2006). https://doi.org/10.1109/TAC.2006.875041

13. Campi, M.C., Garatti, S.: The exact feasibility of randomized solutions of uncertain convex programs. SIAM J. Optim. **19**(3), 1211–1230 (2008). https://doi.org/10.1137/07069821X

14. Campi, M.C., Garatti, S., Prandini, M.: The scenario approach for systems and control design. Annu. Rev. Control. **33**(2), 149–157 (2009). https://doi.org/10.1016/j.arcontrol.2009.07.001
15. Daws, C.: Symbolic and parametric model checking of discrete-time Markov chains. In: Liu, Z., Araki, K. (eds.) ICTAC 2004. LNCS, vol. 3407, pp. 280–294. Springer, Heidelberg (2005). https://doi.org/10.1007/978-3-540-31862-0_21
16. Dehnert, C., et al.: PROPhESY: A PRObabilistic ParamEter SYnthesis tool. In: Kroening, D., Păsăreanu, C.S. (eds.) CAV 2015. LNCS, vol. 9206, pp. 214–231. Springer, Cham (2015). https://doi.org/10.1007/978-3-319-21690-4_13
17. Fang, X., Calinescu, R., Gerasimou, S., Alhwikem, F.: Fast parametric model checking through model fragmentation. In: 2021 IEEE/ACM 43rd International Conference on Software Engineering: ICSE, pp. 835–846. IEEE (2021). https://doi.org/10.1109/ICSE43902.2021.00081
18. Forejt, V., Kwiatkowska, M., Norman, G., Parker, D.: Automated verification techniques for probabilistic systems. In: Bernardo, M., Issarny, V. (eds.) SFM 2011. LNCS, vol. 6659, pp. 53–113. Springer, Heidelberg (2011). https://doi.org/10.1007/978-3-642-21455-4_3
19. Gainer, P., Hahn, E.M., Schewe, S.: Accelerated model checking of parametric Markov chains. In: Lahiri, S.K., Wang, C. (eds.) ATVA 2018. LNCS, vol. 11138, pp. 300–316. Springer, Cham (2018). https://doi.org/10.1007/978-3-030-01090-4_18
20. Garavel, H., Lang, F., Mateescu, R., Serwe, W.: CADP 2011: a toolbox for the construction and analysis of distributed processes. Int. J. Softw. Tools Technol. Transf. **15**(2), 89–107 (2013). https://doi.org/10.1007/s10009-012-0244-z
21. Ghaoui, L.E., Oustry, F., Lebret, H.: Robust solutions to uncertain semidefinite programs. SIAM J. Optim. **9**(1), 33–52 (1998). https://doi.org/10.1137/S1052623496305717
22. Givan, R., Leach, S.M., Dean, T.L.: Bounded-parameter Markov decision processes. Artif. Intell. **122**(1–2), 71–109 (2000). https://doi.org/10.1016/S0004-3702(00)00047-3
23. Hahn, E.M., Han, T., Zhang, L.: Synthesis for PCTL in parametric Markov decision processes. In: Bobaru, M., Havelund, K., Holzmann, G.J., Joshi, R. (eds.) NFM 2011. LNCS, vol. 6617, pp. 146–161. Springer, Heidelberg (2011). https://doi.org/10.1007/978-3-642-20398-5_12
24. Hahn, E.M., Hermanns, H., Zhang, L.: Probabilistic reachability for parametric Markov models. Int. J. Softw. Tools Technol. Transf. **13**(1), 3–19 (2011). https://doi.org/10.1007/s10009-010-0146-x
25. Hahn, E.M., Li, Y., Schewe, S., Turrini, A., Zhang, L.: ISCASMC: a web-based probabilistic model checker. In: Jones, C., Pihlajasaari, P., Sun, J. (eds.) FM 2014. LNCS, vol. 8442, pp. 312–317. Springer, Cham (2014). https://doi.org/10.1007/978-3-319-06410-9_22
26. Hansson, H., Jonsson, B.: A logic for reasoning about time and reliability. Formal Aspects Comput. **6**(5), 512–535 (1994). https://doi.org/10.1007/BF01211866
27. Hensel, C., Junges, S., Katoen, J.-P., Quatmann, T., Volk, M.: The probabilistic model checker Storm. Int. J. Softw. Tools Technol. Transf. **24**(4), 589–610 (2022). https://doi.org/10.1007/s10009-021-00633-z
28. Hopcroft, J.E., Motwani, R., Ullman, J.D.: Introduction to automata theory, languages, and computation, 3rd edn., Pearson International Edition. Addison-Wesley (2007)
29. Jansen, N., et al.: Accelerating parametric probabilistic verification. In: Norman, G., Sanders, W. (eds.) QEST 2014. LNCS, vol. 8657, pp. 404–420. Springer, Cham (2014). https://doi.org/10.1007/978-3-319-10696-0_31

30. Jansen, N., Junges, S., Katoen, J.-P.: Parameter synthesis in Markov models: a gentle survey. In: Raskin, J., Chatterjee, K., Doyen, L., Majumdar, R. (eds.) Principles of Systems Design. LNCS, vol. 13660, pp. 407–437. Springer, Cham (2022). https://doi.org/10.1007/978-3-031-22337-2_20

31. Junges, S., Katoen, J.-P., Pérez, G.A., Winkler, T.: The complexity of reachability in parametric Markov decision processes. J. Comput. Syst. Sci. **119**, 183–210 (2021). https://doi.org/10.1016/j.jcss.2021.02.006

32. Katoen, J.-P., Zapreev, I.S., Hahn, E.M., Hermanns, H., Jansen, D.N.: The ins and outs of the probabilistic model checker MRMC. Perform. Eval. **68**(2), 90–104 (2011). https://doi.org/10.1016/j.peva.2010.04.001

33. Kwiatkowska, M., Norman, G., Parker, D.: PRISM 4.0: verification of probabilistic real-time systems. In: Gopalakrishnan, G., Qadeer, S. (eds.) CAV 2011. LNCS, vol. 6806, pp. 585–591. Springer, Heidelberg (2011). https://doi.org/10.1007/978-3-642-22110-1_47

34. Kwiatkowska, M.Z., Norman, G., Parker, D.: The PRISM benchmark suite. In: QEST 2012: Ninth International Conference on Quantitative Evaluation of Systems, pp. 203–204. IEEE Computer Society (2012). https://doi.org/10.1109/QEST.2012.14

35. Legay, A., Lukina, A., Traonouez, L.M., Yang, J., Smolka, S.A., Grosu, R.: Statistical model checking. In: Steffen, B., Woeginger, G. (eds.) Computing and Software Science. LNCS, vol. 10000, pp. 478–504. Springer, Cham (2019). https://doi.org/10.1007/978-3-319-91908-9_23

36. Li, R., Yang, P., Huang, C., Sun, Y., Xue, B., Zhang, L.: Towards practical robustness analysis for DNNs based on PAC-model learning. In: 2022 ACM/IEEE 44th International Conference on Software Engineering: ICSE, pp. 2189–2201. ACM (2022). https://doi.org/10.1145/3510003.3510143

37. Liu, Y., Turrini, A., Hahn, E.M., Xue, B., Zhang, L.: Scenario approach for parametric Markov models. In: André, É., Sun, J. (eds.) ATVA 2023. LNCS, vol. 14215, pp. 158–180. Springer, Cham (2023). https://doi.org/10.1007/978-3-031-45329-8_8

38. Paigwar, A., Baranov, E., Renzaglia, A., Laugier, C., Legay, A.: Probabilistic collision risk estimation for autonomous driving: validation via statistical model checking. In: 2020 IEEE Intelligent Vehicles Symposium (IV), pp. 737–743. IEEE (2020). https://doi.org/10.1109/IV47402.2020.9304821

39. Puterman, M.L.: Markov Decision Processes: Discrete Stochastic Dynamic Programming. Wiley Series in Probability and Statistics, Wiley (1994). https://doi.org/10.1002/9780470316887

40. Quatmann, T., Dehnert, C., Jansen, N., Junges, S., Katoen, J.-P.: Parameter synthesis for Markov models: faster than ever. In: Artho, C., Legay, A., Peled, D. (eds.) ATVA 2016. LNCS, vol. 9938, pp. 50–67. Springer, Cham (2016). https://doi.org/10.1007/978-3-319-46520-3_4

41. Rockafellar, R.T.: Convex Analysis, vol. 11. Princeton University Press (1997)

42. Spel, J., Junges, S., Katoen, J.-P.: Finding provably optimal Markov chains. In: TACAS 2021. LNCS, vol. 12651, pp. 173–190. Springer, Cham (2021). https://doi.org/10.1007/978-3-030-72016-2_10

43. Xie, J., Tan, W., Fang, B., Huang, Z.: Towards a statistical model checking method for safety-critical cyber-physical system verification. Secur. Commun. Networks **2021**, 5536722:1–5536722:12 (2021). https://doi.org/10.1155/2021/5536722

44. Xue, B., Zhang, M., Easwaran, A., Li, Q.: PAC model checking of black-box continuous-time dynamical systems. IEEE Trans. Comput. Aided Des. Integr. Circuits Syst. **39**(11), 3944–3955 (2020). https://doi.org/10.1109/TCAD.2020.3012251

GPU Accelerating Statistical Model Checking for Extended Timed Automata

Oliver S. Bak[1], Mathias W. B. Christiansen[1], Oliver V. Eriksen[1],
Sergio Feo-Arenis[2], Peter G. Jensen[1], Marcus D. Jensen[1], Simas Juozapaitis[1],
Kim G. Larsen[1], Marius Mikučionis[1(✉)], Marco Muñiz[1],
and Andreas Windfeld[1]

[1] Department of Computer Science, Aalborg University, Aalborg, Denmark
marius@cs.aau.dk
[2] NVIDIA Corp., München, Germany

Abstract. The core component of Statistical Model Checking (SMC) is the repeated sampling of a given system as to estimate statistical measures. To obtain probabilistic estimates with high confidence a significant number of simulations is required, in particular in the presence of *rare events*. In this paper we explore the use of Graphical Processing Unit (GPU) for accelerating SMC for Networks of Stochastic Extended Timed Automata (SXTA). We discuss the many challenges and solutions required to achieve significant speedups on a GPU architecture. In collaboration with NVIDIA we develop a prototype tool for parallel SMC using both GPU and multi-core CPU. Experimental results demonstrate trade-offs in the computation time when utilizing either CPU or GPU. In one case we observed the GPU using 20% of the power of the CPU equivalent while delivering a 2.73 time speedup.

1 Introduction

Statistical model checking (SMC) is a technique where the (statistical) correctness of a given system model is inferred via repeated statistical sampling. SMC is applied for both qualitative and quantitative studies of systems where classical model checking is unpractical due to e.g. the state-space explosion, or impossible e.g. due to intractability of a symbolic analysis [14]. Furthermore, repeated statistical simulation is required for both training and evaluating AI based controllers in a safe environment (see e.g. [7,21]). One formalism for expressing complex stochastic systems is Networks of Stochastic Extended Timed Automata (NSXTA), for which the model checking tool UPPAAL provides an SMC engine. While the SMC technique generally enjoys good scalability, recent applications call for run-time reductions, e.g. training controllers for residential heating systems [21] or simulating large-scale agent-based COVID19-models [5,25]. Additionally, the recent energy cost surges, global warming and increased needs for large-scale AI system training call for more studies of cost of computation [32].

Numerical simulation problems have classically enjoyed good speedups from GPU acceleration, e.g. Computational Fluid Dynamics [2]. We note here that

© The Author(s), under exclusive license to Springer Nature Switzerland AG 2025
N. Jansen et al. (Eds.): Principles of Verification: Cycling the Probabilistic Landscape,
LNCS 15261, pp. 267–292, 2025.
https://doi.org/10.1007/978-3-031-75775-4_12

such classical problems generally enjoy matrix-like descriptions with little or no branching and little or no stochastics, a strong contrast to NSXTA.

In this paper, we study the use of parallel computing via GPUs and CPUs to increase the performance of SMC for NSXTA. Our main contribution is a parallel implementation of SMC for NSXTA on GPU. In addition, our experiments show substantial time and energy savings while using a GPU compared to an equivalent CPU cluster implementation. Another contribution is that estimation of probabilities for large real world scenarios e.g. COVID19-models [5,25] which required a CPU cluster, can now be carried out on workstation or laptop with a suitable GPU.

Relationship to Joost-Pieter Katoen. The SMC engine of Uppaal dates back to the European FP7 project Quasimodo (2008-2011), where Joost-Pieter Katoen was a main contributor representing RWTH Aachen. Aalborg University was a project coordinator and the other partners of the Quasimodo project were ESI, University of Twente, Radboud University, ENS Cachan, Saarland University, University Libre de Bruxelles, Terma A/S, Chess, Inchron, and Hydac.

The objective of the Quasimodo project was to develop theory, techniques and tools for handling quantitative constraints in model-driven development of real-time embedded systems. This involved explicit handling of real-time, hybrid and stochastic constraints to capture use of resources, assumptions about an environment, as well as requirements on the services that the system has to provide. During the project, a large number of tools for probabilistic and real-time analysis were developed, refined, and combined, including MoDEST and Uppaal SMC.

The first presentation of Uppaal SMC was made at a Quasimodo project meeting in February 2011 in Aachen, with Joost-Pieter Katoen being the host and Kim G. Larsen (coauthor of this paper) giving the presentation. At that time Joost-Pieter Katoen was focusing on (exact) model checking of CTMC and stochastic hybrid systems against various specifications (including time automata), the probabilistic model checker MRMC, as well as compositional verification of probabilistic systems. The Quasimodo meetings were characterized by true scientific curiosity and frank discussions, and it is fair to say that the discussion after (and during) this first presentation of Uppaal SMC was *very* frank, with several of the other partners questioning the entire statistical model checking approach. Fortunately, we continued the work with Uppaal SMC becoming part of the standard Uppaal distribution in 2015 [16]. Throughout the years – in line with the core contribution of this paper – there has been a focus on constantly improving the performance of Uppaal SMC with contributions including importance sampling and splitting [24,26] for efficient estimation of rare events as well as distributed statistical model checking [9]. Most importantly, Uppaal SMC has since its introduction been successfully applied to the analysis of a number of highly critical systems ranging from maintenance of railway systems [31], performance analysis of routing protocols [35] to analysis of impact of close-down measures for controlling the spreading of Covid-19 [5,25]. Also, Joost-Pieter Katoen himself has made good use of Uppaal SMC with respect to the modeling and analysis of a microgrid with wind, microturbines, and the main grid as generation resources [10]. We hope all this work inspires Joost-Pieter Katoen and his group to introduce statistical model checking into the STORM model checker [22].

Finally, in 2017 Joost-Pieter Katoen became Honoris doctor causa at Aalborg University in "recognition of his numerous contributions to the research community in model checking including probabilistic model checking and programming in particular".

Related Work. GPUs have been explored in the context of model-checkers, e.g. for accelerating state-space generation [18], probabilistic model-checking [6], improving convergence of value-iteration [11] and speeding up SMT-solvers [28]. Additional examples of model checking using GPUs are GPUExplore [36] and Grapple [17], implemented using CUDA to perform state-space exploration in parallel. ParaFROST [30] uses GPUs to parallelize variable-clause elimination during bounded model checking with CBMC [12]. Closer to our approach is the work of Copik et al. [13] describing the implementation of an extension of *Prism* for statistic probabilistic model checking of Markov decision processes using GPUs, implemented using OpenCL. Similarly, the work of Gainer et al. [20] describes the use of CUDA to speed up model checking of parametric Markov chains. In contrast to previous work we extend the modeling language to Networks of Stochastic Extended Timed Automata and provide two ways of handling discrete data expressions: JIT-compiled C code and interpreted through Polish notation. To the best of our knowledge, this work is the first GPU-based statistical model checking engine for systems with mixed linear and non-linear behavior and complex interleaving stochastics.

The remainder of the paper is structured as follows; Sect. 2 builds up our modeling formalism from variables and automata to its semantics, introduces statistical model checking algorithms and NVIDIA CUDA programming framework, Sect. 3 presents our parallel version of the algorithm followed by a discussion in Sect. 4 on the required technical optimizations. This is followed by experimental findings in Sect. 5, shortly followed by conclusions in Sect. 6.

2   Preliminaries

We use *Timed Automata* [1] extended with discrete variables and given a stochastic semantics just like in statistical model checking (SMC) implemented in UPPAAL [3]. For parallel implementation of SMC algorithm we use NVIDIA CUDA framework.

2.1   Networks of Extended Stochastic Timed Automata (NSXTA)

Clocks and Discrete Variables. Let X be a finite set of *clocks*. A *clock valuation* is a function $\mu : X \to \mathbb{R}_{\geq 0}$. We use $\mathcal{V}(X)$ to denote the sets of all valuations for clocks in X. Let V be a set of *discrete variables*. The function D assigns to each variable $v \in V$ a finite domain $D(v)$. A *variable valuation* is a function

$\nu : V \to \bigcup_{v \in V} D(\iota)$ that maps variables to values such that $\nu(v) \in D(v)$. We use $\mathcal{V}(V)$ to denote the set of all variable valuations. We let μ_0 resp. ν_0 denote the valuation that maps every clock resp. variable to the value 0.

Expressions. We use expr to denote an expression over V. We assume that expressions are well typed. For an expression expr we use $D(\text{expr})$ to denote its domain. Given a variable valuation ν and an expression expr, we use $\text{expr}^\nu \in D(\text{expr})$ to denote the value of expr under ν. We use $V(\text{expr}) \in 2^V$ to denote the set of variables in expr such that if $\nu(v) = \nu'(v)$ for all $v \in V(\text{expr})$ and for all $\nu, \nu' \in \mathcal{V}(V)$ then $\text{expr}^\nu = \text{expr}^{\nu'}$.

Constraints. The set $B(X)$ is the set of *clock constraints* generated by the grammar $\phi ::= x \bowtie \text{expr} \mid \phi_1 \wedge \phi_2$, where $x \in X$, $D(\text{expr})$ is the domain of all natural numbers $\mathbb{N}$ and $\bowtie \in \{<, \leq, \geq, >\}$. The set $B(V)$ is a set of *Boolean variable constraints* over V. The set $B(X, V)$ of constraints comprises $B(X)$, $B(V)$, and conjunctions over clock and variable constraints. Given a constraint $\phi \in B(X, V)$, we use $X(\phi)$ to denote the set of clocks in ϕ, and $V(\phi)$ to denote the set of variables in ϕ. A constraint $\phi \in B(X, V)$ evaluation under ν is denoted as ϕ^ν.

Updates. A *clock update* is of the form $x := \text{expr}$ where $x \in X$, and $D(\text{expr}) = \mathbb{N}$. A *variable update* is of the form $v := \text{expr}$ where $v \in V$ and $D(v) = D(\text{expr})$. The set $U(X, V)$ of *updates* contains all finite, possibly empty sequences of clock and variable updates. Given clock valuation $\mu \in \mathcal{V}(X)$, variable valuation $\nu \in \mathcal{V}(V)$, and update $r \in U(X, V)$, we use r^ν to denote the resulting update after evaluating all expressions in r under ν, we use $X(r)$ to denote the set of clocks in r, and $V(r)$ to denote the set of variables in r. We let $[\![r^\nu]\!] : \mathcal{V}(X) \cup \mathcal{V}(V) \to \mathcal{V}(X) \cup \mathcal{V}(V)$ be a map from valuations to valuations. We use $\mu[r^\nu]$ to denote the updated clock valuation $[\![r^\nu]\!](\mu)$. Analogously, for variable valuation ν', we use $\nu'[r^\nu]$ to denote the updated variable valuation $[\![r^\nu]\!](\nu')$.

Definition 1 (Extended Timed Automata XTA). *An* extended timed automaton $\mathcal{A}$ *is a tuple* $(L, \ell_0, X, V, \Sigma, E, I)$ *where:* L *is a set of locations,* $\ell_0 \in L$ *is the initial location,* X *is the finite set of clocks,* V *is the finite set of variables,* Σ *is a set of actions,* $E \subseteq L \times \Sigma \times B(X) \times B(V) \times U(X, V) \times L$ *is a set of edges between locations with an action, a clock guard, a variable guard, and an update set,* $I : L \to B(X, V)$ *assigns clock and variable invariants to locations.*

Semantics of an XTA. The semantics of an XTA is given by a timed transition system $(S, s_0, \to)$ where $S \subseteq L \times \mathcal{V}(X) \times \mathcal{V}(V)$ is the set of states comprising a location, a clock valuation, and a variable valuation, $s_0 = \langle \ell_0, \mu_0, \nu_0 \rangle$ is the initial state, and $\to \subseteq S \times (\mathbb{R}_{\geq 0} \cup \Sigma) \times S$ is the transition relation defined by:

Delay transitions $\langle \ell, \mu, \nu \rangle \xrightarrow{d} \langle \ell', \mu', \nu \rangle$ with $d \in \mathbb{R}_{\geq 0}$, $\mu' = \mu + d$ and $\mu' \models I(\ell')^\nu$.

Discrete transitions $\langle \ell, \mu, \nu \rangle \xrightarrow{a} \langle \ell, \mu', \nu' \rangle$ if exists $e = (\ell_i, a, \phi, \psi, r, \ell'_i) \in E$ s.t. $\mu \models \phi^\nu$, $\nu \models \psi^\nu$, $\mu' = \mu[r^\nu]$, $\nu' = \nu[r^\nu]$, $\mu' \models I(\ell')^{\nu'}$, and $\nu' \models I(\ell)^{\nu'}$.

Given a transition system $(S, s_0, \to)$ we use $s \xrightarrow{d,a} s'$ as a shorthand for $s \xrightarrow{d} s'' \xrightarrow{a} s'$. A run is a finite (infinite) sequence of transitions $s_0 \xrightarrow{d_1, a_1} s_1 \xrightarrow{d_2, a_2}$

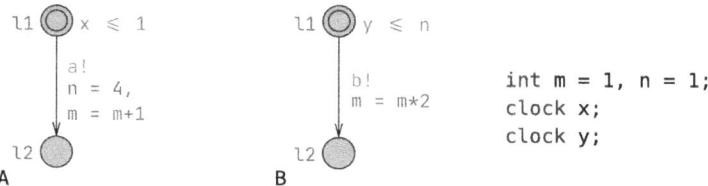

Fig. 1. NSXTA $\mathcal{N}_1$ with components A and B sharing two discrete variables n and m initialized with 1.

s_2 .... The set $\mathsf{En}(s) = \{a \in \Sigma \mid \exists d, s'.\ s \xrightarrow{d,a} s'\}$ is the set of enabled actions at s. Given state s and action a we define $T(s, a) = \{d \in \mathbb{R}_{\geq 0} \mid \exists s'. s \xrightarrow{d,a} s'\}$ and $T(s) = \bigcup_a T(s, a)$.

Definition 2 (Stochastic Extended Timed Automata (SXTA)). *A Stochastic Timed Automaton is a tuple* $(\mathcal{A}, w, r, \mathfrak{u})$ *where* $\mathcal{A}$ *is a timed automaton with local[1] semantics* $(S, s_0, \rightarrow)$, $w : \Sigma \rightarrow \mathbb{N}$ *assigns weights to actions,* $r : L \rightarrow \mathbb{N}$ *assigns rates to locations,* $\mathfrak{u}$ *is a family of probability measures,* $(\mathfrak{u}_s)_{s \in S}$, *such that* $\mathfrak{u}_s(T(s)) = 1$ *and if* $\sup\{T(s)\} < \infty$, *then* $\mathfrak{u}_s$ *is a uniform distribution on* $T(s)$, *otherwise* $\mathfrak{u}_s$ *is an exponential distribution with rate* $r(\ell)$. *For state* $s \in S$. *We assume a probability distribution* γ_s *over actions, such that for every action* $a \in \Sigma$, $\gamma_s(a) = 0$ *iff* $a \notin \mathsf{En}(s)$, *and otherwise* $\gamma_s(a) = w(a) / \sum_{a' \in \mathsf{En}(s)} w(a')$.

Network of Stochastic XTA (NSXTA). A formal definition for NSXTA requires additional notation and long definitions. We refer the reader to [4,15,24] for the precise semantics. In contrast we introduce NSXTA algorithmically and via an example. In a nutshell a network of SXTA $\mathcal{N} = (\mathcal{A}_i, w_i, r_i, \mathfrak{u}_i)$ refines the semantics of a network of XTA [27], non-deterministic time delays are refined by races and stochastic choices induced by $\mathfrak{u}_i$ and discrete non-deterministic choices are refined by probabilistic choices. The semantics of NSXTA assign a probability measure to sets of runs.

Example. As an example consider the network $\mathcal{N}_1$ of SXTA from Fig. 1 with discrete variables n and m with initial value 1. The run $\langle \ell_2, \ell_1, x = y = 0.5, m = 2, n = 4 \rangle \xrightarrow{3,b} \langle \ell_2, \ell_2, x = y = 3.5, m = 4, n = 4 \rangle$ shows that variable m with value 4 can be reached in 3.5 timed units. The run $s_0 = \langle \ell_1, \ell_1, x = y = 0, m = n = 1 \rangle \xrightarrow{0.6,b} \langle \ell_1, \ell_2, x = y = 0.6, m = 2, n = 1 \rangle \xrightarrow{0.1,a} \langle \ell_2, \ell_2, x = y = 0.7, m = 3, n = 4 \rangle$ shows that variable m with value 3 can be reached in 0.7 timed units. In particular we have that the probability of m to have value 4 within 2 time units, i.e. $\mathbb{P}(\mathcal{N}_1 \models \Diamond \ m = 4 \wedge x \leq 2) \approx 0.23$. Similarly, $\mathbb{P}(\mathcal{N}_1 \models \Diamond \ m = 3 \wedge x \leq 2) \approx 0.49$. In fact, the final value of m is decided by the outcome of the initial race between the components A and B for outputting a or b. Following the

---

[1] As opposed to (global) semantics of network of timed automata.

semantics of [15] the component with the smaller delay given by $u_{s_0}^A$ respectively $u_{s_0}^B$ wins the race. In the present case it is a fifty-fifty race given two uniform distributions on $[0, 1]$. Note also, that component A writes on the shared variable n, which is used in the invariant (a uniform distribution) of the initial location of component B. This modification causes bigger delays which makes it less likely to reach $m = 4$ within two time units.

2.2   Statistical Model Checking

The core idea of Statistical Model Checking (SMC) [33] is to generate a number of independent runs for an NSXTA, while monitoring them with respect to a given temporal property. Standard statistics is then used to estimate the probability of system runs satisfying the property with some desired degree of confidence.

To generate a random run according to the stochastic semantics of NSXTA, we assume that the given network has a special clock $\hat{x}$ which is never updated. The clock is used as a time stamp. Algorithm 1 (as in [14,15]) describes the computation of a random run bounded by time horizon c. Line 3 computes the smallest delay (of the component winning the race). A delay can be infinite if no edge is enabled, e.g. a component is only expecting inputs. If the current time plus the smallest delay exceed the given time horizon c the algorithm returns. Otherwise at line 7 time elapses and at Line 8 an enabled action of the winning component is taken. The GPU implementation of Algorithm 1 is complex and a key contribution of this paper.

In this work we focus on the *Quantitative question* for a given NSXTA $\mathcal{N}$ and (time) bounded reachability property φ. Algorithm 2 [23] uses Chernoff-Hoeffding bound to estimate probability $\mathbb{P}(\mathcal{N} \models \varphi)$ by using N runs and providing an interval $p \pm \varepsilon$ with confidence level $1 - \alpha$ (where α is a probability that $\mathbb{P}(\mathcal{N} \models \varphi) \notin [p - \varepsilon, p + \varepsilon]$). Note that each run is sampled independently, therefore random variables derived from runs are independent and identically distributed, and thus Algorithm 2 is suitable for a parallel implementation.

Algorithm 1. Random run for $\mathcal{N} = \|_{i=1}^n (\mathcal{A}_i, w_i, r_i, u_i)$, state $\langle \ell, \mu, \nu \rangle$, bound c

1:    $s := \langle \ell_0, \mu_0, \nu_0 \rangle$, $run := (s)$ ▷ initialize with an initial state
2:    **while** $\mu(\hat{x}) < $ c **do**
3:      $d := min_{i=1}^n(delay(u_i^s))$ ▷ pick smallest delay of component i from s
4:      **if** $\mu(\hat{x}) + d \geq $ c **then**   ▷ beyond time bound
5:        $d := $ c $- \mu(\hat{x})$; **return** $run \oplus (\xrightarrow{d} \langle \ell, \mu + d, \nu \rangle)$ ▷ concatenate remaining delay
6:      **else**
7:        let $\mu_d := \mu + d$ and $s' = \langle \ell, \mu_d, \nu \rangle$ ▷ compute delay
8:        pick $a \in \mathsf{En}(s')$ according to $\gamma_{s'}$ ▷ choose action
9:        $run := run \oplus (\xrightarrow{d} s') \oplus (\xrightarrow{a} s'')$ ▷ concatenate delay and action
10:       $s := s''$
11: **return** run

2.3   The GP-GPU Framework CUDA

CUDA is a programming interface developed by NVIDIA that allows issuing and managing data-parallel computations on specifically NVIDIA *Graphical Processing Unit*s (GPU). It is a language extension of C and C++, however with certain limitations, such as no dynamic recursion or function pointers [29].

The CUDA interface discriminates between CPU and GPU computations, by viewing them as co-processing units named *host* and *device*, respectively. The *device* is viewed as a set of multiprocessors, each of which uses a *Single Instruction, Multiple Data* (SIMD) architecture. In this paradigm, each single sub-processor of a multiprocessor executes the same instruction at the same clock-cycle – although on different data. The *host* issues instructions to the *device* in the form of *kernels* – arbitrarily complex code units expressed as C++ functions. The kernels are executed by a *grid* of parallel threads. The grid is divided into equal size *blocks* with efficient memory sharing among threads within each block. The blocks are divided into SIMD groups called *warps* of synchronous execution where precisely 32 threads within each warp execute the same instruction. If some threads diverge within warp (e.g. due to conditional branching), then their instruction is executed on a different cycle from the rest, thus slowing down the overall progress.

The exact number of blocks and number of threads within a block is configurable upon each kernel launch. An example of a configuration could be 64 blocks with 256 threads per block, which would result in a grid of 16384 threads.

During the execution of a kernel, each *block* is mapped to a multiprocessor. Per clock cycle, the instruction unit of the multiprocessor will issue an instruction to a given *warp* from the set of *blocks* residing on the multiprocessor. This follows the SIMD architecture and allows the GPU a large degree of parallelism for computations where all threads in a given *warp* execute the same instruction. If the threads within a *warp* diverge in their execution path, the performance may be impacted. For example, for a given if-else statement **if (A) then B else C**, if A holds for at least one thread of a given warp, then the multiprocessor will execute the instruction for B, while the remaining threads of the warp will be *stalled*. Afterwards, when C is executed, the threads where A holds idle. By having this thread divergence, the warp may use additional clock cycles to execute instructions, significantly limiting parallelism. This implies that a *device* executes between $\#multiprocessors \cdot 1$ and $\#multiprocessors \cdot 32$ computations in parallel depending on the severity of thread divergence.

Algorithm 2. Prob. estimation of $\mathcal{N} \models \varphi$ with confidence $(1 - \alpha)$ and error ε

1: $N := \ln(2/\alpha)/(2\varepsilon^2)$, $a := 0$
2: **for** $i = 1$ to N **do**
3:     Use Alg. 1 to generate a random *run* and observe random var $x := (run \models \varphi)$
4:     $a := a + x$ ▷ count satisfying runs
5: **return** a/N;   ▷ $\mathbb{P}(\mathcal{N} \models \varphi) \in [a/N - \varepsilon, a/N + \varepsilon]$ with confidence $(1 - \alpha)$

---

3   Statistical Model Checking on GPU

Our tool SMAcc (Statistical Model-checking ACCelerated) [19] accepts NSXTA as a subset of the Uppaal specification language. Initially the input model is parsed in the *host* (CPU) and converted into an internal representation. After this, the model undergoes various optimization steps attempting to minimize thread divergence. These are discussed in detail in Sect. 4. In addition to facilitating computations on the GPU, CUDA facilitates running an almost equivalent code-base directly on the *host* CPU in a parallel fashion. We have utilized this feature to also allow for SMAcc to be executed on multi-core CPU systems.

Internally SMAcc represents an NSXTA as Abstract Syntax Trees and Expression Trees where each semantic component is decomposed into a tree with its leafs being atomic. This representation is designed for fast model traversal in order to perform analysis and optimizations efficiently. This structure further eases the migration of the model from the *host* to the *device* memory.

We utilize expression trees to represent user-supplied values and equations, such as update values, node exponential rates, edge weights, etc. We take particular care in implementing these tree structures such that they can be evaluated through a generic non-recursive post-order tree traversal algorithm using two stacks (one for operations and another for operands). This is particular to work around the limitations of CUDA where dynamic call stacks are not supported. This limitation implies that classical constructs using inheritance and recursion can not be utilized. In practice we determine the size of the required stack-size statically as $\mathcal{O}(depth(\text{expr}))$ given that the expressions are evaluated bottom up. As we shall discuss later, these expression trees make the efficient implementation of a GPU accelerated SMC algorithm challenging, and remain a large source of thread divergence, as illustrated in Figs. 2(a) and 2(b). We shall discuss different strategies of mitigation later in Sect. 4.

3.1   SMC Algorithm for the GPU

In a conventional use-case of SMC, e.g. for simulating disease propagation [5, 25], the main challenge is to obtain a large number of simulations in limited time. For this work we thus focus on the parallelization of drawing a large set of

Fig. 2. Models triggering thread divergence due to: (a) expression complexity, (b) delay re-sampling.

Algorithm 3. CUDA probability estimation for network $\mathcal{N}$, property φ, confidence $(1 - \alpha)$, error ε, and number of threads T

1: $N := \lceil (\ln \frac{2}{\delta})/(2\varepsilon^2) \rceil$; $N_t := \lceil \frac{N}{T} \rceil$; $A := \text{int}[T]\{0, \dots, 0\}$
2: **Cuda parallel** $t \in \{0, \dots, T - 1\}$ **do**   ▷ dispatch threads in warps
3:    **for** $i \in \{1, \dots, N_t\}$ **do**   ▷ batch of simulations per thread
4:       observe $x := (\mathcal{N} \models \varphi)$ using GPU implementation of Alg. 1
5:       $A[t] := A[t] + x$ ▷ count satisfying runs per thread
6: **return** $\frac{1}{N_t \cdot T} \sum_{i=1}^{T} A[i]$ ▷ sum satisfying runs and divide by total

samples from the system. While the challenge of parallelizing a single simulation is interesting we leave that challenge for further work.

The GPU specific version of Algorithm 2 is given in Algorithm 3. The number of simulations each thread executes is predetermined and evenly distributed between all the threads in the execution (line 2), as to not introduce bias in the form of over-representing shorter traces through race-conditions [37]. This has the effect that the total number of simulations must be divisible by the number of threads used. As an example, with a 64-block 256-thread configuration, the total number of simulation runs must be divisible by the minimum number of simulations, which in this case is 16384. These threads are launched concurrently and run independently within their *warp* groups, as can be seen in line 2. A potential side-effect is the creation of *stragglers*: threads generating significantly longer simulations and thus taking longer computation times, which may become a bottleneck for simulation batches, especially when an entire *warp* group can be delayed by one straggler.

The simulation of a single trajectory concludes when one of a few conditions is met; the run can be bounded by time progression or a step counter, the trajectory has met a deadlock, or the monitored random variable has reached its terminal value (i.e. the property holds for the trajectory). This aligns with the semantics of properties as used in UPPAAL [15]. The step-by-step progression of a single simulation trajectory follows the definition of NSXTA closely; for each individual XTA, sample the delay according to the delay distribution then resolve the race between the individual components in the network and conclude with sampling a winning out-edge in the winning XTA. This sampling procedure is also sketched in Algorithm 1. Following this, the results from the individual simulations are aggregated (line 5) using dedicated counter $A[t]$ per thread t and thus avoid race conditions. Finally the result are tallied, normalized and returned (line 6).

3.2   Thread Divergence in SMC for NSXTA

For applications such as Computational Fluid Dynamics [2] and Value Iteration [11] both enjoy little to no thread-divergence, in part due to their roots in linear algebra. In the case of SMC for NSXTA, thread divergence is unavoidable for all but trivial stochastic systems, as traces of different executions naturally diverge, partly due to varied complexity of the expressions used in the system and partly due to the delay computation. In Fig. 2(a) we observe (1) that the complexity of the expressions used in invariants and guards differs and (2) that the out-degree of each location differs. For Algorithm 1 this implies that the number (and sequence) of GPU instructions used for sampling of the *delay* on line 3 will vary depending on the location of the automata, leading to thread divergence. In the model seen in Fig. 2(b) we observe divergence related to the *delay* operation. Consider n threads sampling a delay for location p_0. At the first sample 50% of the threads (on average) will have picked a delay for which an edge can be taken. However, these 50% must await the remainder of the threads to re-sample and find a suitable delay. This re-sampling causes the successful branches to idle until all threads have completed the delay sampling. In the remainder of this work we address the former type of thread divergence and leave the latter to further work.

4   Optimizations

To fully utilize the computational capabilities of the GPU, we have implemented several optimization strategies as to maximize the parallelism and throughput of the simulations when executed on the GPU. The main cause of performance problems in CUDA programs is thread divergence. Our optimization strategies therefore largely focus on reducing thread divergence, either in size or frequency.

Expression Trees. As discussed in Sect. 2.3, expression trees are a source of thread divergence when interpreted naively using the post-order-tree-traversal. Because expressions allow for ease of modeling complex arithmetic operations, these constructions are frequently used in practice. We attempt to combat this issue via two strategies: Just In Time (JIT) compilation of model expressions through CUDA C code, and interpreting the expression trees through Polish notation.

JIT compilation is accomplished through NVIDIA's runtime compilation library NVRTC. This translation is done by a straight-forward conversion of the internal representation of each model expression into a C equivalent formulation. Each expression is given a numerical identifier, and is added to a lookup table, implemented via a `switch` statement. This table is then injected to the source code of the engine, which is compiled at runtime. Using JIT compilation does not directly reduce thread divergence. However, it produces smaller and more uniform branches. In addition, the JIT compiler is at liberty to optimize and re-order the byte-code to be optimized towards the *device* architecture. However, JIT compilation of expressions introduces a significant overhead in pre-processing when running simulations – an effect observed in the experiments in Sect. 5.

Model expression interpretation through Polish notation is an alternative to JIT compilation, where the sequences of expression trees are translated to Polish notation and interpreted during simulation. This avoids having to traverse the expression trees at runtime, which vastly simplifies the evaluation. Furthermore,

Polish notation has the added benefit of entirely eliminating branching caused by varying tree balance, while also limiting the branching caused by varying tree size.

Weakest Preconditions and Expression Simplification. Existing tools such as UPPAAL implement the successor computation by first sampling delays, then applying guards, updates and finally invariants – with a potential reversal of the operation if the invariant is invalidated. This approach thereby has several potential points for thread divergence. This form of divergence can be limited to only a single branching point by "moving" the destination location invariant over to guards over edges that lead to such location: compute the weakest preconditions for the destination invariant after an update execution and add the resulting constraint to the guards. Additionally, we apply a set of identities to further simplify expressions and to remove trivial constraints added by computing weakest preconditions.

Shared Memory. Shared memory is a part of the GPU's L1 cache memory, which can be accessed by all threads in a block and can be controlled by the programmer. The L1 memory bank of the device enjoys faster reading time compared to the global memory of the device. Typically, shared L1 memory is used for intra-block communication, increasing performance of parallel computing through synchronization of thread operations. We utilize this memory for storing the model that each thread will simulate. The L1 cache is though at a limited size, and is further restricted as the number of threads in a block dictates the amount of shared memory available, with up to 32 bytes per thread. Therefore, utilizing shared memory to store the model can be used if $threads \cdot 32B > modelsize$. In the future, the model representation can be further compressed by taking advantage of UPPAAL templates where many processes share the same automata structure.

5   Experiments

We experimentally show the applicability of GPUs for statistical model checking on stochastic systems through its use on seven different model families, whereof four are scalable problem instances. Specifically, our experiments are conducted with the CSMA and Aloha wireless communication protocol models [8], the Agent-Based and CTMC SEIHR Covid models [25], and the Bluetooth, Firewire and Fischer UPPAAL SMC case study models [34]. The Fischer protocol model

Table 1. Configurations of hardware used for the experiments. Experiments pitting different hardware platforms can be found in Appendix A, B and C.

	Power usage	SM/Cores	Clock speed	Release year
NVIDIA A100	250W	108	765 MHz	2020
2 × AMD EPYC 7642	2 × 225W	2 × 48	2.4 GHz	2019

has modified timings s.t. multiple components can reside within the critical section concurrently, thus breaking the mutual exclusion of the protocol. We draw comparison between the performance of running the implementation on the CPU and GPU, using the hardware listed in Table 1, and CUDA version 11.8.

Furthermore, we investigate the impact of using the implemented optimization strategies from Sect. 4. As a final note, all experiments have been conducted with a kernel configuration of 64 blocks and 256 threads. The kernel configuration has significant impact on the GPU performance, and there is no way of deducing the optimal configuration for non-trivial kernel executions a priori. In addition, the optimal kernel configuration is dependent on both the specific model instance and the targeted GPU platform. This specific configuration has been chosen by sweeping through a grid of configurations and picking best performing largest numbers for CTMC Covid model.

The parallel experiments executed on the CPU are conducted by oversubscribing the CPUs with threads; in preliminary experiments we found that a ratio of 10 threads per physical core yields good performance. We hypothesize that this is due to an uneven computational effort between within simulation batches, where the overall simulation time is straggled by a single thread having longer runs. This is similar to the effect observed across threads in the GPU simulation, and thus an artifact of the pipeline of SMAcc for the CPU execution also.

For each problem instance we test 8 different configurations:

- UPPAAL 4.1.26-2 statistical model checker, executed on a single core,
- a **Baseline**, executing SMAcc on a single core,
- a CPU (from Table 1) configuration using post order tree traversal **PO-CPU**, utilizing all the 96 cores of the CPU,
- a GPU (from Table 1) configuration using post order tree traversal **PO-GPU**, configured for 64 blocks of 256 threads,
- versions utilizing the Polish notation optimization for CPU (**PN-CPU**), executed on all 96 CPU cores,
- the GPU version with Polish notation optimization (**PN-GPU**),
- a configuration utilizing the **JIT** optimization – a feature limited to the GPU, vis-á-vis the restrictions of NVRTC framework, and
- a configuration utilizing the shared memory of the GPU (**SM**) when the problem instance fits into memory. Post order tree traversal is used for expression evaluation.

In all experiments we compute exactly 16384 simulations, corresponding to one simulation per GPU thread ($64 \cdot 256$). All experiments are limited to 1 h of computation, and have been run 10 times giving an average runtime. The results have been compared to UPPAAL to guarantee correctness.

A Note on the Scalability of the Models. The scaling method of the scalable systems varies between models with and without local variables. Specifically, Aloha and Agent-Based SEIHR Covid are scaled by the number of components on the

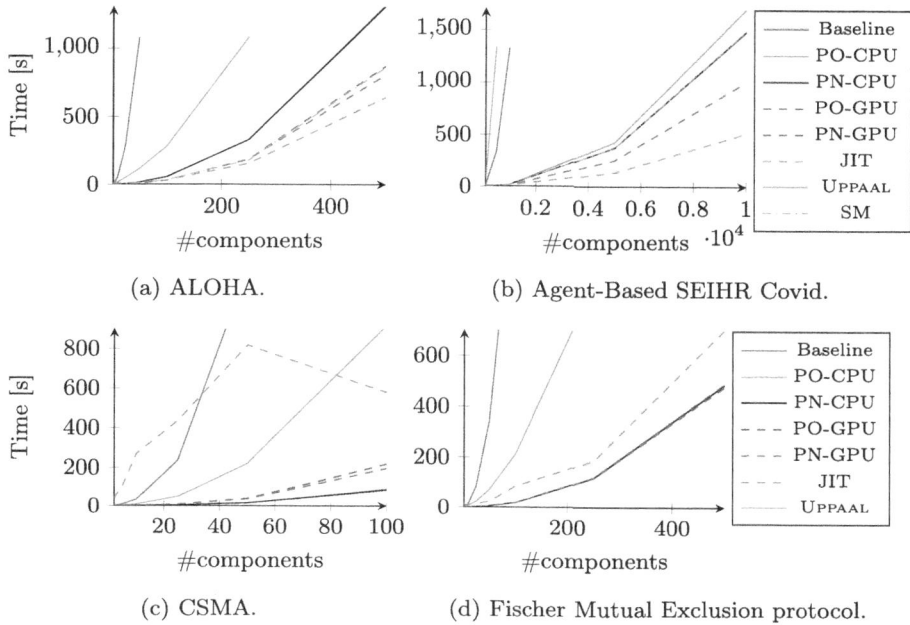

Fig. 3. Simulation computation times (omitted points exceed 1h timeout).

same model, while CSMA and Fischer are scaled by duplicating the model and slightly changing the variables used for each component. Consequently, CSMA and Fischer suffer from increased model size for each added component thus requiring more memory to represent, making the Shared Memory optimization inapplicable. In addition, the Bluetooth and Firewire models are too large on their own to fit into shared memory. In these cases the **SM** configuration is omitted from the experiment. The only model families that fit within the Shared Memory are Agent-Based Covid, Aloha and CTMC Covid.

Discussion. Let us initially compare the performance of UPPAAL to the **Baseline** configuration. In general we observe that these two configurations are incomparable; UPPAAL enjoys significantly lower computation times than the SMACC baseline implementation in the ALOHA (Fig. 3a), CSMA (Fig. 3c), Fischer (Fig. 3d) and Firewire (Table 2) experiments. On the other hand, the **Baseline** configuration outperforms UPPAAL on the remainder. We hypothesize that architectural differences, optimizations and fine-tuning are the cause of this discrepancy and leave it to further work to bring optimizations from UPPAAL into SMACC.

By comparing the **PO-GPU** and the **SM** configuration in Fig. 3a, Fig. 3b and Table 2 we observe marginal differences. We attribute this effect to the efficient memory-caches of the GPUs; for sufficiently small models, cache misses are rare, thus limiting its benefit of allocation directly in the shared memory. The largest improvements over the **Baseline** is enjoyed by the optimization techniques targeting thread divergence. Generally we observe that the Polish notation optimization has an insignificant effect for the CPU (**PN-CPU**) and only rarely a dramatic effect for the GPU (**PN-GPU**). Specifically the **PN-GPU** configuration enjoys good improvements for the Agent-Based SEIHR models (Fig. 3b) as the Bluetooth and Firewire models (Table 2). Importantly, the Polish notation never appears detrimental to the performance.

Contrary to **PN-GPU**, the **JIT** optimization has a varied impact on the performance. Specifically, **JIT** performs well on models where components have identical expressions, as is the case in the Aloha and Agent-Based Covid models.

In the CSMA (Fig. 3c) and Fischer (Fig. 3d) models the **JIT** compilation instead causes a slowdown compared to the post order tree traversal **PO-GPU** implementation. We hypothesize that the effect of **JIT** compilation is especially subject to the number of unique expressions evaluated at a given time. Dissimilar expressions are guaranteed to cause thread divergence for **JIT**, whereas this is not necessarily the case for neither **PO-GPU** nor **PN-GPU**. Furthermore, for the CSMA case study we observe a surprising decrease in run time with increasing problem size. A functional error in the resulting GPU kernel is unlikely, as the obtained SMC results coincide. It is however plausible that larger problem sizes lead to better occupancy[2]. It may be the case that a larger problem results in more concurrent blocks being available, allowing the GPU to schedule interleaved work such that memory access can be coalesced, and that work can be performed on the same multiprocessor while some threads are waiting for data from device memory.

In Fig. 4a and Fig. 4b we see the cactus plots of the speed-up and power-ratio over all the experiments conducted. In these plots, the speedup (power-ratio respectively) is compared to the **PO-CPU** configuration using all 96 cores, sorted individually and then plotted. This implies that a given point in the x-axis may stem from different experiments for a given configuration. We observe in Fig. 4a that the **PN-GPU** configuration delivers the most stable performance compared to the reference with the **JIT** having a more varied effect on the performance. We can also observe that the Polish notation optimization has a generally positive impact on the performance for both GPU and CPU versions, albeit with a point-wise smaller degradation for the CPU-version. Studying instead the power consumption, we see in Fig. 4b that UPPAAL appears to be the most power efficient configuration, however with notable exceptions and an inability to com-

Table 2. Performance measurements for various models in seconds.

Model	Baseline	PO-CPU	PN-CPU	PO-GPU	PN-GPU	JIT	UPPAAL	SM
CTMC Covid	263.633	3.777	3.405	2.080	**1.689**	11.019	565.199	2.295
Bluetooth	4.976	0.191	**0.165**	0.736	0.736	11.284	5.539	-
Firewire	9.315	**0.252**	0.277	0.811	1.689	10.914	1.197	-

---

[2] https://docs.nvidia.com/gameworks/content/developertools/desktop/analysis/report/cudaexperiments/kernellevel/achievedoccupancy.htm.

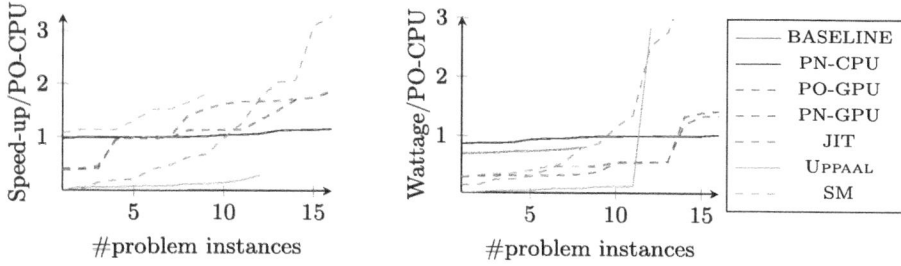

(a) Speed-up relative to **PO-CPU** (b) Power ratio relative to **PO-CPU** (lower is (higher is better).   better).

Fig. 4. Cactus plots for speed-up and power ratio over all experiments. Problems solved by any configurations in < 2*sec* are excluded.

plete the computation within the provided 1 h time limit. Across the majority of examples the **PN-GPU** and **PO-GPU** provide solid reductions in the power-usage, and peaking at a doubling of the power consumption compared to the reference. Studying Table 3, we observe that the degrading efficiency observed in Fig. 4b can be attributed to the CSMA model family. We hypothesize that these models exhibit the re-sampling branch divergence as illustrated by Fig. 2. Such divergence can be reduced by re-sampling only the processes affected by a recent transition, but it requires tracking the dependencies between transitions.

Table 3. Estimated power ratio of the GPU compared to the CPU: (T_{GPU} · P_{GPU}/T_{CPU} · P_{CPU}) where T and P denote the time and power consumption of the CPU and GPU by assuming that devices use max TDP for the entire computation time. The parentheses state the number of components in the scalable models. The best CPU and GPU configuration is chosen for each row.

Model	CPU(s)	GPU(s)	Speed-up	Power ratio
AB Covid (5K)	375.33	137.48	2.73	0.20
Aloha (500)	1306.40	644.42	2.03	0.27
CTMC Covid	2.31	1.69	1.37	0.41
Fischer (500)	484.23	476.94	1.02	0.55
CSMA (100)	84.49	195.65	0.43	1.29
Firewire	0.21	0.81	0.26	2.14
Bluetooth	0.13	0.74	0.18	3.16

6   Conclusion

In this work we show the applicability and advantages of GPU technologies in the context of Statistical Model Checking for Networks of Stochastic Extended

Timed Automata. We presented SMAcc a prototype for performing SMC in NSXTA on the GPU. We have identified and experimented with several optimization and program transformation techniques to better accommodate the *Single Instruction Multiple Data* architecture employed by NVIDIA GPUs. Our experiments show reduced time and energy consumption which demonstrates the potential use of GPU technology for SMC algorithms for larger models. We observe that for one case GPU accelerated SMC uses as little as 20% of the energy of the CPU for completing an equivalent task while conducting the computation 2.73 times faster. Additionally we identify the bottlenecks of the current implementation, exemplified by a worse computation time and power consumption on single model instances.

A   NVIDIA Tesla T4 vs Dual AMD EPYC 7551

Tested using a configuration of 40 blocks and 256 threads, giving us 10240 sims. This has been tested using CUDA version 11.0, which lacks a few optimisations available in newer CUDA versions. These results are from a single run of the experiments (Figs. 5, 6 and Tables 4, 5, 6, 7).

Table 4. Different configurations of hardware used for the experiments.

	Power usage	SM/Cores	Clock speed	Release year
NVIDIA Tesla T4	70W	40	585 MHz	2018
2 × AMD EPYC 7551	2 × 180W	2 × 32	2.0 GHz	2017

Table 5. The model families and their parameters. F indicates whether model fits in GPU shared memory.

Model family	Property	#Components	F
AB Covid	E[<=100;10240] (max: inf)	100,500,1k,5k,10k	✓
Aloha	E[<=100;10240] (max: nt)	2,5,10,25,50,100, 250,500	✓
CSMA	Pr[<=2000;10240](<> Proc(0).SUCCESS)	2,5,10,25,50,100	✗
Fischer	E[<=300;10240] (max:in_critical)	2,5,10,25,50,100, 250,500	✗
CTMC Covid	Pr[<=100;10240](<> I > 1000)	5	✓
Bluetooth	Pr[<=5000;10240](<> receiver1.Reply)	4	✗
Firewire	Pr[<=1000;10240](<> node1.s5)	4	✗

Table 6. Tesla T4 results in seconds.

Model	Baseline	PO-CPU	PN-CPU	PO-GPU	PN-GPU	JIT	Uppaal	SM
Bluetooth	2.718	**0.165**	0.265	0.868	0.969	8.490	5.858	-
CTMC Covid	158.445	3.428	2.818	3.574	**2.772**	10.844	513.376	3.523
Firewire	4.870	0.415	**0.265**	0.818	0.768	11.345	1.112	-

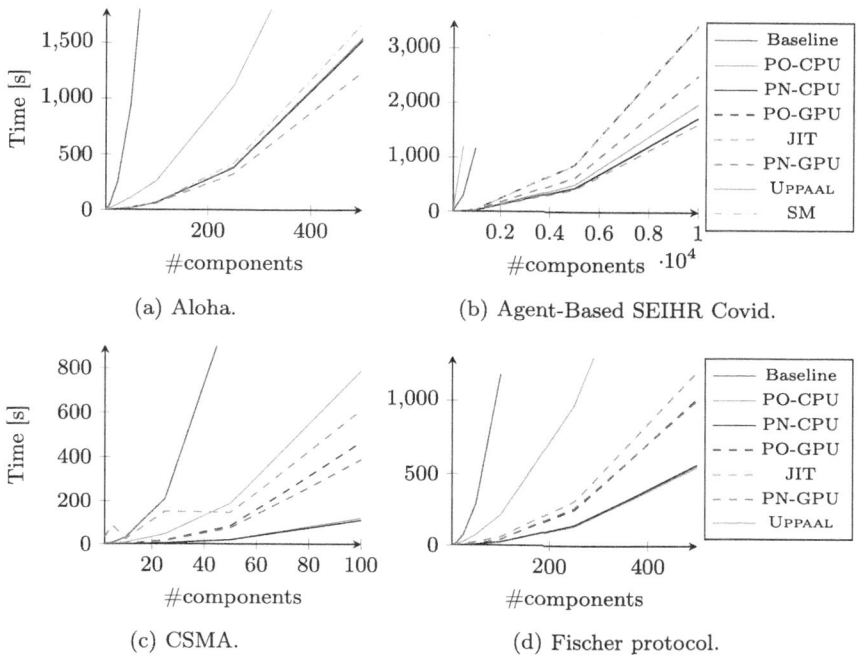

Fig. 5. Tesla T4 results for scalable models (omitted points exceed 1h timeout).

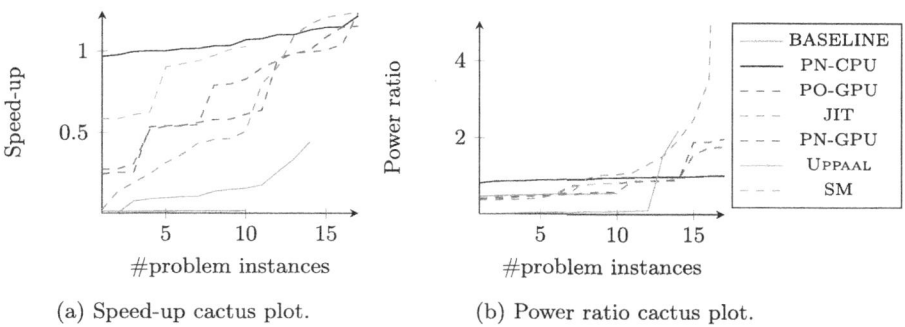

Fig. 6. Speed-up and power ratio comparison of Tesla T4 over PO-CPU.

Table 7. Comparison of CPU vs. GPU, estimating the power ratio of the GPU compared to the CPU: ($T_{GPU} \cdot P_{GPU} / T_{CPU} \cdot P_{CPU}$) where T and P denote the time and power-consumption of the CPU and GPU. The parentheses state the number of components in the scalable systems. The best CPU and GPU configuration is chosen for each row.

Model	CPU(s)	GPU(s)	Speed-up	Power ratio
Aloha (500)	1525.76	1246.60	1.22	0.16
AB Covid (5K)	436.30	412.94	1.06	0.18
CTMC Covid	2.82	2.77	1.02	0.19
Fischer (500)	551.89	1006.87	0.55	0.35
Firewire	0.27	0.77	0.29	0.68
CSMA (100)	109.28	388.67	0.28	0.69
Bluetooth	0.17	0.87	0.20	1.00

B   NVIDIA RTX 3070 vs Dual AMD EPYC 7642

Tested using a configuration of 46 blocks and 256 threads, giving us 11776 sims. This has been tested using CUDA version 11.8. These results are from a single run of the experiments (Figs. 7, 8 and Tables 8, 9, 10, 11).

Table 8. Different configurations of hardware used for the experiments.

	Power usage	SM/Cores	Clock speed	Release year
NVIDIA RTX 3070	220W	46	1500 MHz	2020
2 × AMD EPYC 7642	2 × 225W	2 × 48	2.4 GHz	2019

Table 9. Model families and their parameters. F column indicates whether model fits in GPU shared memory.

Model family	Property	#Components	F
AB Covid	E[<=100;11776] (max: inf)	100,500,1k,5k,10k	✓
Aloha	E[<=100;11776] (max: nt)	2,5,10,25,50,100, 250,500	✓
CSMA	Pr[<=2000;11776](<> Proc(0).SUCCESS)	2,5,10,25,50,100	✗
Fischer	E[<=300;11776] (max:in_critical)	2,5,10,25,50,100, 250,500	✗
CTMC Covid	Pr[<=100;11776](<> I > 1000)	5	✓
Bluetooth	Pr[<=5000;11776](<> receiver1.Reply)	4	✗
Firewire	Pr[<=1000;11776](<> node1.s5)	4	✗

Table 10. RTX 3070 results in seconds.

Model	Baseline	PO-CPU	PN-CPU	PO-GPU	PN-GPU	JIT	Uppaal	SM
CTMC Covid	112.608	1.968	1.781	1.731	**1.378**	9.351	422.666	1.731
Bluetooth	2.220	0.216	**0.166**	0.368	0.368	7.988	4.041	-
Firewire	4.024	0.316	**0.216**	0.418	0.374	8.746	0.891	-

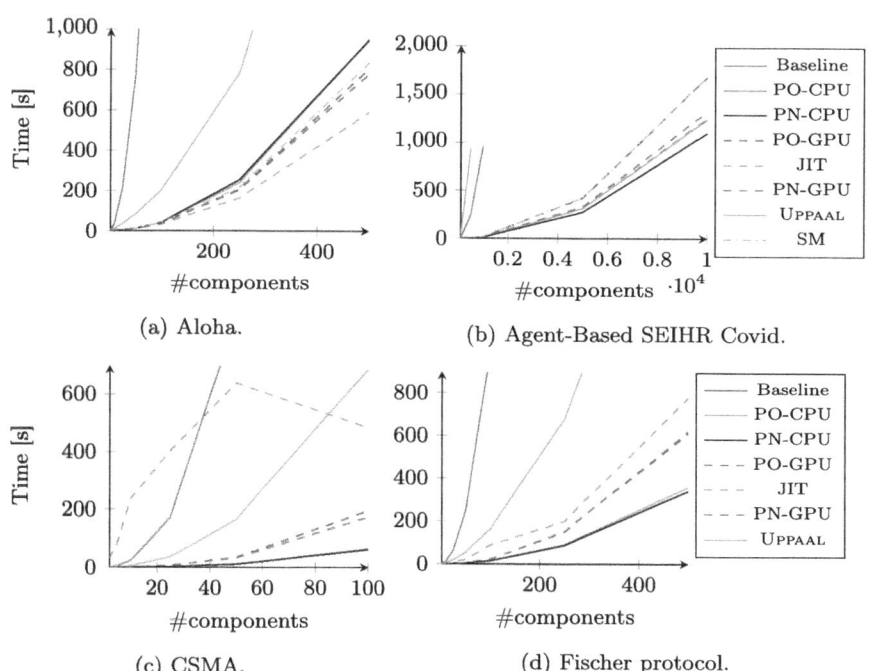

(a) Aloha.

(b) Agent-Based SEIHR Covid.

(c) CSMA.

(d) Fischer protocol.

Fig. 7. RTX 3070 results for scalable models (omitted points exceed 1 h timeout).

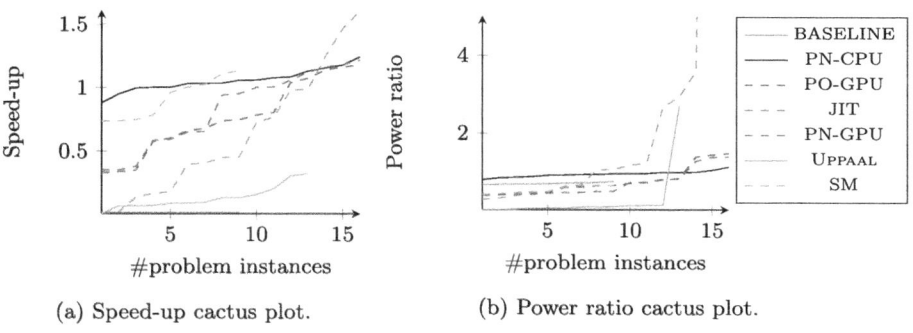

(a) Speed-up cactus plot.

(b) Power ratio cactus plot.

Fig. 8. Speed-up and power ratio comparison of RTX 3070 over PO-CPU.

Table 11. Comparison of CPU vs. GPU, estimating the power ratio of the GPU compared to the CPU: $(T_{GPU} \cdot P_{GPU}/T_{CPU} \cdot P_{CPU})$ where T and P denote the time and power-consumption of the CPU and GPU. The parentheses state the number of components in the scalable systems. The best CPU and GPU configuration is chosen for each row.

Model	CPU(s)	GPU(s)	Speed-up	Power ratio
Aloha (500)	947.96	590.05	1.61	0.30
CTMC Covid	1.78	1.38	1.29	0.38
AB Covid (5K)	272.65	320.45	0.85	0.57
Firewire	0.22	0.37	0.59	0.82
Fischer (500)	337.29	609.41	0.55	0.88
Bluetooth	0.17	0.37	0.46	1.06
CSMA (100)	62.09	173.38	0.36	1.37

C   NVIDIA A100 vs Dual AMD EPYC 7642

Tested using a configuration of 64 blocks and 256 threads, giving us 16384 sims. This has been tested using CUDA version 11.8. These results are from a single run of the experiments (Figs. 9, 10 and Tables 12, 13, 14, 15).

Table 12. Configurations of hardware used for the experiments. Experiments pitting different hardware platforms can be found in Appendix A, B and C.

	Power usage	SM/Cores	Clock speed	Release year
NVIDIA A100	250W	108	765 MHz	2020
2 × AMD EPYC 7642	2 × 225W	2 × 48	2.4 GHz	2019

Table 13. Models and parameters. F indicates if model fits in GPU shared memory.

Model family	Property	#Components	F
AB Covid	E[<=100;16384] (max: inf)	100,500,1k,5k,10k	✓
Aloha	E[<=100;16384] (max: nt)	2,5,10,25,50,100, 250,500	✓
CSMA	Pr[<=2000;16384](<> Proc(0).SUCCESS)	2,5,10,25,50,100	✗
Fischer	E[<=300;16384] (max:in_critical)	2,5,10,25,50,100, 250,500	✗
CTMC Covid	Pr[<=100;16384](<> I > 1000)	5	✓
Bluetooth	Pr[<=5000;16384](<> receiver1.Reply)	4	✗
Firewire	Pr[<=1000;16384](<> node1.s5)	4	✗

Table 14. A100 results in seconds.

	Baseline	PO-CPU	PN-CPU	PO-GPU	PN-GPU	JIT	UPPAAL	SM
CTMC Covid	156.609	2.574	2.418	1.269	**1.119**	12.864	565.199	1.420
Bluetooth	2.972	0.166	**0.165**	0.266	0.265	13.464	5.539	-
Firewire	5.527	0.265	**0.215**	0.266	0.266	12.914	1.197	-

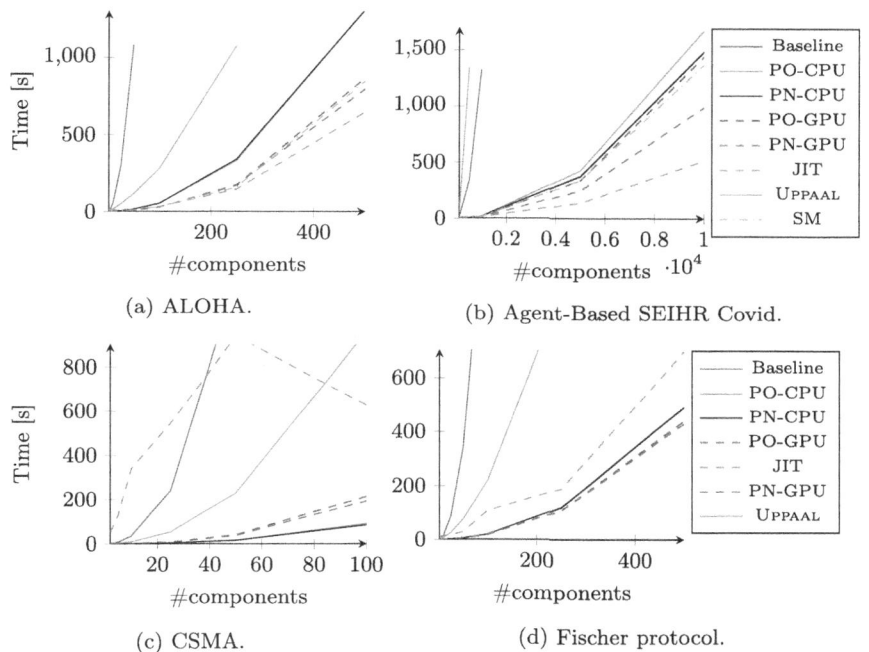

(a) ALOHA.

(b) Agent-Based SEIHR Covid.

(c) CSMA.

(d) Fischer protocol.

Fig. 9. A100 results for scalable models (omitted points exceeds 1 h timeout).

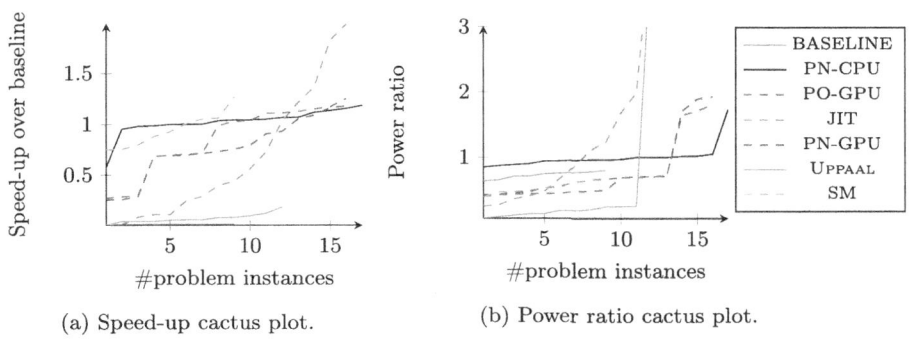

(a) Speed-up cactus plot.

(b) Power ratio cactus plot.

Fig. 10. Speed-up and power ratio for A100 over CPU.

Table 15. Comparison of CPU vs. GPU, estimating the power ratio of the GPU compared to the CPU: $(T_{GPU} \cdot P_{GPU}/T_{CPU} \cdot P_{CPU})$ where T and P denote the time and power-consumption of the CPU and GPU. The parentheses state the number of components in the scalable systems. The best CPU and GPU configuration is chosen for each row.

Model	CPU(s)	GPU(s)	Speed-up	Power ratio
AB Covid (5K)	375.09	139.65	2.69	0.21
CTMC Covid	2.42	1.12	2.16	0.26
Aloha (500)	1311.32	649.20	2.02	0.28
Fischer (500)	491.23	430.13	1.14	0.49
Firewire	0.22	0.27	0.81	0.68
Bluetooth	0.17	0.27	0.63	0.88
CSMA (100)	84.13	194.38	0.43	1.28

D   Kernel Configuration

In order to determine well performing numbers of blocks and threads, we sweep through configurations. Figure 11 shows that 40 blocks of 256 threads is the fastest configuration for CTMC Covid model.

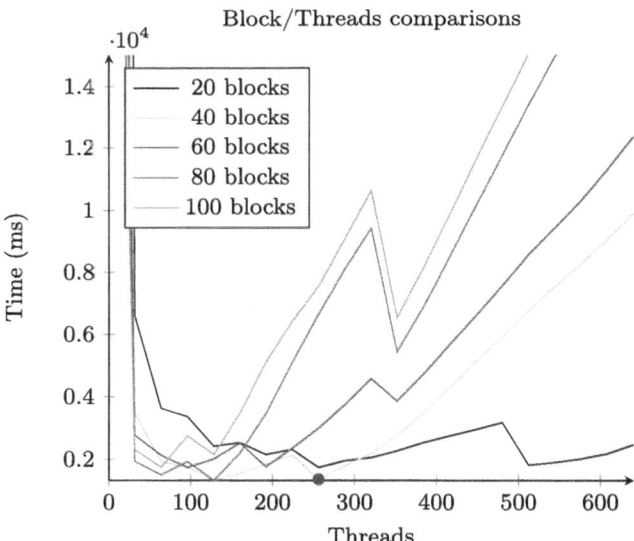

Fig. 11. Performance of various block/thread configurations, using the **PO-GPU** expression evaluation method on the CTMC Covid model. All experiments were run with 10k simulations on the NVIDIA Tesla T4 GPU. The red dot signifies the optimal configuration.

E Parallel Simulation on GPU

Listing 12.1. NVIDIA CUDA GPU C++ encoding of Alg. 3.

```
CPU GPU void simulate_automata(
    const unsigned idx,
    const network* model,
    const result_store* output,
    const sim_config* config)
{
    void* cache = static_cast<void*>(&static_cast<char*>(
        config->cache)[(idx*thread_heap_size(config)) / sizeof(char)]);
    curandState* r_state = &config->random_state_arr[idx];
    curand_init(config->seed, idx, idx, r_state);
    state sim_state = state::init(cache, r_state, model,
        config->max_expression_depth, config->max_backtrace_depth,
        config->max_edge_fanout);
    for (unsigned i = 0; i < config->sim_pr_thread; ++i) {
        const unsigned int sim_id = i + config->sim_pr_thread *
            static_cast<unsigned int>(idx);
        sim_state.reset(sim_id, model, config->initial_urgent,
            config->initial_committed);
        while (true) {
            // model->query->check_query()
            const int process = progress_sim(&sim_state, config);
            if (IS_NO_PROCESS(process))
                break;
            if (sim_state.models.store[process]->type == node::goal)
                break;
            do {
                const node* current = sim_state.models.store[process];
                const edge* e = pick_next_edge_stack(current->edges,
                    &sim_state);
                if (e == nullptr)
                    break;
                sim_state.traverse_edge(process, e->dest);
                e->apply_updates(&sim_state);
                sim_state.broadcast_channel(e->channel, process);
            } while (sim_state.models.store[process]->type == node::branch);
        }
        output->write_output(idx, &sim_state);
    }
}
```

References

1. Alur, R., Dill, D.L.: A theory of timed automata. Theoret. Comput. Sci. **126**(2), 183–235 (1994)
2. Amada, T., Imura, M., Yasumuro, Y., Manabe, Y., Chihara, K.: Particle-based fluid simulation on GPU. In: ACM Workshop on General-Purpose Computing on Graphics Processors, vol. 41, p. 42. Citeseer (2004)
3. Behrmann, G., David, A., Larsen, K.G.: A tutorial on UPPAAL. In: Bernardo, M., Corradini, F. (eds.) SFM-RT 2004. LNCS, vol. 3185, pp. 200–236. Springer, Heidelberg (2004). https://doi.org/10.1007/978-3-540-30080-9_7
4. Bertrand, N., et al.: Stochastic timed automata. Log. Methods Comput. Sci. **10** (2014)

5. Bilgram, A., et al.: An investigation of safe and near-optimal strategies for prevention of Covid-19 exposure using stochastic hybrid models and machine learning. Decis. Anal. J. **5**, 100141 (2022)
6. Bosnacki, D., Edelkamp, S., Sulewski, D., Wijs, A.: Parallel probabilistic model checking on general purpose graphics processors. Int. J. Softw. Tools Technol. Transf. **13**(1), 21–35 (2011)
7. Brockman, G., et al.: Openai gym. arXiv preprint arXiv:1606.01540 (2016)
8. Bulychev, P.E., David, A., Larsen, K.G., Legay, A., Mikučionis, M.: Computing Nash equilibrium in wireless ad hoc networks: a simulation-based approach. Electron. Proc. Theor. Comput. Sci. **78**, 1–14 (2012)
9. Bulychev, P.E., David, A., Larsen, K.G., Mikučionis, M., Legay, A.: Distributed parametric and statistical model checking. In: Barnat, J., Heljanko, K. (eds.) Proceedings 10th International Workshop on Parallel and Distributed Methods in verifiCation, PDMC 2011, Snowbird, Utah, USA, 14 July 2011. EPTCS, , vol. 72, pp. 30–42 (2011)
10. Chakraborty, S., Katoen, J., Sher, F., Strelec, M.: Modelling and statistical model checking of a microgrid. Int. J. Softw. Tools Technol. Transf. **17**(4), 537–554 (2015)
11. Chen, P., Lu, L.: Markov decision process parallel value iteration algorithm on GPU. In: Proceedings of 2013 International Conference on Information Science and Computer Applications, pp. 299–304. Atlantis Press (2013)
12. Clarke, E., Kroening, D., Lerda, F.: A tool for checking ANSI-C programs. In: Jensen, K., Podelski, A. (eds.) TACAS 2004. LNCS, vol. 2988, pp. 168–176. Springer, Heidelberg (2004). https://doi.org/10.1007/978-3-540-24730-2_15
13. Copik, M., Rataj, A., Wozna-Szczesniak, B.: A GPGPU-based simulator for prism: statistical verification of results of PMC (extended abstract). In: Schlingloff, B. (ed.) Proceedings of the 25th International Workshop on Concurrency, Specification and Programming, Rostock, Germany, 28–30 September 2016. CEUR Workshop Proceedings, vol. 1698, pp. 199–208. CEUR-WS.org (2016)
14. David, A., et al.: Statistical model checking for stochastic hybrid systems. Electron. Proc. Theor. Comput. Sci. **92**, 122–136 (2012)
15. David, A., et al.: Statistical model checking for networks of priced timed automata. In: Fahrenberg, U., Tripakis, S. (eds.) FORMATS 2011. LNCS, vol. 6919, pp. 80–96. Springer, Heidelberg (2011). https://doi.org/10.1007/978-3-642-24310-3_7
16. David, A., Larsen, K.G., Legay, A., Mikučionis, M., Poulsen, D.B.: Uppaal SMC tutorial. Int. J. Softw. Tools Technol. Transf. **17**(4), 397–415 (2015)
17. DeFrancisco, R., Cho, S., Ferdman, M., Smolka, S.A.: Swarm model checking on the GPU. Int. J. Softw. Tools Technol. Transf. **22**(5), 583–599 (2020)
18. Edelkamp, S., Sulewski, D.: Efficient explicit-state model checking on general purpose graphics processors. In: van de Pol, J., Weber, M. (eds.) SPIN 2010. LNCS, vol. 6349, pp. 106–123. Springer, Heidelberg (2010). https://doi.org/10.1007/978-3-642-16164-3_8
19. Eriksen, O.V., et al.: GPU accelerating statistical model checking for extended timed automata - artifact (2024)
20. Gainer, P., Hahn, E.M., Schewe, S.: Accelerated model checking of parametric Markov chains. In: Lahiri, S.K., Wang, C. (eds.) ATVA 2018. LNCS, vol. 11138, pp. 300–316. Springer, Cham (2018). https://doi.org/10.1007/978-3-030-01090-4_18
21. Hasrat, I.R., Jensen, P.G., Larsen, K.G., Srba, J.: End-to-end heat-pump control using continuous time stochastic modelling and Uppaal Stratego. In: Aït-Ameur, Y., Crăciun, F. (eds.) TASE 2022. LNCS, vol. 13299, pp. 363–380. Springer, Cham (2022). https://doi.org/10.1007/978-3-031-10363-6_24

22. Hensel, C., Junges, S., Katoen, J., Quatmann, T., Volk, M.: The probabilistic model checker Storm. CoRR, abs/2002.07080 (2020)
23. Hérault, T., Lassaigne, R., Magniette, F., Peyronnet, S.: Approximate probabilistic model checking. In: Steffen, B., Levi, G. (eds.) VMCAI 2004. LNCS, vol. 2937, pp. 73–84. Springer, Heidelberg (2004). https://doi.org/10.1007/978-3-540-24622-0_8
24. Jegourel, C., Larsen, K.G., Legay, A., Mikučionis, M., Poulsen, D.B., Sedwards, S.: Importance sampling for stochastic timed automata. In: Fränzle, M., Kapur, D., Zhan, N. (eds.) SETTA 2016. LNCS, vol. 9984, pp. 163–178. Springer, Cham (2016). https://doi.org/10.1007/978-3-319-47677-3_11
25. Jensen, P.G., Jørgensen, K.Y., Larsen, K.G., Mikučionis, M., Muñiz, M., Poulsen, D.B.: Fluid model-checking in UPPAAL for Covid-19. In: Margaria, T., Steffen, B. (eds.) ISoLA 2020. LNCS, vol. 12476, pp. 385–403. Springer, Cham (2020). https://doi.org/10.1007/978-3-030-61362-4_22
26. Larsen, K.G., Legay, A., Mikučionis, M., Poulsen, D.B.: Importance splitting in Uppaal. In: Margaria, T., Steffen, B. (eds.) ISoLA 2022, Part III. LNCS, vol. 13703, pp. 433–447. Springer, Cham (2022). https://doi.org/10.1007/978-3-031-19759-8_26
27. Larsen, K.G., Mikučionis, M., Muñiz, M., Srba, J.: Urgent partial order reduction for extended timed automata. In: Hung, D.V., Sokolsky, O. (eds.) ATVA 2020. LNCS, vol. 12302, pp. 179–195. Springer, Cham (2020). https://doi.org/10.1007/978-3-030-59152-6_10
28. Li, G., Gopalakrishnan, G.: Scalable SMT-based verification of GPU kernel functions. In: Proceedings of the Eighteenth ACM SIGSOFT International Symposium on Foundations of Software Engineering, FSE 2010, pp. 187–196. Association for Computing Machinery, New York (2010)
29. NVIDIA. CUDA C++ programming guide (2023). https://docs.nvidia.com/cuda/cuda-c-programming-guide/index.html. Accessed 10 Apr 2024
30. Osama, M., Wijs, A.: GPU acceleration of bounded model checking with ParaFROST. In: Silva, A., Leino, K.R.M. (eds.) CAV 2021. LNCS, vol. 12760, pp. 447–460. Springer, Cham (2021). https://doi.org/10.1007/978-3-030-81688-9_21
31. Ruijters, E., Guck, D., van Noort, M., Stoelinga, M.: Reliability-centered maintenance of the electrically insulated railway joint via fault tree analysis: a practical experience report. In: 46th Annual IEEE/IFIP International Conference on Dependable Systems and Networks, DSN 2016, Toulouse, France, 28 June–1 July 2016, pp. 662–669. IEEE Computer Society (2016)
32. Sasha Luccioni, A., Viguier, S., Ligozat, A.-L.: Estimating the carbon footprint of BLOOM, a 176b parameter language model. arXiv e-prints, arXiv:2211.02001 (2022)
33. Sen, K., Viswanathan, M., Agha, G.: Statistical model checking of black-box probabilistic systems. In: Alur, R., Peled, D.A. (eds.) CAV 2004. LNCS, vol. 3114, pp. 202–215. Springer, Heidelberg (2004). https://doi.org/10.1007/978-3-540-27813-9_16
34. UPPAAL. SMC case studies (2007). https://uppaal.org/casestudies/smc/. Accessed 10 Apr 2024
35. van Glabbeek, R.J., Höfner, P., Portmann, M., Tan, W.L.: Modelling and verifying the AODV routing protocol. Distrib. Comput. **29**(4), 279–315 (2016)

36. Wijs, A., Neele, T., Bošnački, D.: GPUexplore 2.0: unleashing GPU explicit-state model checking. In: Fitzgerald, J., Heitmeyer, C., Gnesi, S., Philippou, A. (eds.) FM 2016. LNCS, vol. 9995, pp. 694–701. Springer, Cham (2016). https://doi.org/10.1007/978-3-319-48989-6_42
37. Younes, H.L.S.: Ymer: a statistical model checker. In: Etessami, K., Rajamani, S.K. (eds.) CAV 2005. LNCS, vol. 3576, pp. 429–433. Springer, Heidelberg (2005). https://doi.org/10.1007/11513988_43

Model Checking Markov Chains as Distribution Transformers

Rajab Aghamov[1], Christel Baier[1], Toghrul Karimov[2],
Joris Nieuwveld[2], Joël Ouaknine[2], Jakob Piribauer[1(✉)],
and Mihir Vahanwala[2]

[1] Technische Universität Dresden, Dresden, Germany
{rajab.aghamov,christel.baier,jakob.piribauer}@tu-dresden.de
[2] Max Planck Institute for Software Systems, Saarland Informatics Campus,
Saarbrücken, Germany
{toghs,jnieuwve,joel,mvahanwa}@mpi-sws.org

Abstract. The conventional perspective on Markov chains considers decision problems concerning the probabilities of temporal properties being satisfied by traces of visited states. However, consider the following query made of a stochastic system modelling the weather: given the conditions today, will there be a day with less than 50% chance of rain? The conventional perspective is ill-equipped to decide such problems regarding the evolution of the initial distribution. The alternate perspective we consider views Markov chains as *distribution transformers*: the focus is on the sequence of distributions on states at each step, where the evolution is driven by the underlying stochastic transition matrix. More precisely, given an initial distribution vector μ, a stochastic update transition matrix M, we ask whether the ensuing sequence of distributions $(\mu, M\mu, M^2\mu, \dots)$ satisfies a given temporal property. This is a special case of the model-checking problem for linear dynamical systems, which is not known to be decidable in full generality. The goal of this article is to delineate the classes of instances for which this problem can be solved, under the assumption that the dynamics is governed by stochastic matrices.

1 Introduction

Markov chains are most often regarded by the verification community as a probabilistic means to model the uncertainty inherent to real-world systems. We refer the reader to [4, Chapter 10] for a thorough exposition and a comprehensive set of references on this perspective. A central application is the verification of network protocols, where it must be certified that packets are transmitted with high probability within a certain number of rounds, or that it is exceedingly unlikely that a queue of requests grows longer than a certain threshold. Here, atomic propositions are framed in terms of states of the system, and events are linear- or branching-time properties. The probability of an event is the measure of the set of runs in which the event occurs, and can be obtained by solving

© The Author(s), under exclusive license to Springer Nature Switzerland AG 2025
N. Jansen et al. (Eds.): Principles of Verification: Cycling the Probabilistic Landscape,
LNCS 15261, pp. 293–313, 2025.
https://doi.org/10.1007/978-3-031-75775-4_13

linear programs. The system is deemed correct if events of interest occur with specified probabilities.

The inherent uncertainty plays a more focal role in the study of systems of a more dynamical nature. For instance, consider the weather: it is quite natural to ask whether initialising a forecasting system with the prevalent conditions implies that there will be a day with less than 50% chance of rain, or whether every week will have a day with less than 25% chance of rain. The conventional approach does not resolve such queries: here, atomic propositions refer to *distributions* on states and properties specify their evolution in time. For Markov chains, this evolution is governed by the underlying stochastic matrix M[1]: if the initial distribution is μ, then the ensuing sequence of distributions is $\mu, M\mu, M^2\mu, \ldots$ ad infinitum.

Research on verifying the evolution of distributions against temporal specifications is not as prevalent as that which adopts the conventional perspective. Decidability in the alternative setting has seemed rather inaccessible: [1,6] only present incomplete or approximate verification procedures, while [12,13] owe their model-checking procedures to additional mathematical assumptions. This is not surprising, as the endeavour is fundamentally about solving special instances of the model-checking problem for linear dynamical systems, which is often associated with hard number-theoretic questions.

Formally, a linear dynamical system (LDS) of dimension k is given by an initial vector $v \in \mathbb{Q}^k$ and an update matrix $A \in \mathbb{Q}^{k \times k}$. Its trajectory is the infinite sequence of vectors $(v, Av, A^2v, \ldots)$. Let $\mathcal{T} = \{T_1, \ldots, T_\ell\}$ be a collection of semialgebraic subsets of $\mathbb{R}^k$, i.e. each T_i is defined by a Boolean combination of inequalities involving polynomials with integer coefficients. The characteristic word α of the dynamical system with respect to $\mathcal{T}$ is the infinite word over the alphabet $2^{\mathcal{T}}$ such that for all n, $T \in \alpha(n)$ if and only if $A^n v \in T$. The model-checking problem for LDS takes as input $v, A, \mathcal{T}$, and an ω-regular language $\mathcal{L}$ over the alphabet $2^{\mathcal{T}}$ and asks whether the characteristic word $\alpha \in \mathcal{L}$.

Model checking Markov chains as distribution transformers is a special case of the above where $v = \mu$ is a distribution (all entries are non-negative and sum up to 1), and the update matrix $A = M$ is the (column-)stochastic transition matrix underlying the Markov chain, i.e. the (i,j)-th entry denotes the transition probability to move from state j to state i, and hence each column is a distribution.

The model-checking problem for linear dynamical systems is easily seen to subsume the Skolem problem[2], which is a long-standing number-theoretic problem: given an initial vector v, update matrix A, and normal vector h, the Skolem problem asks whether there is an n such that $h^\top A^n v = 0$. The Skolem problem

---

[1] In this paper, we study a more linear-algebraic perspective than usual, and hence take distributions to be column vectors, and matrices to be left-stochastic, i.e. columns sum up to 1.

[2] The Skolem problem is often formulated equivalently in terms of linear recurrence sequences (LRS) that satisfy a recurrence relation $u_{n+k} = a_{k-1}u_{n+k-1} + \cdots + a_0 u_n$.

has only been solved for dimension $k \leq 4$ [14, 18], and is open for $k \geq 5$. We refer to the Skolem problem in dimension k as Skolem-k.

Recently, Bilu *et al.* [7] gave a decision procedure for the Skolem problem for diagonalisable A; however the guarantee of termination of this procedure is subject to two classical number-theoretic conjectures. A tool that implements the algorithm is available at [8].

It is not uncommon for instances of the model-checking problem for linear dynamical systems to be shown decidable by restricting the matrix A to be diagonalisable [2, 10, 15] or by bounding its dimension k [15, 16]. The natural question for us is whether restricting the update matrix to be stochastic yields any significant spectral or dimensional benefits that make the model-checking problem tractable. The reductions in [17] from the Skolem and closely related problems to the model-checking problem for Markov chains indicate that the answer is not entirely in the affirmative. Nevertheless, there is some nuance, which we comprehensively explore and detail in this article.

Our Contributions

We identify that the dynamics of Markov chains relevant to our model-checking problem play out in a space of dimension lower than that of the ambient space. As an example, consider a 6-state Markov chain with states $A_0, A_1, B_0, B_1, C_0, C_1$. The transition matrix is

$$M = \begin{bmatrix} 1/6 & 1/6 & 0 & 0 & 0 & 0 \\ 1/6 & 1/6 & 0 & 0 & 0 & 0 \\ 1/6 & 1/6 & 0 & 1 & 0 & 0 \\ 1/6 & 1/6 & 1 & 0 & 0 & 0 \\ 1/6 & 1/6 & 0 & 0 & 0 & 1 \\ 1/6 & 1/6 & 0 & 0 & 1 & 0 \end{bmatrix}.$$

From A_0 and A_1, the next state is chosen uniformly at random; B_0 and B_1 always succeed each other; likewise with C_0 and C_1. It is easy to observe that this system has some "redundancy" (A_0 and A_1 behave identically), and has two bottom strongly connected components ($\{B_0, B_1\}$ and $\{C_0, C_1\}$) which are "periodic" (with period 2). The ensuing distributions $\mu = [\mu_1, \ldots, \mu_6]^\top, M\mu, M^2\mu, \ldots$ form a sequence of 6-dimensional vectors.

It is straightforward to show that

$$M^n \mu = \begin{bmatrix} 0 \\ 0 \\ \mu_3 + 1/4(\mu_1 + \mu_2) \\ \mu_4 + 1/4(\mu_1 + \mu_2) \\ \mu_5 + 1/4(\mu_1 + \mu_2) \\ \mu_6 + 1/4(\mu_1 + \mu_2) \end{bmatrix} + \begin{bmatrix} 1/2 \\ 1/2 \\ -1/4 \\ -1/4 \\ -1/4 \\ -1/4 \end{bmatrix} [1/3]^n [u_1 + u_2] \text{ for even } n > 0, \quad (1)$$

$$
M^n \mu = \begin{bmatrix} 0 \\ 0 \\ \mu_4 + {}^1\!/\!4(\mu_1 + \mu_2) \\ \mu_3 + {}^1\!/\!4(\mu_1 + \mu_2) \\ \mu_6 + {}^1\!/\!4(\mu_1 + \mu_2) \\ \mu_5 + {}^1\!/\!4(\mu_1 + \mu_2) \end{bmatrix} + \begin{bmatrix} {}^1\!/\!2 \\ {}^1\!/\!2 \\ -{}^1\!/\!4 \\ -{}^1\!/\!4 \\ -{}^1\!/\!4 \\ -{}^1\!/\!4 \end{bmatrix} [{}^1\!/\!3]^n [u_1 + u_2] \text{ for odd } n. \qquad (2)
$$

Although the ambient space containing the distributions is 6-dimensional, as the above formulae indicate, most of the evolution is "static": the "dynamical" aspect is just 1-dimensional.

In fact, the dynamical dimension is guaranteed to be less than the ambient dimension: each element of the sequence $(\mu, M\mu, M^2\mu, \dots)$ is also a distribution on the probability simplex $\Delta = \{x : x \geq 0 \wedge x_1 + \cdots + x_k = 1\}$. As seen in the above example, other reasons include "redundancy", i.e. states whose behaviours are closely related, as well as periodicity of the transition graph. These reasons can be discerned from the spectrum of the stochastic matrix M, which we use to formalise the notion of dynamical dimension.

Definition 1. *The dynamical dimension of a stochastic matrix M is defined as the number of nonzero eigenvalues (counted with algebraic multiplicity) of M that have modulus strictly less than 1.*

In our example above, M has eigenvalues $1, 1, -1, -1, {}^1\!/\!3, 0$, and thus, by definition, has dynamical dimension 1.

To solve the model-checking problem for Markov chains of dynamical dimension k, we systematically project the problem onto an instance of a linear dynamical system of ambient dimension k. Technically speaking, it is the maximum dimension of the semialgebraic sets involved (see Sect. 2.2) that plays a crucial role in characterising the solvability of the model-checking problem for linear dynamical systems.

Semialgebraic sets come equipped with a notion of *intrinsic dimension* (intuitively, in ambient 3-dimensional space, a point has intrinsic dimension 0, a curve has intrinsic dimension 1, a surface has intrinsic dimension 2, and a solid has intrinsic dimension 3). There is also a notion of *linear dimension*: the dimension of the smallest linear subspace that contains the set in question. In the 3-dimensional world we live in, a rope stretched taut through the origin has linear dimension 1, a rope lying coiled on the ground has linear dimension 2, a rope being tossed as a lasso has linear dimension 3. In all three cases, however, the rope itself is fundamentally a one-dimensional object, and hence has intrinsic dimension 1.

Upon projecting an instance of the model checking problem for a Markov chain of dynamical dimension k onto one for a linear dynamical system of ambient dimension k, it is clear that the attendant semialgebraic sets become at most k-dimensional. We show additionally that the linear dimension necessarily decreases as well:

Theorem 1 (Auxiliary decidability result). *The model-checking problem for Markov chains with instances $(\mu, M, \mathcal{T}, \mathcal{L})$ such that*

(a) M has dynamical dimension k, and
(b) the target sets in $\mathcal{T}$ have intrinsic dimension at most d_1 and linear dimension at most d_2

reduces to the model-checking problem for linear dynamical systems with instances $(v, A, \mathcal{T}', \mathcal{L}')$ such that

(A) A is an invertible $k \times k$ matrix, and
(B) the target sets in $\mathcal{T}'$ have intrinsic dimension at most d_1 and linear dimension at most $d_2 - 1$.

We remark that proving the above requires us to preserve not only the spectral properties of the update matrix but also the rationality of the matrix and the initial vector.

The state of the art motivates us to define a criterion for semialgebraic sets to be considered low-dimensional with respect to our model-checking problem for Markov chains.

Theorem 2 (Main result of [11]). *The model-checking problem $(v, A, \mathcal{T}, \mathcal{L})$ for linear dynamical systems with $\mathcal{T}$ being a collection of semialgebraic sets whose intrinsic dimension is at most 1 or linear dimension is at most 3 is decidable.*

Note that the above result is indeed at the cutting edge of decidability: the open Skolem problem in dimension 5, for example, queries the reachability of a set that has linear dimension 4.

Definition 2. *A semialgebraic set $T \subseteq \mathbb{R}^k$ is said to be Markov-low-dimensional if it has intrinsic dimension at most 1 or is contained in a linear subspace of dimension at most 4.*

Combining Theorems 1 and 2 gives us our main decidability result.

Theorem 3 (Main decidability result). *The model-checking problem for Markov chains restricted to instances $(\mu, M, \mathcal{T}, \mathcal{L})$ such that either*

(a) $\mathcal{T}$ is a collection of Markov-low-dimensional sets, or
(b) the dynamical dimension of M is at most 3

is decidable.

For instances in which both hypotheses (a) and (b) of Theorem 3 fail to hold, we establish hardness through a slightly generalised version of the result of [17]. Recall that semialgebraic sets are defined in terms of polynomial inequalities. We call a set homogeneous if all the polynomials involved are homogeneous, and s-homogeneous if all the polynomials involved would be homogeneous were the origin shifted to s. We refer the reader to Sect. 2.2 for detailed definitions of these terms.

Theorem 4 (First hardness result). *Let $s \in \mathbb{Q}^{k+1}$ be any distribution with strictly positive entries. The model-checking problem for k-dimensional linear dynamical systems with homogeneous target sets reduces to the model-checking problem for $(k+1)$-state ergodic Markov chains with s-homogeneous target sets.*

Theorem 5 (Second Hardness Result). *Skolem-5 Turing-reduces to the reachability problem for ergodic Markov chains and semialgebraic targets of intrinsic dimension at most 2.*

We give the prerequisite mathematical background in Sect. 2, prove our decidability results in Sect. 3, our hardness results in Sect. 4, and finally offer concluding remarks in Sect. 5.

2   Mathematical Background

We will use $\mathbf{0}_k$ to denote the zero vector of dimension k, and $\mathbf{1}_k$ to denote the k-dimensional vector whose entries are all 1. If $v_i \in \mathbb{R}^{d_i}$ for $1 \leq i \leq k$, then by $(v_1, \ldots, v_k)$ we mean the concatenation of $v_1, \ldots, v_k$ belonging to $\mathbb{R}^{d_1 + \cdots + d_k}$.

2.1   Automata over Infinite Words

Let Σ be a finite non-empty alphabet. We use Σ^*, Σ^ω to respectively denote the sets of finite and infinite words over Σ. An ω-language $\mathcal{L}$ over Σ is a subset of Σ^ω. A language $\mathcal{L}$ is ω-regular if and only if it is accepted by a deterministic Muller automaton, which is defined as follows.

Definition 3. *A deterministic Muller automaton $\mathcal{A}$ is given by $(Q, \Sigma, q_0, \delta, \mathcal{F})$ where Q is a finite set of states, Σ is a finite alphabet, q_0 is the initial state, $\delta : Q \times \Sigma \to Q$ is the transition function, and $\mathcal{F} = \{F_1, \ldots, F_a\} \subseteq 2^Q$. Let Inf($\alpha$) denote the set of states visited infinitely often by the run of $\mathcal{A}$ on α. The automaton accepts α if Inf(α) $\in \mathcal{F}$.*

2.2   Semialgebraic Sets

Definition 4. *A set $T \subseteq \mathbb{R}^k$ is called semialgebraic if there is a Boolean combination of finitely many polynomial (in)equalities $p_i(x_1, \ldots, x_k) \sim 0$, where each $p_i \in \mathbb{Z}[x_1, \ldots, x_k]$ (i.e. has integer coefficients) such that T consists exactly of all points satisfying this Boolean combination.*

Definition 5. *A semialgebraic set $T \subseteq \mathbb{R}^k$ is said to be homogeneous if it can be expressed as a Boolean combination of finitely many polynomial (in)equalities $p_i(x_1, \ldots, x_k) \sim 0$, where each p_i is homogeneous, i.e. all its additive monomial terms have the same degree. If there exists $s \in \mathbb{R}^k$ such that each $p_i(x - s)$ is homogeneous, then T is said to be s-homogeneous.*

By definition, we have that for all $\lambda > 0$, and nonzero vectors x, we have $x \in T$ if and only if $\lambda x \in T$ for homogeneous sets T, and $s + x \in T'$ if and only if $s + \lambda x \in T'$ for s-homogeneous sets T'.

Using cell decomposition (see [5, Chapter 5]), a semialgebraic set T can be decomposed into a finite union of semialgebraic sets $T_1, \ldots, T_\ell$, where each T_i is (semialgebraically) homeomorphic to a single point or $(0, 1)^{d_i}$ for some $d_i \geq 1$. The intrinsic dimension d of T is defined to be $\dim(T) = \max_i d_i$; As [5, Chapter 5.3] shows, d is independent of the choice of decomposition and hence well-defined. The linear dimension of T is the dimension of the smallest linear subspace of $\mathbb{R}^k$ that contains T.

Next we define the *Zariski topology* on $\mathbb{R}^d$. An *algebraic set* X is defined by $p(x_1, \ldots, x_d) = 0$ where $p \in \mathbb{Q}[x_1, \ldots, x_d]$. Note that a conjunction

$$\bigwedge_{i \in I} p_i(x_1, \ldots, x_d) = 0$$

of polynomial equalities can be defined by a single polynomial equality

$$\sum_{i \in I} p_i(x_1, \ldots, x_d)^2 = 0.$$

The closed sets in the Zariski topology are exactly the algebraic sets.

Let $f \colon \mathbb{R}^d \to \mathbb{R}^k$ be given by $f(x) = (p_1(x)/q_1(x), \ldots, p_k(x)/q_k(x))$ where each $p_i, q_i \in \mathbb{Q}[x_1, \ldots, x_d]$. Suppose $q_i(x) \neq 0$ for all $x \in \mathbb{R}^d$ and $1 \leq i \leq k$. Consider a Zariski-closed set $X \subseteq \mathbb{R}^d$ defined by a polynomial h. Then $f^{-1}(X)$ is exactly the set defined by $h(p_1(x)q_2(x) \cdots q_k(x), \ldots, p_k(x)q_1(x) \cdots q_{k-1}(x)) = 0$, which is Zariski-closed. It follows that such a function f is continuous in the Zariski topology.

Given a topology, a set X is irreducible if its closure $\overline{X}$ cannot be written as a union of two closed sets different from $\overline{X}$. Irreducibility is preserved under continuous mappings.

2.3   Linear Algebra

We begin by recalling some standard terminology and results. The dimension of a vector space is the smallest number of (necessarily linearly independent) vectors required to span it. Given a matrix A, its rank is equivalently: (a) the size of the largest subset of linearly independent rows (dimension of row space); (b) the size of the largest subset of linearly independent columns (dimension of column space). The kernel of an $m \times n$ matrix A is the vector space of solutions to $Ax = \mathbf{0}_m$. The rank-nullity theorem states that the rank of a matrix plus the dimension of its kernel equals the number of columns.

We follow a standard text [3, Chapter 8] in recording some spectral properties of matrices.

Definition 6. *Let $A \in \mathbb{C}^{k \times k}$. If $\lambda \in \mathbb{C}$ satisfies $\det(A - \lambda I) = 0$, it is called an eigenvalue of A. A nonzero vector $v \in \mathbb{C}^k$ that satisfies $(A - \lambda I)v = \mathbf{0}_k$ is called a (right) eigenvector of λ. A nonzero vector $v' \in \mathbb{C}^k$ that satisfies $v'^\top(A - \lambda I) = \mathbf{0}_k^\top$ is called a left eigenvector of λ.*

If not explicitly specified, an eigenvector means a right eigenvector. We seek to generalise the definition of eigenvectors; the following definition can be made analogously for left eigenvectors too. If not explicitly specified, an eigenvector means an order-1 eigenvector in the sense of the following definition.

Definition 7. *A vector v that satisfies $(A - \lambda I)^j v = \mathbf{0}_k$, but $(A - \lambda I)^{j-1} v \neq \mathbf{0}_k$, is called an order-$j$ generalised eigenvector of λ.*

An eigenvalue λ is called *simple* if all its generalised eigenvectors have order 1. Note that λ has a left order-$(j + 1)$ generalised eigenvector if and only if it has a right order-$(j+1)$ generalised eigenvector if and only if $\mathrm{rank}(A - \lambda I)^{j+1} < \mathrm{rank}(A - \lambda I)^j$.

By definition, we observe that if v_{j+1} is an order-$(j + 1)$ generalised eigenvector, then $A v_{j+1}$ is of the form $\lambda v_{j+1} + v_j$, where $v_j \in \ker(A - \lambda I)^j$ but $v_j \notin \ker(A - \lambda I)^{j-1}$, i.e. $v_j = A v_{j+1} - \lambda v_{j+1}$ is an order-j generalised eigenvector. Given v_j of order j, let $v_j, \ldots, v_1$ be a chain of generalised eigenvectors of λ obtained thus. We can show, by a simple induction on n, that:

$$A^n v_j = \lambda^n v_j + \binom{n}{1} \lambda^{n-1} v_{j-1} + \cdots + \binom{n}{j-1} \lambda^{n-j+1} v_1. \tag{3}$$

The eigenspace $V \subseteq \mathbb{C}^k$ of an eigenvalue λ is defined as the vector space spanned by the generalised eigenvectors of the eigenvalue λ of A. We immediately observe the invariance property of the following result [3, Construction 8.20]:

Lemma 1. *The dimension ℓ of an eigenspace V belonging to an eigenvalue λ is equal to the algebraic multiplicity of λ. The space V is the kernel of $(A - \lambda I)^k$, and a basis can be expressed accordingly. Moreover, V is invariant under A, i.e. if $v \in V$, then $Av \in V$.*

In order to state our next property, we need a notion of composition of vector spaces.

Definition 8 (Sum of vector spaces). *Let $V_1, \ldots, V_m$ be linear subspaces of $\mathbb{C}^k$ with bases $B_1, \ldots, B_m$ respectively. Their sum $V = V_1 + \cdots + V_m$ is the vector space spanned by the set of vectors $B = B_1 \cup \cdots \cup B_m$. Furthermore, if the set B is linearly independent, then the sum is called a direct sum, and is denoted $V_1 \oplus \cdots \oplus V_m$.*

By definition, the dimension of the direct sum of vector spaces is equal to the sum of the dimensions of the vector spaces. The definition of direct sum also implies that $\mathbf{0}_k$ is the only vector common to any pair of subspaces being summed.

Eigenspaces permit a convenient decomposition of $\mathbb{C}$ [3, Theorem 8.22]: they are linearly independent and span the entire space.

Theorem 6. *Let $\lambda_1, \ldots, \lambda_m$ be distinct eigenvalues of $A \in \mathbb{C}^{k \times k}$, with respective eigenspaces $V_1, \ldots, V_m$. Then $V_1 \oplus \cdots \oplus V_m = \mathbb{C}^k$.*

We note the following property.

Lemma 2. *Let λ, η be distinct eigenvalues of $A \in \mathbb{C}^{k \times k}$. Let v_η be a generalised left eigenvector of η and let v_λ be a generalised right eigenvector of λ. Then $v_\eta^\top v_\lambda = 0$.*

Proof. We prove this by induction on the orders i, j of the generalised left and right eigenvectors v_η, v_λ respectively. We have that $(i, j) > (i', j')$ if $i \geq i'$ and $j \geq j'$ with at least one inequality being strict.

We prove the base case (where v_η, v_λ are order-1). Observe by associativity that $v_\eta^\top A v_\lambda = \eta v_\eta^\top v_\lambda = \lambda v_\eta^\top v_\lambda$. Since λ, η are distinct, it must be that $v_\eta^\top v_\lambda = 0$.

Now for the induction step (where v_η, v_λ are of order i, j respectively), we assume that $(v_\eta')^\top v_\lambda' = 0$ for all v_η', v_λ' of orders i', j', with $(i, j) > (i', j')$. Observe by associativity that $v_\eta^\top A v_\lambda = (\eta v_\eta + v_\eta')^\top v_\lambda = v_\eta^\top (\lambda v_\lambda + v_\lambda')$.

We have that v_η' is of order $i - 1$, and v_λ' is of order $j - 1^3$. Thus by the induction hypothesis, $(v_\eta')^\top v_\lambda = v_\eta^\top v_\lambda' = 0$. Substituting into the above equality, we get that $v_\eta^\top A v_\lambda = \eta v_\eta^\top v_\lambda = \lambda v_\eta^\top v_\lambda$ as before: it must be that $v_\eta^\top v_\lambda = 0$. □

2.4   Rational Stochastic Matrices

We use rational (column-)stochastic matrices to specify Markov chains. We shall apply linear-algebraic results to state their important properties.

Definition 9. *A matrix $M \in \mathbb{Q}^{k \times k}$ is said to be stochastic if each entry is non-negative, and $\mathbf{1}_k^\top M = \mathbf{1}_k^\top$, i.e. the entries of each column sum up to 1.*

Very clearly, 1 is an eigenvalue of M: $\det(M - I) = 0$ since by definition, $\mathbf{1}_k^\top (M - I) = \mathbf{0}_k^\top$. The following property holds.

Lemma 3. *Let λ be an eigenvalue of a stochastic matrix M. We have that $|\lambda| \leq 1$. Moreover, if $|\lambda| = 1$, then λ must be a root of unity and a simple eigenvalue (all generalised eigenvectors are of order 1).*

Proof. Consider a left eigenvector $v = (v_1, \ldots, v_k)$ of λ chosen such that the entry of maximum modulus has modulus 1, and let $T \subset \mathbb{C}$ be the bounded polytope defined as the convex hull of the points $v_1, \ldots, v_k \in \mathbb{C}$. Clearly, T is contained in the unit circle centred at the origin. Now, since the entries of each column of M are non-negative and sum up to 1, each coordinate of $v^\top M = (\lambda v_1, \ldots, \lambda v_k)$ is a convex combination of $v_1, \ldots, v_k$, and is hence contained in T, and thus the unit circle. It follows that $|\lambda| \leq 1$.

Moreover, observe that T can only intersect the unit circle at its corners. Now observe that for all $n \geq 1$, $\lambda^n v^\top = v^\top M^n$, and that the entries of each column of M^n are non-negative and sum up to 1. Thus, by the same arguments as above, each entry of $(\lambda^n v_1, \ldots, \lambda^n v_k)$ must be contained in T. Suppose $|v_i| = 1$. Then each $\lambda^n v_i$ must be one of the finitely many corners of the convex hull of $v_1, \ldots, v_k$: this is only possible if λ is a root of unity.

---

[3] If either of i, j is 1, then the proof is even simpler because the corresponding v' is the zero vector.

Now assume that an eigenvalue λ such that $\lambda^d = 1$ were not simple. Then there is an order-2 left eigenvector $v = (v_1, \ldots, v_k)$ of λ chosen such that one of the entries v_i with maximum modulus is 1. Define T as before, and note for all n that each coordinate of $v^\top M^n$ must lie in T and hence the unit circle. However, by Eq. 3 we have $v^\top M^{nd} = v^\top + nd(v')^\top$. The coordinates of $v^\top M^{nd}$ clearly cannot lie in the unit circle for arbitrarily large n: a contradiction.   □

3   Proofs of the Decidability Results

In this section, we establish our decidability results. We start with an instance $(\mu, M, \mathcal{T}, \mathcal{L})$ of the model-checking problem for Markov chains, where M has dynamical dimension d_1, the sets of $\mathcal{T}$ have linear dimension at most d_2 and intrinsic dimension at most d_3. We show how to reduce this instance to an instance $(v, A, \mathcal{T}', \mathcal{L}')$ of the model-checking problem for linear dynamical systems, where A is an invertible $d_1 \times d_1$ matrix, the sets of $\mathcal{T}$ have linear dimension at most $\min(d_1, d_2 - 1)$ and intrinsic dimension at most $\min(d_1, d_3)$. This would precisely be the proof of Theorem 1. Given the state-of-the-art Theorem 2, this implies that instances $(\mu, M, \mathcal{T}, \mathcal{L})$ of the form where M has dynamical dimension at most 3 or the sets of $\mathcal{T}$ have linear dimension at most 4 or intrinsic dimension at most 1 are decidable, thus proving Theorem 3.

We perform the reduction to prove Theorem 1 through three lemmata.

1. Lemma 4 implies that it suffices to consider linear dynamical systems with invertible update matrices.
2. Lemma 5 implies that assuming the update matrix is non-degenerate[4] does not lose any generality.
3. Lemma 6 takes as input an instance of a linear dynamical system model-checking problem obtained upon performing the preprocessing of Lemmata 4 and 5 on $(\mu, M, \mathcal{T}, \mathcal{L})$. It reduces its input into an instance of the model-checking problem with a $d_1 \times d_1$ invertible matrix and semialgebraic sets of lower dimensions.

We remark that the lemmata are elementary, but not immediate, as they preserve both the rationality and the spectra of the involved matrices.

We start with an instance $(\mu, M, \mathcal{T}, \mathcal{L})$, where M is a stochastic matrix, and the eigenvalues of M are $1, \nu_1, \ldots, \nu_{j'}, \gamma_1, \ldots, \gamma_j$, and possibly 0. By Lemma 3, the eigenvalues $\nu_1, \ldots, \nu_{j'}$ of modulus 1 must be roots of unity, and the eigenvalues $\gamma_1, \ldots, \gamma_j$ have modulus less than 1. Furthermore, the eigenvalues $1, \nu_1, \ldots, \nu_{j'}$ must be simple, i.e. their generalised eigenvectors have order 1. We let ℓ_1 be the multiplicity of the eigenvalue 0. The following lemma shows that we can obtain a dynamical system with the same spectral properties as stated above sans the eigenvalue 0.

---

[4]   A matrix A is said to be *non-degenerate* if for every pair of distinct eigenvalues λ, λ', the ratio λ/λ' is not a root of unity.

Lemma 4. *Let* $\mu \in \mathbb{Q}^{k+\ell}$, *and let* $M \in \mathbb{Q}^{(k+\ell) \times (k+\ell)}$ *be a matrix with distinct eigenvalues* $0, \lambda_1, \ldots, \lambda_j$ *with the eigenvalue* 0 *having (algebraic) multiplicity* ℓ. *We can compute a rank-k matrix* $Q \in \mathbb{Q}^{(k+\ell) \times k}$, *an invertible matrix* $B \in \mathbb{Q}^{k \times k}$ *and* $v \in \mathbb{Q}^k$ *such that:*

1. *For all* $n \geq \ell$, *we have* $M^n \mu = QB^n v$.
2. *Let* $n \geq \ell$. *For any semialgebraic set* $T \subseteq \mathbb{R}^{k+\ell}$, $M^n \mu \in T$ *if and only if* $B^n v \in T'$, *where* $T' = \{x \in \mathbb{R}^k : Qx \in T\}$ *and has intrinsic and linear dimensions at most those of* T.
3. *The eigenvalues of* B *are* $\lambda_1, \ldots, \lambda_j$. *Moreover, for any* $i \geq 0$ *and* $\lambda \in \mathbb{C}_{\neq 0}$, y *is a generalised order-i eigenvector of* B *corresponding to* λ *if and only if* Qy *is a generalised order-i eigenvector of* M *corresponding to* λ.

Proof. Let $V_0, V_{\lambda_1}, \ldots, V_{\lambda_j}$ denote the eigenspaces of the respective eigenvalues. Recall that by Theorem 6 we can define the vector space $W = V_{\lambda_1} \oplus \cdots \oplus V_{\lambda_j}$ as a direct sum, and that $V_0 \oplus W = \mathbb{C}^k$. By Lemma 1 and the properties implied by Definition 8, we have that the dimension of V_0 (over $\mathbb{C}$) is ℓ, $V_0 \cap W = \{\mathbf{0}_{k+\ell}\}$, and that the dimension of W is k.

The decomposition into V_0 and W is the key ingredient of the proof because these are invariant subspaces. Indeed, if $z \in V_0$ then by (3) we have $M^\ell z = \mathbf{0}_{k+\ell}$. For a nonzero $w \in W$, we apply Lemma 1 to each of the components V_λ of W to conclude that $Mw \in W$ and that Mw is moreover nonzero since w is not in the eigenspace of 0.

Rational bases for V_0 and W can effectively be computed. A rational basis for V_0 can be obtained by solving the rational homogeneous linear system $M^\ell x = \mathbf{0}_{k+\ell}$, one for W can be obtained by taking k linearly independent columns of M^ℓ. To argue the latter, recall that by Lemma 2, if v' is in the left eigenspace V'_0 of 0 and $w \in W$, then $(v')^\top w = 0$. A rational basis for V'_0 can be obtained similarly to the one for V_0: let its ℓ vectors be the rows of H. By the above observation, W, which has dimension k over $\mathbb{C}$, is also contained in the kernel of H, which, by the rank-nullity theorem, has dimension k. It follows that W is indeed the kernel of H, and a rational basis can be obtained by solving a rational homogeneous linear system.

We take P, Q to respectively be the matrices whose columns form the thusly computed rational bases of V_0, W. Note that the matrix $R = \begin{bmatrix} P \ Q \end{bmatrix}$ is invertible. We take P', Q' such that $R^{-1} = \begin{bmatrix} P' \\ Q' \end{bmatrix}$. This choice establishes that P', Q', P, Q have full rank. In particular, we remark that Q defines an invertible map from $\mathbb{R}^k$ to W, and is inverted by Q', since indeed $Q'Q = I$.

Now, construct $D \in \mathbb{Q}^{(k+\ell) \times (k+\ell)}$ as

$$D = R^{-1}MR = \begin{bmatrix} P' \\ Q' \end{bmatrix} M \begin{bmatrix} P & Q \end{bmatrix}$$

$$= \begin{bmatrix} P' \\ Q' \end{bmatrix} \begin{bmatrix} MP & MQ \end{bmatrix}$$

$$= \begin{bmatrix} P'MP & P'MQ \\ O & Q'MQ \end{bmatrix} \text{ (by definition of } R^{-1})$$

$$= \begin{bmatrix} P'MP & O \\ O & Q'MQ \end{bmatrix} \text{ (since each column of } MQ \text{ is still in } W)$$

$$= \begin{bmatrix} P'MP & O \\ O & B \end{bmatrix} \text{ (defining the bottom right } k \times k \text{ matrix } B = Q'MQ).$$

We observe that for $n \geq \ell$

$$D^n = R^{-1}M^n R = \begin{bmatrix} P'M^n P & O \\ O & B^n \end{bmatrix} = \begin{bmatrix} O & O \\ O & B^n \end{bmatrix}$$

since $M^\ell P = O$ because P spans the eigenspace of 0.

We can compute the unique $u \in \mathbb{Q}^\ell, v \in \mathbb{Q}^k$ such that $\mu = Pu + Qv$. We now observe that for $n \geq \ell$

$$M^n \mu = RD^n R^{-1}\mu = RD^n R^{-1}R \begin{bmatrix} u \\ v \end{bmatrix}$$

$$= R \begin{bmatrix} O & O \\ O & B^n \end{bmatrix} \begin{bmatrix} u \\ v \end{bmatrix} = \begin{bmatrix} P & Q \end{bmatrix} \begin{bmatrix} \mathbf{0}_\ell \\ B^n v \end{bmatrix} = QB^n v.$$

This establishes requirement (1) of the statement.

It is obvious that for $n \geq \ell$, $M^n \mu \in T$ if and only if $B^n v \in \{x : Qx \in T\}$. We observe that for $n \geq \ell$, $M^n \mu \in W$. Thus, $M^n \mu \in T$ if and only if $M^n \mu \in T \cap W$. Since W is a linear subspace, the linear dimension of $T \cap W \subseteq T$ is at most the linear dimension of T, and the intrinsic dimension also cannot increase [5, Proposition 5.28]. Now, recall that Q' is an invertible linear map from W to $\mathbb{R}^k$, and hence a homeomorphism from $T \cap W$ to T'. The linear and intrinsic dimensions of T' are hence the same as those of $T \cap W$. This establishes requirement (2) of the statement.

Finally, we prove that $B = Q'MQ$ has almost the same spectral properties as that of M. We recall that Q is a linear map from $\mathbb{R}^k$ to W, the space W is invariant under M and moreover that M never maps a nonzero $w \in W$ to the zero vector, and Q' inverts Q. This already establishes that $Bx \neq \mathbf{0}$ for nonzero x, and hence the invertibility of B. We shall work with pairs $y \in \mathbb{C}^k, w \in W$ such that $w = Qy, y = Q'w$.

Now, $By = Q'MQy = Q'Mw$. Also, $\lambda y = \lambda Q'w$. If $By = \lambda y$, we also have $Q'(Mw) = Q'(\lambda w)$. The images of two nonzero vectors in W under the invertible Q' are equal: hence the vectors must be equal. We thus have y is an eigenvector of B with eigenvalue λ only if $w = Qy$ is an eigenvector of M with eigenvalue λ.

Conversely, $Q'Mw = Q'MQy = By$, and $Q'(\lambda w) = Q'Q(\lambda y) = \lambda y$. If $Mw = \lambda w$, we must also have $By = \lambda y$. This establishes that B has the same set of eigenvectors as M (for $\lambda \neq 0$), with Q' mapping the eigenvectors of M to those of B.

We can apply the above reasoning in a straightforward induction on the order of generalised eigenvectors to prove that this mapping holds for the entire eigenspaces of each eigenvalue. This establishes requirement (3) of the statement, and completes the proof of Lemma 4. □

Let α be the characteristic word of the dynamical system (M, μ) with respect to $\mathcal{T}$. Denote by mult_0 the (algebraic) multiplicity of the eigenvalue 0 of M, and take $\mathcal{L}_1 = \{\beta : \alpha(0)\alpha(1) \cdots \alpha(\text{mult}_0 - 1) \cdot \beta \in \mathcal{L}\}$. It is clear that $\mathcal{L}_1$ is ω-regular. Lemma 4 thus reduces $(\mu, M, \mathcal{T}, \mathcal{L})$ to $(\mu_1, M_1, \mathcal{T}_1, \mathcal{L}_1)$, where M_1 is invertible, and whose eigenvalues of modulus 1 are all simple and c-th roots of unity. We also have that the dimensions of sets in $\mathcal{T}_1$ are at most those in $\mathcal{T}$. We now convert all eigenvalues that are roots of unity to 1.

Lemma 5. *Let $v \in \mathbb{Q}^k$, let $B \in \mathbb{Q}^{k \times k}$ be an invertible matrix with eigenvalues $\lambda_1, \ldots, \lambda_j$, and let $c \in \mathbb{N} \setminus \{0\}$. Let $\mathcal{T} = \{T_1, \ldots, T_h\}$ be a collection of semialgebraic sets, and let $\mathcal{L}$ be an ω-regular language over $2^{\mathcal{T}}$. The following hold:*

1. *The matrix B^c has eigenvalues $\lambda_1^c, \ldots, \lambda_j^c$. If v is an order-i generalised eigenvector of some eigenvalue λ of B, then it is also an order-i generalised eigenvector of eigenvalue λ^c of B^c, and conversely.*
2. *We can construct $\mathcal{T}'$ and an ω-regular language $\mathcal{L}'$ over $2^{\mathcal{T}'}$ such that the characteristic word α of B, v with respect to $\mathcal{T}$ is in $\mathcal{L}$ if and only if the characteristic word α' of B^c, v with respect to $\mathcal{T}'$ is in $\mathcal{L}'$.*

Proof. It is immediately clear that B^c has $\lambda_1^c, \ldots, \lambda_j^c$ among its eigenvalues. We prove the retention of generalised eigenvectors by induction on the order i. The base case $i = 1$ is trivial: $Bv = \lambda v$ implies $B^c v = \lambda^c v$. For the induction step, suppose the claim holds for i, and let v_{i+1} be an order-$(i+1)$ generalised vector of λ of B. By (3), $B^c v_{i+1} = \lambda^c v_{i+1} + (f_i v_i + \cdots + f_{i-1} v_1)$. The latter summand, by the induction hypothesis, is an order-i generalised eigenvector of λ^c, making v_{i+1} an order-$(i+1)$ generalised eigenvector.

Since we have identified k generalised eigenvectors of B^c, there can be no more. We can also use Lemma 1 to conclude that since a basis of eigenvectors of B is also a basis of eigenvectors of B^c, the multiplicities of $\lambda_1^c, \ldots, \lambda_j^c$ add up to k, and there are no other eigenvalues of B^c. This establishes property (1).

The key observation to prove property (2) is that $B^{qc+r} v = B^r (B^c)^q v$. Thus, for any $n = qc + r$ and semialgebraic set T, we have $B^n v \in T$ if and only if $(B^c)^q v \in T_r = \{x : B^r x \in T\}$. Note that T_r is the pre-image of T under B^r. Since B is invertible, the map from T to T_r is a homeomorphism, and both sets have the same dimensions. Define $\mathcal{T}' = \{T_{1,0}, \ldots, T_{h,0}, \ldots, T_{1,c-1}, \ldots, T_{h,c-1}\}$ where $T_{i,r} = \{x : B^r x \in T_i\}$.

It is now easy to observe that the characteristic word α of B and v is a "flattening" of α' of B^c and v. Formally, $T_i \in \alpha(qc+r)$ if and only if $T_{i,r} \in \alpha'(q)$.

Define $\varphi : 2^{T'} \to \left(2^T\right)^c$ as $\varphi(\sigma') = \sigma_0 \ldots \sigma_{c-1}$, where $T_i \in \sigma_r$ if and only if $T_{i,r} \in \Sigma$. Define the extension $\varphi' : \left(2^{T'}\right)^\omega \to \left(2^T\right)^\omega$ as $\varphi'(\alpha') = \varphi(\alpha'(0))\varphi(\alpha'(1)) \cdots$ and observe that φ' is bijective. Define $\mathcal{L}' = \{\alpha' : \varphi'(\alpha') \in \mathcal{L}\}$. Clearly, $\alpha' \in \mathcal{L}'$ if and only if $\alpha \in \mathcal{L}$. In only remains to show that $\mathcal{L}'$ is ω-regular.

We shall use a deterministic Muller automaton $\mathcal{A} = (Q, 2^T, q_0, \delta, \mathcal{F})$ that accepts $\mathcal{L}$ to give a deterministic Muller automaton $\mathcal{A}' = (Q, 2^{T'}, q_0', \delta', F')$ that accepts $\mathcal{L}'$ in order to do so. Intuitively, $\mathcal{A}'$, upon reading each letter σ' of α' simulates what $\mathcal{A}$ would do upon reading the corresponding $\varphi(\sigma')$. We take

$$Q' = Q \times 2^Q,$$
$$q_0' = (q_0, \{\}) \quad \text{and}$$
$$\delta'((q, S_{\text{prev}}), \sigma') = (\delta(q, \varphi(\sigma')), S_{\text{new}})$$

where S_{new} is the set of states traversed by $\mathcal{A}$ while reading $\varphi(\sigma')$ and going from q to $\delta(q, \varphi(\sigma'))$ along a path of length c. We have that

$$\text{Inf}_{\mathcal{A}}(\alpha) = \bigcup_{(q,S) \in \text{Inf}_{\mathcal{A}'}(\alpha')} S.$$

Thus the acceptance condition

$$F' \in \mathcal{F}' \Leftrightarrow \left(\bigcup_{(q,S) \in F'} S\right) \in \mathcal{F}.$$

This establishes property (2) and completes the proof of Lemma 5. $\qquad\square$

Lemma 5 thus reduces $(\mu_1, M_1, \mathcal{T}_1, \mathcal{L}_1)$ to $(\mu_1, M_2, \mathcal{T}_2, \mathcal{L}_2)$, where M_2 is invertible, and whose only eigenvalue of unit modulus is simple and equal to 1. We also have that the dimensions of sets in $\mathcal{T}_2$ are at most those in $\mathcal{T}$. We get rid of the eigenvalue 1, leaving ourselves with an update matrix M_3 whose dimension is equal to the dynamical dimension of the original stochastic matrix M. We show that in doing so, the linear dimension of the resulting sets in $\mathcal{T}_3$ is less than that of their counterparts in $\mathcal{T}_2$.

Lemma 6. *Let $M \in \mathbb{Q}^{(k+\ell) \times (k+\ell)}$ have nonzero eigenvalues $1, \lambda_1, \ldots, \lambda_j$, such that the eigenvalue 1 is simple, has multiplicity ℓ, and is the only eigenvalue of modulus at least 1. Let $\mu \in \mathbb{Q}^{k+\ell}$, and let $\mathcal{T} = \{T_1, \ldots, T_h\}$ be a collection of semialgebraic sets. We can compute $n_0 \in \mathbb{N}$, $s \in \mathbb{Q}^{k+\ell}$, a rank-$k$ matrix $Q \in \mathbb{Q}^{(k+\ell) \times k}$, an invertible and non-degenerate matrix $A \in \mathbb{Q}^{k \times k}$ with eigenvalues $\lambda_1, \ldots, \lambda_k$, a vector $v \in \mathbb{Q}^k$, and a collection of semialgebraic sets $\mathcal{T}' = \{T_1', \ldots, T_h'\}$ such that the following hold.*

1. *For all n, $M^n \mu = s + QA^n v$.*
2. *The eigenvalues of A are $\lambda_1, \ldots, \lambda_j$. Moreover, for any i, y is a generalised order-i eigenvector of A corresponding to $\lambda \neq 0$ if and only if Qy is a generalised order-i eigenvector of M corresponding to λ.*

3. *Let $n \geq n_0$. For every i, $M^n \mu \in T_i$ if and only if $A^n v \in T_i'$. If T_i has linear and intrinsic dimensions d_1, d_2 respectively, then the corresponding dimensions of T_i' are at most $d_1 - 1, d_2$.*

Proof. The proof of Lemma 4 applies *mutatis mutandis* to establish requirements (1) and (2). In this case, P spans the eigenspace of the simple eigenvalue 1, and we have $MP = P$ and $P'Q = O$. We choose s, v from the unique representation of $\mu = s + Qv$, where s is a linear combination of the columns of P.

Having established requirement (2), we deduce that the Euclidean norm $||A^n v||$ converges to 0 exponentially quickly. We use this observation in computing n_0, T' as required. Let $U_1, \ldots, U_h$ be the smallest subspaces containing $T_1, \ldots, T_h$ respectively. We compute $\varepsilon \in \mathbb{Q}$ such that for all i, if $s \notin U_i$ then neither is any point x in the Euclidean ε-neighbourhood of s. We compute n_0 such that for all $n \geq n_0$, $||A^n v|| = ||M^n \mu - s|| < \varepsilon$.

For all i, we define $T_i' = \{x \in \mathbb{R}^k : s + Qx \in T_i \wedge ||x|| < \varepsilon\}$. Observe that T_i' is non-empty only if $s \in U_i$. It is also straightforward to adapt the reasoning from the proof of Lemma 4(2) to conclude that for $n \geq n_0$, $M^n \mu \in T_i$ if and only if $A^n v \in T_i'$ and that the intrinsic dimension of each T_i' is at most that of the corresponding T_i. It remains to prove that if T_i' is non-empty, then its linear dimension is less than that of T_i.

Consider U_i. Since T_i' is non-empty, we know $s \in U_i$. By definition of a subspace, there exists a $(k + \ell - d) \times (k + \ell)$ matrix H of rank $k + \ell - d$ such that $y \in U_i$ only if $Hy = \mathbf{0}_{k+\ell-d}$. Furthermore, since $s \in U_i$, we have that $Hs = \mathbf{0}_{k+\ell-d}$. We shall now identify a subspace that contains T_i'.

By definition, $x \in T_i'$ if and only if $s + Qx \in T_i$. Thus, $x \in T_i'$ only if $H \cdot Qx = \mathbf{0}_{k+\ell-d}$. Now, recall that the columns of Q span W, the union of eigenspaces of the eigenvalues $\lambda_1, \ldots, \lambda_j$, which is also the k-dimensional kernel of the rank-ℓ matrix $P' \in \mathbb{Q}^{\ell \times (k+\ell)}$. We know that s is an eigenvector of 1, and is hence not in W. Thus, we have at least one row p' of P' such that $p's \neq 0$. This row is thus necessarily linearly independent of the rows of H, for otherwise $Hs = \mathbf{0}_{k+\ell-d}$ would imply $p's = 0$. The fact that $P'Q = O$ by construction guarantees that $P' \cdot Qx = \mathbf{0}_\ell$.

The above argument allows us to append P' to the rows of H, obtaining a matrix G of rank at least $k + \ell - d + 1$ by virtue of its rows H, p' being linearly independent. We can assert a stronger claim: $x \in T_i'$ only if $G \cdot Qx = \mathbf{0}_{k+2\ell-d+1}$. By the rank-nullity theorem, it follows that Qx must lie in a vector space of dimension $d' \leq d - 1$ that is contained in W, the span of the columns of Q.

Finally, we recall that Q has rank k: thus the linear map Q from $\mathbb{R}^k$ to W is invertible via Q'. Thus, $Qx \in \text{span}(v_1, \ldots, v_{d'}) \subseteq W$ (if and) only if $x \in \text{span}(Q'v_1, \ldots, Q'v_{d'})$.

This allows us to conclude that $x \in T$ only if x is contained in a linear subspace of dimension at most $d - 1$, and completes the proof of Lemma 6. □

Finally, Lemma 6 completes the chain of reductions from $(\mu, M, \mathcal{T}, \mathcal{L})$ to $(\mu_2 = v, M_3 = A, \mathcal{T}_3, \mathcal{L}_3)$, where A is invertible and has dimensions equal to the dynamical dimension of M. We have $\mathcal{L}_3 = \{\beta : \alpha(0) \cdots \alpha(n_0 - 1) \cdot \beta \in \mathcal{L}_2\}$, where α is the characteristic word of M_2, μ_1 with respect to $\mathcal{T}_2$. We also have that the linear dimensions of sets in $\mathcal{T}_2$ are at less those of their correspondents in $\mathcal{T}$. This completes the proof of our decidability results.

4   Proofs of the Hardness Results

In this section, we prove Theorems 4 and 5, thus showing that our decidability results are tight, i.e. that further breakthroughs would entail the decidability of Skolem-5. Recall that a Markov chain is ergodic if its transition graph is irreducible (i.e. strongly connected) and aperiodic. Equivalently, for its stochastic matrix M there exists an n_0 such that all entries of M^{n_0} are strictly positive. In our hardness proofs, we shall construct M with $n_0 = 1$.

4.1   First Hardness Result

We first show how to construct, given an arbitrary LDS (v, A), an ergodic Markov chain (μ, M) that captures the dynamics of (v, A).

Corollary 1 (Of Proof of Lemma 6).   *Let $s \in \mathbb{Q}^{k+1}$ be a distribution with strictly positive entries, $A \in \mathbb{Q}^{k \times k}$ and $v \in \mathbb{Q}^k$. We can compute an ergodic Markov chain (μ, M) and constants $\eta, \rho \in \mathbb{Q}$ such that $M^n \mu = s + \eta \rho^n \begin{bmatrix} I \\ -\mathbf{1}_k^\top \end{bmatrix} A^n v$ for all n.*

Proof. Choose Q from Lemma 6 to be $\begin{bmatrix} I \\ -\mathbf{1}_k^\top \end{bmatrix}$. Observe that s is linearly independent of the columns of Q: indeed, we have $\mathbf{1}_{k+1}^\top Q = \mathbf{0}_{k+1}^\top$, but $\mathbf{1}_{k+1}^\top s = 1$. Thus the matrix $R = \begin{bmatrix} s & Q \end{bmatrix}$ is invertible. Moreover, we can easily check that its inverse R^{-1} is of the form $\begin{bmatrix} \mathbf{1}_{k+1}^\top \\ Q' \end{bmatrix}$.

Now we choose η such that the magnitude of the largest entry of $\eta Q v$ is less than the smallest entry of s. We take $\mu = s + \eta Q v$, and observe that all entries of μ are positive, and moreover that $\mathbf{1}_{k+1}^\top \mu = 1$, making μ a distribution. We choose ρ to ensure that the magnitude of the largest entry of $\rho Q A Q'$ is smaller than the smallest entry of s.

Now, we take

$$M = RDR^{-1} = \begin{bmatrix} s & Q \end{bmatrix} \begin{bmatrix} 1 & \mathbf{0}_k^\top \\ \mathbf{0}_k & \rho A \end{bmatrix} \begin{bmatrix} \mathbf{1}_{k+1}^\top \\ Q' \end{bmatrix} = \begin{bmatrix} s & Q \end{bmatrix} \begin{bmatrix} \mathbf{1}_{k+1}^\top \\ \rho A Q' \end{bmatrix} = s \cdot \mathbf{1}_{k+1}^\top + \rho Q A Q'.$$

The choice of ρ ensures that each entry of M is positive, and it is moreover easy to check that $\mathbf{1}_{k+1}^\top M = \mathbf{1}_{k+1}^\top$. This makes M a stochastic matrix. Since all entries of M are positive, (μ, M) is ergodic. It is then straightforward to verify that $M^n \mu = s + \eta \rho^n Q A^n v$. $\qquad\square$

We mention that Corollary 1 generalises the result of [17]. We now prove Theorem 4. Given an instance $(v, A, \mathcal{T}, \mathcal{L})$ of the model-checking problem for linear dynamical systems with $\mathcal{T} = \{T_1, \ldots, T_h\}$ being a collection of homogeneous sets, we apply Corollary 1 to obtain μ, M, and consider Q' from its proof. We note that by homogeneity, for each i, $A^n v \in T_i$ if and only if $\eta \rho^n A^n v \in T_i$. We construct $\mathcal{T}' = \{T_1', \ldots, T_h'\}$ as $T_i' = \{y : \mathbf{1}_{k+1}^\top (y - s) = 0 \wedge Q'(y - s) \in T_i\}$. The first conjunct ensures that $y - s$ is in the space spanned by the columns of Q. The set T_i' is s-homogeneous by construction, and it is straightforward to check that $M^n \mu \in T_i'$ if and only if $\eta \rho^n A^n v \in T_i$ if and only if $A^n v \in T_i$. The equivalent instance $(\mu, M, \mathcal{T}', \mathcal{L}')$ is obtained by taking $\mathcal{L}'$ to be the ω-regular language obtained from $\mathcal{L}$ by simply renaming letters in $2^\mathcal{T}$ to their counterparts in $2^{\mathcal{T}'}$.

4.2 Second Hardness Result

In this section, we take a hard instance (A, v, h) of Skolem-5 and construct an equivalent instance (μ, M, T) of the reachability problem where (μ, M) is an ergodic Markov chain and T is a semialgebraic target with intrinsic dimension at most 2. We will need the following.

Corollary 2 (Of Proof of Lemma 6). *Let $s \in \mathbb{Q}^{k+1}$ be a distribution with strictly positive entries, $B \in \mathbb{Q}^{k \times k}$, and $v \in \mathbb{Q}^k$. Write $Q = \begin{bmatrix} I \\ -\mathbf{1}_k^\top \end{bmatrix}$, and suppose that every entry of $Q^{-1}BQ$ is less than every entry of s in magnitude. Then we can compute an ergodic Markov chain (μ, M) and $\eta \in \mathbb{Q}_{>0}$ such that $M^n \mu = s + \eta QB^n v$ for all n.*

Proof. Same as the proof of Corollary 1, with the difference that ρA is replaced with B, whose entries are already assumed to be sufficiently small. $\square$

Let (A, v, h) be a hard instance of Skolem-5. We have to decide whether there exists n such that $u_n = 0$, where $u_n = h^\top A^n v$ is a rational LRS. As discussed in [9, Sec. 2.3], we can assume the eigenvalues of A are of the form $\lambda, \overline{\lambda}, \gamma, \overline{\gamma}, \rho$ and satisfy $|\lambda| = |\gamma| > |\rho| > 0$. By considering the sequences $(h^\top (A^2)^n v)_{n=0}^\infty$ and $(h^\top (A^2)^n (Av))_{n=0}^\infty$ separately if necessary, we can further assume $\rho > 0$. Since the eigenvalues are the roots of characteristic polynomial of A, we have that $|\lambda|^4 \rho = \lambda \overline{\lambda} \gamma \overline{\gamma} \rho$ is rational. Furthermore, ρ must also be rational. To see this, let σ be a Galois automorphism of the splitting field $\mathbb{Q}(\lambda, \overline{\lambda}, \gamma, \overline{\gamma}, \rho)$ of the characteristic polynomial of A. We have that σ permutes $\lambda, \overline{\lambda}, \gamma, \overline{\gamma}, \rho$. Moreover, $\lambda \overline{\lambda} = \gamma \overline{\gamma}$, and hence $\sigma(\lambda)\sigma(\overline{\lambda}) = \sigma(\gamma)\sigma(\overline{\gamma})$. If σ were to permute any of the other eigenvalues to ρ, this equality would be violated. Thus, ρ is fixed by every automorphism and hence is rational. We conclude that $|\lambda|^4$ must also be rational.

Let s be a distribution with strictly positive entries, and

$$\kappa = \frac{1}{|\rho|} \cdot \frac{|\rho|^{4c}}{|\lambda|^{4c}} \in \mathbb{Q}$$

for c sufficiently large so the condition of Corollary 2 is met with $B := \kappa A$. Then the eigenvalues $\kappa\rho, \kappa\lambda$ of B satisfy $(\kappa|\rho|)^{4c-1} = (\kappa|\lambda|)^{4c}$.

We will next construct an instance $(v, B, \widetilde{T})$ of the model-checking problem such that $\widetilde{T}$ is a semialgebraic set of intrinsic dimension at most 2 and

$$h^\top A^n v = 0 \Leftrightarrow B^n v \in \widetilde{T}$$

for all n. Write $r = |\lambda|$, $H = \{x : h^\top x = 0\}$, and $B = PJP^{-1}$, where J is in real Jordan form. Without loss of generality, we can assume

$$J = \mathrm{diag}(\kappa r \Lambda, \kappa r \Gamma, \kappa\rho)$$

where Λ and Γ are 2×2 rotation matrices.[5] Write Pv as $(v_1, \ldots, v_5)$, $d_1 = \sqrt{v_1^2 + v_2^2}$, and $d_2 = \sqrt{v_3^2 + v_4^2}$. We have

$$\|(\kappa r \Lambda)^n (v_1, v_2)\| = d_1 \cdot (\kappa r)^n = d_1 \cdot ((\kappa r)^{n/(4c-1)})^{4c-1},$$

$$\|(\kappa r \Gamma)^n (v_3, v_4)\| = d_2 \cdot (\kappa r)^n = d_2 \cdot ((\kappa r)^{n/(4c-1)})^{4c-1} \quad \text{and}$$

$$v_5 \cdot (\kappa\rho)^n = (\kappa r)^{4cn/(4c-1)} v_5 = v_5 ((\kappa r)^{n/(4c-1)})^{4c}.$$

It follows that $(J^n Pv)_{n=0}^\infty$ is contained in the set S of all $(x_1, \ldots, x_5) \in \mathbb{R}^d$ satisfying the following equations:

$$(x_1^2 + x_2^2) d_2^2 = (x_3^2 + x_4^2) d_1^2 \quad \text{and}$$

$$((x_1^2 + x_2^2) v_5^2)^{4c} = x_5^{4c-1} \cdot v_5 d_1^{8c}.$$

On the other hand, let $x(t) = \left(\frac{1-t^2}{1+t^2}, \frac{2t}{1+t^2}\right)$, and recall that the unit circle can be parametrised as $\{(-1, 0)\} \cup \{x(t) : t \in \mathbb{R}\}$. We have that $S = S_1 \cup \cdots \cup S_4$, where

$$S_1 = \{(d_1 s^{4c-1} \cdot x(t_1), d_2 s^{4c-1} \cdot x(t_2), v_5 s^{4c}) : s \geq 0, t_1, t_2 \in \mathbb{R}\},$$

$$S_2 = \{(d_1 s^{4c-1} \cdot (-1, 0), d_2 s^{4c-1} \cdot x(t_2), v_5 s^{4c}) : s \geq 0, t_2 \in \mathbb{R}\},$$

$$S_3 = \{(d_1 s^{4c-1} \cdot x(t_1), d_2 s^{4c-1} \cdot (-1, 0), v_5 s^{4c}) : s \geq 0, t_1 \in \mathbb{R}\} \quad \text{and}$$

$$S_4 = \{(d_1 s^{4c-1} \cdot (-1, 0), d_2 s^{4c-1} \cdot (-1, 0), v_5 s^{4c}) : s \geq 0\}.$$

Each of $S_1, \ldots, S_4$ is parametrised by a Zariski-continuous function. The domains $\mathbb{R}_{>0} \times \mathbb{R}^2, \mathbb{R}_{>0} \times \mathbb{R}, \mathbb{R}_{>0}$ are all irreducible, and have dimensions $3, 2, 2, 1$, respectively. Hence each S_i is irreducible, and $\dim(S_1) \leq 3$, $\dim(S_2), \dim(S_3) \leq 2$, and $\dim(S_4) \leq 1$. It can also be shown that $P \cdot H$, which is also irreducible, is not contained in any S_i and vice versa. Hence $\dim(P \cdot H \cap S_i) \leq 2$ and therefore $\dim(P \cdot H \cap S) \leq 2$. We can therefore define $\widetilde{T} = H \cap P^{-1}S$.

Applying Corollary 2, we compute an ergodic Markov chain (μ, M) and $\eta \in \mathbb{Q}_{>0}$ such that $M^n \mu = s + \eta Q B^n v$. Define $T = s + \eta Q \widetilde{T}$. Then $\dim(T) \leq 2$, and

$$M^n \mu \in T \Leftrightarrow B^n v \in \widetilde{T} \Leftrightarrow A^n v \in H.$$

This completes the proof of Theorem 5.

---

[5] This is easily seen: let $v_\lambda, \overline{v_\lambda}, v_\gamma, \overline{v_\gamma}, v_\rho$ be eigenvectors of κA, and take the columns of P to be $(v_\lambda + \overline{v_\lambda}) \cdot i(v_\lambda - \overline{v_\lambda}), (v_\gamma + \overline{v_\gamma}), i(v_\gamma - \overline{v_\gamma}), v_\rho$.

5   Discussion

We conclude by offering perspective on our decidability results and techniques. We observe that our reduction from Markov chains to ordinary linear dynamical systems becomes more powerful as the difference between the order (number of states) and the dynamical dimension of the Markov chain increases. Recall that this difference is attributed to the multiplicity of the eigenvalues of the underlying stochastic transition matrix M that have modulus 0 or 1.

Having the eigenvalue 0 with multiplicity ℓ has a "dependency" effect: all distributions $M^\ell \mu, M^{\ell+1} \mu, \ldots$ will satisfy ℓ homogeneous linear constraints of the form $h_1 x_1 + \cdots + h_k x_k = 0$, where x_i is the probability of being in state i.

Eigenvalues of modulus 1 other than 1 itself are necessarily roots of unity, and hence describe the "periodic" behaviour of the system. They occur if every cycle in a bottom strongly connected component G of the graph has length divisible by some $c > 1$: G can then be partitioned into $G_0, \ldots, G_{c-1}$ such that for each i, all transitions starting in G_i end in G_{i+1}. Thus, the probability mass that lands in G is also cycled between these partitions. By taking M^c to be the transition matrix, we turn each partition into a separate bottom strongly connected component.

The eigenvalue 1 accounts for the "stationary" behaviour of the system, and occurs as many times as there are bottom strongly connected components in the graph of the transition system. This is intuitively because every bottom strongly connected component G corresponds to a unique stationary distribution μ_G which assigns nonzero probability to the states in G and zero probability to all other states. A given initial distribution determines how the probability mass will eventually be distributed between the bottom strongly connected components. Furthermore, if these are aperiodic, then within each component G, the mass that lands in G will inevitably distribute itself in proportion to μ_G

Our reduction extracts the dynamics of the stochastic system by doing away with the redundancy caused by dependencies, partitioning periodicity into phases, and subtracting the stationary behaviour. The sequence of vectors in the resulting linear dynamical system converges to the origin exponentially quickly. In practice:

1. Markov chains might have strong dependencies, be highly periodic, and have several bottom strongly connected components. This could make the dynamical dimension for the model-checking problem small.
2. The sets in $\mathcal{T}$ might not have the limiting distributions on their boundaries, making the resulting sets in $\mathcal{T}'$ empty, and the resulting model-checking problem trivially decidable.

The optimistic practitioner would consider common systems and believe that model checking Markov chains as distribution transformers ought to be easier than arbitrary linear dynamical systems; while a skeptical theoretician would recall ergodic Markov chains and expect that the problems are essentially equivalent. By efficiently distilling the dynamics of Markov chains from their dependencies, periodic nature, and limiting behaviour and quantifying their respective contributions, we formally reconcile these opposing intuitions.

Acknowledgments. This work was funded by DFG grant 389792660 as part of TRR 248 - CPEC (see https://www.perspicuous-computing.science). Joël Ouaknine is also affiliated with Keble College, Oxford as `emmy.network` fellow (https://emmy.network/).

Disclosure of Interests. The authors have no competing interests to declare that are relevant to the content of this article.

References

1. Agrawal, M., Akshay, S., Genest, B., Thiagarajan, P.S.: Approximate verification of the symbolic dynamics of Markov chains. J. ACM (JACM) **62**, 1–34 (2015)
2. Almagor, S., Karimov, T., Kelmendi, E., Ouaknine, J., Worrell, J.: Deciding ω-regular properties on linear recurrence sequences. Proc. ACM Program. Lang. **5**(POPL) (2021)
3. Axler, S.: Linear Algebra Done Right, 4th edn. Springer, Cham (2023). https://doi.org/10.1007/978-3-031-41026-0
4. Baier, C., Katoen, J.-P.: Principles of Model Checking. MIT Press, Cambridge (2000)
5. Basu, S., Pollack, R., Roy, M.-F.: Algorithms in Real Algebraic Geometry. Springer, Heidelberg (2006). https://doi.org/10.1007/3-540-33099-2
6. Beauquier, D., Rabinovich, A., Slissenko, A.: A logic of probability with decidable model checking. J. Log. Comput. **16**, 461–487 (2006)
7. Bilu, Y., Luca, F., Nieuwveld, J., Ouaknine, J., Purser, D., Worrell, J.: Skolem meets schanuel. In: Szeider, S., Ganian, R., Silva, A. (eds.) 47th International Symposium on Mathematical Foundations of Computer Science (MFCS 2022). Leibniz International Proceedings in Informatics (LIPIcs), vol. 241, pp. 20:1–20:15, Dagstuhl, Germany. Schloss Dagstuhl – Leibniz-Zentrum für Informatik (2022)
8. Bilu, Y., Luca, F., Nieuwveld, J., Ouaknine, J., Purser, D., Worrell, J.: The Skolem Tool (2022)
9. Karimov, T.: Algorithmic verification of linear dynamical systems. Ph.D. thesis, Universität des Saarlandes (2024)
10. Karimov, T., Kelmendi, E., Nieuwveld, J., Ouaknine, J., Worrell, J.: The power of positivity. In: 2023 38th Annual ACM/IEEE Symposium on Logic in Computer Science (LICS), pp. 1–11 (2023)
11. Karimov, T., et al.: What's decidable about linear loops? Proc. ACM Program. Lang. **6**(POPL) (2022)
12. Korthikanti, V.A., Viswanathan, M., Agha, G., Kwon, Y.-M.: Reasoning about MDPs as transformers of probability distributions. In: QEST, pp. 199–208 (2010)
13. Kwon, Y.M., Agha, G.: Linear inequality LTL (*iLTL*): a model checker for discrete time Markov chains. In: Davies, J., Schulte, W., Barnett, M. (eds.) ICFEM 2004. LNCS, vol. 3308, pp. 194–208. Springer, Heidelberg (2004). https://doi.org/10.1007/978-3-540-30482-1_21
14. Mignotte, M., Shorey, T.N., Tijdeman, R.: The distance between terms of an algebraic recurrence sequence. Journal für die reine und angewandte Mathematik **349**, 63–76 (1984)

15. Ouaknine, J., Worrell, J.: On the positivity problem for simple linear recurrence sequences. In: Esparza, J., Fraigniaud, P., Husfeldt, T., Koutsoupias, E. (eds.) ICALP 2014. LNCS, vol. 8573, pp. 318–329. Springer, Heidelberg (2014). https://doi.org/10.1007/978-3-662-43951-7_27
16. Ouaknine, J., Worrell, J.: Positivity problems for low-order linear recurrence sequences. In: Proceedings of the Twenty-Fifth Annual ACM-SIAM Symposium on Discrete Algorithms, SODA 2014, Portland, Oregon, USA, 5–7 January 2014, pp. 366–379. SIAM (2014)
17. Vahanwala, M.: Skolem and positivity completeness of ergodic Markov chains. Inf. Process. Lett. **186**, 106481 (2024)
18. Vereshchagin, N.K.: The problem of appearance of a zero in a linear recurrence sequence. Matematicheskie Zametki (in Russian) **38**, 177–189 (1985)

Towards End-to-End GPU Acceleration of PCTL Model Checking

Jan Heemstra[1]ⓘ, Muhammad Osama[2]ⓘ, and Anton Wijs[1](✉)ⓘ

[1] Eindhoven University of Technology, Eindhoven, The Netherlands
{j.h.heemstra,a.j.wijs}@tue.n
[2] Leiden Institute of Advanced Computer Science (LIACS), Leiden University,
Leiden, The Netherlands
m.o.mahmoud@liacs.leidenuniv.nl

Abstract. So far, existing probabilistic model checkers have been programmed to run on a CPU. While earlier work has accelerated some procedures of model checking with GPUs, such as matrix-vector multiplication for probabilistic model checking, we are the first to construct an end-to-end GPU-accelerated probabilistic model checker, where every step of the model checking process, from constructing a Discrete-Time Markov Chain to the verification of a Probabilistic Computation Tree Logic (PCTL) formula, occurs on the GPU, and where all relevant data is located in GPU memory. In this paper, we discuss the challenges imposed by the GPU architecture and memory constraints and how we overcame them, present intermediate performance results for a supported fragment of PCTL, and discuss the challenges that remain to support full PCTL property checking.

Keywords: Temporal logic · PCTL model checking · probabilistic model checking · Discrete-Time Markov Chains · GPU

1 Introduction

This paper was written in honour of Joost-Pieter Katoen on the occasion of his 60th birthday. It addresses a topic that has been at the centre of his research since he was a PhD student: the analysis of probabilistic systems. Already as a PhD student in 1993, he co-authored a paper in which a probabilistic process algebra was proposed with true concurrency semantics [24]. For a topic such as this, developments in both theory and practice are important. To be actually applicable in practice, tools are needed that can effectively and efficiently analyse systems. Joost-Pieter Katoen's research on probabilistic model checking,

This work is supported by NWO grant OCENW.M.21.061 for the GAP project.

ⓒ The Author(s), under exclusive license to Springer Nature Switzerland AG 2025
N. Jansen et al. (Eds.): Principles of Verification: Cycling the Probabilistic Landscape,
LNCS 15261, pp. 314–337, 2025.
https://doi.org/10.1007/978-3-031-75775-4_14

the foundations of which are presented in the book *Principles of Model Checking* [3], led to the development of the *Erlangen-Twente Markov Chain Checker* in 2000 [21], the *Markov Reward Model Checker* in 2005 [23], and the STORM model checker in 2017 [15,20].

The third author of the current paper had the pleasure of collaborating with him in 2013 on parallelising the detection of Strongly Connected Components (SCCs) in graphs, and Maximal End Components (MECs) in directed graphs induced by Markov Decision Processes (MDPs) [48,49]. The targeted computing platform was the *graphics processing unit* (GPU), which offers a way to massively parallelise computations by employing many thousands of threads. MEC detection is relevant for verifying qualitative and quantitative properties of MDPs. Once the induced graph, or *state space*, has been constructed, a MEC detection algorithm can be employed. Although this detection was parallelised, state space construction was still performed sequentially, i.e., by a single CPU thread.

To the best of our knowledge, the very first work in which GPUs were involved in (probabilistic) model checking started with a study in 2006 in which the numerical computation part in the model checker PRISM [26] was accelerated with GPUs [5–7,41]. Also there, they were used to accelerate model checking only partially, leaving state space construction to a single CPU thread. As the numerical part entails the application of one or more matrix-vector multiplications, the use of GPUs was a natural choice. By only accelerating the numerical part, the entire model checking procedure, including state space construction, became up to 18 times faster.

In fact, most papers that combine GPUs with model checking only address part of that procedure, such as successor generation [16], duplicate detection [17], property checking [22], counter-example construction [51], state space decomposition [49], parameter synthesis for stochastic systems [11], and SAT solving (relevant for bounded model checking) [31–36,38,53,54]. VOXLOGICA-GPU applies model checking to analyse (medical) images [9]; state space construction is not applicable in that context.

Whether state space construction can be performed entirely on a GPU for realistic models is a question that was still posed only a few years ago [25]. Acceleration of state space construction is much more complex than, for instance, the numerical computation part in probabilistic model checking, as it is a highly *irregular* problem: the data that a thread needs to access is a priori not known, as this depends on the input. Matrix-vector multiplication, for instance, is a very regular problem: if an $n \times m$ matrix is to be multiplied with an $m \times 1$ vector, and a separate GPU thread is assigned to each matrix column, i.e., we have m threads, then each thread needs to access one predetermined column and the entire vector to perform its part of the computation, resulting in one predetermined entry in the resulting $n \times 1$ vector. In contrast, constructing a state space consists of repeatedly identifying the *successors* of a state reachable from an initial state, and storing them in a hash table, but how those successors should be derived from that state, or even how many successors there are, is a priori not known, and depends on the input model.

Nevertheless, in the last decade, steps have been made to achieve full GPU acceleration of state space construction. In 2014, GPUEXPLORE was the first tool that performed state space construction entirely on a GPU [46], but only for models written in a very restricted language; in particular, it did not support the use of data variables [10,29,45,47,50]. Other GPU-accelerated model checkers followed [4,14,39,40,52], but all had various limitations w.r.t. the types of models they supported; for instance, some were restricted to state vectors of at most 64 bits, and some had similar restrictions related to the encoding of transitions.

With version 3.0 of GPUEXPLORE, support for models with data variables was added in 2023 [43], and by maintaining a tree database [42] and using Cleary compression [13], it was able to keep the memory requirements relatively low, allowing the high-performant construction of state spaces several billions of states in size.

With these recent developments, we are finally in a position to address the question whether probabilistic model checking can be performed *entirely* on a GPU. The two main ingredients are there: state space construction on the one hand, and the numerical computation part on the other hand. However, the first ends with a hash table filled with all the states reachable from the initial state(s), and the second begins with a matrix containing the probabilities associated with the transitions between those states (possibly adjusted for the property to be checked). The gap between these two data structures is considerable. The main contribution of the current paper is therefore a procedure to bridge that gap efficiently, using the thousands of GPU threads at our disposal. By addressing this, moreover, we are the first to present experimental results of end-to-end GPU acceleration of probabilistic model checking, which we compare to the performance of STORM. To reason about probabilistic systems, we have added support for the JANI model format [8] to GPUEXPLORE. While we focus on a fragment of the Probabilistic Computation Tree Logic (PCTL) [18] and Discrete-Time Markov Chains (DTMCs), the same approach is applicable to full PCTL model checking of DTMCs and MDPs, and Continuous Stochastic Logic (CSL) [1] model checking of Continuous-Time Markov Chains (CTMCs) [2]. Furthermore, with the proposed transition (or adjacency) matrix construction procedure, any computation that requires such a matrix as input can be integrated in an end-to-end GPU-based approach, such as CTL model checking [3], bisimulation minimisation [27,28,44] and the detection of SCCs and MECs [48,49].

The remainder of this paper is structured as follows. Section 2 presents the preliminaries, including some of the technical details of GPUEXPLORE's state space construction engine relevant for this paper, and the PCTL model checking of DTMCs. Next, in Sect. 3, we propose a method to construct a transition matrix in parallel, starting with an input model and a hash table to be filled with all the states reachable from the initial state(s) of the model. Section 4 presents the results of our experiments in which we compared PCTL model checking of DTMCs with GPUEXPLORE with the performance of STORM. Finally, conclusions are drawn and possible future work is discussed in Sect. 5.

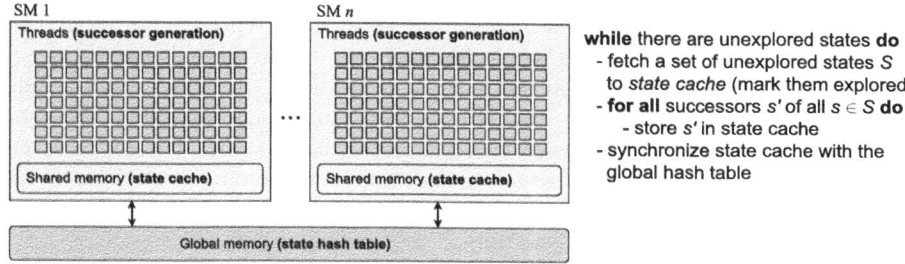

Fig. 1. State space construction, as performed by GPUEXPLORE.

2   Preliminaries

GPUEXPLORE. As GPUEXPLORE is implemented in CUDA C++, the following discussion uses CUDA terminology. A GPU contains a finite number of *streaming multiprocessors* (SM), each containing a number of *cores* (see Fig. 1). The Titan RTX, for instance, has 72 SMs consisting of 4,608 cores in total. GPU threads can run user-defined functions called *kernels*. Parallelism is typically achieved by assigning different parts of the data to each thread, usually determined by their global thread ID.

To execute a kernel, threads are grouped into *blocks*, usually of a size equal to a power of two. GPUEXPLORE uses blocks of 512 threads. All blocks together form a *grid*. A block is executed on an SM, with each SM being able to interleave the execution of many blocks. By default, for instance, GPUEXPLORE runs 3,240 blocks concurrently.

A GPU has a number of different types of memory. *Global memory* is the largest, 24 GB on a Titan RTX. This memory can be used to globally store data, accessible by all the GPU threads. in GPUEXPLORE, a global state hash table is maintained in global memory. It has a high bandwidth, but also a high latency. Having many threads executing a kernel helps in hiding this latency; the cores can rapidly switch contexts to interleave the execution of multiple threads, and whenever a thread is waiting for the result of a memory access, the core uses that time to execute another thread.

Other memory types are *shared memory* and *registers*. Shared memory is very small, but fast on-chip memory with low latency. In GPUEXPLORE, this memory is used by every thread block to store 1) a *work tile* of states that require *exploration*, i.e., construction of their successors, and 2) a local state cache, in which these successors are temporarily stored. Data stored in the shared memory assigned to a thread block is accessible by all threads in that block. In the Titan RTX, each thread block can use up to 64 KB shared memory. The fastest memory is register memory, which is used to store thread-local data. It is very small; allocating too much memory for thread-local variables may result in data spilling over into global memory, which can dramatically limit performance.

On the right in Fig. 1, an overview is given of the state space construction procedure, from the perspective of a thread block. A dedicated explore kernel is implemented, which, when launched, has each block check whether it can retrieve unexplored states from its designated part of the global hash table. If it can, it fetches those states and adds them to its work tile, until there are no more unexplored states or the work tile is full. An important optimisation is called *work claiming*: if, in a previous explore launch, the block has constructed new successors, it can claim these for exploration in the next explore launch, by filling a global memory copy of its work tile. This optimisation tends to prevent a lot of (expensive) hash table scanning.

Next, the block processes its tile. Each thread in the block accesses a designated state, and constructs successors of that state, as defined by the input model. If the model consists of multiple state machines (or automata in JANI terminology), then for each individual state machine, a separate thread computes the successors that can be reached when that state machine fires a transition.

As previously mentioned, each block maintains a local state cache in shared memory. By doing so, repeated accessing of global memory is avoided, with local duplicate detection filtering out any duplicate successors generated at the block-level. Once all the states in the work tile have been explored, the thread block scans the cache, and checks whether the new states are present in the global hash table. If they are not, they are added to the table. In order to support states of arbitrary size, and reduce the memory requirements, states are stored as binary trees. This allows common subtrees of states to be shared. For more information on this, see [42]. Recently, support for the model checking of Linear-Time Temporal Logic (LTL) formulae was added [30].

Probabilistic Model Checking. In the current paper, we use Discrete-Time Markov Chains (DTMCs) to formalise probabilistic system behaviour.

Definition 1 (Discrete-Time Markov Chain). *A DTMC is a tuple* $\mathcal{M} = (S, \mathbf{P}, \iota_{init}, AP, L)$*, with*

- S *a non-empty, finite set of* states;
- $\mathbf{P} : S \times S \to [0, 1]$ *the* transition probability function, *with for all states* $s \in S$:

$$\sum_{s' \in S} \mathbf{P}(s, s') = 1;$$

- $\iota_{init} : S \to [0, 1]$ *the* initial probability distribution, *with* $\sum_{s \in S} \iota_{init}(s) = 1$;
- AP *a finite set of* atomic propositions;
- $L : S \to 2^{AP}$ *a* labelling function.

A *path* through a DTMC $\mathcal{M}$ is an infinite sequence of states $\pi = s_0 s_1 s_2 \cdots \in S^\omega$ such that for all $i \geq 0$, $\mathbf{P}(s_i, s_{i+1}) > 0$. With π_i, we refer to the suffix of π that starts in the i-th state, i.e., $\pi_i = s_i s_{i+1} \cdots$. The set of all paths starting in a state $s \in S$ is referred to as *Paths$_s$*.

PCTL [18] is a probabilistic extension of Computation Tree Logic (CTL) [12]. It can be used to formalise probabilistic behavioural properties of DTMCs. A PCTL formula is composed of state formulae Φ and path formulae φ. However, a PCTL formula itself is always a state formula. The syntax of PCTL is defined as follows.

Definition 2 (Syntax of PCTL formulae). PCTL state formulae Φ *over a set AP of atomic propositions are formed according to the following grammar:*

$$\Phi ::= \textbf{\textit{true}} \mid p \mid \Phi \wedge \Phi \mid \neg \Phi \mid \mathbb{P}_{\bowtie b}(\varphi)$$
$$\varphi ::= \mathsf{X}\,\Phi \mid \Phi\,\mathsf{U}\,\Phi \mid \Phi\,\mathsf{U}^{\leq k}\Phi$$

with $p \in AP$, φ *a path formula,* $b \in [0.0, 1.0]$, *and* $\bowtie\,\in \{\leq, <, \geq, >\}$.

State formulae consist of atomic propositions p combined using the logical operators $\wedge$ and $\neg$, with $\vee$ and $\implies$ being expressible in the usual logical way. In addition, the *probabilistic path operator* $\mathbb{P}_{\bowtie b}(\varphi)$ can be used. Path formulae φ only occur as a parameter of this operator, with $\bowtie\,\in \{\leq, <, \geq, >\}$. A state s satisfies a formula $\mathbb{P}_{\bowtie b}(\varphi)$ iff the probability of following a path from s that satisfies φ is in the interval represented by $\bowtie b$.

Given a PCTL formula Φ and a DTMC $\mathcal{M} = (S, \mathbf{P}, \iota_{init}, AP, L)$, we denote with $s \models \Phi$ that Φ is satisfied in the state $s \in S$. In a similar way, we denote with $\pi \models \varphi$ that the path π through $\mathcal{M}$ satisfies the path formula φ.

For a path π, the semantics of PCTL over DTMCs is as follows.

$$\pi \models \mathsf{X}\,\Phi \iff \pi_1 \models \Phi$$
$$\pi \models \Phi_1 \mathsf{U} \Phi_2 \iff \exists i \geq 0.(\pi_i \models \Phi_2 \wedge \forall j < i.\pi_j \models \Phi_1)$$
$$\pi \models \Phi_1 \mathsf{U}^{\leq k} \Phi_2 \iff \exists i \leq k.(\pi_i \models \Phi_2 \wedge \forall j < i.\pi_j \models \Phi_1)$$

For a state $s \in S$, the semantics of PCTL over DTMCs is as follows.

$$s \models \textbf{true}$$
$$s \models p \iff p \in L(s)$$
$$s \models \Phi_1 \wedge \Phi_2 \iff s \models \Phi_1 \wedge s \models \Phi_2$$
$$s \models \neg \Phi \iff s \not\models \Phi$$
$$s \models \mathbb{P}_{\bowtie b}(\varphi) \iff Pr(s \models \varphi) \bowtie b$$

With $Sat(\Phi)$, we refer to the set $\{s \in S \mid s \models \Phi\}$. We describe how $Pr(s \models \varphi)$ can be computed, which refers to the probability that a path is taken starting from s that satisfies φ.

When $\varphi = \mathsf{X}\,\Phi$, the following holds.

$$Pr(s \models \mathsf{X}\,\Phi) = \sum_{s' \in Sat(\Phi)} \mathbf{P}(s, s')$$

This means that to identify for which states $\mathsf{X}\,\Phi$ holds, the vector $(Pr(s \models \mathsf{X}\,\Phi))_{s \in S}$ can be computed by multiplying the matrix representing $\mathbf{P}$ with the characteristic vector for $Sat(\Phi)$, which is the bit vector $(s \in Sat(\Phi))_{s \in S}$. Computing this requires one matrix-vector multiplication.

For $\varphi = \Phi_1 \mathsf{U}^{\leq k} \Phi_2$, the states in S are partitioned into the three (disjoint) sets S^{no}, S^{yes} and $S^?$, with $S^{no} = S \setminus (Sat(\Phi_1) \cup Sat(\Phi_2))$, $S^{yes} = Sat(\Phi_2)$ and $S^? = S \setminus (S^{no} \cup S^{yes})$. With these sets, the matrix $\mathbf{P}'$ can be defined as follows.

$$\mathbf{P}'(s, s') = \begin{cases} \mathbf{P}(s, s') & \text{if } s \in S^? \\ 1 & \text{if } s \in S^{yes} \wedge s = s' \\ 0 & \text{otherwise} \end{cases}$$

The following computation is needed to compute the set of states satisfying $\Phi_1 \mathsf{U}^{\leq k} \Phi_2$. For $k = 0$, $(Pr(s \models \Phi_1 \mathsf{U}^{\leq 0} \Phi_2))_{s \in S}$ is equal to $(s \in S^{yes})_{s \in S}$. For $k > 0$, $(Pr(s \models \Phi_1 \mathsf{U}^{\leq k} \Phi_2))_{s \in S} = \mathbf{P}' \cdot (Pr(s \models \Phi_1 \mathsf{U}^{\leq k-1} \Phi_2))$. Computing this requires k matrix-vector multiplications.

Finally, for $\varphi = \Phi_1 \mathsf{U} \Phi_2$, again, the sets S^{no}, S^{yes} and $S^?$ can be constructed. Once constructed as defined above, the sets S^{no} and S^{yes} can be extended to include all states for which $Pr(s \models \Phi_1 \mathsf{U} \Phi_2)$ is exactly 0 or 1, respectively, by executing two fix-point precomputation algorithms, typically called PROB0 and PROB1. We do not present these algorithms in pseudo-code. PROB0 removes from S all the states from which a state satisfying Φ_2 can be reached with non-zero probability via states that satisfy Φ_1. PROB1 removes from S the states for which this probability is less than 1.

With the extended sets S^{no} and S^{yes}, it is possible to identify the set of states satisfying $\Phi_1 \mathsf{U} \Phi_2$. For this, the following linear equation system in variables $\{x_s \mid s \in S\}$ must be solved.

$$x_s = \begin{cases} 0 & \text{if } s \in S^{no} \\ 1 & \text{if } s \in S^{yes} \\ \sum_{s' \in S} \mathbf{P}(s, s') \cdot x_{s'} & \text{otherwise} \end{cases}$$

Here, x_s represents $Pr(s \models \Phi_1 \mathsf{U} \Phi_2)$. To solve this with matrix-vector multiplications, let $\mathbf{A} = \mathbf{I} - \mathbf{P}'$, with $\mathbf{I}$ the identity matrix and $\mathbf{P}'$ defined as follows.

$$\mathbf{P}'(s, s') = \begin{cases} \mathbf{P}(s, s') & \text{if } s \in S^? \\ 0 & \text{otherwise} \end{cases}$$

Now, the system $\mathbf{A} \cdot \underline{x} = (s \in S^{yes})_{s \in S}$ should be solved, which can be done with a standard approach, such as the iterative Jacobi or Gauss-Seidel methods. GPUs are particularly well suited for matrix operations, and many libraries and tools exist to perform such calculations. We discuss our use of one such library in Sect. 5.4.

3   From State Hash Table to Transition Matrix

As explained in Sect. 2, for a given model, GPUEXPLORE can fill its global hash table with all the states reachable from the initial state(s). Probabilistic model checking, on the other hand, requires a transition matrix to verify PCTL formulae. In this section, we propose a method to obtain such a transition matrix in a massively parallel way.

Once state space construction has finished in GPUEXPLORE, only information about the states is stored in the global hash table, and no information about transitions is preserved. To still be able to construct a transition matrix, we first reserve extra global memory on the GPU to store the matrix, and furthermore modify the exploration method to store extra information about the states. For the whole procedure, all the states need to be explored three times.

This may seem inefficient, but it should be noted that a single exploration of all states can be accelerated with GPUEXPLORE hundreds of times, compared to state-of-the-art CPU model checkers [30, 42].

Figure 2 presents an overview of the algorithm. In the following subsections, we discuss the individual steps in detail. However, before doing so, we address the format in which the matrix is stored.

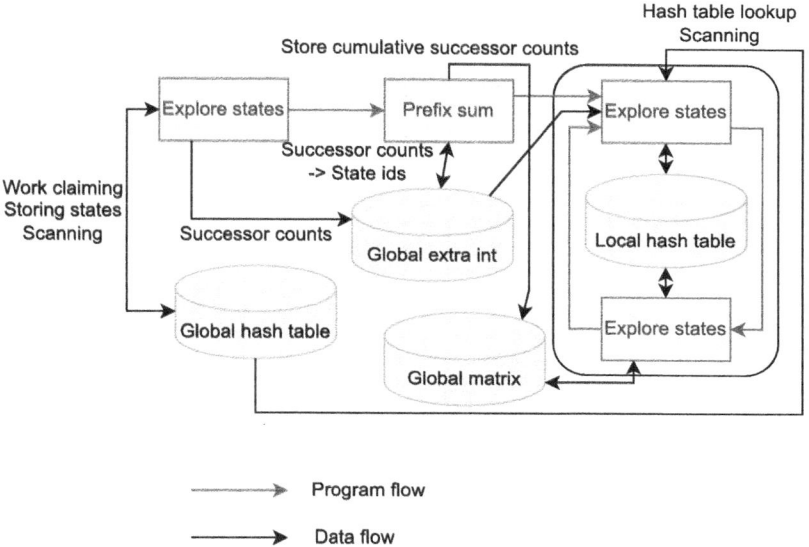

Fig. 2. Overview of matrix construction process.

3.1 Matrix Format

The formats we use to represent the transition matrix are Compressed Sparse Row (CSR) and Compressed Sparse Column (CSC). The CSR representation of a matrix is equivalent to the CSC representation of its transpose. We use this when we need the transpose of the matrix. Since transition matrices tend to be sparse, the use of CSR and CSC effectively reduces the memory requirements.

CSC and CSR are sparse matrix formats, and they represent the matrix by lining up all of the non-zero elements of the columns and rows, respectively. Because this operation loses information about the position of each value in the matrix, two extra lists are added so that this information can be recovered.

Definition 3 (Compressed Sparse Row). *Given an* $m \times n$ *matrix* M *with* nnz *non-zero elements, the* Compressed Sparse Row *(CSR) representation of* M *is a tuple* (R, C, V)*, with*

- R *the list of* row offsets, *containing the cumulative number of non-zero elements of each row of the matrix, starting at* 0 *and ending with* nnz*. As such, this list has* $m + 1$ *elements.*
- C *the list of* column indices, *containing for each value the column it occurs in. The length of the list is* nnz*, and the values are integers ranging from* 0 *to* $n - 1$*.*
- V *the list of* values *of the matrix. For a transition matrix of a probabilistic model, these are in the range* $(0.0, 1.0]$*.*

An example of a matrix in CSR format is given in Fig. 3.

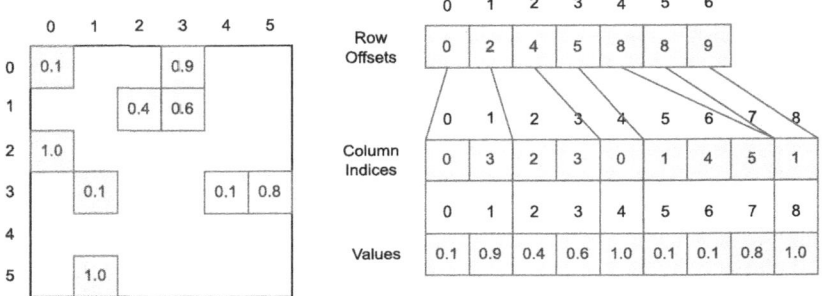

Fig. 3. Example of a matrix in CSR format. The corresponding model has one deadlock at state 4. To turn this into a valid DTMC, a self loop for state 4 could be added.

3.2   First Explore Pass

In the first explore pass (see Fig. 2, the left-most 'Explore states' step), the reachable states are identified, and added to the global hash table, using the already existing procedure in GPUEXPLORE. For this pass, almost no changes were made to the operation of GPUEXPLORE. The only adjustment consists of counting the number of successors of each state. An extra 32-bit integer is therefore reserved for each entry of the global hash table to keep track of this information. This is indicated in the overview by 'Global extra int'.

3.3   Prefix Sum Procedure

Next, a prefix sum procedure is performed, which computes the cumulative sum of an array of values using parallel computation. This procedure serves two purposes. First, to construct the matrix it is required to assign to every state a

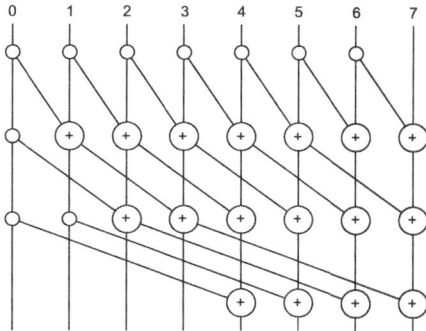

Fig. 4. Circuit representation of a simple prefix sum, for an array of size 8.

unique and consecutive ID. These IDs will correspond to the rows and columns of the matrix. The process of achieving this using a prefix sum is called *stream compaction*. Second, a prefix sum of the successor counts is needed to populate the row offsets. We present an algorithm to efficiently perform both of these tasks at the same time, while using a minimal amount of extra memory.

A simple prefix sum algorithm, where every thread is assigned to a single index of the input array, is presented in Algorithm 1. In each of the $log_2(n)$ steps, every thread adds a particular preceding element of the array to the element assigned to that thread, unless the index of the preceding element is out of bounds. At the end of step i, each array element thus contains the sum of itself and the preceding $2^i - 1$ elements. The barrier() function needs to be reached by every single thread before any thread can start executing succeeding instructions.[1] This barrier() function is used in conjunction with a buffer variable b to prevent race conditions when reading the preceding values of a. An exclusive scan, where the initial value of a_i does not contribute to the sum finally in a_i, can be achieved by shifting all elements of the resulting array one position to the right, and prepending the array with 0. In Fig. 4, a circuit representation of the prefix sum algorithm for an input of size 8 is displayed.

The total size of the GPUEXPLORE hash table can exceed one billion elements. This is too large to be processed by a single thread block. Since there are no explicit inter-block synchronisation barriers, we will have to introduce synchronisation via a succession of kernel launches, as the starting and terminating of kernel executions act as global synchronisation points. We divide the hash table into 3,240 chunks, and assign a block to each chunk. This number is chosen as it is also the grid size of the state space construction procedure of GPUEXPLORE, and it is large enough to ensure sufficient parallelism, but small enough to still take advantage of consecutive memory addressing. Furthermore, each chunk is subdivided in mini-chunks, with each mini-chunk having a size

---

[1] As global barriers for threads across multiple blocks do not exist in CUDA, the given prefix sum algorithm only works for threads that are part of the same block. Subsequent algorithms use this block-local prefix sum algorithm.

Algorithm 1: Simple prefix sum

```
   // t is current thread
   // a is array of values
   // n is length of array
   // e is true iff we perform an exclusive scan
 1 Procedure prefixSum(t, a, n, e)
 2     i ← 1;
 3     while i < n do
 4         barrier();
 5         if t − i ≥ 0 then
 6             b ← a_{t−i};
 7         barrier();
 8         if t − i ≥ 0 then
 9             a_t ← b;
10         i ← 2 ∗ i;
11     barrier();
12     if e then
13         if t > 0 then
14             b ← a_{t−1};
15         else
16             b ← 0;
17         barrier();
18         a_t ← b;
19     barrier();
```

---

equal to the number of threads in a block, i.e., by default 512. For each block, a prefix sum is performed on each of the mini-chunks in its chunk, with the mini-chunks being processed in sequence, as shown in Algorithm 2. Computing a prefix sum in a sequential context is trivial, and furthermore the sequential access of the global memory makes better use of the wide memory bus. The prefix sum of the state count is performed on the values in the 'Global extra int' memory space. At the same time, the prefix sum for computing the state IDs is performed using the shared memory and the registers of each thread.

After the state count and the sum of the successors of each chunk has been computed, these values are stored in two special global memory arrays, each with $3,240$ elements, referred to in Algorithm 2 with z^{state} and z^{suc}. Once Algorithm 2 has terminated, another kernel is launched to perform a prefix sum on the elements of these arrays, yielding the overall prefix state and successor counts of the first elements of each chunk. The pseudocode for that operation is given in Algorithm 3.

Algorithm 2: Step 1 of assigning state IDs and counting successors

---

```
// t is the thread index within the block
// b is the block index
// s is the block size
// g is the global hash table
// e is the global extra int array
// l^state is the local array of states for stream compaction
// l^suc is the local array of successor counts
// n is the size of the global hash table
// z^state and z^suc are the two 3,240-wide global prefix sum buffer
   arrays
```

1 **Procedure** $Kernel1(t, b, s, g, n, l, z)$
    `// For readability purposes, it is assumed that chunkStart returns`
    `   multiples of the block size.`
2      $x \leftarrow \mathsf{chunkStart}(b, n)$;
3      $y \leftarrow \mathsf{chunkStart}(b + 1, n)$;
4      $stateCount \leftarrow 0$;
5      $successorCount \leftarrow 0$;
6   **for** $j \leftarrow x; j < y; j \leftarrow j + s$ **do**
7          $l_t^{state} \leftarrow 1$ **if** $\mathsf{containsState}(g_{j+t})$ **else** 0;
8          $l_t^{suc} \leftarrow e_{j+t}$;
9          $\mathsf{prefixSum}(t, l^{state}, s, \mathbf{false})$;
10         $\mathsf{prefixSum}(t, l^{suc}, s, \mathbf{false})$;
11   **if** $t = s - 1$ **then**
12             $stateCount \leftarrow stateCount + l_t^{state}$;
13             $successorCount \leftarrow successorCount + l_t^{suc}$;
14      $z_b^{state} \leftarrow stateCount$;
15      $z_b^{suc} \leftarrow successorCount$;

At the end of the prefix sum process, a final kernel is launched, which again dedicates a separate block to each of the 3,240 chunks, further separated into mini-chunks. Once more, each block traverses the mini-chunks in order. The global prefix sum of the successor counts can be readily computed using the chunk sums stored by the previous kernel, and the value in the 'Global extra int' memory space. This is then stored in the 'Global matrix', to be later used as the row offsets of the CSR matrix. For the state IDs, the prefix sum has to be repeated, and after the successor counts have been computed and stored away as row offsets, the memory space in 'Global extra int' is reused to store the state IDs. The pseudocode for this step is shown in Algorithm 4. The overall process described in this section is visualised in Fig. 5.

3.4 Final Explore Passes

In the final step of the matrix construction, the column indices and values are inserted into the matrix at their respective positions. The challenge for this step is that in GPUEXPLORE, at no point during state space construction, the global

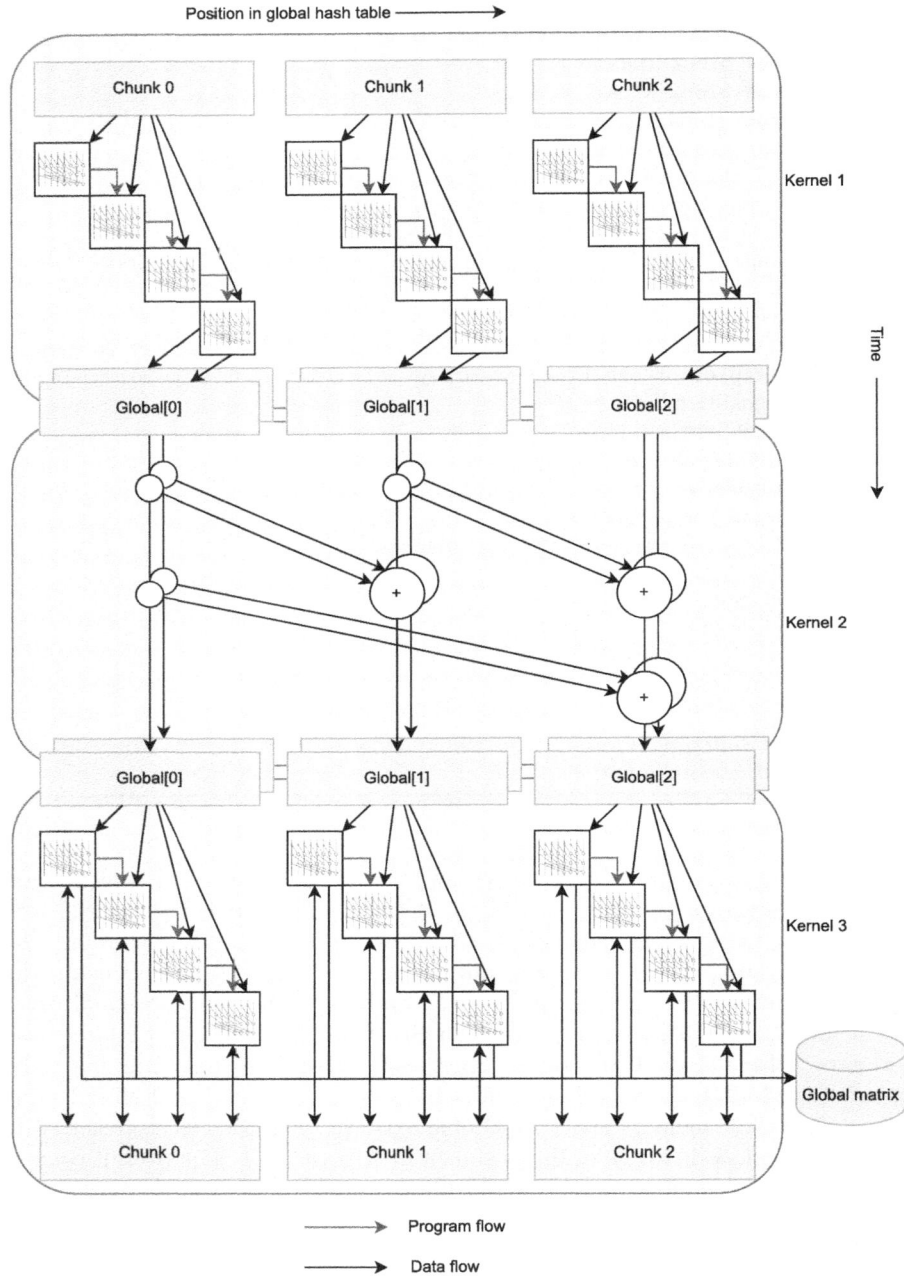

Fig. 5. An overview of the prefix sum procedure used to compute the cumulative successor counts and unique state IDs.

Algorithm 3: Step 2 of assigning state IDs and counting successors

---

```
   // t is the thread index
   // z^state and z^suc are the two 3,240-wide global prefix sum buffers
 1 Procedure Kernel2(t, z)
 2     prefixSum(t, z^state, 3,240, true);
 3     prefixSum(t, z^suc, 3,240, true);
```

IDs of the source and target state of a transition are available at the same time. For performance reasons, as described in Sect. 2, successor generation is done using shared memory to store the successors in a local state cache. By the time these successors are synchronised with the global memory hash table, it is no longer known which source state(s) led to which target, i.e., successor, states.

However, for each cache entry, a separate 32-bit field is reserved in the cache, free to be used for various purposes.[2] At the end of the second explore pass, when the successors in the cache are synchronised with the global hash table, the encountered IDs of those successors, which have been stored in global memory by the prefix sum procedure, are copied into these fields in the cache. While running the third and final explore pass, this helps to identify for each source state the IDs of its successor states, without having to access global memory again. At this stage, each time an enabled transition has been identified, the IDs of its source and target states can be obtained, and the corresponding entry in the matrix can be filled. Hence, after this pass, the construction of the CSR matrix is finished.

3.5   Label Construction

After matrix construction, PCTL *label bitvectors* are generated, for and using the states in the hash table. In Definition 2, φ represents the path formulae, and Φ represents the state formulae. The truth values for some of the latter can be checked state locally, and stored as Boolean labels. More precisely, the state formulae that can be represented without further computation are those that do not contain the probabilistic path operator $\mathbb{P}_{\bowtie b}(\varphi)$.

While support is planned for full PCTL (see Sect. 5.2), currently, only a fragment is supported. However, this fragment already requires the core numerical computation steps. We present the fragment in Definition 4.

---

[2] For LTL model checking, for instance, this field is used to store a pointer to an accepting state, see [30].

Definition 4 (Syntax of PCTL fragment supported by GPUEXPLORE).
PCTL state formulae Φ currently supported by GPUEXPLORE *over a set AP*
of atomic propositions are formed according to the following grammar:

$$\Phi ::= \mathbb{P}(\varphi)$$
$$\varphi ::= \psi \mathsf{U}\, \psi \mid \psi \mathsf{U}^{\leq k}\psi$$
$$\psi ::= \textbf{\textit{true}} \mid p \mid \psi \wedge \psi \mid \neg\psi$$

with $p \in AP$, φ a path formula, and ψ a state formula.

Algorithm 4: Step 3 of assigning state IDs and counting successors

---

```
   // t is the thread index within the block
   // b is the block index
   // s is the block size
   // g is the global hash table
   // e is the global extra int array
   // l^state is the local array of states for stream compaction
   // l^suc is the local array of successor counts
   // n is the size of the global hash table
   // z^state and z^suc are the two 3,240-wide global prefix sum buffers
   // m is the row offsets array
 1 Procedure Kernel3(t, b, s, g, n, l, z, m)
       // For readability purposes, it is assumed that chunkStart returns
           multiples of the block size
 2     x ← chunkStart(b, n);
 3     y ← chunkStart(b + 1, n);
 4     stateCount ← z_b^state;
 5     successorCount ← z_b^suc;
 6     for j ← x; j < y; j ← j + s do
 7         l_t^state ← 1 if containsState(g_{j+t}) else 0;
 8         l_t^suc ← e_{j+t};
 9         prefixSum(t, l^suc, s, false);
10         prefixSum(t, l^state, s, false);
11         if containsState(g_{j+t}) then
12             m_{stateCount+l_t^state} ← successorCount + l_t^suc
13         barrier();
14         if t = s − 1 then
15             successorCount ← successorCount + l_t^suc;
16             stateCount ← stateCount + l_t^state;
17         barrier();
18         e_{j+t} ← l_t^state;                    // Populate extra int with id
```

For a formula $\mathbb{P}(\varphi)$, GPUEXPLORE computes $Pr(s \models \varphi)$ for each state s.
Thus, the value of a property is always a probability, in practice produced in
floating point format. Furthermore, φ may be either of the form $\psi \mathsf{U}\, \psi$ or $\psi \mathsf{U}^{\leq k}\psi$,

with ψ being a state formula that does not contain $\mathbb{P}_{\bowtie b}(\varphi)$. This means that in our fragment, X does not occur, nor are there nested occurrences of $\mathbb{P}_{\bowtie b}$, U or $\mathsf{U}^{\leq k}$.

4   Experimental Results

Hardware. GPU and CPU hardware is generally hard to compare, due to their different architectures, power draw, and system integration. Where a GPU generally comes pre-installed on a graphics card with cooling, RAM, power delivery, and data connectivity already taken care of, a CPU can be paired with different motherboards and memory configurations. Thus, comparing GPUEXPLORE with CPU-based model checkers can never truly be an apples to apples comparison. In this section we list the hardware used, and describe its strengths and weaknesses.

The CPU used to benchmark STORM is an AMD Ryzen^{TM} 7 5800X, installed on an MSI MPG x570 Gaming Pro Carbon Wi-Fi motherboard, with 2 sticks of 16GB DDR4 3200MHz RAM memory, for a total of 32GB of dual-channel memory with an effective bus width of $64 \times 2 = 128$ bits. The CPU was launched in November 2020 and was initially available in the Netherlands for about €500. By August 2024 the price had dropped to about €175. The thermal design power (TDP) of the CPU is 105 W. With modern processors, however, the actual power use can spike to multiple times the official TDP rating. Even though this is more extreme in Intel processors, AMD processors can exhibit similar behaviour when having sufficient cooling installed. We used an Aqua Elite 240 White V3 AIO water cooling loop.

The system used to test GPUEXPLORE has two Titan RTX GPUs connected with an SLI-bridge, but since the PCTL model checking mode does not support multiple GPUs, our tests are run on a single Titan RTX. The GPUs contain 24GB of GDDR6 VRAM, running at 1350MHz with a bus width of 384 bits. The thermal design power of the Titan RTX is 280W. The `nvidia-smi` tool reports that the GPU does not exceed the TDP. The CPU on this system is an i5 6600k, with 32 GB of RAM installed.

In the Netherlands in 2020 these GPUs would cost roughly €3,000. However, in August 2024, the RTX4090, which is over twice as fast as the Titan RTX, is available for under €1,750.

Models. We ran benchmarks using JANI models from the quantitative verification benchmark set [19], which amongst others, contains models exported from PRISM. As such, we are able to test these models in all model checkers that support either the PRISM language or JANI. The models have been tested using GPUEXPLORE 3.0 and STORM 1.8.1 built from commit 3f74f3e of the stable branch [15,20]. We chose in particular DTMC models that have a state count that can be contained within the 24GB memory constraint imposed by our GPU. Since we have to store both states and transitions, no models with more than a billion states can be considered, and problems can already appear earlier. The largest models we have tested contain about 50 million states.

Current limitations in our parser for the JANI language along with the previously mentioned memory constraints and incomplete PCTL support limit our selection of models. Since our checker is only advantageous over the conventional approach starting from a certain explicit model size, we opted to focus on the Crowds model, whose chosen configurations yield state counts from several thousand to tens of millions of states. We also attempted to run the checker on the bounded retransmission protocol (BRP) model, but found that due to missing 64-bit support GPUEXPLORE is not yet viable for the configurations where it is competitive.

Table 1. Tested configurations for BRP model.

MAX	N	states	transitions	$\Phi = \mathbb{P}(\mathbf{true}\mathsf{U}\,(s = 5))$
2	16	6,025	8,067	$1.335653548 \times 10^{-9}$
10	64	1,347,687	1,861,635	$8.056429821 \times 10^{-152}$

The values for the properties of the BRP model, for which the tested configurations are shown in Table 1, can get very low very quickly. Since GPUEXPLORE currently uses 32-bit floats, values below $1.17549435 \times 10^{-38}$ cannot be represented or computed by GPUEXPLORE, and instead it reports the value to be 0. Support is planned for 64-bit floats.

Table 2. Tested configurations for the Crowds model.

total runs	crowd size	states	transitions	$\Phi = \mathbb{P}(\mathbf{true}\mathsf{U}\,(observe0 > 1))$
3	10	6,563	15,143	0.03679081148
4	10	30,070	70,110	0.06798654506
5	10	111,294	261,444	0.1047867889
6	10	352,535	833,015	0.145485201
7	10	990,601	2351,961	0.1886943257
8	10	2,529,567	6,030,207	0.2332947525
9	10	5,971,863	14,285,883	0.2783917593
10	10	13,201,657	31,677,257	0.323278389
11	10	27,595,829	66,394,589	0.3674040521
12	10	54,964,911	132,562,431	0.4103478733

The tested configurations of the Crowds model are shown in Table 2. We benchmarked on configurations with state counts ranging between $6,563$ and $54,964,911$ and transition counts between $15,143$ and $132,562,431$, so that we can determine when our approach becomes advantageous.

Data. We benchmarked GPUEXPLORE and STORM on the BRP and Crowds models. STORM reports times for both model construction (listed in the tables as 'explore'), and property checking (listed in the tables as 'checking'). GPU-EXPLORE reports running times for the initialisation of the hash table ('initial'), the explore steps ('explore'), the prefix sum for stream compaction and cumulative successor IDs ('compaction'), and the matrix multiplication for the PCTL property checking ('checking'). The checking step consists of 400 matrix-vector multiplications, which we found to be sufficient to approximate the value as far as the 32-bit floating point precision allowed.

Table 3. Running times of STORM and GPUEXPLORE on the configurations of the BRP model in seconds.

constants		STORM		GPUEXPLORE			
total runs	crowd size	explore	checking	initial	explore	compaction	checking
2	16	0.034	0.002	0.108	0.056	0.172	0.170
10	64	4.789	0.622	0.108	0.222	0.147	0.285

In Table 3, the running times for the BRP model are shown. GPUEXPLORE is not yet able to compute the outcome for the latter property in this list, as it is too small to be represented by a 32-bit float. It instead outputs a value of 0.

Table 4. Running times of STORM and GPUEXPLORE on configurations of the Crowds model in seconds.

constants		STORM		GPUEXPLORE			
total runs	crowd size	explore	checking	initial	explore	compaction	checking
3	10	0.022	0.000	0.103	0.031	0.172	0.171
4	10	0.063	0.003	0.107	0.039	0.151	0.177
5	10	0.211	0.019	0.114	0.050	0.159	0.206
6	10	0.643	0.115	0.124	0.086	0.167	0.308
7	10	1.748	0.756	0.102	0.199	0.172	0.714
8	10	4.281	4.731	0.117	0.379	0.154	1.980
9	10	10.208	27.485	0.098	0.733	0.135	5.062
10	10	21.511	220.922	0.115	1.525	0.124	11.726
11	10	44.252	1,097.049	0.100	3.627	0.122	25.084
12	10	87.663	5,137.711	0.099	7.302	0.126	50.824

In Table 4, the running times for the Crowds model are displayed. Figure 6 compares the total running time of GPUEXPLORE and STORM for the configurations. Both the initial and compaction times do not seem to be affected by the size of the model. This makes sense, as these times mostly result from the size of the hash table itself, which we did not change throughout these tests.

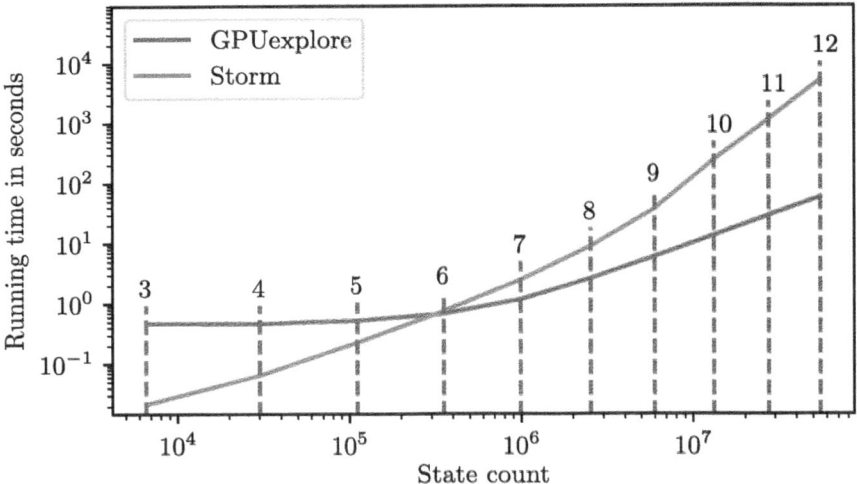

Fig. 6. Performance of GPUEXPLORE with respect to STORM on the **Crowds** model (`crowds.jani`). The *total runs* model constant ranges from 3 to 12, while *crowd size* is 10; each configuration is indicated by a blue dashed line.

5   Conclusions and Future Work

5.1   Conclusions

The results demonstrate a real-world advantage for our prover over STORM when dealing with state spaces consisting of at least 10^6 states. In the most advantageous conditions, GPUEXPLORE achieves a 90× speedup over STORM, performing the full initialisation, state space construction, matrix construction, and property computation in less than half the time it takes STORM to construct the explicit state model. While these results look promising, they also may paint a picture that is too positive. The CPU used was both cheaper at launch, and on top of that it uses less power. However, as mentioned before, the differences in hardware make it nearly impossible to do a true apples to apples comparison, and even if a 90× improvement may be an overstatement in some sense, it still shows the potential of an end-to-end GPU-accelerated probabilistic model checker. We expect that once full PCTL is supported, the verification of more complex PCTL formulae will demonstrate greater speed-ups.

5.2 Full PCTL Support

Currently, only a fragment of PCTL is supported. Firstly, the creation of new labels to store the result of verifying a $\mathbb{P}_{\bowtie p}(\varphi)$ formula is not yet supported. This means that formulae with nested use of the probabilistic path operator cannot at the moment be verified, as described in Sect. 3.5. The same holds for nested use of U and $\mathsf{U}^{\leq k}$. Creating new labels poses challenges with respect to memory management. For each label, a bitvector the size of the state space has to be made available, as each state in the hash table requires the label. Currently, a single 32-bit memory address for each state is reserved for labels. For models that require more than 32 labels in total, either the reserved space has to be expanded, or the existing memory has to be re-used. Optimally, both of these techniques would be applied to achieve minimal memory requirements while ensuring large model and property compatibility.

Lastly, the next-state operator X is not yet supported. As computing the result for a property $\mathsf{X}\,\phi$ only entails a single matrix-vector multiplication, supporting this operator is likely straightforward. Since none of the benchmarked properties used the operator, and since it is the least performance critical of the path formula operators, implementing it was not a priority for this paper.

5.3 Floating Point Precision

The matrix multiplication algorithm currently uses 32-bit floating point vectors to represent the probabilities. This limits the properties that can be effectively checked, as some (configurations of) models produce smaller values than the minimum 32-bit floating point value of 1.175×10^{-38}. Upgrading to double precision 64-bit floating point vectors would lower that value to 2.225×10^{-308}. The matrix values are based on model values and are unlikely to occur out of the viable range for 32-bit floating points, so double precision would only have to be implemented for the state probability vectors. This is convenient, because these vectors only have to be reserved after the matrix construction has completed, and so they do not interfere with the tight memory budget during that procedure.

Double precision would make it viable to check a greater range of properties, as some results are too small to be distinguished from 0 by single precision floating point numbers. Where the smallest floating point number is 1.175×10^{-38}, the smallest positive double is 2.25×10^{-307}. Due to high step sizes values at or near this limit should be avoided, but properties such as those in Table 1 lead to results that are well within the testable range.

5.4 Matrix Equation System

For the unbounded until operator U, computation currently involves traversing the state space in reverse order using the transpose of the transition matrix. Between each traversal step, the labels of the arguments of the until operator are used to filter the state probability vector.

For $a \cup b$, if there are long paths that involve many states in which a holds before a state is reached in which b holds, the above method converges slowly, and requires many matrix-vector multiplications. Since PCTL model checking of the unbounded until operator can be reduced to a system of linear equations (see Sect. 2 and [37]), we could use the built-in linear solver of cuSPARSE, the CUDA sparse matrix library.[3] However, in such a system of linear equations, many values of the matrix are typically set to 0. Particularly when dealing with larger PCTL formulae, this can pose a challenge, as all of the matrix values must be preserved somewhere in memory for later use.

References

1. Aziz, A., Singhal, V., Balarin, F., Brayton, R.K., Sangiovanni-Vincentelli, A.L.: It usually works: the temporal logic of stochastic systems. In: Wolper, P. (ed.) CAV 1995. LNCS, vol. 939, pp. 155–165. Springer, Heidelberg (1995). https://doi.org/10.1007/3-540-60045-0_48
2. Baier, C., Haverkort, B., Hermanns, H., Katoen, J.P.: Model checking algorithms for continuous time Markov chains. IEEE Trans. Software Eng. **29**(6), 524–541 (2003). https://doi.org/10.1109/TSE.2003.1205180
3. Baier, C., Katoen, J.: Principles of Model Checking. MIT Press, Cambridge (2008)
4. Bartocci, E., DeFrancisco, R., Smolka, S.A.: Towards a GPGPU-parallel SPIN model checker. In: SPIN 2014, pp. 87–96. ACM, New York (2014). https://doi.org/10.1145/2632362.2632379
5. Bošnački, D., Edelkamp, S., Sulewski, D., Wijs, A.: Parallel probabilistic model checking on general purpose graphics processors. STTT **13**(1), 21–35 (2011). https://doi.org/10.1007/s10009-010-0176-4
6. Bošnački, D., Edelkamp, S., Sulewski, D.: Efficient probabilistic model checking on general purpose graphics processors. In: Păsăreanu, C.S. (ed.) SPIN 2009. LNCS, vol. 5578, pp. 32–49. Springer, Heidelberg (2009). https://doi.org/10.1007/978-3-642-02652-2_7
7. Bošnački, D., Edelkamp, S., Sulewski, D., Wijs, A.: GPU-PRISM: an extension of PRISM for general purpose graphics processing units. In: PDMC, pp. 17–19. IEEE (2010). https://doi.org/10.1109/PDMC-HiBi.2010.11
8. Budde, C.E., Dehnert, C., Hahn, E.M., Hartmanns, A., Junges, S., Turrini, A.: JANI: quantitative model and tool interaction. In: Legay, A., Margaria, T. (eds.) TACAS 2017. LNCS, vol. 10206, pp. 151–168. Springer, Heidelberg (2017). https://doi.org/10.1007/978-3-662-54580-5_9
9. Bussi, L., Ciancia, V., Gadducci, F.: Towards a spatial model checker on GPU. In: Peters, K., Willemse, T.A.C. (eds.) FORTE 2021. LNCS, vol. 12719, pp. 188–196. Springer, Cham (2021). https://doi.org/10.1007/978-3-030-78089-0_12
10. Cassee, N., Neele, T., Wijs, A.: On the scalability of the GPUexplore explicit-state model checker. In: GaM. EPTCS, vol. 263, pp. 38–52. Open Publishing Association (2017). https://doi.org/10.4204/EPTCS.263.4

---

[3] See https://docs.nvidia.com/cuda/cusparse, visited 21 June 2024.

11. Češka, M., Pilař, P., Paoletti, N., Brim, L., Kwiatkowska, M.: PRISM-PSY: precise GPU-accelerated parameter synthesis for stochastic systems. In: Chechik, M., Raskin, J.-F. (eds.) TACAS 2016. LNCS, vol. 9636, pp. 367–384. Springer, Heidelberg (2016). https://doi.org/10.1007/978-3-662-49674-9_21

12. Clarke, E., Emerson, E.: Design and synthesis of synchronization skeletons using branching time temporal logic. In: Kozen, D. (ed.) Logic of Programs. LNCS, vol. 131, pp. 52–71. Springer, Heidelberg (1981). https://doi.org/10.1007/BFb0025774

13. Cleary, J.: Compact hash tables using bidirectional linear probing. IEEE Trans. Comput. **c-33**(9), 828–834 (1984). https://doi.org/10.1109/TC.1984.1676499

14. DeFrancisco, R., Cho, S., Ferdman, M., Smolka, S.A.: Swarm model checking on the GPU. Int. J. Softw. Tools Technol. Transf. **22**(5), 583–599 (2020). https://doi.org/10.1007/s10009-020-00576-x

15. Dehnert, C., Junges, S., Katoen, J.-P., Volk, M.: A storm is coming: a modern probabilistic model checker. In: Majumdar, R., Kunčak, V. (eds.) CAV 2017. LNCS, vol. 10427, pp. 592–600. Springer, Cham (2017). https://doi.org/10.1007/978-3-319-63390-9_31

16. Edelkamp, S., Sulewski, D.: Efficient explicit-state model checking on general purpose graphics processors. In: van de Pol, J., Weber, M. (eds.) SPIN 2010. LNCS, vol. 6349, pp. 106–123. Springer, Heidelberg (2010). https://doi.org/10.1007/978-3-642-16164-3_8

17. Edelkamp, S., Sulewski, D.: External memory breadth-first search with delayed duplicate detection on the GPU. In: van der Meyden, R., Smaus, J.-G. (eds.) MoChArt 2010. LNCS (LNAI), vol. 6572, pp. 12–31. Springer, Heidelberg (2011). https://doi.org/10.1007/978-3-642-20674-0_2

18. Hansson, H., Jonsson, B.: A logic for reasoning about time and probability. Formal Aspects Comput. **6**(5), 512–535 (1994). https://doi.org/10.1007/BF01211866

19. Hartmanns, A., Klauck, M., Parker, D., Quatmann, T., Ruijters, E.: The quantitative verification benchmark set. In: Vojnar, T., Zhang, L. (eds.) TACAS 2019. LNCS, vol. 11427, pp. 344–350. Springer, Cham (2019). https://doi.org/10.1007/978-3-030-17462-0_20

20. Hensel, C., Junges, S., Katoen, J.P., Quatmann, T., Volk, M.: The probabilistic model checker storm. STTT **24**(4), 589–610 (2022). https://doi.org/10.1007/s10009-021-00633-z

21. Hermanns, H., Katoen, J.-P., Meyer-Kayser, J., Siegle, M.: A Markov chain model checker. In: Graf, S., Schwartzbach, M. (eds.) TACAS 2000. LNCS, vol. 1785, pp. 347–362. Springer, Heidelberg (2000). https://doi.org/10.1007/3-540-46419-0_24

22. Barnat, J., Brim, L., Češka, M.: DiVinE-CUDA - a tool for GPU accelerated LTL model checking. In: PDMC. EPTCS, vol. 14, pp. 107–111. Open Publishing Association (2009). https://doi.org/10.4204/EPTCS.14.8

23. Katoen, J.P., Khattri, M., Zapreev, I.: A Markov reward model checker. In: QEST, pp. 243–244. IEEE Computer Society Press (2005). https://doi.org/10.1109/QEST.2005.2

24. Katoen, J.P., Langerak, R., Latella, D.: Modeling systems by probabilistic process algebra: an event structures approach. In: FORTE. IFIP Transactions, vol. C-22, pp. 253–268. North-Holland (1993)

25. Khan, M.H., Hassan, O., Khan, S.: Accelerating SpMV multiplication in probabilistic model checkers using GPUs. In: Cerone, A., Ölveczky, P.C. (eds.) ICTAC 2021. LNCS, vol. 12819, pp. 86–104. Springer, Cham (2021). https://doi.org/10.1007/978-3-030-85315-0_6

26. Kwiatkowska, M., Norman, G., Parker, D.: PRISM: probabilistic symbolic model checker. In: Field, T., Harrison, P.G., Bradley, J., Harder, U. (eds.) TOOLS 2002. LNCS, vol. 2324, pp. 200–204. Springer, Heidelberg (2002). https://doi.org/10.1007/3-540-46029-2_13

27. Martens, J., Groote, J.F., van den Haak, L., Hijma, P., Wijs, A.: A linear parallel algorithm to compute bisimulation and relational coarsest partitions. In: Salaün, G., Wijs, A. (eds.) FACS 2021. LNCS, vol. 13077, pp. 115–133. Springer, Cham (2021). https://doi.org/10.1007/978-3-030-90636-8_7

28. Martens, J., Groote, J., van den Haak, L., Hijma, P., Wijs, A.: Linear parallel algorithms to compute strong and branching bisimilarity. Softw. Syst. Model. **22**, 521–545 (2022). https://doi.org/10.1007/s10270-022-01060-7

29. Neele, T., Wijs, A., Bošnački, D., van de Pol, J.: Partial-order reduction for GPU model checking. In: Artho, C., Legay, A., Peled, D. (eds.) ATVA 2016. LNCS, vol. 9938, pp. 357–374. Springer, Cham (2016). https://doi.org/10.1007/978-3-319-46520-3_23

30. Osama, M., Wijs, A.: Hitching a ride to a lasso: massively parallel on-the-fly LTL model checking. In: Finkbeiner, B., Kovács, L. (eds.) TACAS 2024. LNCS, vol. 14571, pp. 23–43. Springer, Cham (2024). https://doi.org/10.1007/978-3-031-57249-4_2

31. Osama, M.: GPU enabled automated reasoning. Ph.D. thesis, Eindhoven University of Technology (2022). ISBN: 978-90-386-5445-4

32. Osama, M., Gaber, L., Hussein, A.I., Mahmoud, H.: An efficient SAT-based test generation algorithm with GPU accelerator. J. Electron. Test. **34**(5), 511–527 (2018). https://doi.org/10.1007/s10836-018-5747-4

33. Osama, M., Wijs, A.: Parallel SAT simplification on GPU architectures. In: Vojnar, T., Zhang, L. (eds.) TACAS 2019. LNCS, vol. 11427, pp. 21–40. Springer, Cham (2019). https://doi.org/10.1007/978-3-030-17462-0_2

34. Osama, M., Wijs, A.: SIGmA: GPU accelerated simplification of SAT formulas. In: Ahrendt, W., Tapia Tarifa, S.L. (eds.) IFM 2019. LNCS, vol. 11918, pp. 514–522. Springer, Cham (2019). https://doi.org/10.1007/978-3-030-34968-4_29

35. Osama, M., Wijs, A.: GPU acceleration of bounded model checking with ParaFROST. In: Silva, A., Leino, K.R.M. (eds.) CAV 2021. LNCS, vol. 12760, pp. 447–460. Springer, Cham (2021). https://doi.org/10.1007/978-3-030-81688-9_21

36. Osama, M., Wijs, A., Biere, A.: SAT solving with GPU accelerated inprocessing. In: TACAS 2021. LNCS, vol. 12651, pp. 133–151. Springer, Cham (2021). https://doi.org/10.1007/978-3-030-72016-2_8

37. Parker, D.: Implementation of symbolic model checking for probabilistic systems. Ph.D. thesis, University of Birmingham (2002)

38. Prevot, N., Soos, M., Meel, K.S.: Leveraging GPUs for effective clause sharing in parallel SAT solving. In: Li, C.-M., Manyà, F. (eds.) SAT 2021. LNCS, vol. 12831, pp. 471–487. Springer, Cham (2021). https://doi.org/10.1007/978-3-030-80223-3_32

39. Wei, H., Chen, X., Ye, X., Fu, N., Huang, Y., Shi, J.: Parallel model checking on pushdown systems. In: ISPA/IUCC/BDCloud/SocialCom/SustainCom, pp. 88–95. IEEE (2018). https://doi.org/10.1109/BDCloud.2018.00026

40. Wei, H., Ye, X., Shi, J., Huang, Y.: ParaMoC: a parallel model checker for pushdown systems. In: Wen, S., Zomaya, A., Yang, L.T. (eds.) ICA3PP 2019. LNCS, vol. 11945, pp. 305–312. Springer, Cham (2020). https://doi.org/10.1007/978-3-030-38961-1_26

41. Wijs, A.J., Bošnački, D.: Improving GPU sparse matrix-vector multiplication for probabilistic model checking. In: Donaldson, A., Parker, D. (eds.) SPIN 2012. LNCS, vol. 7385, pp. 98–116. Springer, Heidelberg (2012). https://doi.org/10.1007/978-3-642-31759-0_9

42. Wijs, A., Osama, M.: A GPU tree database for many-core explicit state space exploration. In: Sankaranarayanan, S., Sharygina, N. (eds.) TACAS 2023. LNCS, vol. 13993, pp. 684–703. Springer, Cham (2023). https://doi.org/10.1007/978-3-031-30823-9_35

43. Wijs, A., Osama, M.: GPUexplore 3.0: GPU accelerated state space exploration for concurrent systems with data. In: Caltais, G., Schilling, C. (eds.) SPIN 2023. LNCS, vol. 13872, pp. 188–197. Springer, Cham (2023). https://doi.org/10.1007/978-3-031-32157-3_11

44. Wijs, A.: GPU accelerated strong and branching bisimilarity checking. In: Baier, C., Tinelli, C. (eds.) TACAS 2015. LNCS, vol. 9035, pp. 368–383. Springer, Heidelberg (2015). https://doi.org/10.1007/978-3-662-46681-0_29

45. Wijs, A.: BFS-based model checking of linear-time properties with an application on GPUs. In: Chaudhuri, S., Farzan, A. (eds.) CAV 2016. LNCS, vol. 9780, pp. 472–493. Springer, Cham (2016). https://doi.org/10.1007/978-3-319-41540-6_26

46. Wijs, A., Bošnački, D.: GPUexplore: many-core on-the-fly state space exploration using GPUs. In: Ábrahám, E., Havelund, K. (eds.) TACAS 2014. LNCS, vol. 8413, pp. 233–247. Springer, Heidelberg (2014). https://doi.org/10.1007/978-3-642-54862-8_16

47. Wijs, A., Bošnački, D.: Many-core on-the-fly model checking of safety properties using GPUs. STTT **18**(2), 169–185 (2016). https://doi.org/10.1007/s10009-015-0379-9

48. Wijs, A., Katoen, J.-P., Bošnački, D.: GPU-based graph decomposition into strongly connected and maximal end components. In: Biere, A., Bloem, R. (eds.) CAV 2014. LNCS, vol. 8559, pp. 310–326. Springer, Cham (2014). https://doi.org/10.1007/978-3-319-08867-9_20

49. Wijs, A., Katoen, J.P., Bošnački, D.: Efficient GPU algorithms for parallel decomposition of graphs into strongly connected and maximal end components. Formal Methods Syst. Des. **48**(3), 274–300 (2016). https://doi.org/10.1007/s10703-016-0246-7

50. Wijs, A., Neele, T., Bošnački, D.: GPUexplore 2.0: unleashing GPU explicit-state model checking. In: Fitzgerald, J., Heitmeyer, C., Gnesi, S., Philippou, A. (eds.) FM 2016. LNCS, vol. 9995, pp. 694–701. Springer, Cham (2016). https://doi.org/10.1007/978-3-319-48989-6_42

51. Wu, Z., Liu, Y., Liang, Y., Sun, J.: GPU accelerated counterexample generation in LTL model checking. In: Merz, S., Pang, J. (eds.) ICFEM 2014. LNCS, vol. 8829, pp. 413–429. Springer, Cham (2014). https://doi.org/10.1007/978-3-319-11737-9_27

52. Wu, Z., Liu, Y., Sun, J., Shi, J., Qin, S.: GPU accelerated on-the-fly reachability checking. In: ICECCS, pp. 100–109 (2015). https://doi.org/10.1109/ICECCS.2015.21

53. Youness, H., Osama, M., Hussein, A., Moness, M., Hassan, A.M.: An effective SAT solver utilizing ACO based on heterogenous systems. IEEE Access **8**, 102920–102934 (2020). https://doi.org/10.1109/ACCESS.2020.2999382

54. Youness, H.A., Ibraheim, A., Moness, M., Osama, M.: An efficient implementation of ant colony optimization on GPU for the satisfiability problem. In: PDP, pp. 230–235. IEEE (2015). https://doi.org/10.1109/PDP.2015.59

Model Checking of PLC Code Specifications: Impact of GRAFCET Features to State Space Size

Robin Mroß[1]([✉])(iD), Marcus Völker[1]([✉])(iD), Stefan Kowalewski[1]([✉])(iD), Aron Schnakenbeck[2](iD), and Alexander Fay[3](iD)

[1] Embedded Software (Informatik 11), RWTH Aachen University, 52056 Aachen, Germany
{mross,voelker,kowalewski}@embedded.rwth-aachen.de
[2] Institut für Automatisierungstechnik, Helmut-Schmidt-Universität, 22043 Hamburg, Germany
aron.schnakenbeck@hsu-hh.de
[3] Lehrstuhl für Automatisierungstechnik, Ruhr-Universität Bochum, Universitätsstraße 150, 44801 Bochum, Germany
alexander.fay@rub.de

Abstract. Formal methods can help make safety-critical systems safer by detecting problems before they occur. In general, the earlier a problem is caught during development, the better. Therefore, applying formal methods not to the actual code, but to its specification, before a line of code is even written, can make fixing problems much easier. A property of formal verification, however, is that the state space tends to scale exponentially with the size of the analysed system, which applies to verification of specifications as much as it applies to verification of code. In this work, we take previous work to translate the specification language GRAFCET to GAL for verification purposes and analyse which components of GRAFCET especially impact the size of the resulting state space. Our approach is to construct families of GRAFCET that vary specific parameters while leaving other parameters the same, then feed the resulting GAL models into the model checker ITS-tools and query the size of the state space to draw conclusions about the impact of the different structures in GRAFCET.

Keywords: Programmable logic controllers · Model checking · GRAFCET

1 Introduction

It is self-evident that, when it comes to software systems used in an industrial context, the safety of these systems is much more of a concern than software running on a typical desktop computer or smartphone. After all, if a word processor crashes, the potential dangers are much less dire than if the software controlling the heating element of a big chemical tank malfunctions. Therefore, it is of utmost importance

© The Author(s), under exclusive license to Springer Nature Switzerland AG 2025
N. Jansen et al. (Eds.): Principles of Verification: Cycling the Probabilistic Landscape,
LNCS 15261, pp. 338–359, 2025.
https://doi.org/10.1007/978-3-031-75775-4_15

to ensure that industrial software behaves in the way that it is supposed to. However, ensuring the safety of a system is difficult, especially the more complex and interconnected the components of the system become. This is where model checking can help by providing a mathematically rigorous framework to verify the correctness of control code. One notable idiosyncrasy of the industrial domain though is that the code is often run on specialised hardware and in languages not commonly used outside of this domain. Of note here are Programmable Logic Controllers (PLCs), which are industrial computers specifically designed to control manufacturing processes. The code running on PLCs is typically written in one of the languages standardised by IEC 61131-3 [11], for which few analysis tools exist. Therefore, to tackle problems in this domain, specialised tools need to be developed. Another relevant point pertains to the nature of the development process itself; the earlier problems are identified, the better. This means that ideally, we would like to fix problems before the first line of code is even written, while the system is still being designed. This, of course, requires that the design process is done in a formal way itself, as informal descriptions are inherently ambiguous and difficult to combine with a formal verification process. A way to specify the behaviour of PLC systems is with the specification language GRAFCET [10]. GRAFCET is a graphical language, similar to the programming language SFC [11] or to Petri nets. For our purposes of formal verification, GRAFCET sits at an interesting point: While it is standardised and offers some notion of defined syntax and semantics, the semantics are not fully defined and there are ambiguities in the standard that the community of GRAFCET users and researchers does not fully agree on. This means that for formal verification, a specific interpretation of the standard must be chosen [19]. In previous work [18], we already showed how to translate GRAFCET models into Guarded Action Language (GAL), the input language of the model checker ITS-tools [29], allowing verification according to our interpretation of the standard. Of course, model checking has an inherent problem with complexity. The state space of a model tends to grow exponentially with the size of the system it is modelling (e.g. number of variables). Therefore, it is important to understand where model complexity comes from. In this paper, we aim to identify the factors in GRAFCET that contribute to state space explosion of the generated GAL models, based on the translation presented in [18]. To this end, we have created multiple parametrised GRAFCET instances specifically to vary certain parameters while keeping other parameters constant, in order to evaluate the sizes of the resulting state spaces. We hope this work will allow for future work to develop specific analysis techniques to tackle the exact source of complexity in GRAFCET models.

2   Safety Verification of PLC Code: Related Work

2.1   Programmable Logic Controllers

PLCs were introduced to the industry in the late 1960s. They were originally either programmed in assembly language or, as they replaced hard-wired switching circuits, the programming languages resembled electric and electronic circuit representations. For economical reasons in the presence of huge amounts of legacy code, this situation has never really changed in the last fifty years. When the international standard [11] harmonized the existing PLC languages, a high level language *Structured Text* was introduced which is based on PASCAL and has been gaining increasing popularity. PLCs also differ in their execution scheme, the so-called *cyclic scanning mode*: After copying the current sensor inputs to a dedicated input memory, the program is executed once, then the newly determined output values are copied from a dedicated output memory to the actuators and the cycle starts again. During the program execution, only the memory is accessed while the physical interfaces to the sensors and actuators are ignored.

2.2   Safety Verification of PLC Code

The pioneering work of formal verification of PLC code goes back to Moon and Powers from the Chemical Engineering Dept. at Carnegie Mellon University who translated Ladder Diagram programs into the input language of Clarke's model checker SMV [16,17] already in the early 1990s. Their basic approach - re-modeling the program behavior in a formal representation for which a verification tool exists - has been picked up by various other researchers since then. The model checkers SMV, NuSMV, and nuXmv have been particularly popular in this respect and were applied to the following PLC languages: Sequential Function Charts [1,4], Instruction List (IL) [22], Structured Text [8,9], Function Block Language [23], and Ladder Diagram, again [13]. Other approaches chose, e.g., Petri nets [15] or Condition/Event systems [30] as alternatives to state transition systems. Schlich et al. [24] omit the translation step by generating directly a data structure for the state transition systems from the PLC code and performing explicit state model checking. All mentioned approaches generally differ in the way how the transformation can be efficient in the size of the resulting transition system. To overcome the shortcomings of model checking, further safety verification techniques less prone to state space explosion have been applied to PLC programs, too, e.g. Theorem Provers [3], Abstract Interpretation [5], and Static Analysis, either as a proof method or for reducing the state space before model checking [2].

Joost-Pieter Katoen's group's contributions to the field of PLC code verification fall mainly into the latter category. In Lange et al. [14] a safety verification approach for IL programs based on Bounded Model Checking is presented. To deal with address arithmetics in the PLC program, the properties go beyond propositional logic and can be expressed in quantifier free first order formulae over bit vector theories. Consequently, an SMT solver is used. To improve efficiency, the IL program is mapped to a simpler intermediate representation to which a property-guided slicing is applied, leading to considerable speed-ups in realistic examples compared to existing approaches.

2.3   Verification of IEC 60848 GRAFCET

Throughout this work, the term *Grafcet* refers to a specification written in IEC 60848, while *GRAFCET* refers to the standard itself. With respect to the topic of the remainder of this paper, i.e., the verification of GRAFCET specifications for

PLC programs, the following work is relevant. In ongoing research, analysis techniques tailored to IEC 60848 are developed in order to potentially find errors in the early development stage of specification, motivated by the practical relevance of GRAFCET. To this end, an existing meta model for GRAFCET [12] has been extended and invariants formulated in object constraint language (OCL) have been established that can be used to ensure that a given specification formulated in IEC 60848 is syntactically correct [18]. In order to analyse the semantics of a given model, two methods have been applied: Static analysis and model checking. Regarding the former, value set analysis [21] using interval domain [7] is employed [26]. Further techniques determining an approximation of steps that can be active in parallel have been researched [27]. With respect to model checking, a translation from GRAFCET to GAL has been established in a previous work [18], enabling the verification of specification formulated in IEC 60848 using ITS-tools. The translation considers all elements of the standard except for timed artefacts, such as time sensitive transition conditions and continuous actions. While the approach allows for the specification of Boolean and integer input variables, the work focuses on the former since early experiments indicate that integer variables, even when limited to a fixed width, increase the state space to an unfeasible extent. This is due to the assumed independence of these input signals, meaning that their values can change to any possible value. Note that the introduced translation makes no assumption regarding the environment, i.e., even for Boolean input variables, their values are assigned non-deterministically to any possible value. The resulting GAL system simulates all possible behaviors of the GRAFCET instance by non-deterministically assigning values to all input variables and computing the reaction of the Grafcet to this event, after which another input event is simulated. More precisely, after setting values to input variables it is tested which transitions and actions on events can be triggered. All of those that can subsequently do so simultaneously. Such a reaction usually leads to a change of situation and it can cause a different set of transitions to be fireable without another input event, possibly yielding yet another situation. The intermediate situation is considered *transient* or *unstable*. When no transition is able to be cleared the reached situation is considered *stable* and a new input event is simulated. An overview of this behavior is illustrated in Fig. 2.

Regarding the verification flow, a Grafcet is first translated into GAL, which is then used for verification via ITS-tools. When the properties to be verified are known prior to the translation, reduction techniques [20], based on [31,32], can be used to obtain a GAL instance tailored to the respective verification task. The transformation can be configured. For example, it is possible to hide unstable situations in the state space and to set details of the interpretations as the standard is written in a semi-formal way and therefore leaves room for interpretation. A literature research regarding ambiguities in IEC 60848 has been conducted in the context of this research project [19]. More recently, we have started to consider the environment in the context of the analysis techniques for the possibility of more precise results by modeling information of the plant directly using GRAFCET itself or by integrating constraints on for example input variables in the GAL translation [25].

3   Preliminaries

3.1   IEC 60848 GRAFCET

GRAFCET, internationally standardized in IEC 60848 [10], is a graphical language for the specification of logic control systems. Similar to place transition Petri nets, Grafcets contain so-called steps and transitions alternately connected. A step is depicted by a square and at any given time is either active or inactive. An initial step is visualized using a double bordered square and is active in the initial situation. Transitions are connected with steps using directed links. To each transition a Boolean condition is associated concerning input (or internal) variables of the Grafcet. A rising ($\uparrow$) or falling ($\downarrow$) edge operator can be used in the context of these conditions that evaluate to *true* whenever its operand changes its value from *false* to *true* in the rising edge or from *true* to *false* in the falling edge case. For example, given sensor inputs *buttonA* and *lightBarrierA*, the expression *buttonA* $\wedge \uparrow$ (*lightBarrierA*) evaluates to *true* whenever the *lightBarrierA* starts to register an object while *buttonA* is pressed. A transition can fire when all preceding steps are active while its associated condition evaluates to *true*, deactivating all preceding and activating all succeeding steps in the process. Transitions that can fire simultaneously do so, i.e., the behavior is synchronous. A step can have multiple preceding and multiple succeeding transitions. In the latter case, the transitions have to be mutually exclusive with respect to clearing according to the standard, referred to as alternative junction. A transition can have multiple preceding and multiple succeeding steps, referred to as parallel branches and synchronization. The set of all currently active steps is referred to as the current situation of a Grafcet.

IEC 60848 defines different kinds of actions that can be used to modify internal and output variables, all of which are connected to steps. A continuous action sets the specified Boolean variable to *true* as long as the associated step is active, otherwise it is set to *false*. Such an action can be supplied with a condition such that the output variable is only set to *true* while additionally that condition is currently met. Note that this condition can not depend on an edge operator. Another class of actions are stored actions on step activation and deactivation, which may set specified values to not only Boolean variables. Such an action is executed whenever the associated step becomes active or inactive respectively. Finally, actions on events are executed while the associated step is active and the associated condition evaluates to *true*. Note that this condition is supposed to describe an event and therefore must depend on an edge operator.

Figure 1 shows an illustrative example of a Grafcet controlling a filling system with a valve to fill and a valve to empty a tank. The Grafcet consists of two steps of which step 1 is an initial step. Associated to the steps there are two continuous actions that open the valves if the respective step is active and a stored action on activation (indicated by upwards pointing arrow) that increases a counter when step 2 is activated. The two transitions fire when a certain fill level of the tank is exceeded or undershoot.

Note that a Grafcet can contain several so-called partial Grafcets, each of which comprises a certain part of the model to structure the model in a composite, concurrent or hierarchical way. The term situation refers to the set of active steps in the complete Grafcet. In the following, the term local situation refers to the set of active steps within a given partial Grafcet. The standard [10] defines enclosures and forcing orders: An enclosed partial Grafcet is activated when the enclosing step becomes active and is completely deactivated when the enclosing step becomes inactive. The steps that are activated in an enclosure are marked with an asterisk. A forcing order is a special action attached to a step which forces the controlled partial Grafcet into the defined local situation for as long as the associated step is active. When the step becomes inactive, the enforced Grafcet can continue to evolve freely according to the standard, given that no other forcing order controls the same partial Grafcet. The interested reader is referred to the standard for more details.

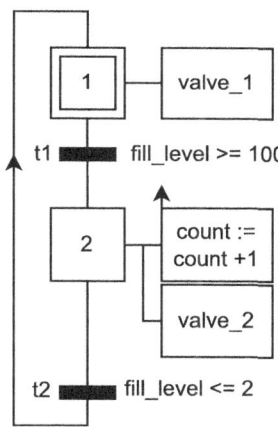

Fig. 1. Example Grafcet

3.2   Guarded Action Language and ITS-Tools

GAL [28] can be regarded as a formalism that can describe large transition systems in a rather compact way. In its core, it consists of integer variables and transition templates with valuations of variables defining the states of the system and transition templates defining how their valuations can change, typically subject to some conditions. It is intended to be a target language for model to model transformations [28]. ITS-tools [29] is a model checker that uses GAL as input language and allows for the verification of properties specified in, e.g., Computation Tree Logic (CTL) [6] with respect to the model described in GAL. It also offers a functionality, *its-reach*, that specifically computes the size of the state space of a model while also evaluating simple reachability and invariant properties. ITS-tools is a symbolic model checker that makes use of Data Decision Diagrams and Set Decision Diagrams for efficient encoding of transition systems and it employs procedures such as automatic saturation [28].

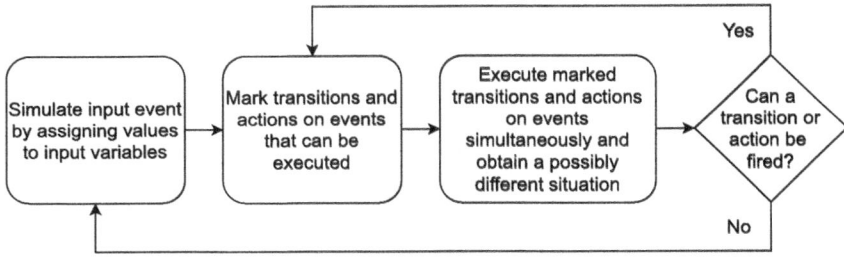

Fig. 2. Overview of the behavior in GAL obtained by the transformation from [18]

4   Evaluation Model and Results

Even when making use of the reduction techniques described in [20], verification of IEC 60848 using model checking based on the translation to GAL [18] often remains infeasible, serving as a motivation to develop additional techniques. In order to determine which elements of IEC 60848 are useful targets for these techniques, we aim to determine the causes for large state spaces in GRAFCET in the following, by employing the translation [18] and making use of ITS-tools option to explicitly compute the state space sizes. This work specifically aims at evaluating GAL instances obtained by [18]. The number of GRAFCET instances in literature appears to be comparably low, such that a statistical evaluation based on these suffers from a sample size too low to produce reliable results. Since this work aims to identify significant factors for large state spaces in the context of IEC 60848 in general, we make use of a specifically constructed IEC 60848 specification that serves as a basis for the evaluation. The structure of the model is depicted in Fig. 3 and comprises the different kinds of branches introduced by the standard: A linear segment which has no branching at all, a parallel segment which makes use of parallel branches that leads to areas of the GRAFCET instance that run in parallel, and a segment of alternative branches. In an alternative branching, the standard demands that the transitions are mutually exclusive with respect to firing [10], guaranteeing that at most one of the branches in this model is active at any given time. This model has five parameters that to a large degree describe the size of the partial Grafcet: The length L_l of the linear part, the length L_p of the parallel part, the number of branches B_p in the parallel part, the length L_a of the alternative part and the number of branches B_a of the alternative part. Here, the length refers to the number of steps in sequence within a given branch. Conditions associated to transitions, continuous actions and actions on events are generated to be mutually exclusive, depending only on input variables. When in total n of these artefacts exist, $\lceil \log_2(n) \rceil$ input variables are introduced and conditions of the form of, e.g., $in_0 \wedge in_1 \wedge in_2...$ and $\neg in_0 \wedge in_1 \wedge in_2...$ are generated which are subsequently used. When, e.g., increasing L_l step by step, an additional transition will be generated in each iteration and at some points a new input variable will be required to guarantee mutual exclusivity. As discussed later, additional Boolean input variables increase the state space. In the following experiments, only the parameter explicitly mentioned is varied. Further, the translations from the given GRAFCET instances to GAL all follow [18] and the invocations of ITS-tools all use the same configurations, more precisely ITS-tools is invoked using *-quiet -reach -timeout 900 -itsflags "-quiet"* along the input GAL file location, which in turn invokes *its-reach* with the parameters *–gc-threshold 2000000 –quiet -t CGAL –quiet* next to providing locations for the input GAL files.

In the following, the aforementioned model is evaluated by explicitly computing the state space size using *its-reach* of differently configured instances. We begin the discussion by considering structural properties of the Grafcet and the introduction of additional variables of different kinds that are not used in the context of conditions and not controlled by actions. Afterwards, the impact of different kinds of actions and hierarchical constructs is investigated. The tests are run on a 64-bit-system using Windows 10, equipped with an AMD Ryzen 5 PRO 4650U (2.10 GHz) CPU and 16 GB RAM. The experiments are set to time out after 900 s. The GAL instances are available under[1].

4.1   Structure and Variables

To assess the impact of each of the parameters L_l, L_p, B_p, L_a and B_a, four of them are fixed to the value 0 while the fifth is increased. Note that B_p or B_a set to zero means that the whole substructure is replaced with a simple arc to ensure connectedness. If B_p or B_a is evaluated, the corresponding length is set to 3. Likewise, when evaluating different values for L_p or L_a, the corresponding

---

[1] https://github.com/robmro/GRAFCET_GAL_State_Space_Evaluation_Models.

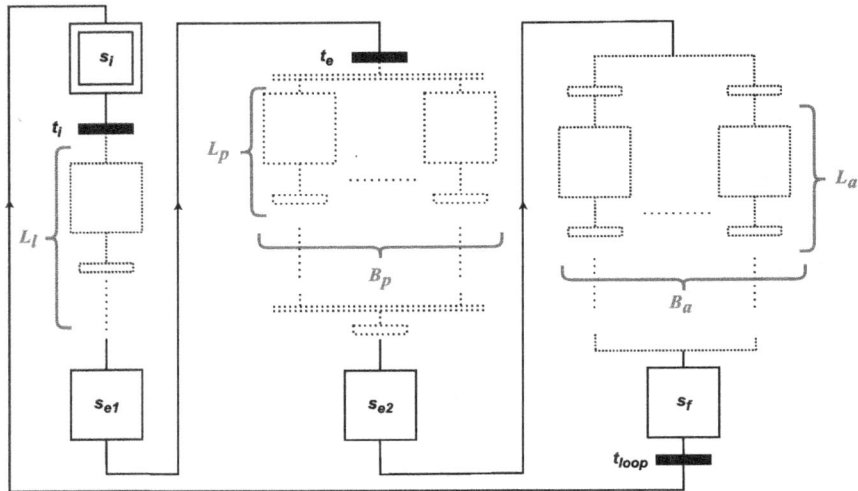

Fig. 3. General structure of the evaluated Grafcets

breadth is set to 3. The results, depicted in Fig. 4 and Fig. 5, indicate that parallel branches contribute greatly to large state spaces, whereas non-parallel linear segments are low factors.

Having multiple instances of the base model in parallel is a major factor, though this is unsurprising as it leads to increases in number of steps, transitions and therefore to further input variables. Indeed, with all five structural parameters set to 2, the state space of a single such partial Grafcet is determined to be 417, while one additional copy increases it to 11649 states. A third iteration is met with a time out. Further tests show that these parallel partial Grafcets essentially exhibit the same state space sizes as a model in which these partial Grafcets are explicitly run in parallel using a respective branching construct: The initial steps of the parallel Grafcets can be transformed into a regular step while being the target of a transition which has as a single preceding step as new initial step. The associated transition condition is *true* such that it can fire immediately. An illustration of this construction is given in Fig. 6. In an abstract way, parallel partial Grafcets can thus be considered to be a special case of parallel branches.

The model can be configured to either include a transition that loops back to the initial state or not, i.e., whether t_{loop} and the related connections to s_f and s_i are generated. Results show that for these Grafcets that do not have actions the state space sizes are identical in either case, albeit for a state more in the looping case since then it is not possible to have every valuation of input variables in the otherwise sink state of the partial Grafcet. The model as depicted in Fig. 3 has an explicit ordering of the three sections: The linear segment is first, followed by the parallel area and thereafter the alternative branches. This ordering can be set to any of the six possible options and results show that all of these variants exhibit

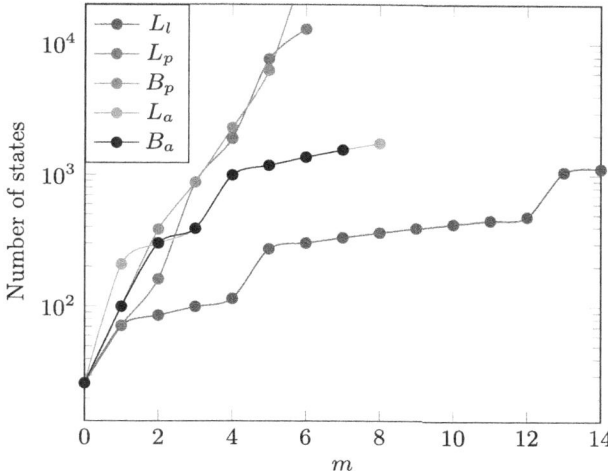

Fig. 4. State space sizes for the Grafcet depicted in Fig. 3 when increasing one of the parameters. The sudden jumps, e.g. between 12 and 13 for L_l, are due to the introduction of additional input variables. Missing data points indicate time outs.

identical state space sizes. Finally, the model can be extended to have additional output and internal and Boolean input variables. The results of increasing the number of these variables are depicted in Fig. 7 and Fig. 8. In its base form, every Boolean input variable is set non-deterministically when an input event occurs [18]. This explains the exponential increase of states in the model, though it should be noted that these variables can be constrained by, e.g., a technique presented in [20]. Further, the low computation times required even for additional input variables indicate that the tool performs optimizations, likely due to these input variables being set but not used in, e.g., transition conditions. However, as other experiments indicate (c.f. Fig. 4 and Fig. 5), additional input variables which are used in the model do increase computation times. Unused internal and output variables keep their initial value 0 and it is therefore reasonable that more of these variables do not change the state space at all.

4.2   Continuous Actions

The model has been extended by continuous actions with and without conditions in order to assess their impact on the state space and results, depicted in Fig. 9, indicate that when adding continuous actions without conditions the state space is not changed at all. This appears reasonable since such an action sets the controlled output variable to *true* if, and only if, the associated step is currently active. Since the model already contained a variable that is set to 1 precisely when the step is currently active, the state of the controlled output variable is logically implied by that value. Introducing continuous actions with conditions to the model can increase the overall number of required input

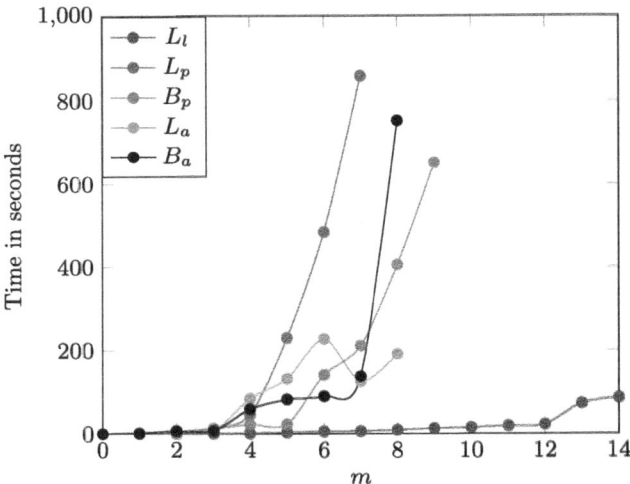

Fig. 5. Computation times for the Grafcet depicted in Fig. 3 when increasing one of the parameters. Each data point represents the average time of five executions. Missing data points indicate time outs.

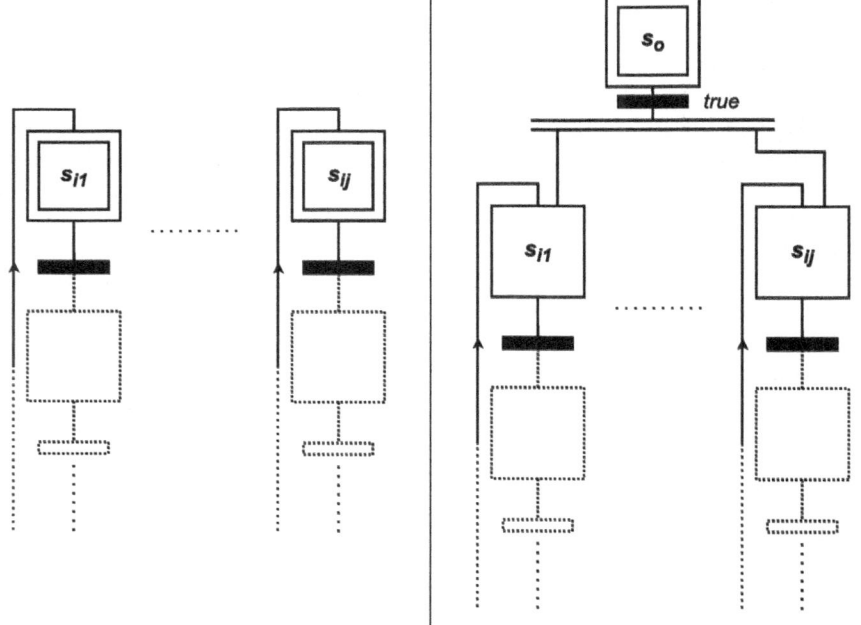

Fig. 6. Equivalence of partial Grafcets and parallel Grafcets

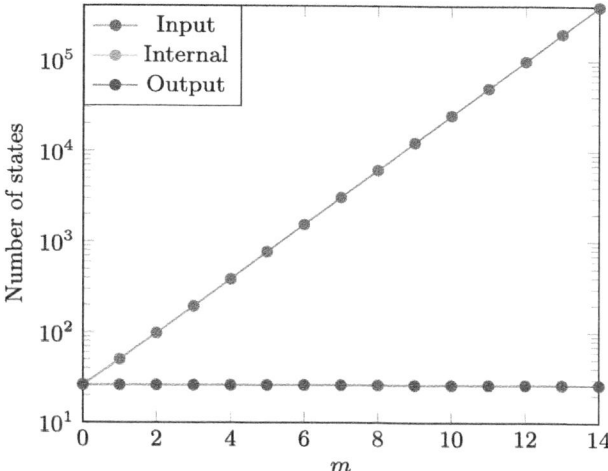

Fig. 7. State space sizes for the Grafcet depicted in Fig. 3 when adding additional variables to the model. Note that adding internal and output variables does not increase the state space size.

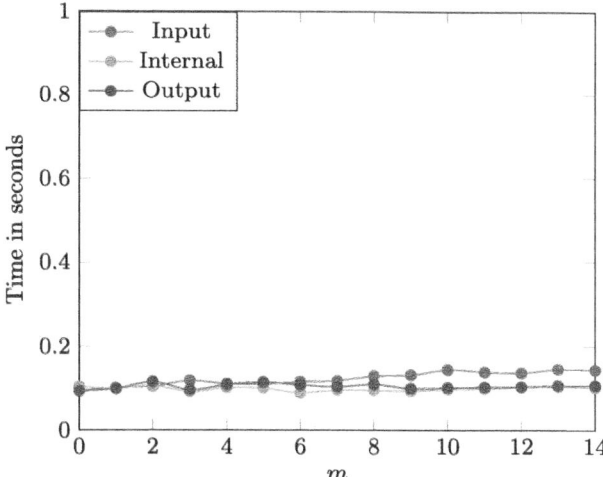

Fig. 8. Computation times for the Grafcet depicted in Fig. 3 when adding additional variables to the model. Each data point represents the average time of five executions.

variables as described in a previous subsection, which in turn can increase the number of states. However, the valuation of these input variables together with the valuation of the variable indicating the activity state of the associated step completely determine the value of the controlled Boolean variable and therefore, in itself, continuous actions with conditions also do not increase the state space.

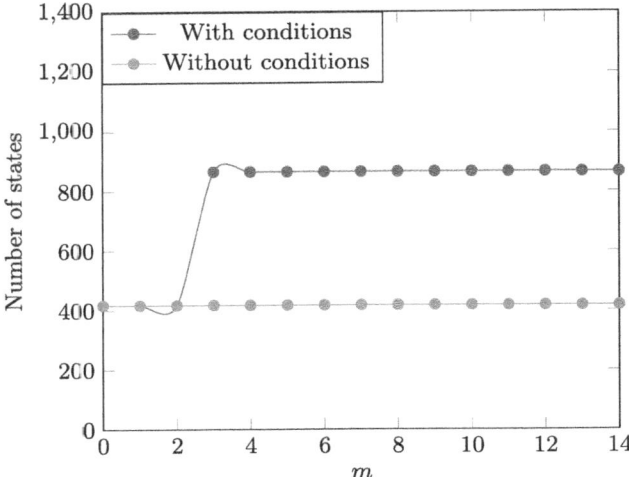

Fig. 9. State space sizes for the Grafcet depicted in Fig. 3 when adding continuous actions, either with an associated condition or without. The sudden jump is due to the introduction of an additional input variable.

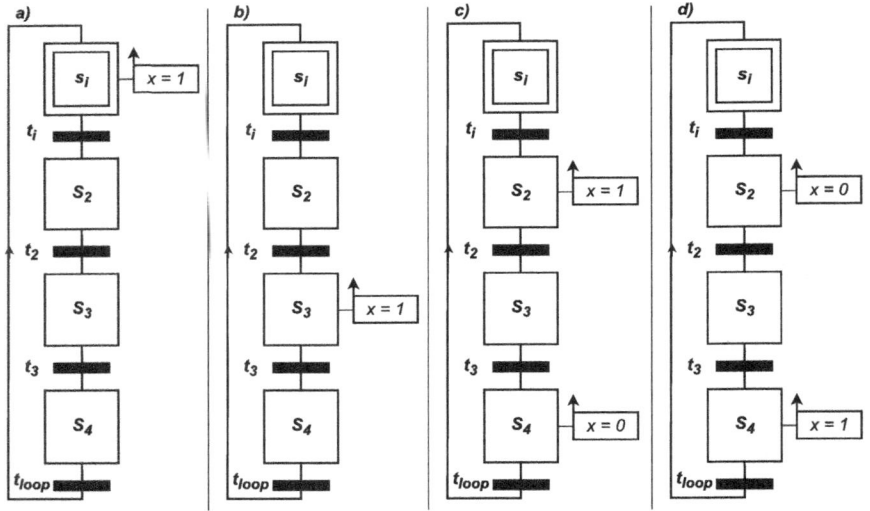

Fig. 10. Different action distributions on the same Grafcet exhibiting a simple linear structure

4.3 Actions on Events

Introducing an action that triggers upon on event and sets an internal variable to 1 does increase the number of states of the system by a factor of about 2, independent of where this action is placed, assuming that the loop construction is

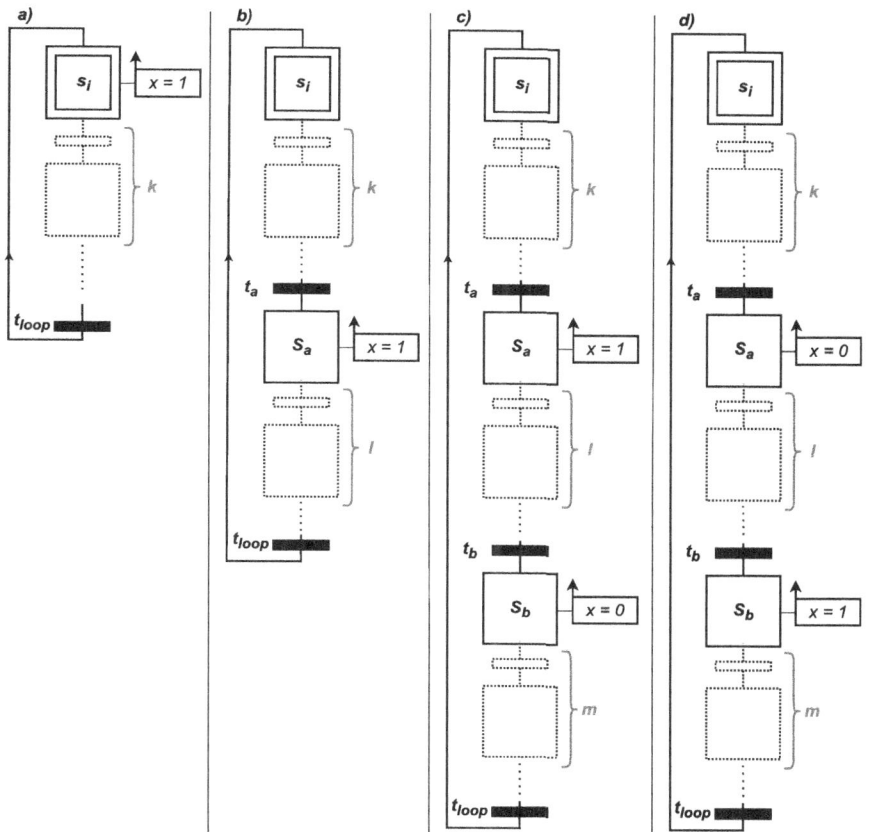

Fig. 11. Different action distributions with added steps in between

enabled. Since the condition associated to the action is independent of all other conditions used by transitions it is the case that every situation is reachable with the internal variable retaining its original value 0 and that every situation is reachable when the internal variable was set to 1 by the action. Note that the choice of setting the variable to 1 instead of any other value is arbitrary. When disabling the loop, the position of the step that is associated with the action that sets the controlled variable to 1 plays a role in the resulting state space: For the model that has L_p, B_p, L_a and B_a set to 2 and L_l set to 6, the resulting state space size is 2165, 2103, 2041, 1979, 1917, 1855 when the action is associated to the first, second, third, fourth, fifth or sixth linear step, starting from the step that is directly following the initial step, respectively. In particular, the later the action appears in the control flow, the lower the state space count is. This is reasonable, since the missing loop guarantees that the situations that occur before the step having the action can be active can not have the controlled variable set to 1, i.e., their valuations are unique. For every following situation however, there exists a state in which the controlled variable is set to 1 by the action or still has its initial value 0 since the action is not guaranteed to be executed.

4.4   Stored Actions

Unlike continuous actions, actions on step (de)activation can set values to variables that are retained until set to another value later on and unlike actions on events, these actions are guaranteed to execute whenever their associated step (de)activates. Results indicate that their effect on the state space size is highly dependent on their positioning. Further depending on their positioning, actions that set their controlled variable to a value other than the initial value 0 can also greatly increase the state space. In the following, the *base case* is the respective Grafcet which has no actions but is otherwise identical and will be used for comparisons. To this end, occasionally the notation $x : y$ will be used, with x describing the state space size of the respective base case and y describing the number of states in the complete model. Considering the Grafcets in Fig. 10, all of which have a state space size of 9 in its base case:

- The state space size is 9. The initial value of the internal variable x is 0, but since it is set to 1 in the initial moment and never set to any other value only the value 1 is present in observable states of the model.
- The state space size is 12. Even though there is no action that sets the value of x back to its initial value 0, there are states present in which x still is 0. In particular, every step prior to s_3 can be active while x is 0 and while x is 1, while at step s_3 and steps after s_3 and before the initial step s_i only allow for x to have the value 1.
- The state space size is 9. At every active step, the valuation of x is unique since the final action on activation sets the value of x back to 0.
- The state space size is 10. In the initial step s_i the variable x can be either 0 (initial) or 1 (after the first iteration of the loop).

The instances depicted in Fig. 10 can be generalized further, as shown in Fig. 11. This generalization takes into consideration a number of steps between, e.g., the actions and the initial step:

- Starting with $k = 0$ and increasing it by one in each iteration leads to state space sizes $3 : 3, 5 : 5, 7 : 7, 9 : 9, 11 : 11, 13 : 13, 15 : 15, ...$
- Setting $k = 0$, $l = 1$ and increasing k by one in each iteration leads to state space sizes $7 : 8, 9 : 12, 11 : 16, 13 : 20, 15 : 24, 17 : 28, 19 : 32, ...$ Keeping $k = 0$ fixed and increasing l results in $7 : 10, 9 : 12, 11 : 14, 13 : 16, 15 : 18, 17 : 20, 19 : 22, ...$, i.e., the difference is constant.
- For all tested values for k, l and m the state space sizes were equal to the base cases.
- Only increasing k while keeping the other parameters set to 1 leads to state space that increases as k is increased by one in every iteration: $13 : 16, 15 : 20, 17 : 24, 19 : 28, 21 : 32, ...$, i.e., the difference in state space sizes increases.

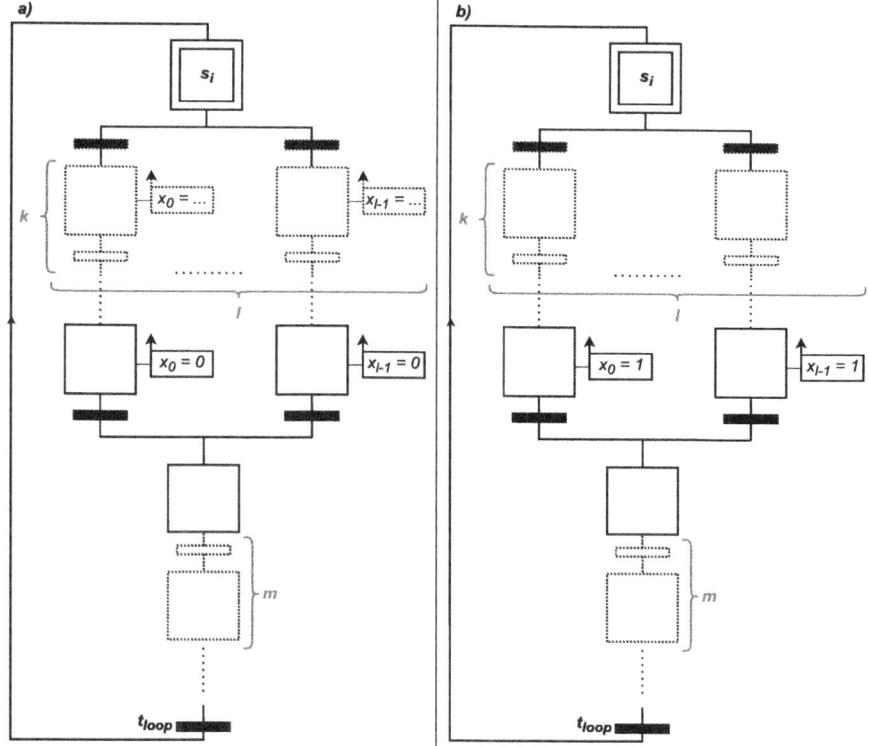

Fig. 12. Different actions in alternative branches

Evaluating the other parameters l and m the same way results in constant differences with respect to the corresponding base case. The constant difference is due to the initial step and the step created by $k = 1$, since x is not uniquely defined in these cases.

It should be noted that, with respect to the instances shown in Fig. 11, when leaving out the looping construct, the state space sizes are identical to the respective base cases. The results for these linear Grafcets translate to some degree to alternative and parallel junctions, as they can be thought of single branches within these areas. Consider the Grafcets in Fig. 12:

- Every branch writes to its own variable while the last step of each branch sets the respective variable to its initial value 0. All tested positive values for k, l and m result in state space sizes that are identical to their respective base cases.
- Every branch writes to its own variable only in the last step of the respective branch, setting its value to 1. Increasing k by one in each iteration, starting with $k = 1$ while keeping $l = m = 3$ leads to the state space sizes 89 : 571, 113 :

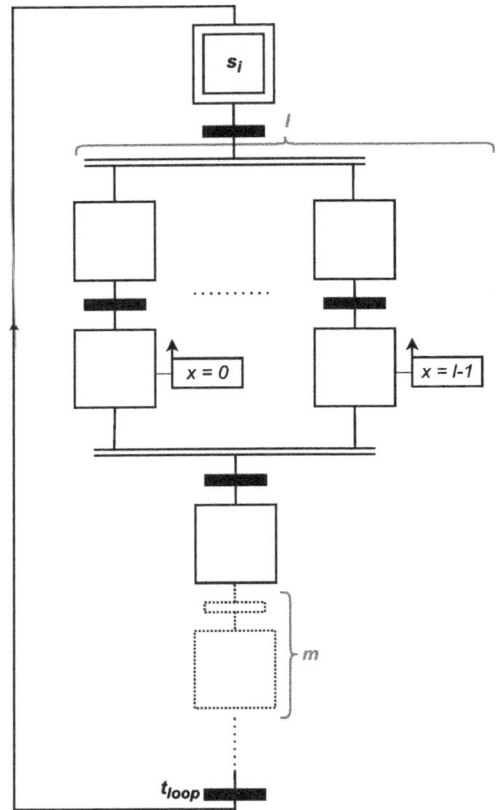

Fig. 13. Different actions in parallel branches

$763, 137 : 955, 161 : 1147, 185 : 1339, 209 : 1531, ...$ Setting $k = m = 3$ and increasing l by one in each iteration leads to $37 : 51, 54 : 174, 137 : 955, 170 : 2394, 401 : 11447, 465 : 26549, ...$ Finally for $k = l = 3$ and increasing m we obtain $121 : 843, 129 : 899, 137 : 955, 145 : 1011, 153 : 1067, 161 : 1123, ...$ The increase along all three parameters are primarily due to the non-deterministic choice for the order of the branches that are executed. In particular, it is possible for the steps in the linear segment following the alternative branches that only one of the variables is set to 1, but also, after further iterations due to the loop, more of these variables are set, until all of them are. The same effect happens with respect to the steps within the branches, explaining why increasing k also increases the state space.

Unlike in the purely linear cases, even when not using a loop, the state space size increases for $m > 0$ since the steps after the alternative junction can be active after any of the branches was chosen non-deterministically. Note that these models are designed in a way that at most one branch of the alternative

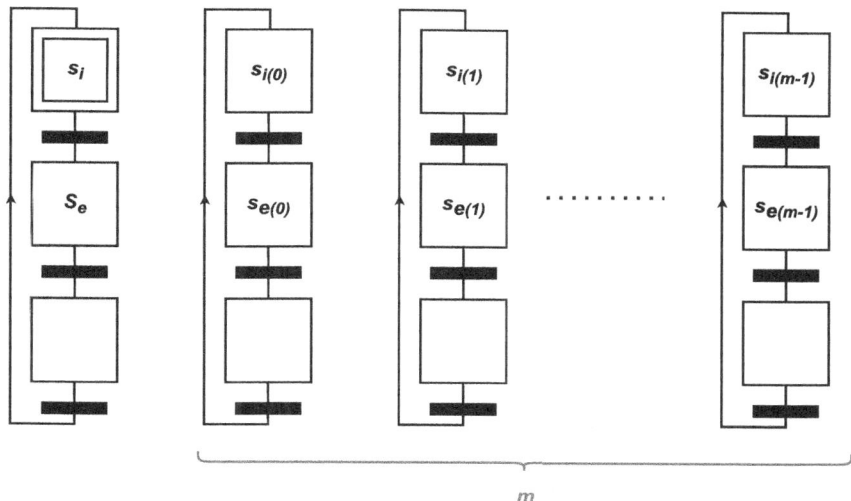

Fig. 14. Grafcet with different possible hierarchical structures

junction is active at any given time. It is possible to construct Grafcets in which that is not given, since the standard only requires the branching transitions to be mutually exclusive with respect to firing. An alternative branching in which, for structural reasons, more and more branches can become active are similar to, but not the same as, explicit parallel branches, which are investigated next. Consider the Grafcet depicted in Fig. 13. It has a configurable number of parallel branches, each containing two steps. The conditions for the transitions within these branches are mutually exclusive, such that the branches can progress independently of each other. There is only one internal variable which attains a value depending on which step within the parallel section was activated last. Setting $l = 3$ and increasing m iteratively by 1, results in sizes $71 : 169, 79 : 193, 87 : 217, 95 : 241, 103 : 265, 111 : 289, ...$ The increase comes from the issue that it is possible for any of the actions on step activation within the parallel branches to be executed last, such that respectively written value is retained for the linear part that follows. Therefore, the state space contains for every step in the lower half of the Grafcet the possible valuations $x \in \{0, ..., l - 1\}$.

4.5 Enclosures and Forcing Orders

Elements discussed so far arguably concern only the basic features of IEC 60848 and so far the number of steps and more precisely the possible situations appear to play a major role in the resulting state space sizes. The standard allows to structure a Grafcet using different partial Grafcets and to hierarchically relate these parts by special structures such as enclosures and forcing orders. Both of these allow one partial Grafcet to directly influence the local situation of another. In the following, experiments regarding these hierarchical Grafcets are discussed

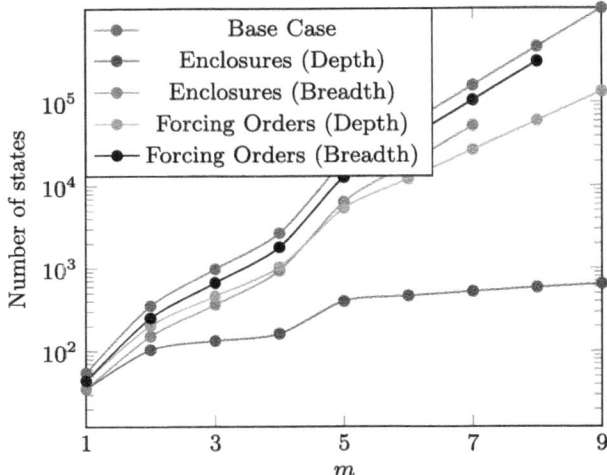

Fig. 15. State space sizes for the Grafcet depicted in Fig. 14 when increasing the number of additional partial Grafcets. Missing data points indicate time outs.

while not employing any of the actions described in the previous subsections in order to determine the number of possible situations compared to the case of having these partial Grafcets run in parallel, referred to as the *base cases* in this scenario. Consider the Grafcet in Fig. 14. In the base case, for each partial Grafcet $x \in \{0, ..., m-1\}$, the step $s_i(x)$ is set to be an initial step. When testing for enclosures, the steps $s_i(x)$ are marked with an asterisk, i.e., are the steps that get activated when the enclosing step becomes active. For forcing orders, the steps $s_i(x)$ are the only steps in the respective partial Grafcet that is set due to the forcing command. The model can be configured to form a wide or a deep hierarchy. In the wide case, the step S_e encloses all other partial Grafcets when evaluating enclosures, while for each other partial Grafcet a forcing order is attached to S_e when evaluating forcing orders. In particular, in the wide case, one partial Grafcet directly controls all the others. In the deep case, each partial Grafcet controls one other, except for the last one: For enclosures, s_e encloses the partial Grafcet containing $S_{i(0)}$, the step $s_{e(0)}$ encloses the partial Grafcet containing $S_{i(1)}$ and so on. Similarly, forcing orders are attached to S_e and to each $S_{e(x)}$ for $x \in \{0, ..., m-2\}$, each ordering the next partial Grafcet in the chain. The results are depicted in Fig. 15. The base case has the largest state space size for all tested configurations, while in particular chained enclosures have comparable low state spaces. The reason for this appears to be that both commands realize implications with respect to the situations: The local situation of a partial Grafcet is uniquely defined by all steps being inactive whenever the enclosing step is inactive and the local situation for a forcing order is uniquely defined by the issued command whenever the enforcing step is active. For the latter, an exception is the freeze command [10] which appears to not generate an implication for local situations.

5   Conclusion

In this work a parameterized Grafcet has been evaluated with respect to the resulting state space size, according to the transformation in GAL as discussed in [18]. The analysis differentiated between situations which take into consideration only step activity variables, actions and hierarchical constructs. Primary reasons for state space explosion in the context of GRAFCET appear to be the number of input variables, certain actions and the number of steps in particular parallel sections of the Grafcet, e.g., in parallel branches or parallel active partial Grafcets. Other elements appear to have no or very little influence on the state space, such as continuous actions. The choice of the evaluation examples can be criticized, since they consider only a small fraction of possible Grafcet structures. However, based on experience, they do reflect common artifacts found in several Grafcets in literature. Further, the choice that all transition conditions and conditions associated with actions are mutually exclusive does not necessarily reflect all real world scenarios. However, mutually exclusive conditions tend to increase the size of the state space, since overlap between them would keep some situations from being reachable in the resulting state space. As the goal is to identify aspects of IEC 60848 that can lead to stark increases of state space sizes, this approach seems justified since it roughly represents worst case scenarios. Future work aims to develop additional techniques in order to reduce the state space for evaluation of some properties by, if possible, mitigating some of these factors. For example, considering *a)* in Fig. 12, resetting variables early when not used subsequently can be beneficial for the state space size.

Acknowledgement. This work was supported by the Deutsche Forschungsgemeinschaft through the project "Analyse von GRAFCET-Spezifikationen zur Erkennung von Entwurfsfehlern" (AGRAFE2).

Disclosure of Interests. The authors have no competing interests to declare that are relevant to the content of this article.

References

1. Beckert, B., Ulbrich, M., Vogel-Heuser, B., Weigl, A.: Regression verification for programmable logic controller software. In: Butler, M., Conchon, S., Zaïdi, F. (eds.) ICFEM 2015. LNCS, vol. 9407, pp. 234–251. Springer, Cham (2015). https://doi.org/10.1007/978-3-319-25423-4_15
2. Biallas, S., Bohlender, D., Kowalewski, S.: Boolean and modular abstraction for programmable logic controllers. In: Dependable Control of Discrete Systems (DCDS), pp. 97–102. IEEE (2013)

3. Blech, J.O., Ould Biha, S.: Verification of PLC properties based on formal semantics in coq. In: Barthe, G., Pardo, A., Schneider, G. (eds.) SEFM 2011. LNCS, vol. 7041, pp. 58–73. Springer, Heidelberg (2011). https://doi.org/10.1007/978-3-642-24690-6_6

4. Bornot, S., Huuck, R., Lakhnech, Y., Lukoschus, B.: Verification of sequential function charts using SMV. In: International Conference on Parallel and Distributed Processing Techniques and Applications, Monte Carlo Resort, Las Vegas, Nevada, USA, 26–29 June 2000, vol. V, pp. 2987–2993. CSREA Press (2000). ISBN 1-892512-51-3

5. Bornot, S., Huuck, R., Lakhnech, Y., Lukoschus, B.: Utilizing static analysis for programmable logic controllers. In: 4th International Conference on Automation of Mixed Processes: Hybrid Dynamic Systems (ADPM), Dortmund, Germany, 18–19 September 2000, Aachen, Germany, pp. 183–187. Shaker Verlag (2000). ISSN 0945-4659. ISBN 3-8265-7836-8

6. Clarke, E.M., Emerson, E.A., Sistla, A.P.: Automatic verification of finite-state concurrent systems using temporal logic specifications, vol. 8, no. 2, pp. 244–263 (1986). https://doi.org/10.1145/5397.5399

7. Cousot, P., Cousot, R.: Static determination of dynamic properties of programs. In: Proceedings of the 2nd International Symposium on Programming, Paris, France, Dunod, pp. 106–130 (1976)

8. Darvas, D., Fernández Adiego, B., Vörös, A., Bartha, T., Blanco Viñuela, E., González Suárez, V.M.: Formal verification of complex properties on PLC programs. In: Ábrahám, E., Palamidessi, C. (eds.) FORTE 2014. LNCS, vol. 8461, pp. 284–299. Springer, Heidelberg (2014). https://doi.org/10.1007/978-3-662-43613-4_18

9. Gourcuff, V., De Smet, O., Faure, J.-M.: Efficient representation for formal verification of PLC programs. In: 8th International Workshop on Discrete Event Systems, Ann Arbor, MI, USA, pp. 182–187 (2006). https://doi.org/10.1109/WODES.2006.1678428

10. GRAFCET Specification Language for Sequential Function Charts, Standard IEC 60848 (2013)

11. Programmable controllers - Part 3: Programming languages, Standard IEC 61131-3 (2013)

12. Julius, R., Trenner, T., Fay, A., Neidig, J., Hoang, X.L.: A meta-model based environment for GRAFCET specifications. In: Proceedings of IEEE International Systems Conference (SysCon), Piscataway, NJ, USA, pp. 1–7 (2019)

13. Kuzmin, E.V., Sokolov, V.A., Ryabukhin, D.A.: Construction and Verification of PLC-programs by LTL-specification. Model. Anal. Inform. Sist. 20(4), 5–22 (2013)

14. Lange, T., Neuhäußer, M.R., Noll, T.: Speeding up the safety verification of programmable logic controller code. In: Bertacco, V., Legay, A. (eds.) HVC 2013. LNCS, vol. 8244, pp. 44–60. Springer, Cham (2013). https://doi.org/10.1007/978-3-319-03077-7_4

15. Mertke, T., Frey, G.: Formal verification of PLC programs generated from signal interpreted Petri nets. In: 2001 IEEE International Conference on Systems, Man and Cybernetics, Tucson, AZ, USA, vol. 4, pp. 2700–2705 (2001). https://doi.org/10.1109/ICSMC.2001.972974

16. Moon, I., Powers, G.J., Burch, J.R., Clarke, E.M.: Automatic verification of sequential control systems using temporal logic, in A.I.Ch.E. Journal 38, 67–75 (1992)

17. Moon, I.: Modeling programmable logic controllers for logic verification. In: IEEE Control Systems Magazine, vol. 14, no. 2, pp. 53–59 (1994). https://doi.org/10.1109/37.272781

18. Mross, R., Schnakenbeck, A., Völker, M., Fay, A., Kowalewski, S.: Transformation of GRAFCET into GAL for verification purposes based on a detailed meta-model. IEEE Access **10**, 125652–125665 (2022). https://doi.org/10.1109/ACCESS.2022.3225736

19. Mroß, R., Schnakenbeck, A., Völker, M., Fay, A., Kowalewski, S.: Unambiguous interpretation of IEC 60848 GRAFCET based on a literature review. In: 28th International Conference on Emerging Technologies and Factory Automation (ETFA) (2023)

20. Mroß, R., Schnakenbeck, A., Völker, M., Fay, A., Kowalewski, S.: GRAFCET reduction techniques for model checking. In: 21st International Conference on Industrial Informatics (INDIN) (2023)

21. Nielson, F., Nielson, H.R., Hankin, C.: Principles of Program Analysis. Springer, Heidelberg (2010). https://doi.org/10.1007/978-3-662-03811-6. ISBN 3642084745

22. Pavlovic, O., Pinger, R., Kollmann, M.: Automation of formal verification of PLC programs written in IL. In: 4th International Verification Workshop (VERIFY), Bremen, Germany, CEUR Workshop Proceedings, vol. 259, pp. 152–163 (2007)

23. Pavlovic, O., Ehrich, H.-D.: Model checking PLC software written in function block diagram. In: 3rd International Conference on Software Testing, Verification and Validation, Paris, France, pp. 439–448 (2010). https://doi.org/10.1109/ICST.2010.10

24. Schlich, B., Brauer, J., Wernerus, J., Kowalewski, S.: Direct model checking of PLC programs in IL. In: Dependable Control of Discrete Systems (DCDS), IFAC Proceedings, vol. 42, no 5, pp. 28–33 (2009). https://doi.org/10.3182/20090610-3-IT-4004.00010

25. Schnakenbeck, A., Mroß, R., Völker, M., Kowalewski, S., Fay, A.: Ansätze für die Modellierung von Streckeninformationen zur Verifikation im Steuerungsentwurf. Tagung "Entwurf komplexer Automatisierungssysteme" (EKA), 14.-15.05.2024, Magdeburg, Germany (2024). https://doi.org/10.25673/116044

26. Schnakenbeck, A., Mroß, R., Völker, M., Kowalewski, S., Fay, A.: A control flow based static analysis of grafcet using abstract interpretation. In: 21st International Conference on Industrial Informatics (INDIN) (2023)

27. Schnakenbeck, A., Mroß, R., Völker, M., Kowalewski, S., Fay, A.: Structural analysis of GRAFCET control specifications. In: 28th International Conference on Emerging Technologies and Factory Automation (ETFA) (2023)

28. Thierry-Mieg, Y.: From Symbolic Verification To Domain Specific Languages. Habilitation à diriger desrecherches, Sorbonne Université, UPMC; Laboratoired'informatique de Paris 6 [LIP6] (2016)

29. Thierry-Mieg, Y.: Symbolic model-checking using ITS-tools. In: Baier, C., Tinelli, C. (eds.) TACAS 2015. LNCS, vol. 9035, pp. 231–237. Springer, Heidelberg (2015). https://doi.org/10.1007/978-3-662-46681-0_20

30. Treseler, H., Bauer, N., Kowalewski, S.: Verification of IL programs with an explicit model of their PLC execution. In: Proceedings of 5th Workshop on Discrete Event Systems (WODES 2000), Ghent, Belgium, 21–23 August 2000, pp. 283–289. Kluwer Academic Publishers (2000)

31. Weiser, M.: Program slicing. IEEE Trans. Softw. Eng. **SE-10**(4), 352–357 (1984). https://doi.org/10.1109/TSE.1984.5010248

32. Zaytoon, J.: A contribution to the validation of grafcet controlled systems. Eur. J. Control **6**(6), 488–506 (2000). https://www.sciencedirect.com/science/article/pii/S0947358000711113

Model Checking and Strategy Synthesis with Abstractions and Certificates

Alessandro Abate[1]([✉]), Mirco Giacobbe[2], Diptarko Roy[1], and Yannik Schnitzer[1]

[1] University of Oxford, Oxford, UK
aabate@cs.ox.ac.uk
[2] University of Birmingham, Birmingham, UK

Abstract. We survey a broad line of research concerned with the application of concepts and techniques from formal verification to the model checking of reactive systems and of dynamical models, and to the synthesis of strategies for control objectives. The models and techniques discussed in this contribution are of interest to the research area concerned with heterogeneous models and are of relevance for applications dealing with cyber-physical systems. The models under consideration encompass differences in state/variable type—finite vs. (un-)countably infinite—and in model semantics—(non-)deterministic vs. probabilistic. We categorise the discussed techniques into two main approaches: on the one hand, the derivation and use of formal abstractions; and on the other, the synthesis of certificates. We also distinguish between the separate-yet-related objectives of model checking and of strategy synthesis.

Keywords: Model checking · strategy synthesis · reactive systems · dynamical and control models · formal abstractions · certificate synthesis

1 Introduction

This contribution is structured as follows. In Sect. 2 we discuss a unified modelling framework for reactive systems and dynamical models, evolving in discrete time, and in particular we distinguish notions of non-determinism (in its various semantics) and of probability. This section also presents requirements on these models, expressed as appropriate formulae in temporal logic, and lays out the two overall problem statements depending on how non-determinism is conceived, namely that of model checking and that of strategy synthesis. We tackle both objectives with two general approaches: via formal abstractions and via synthesis of certificates. These two alternative approaches will be discussed in the following two parts of the work, namely Sects. 3 and 4, respectively. Within these two sections, we first analyse deterministic models, then extend the above results to models with probability and with the possible presence of non-determinism. Special instances, namely purely non-deterministic and probabilistic models, can be analysed accordingly. Throughout both sections, we emphasise and distinguish the model-checking from the strategy synthesis problem.

© The Author(s), under exclusive license to Springer Nature Switzerland AG 2025
N. Jansen et al. (Eds.): Principles of Verification: Cycling the Probabilistic Landscape,
LNCS 15261, pp. 360–391, 2025.
https://doi.org/10.1007/978-3-031-75775-4_16

Throughout this contribution and finally in Sect. 5, we discuss how Joost-Pieter's work has been influential across these areas. His contributions in model checking have indeed witnessed relevant repercussions in the area of hybrid systems, and been put to good use to understand and analyse control models, particularly in the presence of probabilistic dynamics, namely for general stochastic processes. An exemplar problem is the deep connection between Bellman's dynamic programming, a paradigm from control theory, and algorithms for probabilistic model checking, core to Joost-Pieter's work, which has led to a plethora of new results for stochastic hybrid models - for the latter formalism, his more recent work on probabilistic models is similarly very insightful. As a second instance, his work on formal abstractions of reactive models has been translated to the analysis and policy synthesis for general control models. But other areas of work, which are external to this very contribution, such as statistical model checking or the good use of learning techniques, could as well be ascribed to his body of literature, which has been broad and impactful in areas across computer science and information engineering.

2   Models and Specifications

We present a unified framework for modeling the various classes of systems addressed in this paper, ranging from reactive software to probabilistic control systems. We start by introducing the simplest model class for deterministic systems, and progressively expand its scope, by encompassing more complex models describing richer behaviour involving (both) nondeterminism and probability, respectively. For each of these model classes, we introduce corresponding temporal logic specification languages, which are used for encoding properties that we wish to be verified.

2.1   Deterministic Models

A model $\mathcal{M}$ is defined over variables X taking values over a set $\mathcal{X}$. It is initialised to values X_0 from a set Init, and it evolves over discrete time steps according to a function Update. In a deterministic model, the next valuation is unique and solely depends on the current state (value of the variable), without any additional internal or external influences:

$$X_{t+1} = \mathsf{Update}(X_t), \qquad X_0 \in \mathsf{Init}. \tag{1}$$

A trajectory of $\mathcal{M}$ is an infinite sequence of states $\tau = X_0, X_1, X_2, \ldots$ such that $X_{i+1} = \mathsf{Update}(X_i)$ for all $i \geq 0$.

Remark 1. Notice that we allow for non-determinism in initial condition, which can be selected within a non-trivial set. This is a *non-branching* form of non-determinism (cf. semantics in (2) for more generality) that is important in the context of certificate synthesis (cf. Sect. 4). Pure determinism can be easily distilled from imposing that the initial set Init collapses to a single point.   □

The model definition in (1) provides a versatile and unified framework for reactive systems endowed with dynamical behaviour, such as deterministic transition systems, and encompasses various dynamical systems that differ in the type of their variables. For instance, if the variables X are discrete, this formalism can effectively model software programs that perform deterministic computations from a given set of inputs. Conversely, if the variables X are continuous, the model defines dynamical systems described by ordinary difference equations, where Update is also known as a vector field.

A model as in (1) can include a *labeling function* $L \colon \mathcal{X} \to 2^{AP}$, which assigns a set of labels $L(X)$ to any variable valuation X. Labels are taken from a finite alphabet, or set of atomic propositions, denoted as AP. They serve for the specification of requirements on the model's behavior. Requirements will be upheld over *traces* of the models, which are mappings of model trajectories through the labelling function L - they are the 'observables' - or the 'outputs' - of the model.

As an alternative to their rather syntactical definition using Update and Init, systems can be characterised by their semantics. For deterministic systems this is given as *deterministic transition systems*:

Definition 1 (Deterministic Transition Systems). *A transition system $\mathcal{M}$ consists of*

- *a state space $\mathcal{X}$,*
- *an initial region $\mathcal{X}_{\mathcal{I}} \subseteq \mathcal{X}$,*
- *a non-blocking transition function $T \colon \mathcal{X} \to \mathcal{X}$, and*
- *a labelling function $L \colon \mathcal{X} \to 2^{AP}$,*

for a set of atomic propositions AP, and where $T(x) = \mathsf{Update}(x)$ and $\mathcal{X}_I = \mathsf{Init}$.

The definition of T, as a non-blocking, total transition function ensures that every state has a successor, much like the case for the function/vector field Update. Hence, models emit necessarily infinite trajectories. We raise requirements, or define properties, over the set of infinite traces - the mapping of trajectories across the labelling function. The standard specification language for properties of deterministic models is Linear Temporal Logic (LTL) [21, 101]. Below, we introduce LTL and the corresponding model checking problem.

Definition 2 (Linear Temporal Logic). *LTL formulas are constructed according to the following grammar:*

$$\varphi ::= true \mid a \in AP \mid \varphi \wedge \varphi \mid \neg \varphi \mid \bigcirc \varphi \mid \varphi \, U \, \varphi$$

The model checking problem for LTL consists in deciding whether a given transition system $\mathcal{M}$ satisfies a given LTL formula φ. A satisfaction relation $\models$ for trajectories of $\mathcal{M}$ is defined as follows:

$$\tau, i \models true$$

$$\tau, i \models a \qquad \textit{iff } a \in L(x_i) \textit{ where } \tau = x_0, x_1, x_2, \dots$$

$$\tau, i \models \varphi_1 \wedge \varphi_2 \quad \textit{iff } \tau, i \models \varphi_1 \textit{ and } \tau, i \models \varphi_2$$

$$\tau, i \models \neg\varphi \qquad \textit{iff } \tau, i \not\models \varphi$$

$$\tau, i \models \bigcirc\varphi \qquad \textit{iff } \tau, i+1 \models \varphi$$

$$\tau, i \models \varphi_1 \, U \, \varphi_2 \quad \textit{iff for a finite } k \geq i, \ \tau, k \models \varphi_2 \textit{ and } \tau, j \models \varphi_1 \textit{ for all } j = i, \dots, k-1,$$

where $i \in \mathbb{N}$ is any index on the infinite trajectory τ. The relation can be lifted to the entire model by requiring that every trajectory initialised within $\mathcal{X}_I$, satisfies φ, namely:

$$\mathcal{M} \models \varphi \textit{ iff } \tau, 0 \models \varphi \textit{ for all trajectories } \tau \textit{ of } \mathcal{M}.$$

We also introduce the derived and widely-used temporal operators *eventually* $\Diamond$ and *globally* $\Box$ next. The formula $\Diamond\varphi := true \, U \, \varphi$ states that φ must be true in some state of a considered trajectory. Dually, the formula $\Box\varphi := \neg(\Diamond\neg\varphi)$ requires that φ holds true in all states of the trajectory. If we do not include the *next* operator $\bigcirc$ from full LTL, we obtain the fragment $\text{LTL}_{\backslash\bigcirc}$: this will be of relevance in Sect. 3, where we are interested only in the model's reachability properties, rather than in its exact stepwise behaviour.

Non-deterministic Models. Non-determinism can affect a dynamical model in a number of ways. Mathematically, the model can be written as follows:

$$X_{t+1} = \mathsf{Update}(X_t, U_t), \qquad X_0 \in \mathsf{Init}. \tag{2}$$

where $U_t \in \mathcal{U}$ is a valuation of non-deterministic input variables. Whilst for a deterministic model one initial condition results in a *single trajectory*, for a non-deterministic model one initial condition results in a *tree of possible/allowable runs* - which trajectory is in the end selected (or executed), depends on how non-determinism is "resolved", as discussed next. Semantically, we distinguish the following alternative ways to handle a non-deterministic signal/variable U_t:

- it can be due to non-controllable (external) environmental circumstances. Its correspondingly adversarial handling results in conservative/pessimistic model checking approaches to verification;
- it can be otherwise agential, namely due to a (internal) controllable input, resulting in an optimistic synthesis approach to "resolve" it.

For non-deterministic models, computations do not necessarily evolve linearly but can "branch" (cf. "tree" of possible runs above). Therefore, specifications on model traces require a logic that is able to explicitly account for non-deterministic behavior, and is such that its satisfaction is defined over states (branching semantics), as opposed to the case of LTL specifications, where satisfaction is defined over trajectories (linear semantics). In the following, we define

Computation tree logic (CTL) [44] and its corresponding model checking problem.

Definition 3. *CTL distinguishes between state formulas φ and path formulas ψ, defined by the grammar:*

$$\varphi ::= \text{true} \mid a \in AP \mid \varphi \wedge \varphi \mid \neg\varphi \mid \exists\psi \mid \forall\psi$$
$$\psi ::= \bigcirc \varphi \mid \varphi \, U \, \varphi$$

The semantics for $\bigcirc$ and for U are as before, and the semantics for true, *a,* $\wedge$, *and* $\neg$ *are also identical except for being defined with reference to a state s, instead of a trajectory τ. The new branching operators $\exists$ and $\forall$ come with existential or universal path semantics over the runs originating in state x:*

$$x \models \exists\psi \text{ iff } \exists\tau: \tau(0) = x \text{ and } \tau, 0 \models \psi,$$
$$x \models \forall\psi \text{ iff } \forall\tau: \tau(0) = x \text{ implies } \tau, 0 \models \psi.$$

Remark 2. We note that the control literature has so far *not* developed bespoke algorithms for general CTL model checking over continuous-space models, beyond reachability verification. We believe that it is quite natural to specify requirements for control models in CTL, and correspondingly of great interest to re-develop the standard CTL model checking algorithms for finite-state transition systems, to control models evolving over continuous spaces. A contribution in this direction is [59]. □

In this contribution we have solely introduced model classes and relevant specifications, and do not do justice to the rich landscape of results in model checking and control synthesis for such models. We refer to Joost-Pieter's renowned monograph [21] for a broader technical overview of the field.

2.2 Probabilistic Models

Probabilistic (or equivalently, stochastic) models describe systems with uncertainty that entails probabilistic behaviour. Whilst for a deterministic model one initial condition results in a single run, for a probabilistic model, one initial condition results in a distribution over runs. Notice that this is a fine-grained form of uncertainty that is distinguished from the discussed external non-determinism: indeed, whilst we again witness branching behaviour, we now have a distribution over the branching - accordingly, we shall see that behaviours' specification will require a bespoke logic, since quantifying existentially or universally over branching (as in CTL) might be overly conservative.

Mathematically, a probabilistic model can be defined in terms of an update of the state $X_t \in \mathcal{X}$, which now depends on an additional stochastic input W_t, sampled i.i.d. from a probability distribution at each step:

$$X_{t+1} = \text{Update}(X_t, W_t), \qquad X_0 \in \text{Init.} \tag{3}$$

This model encompasses without loss of generality any time-homogeneous Markov process, that is, any such system where the distribution of states at time X_{t+1} is solely determined by the current state X_t.

A probabilistic model, as described by the difference equation above, defines a discrete-time Markov chain (DTMC) over a general (possibly infinite or continuous) state space, which characterises the semantics of the model [21]. The formalism of Markov chains will also be useful as abstract, finite-state models in the sequel. In order to define the semantics of the probabilistic model in (3) as a discrete-time Markov chain, we require that $\mathcal{X}$ is measurable with Σ being the associated σ-algebra, and that W_t is sampled from a measurable disturbance space $\mathcal{W}$. We delegate the probabilistic foundations of these models and the required measure-theoretic underpinnings to specialised monographs [21,26,68,95] and journal articles [8,78].

Definition 4 (Discrete-time Markov Chain). *A discrete-time Markov chain $\mathcal{M}$ consists of*

- *a Σ-measurable state space $\mathcal{X}$,*
- *an initial region $\mathcal{X}_\mathcal{I} \subseteq \mathcal{X}$, and*
- *a transition kernel $P \colon \mathcal{X} \times \Sigma \to [0,1]$.*

As for (non-)deterministic models, a state is a valuation for the variables X, and $\mathcal{X}$ is the set of possible valuations. This kernel fully characterises the probability to transition from a given state s to any (measurable) set T within $\mathcal{X}$, and is defined as follows:

$$P(s,T) = \int_{\mathcal{W}} \mathbf{1}_T(\mathsf{Update}(s,w)) \cdot \Pr(\mathrm{d}w), \tag{4}$$

where $\mathbf{1}_T(\cdot)$ denotes the indicator function of T, which takes value 1 on elements in T and 0 otherwise.

For probabilistic models, properties of interest can be expressed in Probabilistic Computation Tree Logic (PCTL) [43]. As we anticipated earlier, PCTL differs from CTL in that, instead of specifying properties over the computation tree originating from a state and resulting from non-determinism, it instead reasons over probability measures associated with distributions over outgoing paths that are induced by the stochastic dynamics. Consequently, PCTL replaces the universal and existential path quantifiers of CTL with a probabilistic operator ($\mathbb{P}$), allowing for quantitative reasoning over the outgoing paths that satisfy a given temporal requirement from a state.[1]

Definition 5 (Probabilistic Computation Tree Logic). *The syntax of (PCTL) formulae is defined recursively using the following operators:*

$$\varphi ::= \mathsf{true} \mid a \in AP \mid \varphi \wedge \varphi \mid \neg\varphi \mid \mathbb{P}_{\sim p}[\psi]$$
$$\psi ::= \bigcirc \varphi \mid \varphi \, U \, \varphi$$

---

[1] We mention just in passing that it is also possible to express and model check linear-time properties over stochastic models, and leave the reader to the following pointers for more details, [6,21,126,127].

Here $\sim \in \{<, \leq, \geq, >\}$ *and* $p \in [0, 1]$. *The semantics for operators inherited from CTL are unchanged, and again the model checking problem for formulae* φ *is defined over states* $x \models \varphi$. *The satisfaction semantics for the expression* $x \models \mathbb{P}_{\sim p}[\psi]$ *is defined as follows:*

$$\Pr(\{\tau \in \Sigma^{\omega} \mid \tau(0) = x \text{ and } \tau, 0 \models \psi\}) \sim p,$$

where $\Pr$ *is the probability distribution over the infinite paths through* $\mathcal{X}$ *induced by the stochastic dynamics.*

Joost-Pieter has played a core rôle in the development of algorithms and tools for model checking of probabilistic systems - the contribution in [71] provides a survey of this rich landscape.

2.3   Stochastic Control Models

Stochastic control models combine probabilistic behaviours with decisions, a form of resolution of non-determinism. A stochastic control model extends the update function with an additional control input U_t at each time step t. A state update is therefore determined by the current state, a control input U_t (a decision) determined by a control strategy, and a probabilistic disturbance W_t sampled i.i.d. from a probability distribution. Mathematically, the update equations can be written as:

$$X_{t+1} = \mathsf{Update}(X_t, W_t, U_t), \qquad X_0 \in \mathsf{Init}. \tag{5}$$

This model describes a Markov Decision Processes on general state space, as defined in the following [26, 65].

Definition 6 (Markov Decision Process). *A Markov Decision Process* $\mathcal{M}$ *consists of*

– *a* Σ-*measurable state space* $\mathcal{X}$,
– *an input space* $\mathcal{U}$,
– *an initial region* $\mathcal{X}_{\mathcal{I}} \subseteq \mathcal{X}$, *and*
– *a conditional transition kernel* $P: \mathcal{X} \times \mathcal{U} \times \Sigma \rightarrow [0, 1]$

The transition kernel of an MDP extends the transition kernel of a Markov chain with a control input, which determines the probability of transitioning into a set of states T based on the current state s and input u:

$$P(x, u, T) = \int_{\mathcal{W}} \mathbf{1}_T(\mathsf{Update}(x, w, u)) \cdot \Pr(\mathrm{d}w). \tag{6}$$

While for a purely probabilistic model every transition consists of a distribution over successor states, with a control model every transition consists of family of distributions over successor states, one for each control input. Alternatively seen, but equivalently, a distributions over successor states is associated to state-action pairs. A control policy (also known as a control strategy) selects the available input and thus induces the probability distribution of successor states. In particular, a memory-less and deterministic control policy $\pi \colon \mathcal{X} \to \mathcal{U}$ decides the next control input solely based on the current state. Once a policy is fixed, the model behaves as a purely probabilistic model, and if the policy is memory-less then it behaves as a Markov chain, whose transition kernel is as follows:

$$P(x, T) = \int_{\mathcal{W}} \mathbf{1}_T(\mathsf{Update}(x, \pi(x), w)) \cdot \Pr(dw). \tag{7}$$

Specifications for stochastic control models can also be expressed using PCTL. However, satisfaction depends on states, stochastic disturbances, and the employed control policy π. Consequently, the verification of PCTL formulae and the synthesis of optimal control policies that maximise or minimise the probability of satisfying temporal requirements are inseparable. The satisfaction semantics for the expression $x \models \mathbb{P}_{\sim p}[\psi]$ is commonly quantified universally over all policies:

$$\max_{\pi} \Pr^{\pi}(\{\tau \in \Sigma^{\omega} \mid \tau(0) = x \text{ and } \tau, 0 \models \psi\}) \sim p, \text{ for } \sim \in \{<, \leq\}, \text{ and}$$

$$\min_{\pi} \Pr^{\pi}(\{\tau \in \Sigma^{\omega} \mid \tau(0) = x \text{ and } \tau, 0 \models \psi\}) \sim p, \text{ for } \sim \in \{>, \geq\},$$

where $\Pr^{\pi}$ is the probability distribution over infinite paths induced by the stochastic dynamics under control policy π.

Joost-Pieter has, over the past few years, spearheaded a research initiative on probabilistic programs, for which the operational semantics in (3) and in (5) are special models. His broad surveys on probabilistic programs can be found in [70] and [23]. His work on the analysis of such models concerns both their theoretical foundations and the development of specific tools [90,91]. This theoretical work is quite broad, but it includes techniques that are well aligned with the two main approaches discussed in Sects. 3–4 of this contribution.

3 Abstractions

Abstractions serve as a powerful technique for reducing a *concrete* model to a simpler *abstract* model while preserving properties of interest that can be expressed in temporal logic [49,61,88,98]. Any preserved properties verified on the abstract model carry over to the original concrete model. In the following, we give a general overview of abstractions for the different kinds of models introduced earlier, and address their connection to temporal logics [88,89].

3.1 Abstractions for Deterministic Models

Most generally abstractions are equivalence relations $\simeq \subseteq \mathcal{X} \times \mathcal{X}$ inducing a partition $\mathcal{X}/_{\simeq}$ of equivalent states on a model's state space – the *quotient space*. An abstraction groups states into equivalence classes, with each class comprising states that exhibit similar behavior. The specific conditions defining this similarity characterise different types of abstractions and determine which properties are preserved [29]. An abstraction induces an *abstract* model, where each equivalence class is merged into a single state that aggregates the behavior of all states within the class. The abstract model is also referred to as the *quotient*:

Definition 7 (Quotient). *The quotient of $\mathcal{M}$ under the partition $\simeq$ is the transition system $\mathcal{M}/_\simeq$ with*

- *state space $\mathcal{X}/_\simeq$,*
- *initial region $\mathcal{X}_I/_\simeq$ where $R \in \mathcal{X}_I/_\simeq$ iff $R \cap I \neq \emptyset$, and*
- *transition function $T/_\simeq$, where*
  1. *$R \neq Q \in T/_\simeq(R)$ iff $T(x) \in Q$ for some $x \in R$,*
  2. *$R \in T/_\simeq(R)$ iff $T(x) \in R$ for all $x \in R$.*

Depending on the specific abstraction, the resulting partition may be coarse, resulting in an abstract model that is significantly smaller than the concrete model. Consequently, it becomes more feasible to apply model checking techniques to the quotient. However, there is an inherent trade-off between the coarseness and the preserved properties. In the following, we focus on *bisimulation*, an equivalence relation that is common in many fields of computer science, which allows preserving both linear- and branching-time properties [29,64].

Definition 8 (Bisimulation). *A partition $\sim$ is a bisimulation if $x \sim y$ implies $L(x) = L(y)$, and for all states $x, x', y \in \mathcal{X}$ such that $x \sim y$ and $x' \in T(x)$, it holds that $x' \sim y'$, for some $y' \in T(y)$.*

Bisimulation owns the elegant property of depending on a purely local condition for states, which co-inductively ensures their unbounded temporal equivalence [89]. Intuitively, bisimulation requires two related states to share the same label, and that for any transition one can take, the other must be able to match it with a transition such that both successors are again in relation (see Fig. 1).

$$
\begin{array}{ccc}
x \longrightarrow x' & & x \longrightarrow x' \\
\text{\tiny R} & \text{can be completed to} & \text{\tiny R} \quad\quad \text{\tiny R} \\
y & & y \longrightarrow y'
\end{array}
$$

Fig. 1. Local bisimulation condition – every transition of related states can be matched.

Theorem 1 ([29]). *Let $\mathcal{M}$ be a labelled transition system. If $\sim$ is a bisimulation on $\mathcal{M}$, then $\mathcal{M} \models \varphi$ if and only if $\mathcal{M}/_\sim \models \varphi$ for any LTL formula φ.*

Preserving the $\bigcirc$-operator requires accounting for a state's stepwise behavior, potentially resulting in large quotients. This is especially challenging for infinite-state models with non-repeating trajectories (periodic behaviours), leading to infinite quotients that are unsuitable for verification [27]. However, many interesting specifications, such as reachability, or invariance, do not require the $\bigcirc$-operator [76]. Therefore, we consider a weaker form of bisimulation that abstracts from *stuttering*, i.e., transitions between states that appear identical to an observer (see Fig. 2).

Definition 9 (Stutter-insensitive Bisimulation). *A partition $\simeq$ is a stutter-insensitive bisimulation if $x \sim y$ implies $L(x) = L(y)$, and for all states $x, x', y \in \mathcal{X}$ such that $x \simeq y$ and $x \not\simeq x' \in T(x)$, there exists a finite trajectory $y_0, y_1, \ldots, y_k$ such that $y_0 = y$, $y_i \simeq x$ for all $i = 1, \ldots k - 1$, and $y_k = y'$ for some $y' \simeq x'$.*

$$x \longrightarrow x' \qquad \text{with } x \not\simeq x' \qquad x \qquad x \qquad \ldots \qquad x \longrightarrow x'$$
$$\scriptstyle R \qquad\qquad\qquad \text{can be completed to} \qquad \scriptstyle R \qquad\quad \scriptstyle R \qquad\qquad\qquad \scriptstyle R \qquad\quad \scriptstyle R$$
$$y \qquad\qquad\qquad\qquad\qquad\qquad\qquad\qquad y \longrightarrow y_1 \longrightarrow \ldots \longrightarrow y_{k-1} \longrightarrow y'$$

Fig. 2. Trajectory-based representation of the stutter-insensitive stability condition.

Intuitively, stutter-insensitive bisimulation weakens the definition of bisimulation by requiring that the matching transition can be preceded by a finite sequence of *stutter steps*, which are such that the path does not leave the equivalence class. This abstraction disregards exact stepwise behavior, but preserves still its reachability properties. Therefore, stutter-insensitive bisimulation quotients can be much smaller (coarser) than their strong counterparts while preserving temporal logics without $\bigcirc$-operator.

Theorem 2 ([29]). *If $\simeq$ is a stutter-insensitive bisimulation, then $\mathcal{M} \models \varphi$ if and only if $\mathcal{M}/\simeq \models \varphi$ for any $LTL_{\backslash \bigcirc}$ formula φ and deterministic model $\mathcal{M}$.*

There exist models which do not admit a finite bisimulation but have a finite stutter-insensitive bisimulation quotient. Figure 3(a) shows the Euclidean algorithm, which does not terminate for any two unequal non-positive inputs [13]. While there does not exist a finite bisimulation, Fig. 3(b) shows the finite stutter-insensitive bisimulation quotient. This quotient distinguishes between states that eventually terminate in a state where x = y and the greatest common divisor is found, and the states that will never terminate, remaining in the class of non-terminating states indefinitely.

In the following, we survey two algorithms for computing bisimulation and, stutter-insensitive bisimulation quotients: the standard Paige-Tarjan algorithm for iterative partition refinement [66, 94] and a recent data-driven *bisimulation learning* approach based on counterexample-guided inductive synthesis [13].

Partition Refinement. To arrive at a valid bisimulation, partition refinement starts from the *label partition* $\simeq_L = \{(x, y) \mid L(x) = L(y)\}$ and iteratively refines the equivalence classes by identifying *splitters*. A splitter for a partition $\simeq$ is an

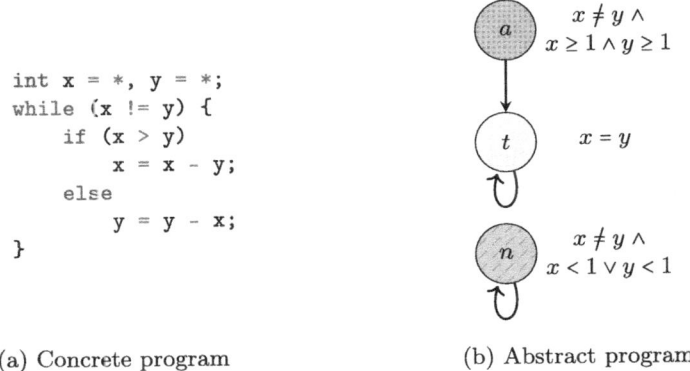

```
int x = *, y = *;
while (x != y) {
        if (x > y)
                x = x - y;
        else
                y = y - x;
}
```

(a) Concrete program   (b) Abstract program

Fig. 3. Stutter-insensitive bisimulation of the Euclidean algorithm, adapted from [13].

equivalence class C, where there exist two states $x \simeq y$ such that $T(x) \in C$ and $T(y) \notin C$. A splitter indicates that two related states exhibit dissimilar behavior and should not be in the same equivalence class. Therefore, the equivalence class $B \ni x, y$ is refined with respect to splitter C:

$$\text{Refine}(B, C) = \{B \cap \text{Pre}(C), B \setminus \text{Pre}(C)\} \setminus \emptyset,$$

where $\text{Pre}(C) = \{x \mid T(x) \in C\}$. Partition refinement iteratively refines the current partition until it is *stable* and no more splitters exist. The resulting partition is both valid and the coarsest bisimulation. Partition refinement runs in time linear to the size of the model. However, for large models, this can quickly become infeasible. For that reason, partition refinement was improved with on-the-fly partition refinement of the reachable state space and parallelisation [51, 80,81,84]. However, when adapted to stutter-insensitive bisimulation, partition refinement requires the computation of exact unbounded preimages through the transition function, which can be very costly. Therefore, we consider a data-driven approach specifically targeted to stutter-insensitive bisimulations, aiming to learn a valid partition by generalising from a small, finite set of sample states.

Bisimulation Learning. Bisimulation learning is a recent approach to computing stutter-insensitive bisimulations [13]. It builds on the observation that finite partitions can be characterised as state classifiers $f \colon \mathcal{X} \to \mathcal{C}$ from states to a finite set of classes, and finite stuttering as a *ranking functions* $h \colon \mathcal{X} \to \mathbb{N}$ which are bounded from below and strictly decrease along trajectories.

Theorem 3 ([13]). *Let $\mathcal{M}$ be a deterministic model. Suppose that there exist functions $f \colon \mathcal{X} \to \mathcal{C}$, $g \colon \mathcal{C} \to \mathcal{C}$, and $h_c \colon \mathcal{X} \to \mathbb{N}$ for each $c \in \mathcal{C}$ such that, $f(x) = f(y)$ implies that $L(x) = L(y)$, and for every $c \neq d \in \mathcal{C}$ and $x \in \mathcal{X}$, it holds that:*

$$f(x) = c \wedge g(c) = d \implies f(T(x)) = d \vee [f(T(x)) = c \wedge h_c(x) > h_c(T(x))], \quad (8)$$
$$f(x) = c \wedge f(T(x)) = d \implies g(c) = d. \quad (9)$$

Then, $\simeq_f$ defined as $\simeq_f = \{(x, y) \mid f(x) = f(y)\}$ is a stutter-insensitive bisimulation on $\mathcal{M}$ and $T_{\simeq_f}(f^{-1}[c]) = \{f^{-1}[g(c)]\}$.

Functions f and g in Theorem 3 describe the quotient space and transition function. The ranking functions $\{h_c\}_{c \in \mathcal{C}}$ ensure that for each equivalence class, all states eventually enter the same equivalence class after stuttering for a finite amount of time or remain within their equivalence class indefinitely. To derive suitable functions, bisimulation learning employs a *learner* and a *verifier*, implementing a counterexample-guided inductive synthesis (CEGIS) loop [118]. Both components use an SMT solver, and the algorithm maintains a finite set of sample states. The learner seeks parameters for function templates for f, g, and $\{h_c\}_{c \in \mathcal{C}}$ such that Conditions 8 and 9 are satisfied for the sample set. The verifier seeks an assignment for a counterexample state for which the current functions violate the conditions. If a counterexample is found, it is added to the sample set and the learner is retrained. If no counterexample can be found, the verifier proves that the functions provided by the learner induce a valid stutter-insensitive bisimulation quotient.

Figure 4 shows the iterative process of bisimulation learning for the Euclidean algorithm from Fig. 3. While bisimulation learning is not guaranteed to be more efficient than partition refinement, it has been shown to be beneficial for large or infinite state models with long stuttering intervals, which are challenging for partition refinement or classical verification algorithms alone [13].

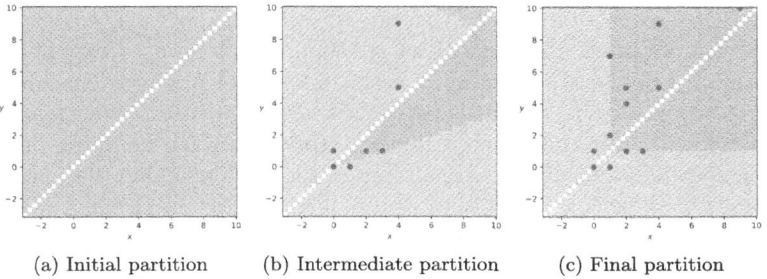

(a) Initial partition   (b) Intermediate partition   (c) Final partition

Fig. 4. Iterative process of bisimulation learning, adapted from [13].

Abstractions for Non-deterministic Models. Although we introduced the concepts of abstraction and (stutter-insensitive) bisimulation in the context of deterministic models, these definitions also apply to non-deterministic models. In fact, bisimulation (stutter-insensitive bisimulation) serves as the abstraction that precisely preserves all branching-time properties that can be expressed in CTL

(CTL$_{\backslash \bigcirc}$) [29,44]. Partition refinement naturally extends to non-deterministic models, while bisimulation learning, as presented above, is only applicable to deterministic models. However, by restricting the ranking functions to constants and effectively turning the definition into standard bisimulation, the procedure becomes applicable to non-deterministic models [13].

Abstractions are applied to various kinds of non-deterministic models to reduce their complexity and to enable their efficient analysis. Relevant instances are Joost-Pieter's contributions to models of concurrent systems, applying notions of bisimulation to show the linearisability of multi-thread models [134–136].

3.2   Abstractions for Stochastic Control Models

There has been substantial work in the area of formal methods concerning the development of different types of stochastic similarity relations, which are employed to associate the probabilistic behaviour of a concrete model to that of its abstraction, and have been more recently studied for continuous-space models [1,95]. Early on, similarity relations over finite-state stochastic models via exact notions of probabilistic bisimulation relations have been introduced by [67,77].

One can construct finite abstractions of probabilistic models in the form of finite MDPs (see Sect. 2.3). These abstractions are approximate descriptions of the concrete models, in which each discrete state corresponds to a set of continuous states of the concrete models. As it will be discussed below, quantitative notions of approximate bisimulation can be drawn between the abstract model and its concrete counterpart [9,125]. Notions of formal abstractions of probabilistic models are well known in the finite-state context: [69,72] are instances of Joost-Pieter's contributions to this line of research.

Since the obtained abstractions of continuous MDPs are actually finite in the cardinality of the state space, one can employ algorithmic machinery and existing software tools to automatically synthesise controllers, which can then be applied (refined) over the concrete models, thus enforcing complex properties, including specifications expressed as temporal logical formulae (e.g., in PCTL). One modern and elegant instance of probabilistic model checker is STORM [50], which Joost-Pieter has co-developed.

Let us now provide a few technical details. A concrete model $\mathcal{M}$ is approximated by a *finite* $\widehat{\mathcal{M}}$, albeit at the cost of quantifiable approximation errors. To construct such an approximation, one first constructs a finite partition of the state set $\mathcal{X} = \bigcup \mathsf{X}_i$ and the input set $\mathcal{U} = \bigcup \mathsf{U}_i$. Then arbitrary "representative points" $\bar{x}_i \in \mathsf{X}_i$ and $\bar{\nu}_i \in \mathsf{U}_i$ are selected as abstract states and inputs. Finally, the transition probabilities p_{ij} in the finite MDP $\widehat{\mathcal{M}}$ are computed according to the marginalisation of the transition kernel over partitions X_j, conditioned over pairs of representative points $(\bar{x}_i, \bar{\nu}_i)$.

We now present bounds on the difference between the satisfaction probability of logic properties over a given model $\mathcal{M}$ and its corresponding finite abstraction $\widehat{\mathcal{M}}$. This type of probabilistic closeness requires some assumptions on $\mathcal{M}$ that can be potentially relaxed, as comprehensively discussed in [119, 125]. We start with a Lipschitz continuity assumption on the stochastic kernel of the MDP.

Definition 10. *The MDP* $\mathcal{M}$ *endowed with a Lipschitz continuous stochastic kernel, namely* $P(x, u, \cdot)$ *admits a density function* $t_s(\bar{x}|x, u)$ *satisfying the following inequality for some constant* $\mathscr{H} \geq 0$:

$$|t_s(\bar{x} \,|\, x, u) - t_s(\bar{x} \,|\, x', u')| \leq \bar{\mathscr{H}}(\|x - x'\| + \|u - u'\|), \tag{10}$$

for all $x, x', \bar{x} \in \mathcal{X}$ *and all* $u, u' \in \mathcal{U}$. *If the policy for the MDP is instead given as* $\nu : \mathcal{X} \to \mathcal{U}$, *we simply define the Lipschitz constant of the stochastic kernel by* $\mathscr{H}$, *where*

$$|t_s(\bar{x} \,|\, x, \nu(x)) - t_s(\bar{x} \,|\, x', \nu(x'))| \leq \mathscr{H}\|x - x'\|, \tag{11}$$

for all $x, x', \bar{x} \in \mathcal{X}$.

Theorem 4. *Let* $\mathcal{M}$ *be a continuous-space MDP and* $\widehat{\mathcal{M}}$ *be its finite-state abstraction, as introduced above. Assume that the original model* $\mathcal{M}$ *is Lipschitz continuous, as per Definition 10. For a given PCTL logic specification* φ, *and for any policy* $\hat{\nu}$ *that preserves the Markov property for the closed-loop* $\widehat{\mathcal{M}}$ *(i.e., model* $\widehat{\mathcal{M}}$ *fed by input* $\hat{\nu}(\cdot)$, *which is denoted by* $\widehat{\mathcal{M}}_{\hat{\nu}}$), *the probabilistic closeness between two models is as follows:*

$$|\mathbb{P}(\mathcal{M}_{\hat{\nu}} \vDash \varphi) - \mathbb{P}(\widehat{\mathcal{M}}_{\hat{\nu}} \vDash \varphi)| \leq \lambda, \tag{12}$$

with $\lambda = T_d \delta \mathscr{H} \mathscr{L}_b$, *where* T_d *is the finite-time horizon of the formula,* δ *is the state discretisation parameter,* $\mathscr{H}$ *is the Lipschitz constant of the density* t_s *of the stochastic kernel under policy* $\hat{\nu}$ *as in* (11), *and* $\mathscr{L}_b$ *is the Lebesgue measure (the "volume") of the state space. Moreover, the difference between the optimal probabilities of satisfying a given LTL specification* φ *by the two models is bounded by*

$$\left| \sup_{\nu} \mathbb{P}(\mathcal{M}_\nu \vDash \varphi) - \sup_{\hat{\nu}} \mathbb{P}(\widehat{\mathcal{M}}_{\hat{\nu}} \vDash \varphi) \right| \leq \bar{\lambda}, \tag{13}$$

with $\bar{\lambda} = T_d \delta \bar{\mathscr{H}} \mathscr{L}_b$, *where* $\bar{\mathscr{H}}$ *is the Lipschitz constant of the density* t_s *of the stochastic kernel over the state* x *and input* ν *as in* (10).

Notice that in establishing the relationship in (13), we provide a way to synthesise policies over the abstract model, that can be refined over the concrete $\mathcal{M}$, whereas in (12) we assume to be using the very same controller $\hat{\nu}$ (in closed loop), hence such relationship can be useful for verification goals. Broader results on controller synthesis can be found in [63].

Remark 3. The results in Equations (12)–(13) clearly are meaningful solely for finite-horizon specifications: the work in [125] extends them to infinite-horizon ones. The bounds in (12)–(13) are of practical use only when tight: work in [119] looks at computational implementation of tighter bounds, or of bounds under weaker assumptions on $\mathcal{M}$. These abstraction procedures have been implemented in a number of software tools [10], such as FAUST [120] and StocHy [30] - the latter employing interval Markov chains as the model class for the abstraction. Alternative algorithms are discussed in [10, 78]. Ongoing recent work pursues abstractions based on samples, which relax the assumed knowledge of the dynamics of $\mathcal{M}$ [78]. □

We next tailor the statement in (12) to frame the abstraction we have put forward as an approximate probabilistic bisimulation [9], a notion that aligns with the early concept introduced in [77] and that has more recently been much extended in [63] towards stochastic models with inputs and partial observations.

Corollary 1. *Pick* $\varphi = \bigcirc \mathsf{X}_i$, *for any* i. *Then Eq.* (12) *becomes*

$$|P(x, \mathsf{X}_i) - \mathbb{P}(\bar{x}_j, \mathsf{X}_i)| \leq \lambda,$$

for any j *and where* $x \in \mathsf{X}_j$. *This says that* $\widehat{\mathcal{M}}$ *is a* λ-*approximate (forward) probabilistic bisimulation of* $\mathcal{M}$, *as per [9, 77].*

The construction of finite abstractions of SHSs has been initially proposed by [7] and used for formal verification and synthesis. This work investigates probabilistic safety and reachability over a finite-time horizon for a general class of discrete-time SHS with control inputs. The proposed framework characterises the set of initial conditions providing a certain probabilistic guarantee that the model will keep evolving within a desired 'safe' region of the state space in terms of a value function, and determines 'maximally safe' Markov policies via dynamic programming over the finite abstract MDP. An improved gridding scheme, which is adaptive and sequential, for the abstraction and verification of stochastic processes is proposed by [119]. The abstract model is constructed as a Markov chain using an adaptive gridding algorithm that conforms to the underlying dynamics of the model and thus mitigates the curse of dimensionality unavoidably related to the partitioning procedure.

We have mentioned that [7] was the first work to introduce a formal, finite approximation of a continuous-space probabilistic model, to be employed for model checking goals. This contribution put to good use the insight of Joost-Pieter in formal verification, by proposing a new algorithm to approximately model check the concrete model, via its abstraction, over PCTL formulae. This abstraction was later framed as an *approximate probabilistic bisimulation*, as we mentioned before. The subsequent work in [6] introduced the notion of product construction between a continuous-space probabilistic model and a deterministic finite automaton (DFA), later extended to a policy synthesis problem over a fragment of omega-regular properties in [126]. Effectively, the product construction entails a stochastic hybrid system (SHS), a known modelling framework widely studied at those time. Work on controller synthesis for infinite-horizon specifications over stochastic and hybrid models was then generalised in [127]. The verification underpinnings of all these work have been bolstered by Joost-Pieter's contributions.

Similarly, the work in [52] studied robust PCTL model checking algorithms, implicitly employing *interval* Markov models (mentioned above) as approximate abstractions of concrete MCs. This idea was later pursued in numerous approaches for abstractions, such as [31], and in the software tool StocHy [30].

4   Proof Certificates

The behavioural properties of a dynamical model, as in (1), can be investigated from different perspectives and with diverse approaches: either analytical (e.g., via local linearisation, evaluation of eigenvalues), or computational ones (e.g., via reach-set computation, or via formal abstractions, as pursued in the previous section). In general, non-linearity in dynamical models is difficult to deal with analytically and automatically, whereas abstraction-based techniques are known to be prone to state-space explosion. On account of these possible limitations, alternative approaches that are *indirect* or *sufficient* can mitigate stated shortcomings: they provide a proof that the model actually fulfils a given requirement in the form of a *certificate*. The onus thus shifts to finding, or to synthesising, a real-valued function defined over the state space with proper characteristics. In control theory, a celebrated instance of indirect methods is the synthesis of Lyapunov functions [3,15], whereby one ought to hand-craft a bespoke energy function, oftentimes based on intuition and on physical properties of the underlying dynamical model.

Proof certificates offer a direct approach to model checking that avoids the construction of finite abstractions, and as such avoids the state space explosion that is intrinsically associated to it. While abstractions (simulations and bisimulations) construct finite graphs that are in correspondence with the original model, and enable their analysis via graph algorithms, proof certificates seek to construct functions that constitute sufficient conditions for the model to satisfy a property of interest. For diverse models and properties, different certificates exist, and different algorithms are correspondingly available to compute such functions, which include methods based on computational algebraic geometry (including sum-of-squares [99] and Positivstellensätze [35,115], which are techniques recently employed by Joost-Pieter and colleagues [129]) as well as recent machine-learning methods based on neural certificates [5,11,20,39,79,138–140].

In [54], we have presented a number of properties (or requirements) for dynamical models defined over their trajectories, alongside definitions of corresponding certificates, whose existence serve as *sufficient conditions* for the satisfaction of the desired properties. Synthesis was in practice pursued via a data-driven approach, grounded on neural network training.

In Sect. 4.1 we zoom in on certificates for *safety* certification in *deterministic models* (cf. Definition 1 and Eq. (2)), which include *barrier certificates*, and then discuss certificates for *liveness*, focusing on non-deterministic software models. In Sect. 4.2, we examine certificates for probabilistic models, including probabilistic and control-theoretic generalisations of barrier certificates, as well as supermartingale proof rules for liveness properties.

4.1   Proof Certificates for Deterministic Models

Barrier Certificates for Safety Certification of Deterministic Models.
We consider models $\mathcal{M}$ described by Eq. (1), where $X \in \mathcal{X} \subseteq \mathbb{R}^n$ is a variable
representing the state of the model, and where $X_0 \in \mathcal{X}_\mathcal{I} \subseteq \mathcal{X}$, a set of initial
conditions, and where we require $\mathsf{Update} : \mathcal{X} \to \mathcal{X}$ to be a transition function describing the model's dynamics. We define properties over trajectories of
dynamical models, and exemplify this with the case of *safety*.

Safety properties specify that no trajectory starting from an initial set $\mathcal{X}_\mathcal{I}$
may enter some unsafe set $\mathcal{X}_\mathcal{U}$; for continuous-time and discrete-time deterministic models, safety over an unbounded time horizon can be proved via *barrier*
certificates [107,108]. Here, we consider an unbounded-time safety specification,
again over discrete-time models - formally, trajectories ought to fulfil the following property:

$$\forall X_0 \in \mathcal{X}_\mathcal{I}, \, \forall t \in \mathbb{N} \colon X_t \in \mathcal{X}_\mathcal{U}^{\mathsf{C}}. \tag{14}$$

Consider a dynamical model, a compact unsafe set $\mathcal{X}_\mathcal{U}$ and compact initial
set $\mathcal{X}_\mathcal{I}$. A function $B : \mathcal{X} \subset \mathbb{R}^n \to \mathbb{R}$ is a barrier certificate if the following holds:

$$
\begin{align}
B(X) &\leq 0 & \forall X \in \mathcal{X}_\mathcal{I}, \tag{15a} \\
B(X) &> 0 & \forall X \in \mathcal{X}_\mathcal{U}, \tag{15b} \\
B(\mathsf{Update}(X)) &\leq B(X) & \forall X \in \mathcal{X} \setminus (\mathcal{X}_\mathcal{I} \cup \mathcal{X}_\mathcal{U}). \tag{15c}
\end{align}
$$

Put informally, we require that the function B is initially negative, is strictly positive within the unsafe set and is non-increasing across transitions from outside
of the (initial and) unsafe set. If a barrier certificate is found, then no trajectory
of the deterministic transition system $\mathcal{M}$ can reach the unsafe set when started
within the initial set (Theorem 5).

Theorem 5 (Soundness of Barrier Certificates for Safety). *Consider a
deterministic transition system $\mathcal{M}$ and let a corresponding barrier certificate B
be given (or found). Then the trajectory of $\mathcal{M}$ satisfies the safety requirement in
(14), namely the solution, starting from any initial state $X_0 \in \mathcal{X}_I$, does not ever
reach $\mathcal{X}_U$ within any time $t \in \mathbb{N}$.*

Barrier certificates admit extensions to non-deterministic models, specified according to Eq. (2). Under an agential/angelic interpretation of non-
deterministic inputs, *control certificates* (e.g. control barrier certificates, or control Lyapunov functions) can be synthesised [124]. We shall discuss details of this,
along with model extensions from deterministic transition systems to stochastic
control models, in Sect. 4.2.

Liveness Certificates for Non-deterministic Models. We now consider
proof certificates for liveness properties of non-deterministic models, focusing on
non-deterministic software where the program state X_t (cf. Eq. (2)) ranges over
a countably infinite state space (the space of valuations of program variables),

and non-deterministic inputs U_t reflect external factors outside the program's control (e.g. the behaviour of the operating system). As a concrete example, we might consider a device driver that invokes an operating system function to acquire a spin lock, and this function can either succeed (granting the device driver the resource), or fail, with the device driver executing a busy-waiting loop until it acquires the lock.

Ranking functions are a classic proof certificate for establishing that a program terminates for *all* non-deterministic inputs [16,46,48,58,103], but when applied directly, may be too conservative for practical verification of non-deterministic software. Since a program's temporal behaviour depends on its non-deterministic environment (e.g., the operating system), it may not meet a liveness specification, such as termination, against every possible behaviour of this environment. For example, a device driver may fail to terminate if the operating system indefinitely withholds a spin lock. Therefore, liveness properties must typically be qualified by *compassion requirements* upon the behaviour of the environment [47,102], which often constitute a reactivity assumption (e.g. repeated attempts to acquire a spin lock will eventually succeed).

An influential technique for verifying fair termination under compassion requirements (which subsumes verification of LTL properties) is the use of disjunctively well-founded transition invariants [47,104]; these consist of finitely many well-founded relations that cover the transitive closure of the transition relation of a suitably instrumented program derived from the product of the non-deterministic model, and an automaton representing the temporal property [47,128]. We note that constructing such an invariant uses a ranking function synthesis procedure to certify the well-foundedness of the relations within the transition invariant (cf. [47, Figure 6] and [62,82]).

4.2 Proof Certificates for Probabilistic Models

Control Barrier Functions for Safe Control of Stochastic Models. In this section we discuss discretisation-free approaches to the safe control of Markov decision processes, based on barrier certificates that have been proposed in recent literature.

Work in this domain follows seminal theoretical [106] and computational [2, 55] contributions. We first formally define control barrier certificates [78, Definition 6.1] for finite-horizon safe control of Markov decision processes.

Definition 11 ([78]). *Consider an MDP $\mathcal{M}$ with sets $\mathcal{X}_I, \mathcal{X}_U \subseteq X$ that are respectively the initial and unsafe sets of the model. A function $B : \mathcal{X} \to \mathbb{R}_{\geq 0}$ is called a control barrier certificate (CBC) for $\mathcal{M}$ if there exist constants $\eta, \beta \in \mathbb{R}_{\geq 0}$ with $\beta > \eta$ such that*

$$B(X) \leq \eta, \qquad \forall X \in \mathcal{X}_I, \tag{16}$$

$$B(X) \geq \beta, \qquad \forall X \in \mathcal{X}_U, \tag{17}$$

and $\forall X \in \mathcal{X}$, $\exists \nu \in \mathcal{U}$, such that

$$\int_{\mathcal{X}} P(X, \nu, \mathrm{d}y) \ B(y) \leq \max\left\{\kappa B(X), c\right\} \qquad (18)$$

for constants $0 < \kappa \leq 1$ and $c \in \mathbb{R}_{\geq 0}$.[2]

Remark 4. Note that the existential quantifier for the condition in (18) implies the presence of a memory-less deterministic feedback controller $\nu(\cdot) : \mathcal{X} \to \mathcal{U}$ for a model satisfying the conditions, namely, one that maps a given state $X \in \mathcal{X}$ to an input $\nu(X) \in \mathcal{U}$ that witnesses Eq. (18). This certificate can be thus tailored to (input-less) Markov chains, by disregarding the existential quantification over the non-determinism in the update function (i.e. by treating $\mathcal{U}$ as trivially containing a single point at each state).   □

Employing Definition 11, one can propose an upper bound on the probability that the MDP reaches an unsafe region over a finite time horizon, as presented in the next theorem. Note that the requirement $\beta > \eta$ is needed in order to propose meaningful probabilistic bounds.

Theorem 6 ([78]). *Consider an MDP $\mathcal{M}$ and let a CBC B be given. Then the probability that a trajectory of $\mathcal{M}$, starting from any initial state $X_0 \in \mathcal{X}_I$ and reaches $\mathcal{X}_U$ under the policy $\nu(\cdot)$ (associated with the CBC B) within the time interval $[0, T_d]$ is bounded by $\bar{\delta}$, namely*

$$\mathrm{Pr}^{\nu}\left(X_k \in \mathcal{X}_{\mathcal{U}} \text{ for some } 0 \leq k \leq T_d \mid X_0 \in \mathcal{X}_I\right) \leq \bar{\delta}, \qquad (19)$$

where $\bar{\delta} = \frac{\eta + c T_d}{\beta}$.

The statement above provides an upper bound on the probability that the solution process of $\mathcal{M}$ reaches unsafe regions within a *finite* time horizon. One can generalise the proposed results to an *infinite* time horizon (as aligned with the result in Sect. 4.1), provided that the constant $c = 0$, as stated in the following corollary.

Corollary 2. ([78]) *Let $\mathcal{M}$ be an MDP and suppose B is a CBC for $\mathcal{M}$ with $c = 0$ in (18). Then the probability that the trajectory of $\mathcal{M}$ starts from any initial state $X_0 \in \mathcal{X}_I$ and reaches $\mathcal{X}_U$ under the policy $\nu(\cdot)$ is bounded by*

$$\mathrm{Pr}^{\nu}\left(X_k \in \mathcal{X}_{\mathcal{U}} \text{ for some } k \geq 0 \mid X_0 \in \mathcal{X}_I\right) \leq \frac{\eta}{\beta}. \qquad (20)$$

The bounds in (19) and (20) are obtained by leveraging supermartingale inequalities [78], which is what condition (18) induces. Closely related to barrier certificates for stochastic models are supermartingale proof rules for infinite-horizon safety properties developed in the context of probabilistic (randomised) programs, such as repulsing supermartingales and variants thereof

---

[2] We note that the notation $P(X, \nu, \mathrm{d}y)$ denotes the density function of the measure $P(X, \nu, \cdot)$ as defined by Eq. (6), and refer the reader to [53, Section 1.2, Example 1.2.4, p.7] for more details.

[25, 37, 40, 73, 122], which build upon results in the theory of general state-space Markov chains (e.g. [53, Corollary 4.4.7, p.87]). Such certificates may be applied to certifying quantitative upper- and lower-bounds on the probability that a trajectory will leave a particular subset of the state space. While such bounds may be useful in their own right, they may also be integrated with proof certificates for co-safety properties, e.g. to establish lower bounds on the probability of probabilistic reachability, cf. Remark 5. We thus turn to certificates for more general liveness properties, starting with proof certificates for almost-sure reachability, and then extending towards obligation properties, recurrence, persistence, and finally towards arbitrary reactivity and ω-regular properties.

Ranking Supermartingales for Almost-Sure Reachability. While barrier certificates establish safety properties (namely, that *globally* an unsafe state is not visited), different certificates are needed to prove liveness properties. The most primitive liveness property that one might try to verify is that of almost-sure reachability, namely the property that *eventually*, the Markov chain enters a desirable "target" subset $\mathcal{X}_T$ of its state space $\mathcal{X}$. In the context of probabilistic (randomised) programs, a natural property of this flavour is *almost-sure termination* (AST) [32, 86], namely, the question of whether a probabilistic program will halt with probability 1. For a probabilistic program that halts with probability 1, we may further ask the question of whether the number of execution steps prior to halting is finite in expectation (which is called *positive almost-sure termination* (PAST), [57, Definition 5.3]).

To prove that a Markov chain eventually reaches a subset of the state space with probability 1, it suffices to provide a *ranking supermartingale* (Definition 12). This is a function V mapping any state $X \in \mathcal{X}$ of the Markov chain into a non-negative real $V(X)$, additionally satisfying the condition that its expected value at the next time step must be sufficiently lower than its current value:

Definition 12 (Ranking Supermartingale). *For a discrete-time Markov chain $\mathcal{M}$ with transition kernel P, for a constant $\epsilon > 0$ the function $V : \mathcal{X} \to \mathbb{R}_{\geq'}$ is an ϵ-ranking supermartingale for the target set $\mathcal{X}_T \subseteq S$*

$$\int_{\mathcal{X}} P(x, \mathrm{d}y)V(y) \leq V(X) - \epsilon, \quad \forall X \in \mathcal{X} \setminus \mathcal{X}_T. \tag{21}$$

Intuitively, the existence of such a function suggests that a trajectory of the Markov chain cannot remain outside of $\mathcal{X}_T$ indefinitely, thus proving the property of interest. Formally, one may leverage classic results relating to non-negative supermartingales [105, Theorem 22, p.148] to establish the following theorem (cf. [57, Lemma 5.5]):

Theorem 7 (Soundness of Ranking Supermartingales). *Let V be an ϵ-ranking supermartingale for the discrete-time Markov chain $\mathcal{M}$ for the target set $\mathcal{X}_T$. Then,*

1. with probability 1, a trajectory of $\mathcal{M}$ visits the set $\mathcal{X}_T$;

2. *the expected number of steps prior to the first visit to $\mathcal{X}_T$ of a trajectory initialised at state $X \in \mathcal{X}$ is no greater than $V(X)/\epsilon$.*

Remark 5. We remark that if we enforce requirement Eq. (21) over a subset $\mathcal{X}_{\mathrm{Inv}} = \mathcal{X} \setminus \mathcal{X}_{\mathcal{U}}$, where the probability of exiting $\mathcal{X}_{\mathrm{Inv}}$ (equivalently of entering $\mathcal{X}_U$) is bounded from above by $p \in (0,1)$ (e.g. via a suitable certificate for infinite-horizon safety yielding an upper bound similar to Corollary 2), then a trajectory remains within $\mathcal{X}_{\mathrm{Inv}}$ with probability at least $1 - p$. A certificate function V that satisfies the requirement Eq. (21) except quantified over states $X \in (\mathcal{X} \setminus \mathcal{X}_T) \cap \mathcal{X}_{\mathrm{Inv}}$ establishes that the set $\mathcal{X}_T$ is reached with probability at least $1 - p$ [37,40]. □

The existence of a ranking supermartingale establishes the property of *positive almost-sure termination*, namely, that the set $\mathcal{X}_T$ is reached in finite expected time. This fact by itself suffices to establish that the set $\mathcal{X}_T$ is reached with probability 1: namely, PAST implies AST ([105, Lemma 26, p.33]). It is also well known that the converse is not true [87, Eq. 1] and a Markov chain may reach a subset of the state space with probability 1, albeit requiring an infinite time to do so in expectation (which precludes the existence of a ranking supermartingale of the form of Definition 12 for certifying almost-sure reachability). In other words, while the proof rule (Definition 12) is known to be *complete* for the PAST problem [57, Theorem 5.8], it is *incomplete* for the question of AST.

This deficiency of the proof rule (Definition 12) as a technique for establishing almost-sure reachability has led to numerous extensions. One the one hand, extensions have attempted to devise more fine-grained ways of applying the result of Theorem 7, e.g. via *lexicographic* proof rules [14,38,123], which require one to provide multiple ranking supermartingales in a manner that exhibits a lexicographic decrease in expectation, which extends the completeness of the basic ranking supermartingale rule (cf. [14, Example 4.8]). A second strategy for addressing the incompleteness of the ranking supermartingale proof rule has been to consider alternative proof rules for almost-sure termination, which weaken the proof obligation of Eq. (21) and thus enjoy a greater degree of completeness: an example is with *antitone* ranking supermartingales [74], a direction which has seen key contributions from Joost-Pieter and colleagues [87].

Streett Supermartingales for Almost-Sure Reactivity. Proof rules based on ranking supermartingales have also been developed for stochastic control models in the form of Markov decision processes with demonic and angelic non-determinism [36,57], as introduced above. We also note that supermartingale-based proof rules have been devised for further linear-time properties, including reach-avoid (constrained reachability, or 'bounded until') requirements [20,140]. Although prior work has introduced supermartingale proof rules for almost-sure persistence and recurrence [33], these are too conservative for general reactivity properties (cf. [12, Example 1]).

A recent supermartingale proof rule (termed the *Streett supermartingale*, cf. [12, Theorem 2]) may be used to certify probability 1 satisfaction of an arbitrary ω-regular property (which subsume the LTL properties) for discrete-time

Markov chains over general state spaces. By representing the ω-regular property of interest as a deterministic Streett automaton (DSA, cf. [128, Section 2.1]), we reduce the almost-sure LTL verification problem to that of certifying almost-sure acceptance of a finite number of Streett pairs over a product Markov chain [6]. A Streett pair $(\mathcal{X}_A, \mathcal{X}_B)$ consists of two regions $\mathcal{X}_A, \mathcal{X}_B \subseteq \mathcal{X}$ of the state space $\mathcal{X}$ of the product Markov chain. A trajectory is accepted by a Streett pair if it either visits $\mathcal{X}_A$ finitely many times or it visits $\mathcal{X}_B$ infinitely often, which may be proved using a Streett supermartingale.

Definition 13 (Streett Supermartingale [12]). *For a discrete-time (product) Markov chain $\mathcal{M}$ with transition kernel P, for constants $\epsilon, M > 0$ the function $V : S \to \mathbb{R}_{\geq 0}$ is an $(\mathcal{X}_A, \mathcal{X}_B)$-Streett supermartingale if*

$$\int_{\mathcal{X}} P(x, \mathrm{d}y) V(y) \leq V(x) - \epsilon \cdot \mathbf{1}_{\mathcal{X}_A \setminus \mathcal{X}_B}(x) + M \cdot \mathbf{1}_{\mathcal{X}_B}(x), \quad \forall x \in \mathcal{X}. \qquad (22)$$

A Streett supermartingale has the property that it may *increase in expectation* over certain regions of the state space, dictated by the Streett pairs that were derived from the ω-regular property. Therefore, technically, it is a *nonnegative almost supermartingale* (cf. [113] and [12, Theorem 1]) that is sufficient to prove that, with probability 1, that a trajectory either visits $\mathcal{X}_A$ finitely often, or $\mathcal{X}_B$ infinitely often. A general Streett acceptance condition consists of a finite number of Streett pairs, with the requirement that a trajectory must be accepted by all of the Streett pairs. Thus, a general Streett acceptance condition is established by providing a Streett supermartingale for each Streett pair:

Theorem 8 (Soundness of Streett Supermartingales). *Let $\mathcal{M}$ be a discrete-time Markov chain and let $\{(\mathcal{X}_{A_i}, \mathcal{X}_{B_i}) : i = 1, \ldots, k\}$ be a Streett acceptance condition. If every Streett pair admits a Streett supermartingale, then $\mathcal{M}$ satisfies the acceptance condition almost surely:*

$$\Pr\left(\bigwedge_{i=1}^{k} \left(\sum_{t=0}^{\infty} \mathbf{1}_{\mathcal{X}_{A_i}}(X_t) < \infty \vee \sum_{t=0}^{\infty} \mathbf{1}_{\mathcal{X}_{B_i}}(X_t) = \infty \right) \right) = 1. \qquad (23)$$

While Streett supermartingales are, in theory, applicable to general stochastic processes and admit efficient proof construction given restrictions upon the model (cf. Sect. 4.3), the general question of whether a given general state-space Markov chain and ω-regular property admit a Streett supermartingale is undecidable. Over the past few decades, effort has been devoted to analysing classes of (finitely presented) discrete-time Markov chains, over countably infinite statespaces, for which ω-regular verification enjoys stronger decidability properties, such as recursive Markov chains (RMC) [56,137] and probabilistic pushdown automata (pPDA) [28,75,130]. Joost-Pieter and his colleagues have recently been at the forefront of analysing these questions, by developing decidability results for the quantitative ω-regular model checking problem for pPDA [131], and certificates for proving upper- and lower-bounds on quantitative properties of pPDA [132,133]. Relatedly, Joost-Pieter and colleagues have studied the question of strategy synthesis in infinite-state Markov decision processes represented by probabilistic programs with non-determinism [24].

4.3   Algorithmic Construction of Proof Certificates

As established in the previous sections, direct methods inspired by Lyapunov and supermartingale theory offer sufficient conditions for a wide range of specifications. These approaches translate the challenges of model checking and strategy synthesis to the alternative objective of identifying a function V that certifies a model's compliance with its specifications. Typically, these functions are represented as parameterised templates, thus reducing the search problem to finding a set of parameters that ensure that the corresponding function adheres to the relevant proof rules. Accordingly, given a template function $V : \mathcal{X} \times \Theta \to \mathbb{R}$, with parameter space Θ, constructing a proof certificate in the form of a potential function amounts to solving the following problem:

$$\exists \text{ parameter } \theta \in \Theta \ \forall \text{ states } x \in \mathcal{X} \ : \ \text{proof rule holds for } V(x; \theta).$$

Various numerical optimisation methods have been used for the synthesis of certificates, employing templates, e.g. polynomial templates for sum-of-squares convex problems [96,97] These techniques require models with polynomial dynamics and convexity assumptions. Alternative formulations include linear programs [114] and semi-algebraic computations [117]. The practical implementations of the mentioned synthesis approaches are numerically sensitive and the efficient implementations tend to be unsound.

Interest has thus grown in approaches for synthesis that can yield *provably-correct* certificates. A powerful technique to reason formally about correctness involves SMT-solving [22], which extends satisfiability (SAT) solving to richer algebraic theories, e.g., (non-)polynomial arithmetics. We remark upon the close connection between barrier certificates for (non-)deterministic transition systems and the notion of pure invariants, as the zero level-set of a barrier certificate is precisely a pure invariant for the model, and similar template-based strategies have been applied in this context [45]. *Counterexample-guided Inductive Synthesis* approaches (CEGIS) [118], leveraging SMT, have been used to synthesise certificates [111] and controllers [4] for dynamical models. Such techniques have been used first for stability certification of dynamical models using polynomial Lyapunov functions and later extended to more general requirements [15,111]. See [54] for an up-to-date survey. We should note that recent work by Joost-Pieter has also looked at leveraging inductive synthesis approaches across areas, both in the context of programs [18] and of controllers for Markov Decision Processes [19].

Neural certificates extend CEGIS approaches with templates based on neural networks, which are both amenable to efficient stochastic gradient descent learning algorithms and compatible with symbolic reasoning algorithms for their formal verification. Seminal work introduced the idea of using neural networks to represent Lyapunov functions [83,109]. This concept led the development of numerous numerical algorithms for the training of Lyapunov functions represented as neural networks [93,100,110,112,116,121], and subsequently their coupling with symbolic reasoning algorithms to guarantee soundness of the result [3,34]. Formal verification with neural certificates has been applied to the stability, reachability and safety analysis of continuous- and discrete-time systems [17,41,42,92], as well as to the termination analysis of computer programs [60]. Neural certificate approaches for probabilistic reasoning operate on a similar principle, extending it to supermartingale-like proof rules, as discussed in the previous sections. Initially introduced for the almost-sure termination analysis of probabilistic programs [5], neural supermartingale certificates have since been successfully applied to almost-sure stability verification and control [20,79], and extended to quantitative safety and reach-avoidance verification [11,85,139,140].

5   Reflections on the Work by Joost-Pieter Katoen

This contribution has attempted to provide a crisp presentation of a unified view of models and of analytical techniques across the areas of formal verification and control theory. In particular, we have provided models that have been useful to describe both certain classes of reactive software programs, as well as general dynamical and control systems - as such, this modelling framework has been relevant for work in the area of Cyber-Physical Systems. We have furthermore presented two alternative verification approaches, namely one based on computing quantitative finite abstractions (which allow leveraging off-the-shelf model checking tools), and a second one that aims at synthesising sufficient proofs (certificates) for the validity of given specifications. Both of these approaches inherit ideas from the areas of model checking and of control theory, and indeed can be used under different semantics of non-determinism, whether demonic (model checking) or angelic (strategy synthesis).

The work of Joost-Pieter Katoen, stemming from the model checking community, has been instrumental to bridge across the two areas of formal methods and control theory, and has proven to be influential on multiple fronts in the context of work on quantitative model checking and synthesis of hybrid systems and CPS. We have detailed specific contributions that are exemplar of his cross-disciplinary work, with particular emphasis on uncertain models with probabilistic behaviour.

References

1. Abate, A.: Approximation metrics based on probabilistic bisimulations for general state-space Markov processes: a survey. Electron. Notes Theor. Comput. Sci. **297**, 3–25 (2013)
2. Abate, A., Ahmed, D., Edwards, A., Giacobbe, M., Peruffo, A.: FOSSIL: a software tool for the formal synthesis of Lyapunov functions and barrier certificates using neural networks. In: Proceedings of HSCC, pp. 1–11 (2021)
3. Abate, A., Ahmed, D., Giacobbe, M., Peruffo, A.: Formal synthesis of Lyapunov neural networks. IEEE Control Syst. Lett. **5**(3), 773–778 (2021)
4. Abate, A., et al.: Automated formal synthesis of provably safe digital controllers for continuous plants. Acta Informatica **57**(3), 223–244 (2020)

5. Abate, A., Giacobbe, M., Roy, D.: Learning probabilistic termination proofs. In: Silva, A., Leino, K.R.M. (eds.) CAV 2021. LNCS, vol. 12760, pp. 3–26. Springer, Cham (2021). https://doi.org/10.1007/978-3-030-81688-9_1

6. Abate, A., Katoen, J.P., Mereacre, A.: Quantitative automata model checking of autonomous stochastic hybrid systems. In: Proceedings of the 14th ACM International Conference on Hybrid Systems: Computation and Control, Chicago, IL, pp. 83–92 (2011)

7. Abate, A., Katoen, J., Lygeros, J., Prandini, M.: Approximate model checking of stochastic hybrid systems. Eur. J. Control. **16**(6), 624–641 (2010)

8. Abate, A., Prandini, M., Lygeros, J., Sastry, S.: Probabilistic reachability and safety for controlled discrete time stochastic hybrid systems. Automatica **44**(11), 2724–2734 (2008)

9. Abate, A., Kwiatkowska, M., Norman, G., Parker, D.: Probabilistic model checking of labelled Markov processes via finite approximate bisimulations. In: van Breugel, F., Kashefi, E., Palamidessi, C., Rutten, J. (eds.) Horizons of the Mind. A Tribute to Prakash Panangaden. LNCS, vol. 8464, pp. 40–58. Springer, Cham (2014). https://doi.org/10.1007/978-3-319-06880-0_2

10. Abate, A., et al.: ARCH-COMP21 category report: stochastic models. In: 8th International Workshop on Applied Verification of Continuous and Hybrid Systems, pp. 55–89 (2021)

11. Abate, A., Edwards, A., Giacobbe, M., Punchihewa, H., Roy, D.: Quantitative verification with neural networks. In: CONCUR. LIPIcs, vol. 279, pp. 22:1–22:18. Schloss Dagstuhl - Leibniz-Zentrum für Informatik (2023)

12. Abate, A., Giacobbe, M., Roy, D.: Stochastic omega-regular verification and control with supermartingales. In: Gurfinkel, A., Ganesh, V. (eds.) CAV 2024. LNCS, vol. 14683, pp. 395–419. Springer, Cham (2024). https://doi.org/10.1007/978-3-031-65633-0_18

13. Abate, A., Giacobbe, M., Schnitzer, Y.: Bisimulation learning. In: Gurfinkel, A., Ganesh, V. (eds.) CAV 2024. LNCS, vol. 14683, pp. 161–183. Springer, Cham (2024). https://doi.org/10.1007/978-3-031-65633-0_8

14. Agrawal, S., Chatterjee, K., Novotný, P.: Lexicographic ranking supermartingales: an efficient approach to termination of probabilistic programs. CoRR abs/1709.04037 (2017)

15. Ahmed, D., Peruffo, A., Abate, A.: Automated and sound synthesis of lyapunov functions with SMT solvers. In: TACAS 2020. LNCS, vol. 12078, pp. 97–114. Springer, Cham (2020). https://doi.org/10.1007/978-3-030-45190-5_6

16. Alias, C., Darte, A., Feautrier, P., Gonnord, L.: Multi-dimensional rankings, program termination, and complexity bounds of flowchart programs. In: Cousot, R., Martel, M. (eds.) SAS 2010. LNCS, vol. 6337, pp. 117–133. Springer, Heidelberg (2010). https://doi.org/10.1007/978-3-642-15769-1_8

17. Anand, M., Zamani, M.: Formally verified neural network control barrier certificates for unknown systems. IFAC-PapersOnLine **56**(2), 2431–2436 (2023). 22nd IFAC World Congress

18. Andriushchenko, R., Češka, M., Junges, S., Katoen, J.-P., Stupinský, Š: PAYNT: a tool for inductive synthesis of probabilistic programs. In: Silva, A., Leino, K.R.M. (eds.) CAV 2021. LNCS, vol. 12759, pp. 856–869. Springer, Cham (2021). https://doi.org/10.1007/978-3-030-81685-8_40

19. Andriushchenko, R., Češka, M., Junges, S., Katoen, J.P.: Inductive synthesis of finite-state controllers for pomdps. In: Cussens, J., Zhang, K. (eds.) Proceedings of the Thirty-Eighth Conference on Uncertainty in Artificial Intelligence. Proceedings of Machine Learning Research, vol. 180, pp. 85–95 (2022)

20. Ansaripour, M., Chatterjee, K., Henzinger, T.A., Lechner, M., Zikelic, D.: Learning provably stabilizing neural controllers for discrete-time stochastic systems. In: André, É., Sun, J. (eds.) ATVA 2023. LNCS, vol. 14215, pp. 357–379. Springer, Cham (2023). https://doi.org/10.1007/978-3-031-45329-8_17
21. Baier, C., Katoen, J.: Principles of Model Checking. MIT Press, Cambridge (2008)
22. Barrett, C., Stump, A., Tinelli, C., et al.: The SMT-LIB standard: version 2.0. In: Proceedings of the 8th International Workshop on Satisfiability Modulo Theories (Edinburgh, UK), vol. 13, p. 14 (2010)
23. Barthe, G., Gordon, A., Katoen, J.P., McIver, A.: Challenges and trends in probabilistic programming: (dagstuhl seminar 15181). Dagstuhl Reports 5(4), 123–141 (2015)
24. Batz, K., Biskup, T.J., Katoen, J., Winkler, T.: Programmatic strategy synthesis: resolving nondeterminism in probabilistic programs. Proc. ACM Program. Lang. 8(POPL), 2792–2820 (2024)
25. Batz, K., Chen, M., Junges, S., Kaminski, B.L., Katoen, J., Matheja, C.: Probabilistic program verification via inductive synthesis of inductive invariants. In: Sankaranarayanan, S., Sharygina, N. (eds.) TACAS 2023. LNCS, vol. 13994, pp. 410–429. Springer, Cham (2023). https://doi.org/10.1007/978-3-031-30820-8_25
26. Bertsekas, D.P., Shreve, S.E.: Stochastic Optimal Control: The Discrete-Time Case. Athena Scientific (1996)
27. Bouajjani, A., Fernandez, J.-C., Halbwachs, N.: Minimal model generation. In: Clarke, E.M., Kurshan, R.P. (eds.) CAV 1990. LNCS, vol. 531, pp. 197–203. Springer, Heidelberg (1991). https://doi.org/10.1007/BFb0023733
28. Brázdil, T., Esparza, J., Kiefer, S., Kucera, A.: Analyzing probabilistic pushdown automata. Formal Methods Syst. Des. 43(2), 124–163 (2013)
29. Browne, M.C., Clarke, E.M., Grumberg, O.: Characterizing finite kripke structures in propositional temporal logic. Theor. Comput. Sci. 59, 115–131 (1988)
30. Cauchi, N., Abate, A.: StocHy: automated verification and synthesis of stochastic processes. In: Vojnar, T., Zhang, L. (eds.) TACAS 2019. LNCS, vol. 11428, pp. 247–264. Springer, Cham (2019). https://doi.org/10.1007/978-3-030-17465-1_14
31. Cauchi, N., Laurenti, L., Lahijanian, M., Abate, A., Kwiatkowska, M., Cardelli, L.: Efficiency through uncertainty: scalable formal synthesis for stochastic hybrid systems. In: Proceedings of HSCC, pp. 240–251 (2019)
32. Chakarov, A., Sankaranarayanan, S.: Probabilistic program analysis with martingales. In: Sharygina, N., Veith, H. (eds.) CAV 2013. LNCS, vol. 8044, pp. 511–526. Springer, Heidelberg (2013). https://doi.org/10.1007/978-3-642-39799-8_34
33. Chakarov, A., Voronin, Y.-L., Sankaranarayanan, S.: Deductive proofs of almost sure persistence and recurrence properties. In: Chechik, M., Raskin, J.-F. (eds.) TACAS 2016. LNCS, vol. 9636, pp. 260–279. Springer, Heidelberg (2016). https://doi.org/10.1007/978-3-662-49674-9_15
34. Chang, Y.C., Roohi, N., Gao, S.: Neural Lyapunov control. In: Advances in Neural Information Processing Systems, vol. 32 (2019)
35. Chatterjee, K., Fu, H., Goharshady, A.K.: Termination analysis of probabilistic programs through positivstellensatz's. In: Chaudhuri, S., Farzan, A. (eds.) CAV 2016. LNCS, vol. 9779, pp. 3–22. Springer, Cham (2016). https://doi.org/10.1007/978-3-319-41528-4_1
36. Chatterjee, K., Fu, H., Novotný, P., Hasheminezhad, R.: Algorithmic analysis of qualitative and quantitative termination problems for affine probabilistic programs. In: POPL, pp. 327–342. ACM (2016)

37. Chatterjee, K., Goharshady, A.K., Meggendorfer, T., Žikelić, D.: Sound and complete certificates for quantitative termination analysis of probabilistic programs. In: Shoham, S., Vizel, Y. (eds.) CAV 2022. LNCS, vol. 13371, pp. 55–78. Springer, Cham (2022). https://doi.org/10.1007/978-3-031-13185-1_4

38. Chatterjee, K., Goharshady, E.K., Novotný, P., Zárevúcky, J., Zikelic, D.: On lexicographic proof rules for probabilistic termination. CoRR abs/2108.02188 (2021)

39. Chatterjee, K., Henzinger, T.A., Lechner, M., Zikelic, D.: A learner-verifier framework for neural network controllers and certificates of stochastic systems. In: Sankaranarayanan, S., Sharygina, N. (eds.) TACAS 2023. LNCS, vol. 13993, pp. 3–25. Springer, Cham (2023). https://doi.org/10.1007/978-3-031-30823-9_1

40. Chatterjee, K., Novotný, P., Žikelić, D.: Stochastic invariants for probabilistic termination. In: POPL, pp. 145–160. ACM (2017)

41. Chen, S., Fazlyab, M., Morari, M., Pappas, G.J., Preciado, V.M.: Learning lyapunov functions for hybrid systems. In: HSCC, pp. 13:1–13:11. ACM (2021)

42. Chen, S., Fazlyab, M., Morari, M., Pappas, G.J., Preciado, V.M.: Learning region of attraction for nonlinear systems. In: 2021 60th IEEE Conference on Decision and Control (CDC), pp. 6477–6484. IEEE (2021)

43. Ciesinski, F., Größer, M.: On probabilistic computation tree logic. In: Baier, C., Haverkort, B.R., Hermanns, H., Katoen, J.-P., Siegle, M. (eds.) Validation of Stochastic Systems. LNCS, vol. 2925, pp. 147–188. Springer, Heidelberg (2004). https://doi.org/10.1007/978-3-540-24611-4_5

44. Clarke, E.M., Emerson, E.A.: Design and synthesis of synchronization skeletons using branching-time temporal logic. In: Kozen, D. (ed.) Logic of Programs. LNCS, vol. 131, pp. 52–71. Springer, Heidelberg (1981). https://doi.org/10.1007/BFb0025774

45. Colón, M.A., Sankaranarayanan, S., Sipma, H.B.: Linear invariant generation using non-linear constraint solving. In: Hunt, W.A., Somenzi, F. (eds.) CAV 2003. LNCS, vol. 2725, pp. 420–432. Springer, Heidelberg (2003). https://doi.org/10.1007/978-3-540-45069-6_39

46. Colóon, M.A., Sipma, H.B.: Synthesis of linear ranking functions. In: Margaria, T., Yi, W. (eds.) TACAS 2001. LNCS, vol. 2031, pp. 67–81. Springer, Heidelberg (2001). https://doi.org/10.1007/3-540-45319-9_6

47. Cook, B., Gotsman, A., Podelski, A., Rybalchenko, A., Vardi, M.Y.: Proving that programs eventually do something good. In: POPL, pp. 265–276. ACM (2007)

48. Cook, B., See, A., Zuleger, F.: Ramsey vs. lexicographic termination proving. In: Piterman, N., Smolka, S.A. (eds.) TACAS 2013. LNCS, vol. 7795, pp. 47–61. Springer, Heidelberg (2013). https://doi.org/10.1007/978-3-642-36742-7_4

49. Cousot, P., Cousot, R.: Abstract interpretation: a unified lattice model for static analysis of programs by construction or approximation of fixpoints. In: POPL, pp. 238–252. ACM (1977)

50. Dehnert, C., Junges, S., Katoen, J.-P., Volk, M.: A storm is coming: a modern probabilistic model checker. In: Majumdar, R., Kunčak, V. (eds.) CAV 2017. LNCS, vol. 10427, pp. 592–600. Springer, Cham (2017). https://doi.org/10.1007/978-3-319-63390-9_31

51. van Dijk, T., van de Pol, J.: Multi-core symbolic bisimulation minimisation. Int. J. Softw. Tools Technol. Transf. **20**(2), 157–177 (2018)

52. D'Innocenzo, A., Abate, A., Katoen, J.P.: Robust PCTL model checking. In: Proceedings of the 15th ACM International Conference on Hybrid Systems: Computation and Control, Beijing (PRC), pp. 275–285 (2012)

53. Douc, R., Moulines, E., Priouret, P., Soulier, P.: Markov Chains. Springer Series in Operations Research and Financial Engineering. Springer, Cham (2018). https://doi.org/10.1007/978-3-319-97704-1
54. Edwards, A., Peruffo, A., Abate, A.: A general verification framework for dynamical and control models via certificate synthesis. arXiv:2309.06090 (2023)
55. Edwards, A., Peruffo, A., Abate, A.: FOSSIL 2.0: formal certificate synthesis for the verification and control of dynamical models. In: Proceedings of HSCC (2024). arXiv:2311.09793
56. Etessami, K., Yannakakis, M.: Recursive Markov chains, stochastic grammars, and monotone systems of nonlinear equations. J. ACM **56**(1), 1:1–1:66 (2009)
57. Fioriti, L.M.F., Hermanns, H.: Probabilistic termination: soundness, completeness, and compositionality. In: POPL, pp. 489–501. ACM (2015)
58. Floyd, R.W.: Assigning meanings to programs. In: Colburn, T.R., Fetzer, J.H., Rankin, T.L. (eds.) Program Verification: Fundamental Issues in Computer Science. Studies in Cognitive Systems, vol. 14, pp. 65–81. Springer, Dordrecht (1993). https://doi.org/10.1007/978-94-011-1793-7_4
59. Gao, Y., Johansson, K., Abate, A.: CTL model checking of Markov decision processes over the distribution space. In: Proceedings of 27th ACM International Conference on HSCC, pp. 1–12 (2024)
60. Giacobbe, M., Kroening, D., Parsert, J.: Neural termination analysis. In: ESEC/SIGSOFT FSE, pp. 633–645. ACM (2022)
61. Glabbeek, R.J.: The linear time — branching time spectrum II. In: Best, E. (ed.) CONCUR 1993. LNCS, vol. 715, pp. 66–81. Springer, Heidelberg (1993). https://doi.org/10.1007/3-540-57208-2_6
62. Grumberg, O., Francez, N., Makowsky, J.A., de Roever, W.P.: A proof rule for fair termination of guarded commands. Inf. Control **66**(1/2), 83–102 (1985)
63. Haesaert, S., Soudjani, S., Abate, A.: Verification of general Markov decision processes by approximate similarity relations and policy refinement. SIAM J. Control Optimisation **55**(4), 2333–2367 (2017)
64. Hennessy, M., Milner, R.: Algebraic laws for nondeterminism and concurrency. J. ACM **32**(1), 137–161 (1985)
65. Hernández-Lerma, O., Lasserre, J.B.: Discrete-Time Markov Control Processes. Springe, New York (1996). https://doi.org/10.1007/978-1-4612-0729-0
66. Hopcroft, J.: An n log n algorithm for minimizing states in a finite automaton. In: Kohavi, Z., Paz, A. (eds.) Theory of Machines and Computations, pp. 189–196. Academic Press (1971)
67. Jonsson, B., Larsen, K.G.: Specification and refinement of probabilistic processes. In: LICS, pp. 266–277. IEEE Computer Society (1991)
68. Kallenberg, O.: Foundations of Modern Probability. Springer, New York (1997). https://doi.org/10.1007/978-3-030-61871-1
69. Katoen, J.-P.: Abstraction of probabilistic systems. In: Raskin, J.-F., Thiagarajan, P.S. (eds.) FORMATS 2007. LNCS, vol. 4763, pp. 1–3. Springer, Heidelberg (2007). https://doi.org/10.1007/978-3-540-75454-1_1
70. Katoen, J.-P.: Probabilistic programming: a true verification challenge. In: Finkbeiner, B., Pu, G., Zhang, L. (eds.) ATVA 2015. LNCS, vol. 9364, pp. 1–3. Springer, Cham (2015). https://doi.org/10.1007/978-3-319-24953-7_1
71. Katoen, J.P.: The probabilistic model checking landscape. In: Proceedings of the 31st Annual ACM/IEEE Symposium on Logic in Computer Science, pp. 31–45. Association for Computing Machinery (2016)

72. Katoen, J.-P., Kemna, T., Zapreev, I., Jansen, D.N.: Bisimulation minimisation mostly speeds up probabilistic model checking. In: Grumberg, O., Huth, M. (eds.) TACAS 2007. LNCS, vol. 4424, pp. 87–101. Springer, Heidelberg (2007). https://doi.org/10.1007/978-3-540-71209-1_9

73. Katoen, J.-P., McIver, A.K., Meinicke, L.A., Morgan, C.C.: Linear-invariant generation for probabilistic programs. In: Cousot, R., Martel, M. (eds.) SAS 2010. LNCS, vol. 6337, pp. 390–406. Springer, Heidelberg (2010). https://doi.org/10.1007/978-3-642-15769-1_24

74. Kenyon-Roberts, A., Ong, C.L.: Supermartingales, ranking functions and probabilistic lambda calculus. In: LICS, pp. 1–13. IEEE (2021)

75. Kucera, A., Esparza, J., Mayr, R.: Model checking probabilistic pushdown automata. Log. Methods Comput. Sci. 2(1) (2006)

76. Lamport, L.: What good is temporal logic? In: IFIP Congress, pp. 657–668. North-Holland/IFIP (1983)

77. Larsen, K.G., Skou, A.: Bisimulation through probabilistic testing. In: POPL, pp. 344–352. ACM Press (1989)

78. Lavaei, A., Soudjani, S., Abate, A., Zamani, M.: Automated verification and synthesis of stochastic hybrid systems: a survey. Automatica 146 (2022)

79. Lechner, M., Zikelic, D., Chatterjee, K., Henzinger, T.A.: Stability verification in stochastic control systems via neural network supermartingales. In: AAAI, pp. 7326–7336. AAAI Press (2022)

80. Lee, D., Yannakakis, M.: Online minimization of transition systems (extended abstract). In: STOC, pp. 264–274. ACM (1992)

81. Lee, I., Rajasekaran, S.: A parallel algorithm for relational coarsest partition problems and its implementation. In: Dill, D.L. (ed.) CAV 1994. LNCS, vol. 818, pp. 404–414. Springer, Heidelberg (1994). https://doi.org/10.1007/3-540-58179-0_71

82. Lehmann, D., Pnueli, A., Stavi, J.: Impartiality, justice and fairness: the ethics of concurrent termination. In: Even, S., Kariv, O. (eds.) ICALP 1981. LNCS, vol. 115, pp. 264–277. Springer, Heidelberg (1981). https://doi.org/10.1007/3-540-10843-2_22

83. Long, Y., Bayoumi, M.: Feedback stabilization: control Lyapunov functions modelled by neural networks. In: Proceedings of 32nd IEEE Conference on Decision and Control, pp. 2812–2814. IEEE (1993)

84. Martens, J., Groote, J.F., van den Haak, L., Hijma, P., Wijs, A.: A linear parallel algorithm to compute bisimulation and relational coarsest partitions. In: Salaün, G., Wijs, A. (eds.) FACS 2021. LNCS, vol. 13077, pp. 115–133. Springer, Cham (2021). https://doi.org/10.1007/978-3-030-90636-8_7

85. Mathiesen, F.B., Calvert, S.C., Laurenti, L.: Safety certification for stochastic systems via neural barrier functions. IEEE Control. Syst. Lett. 7, 973–978 (2023)

86. McIver, A., Morgan, C.: Abstraction, Refinement and Proof for Probabilistic Systems. Monographs in Computer Science. Springer, New York (2005). https://doi.org/10.1007/b138392

87. McIver, A., Morgan, C., Kaminski, B.L., Katoen, J.: A new proof rule for almost-sure termination. Proc. ACM Program. Lang. 2(POPL), 33:1–33:28 (2018)

88. Milner, R.: A Calculus of Communicating Systems. Lecture Notes in Computer Science, vol. 92. Springer, Heidelberg (1980). https://doi.org/10.1007/3-540-10235-3

89. Milner, R.: Communication and Concurrency. PHI Series in Computer Science. Prentice Hall (1989)

90. Moosbrugger, M., Bartocci, E., Katoen, J.-P., Kovács, L.: Automated termination analysis of polynomial probabilistic programs. In: ESOP 2021. LNCS, vol. 12648, pp. 491–518. Springer, Cham (2021). https://doi.org/10.1007/978-3-030-72019-3_18

91. Moosbrugger, M., Bartocci, E., Katoen, J.-P., Kovács, L.: The probabilistic termination tool amber. In: Huisman, M., Păsăreanu, C., Zhan, N. (eds.) FM 2021. LNCS, vol. 13047, pp. 667–675. Springer, Cham (2021). https://doi.org/10.1007/978-3-030-90870-6_36

92. Nadali, A., Murali, V., Trivedi, A., Zamani, M.: Neural closure certificates. In: AAAI, pp. 21446–21453. AAAI Press (2024)

93. Noroozi, N., Karimaghaee, P., Safaei, F., Javadi, H.: Generation of Lyapunov functions by neural networks. In: Proceedings of the World Congress on Engineering, vol. 2008 (2008)

94. Paige, R., Tarjan, R.E.: Three partition refinement algorithms. SIAM J. Comput. 16(6), 973–989 (1987)

95. Panangaden, P.: Labelled Markov Processes. Imperial College Press, London (2009)

96. Papachristodoulou, A., Prajna, S.: On the construction of lyapunov functions using the sum of squares decomposition. In: Proceedings of the 41st IEEE Conference on Decision and Control, vol. 3, pp. 3482–3487 (2002)

97. Papachristodoulou, A., Anderson, J., Valmorbida, G., Prajna, S., Seiler, P., Parrilo, P.: SOSTOOLS Version 3.00 Sum of Squares Optimization Toolbox for MATLAB. arXiv:1310.4716 (2013)

98. Park, D.: Concurrency and automata on infinite sequences. In: Deussen, P. (ed.) GI-TCS 1981. LNCS, vol. 104, pp. 167–183. Springer, Heidelberg (1981). https://doi.org/10.1007/BFb0017309

99. Parrilo, P.: Structured semidenite programs and semialgebraic geometry methods in robustness and optimization. Ph.D. thesis (2000)

100. Petridis, V., Petridis, S.: Construction of neural network based Lyapunov functions. In: IJCNN, pp. 5059–5065. IEEE (2006)

101. Pnueli, A.: The temporal logic of programs. In: FOCS, pp. 46–57. IEEE Computer Society (1977)

102. Pnueli, A., Podelski, A., Rybalchenko, A.: Separating fairness and well-foundedness for the analysis of fair discrete systems. In: Halbwachs, N., Zuck, L.D. (eds.) TACAS 2005. LNCS, vol. 3440, pp. 124–139. Springer, Heidelberg (2005). https://doi.org/10.1007/978-3-540-31980-1_9

103. Podelski, A., Rybalchenko, A.: A complete method for the synthesis of linear ranking functions. In: Steffen, B., Levi, G. (eds.) VMCAI 2004. LNCS, vol. 2937, pp. 239–251. Springer, Heidelberg (2004). https://doi.org/10.1007/978-3-540-24622-0_20

104. Podelski, A., Rybalchenko, A.: Transition invariants. In: LICS, pp. 32–41. IEEE Computer Society (2004)

105. Pollard, D.: A User's Guide to Measure Theoretic Probability. Cambridge Series in Statistical and Probabilistic Mathematics. Cambridge University Press, Cambridge (2001)

106. Prajna, S., Jadbabaie, A., Pappas, G.J.: A framework for worst-case and stochastic safety verification using barrier certificates. IEEE Trans. Autom. Control 52(8), 1415–1428 (2007)

107. Prajna, S., Jadbabaie, A., Pappas, G.: Stochastic safety verification using barrier certificates. In: 2004 43rd IEEE Conference on Decision and Control (CDC) (IEEE Cat. No.04CH37601), vol. 1, pp. 929–934 (2004)

108. Prajna, S.: Barrier certificates for nonlinear model validation. Automatica (J. IFAC) **42**(1), 117–126 (2006)
109. Prokhorov, D.V.: A Lyapunov machine for stability analysis of nonlinear systems. In: 1994 IEEE World Congress on Computational Intelligence, 1994 IEEE International Conference on Neural Networks, vol. 2, pp. 1028–1031. IEEE (1994)
110. Qin, Z., Zhang, K., Chen, Y., Chen, J., Fan, C.: Learning safe multi-agent control with decentralized neural barrier certificates. In: ICLR. OpenReview.net (2021)
111. Ravanbakhsh, H., Sankaranarayanan, S.: Counterexample Guided Synthesis of Switched Controllers for Reach-While-Stay Properties. arXiv:1505.01180 (2015)
112. Richards, S.M., Berkenkamp, F., Krause, A.: The Lyapunov neural network: adaptive stability certification for safe learning of dynamical systems. In: Conference on Robot Learning, pp. 466–476. PMLR (2018)
113. Robbins, H., Siegmund, D.: A convergence theorem for non negative almost supermartingales and some applications. In: Optimizing Methods in Statistics, pp. 233–257 (1971)
114. Sankaranarayanan, S., Chen, X., Ábrahám, E.: Lyapunov function synthesis using handelman representations. IFAC Proc. Vol. **46**(23), 576–581 (2013)
115. Schreuder, A., Ong, C.L.: Polynomial probabilistic invariants and the optional stopping theorem. CoRR abs/1910.12634 (2019)
116. Serpen, G.: Empirical approximation for Lyapunov functions with artificial neural nets. In: Proceedings of 2005 IEEE International Joint Conference on Neural Networks, vol. 2, pp. 735–740. IEEE (2005)
117. She, Z., Li, H., Xue, B., Zheng, Z., Xia, B.: Discovering polynomial lyapunov functions for continuous dynamical systems. J. Symb. Comput. **58**, 41–63 (2013)
118. Solar-Lezama, A., Tancau, L., Bodík, R., Seshia, S.A., Saraswat, V.A.: Combinatorial sketching for finite programs. In: ASPLOS, pp. 404–415. ACM (2006)
119. Soudjani, S., Abate, A.: Adaptive and sequential gridding procedures for the abstraction and verification of stochastic processes. SIAM J. Appl. Dyn. Syst. **12**(2), 921–956 (2013)
120. Soudjani, S.E.Z., Gevaerts, C., Abate, A.: FAUST²: Formal Abstractions of Uncountable-STate STochastic processes. In: Baier, C., Tinelli, C. (eds.) TACAS 2015. LNCS, vol. 9035, pp. 272–286. Springer, Heidelberg (2015). https://doi.org/10.1007/978-3-662-46681-0_23
121. Sun, D., Jha, S., Fan, C.: Learning certified control using contraction metric. In: CoRL. Proceedings of Machine Learning Research, vol. 155, pp. 1519–1539. PMLR (2020)
122. Takisaka, T., Oyabu, Y., Urabe, N., Hasuo, I.: Ranking and repulsing supermartingales for reachability in randomized programs. ACM Trans. Program. Lang. Syst. **43**(2), 5:1–5:46 (2021)
123. Takisaka, T., Zhang, L., Wang, C., Liu, J.: Lexicographic ranking supermartingales with lazy lower bounds. In: Gurfinkel, A., Ganesh, V. (eds.) CAV 2024. LNCS, vol. 14683, pp. 420–442. Springer, Cham (2024). https://doi.org/10.1007/978-3-031-65633-0_19
124. Tkachev, I., Abate, A.: A control Lyapunov function approach for the computation of the infinite-horizon stochastic reach-avoid problem. In: Proceedings of the 52nd IEEE Conference on Decision and Control, Florence (IT), pp. 3211–3216 (2013)
125. Tkachev, I., Abate, A.: Characterization and computation of infinite horizon specifications over Markov processes. Theoret. Comput. Sci. **515**, 1–18 (2014)

126. Tkachev, I., Mereacre, A., Katoen, J.P., Abate, A.: Quantitative automata-based controller synthesis for non-autonomous stochastic hybrid systems. In: Proceedings of the 16th ACM International Conference on Hybrid Systems: Computation and Control, pp. 293–302 (2013)
127. Tkachev, I., Mereacre, A., Katoen, J.P., Abate, A.: Quantitative model-checking of controlled discrete-time Markov processes. Inf. Comput. **253**, 1–35 (2017)
128. Vardi, M.Y.: Verification of concurrent programs: the automata-theoretic framework. In: LICS, pp. 167–176. IEEE Computer Society (1987)
129. Wang, Q., Chen, M., Xue, B., Zhan, N., Katoen, J.-P.: Synthesizing invariant barrier certificates via difference-of-convex programming. In: Silva, A., Leino, K.R.M. (eds.) CAV 2021. LNCS, vol. 12759, pp. 443–466. Springer, Cham (2021). https://doi.org/10.1007/978-3-030-81685-8_21
130. Winkler, T., Gehnen, C., Katoen, J.-P.: Model checking temporal properties of recursive probabilistic programs. In: FoSSaCS 2022. LNCS, vol. 13242, pp. 449–469. Springer, Cham (2022). https://doi.org/10.1007/978-3-030-99253-8_23
131. Winkler, T., Gehnen, C., Katoen, J.: Model checking temporal properties of recursive probabilistic programs. Log. Methods Comput. Sci. **19**(4) (2023)
132. Winkler, T., Katoen, J.: Certificates for probabilistic pushdown automata via optimistic value iteration. In: Sankaranarayanan, S., Sharygina, N. (eds.) TACAS 2023. LNCS, vol. 13994, pp. 391–409. Springer, Cham (2023). https://doi.org/10.1007/978-3-031-30820-8_24
133. Winkler, T., Katoen, J.: On certificates, expected runtimes, and termination in probabilistic pushdown automata. In: LICS, pp. 1–13. IEEE (2023)
134. Yang, X., Katoen, J., Lin, H., Liu, G., Wu, H.: Branching bisimulation and concurrent object verification. In: DSN, pp. 267–278. IEEE Computer Society (2018)
135. Yang, X., Katoen, J., Lin, H., Wu, H.: Proving linearizability via branching bisimulation (2016)
136. Yang, X., Katoen, J.P., Wu, H.: Verifying concurrent stacks by divergence-sensitive bisimulation (2024)
137. Yannakakis, M., Etessami, K.: Checking LTL properties of recursive Markov chains. In: QEST, pp. 155–165. IEEE Computer Society (2005)
138. Zhi, D., Wang, P., Liu, S., Ong, C.L., Zhang, M.: Unifying qualitative and quantitative safety verification of DNN-controlled systems. In: Gurfinkel, A., Ganesh, V. (eds.) CAV 2024. LNCS, vol. 14682, pp. 401–426. Springer, Cham (2024). https://doi.org/10.1007/978-3-031-65630-9_20
139. Zikelic, D., Lechner, M., Henzinger, T.A., Chatterjee, K.: Learning control policies for stochastic systems with reach-avoid guarantees. In: AAAI, pp. 11926–11935. AAAI Press (2023)
140. Zikelic, D., Lechner, M., Verma, A., Chatterjee, K., Henzinger, T.A.: Compositional policy learning in stochastic control systems with formal guarantees. In: NeurIPS (2023)

Author Index

© The Editor(s) (if applicable) and The Author(s), under exclusive license
to Springer Nature Switzerland AG 2025
N. Jansen et al. (Eds.): Principles of Verification: Cycling the Probabilistic Landscape, LNCS 15261, pp. 393–395, 2025.
https://doi.org/10.1007/978-3-031-75775-4

SPRINGER NATURE

GPSR Compliance

The European Union's (EU) General Product Safety Regulation (GPSR) is a set of rules that requires consumer products to be safe and our obligations to ensure this.

If you have any concerns about our products, you can contact us on ProductSafety@springernature.com

In case Publisher is established outside the EU, the EU authorized representative is:

Springer Nature Customer Service Center GmbH
Europaplatz 3
69115 Heidelberg, Germany

The manufacturer's authorised representative in the EU is Springer
Nature Customer Service Centre GmbH, Europaplatz 3, 69115 Heidelberg,
Germany. If you have any concerns regarding our products, please
contact ProductSafety@springernature.com

Printed and bound by CPI Group (UK) Ltd, Croydon, CR0 4YY
24/04/2026
02096364-0003